A SAVAGE WAR

A SAVAGE WAR

A Military History of the Civil War

Williamson Murray and Wayne Wei-siang Hsieh

PRINCETON UNIVERSITY PRESS

Princeton & Oxford

Library of Congress Cataloging-in-Publication Data

Names: Murray, Williamson, author. | Hsieh, Wayne Wei-siang, author.
Title: A savage war : a military history of the Civil War /
Williamson Murray and Wayne Hsieh.
Description: Princeton : Princeton University Press, 2016. | Includes
bibliographical references and index.
Identifiers: LCCN 2016008730 | ISBN 9780691169408 (hardback : alk. paper)
Subjects: LCSH: United States—History—Civil War, 1861–1865—Campaigns.
Classification: LCC E470 .M88 2016 | DDC 973.7/3—dc23
LC record available at http://lccn.loc.gov/2016008730

British Library Cataloging-in-Publication Data is available

This book has been composed in Baskerville 10 Pro, Clarendon LT Std,
and John Sans White Pro

Printed on acid-free paper. ∞

Printed in the United States of America

1 3 5 7 9 10 8 6 4 2

This country will be drenched in blood. God only knows how it will all end. . . . O, it is all folly, madness, a crime against civilization! . . . You people speak so lightly of war. You don't know what you are talking about. War is a terrible thing. . . . You mistake, too, the people of the North. They are a peaceable people, but an earnest people, and will fight, too; and they are not going to let this country be destroyed without a mighty effort to save it. Besides, where are your men and appliances of war to contend against them? . . . The North can make anything it needs; you can make scarcely anything you need. You can't make a steam engine, locomotive, or railway car; hardly a yard of cloth or pair of shoes can you make. Yet you are rushing into war with one of the most powerful, ingeniously mechanical, and determined people on earth right at your doors. You are bound to fail. Only in your spirit and determination are you prepared for war. In all else are you totally unprepared, with a bad cause to start with. At first you will make headway; but as your limited resources begin to fail, and, shut out from the markets of Europe by blockades, as you will be, your cause will begin to wane. . . . If your people will but stop to think, they must see that in the end you will surely fail.

—William Tecumseh Sherman (Boyd, "Gen. W. T. Sherman")
Christmas Eve, 1860

CONTENTS

MAPS

PREFACE

We have found ourselves interested in the American Civil War from our earliest readings in the past. And that fact explains much about how and why we came to write this book. Yet, the reader should understand that this great war has not been the exclusive focus of our academic interests and writing. The elder of us has spent much of his career as a student of European strategic and academic history in the twentieth century, while taking time off to write a history of the Iran-Iraq War. The other is a student of American military history in the nineteenth century with a much wider perspective than just the military events that occurred between 1861 and 1865, and whose own dissertation advisors were originally trained as historians of the American South—although both later became important Civil War scholars. Moreover, both of us have had extensive experience with the American military, one as an officer and consultant, the other as a provincial advisor in Iraq.

Moreover, both of us in our various careers as students and teachers at Yale found ourselves under the spell and writings of Donald Kagan and his examination of the Peloponnesian War and the brilliant account of that catastrophic war by that greatest of all strategic historians, Thucydides. Our Athenian inspiration described his own war as "the greatest disturbance in the history of the Hellenes."[1] So too we believe that the Civil War was "the greatest disturbance in the history of the Americans" and for that reason deserves the closest attention of those who have inherited this great Republic.

A SAVAGE WAR

Introduction

Why another history of a war that has so fascinated so many Americans and led to so much spilled ink over the century and a half since its ending? Quite simply, as with all great events, new perspectives continue to influence our understanding of the war that ripped apart the American Republic in the mid-nineteenth century. The Civil War combined an unprecedented movement and projection of military forces across a continent on a scale made possible by the Industrial Revolution with the psychic mobilization of two contending nations that the French Revolution had foreshadowed. It represented a momentous change in the character of war from the conflicts of the previous century and a half. Nevertheless, the American Civil War forms an integral element in the overall development of the Western way of war, influenced undoubtedly by the peculiarities of geography, politics, economics, and intellectual perceptions that shaped the developing nation at that time.

Thus, one cannot judge the war as an exceptional event separate from the powerful influences of what was also occurring in Europe. Instead its American participants found themselves influenced by the wider patterns of social, political, and military revolutions that for a brief, short-lived period in history gave the Western world global dominance in terms of its military and strategic power. Despite the war's revolutionary aspects, its belligerents, and, most importantly, its leaders, still faced the same inherent uncertainties in armed conflict Thucydides would have recognized over two millennia before and which Clausewitz described as "friction" several decades before the American conflict.

The far-reaching implications of that era of Western military dominance remain with us to this day, even as that supremacy has faded considerably since the end of the world wars. Indeed, an historically inaccurate belief that Western military dominance came about exclusively from technological changes in warfare continues to haunt American defense policy. Recently, Donald Rumsfeld's vision of network-centric warfare sought to remove much of war's uncertainties through the innovations of late twentieth-century information and communications technologies, along with a proliferation of precision-guided munitions embedded in new surveillance technologies. In the aftermath of the 1991 Gulf War, military and civilian pundits even argued enthusiastically that the technological sophistication of America's military had caused a revolution in war that would alter not only the character of war but its fundamental nature as well.

The penchant of Barack Obama's administration to employ drone strikes and commando raids in place of serious strategic choices follows in Rumsfeld's footsteps in its desire to use technology to banish uncertainty from warfare, albeit from a different ideological viewpoint. Both Obama and Rumsfeld, as well as too many others, have subscribed to a special conceit of our era—that technological change provides the primary motive force for historical change. Unfortunately, a version of this belief has remained prevalent among historians who continue to cite the introduction of the rifle musket as the primary factor in explaining why Civil War battles tended to be indecisive and why the war dragged on as long as it did.

Regardless of the aspirations of modern military futurists and technicians, military historians have actually examined at some length periods of great change in the waging and conduct of war in the West since the seventeenth century. In a conference at the end of the 1990s examining "revolutions in military affairs" since the seventeenth century, and in the wake of the US military's decisive defeat of Saddam Hussein's invasion of Kuwait, a group of historians—including well-known scholars such as Geoffrey Parker, Holger Herwig, MacGregor Knox, and Clifford Rogers as well as one of this volume's authors—found technological change to be only one of a number of factors in explaining the seismic changes in Western military practice at certain points in history. They presciently warned American policy makers of the dangers in assuming technology by itself "would confer upon America an effortless superiority over all potential opponents in the coming century."[1]

Even in our own more anxious era, American military policy remains wedded to technical solutions for challenges as diverse as Islamist terrorists, cybersecurity threats, and rising tensions with the People's Republic of China. The Civil War's important place in the larger evolution of Western warfare provides no obvious and simple solutions to early twenty-first-century security problems, but by showing how technological change did and did *not* affect the course and outcome of a major war, it can help the reader build a framework for a more subtle understanding of how technology might affect future American conflicts.

The aforementioned historians also argued that there were two related phenomena driving the increasingly sophisticated and lethal approaches to wars among Western states, which eventually manifested themselves in the great American conflict. The first of these phenomena were the great changes in political, social, economic, and/or military patterns that have shattered the European framework of military and economic power at various times from 1610 to the twentieth century. One might best term them "military-social revolutions" which changed states and societies in addition to their armed forces. The second of these phenomena are "revolutions in military affairs," which formed a part of the larger military-social revolutions. Revolutions in military affairs have been more specific and constrained, and in their tactical or organizational innovations fundamentally altered the military capabilities of the major powers and their armies and navies, and later their air forces.

The first of the great "military-social revolutions" occurred in the seventeenth century and involved the creation of the modern state with its attendant bureaucratic and disciplined military organizations. On the other hand, the "revolutions in military affairs" of the time remained particularly important because with the reintroduction of the Roman system and discipline (modern parade ground commands are all derived from Roman commands), for example, European armies became directly responsive to the early modern states of Europe and as such they could be of use for both internal and external purposes.

Accompanying the creation of the modern state and its bureaucratic structure were lesser pre- and postquake shocks that altered the ability of the European powers to make war. In the intensely competitive framework of European politics and warfare in the seventeenth and early eighteenth centuries, the improvements by one army or navy were followed almost immediately by similar adaptations by their competitors. For example, Gustavus Adolphus's tactical innovations with infantry and artillery in a disciplined tactical framework destroyed the dominance of the Hapsburg armies in Central Europe in the Thirty Years' War. The major European powers then immediately copied and improved on those innovations. Similarly, in its adaptation to the Second Hundred Years' War with the French (1689–1815), Great Britain, successor to the medieval English kingdom, developed far more effective methods of financing wars than had been the case in the past. That enabled the British to project their naval power on a global scale, while at the same time supporting continental commitments with substantial military and financial aid to their allies. The result was that Britain, weaker in terms of its economy and population, was able to defeat the French and dominate the global commons. Some powers, such as Spain with its decrepit finances, failed to adapt to the changes and soon fell by the wayside by comparison.

The second and third of the great "military-social revolutions" that transformed the character of war occurred in the second half of the eighteenth century: the beginnings of the Industrial Revolution in Britain and the French Revolution, first in France, then across the Continent. The Industrial Revolution allowed the British to dominate global trade throughout the quarter century of wars with Revolutionary and Napoleonic France, while supporting major military forces in Portugal and Spain and providing major subsidies that finally enabled their allies to mobilize sufficient military force to break Napoleon's armies in Central Europe in 1813. The enormous wealth generated by Britain's industrializing economy provided the British with the wherewithal needed to overwhelm Napoleon's battlefield genius indirectly. Moreover, the Industrial Revolution channeled much of Britain's growing population into industrial concerns and not revolutionary activities as was occurring in France.

Across the Channel, the French Revolution provided the ideology and ruthlessness to mobilize France's population and resources to carry on wars against the rest of Europe for a period that lasted almost twenty-five years. The French Revolutionary armies won relatively few battles, but with an almost endless source of manpower, the populous French Nation, they were able to batter their opponents into surrender. The continuation of the *levée en masse* between 1800 and 1814, with its conscription of young men, allowed Napoleon to rally two million

Frenchmen to his banners and destroy his opponents until they finally were willing to unite against the Corsican ogre.

But while those two "military-social revolutions" were altering the framework of European politics and strategy in profound ways, they did not merge. The British army on the Iberian Peninsula was in almost every respect an army of the ancient régime. The Duke of Wellington's soldiers possessed infantry weapons that differed little from those carried by the Duke of Marlborough's redcoats in the War of Spanish Succession a century earlier. On the other hand, Britain's immense wealth, largely supported by the Industrial Revolution, allowed the Royal Navy to dominate the world's oceans, created a cancer for the French and Napoleon by deploying Wellington's Army to Spain, and supported the European armies on the Continent with major subventions. In 1813 British financial support played a significant role in allowing the Russians, Austrians, and Prussians to mobilize their manpower from their weak economic bases.

The fourth great "military-social revolution" occurred with the coming of the American Civil War and the First World War. Over the course of those two wars, the combination of the effects of the Industrial Revolution and French Revolution allowed the opposing sides to mobilize immense numbers of soldiers while projecting military power over great distances. Thus, the American Civil War represented the first incidence of a profound change in the character of war. In every respect, both sides in the American conflict drew on social and political forces similar to the French Revolution's ability to mobilize popular sentiment for the purposes of war. Moreover, the advances of the Industrial Revolution provided not only the equipment to support great armies but also contributed directly to the battlefield, particularly in its logistical and transportation support.

By 1864 the Americans had in effect stumbled into modern war, the conduct of which had by that point in many respects come to resemble what was to happen in 1914. The Union had mobilized mass armies in the Eastern and Western theaters of operations that possessed, in historical terms, an unprecedented capacity in logistics, transportation, and communications. It was that combination of industrial power with the mobilization of manpower that allowed the North to bring the war home to almost every hamlet in the South. The mobilization of this power was not inevitable. The military potential of this combination of the Industrial Revolution with the French Revolution could find fruition only if competent leaders emerged to guide the North's war effort. It depended to a great extent on political leadership at the top; imaginative financial innovation, at least in American terms; and military leaders who understood the connection between combat power and logistics.

In the mid-nineteenth century, the Europeans, on the other hand, remained locked in the framework of limited conflicts, or at least that is how they interpreted their experiences. One is struck by the differences between the American Civil War, the Crimean War (1853–56), and the German Wars of Unification (1866–71) that occurred during the same years in Europe. Admittedly, the Europeans came perilously close to seeing the results of a marriage between the two revolutions. In 1870 Otto von Bismarck, the iron chancellor of the emerging German state, unleashed German nationalism and popular enthusiasm against the French, who replied in kind. But a combination of the gross incompetence of French military leadership and the competence of the German general staff destroyed France's professional army within a matter of months, long before the French could effectively integrate the new levies with the regulars. So Europe's military-social revolution in modern warfare had to wait until war broke out in 1914.

In North America, the fruits of the Industrial Revolution created the North's ability to project military power over continental distances. Those combat and logistical capabilities allowed Union armies to drive deep into the Confederacy's heartland and break the will of Southern whites to continue the struggle. Here it is important to emphasize a factor that far too many historians of the war have ignored—namely, that the Confederacy controlled, especially by European standards, immense territory. For example, the distance from Baton Rouge to Richmond exceeds that from the Franco-German frontier to Moscow, and even Napoleon's invasion of Russia, launched from bases in East Prussia and Poland far removed from metropolitan France, did not have to control the vast territory Union armies needed to conquer and hold.

One of the major problems Union strategists confronted in the conduct of military operations lay in the projection of military power over continental distances rarely seen elsewhere to that time. Furthermore, despite its relative weakness when compared to the Union in terms of its industrial potential and capacity, the Confederacy mustered enough of a manufacturing base to force the Union to fight a costly war for four long years. The contribution of the Industrial Revolution, namely railroads, steamboats, and the telegraph, allowed the Union forces to overcome the tyranny of distance, which had defeated even the great Napoleon in his invasion of Russia.

The creation of that logistical infrastructure took a sustained period of time, and it was not until 1864 that Union armies, particularly in the West, possessed the necessary logistical means to conduct operations over continental distances. Yet one should not underestimate the importance of Union industrial strength in the early war years. The creation of an armored, steam-driven riverine fleet by late 1861 enabled Ulysses S. Grant, a then-obscure Union commander with a checkered prewar history, to launch the war's most important strategic move in February 1862, the strike at Forts Donelson and Henry in Tennessee, which gave the Union control of the Tennessee and Cumberland Rivers and central and western Tennessee with its agricultural bounty and its iron-producing facilities. The move represented a success from which Confederate forces in the West never fully recovered.

That brings us to another essential point. To wage this great war, the contending sides had to create everything out of whole cloth. None of the vast structure and production necessary to equip and prepare the massive Union armies of 1864 for the great campaigns of that year existed at the war's outset. In 1860 the Army of the United States was little more than a minuscule constabulary force, the purpose of which was nothing more than to kill Indians, keep the peace among the fractious settlers, and maintain small garrisons in the forts scattered along the coasts of the United States. Staff functions, particularly in logistics, to coordinate and support the huge Union armies dispersed over the vast distances of the Confederacy did not exist. Indeed, the creation of a million-man army, 600,000 in the field, by 1864 represented a massive mobilization of citizens and industrial production the likes of which the world had never before seen. Given the fact that the opponents had to support those armies over continental distances, one gains an appreciation for the unprecedented accomplishment of Northern leaders in beating plowshares into cannon and muskets.

That success—the creation of the forces to build and sustain a successful four-year, continent-wide war which by itself was not inevitable—required skillful political and military leadership. In the end Union victory was a monument to the ability of the American people and their political system to innovate and adapt. It should also have represented a dark warning to the Germans of 1917 and 1941, who paid not the slightest attention to the implications of what the Americans had done from 1861 to 1865 in creating massed armies supported with all the accoutrements of war out of the Old Army, which displayed little of the basic requirements for a modern army. Thus, with nary a thought, the Germans brought an unwilling United States into both world wars.

Adding to both the North's and the Confederacy's problems, for that matter, was that the American leaders and populace found themselves misled by two basic assumptions at the war's outset. Each side believed that their opponents had little stomach for the fight. Northerners thought white Southerners remained at heart Unionists, while most Confederates had nothing but contempt for the human products of the industrializing North. Reinforced by a misreading of the Napoleonic wars a mere fifty years earlier, most soldiers and politicians also believed that one decisive victory on the battlefield would either end secession or gain the Confederacy its independence. In reality, decisive victory even in the last years of the Napoleonic wars had been a thing of the past, and it was even less likely in the age of rapid industrialization and the mobilization and equipping of great, massed armies.

The mobilization in 1861, in many respects seemingly ill-thought out, decentralized in the raising of volunteer regiments by the states, and led by officers who had no real preparation for the strategic and operational complexity of the conflict, created much confusion, some corruption, and processes that resulted in considerable difficulties in creating an effective strategic approach. Lincoln proved to be a fast learner, but even he made serious mistakes in his initial assumptions. None of the generals at any point in the war, except Grant and William Tecumseh Sherman in the North, grasped the war's larger strategic framework or its continental canvas. At every level it was amateur hour at the war's beginning. Only slowly and at great cost did a winning formula emerge. Learning on the fly on the battlefield is an expensive way to come to terms with the business of a major war. Thus, it is not surprising that extraordinarily high casualties resulted—casualties that demographers have recently raised to close to three-quarters of a million deaths from a population of thirty million.

A second aspect of the Union and Confederate deployments in the Eastern and Western theaters of operation is worth noting. One of the crucial aspects of military effectiveness—the ability of military organizations to defeat their enemies at minimum cost to their soldiers and marines—that historians have not given sufficient attention to is that of the culture of particular armies, navies, and air forces. Not surprisingly, "military effectiveness" is a subject of great interest to the modern American military, which sponsored important scholarship on the topic during the 1980s by the more senior of this volume's authors. In that larger multiauthor project, the authors defined military effectiveness as "the process by which armed forces convert resources into fighting power. A fully effective military is one that derives maximum combat power from the resources physically and politically available."[2]

In the Civil War, each of the major armies developed particular cultures, which helped determine their battlefield prowess. For example, two factors helped to shape the Army of the Potomac: the dominance of career regular army officers at all the higher levels and the choices that its first commander, George McClellan, made in selecting that army's brigade and division commanders. Thus, its army's commanders throughout the war were generals who rarely, if ever, took risks, and who suffered more often than not from the bureaucratic mind set of the Old Army. It was not necessarily that most of the Army of the Potomac's leaders were West Pointers. After all, academy graduates held nearly all of the highest positions in the major Civil War armies. Rather, it was the case that the Army of the Potomac acquired and maintained throughout the war the Old Army's worst habits as embodied in McClellan's makeup: a prideful preoccupation with status and rank, a confusion of administrative consistency with military effectiveness, and an overly cautious and engineering orientated style of command. Exacerbating the Army of the Potomac's proclivities was the fact that chance intervened with the result that its most aggressive generals died in battle: Philip Kearny at Second Bull Run, Jesse L. Reno at South Mountain, Israel B. Richardson at Antietam, and John F. Reynolds at Gettysburg.

The Union's opponent in the Eastern campaigns, the Confederate Army of Northern Virginia, possessed an extraordinarily different culture, not because the makeup of its rank and file was different from that of its opponent, but rather because Robert E. Lee and his major corps commanders were aggressive risk takers who never failed to take advantage of what they regarded as an opportunity.

Ironically, given that historians have spilled so much ink over the battles in Virginia, Maryland, and Pennsylvania, the Union won the war in the West. There, Grant molded his Army of the Tennessee into a military force that bore little resemblance in terms of its leadership to that of its Union counterparts in the Eastern theater of operations. Grant's division and corps commanders in the Army of the Tennessee moved aggressively, took risks, and for the most part seized the initiative, just as Lee and his generals did in the East. Grant took advantage of his relative distance from politicized Washington to foster among his subordinates a sense of mutual trust and loyalty. Its leaders wore the same uniforms as the Army of the Potomac, but their approach to operations represented a military culture of command that was night-and-day different from that of Union forces in the East.

On the other hand, the Confederate opponents of Union armies in the West showed little of the imaginative aggressiveness that marked Lee's leadership in the east. Confederate General Braxton Bragg displayed a perversely cantankerous personality in commanding the Army of Tennessee that drove his subordinates to mutiny. His superior, Jefferson Davis, only exacerbated matters by refusing to resolve the conflict between Bragg and his subordinates until the catastrophe at Chattanooga in late 1863 forced his hand. To add insult to injury for this hardest luck of American armies, in the middle of the Atlanta campaign in 1864, Davis replaced the competent Joe Johnston with John Bell Hood, who managed through reckless offensives to destroy the once proud Confederate Army of Tennessee by the end of 1864 in a series of costly and hopeless attacks.

The Confederate Army of Tennessee's less famous adversary, the Union Army of the Cumberland (originally the Army of the Ohio), had its own problems with a fractious command culture, including the notorious murder of a corps commander by a division commander during Don Carlos Buell's tenure as army commander, while the pettiness between William Rosecrans and Thomas J. Wood created a hole in Union lines that James Longstreet smashed through at Chickamauga in northern Georgia in September 1863. For all its faults, the Army of the Cumberland eventually produced a competent commander in George Thomas, and even the murderous subordinate division commander mentioned earlier, Jefferson Davis (no relation to the Confederate president), later proved a militarily successful corps commander himself.[3] These very different leadership cultures played a key role on the course of increasingly complex campaigns.

Too much of the writing of the Civil War has been and remains dominated by the Southern white or "Lost Cause" narrative. Developed in response to the catastrophic smashup of 1864 and 1865, that narrative argued that the Confederate cause was hopeless, overwhelmed by the masses of inept Union soldiers drawn from the dregs of the North's cities fighting against the incredibly skilled yeomen farmers of the Confederacy; that white Southerners bore little responsibility for the outbreak of the "War of Yankee Aggression"; and that Grant triumphed over Lee and the Army of Northern Virginia only as a result of a campaign of butchery with no skill. The segregationists who fought a rear-guard action against the twentieth-century civil rights movement even appropriated for themselves a somewhat historically inaccurate version of the old Confederate battle flag as their standard, and whose presence at public buildings throughout the South remains a point of controversy into our own century. In retrospect, Grant was a particular target not just for his role in crushing the Confederacy militarily, but because of his role in sponsoring political Reconstruction, the effort to bring some measure of justice to the blacks of the South. Little of this "Lost Cause" narrative focuses on what happened in the Western campaigns, where the performance of Confederate armies rivaled that of the Army of the Potomac in terms of sheer incompetence and where the Northern armies were skillfully dominant.

Over the past four decades, academic historians have demolished many of these myths. Nevertheless, too many of them remain alive among the great American public. The idea that white Southern armies consisted of hardy country folk up against the riffraff of Northern city dwellers has finally disappeared. So too has the overemphasis on the Eastern theater of operations with an understanding that the Union won the war in the West. Perhaps, most importantly, historians have consigned to the garbage dump the notion that the war was about "states' rights" and not about slavery. We are delighted to add our voices to those historians, like James McPherson, who have done so much to restore some balance to the history of the Civil War, and in this work we hope to help make accessible this significant body of scholarship to a larger reading public.

Lastly, from the Civil War there emerged a particularly American way of war, which goes beyond the historian Russell Weigley's formulation that after the Civil War American war-making tended toward the complete destruction of an opponent's military forces in the service of absolute victory. Instead, the American way of war that emerged from the conflict emphasized the logistical and operational projection of military power over continental distances along with a ruthless desire to bring the consequences of secession home to every hamlet in the Confederacy. That American approach would show in great clarity in both of the world wars, although in the first the Americans and their allies failed to bring the consequences of the Reich's murderously flawed approach to the war home to the German people. And despite the frustrating and insurgency-laden aftermaths, the United States achieved the complete destruction of the relatively unified and cohesive Taliban and Baathist states that governed Afghanistan and Iraq in the early twenty-first century. Even in the present day of lawyer-approved drone strikes, the signature characteristic of American military might is its ability to project power across the globe with land, air, and sea forces.

This is not a history of the social and economic consequences of the war. Rather, its purpose is to examine the major factors that explain the course of the military campaigns and operations in the widest sense. The battles of the Civil War mattered; in the end they determined the winners and the losers and drove the course of world history. The breakup of the United States in the early 1860s would have had the most dismal consequences for the fate of Europe in the first decades of the twentieth century. Thus, not surprisingly, we are interested in military leadership, effective and ineffective leadership, and in critiquing the strategic and operational choices made by the political and military leaders of the opposing sides. Above all, we do not take a deterministic view of the war; the North confronted an almost insoluble task in crushing Confederate resistance because of both the distances involved and the tenacious nature of white Southern resistance. In the end the Union succeeded, but only by the barest of margins.

CHAPTER 1

The Origins

In times of peace and prosperity cities and individuals alike follow higher standards, because they are not forced into a situation where they have to do what they do not want to do. But war is a stern teacher; in depriving them of the power of satisfying their daily wants, it brings most people's minds down to the level of their actual circumstances.

—Thucydides, *The History of the Peloponnesian War*

At the end of the Peloponnesian War in the late fifth century BC, that greatest of all strategic and military historians, Thucydides, noted the following as the overarching cause of the terrible conflict that had destroyed so much of his world: "What made war inevitable was the growth of Athenian power and the fear which this caused in Sparta."[1] So too might we not attribute the outbreak of the American Civil War to the growth of Northern power and the fear that it occasioned throughout much of the South? Indeed, John C. Calhoun's proposal for a dual executive to allow the slave South to counterbalance growing Northern power cited as one precedent the classical examples of Sparta's two kings.[2]

In the case of the Peloponnesian War, the opposing sides had developed starkly different social systems: Spartan power rested firmly on the enslavement of its Helot population; the Athenians, on the other hand, had developed into a vibrant and seaborne empire, the economic impulses of which rested on trade and industry. So too, wealth, social status, and the political framework of the southern American states rested on the institution of slavery, which had allowed them to produce the millions of bales of cotton on which the clothing mills of old and New England depended, but which had also retarded the growth of the South in other sectors. Meanwhile, the fruits of continental expansion, which by the late 1850s had reached the territories of the Dakota Sioux, and the opening up of unimagined agricultural wealth, had combined with the Industrial Revolution to provide the North with a rapidly increasing advantage in wealth and power over the slave states. The growing disparity between the two regions had not gone unnoticed among white Southerners, despite the shrillness of their declarations about the vibrancy of their civilization and the future potential of slavery.

Even in areas where the South made strides, such as the near quadrupling of the mileage of its railroad tracks in the 1850s, it fell further behind the North's total. In that decade, Northern railroads laid down almost double the mileage than did those of the South,[3] as the tentacles of those tracks knit the Midwest ever more closely to the eastern seaboard. Not only did this have a profound impact on the industrialization of the North, but it was also to provide the transportation necessary for the agricultural bounty that was to feed the explosive growth of the North's population. In the South the Industrial Revolution lagged behind. The Southern slave economy remained dependent on the production of agricultural staples—tobacco, rice, sugar, and particularly "king cotton," but like modern economies over reliant on a single natural resource such as oil, the South's specialization in staple agriculture retarded the growth of an indigenous industrial economy.

Indeed, it was slavery, and slavery alone, that accounted for the steadily growing gap in the culture and attitudes between the two sections of the American state that the revolution of the colonies against Britain in 1775 had created. While both the free and slave states played important roles in a larger Industrial Revolution, so far based mostly in Britain, the slave society of the South set it apart from its Northern brethren. Contrary to popular imagination, the antebellum South fully participated in the rapid social and economic changes the Western world saw in the mid-nineteenth century. By Western European standards, the future states of the Confederacy possessed an impressive railroad network, high rates of literacy, a thriving civil society, and a vibrant political democracy (albeit one strictly restricted to white men). Nevertheless, free labor and the absence of a dominant agricultural staple facilitated the growth of Northern industry, agriculture, and transportation which justified growing Southern fears that they would at some date in the future find themselves submerged under the weight of Northern economic and political power.

Furthermore, rapid social changes in the North enabled the rise of an antislavery reform movement that aimed a dagger at the heart of the Southern social and racial order. While many Southern slaveholders believed with conviction that they had Christianized chattel slavery into a benign and godly institution (indeed, some had criticized the Spartans for excessive cruelty toward the Helots), the violent examples of slave revolts in the Haitian Revolution (1791–1804) and Nat Turner's Rebellion in Virginia (1831) appeared to pose serious threats to the very fabric of Southern white society. Roughly a year before the 1860 presidential election that sent Lincoln to the White House with exclusively Northern votes, John Brown's aborted raid on Harper's Ferry on 16 October 1859, raised the alarm among white Southerners to a fevered pitch. Brown had earned a notorious reputation in the guerrilla warfare between free soil and proslavery settlers in "Bleeding Kansas," and he stormed the Harper's Ferry armory in the failed hope of raising and arming a slave rebellion. While responsible Northern politicians such as Lincoln condemned the raid, a significant and vocal Northern minority (including antiwar activist Henry David Thoreau) hailed Brown as a hero. Just as the Spartans in the midst of hostile Helot slaves saw Athenian ideas about Radical Democracy as a threat to their physical survival (fears eventually justified by the successful Theban effort to free the Helots and break Spartan power), Confederates saw similar perils if they remained coupled to an increasingly antislavery North.

Only the coming Civil War would reveal the true importance of Northern industrial superiority, but the Confederate nation-in-waiting had found threatening enough a changing American political system less willing to protect slavery. Not only did future Confederates see the free states gain an increasing advantage in sheer numbers—an important component of political power in the federal Union's representative system of government—but it also saw the gradual collapse of a political system based around two *national* political parties, each of which needed both Northern *and* Southern votes to succeed. That fear, combined with a deep sense of the uniqueness of the South's civilization and a belief that the Southern way of life was under siege resulted in the steady growth in the numbers of those who either tacitly or actively supported the movement toward secession. Yet there was considerable irony in such attitudes, for in terms of the nation's political life, white Southerners controlled the Supreme Court; along with Northern sympathizers, they dominated the Senate; and they had maintained a solid control over the presidency for most of the two decades before the Civil War with either white Southerners or Southern sympathizers holding the office. And even the popularly elected House of Representatives was controllable as long as Northern and Southern Democrats retained a semblance of unity.

Nevertheless, the shrillness with which white Southerners defended their rights only served to underline their fear that they were losing control of their destiny. And they intimately tied that destiny to the continuation of slavery, the most inhumane of all of the institutions that marked the republic's expansion across North America. William Seward, who eventually became a Republican Party political boss and served as secretary of state to Lincoln, caught that inhumanity in a chilling note in which he described a scene that he, his wife, and son witnessed in their progress through Virginia: "Ten naked little boys, between six and twelve years old, tied together, two and two, by their wrists, were all fastened to a long rope, and followed by a tall, gaunt white man, who, with his long lash, whipped up the sad and weary little procession, drove it to the horse-trough to drink, and thence to a shed, where they lay down on the ground and sobbed and moaned themselves to sleep."[4] All, purchased that day, were headed south to the slave markets of Richmond—most eventually to journey on to the plantations of the Deep South. That was the reality of an economic and political system which rested on the enslavement of human beings, whose labor it obtained with the whip and the lash.

The Founding Fathers had attempted to avoid or disguise the issue of slavery, at least in their most important political documents. They could do so, because while slavery existed in the North, and some Northern communities benefited from the slave trade, the institution did not form a crucial pillar of the social order—to use the terms of a modern historian, the North was a "society *with* slaves" before the Revolution, while the Southern colonies were true "*slave societies*."[5] Moreover, the distances between the individual colonies, as well as the parochialism of the new nation, made it relatively easy for Northerners to ignore the implications of the institution. And some of the Founding Fathers from the South hoped that the institution would gradually disappear. George Washington on his deathbed had freed his slaves. Few at the time were willing to defend the institution in public as a positive good in and of itself.

But two major contributions of the Industrial Revolution changed the status of and the attitudes toward slavery throughout the South. The first was Eli Whitney's invention of the cotton gin, which by eliminating the obnoxious seeds in the cotton balls quickly made cotton a viable cash crop. Second was the rapid growth of the Industrial Revolution's textile mills in Britain, and to a lesser extent in New England, which possessed an insatiable hunger for cotton to mass produce cloth in unheard of amounts. Thus, slavery became immensely profitable throughout the Deep South along the lowlands of the many rivers that drained into the Mississippi River and Gulf of Mexico. With fortunes at stake, slavery spread throughout the richest delta lands of Georgia, Tennessee, Alabama, Louisiana, Mississippi, and then into Texas.

But at the same time, revolutions in transportation, communications, and cultural values knitted together the United States in an unprecedented manner. Moreover, the telegraph reported events almost instantaneously to a literate and increasingly informed population, while transportation by rail and steamboat allowed many to see what others reported. No longer were the realities of slavery something Northerners could ignore. Some, particularly in the Democratic Party, supported the white Southern myth about the happiness of the slaves under the "benevolent" tutelage of their plantation masters. Some in the North hoped the problem would go away. Others came to believe that, if slavery were not an evil, then it represented a serious impediment to their interests and the economic growth of the nation. Finally, particularly in New England, a growing number of abolitionists decried slavery as an unmitigated evil. But at least until the 1840s that group remained relatively small, however socially prominent its leaders, and for the most part ineffective—a group confined largely to the states farthest from the South.

Toward the Abyss: The Political Origins of the War

Besides setting the overarching cause for the Peloponnesian War—the growing fear in Sparta of Athenian power—that made war inevitable, Thucydides set out for his readers the tangled course of events that contributed directly to the outbreak of the war in 431 BC, rather than any other year. Thus, to understand the American Civil War one must understand the contributing factors and events the led to *the* Civil War that eventually broke the Confederacy and redefined the relationship between the Federal government and the states—in other words the war that began in April 1861. The rapid expansion of American territory between independence and the outbreak of the Civil War provided the primary points of conflict between free soil and proslavery forces. American constitutional practice saw slavery as falling within the general police powers of individual states; the main questions centered on slavery's status in new territories and states. Did Congress have the authority to prohibit slavery in territories before they achieved statehood? And how would the incorporation of new states affect the sectional balance of power in the Federal system, particularly in the Senate with its equal representation allotted to every state?

Before 1800, Tennessee and Kentucky had joined the Union as slave states, while the admission of Vermont had equalized the number of slave and nonslave states. Then, the Louisiana Purchase made available for settlement a wide span of territory ranging from Louisiana to Montana, but it was the southern portions of that purchase with its climate and soil particularly suitable for cultivation of cotton that attracted those willing to carve plantations out of the wilderness. Meanwhile, the soil and climate of the old Northwest territories (eventually Ohio, Michigan, Indiana, and Illinois), where Congress had prohibited slavery in the territorial phase of organization, attracted farmers from the North's free states as well as from abroad. The Compromise of 1820 seemingly laid to rest the issue of slavery in the western and southern territories for the immediate future. With the exception of Missouri, admitted as a slave state in 1821, largely because its settlers had come up the Mississippi River from the south rather from the east and north, those territories lying north of the line 36°30' were to be free, while those lying to the south would become slave states. Both North and South seemed willing to accept the agreement as a reasonable solution to what, even in 1820, was becoming a troubling issue. For the next two-and-a-half decades Americans got on with the business of continental expansion without too much friction over issues associated with slavery.

The Mexican Cession that resulted from the Mexican War broke the domestic truce between free and slave states, because it once again raised the question of slavery's status in newly acquired territory. Sagacious politicians, North and South, had earlier avoided conflict with Mexico over the newly independent Republic of Texas, rightly fearing that the acquisition of Texas and other Mexican territories would reopen questions that the Missouri Compromise had seemed to resolve. Nevertheless, the sudden death of William Henry Harrison in 1841 led to the presidency of John Tyler, who had been selected by the Whigs as a cynical sop to planter interests in the Whig presidential ticket of 1840—a cynicism that came back to haunt the Whigs, because Tyler proved indifferent to Whig economic policies and defied the party's leadership. Indeed, the leading Whig, Henry Clay, opposed Texas annexation precisely because he feared the consequences of another political debate over slavery in newly acquired American territory. Tyler failed in his bid to build a political base of support independent of both the Whigs and the Democrats, but the winner of the 1844 election, Democrat James K. Polk, set the acquisition of California as one of his top priorities—even if it required war with Mexico.

In Mexico, the young republic found an impediment to expansion more serious than what had previously hindered western expansion. Instead of fragmented Indian tribes bereft of imperial sponsorship, the United States would have to defeat a nation-state army fighting on its own terrain and a government determined to avoid humiliation. Fortunately for American arms, although not for the Union's sectional balance, a newly professionalized officer corps showed its worth in Mexico. It was in Mexico where the post–War of 1812 officer corps, now mostly trained at a reinvigorated and reformed West Point, showed their worth as talented junior officers serving under the stolid Zachary Taylor and the brilliant Winfield Scott. These junior officers would later go on to serve as senior commanders during the Civil War. For example, Grant modeled his military bearing on the bluff and stolid persona of Taylor, while his own triumph at Vicksburg echoed the bold flanking movements of Scott during the Vera Cruz campaign. At the same time, Lee so impressed Scott with his daring reconnaissance missions and intellect that on the eve of the Civil War he would ask Lee to command what would become the Union Army of the Potomac—an offer Lee refused, with fateful consequences. However, Lee's later campaign style would also show some of the boldness exhibited by his former commander.

The quick victories achieved by American arms had all the more importance because of the war's controversial nature at home, especially in the North. Henry David Thoreau would spend a night in jail for refusing to pay taxes that he believed supported the war effort—an act of civil disobedience that would inspire future dissidents both at home and abroad. White Southerners supported the war for obvious reasons, but the strongly expansionist Jacksonians also believed in an economical and limited Federal government, which meant the war had to be won on the cheap. Furthermore, even within the officer corps, especially among Northerners, U. S. Grant was not alone in the sentiment he later reported in his memoirs, that "the war that resulted [was] one of the most unjust wars ever waged by a stronger nation against a weaker nation."[6] Moreover, as he rightly pointed out: "the Southern rebellion was largely the outgrowth of the Mexican War."[7]

Why so? Basically, the war with Mexico upset a delicate political equilibrium between North and South, because slave-holding white Southerners, the most vociferous supporters for the war, had appeared to aim at the creation of a number of slave states out of the territorial gains made at Mexico's expense. Taylor's early victories on the Texas border had made him a household name. Fearful that Taylor might run for president, Polk dispatched Winfield Scott to Mexico to command the Vera Cruz campaign. The ensuing military operations, in which Scott's army took Mexico City and forced the Mexicans to agree to the exorbitant American demands, were even more brilliant than those of Taylor. Scott's victories insured the United States would acquire vast tracks of territory that had hitherto been Mexican.

Even before the passage of the peace treaty with Mexico, Congress had lit the fuse of a furious debate as to whether it should extend slavery to the new territories. Northern resentment at the white South's enthusiastic support for the war boiled into the open—especially since there was increasing suspicion the slave South aimed at using the new territories as a means to tip the sectional balance in its favor. From the territories added to the United States since its creation only one had come in as a free state (Iowa), while Florida, Alabama, Mississippi, Louisiana, Arkansas, and Missouri had been admitted as slave states from the Louisiana Purchase, plus Texas after its annexation in 1845 (the free states admitted during this period had been part of the territory claimed by the United States after the revolution). With the additional territories accruing, the question of slavery in the territories exploded.

On a dark, humid night in early August 1846, an otherwise undistinguished congressman from Pennsylvania, David Wilmot, proposed an amendment to the appropriations bill for the still ongoing war.

His amendment baldly stated "that, as an express and fundamental condition of the acquisition of any territory from the Republic of Mexico . . . neither slavery nor involuntary servitude shall ever exist in any part of said territory."[8] This famous Wilmot Proviso sharply divided the Union among sectional lines, and while the Compromise of 1850 in the end preserved the Union, white Southerners now had more reason to distrust free-soil Northerners. Nevertheless, led by Henry Clay and Daniel Webster, while opposed by a dying John C. Calhoun acting as the dark shade of Christmases yet to come, the Compromise of 1850 slowly came into being. The sudden death of President Zachary Taylor after eating and drinking huge quantities of cherries and chilled milk at the Fourth of July ceremony in Washington helped prevent a confrontation between the South and an aggressive president cut in the Andrew Jackson mold. His successor, Millard Fillmore, a New York political hack, had little stomach for standing up to proslavery partisans. Fillmore was the first of three of the worst presidents the United States has ever endured—all to contribute to the coming catastrophe. The final compromise largely resulted from the efforts of a politician relatively new to the Washington stage, Senator Stephen A. Douglas of Illinois, who by his legislative skills assembled coalitions that passed various provisions of the Compromise of 1850 separately.

Over the Precipice

The Compromise of 1850 admitted California as a state, prohibited the slave trade in the District of Columbia, and enacted a stronger fugitive slave law, while setting no restrictions on slavery in the Utah and New Mexico territories. The compromise seemingly satisfied everyone except radical abolitionists and proslavery Southern nationalists. But the country as a whole, including most white Southerners, welcomed the political settlement with enthusiasm in the belief Congress had achieved a satisfactory compromise over slavery. In fact, the compromise only papered over a dangerous rift that was eating away at the nation's soul.

The fugitive slave law, one of the least controversial items under dispute between Northern and Southern representatives at the time, proved the most disastrous of the Compromise's provisions. It exacerbated negative attitudes toward slavery throughout the North, because its provisions and enforcement rubbed raw salt into sectional wounds. It gave slavery a dark face throughout the North that had not existed before. Here common sense played no role in the slave-holding South's actions and reactions. The most vociferous supporters of the law were the representatives of the deep southern cotton states, which were losing few, if any, slaves, while the numbers of slaves escaping from Virginia, Kentucky, and Missouri each year numbered barely a thousand at most—hardly a threat to the institution.

Within a year of the compromise, Northerners viewed spectacles such as the one in Boston, where 300 US marshals and soldiers marched a single runaway slave from the courthouse to the Boston Navy Yard, that institution guarded by a further 250 soldiers, so the government could ship the runaway back to bondage. What such an assemblage of governmental power underlined was that Northerners were now willing to threaten with force those trying to enforce the laws of the United States regarding slavery. Through all of this Fillmore provided support for the fugitive slave law to include mobilizing the power of the Federal government. Fillmore's successor, Franklin Pierce, proved willing to go further in appeasing white Southerners in rigorously enforcing the Fugitive Slave Act. In March 1854, he sent the marines, cavalry, artillery, and a revenue cutter to hold and then ship a single escaped slave back to bondage, even though his owner was willing to sell the individual to Northern abolitionists, who then planned to set him free. Only with the flight of virtually all escaped slaves from their Northern refuges to Canada did the furor over the law begin to subside in the mid-1850s.

Nevertheless, in 1852 the tensions of sectional strife widened. Perhaps the most influential novel in American history exploded on the political scene. Harriet Beecher Stowe's *Uncle Tom's Cabin*, whatever its inaccuracies, focused on the human face of slavery. It depicted a world of callousness, cruelty, and unregenerate evil, all reflective of much of the harsh reality of slavery. Within a year it had sold over 300,000 copies in the United States alone, a runaway best seller. With considerable justification, Lincoln was to greet Stowe at a reception during the war as the woman whose book had started the war. Not surprisingly, most white Southerners were outraged not only at the novel's exaggerations, but also at its truths. However, they were helpless, except to ban the novel throughout the South.

Equally important was Douglas's political error in contributing to the destruction of the Missouri Compromise of 1820, which opened up the Kansas-Nebraska territory to troubles that verged on civil war. In the early 1850s, the senator from Illinois had amassed a considerable fortune from real estate dealings in the building of the Chicago to Mobile railroad. In 1852 he set in motion efforts to organize the Nebraska territory as the first step toward building the transcontinental railroad. To do so he needed the support of a powerful cabal of Southern senators. Their price was high: the overturning of the Missouri Compromise. By dividing the Kansas-Nebraska territory and repealing the ban on slavery above 36°30', Douglas's Southern allies hoped to set the stage for Missouri slave owners to make Kansas a slave state. Douglas became their willing ally. In January 1854 he, the "F Street Mess," as his Southern allies called themselves, and Jefferson Davis, the administration's secretary of war, cajoled a dubious but weak president into supporting a bill that would allow slavery above 36°30' in spite of the objections of most of the cabinet. Pierce thereby proved himself almost completely under the control of the proslavery partisans. In the end, only stringent application of Democratic Party discipline in the two houses of Congress pushed the bill through. But in doing so, Douglas and his friends destroyed the Whig Party and opened the way for the creation of the Republican Party, a party far more antithetical to the slave-holding South and its interests. Moreover, they unleashed anger in the North at what most Northerners saw as a duplicitous political deal.

Immediate payback came in the fall congressional elections: the Democratic Party lost seventy House seats in the North. For the short term, the Know-Nothing Party, which advocated opposition to America's new immigrants and especially Catholics, were the gainers, but in the long run the Republicans would benefit most from the Democratic Party's collapse and the disappearance of the Whigs in the North. Abraham Lincoln succinctly characterized what the Know-Nothings stood for: "As a nation, we began by declaring that '*all men are equal.*' We now practically read it 'all men are equal, *except negroes.*' When the Know-Nothings get control, it will read 'all men are created equal, except *negroes and foreigners, and catholics.*'"[9]

If Douglas's miscalculations had a serious impact on American politics, they resulted in a virtual civil war in Kansas. Free-soilers and proslavery elements contested the establishment of a territorial government with outright violence. The proslavery faction fell back on using Missouri slave owners and their supporters to tip the electoral balance in their favor. Moreover, the territorial governors appointed by Washington found the ground cut out from underneath them by the insipid, weak Pierce. The first governor, Andrew Reeder, a firm supporter of slavery, found himself appalled by the electoral shenanigans of proslavery elements in Kansas. Within less than a year Pierce replaced Reeder with Wilson Shannon, whom the president ordered to support the sham proslavery legislature. By fall 1855 the territory was on the brink of violent conflict between contending factions, which Shannon prevented from turning into a civil war only by strenuous efforts.

But the confrontational nature of politics in Kansas soon spilled over into national politics. In May 1856 Senator Charles Sumner of Massachusetts gave an intemperate speech, titled "The Crime against Kansas," in which he denounced not only what was happening in Kansas, but also personally attacked a number of Southern politicians. Two days later Preston S. Brooks, a representative from South Carolina, viciously assaulted Sumner with his cane in a cowardly attack against the senator, who, seated at his desk, could not rise to defend himself. It was not so much the attack on Sumner that outraged Northerners, but rather the intemperate and delighted commendations that Brooks received from white Southerners. The *Richmond Examiner*'s comments were all too typical of the Southern response: "when caned for cowardly vituperation, [Sumner] falls to the floor an inanimate lump of incarnate cowardice."[10]

The episode also starkly highlighted the growing cultural rift between North and South. While even by the Southern code of honor, Brooks had gone too far (a point forgotten by his partisans), part of the confrontation stemmed from Sumner's principled opposition to dueling—a practice that survived in the South, in part due to its agrarian values (although even there it had its critics, particularly among evangelicals). For proslavery white Southerners, Sumner represented a dangerous breed of radical moral extremism, willing to slander Southern gentlemen but also unwilling to answer the gentleman's obligation to answer for his actions on a dueling field with honor. For Northerners, Brooks represented an un-Christian form of barbarism where men settled their disputes with violence and tainted the concept of honor with undisciplined rage—and most dangerously, in Sumner's caning, they saw a "slave power" that viewed Northern white men not as a freeborn fellow Americans, but as slaves to be flogged.

Not all Northern opponents of slavery held themselves to a nonviolent standard, however. In Kansas a ferocious and slightly crazed abolitionist, John Brown, replied to Sumner's caning by kidnaping and then murdering with a broadsword five proslavery settlers. Violence beget violence. Disgusted at the Pierce administration's unwillingness to enforce the laws of the United States in Kansas, much less provide him the support he needed, Shannon resigned as territorial governor in August 1856. Recognizing that, if some order were not brought to the conflict in Kansas, the Republicans would elect John C. Frémont as the next president, Pierce appointed a new governor, John W. Geary, and provided him with sufficient backing to quell the troubles for a time.

The election of 1856 turned on Kansas and the lack of familiarity most Northerners had for the new Republican Party. It involved a three-cornered race involving Frémont, the retread Fillmore, and James Buchanan. The last rightly gained the title of "Old Public Functionary," for he had held a large number of federal positions: congressman, senator, diplomat, secretary of state, none with particular distinction.[11] That fact was what made him attractive to many of his countrymen, North as well as South. He won the slave states solidly and enough states in the North and border states to win the election handily. If Fillmore and Pierce had proven inept, indecisive, and incompetent during their terms, Buchanan fully lived up to their standards. But he also displayed a penchant to play hardball politics in pursuit of appeasement while seeking to provide every advantage to proslavery partisans. By its political ineptness and proslavery maneuvers his presidency ensured war would come in spring 1861.

Early in Buchanan's administration, the Supreme Court rendered its decision in the Dred Scott case—a case involving a slave whose master, an army surgeon, had taken him north from Missouri to Illinois and eventually into the Wisconsin territory, both of which banned slavery. Scott sued for his freedom, and by 1856 the case had ended up in Washington before the Supreme Court. The justices might have determined the case on narrow grounds and refused to consider the controversial issues of whether a black man had the right to redress before federal courts or, more importantly, whether Congress in the Missouri Compromise of 1820 had possessed the legal right to bar slavery in the territories. However, the chief justice, Roger Taney, along with a majority of justices, issued a comprehensive ruling representing extraordinary judicial interference in legislative and political matters. Buchanan seconded Taney's efforts by bringing improper influence to bear on one of the two Northern justices, so that the court's opinion, written by Taney, had a Northern supporter as well as five Southern justices.

Taney's opinion not only denied slaves the right to sue but also argued that even freed blacks were not citizens and thus possessed no rights under the Constitution. Not surprisingly, Taney also denied Congress the right to legislate on the matter of slavery in the territories. In every respect, the ruling represented judicial arrogance combined with political ineptitude—a ruling that deliberately misconstrued the actual words of the Constitution. As Lincoln warned, the Supreme Court's decision represented the opening round in what might have been further pronouncements by the Taney court that *Northern* states did not have the right to free slaves brought by their masters within their territorial jurisdiction.

Some historians have argued that the Dred Scott decision represented an effort of statesmanship to remove slavery from the political arena. The foremost historian of the case, however, notes: "Taney's opinion, carefully read, proves to be a work of unmitigated partisanship, polemical in spirit though judicial in its language, and more like an ultimatum than a formula for national accommodation."[12] That was certainly how proslavery white Southerners saw it. The *Constitutionalist* of Augusta, Georgia, commented that "Southern opinion upon the subject of southern slavery . . . is now the supreme law of the land . . . and opposition to southern opinion upon this subject is now opposition to the Constitution, and morally treason against the Government."[13] Yet as was the case with so many of the slave-holding South's political "triumphs" before the war, this judicial "victory" also proved pyrrhic.

If Taney and Buchanan had believed the Dred Scott decision would settle the matter of slavery, reaction throughout the North should have disabused them. But no matter how angry Northern opinion might have been, the Taney decision was now the law of the land. Meanwhile, events in Kansas continued to feed Northern anger. Like his predecessor, Geary arrived in Kansas sympathetic to the proslavery side and antithetical to Free Soilers. Yet angered at a lack of support from Washington and infuriated at the dishonesty and criminal behavior of the proslavery cabal, Geary resigned his position in March 1857. He eventually became a Republican and then a Union general. Buchanan replaced Geary with a Mississippian, Robert J. Walker. Unfortunately for the president, Walker also proved a man of integrity, a quality for which the president had little use. Nevertheless, the proslavery supporters in Kansas put together a constitution—the Lecompton Constitution—which not only protected slavery but also prohibited any amendments for the next seven years.

Walker then denounced the Lecompton effort and the frauds accompanying its creation, but almost immediately found the ground cut from beneath him, as Buchanan buckled under proslavery pressure. In early February 1858, the president, ignoring the advice of his representative in the state, sent the Lecompton Constitution to Congress and urged the admission of Kansas as a slave state. Moreover, without reference to the voters in Kansas, Buchanan announced by virtue of the Dred Scott decision that "Kansas is therefore at this moment as much a slave state as Georgia or South Carolina."[14] As with the crisis of 1854, the supporters of the Lecompton Constitution confronted the need to cobble together a coalition of white Southerners and Northern Democrats in Congress to railroad Kansas into the union as a slave state. But this time there was one important difference. Stephen Douglas recognized that his political future in the North depended on his opposing the administration on Lecompton. Buchanan explicitly warned Douglas in a face-to-face confrontation that he would make the Illinois senator pay, if he failed to support the constitution. Only by the strongest measures could the administration persuade the Senate to vote favorably on admitting Kansas as a slave state. However, the measure then failed in the House of Representatives. Not surprisingly, Buchanan and his Southern friends would not deny themselves their revenge on Douglas, when it came time to nominate the Democratic Party's candidate for president in 1860.

While Douglas successfully held on to his senate seat against Abraham Lincoln in the fall election of 1858, he returned to Washington to discover that Buchanan's supporters in the Senate had removed him from his chairmanship of the committee on territories. In 1860, as the Democratic Party's nominating convention approached, he confronted the unforgiving Democrats of the South, who had the president's full support. The president used his powers of patronage to woo Northern democrats away from Douglas, and the combination of Southern anger and the president's actions not only denied the Illinois senator the nomination of a united Democratic Party but also sabotaged his chances of gaining the South's electoral votes. The result of these efforts facilitated Lincoln's election as the first Republican president of the United States, a spark that fired the tinder of civil war.

The last years of the old compact among the states passed with ever-darkening clouds. Efforts by Northerners to pass legislation, such as a transcontinental railroad, a Homestead Act, and a Land Grant College Act failed due to the virulent opposition of Southern representatives or, in the case of the last measure, ran into a presidential veto. These acts added to the growing sense of frustration in the North that led its citizens in 1860 to vote into power an administration that would have no truck with the further appeasement of the slave South. Added to their antagonism to Buchanan's presidency was the fact that his administration proved one of the more corrupt in American history. In 1860 a House committee revealed the extent of that corruption, a fact to which the Republicans gave maximum publicity during the presidential campaign.

Then another major crisis presaged the coming maelstrom—John Brown's inept raid on Harper's Ferry in October 1859. Leading eighteen blacks and whites into Harper's Ferry, which possessed little access to the slave-owning areas of the South, Brown and his accomplices seized the arsenal, their first victim a black watchman. But their hopes of sparking a servile revolution were entirely misguided, and Frederick Douglass himself had counseled Brown against such a foolhardy gesture. Nor were there any escape routes for the raiders or any slaves who might have joined them. Within a day those raiders, whom the local militia, with the support of a small group of marines, led by Colonel Robert E. Lee and Lieutenant Jeb Stuart, had not killed, were in the hands of the authorities. Two months later the Commonwealth of Virginia tried and hanged Brown after a trial in which the authorities allowed Brown to express his views on slavery. Among the witnesses to his execution were a young actor, John Wilkes Booth; the future Confederate general, Thomas Jackson; and the radical agitator and pro-secessionist Virginian, Edmund Ruffin. The representatives of the Commonwealth of Virginia hanged expeditiously the rest of the participants in the Harper's Ferry fiasco shortly thereafter.

But while Brown's life had been one of failure, violence, and miscalculation, his conduct at his trial and during his execution was so exceptional that even the governor of Virginia, Henry Wise, could not help but admire his captive's conduct. Brown's words at his trial were to find an ever-deepening response on the part of Northerners: "Now, if it is deemed necessary that I should forfeit my life for the furtherance of the ends of justice, and mingle my blood further with the blood of my children [one of Brown's sons had been killed in the raid on Harper's Ferry] and with the blood of millions in this slave country, whose rights are disregarded by wicked, cruel and unjust enactments, I say let it be done."[15] In the North, the initial reaction to Brown's raid had been one of bemusement, if not outright hostility, but within a few months many declared him a martyr. Henry David Thoreau put it in the following terms: "The momentary charge at Balaclava, in obedience to a blundering command, proving what a perfect machine the soldier is, has, properly enough, been celebrated by a poet laureate; but the steady, and for the most part successful, charge of this man [Brown], for some years, against the legions of Slavery, in obedience to an infinitely higher command, is as much more memorable than that as an intelligent and conscientious man is superior to a machine. Do you think that that will go unsung"?[16]

The willingness of the pacific Thoreau, later hero to Martin Luther King Jr and Mahatma Gandhi, to endorse a figure like Brown showed how far many Northerners were now willing to go to oppose the "slave power." However, Thoreau's remarks also highlight his long-standing distaste for the regimented world of military organizations—associated in his view with slavery—and the hostility of the most enthusiastic antislavery advocates toward military professionalism would foretell serious civil-military conflicts in the North during the Civil War.

For white Southerners, Brown represented proof of a dangerous Northern radicalism that aimed to foment slave insurrection, threatening the physical security of every white man, woman, and child in the slave South. They heard with trepidation Brown's dark words, handed in a note to a guard on the day of his execution, where he foresaw the price that expunging slavery would entail: "I John Brown am now quite *certain* that the crimes of this *guilty land*: will never be purged *away*; but with Blood. I had *as I now think*: vainly flattered myself without *very much* bloodshed; it might be done."[17]

The Election of 1860

The final hammering of nails into the old Union's coffin began with the national convention of the Democratic Party, held in Charleston, South Carolina. The majority of Southern delegates aimed at denying Douglas the nomination as punishment for his failure to support the Lecompton Constitution and the admission of Kansas as a slave state. By his actions Douglas had proven that as president he would be neither a Fillmore nor a Pierce, much less a Buchanan in the future appeasement of the slave-holding South. A number of Northern Democrats, enthusiastically supported by the mean-spirited president, furthered Southern efforts to deny Douglas the nomination in a raucous convention. Intermingled with those of obdurate and shorted-sighted views were a group of secessionists who deliberately aimed at sundering the Democratic Party and bringing about a Republican victory in the upcoming election. To accomplish their goal of denying Douglas the support of a united Democratic Party, these Southern radicals pushed for a slave code for the territories in the party's platform that would prevent either Congress or a territorial legislature from forbidding a slave owner from taking his human property into territories controlled by the United States. Support for such a provision would have guaranteed the Democratic Party's defeat in most Northern states in the election.

But that was precisely what Southern radicals hoped to achieve. They believed that election of a Republican would immediately lead to the secession of the Southern states—an aim many of them had worked assiduously for over the course of the previous decade. Moreover, they demanded that the Democratic Party pronounce that slavery was justified and its expansion should be encouraged. The end result was that the Charleston convention failed to nominate anyone, and the Democratic Party broke irrevocably apart. In the words of historian Allan Nevins, "The bright smiles and handclappings which Charleston ladies bestowed upon the receding delegates were applause for an irrevocable step toward war; the bouquets which they brought next day to fill the empty seats of the seceders were symbolic of the flowers soon to be cast upon multitudinous Southern graves."[18]

Thus, there was to be a Northern candidate of the Democratic Party, Douglas, nominated by a rump convention of Northern Democrats in Baltimore and a Southern Democratic candidate, John C. Breckinridge, Buchanan's vice president. If that were not sufficient to insure the election of a Republican president in the fall, a new party, the Constitutional Union Party, largely consisting of moderates from the border states, nominated John Bell on a platform that had as its foremost aim the removal of sectional disputes from the national debate—by this point a hopeless dream.

The question then was who was to be the Republican Party's nomination. The leading candidate was William Seward from upstate New York, who had at the time held a reputation as an antislavery radical for describing the sectional conflict as "irrepressible." There were other potential candidates, each with substantial drawbacks. The foremost was Abraham Lincoln, a dark horse with substantial support throughout the old Northwest (Indiana, Illinois, Wisconsin, Iowa, and Minnesota). He had emerged as a national figure in his run for senator against Stephen Douglas, a race Lincoln had narrowly lost. But his eloquence during his debates with Douglas had burnished his image. In that effort he had calmly, but thoroughly, attacked the idea of further appeasement of the slave-holding South. Nevertheless, Lincoln also made clear that he had no intention of interfering with the continuation of slavery in those states where it currently existed, which suggested that he, instead of Seward or Salmon Chase of Ohio, might prove more acceptable to those in the North afraid of confrontation with the "slave power."

Lincoln enjoyed a number of advantages at the Republican convention. It was taking place in Chicago, his home ground, where his managers packed the galleries. Perhaps his greatest advantage lay in the tendency of his opponents to underestimate his extraordinary intelligence—a factor exacerbated by his gawky appearance, his emergence from the backwoods of Kentucky, and his almost total lack of formal education. Moreover, the politicians who ran his nomination and campaign did an extraordinary job in lining up support in Lincoln's march to the nomination, which he achieved on the third ballot. Thereafter, Lincoln sat in his house in Springfield, Illinois, as was the custom for an age that believed politicians should mask their ambition, while others ran his campaign throughout the North and what is today known as the Midwest. Douglas desperately attempted to pull support from the South, but the presence of Breckinridge and Bell in the race split the Democratic vote and doomed his candidacy. The great danger was that Lincoln would not achieve a majority of electoral votes, which would throw the election into the House.

In November 1860 the American people spoke. Lincoln won all of the electoral votes in the North with the exception of three from New Jersey. His total of 180 was well over the 152 needed for a clear majority. He totaled 54 percent of the popular vote north of the Mason-Dixon Line. The North had thrown down an electoral challenge. Charles Francis Adams, the direct descendant of two presidents, noted: "The great revolution has actually taken place. . . . The country has once and for all thrown off the domination of the Slaveholders."[19]

On 20 December, the slave-holding Deep South replied with its counterrevolution. On that day by a vote of 169 to 0 the convention called by the South Carolinian legislature passed the ordinance of secession separating their state from the United States. Within a matter of two months, Georgia, Florida, Alabama, Mississippi, Louisiana, and Texas had joined the Palmetto State in declaring their independence. In February 1861 the representatives of those states approved a new constitution, one which explicitly placed slavery at the center of its framework. That document, largely copied from the old Federal Constitution, did limit the president of the nascent state to a single, six-year term. On 18 February 1861, in Montgomery, Alabama, Jefferson Davis, West Point graduate, veteran of the Mexican War, former secretary of war, and US senator from Mississippi, took the oath of provisional president to head the Confederate States of America.

Southern revolutionaries had now responded to the Northern political challenge by throwing down an armored gauntlet. In a speech to the assembled multitudes in Montgomery upon his arrival in the Alabama capital on 16 February, Davis made clear that his expectations were for war. "If war should come, if we must again baptize in blood the principles for which our fathers bled in the Revolution, we shall show that we are not degenerate sons, but will redeem the pledges they gave, preserve the rights they transmitted to us, and prove that Southern valor still shines as bright as in the days of '76—in 1812, and in every other conflict."[20] It remained to be seen whether the North would accept the challenge.

Conclusion

The storm now burst with Lincoln's election. All too many Americans, particularly in the American South, and later in the North, had delightedly courted the confrontation. They might have remembered with profit the chilling words of the Spartan king, Archidamus, in the days immediately before the outbreak of the Peloponnesian War: "Spartans, in the course of my life I have taken part in many wars, and I see among you people of the same age I am. They and I have had experience, and so are not likely to share in what may be a general enthusiasm for war, nor to think that war is a good thing or a safe thing."[21] And that was precisely the problem: few in either the South or North had experience in a real war, much less a war of length and ferocity. Thus, in terms of violent sectional political conflict, it seemed that war might bring an end to what appeared to be insoluble political troubles. How far removed Americans were from the realities of *civil war* would soon be clear in the ferocious battles and conduct of the campaigns that had crossed the South's landscape by 1865.

One must count the deep fears of the slave-holding South and the aggressive manifestation of those fears as the primary factor in the outbreak of war. Added to that fear was a strongly held belief in the institution of slavery—to the point where some white Southerners were advocating not only outlawing the practice of manumission but were also urging the expulsion or enslavement of the entire population of free blacks. Moreover, many in the South were urging the renewal of the slave trade and further territorial expansion in the Caribbean and Latin America, actions that would have inevitably aroused the opposition of the British, who had taken a firm moral position as early as the Napoleonic Wars to outlaw this vicious international trade in human beings.

The *Richmond Examiner* summed up the attitude of most white Southerners toward slavery: "It is all an hallucination to suppose that we are ever going to get rid of slavery, or that it will ever be desirable to do so. It is a thing we cannot do without; that is righteous, profitable, and permanent, and that belongs to Southern society as inherently, intrinsically, and durably as the white race itself. Southern men should act as if the canopy of heaven were inscribed with a covenant, in letters of fire, that the negro is here, and here forever—is our property, and ours forever—is never to be emancipated—is to be kept at hard work and in rigid subjection all his days."[22]

Individuals as well as great themes and issues determine the course of history. Here the actions of presidents Fillmore, Pierce, and particularly Buchanan contributed enormously to the crisis of 1861. Their intellectual dishonesty, political ineptness, and pusillanimity all serve to rank them among the worst presidents in American history. They were aided and abetted by those in the South, who fiercely defended slavery. The Fugitive Slave Act, the Lecompton Constitution, the caning of Sumner, and the general demeanor of Southern politics slowly but steadily poisoned the national polity. By 1860 a majority in the North had had enough. While many of those who voted for Lincoln did not believe war to be inevitable, they were now willing to take the risk. They had reached the point of the German proverb: "Better a terrible end, than endless terror."

What is indeed astonishing and yet not surprising was the refusal of proslavery white Southerners to recognize that by seceding from the Union, they were in effect placing themselves in a dangerous situation. Almost as soon as the Southern senators and congressmen had returned to their states after secession, the lame duck Congress and its successor passed virtually all of the acts Southern representatives had been sabotaging over the past decade—such as the Homestead Act, the transcontinental railroad, the Land Grant College Act, and higher tariffs. Moreover, Congress proceeded to admit Kansas as a free state on 29 January 1861. These factors would inevitably have contributed to a North that would have continued in its growth and power to overawe the Confederacy, had the separation so devotedly desired by secessionists come about peacefully. Alternatively, the great danger that some like William Tecumseh Sherman saw was that, if the South separated from the Union, other states would split away, thus creating a group of fractious republics that would have engaged in constant conflict. In the antebellum period, the "Old Army" had spent most of its time policing a chronically chaotic frontier, filled with Indians, freebooting whites, and even filibusters fomenting trouble with the Union's neighbors, ranging from Canada to Mexico. The tenuous Federal authority they represented might have been irrevocably weakened by secession, leading to further political fragmentation in North America.

Finally, a hostile North would never have agreed to enforce the Fugitive Slave Act, while the North's very existence as a nation where there was no slavery would have served as a beacon of hope to slaves seeking to escape their bondage. And most important, war itself was to act as a disruptive and violent agent, which by its nature would inevitably damage the institution of slavery—a lesson Confederates should have learned from the Revolution. Most newly minted

Confederates could see none of this as they joyously hurtled off the cliff. All they could perceive was a few short, decisive victories over the cowardly, slum-dwelling soldiers of the North, led by their greedy, uncultured capitalists. Few of them were willing to see the wisdom in Spartan king Archidamus's warning that war "is not a good thing or a safe thing."[23]

CHAPTER 2

The War's Strategic Framework

And war is not so much a matter of armaments as of the money [and the resources] which make armaments effective: particularly is this true in a war fought between a land power and a sea power. So let us first of all see to our finances and, until we have done so, avoid being swept away by speeches.

—Thucydides, *The History of the Peloponnesian War*

The North can make a steam-engine, locomotive, or railway car; hardly a yard of cloth or shoes can you make. You are rushing into war with one of the most powerful, ingeniously mechanical and determined people on earth—right at your doors. You are bound to fail. Only in your spirit and determination are you prepared for war. In all else you are totally unprepared, with a bad cause to start with. . . . If your people would but stop and think, they must see that in the end you will surely fail.

—William T. Sherman (Simpson and Berlin, *Sherman's Civil War*)

The Industrial Revolution had begun in Britain in the last decades of the eighteenth century. The use of steam power to perform tasks which for the most part only the muscle power of men and animals had hitherto performed, represented a revolutionary break with the past. As James Watt, eighteenth-century inventor and capitalist, suggested to a potential buyer: "I sell, Sir, what all the world desires to have—power."[1] That revolution's economic consequences provided Britain with the financial clout to support the great coalitions, which finally defeated the Napoleonic empire in the great battles between 1813 and 1815. However, in the first decades of the nineteenth century, the Industrial Revolution had yet to significantly influence the armaments of the opposing sides, and thus, the tactics and the conduct of military campaigns. Nevertheless, the war showed the importance of financial resources, as British economic strength helped overwhelm Napoleon's potent mix of military genius and nationalist enthusiasm.

Indeed, the economic fruits of Britain's Industrial Revolution contributed to the coming of the Civil War, because the wealth the American South gained from providing cotton to hungry English textile mills in Lancashire provided much of the self-confidence and wealth that made secession possible. Some overconfident Confederates even believed that "King Cotton" would force Britain to intervene on their behalf, lest the British economy starve in the absence of Southern cotton. What they instead discovered was that Britain's dynamic economy would make it resistant to such crude coercion, and that the economic dynamism of a North engaged in its own process of industrialization would eventually doom the Confederate war effort. However, while the Confederacy eventually found its material resources wanting, it mobilized an especially potent nationalism that traced its origins to both the American and French revolutions.

The American Revolution had shown both the world and Confederates a model for building a new nation based on an idea, but the French Revolution's mass mobilization of an entire nation had greater military significance for the American Civil War. Confronted with an invasion of Austrian and Prussian armies and by the collapse of the French Army with the flight of its noble officers, the French National Assembly in 1792 had shrilly declared a *levée en masse* in terms recalling the days of Republican Rome: "From this moment, until our enemies have been driven from the territory of the Republic, the entire French nation is permanently called to the colors. The young men will go into battle; married men will forge weapons and transport supplies; women will make tents and uniforms, and serve in the hospitals; children will make old cloth into bandages; old men will have themselves carried into the public squares to rouse the courage of the warriors and preach hatred of kings, and the unity of the Republic."[2]

The imposition of the *levée*, however, was anything but quaint, as the ancien régimes of Europe soon discovered. France could now deploy far greater armies than had been the case before 1789. Moreover, those armies could suffer enormous casualties and still continue fighting, which had never been the case with the armies of the ancien régime. The ancien régime armies depended on highly trained, and therefore difficult to replace, soldiers. The result was a spectacular alteration of the political and military framework within which Europeans had conducted war over the past century and a half. As the military theorist Carl von Clausewitz noted, "Suddenly war again became the business of the people—a people of thirty millions, all of whom considered themselves to be citizens. . . . The people became a participant in war; instead of government and armies as heretofore, the full weight of the nation was thrown into the balance. The resources and efforts now available for use surpassed all conventional limits; nothing now impeded the vigor with which war could be waged, and consequently the opponents of France faced the utmost peril."[3]

It was not until the ancien régimes of Prussia, Austria, and Russia adapted to the French approach and mobilized their population and resources that Napoleon's enemies could defeat the Corsican ogre. In 1805 and 1806 Napoleon had not only destroyed his opponents militarily in his victories at Austerlitz and Jena-Auerstedt but had also obliterated their political will to continue the struggle. But in 1813 a series of great battlefield victories, Bautzen, Lutzen, and Dresden, all won in decisive fashion by the French emperor, commanding an army reconstituted after the Russian campaign, no longer sufficed against opponents who possessed massive, new-style armies mobilized from their whole populations and backed financially by the wealth of Britain's Industrial Revolution. As a result, what mattered most in the last years of the Napoleonic Wars was the number of troops the powers could put in the field. By 1813–14, the Allies—Austria, Russia, Prussia, Sweden, and Britain—could deploy far greater numbers in the field than could Napoleon's French Empire fighting alone. "Not until statesmen had at last perceived the nature of the forces that had emerged in France, and had grasped that new political conditions now obtained in Europe, could they foresee the broad effect all this would have on war; and only in that way could they appreciate the scale of the means that would have to be employed."[4] Napoleon is reputed to have once said that God was on the side with the biggest battalions. By the time of the Civil War, he was on the side with the greatest resources as well.

In 1861, unknown to the contesting sides in the Civil War, these two revolutionary currents—popular mobilization and the effects of the Industrial Revolution—would collide and combine across a continent. In time that combination would significantly increase the lethality of the battlefield and at the same time enable the Union and the Confederacy to mobilize their populations and resources to meet the demands of a war that would take place over vast distances. Therein lay the greatest strategic problems confronting the North during the war, which it would not satisfactorily solve until 1864. The great strategic question was how would the Union not only raise great armies but then also project and support those armies over the continent-sized distances of the American South against a white population firmly in support of secession? And how could the North organize the *logistical capabilities* necessary to make such a strategy possible? Thus, military operations over continental distances presented difficulties that no one in America, or Europe for that matter, could have conceived of, much less addressed in 1861. Nearly three long years elapsed before Union forces could find solutions to the problems raised by that strategic framework.

Much of the problem of why it took the North with its greater population and industrial resources so long to defeat the Confederacy lies in the spatial distance over which its military forces had to conduct operations. In European terms the distance from central Georgia to northern Virginia was approximately the distance from Tilsit in East Prussia to Moscow. The distance from Baton Rouge to northern Virginia is almost equal to that from central Germany to Moscow. Napoleon's one attempt to operate at such distances, his invasion of Russia in 1812, had collapsed in failure. Furthermore, neither Napoleon nor his opponents had faced as an opponent a unified nation-state that controlled the human and material resources of a continental-sized land mass.

Exacerbating the challenge of distance was the fact that primeval wilderness covered substantial portions of the South, particularly in the west. Nor was there anything that resembled a reasonable road system throughout much of the South's vast area. The Union general Philip Sheridan, who accompanied the Prussian high command for the key period of the Franco-Prussian War, noted the vivid contrast between the modern, macadamized road systems of France and the primitive road system even in Virginia, over which his troops had to march during the Civil War. Moreover, while the Eastern theater was relatively close to the centers of Northern industrial power, the starting point in the west for Union armies—Cairo, Illinois—was nearly a thousand miles from the North's main industrial centers.

Railroads could alleviate some of the difficulties the miserable state of the road system posed, but unlike rivers, they remained vulnerable to Confederate raiding parties and required major efforts to protect them as well as to rebuild them. In the west the Mississippi, Ohio,

Cumberland, and Tennessee Rivers provided access to nearly all of Tennessee and Kentucky, as well as parts of northern Alabama and Mississippi, or at least the parts that mattered. For its part, the great Mississippi River controlled a vast swath of territory, and its storied place in American history as the "Father of Waters" made its possession an important psychological marker of Federal progress. In the long run, the steam engines that powered railroad trains and the steamboats that cruised not only the South's coasts but also its rivers would prove to be the crucial enabler of the North's victory, because they shrank the tyranny of distance.

Nevertheless, Northern armies could only take advantage of the fruits of industrialization if they could develop the military organizations necessary to convert industrial capacity into combat power. Both the Union and Confederacy had to create military institutions capable of waging war on a truly continental scale, but the Union had the additional burdens of waging a war of conquest against a Southern white population willing to see one in five men of military age perish. By the end of the war, highly motivated, battle-hardened Confederate veterans fighting behind entrenched positions would present tactical challenges to the Federal war effort that only inspired operational and strategic leadership could overcome. While the ragtag armies of ill-trained volunteers the opposing sides put in the field in 1861 resembled the enthusiastic but green armies of Revolutionary France in 1792, the hard survivors who fought the battles of 1864 and 1865 foreshadowed the Western Front of 1914 and 1915.

Before the war the American military had constructed no sophisticated mechanisms or systems of lessons-learned analyses to enable successful adaptation, because of a fear of standing armies, and the technological changes of the railroad, steamboats, telegraph, and mass production represented such new aspects of combat effectiveness that they overwhelmed the institutions that did exist. Thus, to paraphrase General James Mattis, USMC, ret., battlefield adaptation was inevitably a matter of "winging it" and "filling body bags as [the opposing sides] sorted out what work[ed]."[5] Worse yet, the hoary myths of the Revolutionary War framed the American view of war in both the North and South, myths in which untrained Minutemen had bested the trained professionals of the British Army. Institutional reforms before the Mexican War had inculcated some degree of military expertise into the regular army's officer corps, who then faced Mexicans even

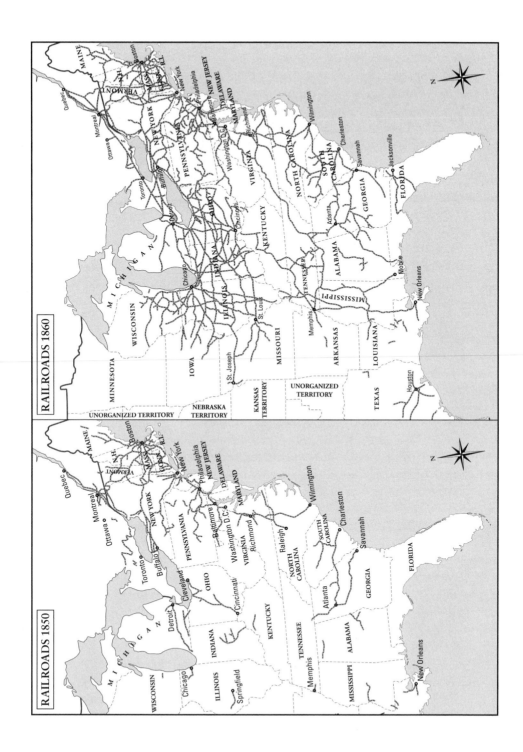

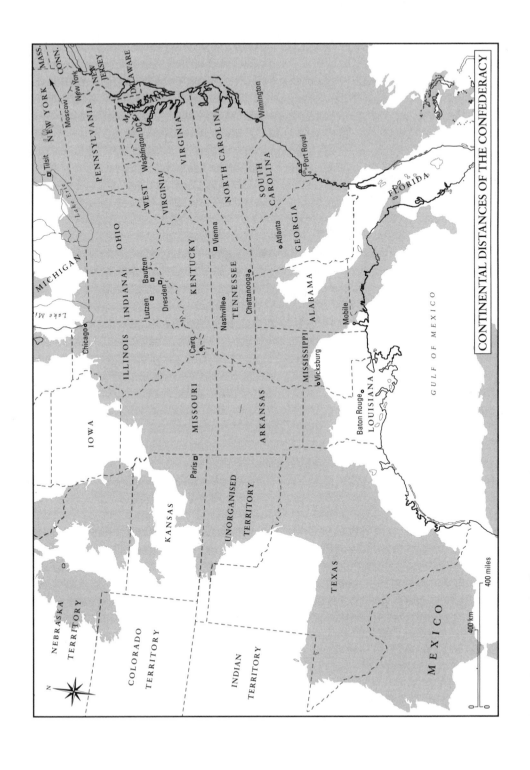

CONTINENTAL DISTANCES OF THE CONFEDERACY

less professional and prepared for war than the victorious Americans. The possession of a trained cadre of officers, most educated at West Point, had provided the American armies with a substantial advantage. Nevertheless, the relatively small size of the forces required to defeat the Mexicans and the limited logistic support required in that conflict misled both sides in 1861 as to the complexity of the tasks they would face in the Civil War.

Still, in place of the few large-scale wars in North America—the French and Indian War being the first and the American Revolution being the second—the Napoleonic Wars influenced most of what passed for thinking about military affairs in the United States. The collapse of Austria and Prussia in the immediate aftermath of the emperor's stunning victories at Austerlitz (1805) and Jena-Auerstedt (1806) exercised a profound influence over European and, hence, American thinking. In fact, the search for a Napoleonic "decisive" victory has bedeviled politicians and generals down to the present, as recently as Operation Iraqi Freedom. In reality, the mobilization of whole populations as well as the nation's resources, even in the last years of Napoleonic warfare, had rendered the search for a decisive, swift victory an illusory quest. But the politicians and generals who led the opposing sides in the Civil War could not see this. Thus, their belief in and their search for a climactic battlefield decision marked their expectations of military operations—a search only exacerbated by a general underestimation of the enemy. It certainly marked Jefferson Davis's view of the war and his understanding of strategy throughout the conflict. Grant clung to the belief that a decisive victory would suffice to defeat the Confederacy until the Battle of Shiloh disabused him of that notion. As has been the case of most major wars since 1807, the Civil War turned into a war of attrition, one in which victory rested on which side could take the most punishment and remain standing at the end.

A Net Assessment of the Opposing Sides

THE ECONOMIC AND POPULATION BALANCE

Simply in terms of contending populations, the North possessed an obvious and important advantage, which would be amplified the longer the war lasted. The population of the North in 1860 was approximately 23,000,000, while that of the South was barely 9,000,000, nearly 40 percent of whom were slaves. Initially, slaves benefited the Confederate war effort, because they could bear much of the burden of farm work, while the white men went off to war. But the longer the war lasted and the farther Northern forces advanced into the South, the more slaves became a wasting asset, if not an advantage, to the Union, because of the valuable intelligence and, by war's end, direct military service, they provided Federal forces. Of course, what really mattered was the quality of manpower available to the opposing sides, and here there was little to differentiate the raw material from which the contending sides would make their armies. Northerners were not all city boys who had never fired a weapon as many white Southerners believed. In fact, most lived on farms or in small villages, just as their Confederate opponents did.

The North's greatest advantage in the coming struggle lay in the explosion of industrial and agricultural growth that had occurred between 1820 and 1860 throughout the northern and midwestern states—an explosion which fueled, and which in turn was fueled by, the Industrial Revolution. Accompanying the transportation revolution on land was one of equal importance in terms of the arrival of the steamboat as the primary means not only for riverine traffic—of huge importance for the United States—but for oceanic travel as well. And finally, the invention of the telegraph allowed for an unprecedented ability to coordinate transportation capabilities in support of military forces.

The greatest change in the American landscape, since the beginning of the nineteenth century, lay in what some historians have termed the *transportation revolution*. By 1850 the United States possessed nearly 10,000 miles of railroads. Over the course of the next ten years, the trackage across the expanses east of the Mississippi increased three-fold to slightly over 30,000 miles, much of that located in the North. The rapid expansion of railroads tied the northeast and Midwest into an economic whole. By 1860 three major routes linked the East Coast to Chicago, while another reached all the way to St. Louis. Moreover, a number of smaller routes connected major and middle-sized cities throughout the North and Midwest with lines that stretched all the way to Iowa, Wisconsin, and the border of Minnesota. While one might think that the river system west of the Alleghenies, with the Ohio, Cumberland, Tennessee, and Mississippi Rivers, might have favored transportation by water rather than land, low water in summer and ice in winter made railroads a more reliable and thus more attractive means for the transshipment of the vast produce of Midwest farmers to eastern and international markets. Thus, Chicago, with its position on Lake Michigan and its proximity to the great farming lands to its west, south, and north, became a burgeoning city.

Accompanying the transportation revolution was the development of the telegraph. In May 1844, the inventor and painter Samuel Morse and his partners sent a message from the US capitol to Baltimore. The simple message—"what hath God wrought"—represented a revolution in communications every bit as important as the railroad and steamship were for transport. The first commercial use of the telegraph in 1851 coordinated the movement of trains between different sections of line. By the end of the decade telegraph lines helped coordinate increasing railroad traffic that moved people and goods between cities and countryside, especially in the North. Furthermore, the telegraph launched a communications revolution on which the increasing reach and sophistication of newspapers and magazines depended. Throughout the war newspaper readers could read accounts of battles within a matter of days of their happening—a factor of political importance almost entirely new to the conduct of war by states.

The antebellum South fully participated in these transportation and communication revolutions. The ever-expanding railroad network opened up lands far removed from river transportation to plantation agriculture and increased the profitability of cotton cultivation. Unlike the North, Southern railroads also made extensive use of slave labor, which when combined with expanding cotton production drove the market price of slaves to new highs. Indeed, the president of the Mississippi Central Railroad could even claim in 1855 "that in ease of management, in economy of maintenance, in certainty of execution of work—in amount of labor performed—in absence of [the] disturbance of riotous outbreaks, the slave is preferable to free labor, and far better adapted to the construction of railways in the south."[6] Telegraph lines also followed the expanding Southern railroad network, allowing the future states of the Confederacy to participate fully in the vibrant newspaper culture of antebellum America. Southern planters also looked outward and saw themselves as a cosmopolitan-minded group worthy of standing on the international stage as a legitimate nation-state. Not only did they see themselves as part of a larger planter class based in the Western Hemisphere, they also maintained links to European banking houses based in London, Paris, and Frankfurt. Indeed, European investors held many of the public and private bonds that funded railroad construction throughout the South.[7]

The Confederacy's impressive railroad net and deep links with a larger global economy centered on England should disabuse us of the notion that the new nation was a primitive backwater, but the South's economy remained focused on the production of an agricultural staple—cotton. As a consequence, unlike the North, the Confederacy had little domestic industrial capacity to produce the complex machinery associated with railroads and steamboats. For Confederates, as one politician boldly announced, cotton was king. As a result, Southern railroad infrastructure and equipment went into a steady, irrevocable decline from the minute the war began, because the Confederacy had so little manufacturing capacity and what little there was had to support Southern armies in the field. Ironically, 25 percent of the Confederacy's iron production went to the construction of ironclads—a disastrous mistake given the general failure of the Confederate navy to make use of such vessels. That iron could have been put to far better use repairing the South's railroads. In contrast, the North would steadily improve and expand its infrastructure of railroads as well as the equipment on which its transportation system depended in spite of the pressures of war.

Furthermore, Northern industrial superiority provided the Union with a massive superiority in naval power. Not only did this provide the North with the naval resources necessary to impose a gradually constricting blockade on the Confederacy, it also provided the innovative brown-water fleets in the West that helped enable the success of the Union's most efficient field armies. Despite an impressive and at times heroic Confederate effort at naval improvisation, the near complete absence of a domestic manufacturing base and limited maritime traditions placed the Confederate cause at a severe disadvantage in a crucial area of military power. While geography limited Father Neptune's reach, even railroads could not come close to matching the efficiency by which military power could move via water, due to the inherent physics of waterborne transportation. Like the Spartans, the Confederates looked to third parties for naval succor. However, while the diplomatic interests of the Persians would cause them to provide Sparta with the naval power it needed to defeat Athens, the Confederates would find no such assistance from the British. In contrast, as with the Athenians, Union dominance at sea gave Federal arms a flexibility and reach that made possible (but did not make inevitable) its eventual victory.

Moreover, railroads and steamships represented only the most obvious manifestation of the North's advantage in industrial strength. It possessed over 100,000 factories compared to fewer than 20,000 in the South. There was also a considerable difference in scale between those establishments. More than ten times the number of industrial workers filled the factories in the North, and as soon as the war broke out that economic advantage substantially increased as most Southern white men quickly found themselves in uniform. The factories in New York State alone produced more than twice the total industrial production of the South, Pennsylvania produced twice as much, and the little state of Massachusetts produced 60 percent of Southern output. The North thus possessed far more manufacturing potential to produce military necessities such as armaments, clothing, and uniforms. Nevertheless, the Union would still have to translate material potential into actual military power. And that would prove to be no easy task.

Equally important, farming in the North was more up to date with widespread use of fertilizers and farming machinery, like the Mc-Cormick reaper, which significantly improved productive capacity per acre. While the Industrial Revolution had yet to provide direct power to farm machinery, the production of no less than 233,000 reapers during the war years increased Northern food production enormously. Moreover, a number of other pieces of machinery came into use, all the product of Northern industry. As one state's board of agriculture noted: "without drills, corn-planters, reapers and mowers, horse rakes, hay elevators, and threshing machines, it would have been impossible to have seeded and gathered the crops of 1863 with the implements in use forty or fifty years ago."[8]

At the same time an inflow of immigrants and easterners moving west created 430,000 new farms and added 2,700,000 acres of land to production. The development of new methods of agriculture served to maximize the yield of some of the richest soil in the world, providing unprecedented bounty. Economically, agriculture lay at the heart of the North's wealth. The total dollar value of its agricultural production was greater than that of the South's cotton—the difference being that much of that production was for internal use throughout the Midwest and Northern states. Nevertheless, export markets for American grain added to Northern prosperity, and access to the railroads and the passage through the Great Lakes was of crucial importance to the development of the Midwest, as was passage down the Mississippi River. All of this figured in the political and strategic calculations of Union leaders, particularly Lincoln, early in the war.

However, in terms of what could eventually be transformed into military power, manufacturing provided the North with its greatest advantage. In 1850 the South had possessed only 18 percent of the nation's manufacturing capabilities, and half of that was in the border states, which found themselves increasingly interconnected with the North. In the decade before the outbreak of the Civil War, investments in manufacturing in the United States increased nearly 90 percent—from $533,200,000 to $1,009,000,000—again virtually all in the North. Moreover, a substantial portion of the gold from California undergirded the North's explosive growth in industry. Nor should one discount the fact that American inventiveness, which the Constitution had encouraged with its provision for the patenting of inventions, led to manufacturing and transportation innovations that placed the North's manufacturers on a par with, and in some cases ahead of, European competition.

Further aiding the extraordinary increase in manufacturing and agricultural wealth in the United States was a flood of immigrants who populated the cities, towns, and farms of the nonslave states. In the 1830s nearly 600,000 immigrants had arrived on America's shores, but that was merely a harbinger. In the 1840s immigration, driven by the potato famine in Ireland and the failed revolutions of central Europe in 1848 and 1849, almost tripled to 1,713,251. Numbers of immigrants again rose in the 1850s to over two and a half million. Even during the worst years of the Civil War, the flood of immigrants abated only slightly. Significantly, nearly all went to the North—Europe's poor drawn by the jobs and opportunities of that region's rapidly expanding cities and factories, while relatively more prosperous immigrants from Germany, Scandinavia, and Central Europe chose the North because of their distaste for slavery.

The bottom line was that although the South was first and foremost a slave society, we should not see the Confederacy as an agrarian throwback to some earlier feudal era, even though former Confederates after the war took refuge in such a romanticized and bucolic vision to explain their bitter defeat. Instead, before and during the war, Confederates fully participated in many of the revolutions of the mid-nineteenth century associated with the rise of the modern world. White Southerners saw themselves as part of the forward momentum of history, and this inspired much of the confidence they associated with their cause. Some of that confidence proved mistaken—for example, the belief of some Confederates that their control over cotton could coerce Britain into intervention on their behalf—but some of it was rooted in material fact, and the ability of the Confederacy to sustain a long and prolonged war effort simply does not square with the idea of a feudal and agrarian "Old South."

Nevertheless, for all their outward confidence, like the Spartans, the Confederates recognized both the strengths and weaknesses of slavery at the root of their social order, but unlike the Spartans, Confederates had to contend with a rising tide of antislavery sentiment on both sides of the Atlantic. By creating an independent nation, they hoped to continue the antebellum project of modernizing slavery and fending off a dreaded servile insurrection similar to the Haitian Revolution, and potentially presaged in Nat Turner's revolt and John Brown's raid. Like other nationalist movements in Europe—such as those of the Italians, Greeks, Irish, and Poles—they put their trust not in the material forces of industrialization but in moral and psychological forces rooted in a potent sense of national identity. They wagered that, like the Americans of the Revolutionary War era, or the Italians who fought the Austrians, the strength of their moral commitment to Confederate nationhood would trump their opponents' material superiority. In the end, they underestimated the combined power of Northerners' moral commitment to the idea of Union and their more plentiful material resources. Nevertheless, the Confederacy came close enough to victory that we should never dismiss its defeat as economically predetermined.

THE MILITARY PROBLEM

The sheer military amateurism both contending sides brought to the battlefield at the start of the war exacerbated the challenges posed by American geography and by newly industrialized technology. Isolated by two great oceans, the United States required minimal military forces from its birth in 1788 through 1861. In 1860 a constabulary force of a little over 16,000 officers and men sufficed to maintain Federal control over hostile Indian tribes and disorderly white settlers on the western frontier. Only the Mexican War provided American military officers any experience with major military operations, and almost all of the Civil War's generals had only served in subordinate roles as junior officers in that earlier conflict. Indeed, the most gifted commander of that war—Winfield Scott—was now too old to take the field.

The official reports of the secretary of war in the first years of the conflict underline the problem the opposing sides faced in creating vast armies with such a miniscule training cadre. In April 1861 Lincoln issued his proclamation calling for 75,000 volunteers. Two years later, with an army that was approaching 1,000,000 in strength, the War Department reported that over the course of 1862 it had procured: 1,577 field, siege, and seacoast cannons, with carriages, caissons, and other implements; 1,082,841 muskets and rifles for foot soldiers; 282,389 carbines and pistols for mounted troops; 1,251,995 cannon balls and shells; 48,719,862 pounds of lead and lead bullets; 1,435,046 cartridges for artillery; 259,022,216 cartridges for small arms; 347,276,400 percussion caps; 3,925,369 friction primers; 5,764,768 pounds of gun powder; 919,676 sets of accouterments for men; 94,639 sets of equipment for cavalry horses; and 3,281 sets of artillery harnesses.

Those figures suggest the extent of the North's mobilization of its manpower and resources to fight the war, and why confusion and inexperience better explain the War Department's early floundering in procuring uniforms and equipment in the required quantities, rather than incompetence or corruption, although those two perennial aspects of human behavior certainly contributed to the difficulties. Matters in the South proceeded even less smoothly, given the weaknesses of its industrial and manufacturing base. Nevertheless, the Confederacy's logistical apparatus drew on the same antebellum US Army models, which had procured, organized, and transported the supplies required by the army's far-flung detachments across the frontier and along the seacoasts. The Mexican War had already proven the worth of the US Army's administrative apparatus, and the experience added to a base of knowledge that would prove invaluable to both sides of the sectional conflict, and which would help solidify the importance of West Point–trained officers to both newly organized armies. Nevertheless, whatever their antebellum sophistication, Civil War logisticians faced an unprecedented task in both the Union and the Confederacy.

At the start of the Civil War most of the army's officers were graduates of West Point, which had been built on one of the key geographic features of the Revolutionary War. However, Sylvanus Thayer, the crucial figure in West Point's early history who had shaped the curriculum that produced the Civil War's generals, had seen military engineering as identical to military science, and part of West Point's social support stemmed from the civil engineering expertise it produced, as opposed to a rigorous form of military professionalism. While the academy produced the best-trained engineers of antebellum America, it neglected other crucial subjects such as military history and strategy. And while its disciplinary regime produced obedient junior officers well versed in tactics up to the regimental level, such a restrictive environment was not necessarily conducive to innovation and risk taking. Indeed, while Lee had excelled as a cadet and as a Civil War general, Sherman had rebelled to some degree against the Thayer system, while Grant found the whole experience tedious and uninspiring. As he dryly noted in his memoirs, a year at the academy "still seemed about five times as long as Ohio years."[9]

Although the American military establishment boasted a secretary of war and a commanding general, in reality it possessed little sense of what we understand today as serious military professionalism. There was no real staff. No systematic program of professional military education existed beyond West Point, much less a real understanding of strategy and operational execution. The Swiss thinker Baron d'Jomini had written a number of treatises on war, but few officers had bothered to read his writings. Even fewer had examined the more obscure writings of Carl von Clausewitz. The pedantic soldier Henry Halleck had drawn on Jomini's ideas for his own derivative treatise on strategy, but his writings had little influence, and he himself proved a mediocre general. In other words, nearly everyone on both sides, including those with experience in the regular army, were rank amateurs in the business to come, and almost everything above the level of regimental operations, including operational and logistical planning, deploying large forces in combat, and the complex staff work required to run large armies, had to be learned from the ground up on the battlefield.

At the small unit level, West Point and service in the regular army imparted useful military knowledge to the republic's officers. Certainly the improved performance of the army in the Mexican War, compared to its egregious incompetence in the War of 1812, reflected an increased professionalization. Furthermore, the Old Army acquired a real facility for constabulary operations on the frontier where it maintained a crucial measure of order among various groups prone to violence, including Indian tribes, white settlers, and extralegal American filibusters, who aimed at overthrowing foreign governments in direct opposition to the republic's foreign policy. Nevertheless, peacetime service could not help but exercise a deadening hand on much of the officer corps, many of whom turned to drink or fractious behavior to escape the bureaucracy and discipline. General Alpheus Williams, not a graduate of West Point, graphically described the prewar army in the following terms: "At least fifteen years as a clerk in an army bureau or on duty at a frontier post as a lieutenant to a command of a dozen men, where there are no books, no drill, no military duty, nothing but a vast amount of whiskey drinking, card playing, and terrific profane swearing; and where as a consequence, men forgot in a year or so all they could learn in four years, and acquire habits of the most indolent, unambitious, and dissolute kind."[10]

Both sides thus faced the major challenge of turning the raw material of manpower and resources into military power. Given the size of the armies and American traditions of decentralized governance as well as the complex problems associated with a massive mobilization, with which the Federal government much less the Confederacy was in no fashion prepared to deal, it was inevitable that the individual states would play a considerable role in the processes of mobilization. In a theoretical world, if the North's leaders understood that they were confronting a long-drawn-out conflict, it might have been possible to focus the Union's mobilization on the regular army. But in the real world, Northern leaders possessed neither the foresight nor the ability to build up a truly national army. Such a task would have required time and patience, as American experience in two world wars underlined, and the North's population possessed neither.

Northern public demanded action against the Confederate states immediately, and any hesitation would have inevitably raised serious political difficulties. The Confederacy confronted the same problem in a slightly different form. With a war for its independence a distinct possibility, it needed to form military forces as quickly as possible. Since both sides underestimated their opponents, a quick mobilization organized in large part by state governors seemed reasonable for military as well as political reasons. As with so much Civil War history the process of raising and maintaining volunteer regiments appears messy, inefficient, and at times even corrupt, especially from the point of view of the twenty-first century. Nevertheless, our view misses the latent strength of a fractious political culture, the very disorderliness of which reflected a democratically dispersed but powerful level of popular commitment.

THE SOLDIERS

At the most fundamental level, the problem was how to create effective military organizations out of nothing. Both sections indulged in harsh stereotypes of each other; Northerners believed the Confederacy a feudal society dominated by planters who overawed degraded poor whites. Many Northerners (including Lincoln at the war's start) believed those poor whites to be closet Unionists—a delusion Lincoln would discard forthwith as events progressed. Confederates saw Northern troops as mudsills, the dregs of Yankee slums, as opposed to their supposed yeoman farmer class raised around weapons and led by an honor-bound plantation gentry. In fact, city boys make just as competent soldiers as those from the countryside. Who can doubt that the tough Irish kids from the slums of New York and Boston who formed the Irish brigade could fight just as hard as farm boys from the Shenandoah Valley. While more urbanized than the Confederacy, 80 percent of the North's population still lived on farms or in small villages. Regardless of their mutual misconceptions, the Civil War bit most deeply of all the wars Americans have fought, and given the casualties, it took an extraordinary commitment on the part of both sides' rank and file to see the war through to its end. Furthermore, Americans' self-organizing impulses, so well immortalized by Alexis de Tocqueville before the war, combined with the rough professional scaffolding created by the antebellum US Army's West Point–trained professionals to put in the field disciplined effective military forces on a scale never before seen in North America.

Despite the broadly similar raw material that made up both section's military forces, each of the major field armies deployed in their different theaters developed peculiar and substantially different subcultures, even among their separate forces. The Army of the Potomac was renowned for its spit and polish in sharp contrast to the generally casual, if not downright sloppy, appearance of the Union's Western armies. The less well-supplied Confederates also could not afford any resemblance to the "looking good" formations of Europe. One observer of the soldiers in Sherman's army group in his campaign through Georgia into South Carolina noted: "Strange, rough-looking, unshaven, and badly dressed: they seem like a gang of coal-heavers, when compared with the trim and snug fellows here [Union troops already in Beaufort, South Carolina], who have nothing to do but guard-duty with white gloves. These western marauders came trooping through the streets, roaring out songs and jokes, making sharp comments on all the tidy civilians, and over-flowing with merriment and good-nature. Their clothes were patched like Scripture—Joseph's. Hats without rims, hats without crowns, some with no hats at all."[11]

More importantly, different armies developed different command cultures and temperaments, especially when a general with a strong personality commanded an army during its crucial formative phase and imparted his own persona and values onto the organization. For example, in George B. McClellan's Army of the Potomac, the general's cautious and engineering-oriented temperament discouraged improvisation and initiative among subordinate commanders, leading to a cautious and even passive style of command. In contrast, Ulysses S. Grant's "style of command, characterized by a steady promotion of gifted leaders who also exhibited loyalty and the ability to work as a team, became a hallmark of the Army of the Tennessee's top command," which in turn encouraged a culture of proactive initiative among subordinates in that important Union army.[12] Robert E. Lee remade the Confederacy's most effective military organization, the Army of Northern Virginia, in his own image during and after the Seven Days battles. Lee built an aggressive mindset among his subordinates to seize opportunities by offensive military action. In contrast, the war's most woeful army, the Confederate Army of Tennessee, possessed a command culture marked by bitter infighting and internal dysfunction, reflecting in many ways the personality and temperament of its most important commander, Braxton Bragg.

Finally, what started off as the Union's Army of the Ohio and then became the Army of the Cumberland had inauspicious origins in the failed command of Don Carlos Buell. While Buell was not able to imprint his style on the army as had McClellan, so badly riven was its command structure that Brigadier General Jefferson Davis (no relation to the Confederate president) in the fall of 1862 murdered his fractious superior, Major General William Nelson—and found defenders among his colleagues. He eventually commanded a corps in Sherman's March to the Sea. Buell's successor, William Rosecrans, inspired such dissension that a subordinate obeyed a clearly erroneous order out of mere spite at Chickamauga, contributing directly to the Union defeat in that battle. This hard-luck army finally found a competent leader in George H. Thomas, but both Grant and Sherman would still find the army sluggish and insufficiently aggressive. The Army of the Cumberland's checkered history showed that a strong sense of solidarity and mutual trust was vital during an army's early history and that such could not be inculcated in its leadership late in the game.

Returning to the war's first year, only volunteers composed the armies, with the Confederacy introducing conscription in 1862 followed by the Union a year later. For virtually the first time in history, these were literate armies. Even the majority of the privates, no matter how bad their spelling or atrocious their grammar, could express their ideas and experiences in letters back home or in diaries. As Gary Gallagher and James McPherson have underlined, the Northern armies taken as a whole bore a deep ideological commitment to the cause of the Union, as best seen in a reenlistment rate of close to 60 percent for those battle-hardened Union soldiers whose three-year enlistments expired in 1864. While the Confederacy relied on conscription and so never faced a reenlistment problem, the fact remains that one in five Southern white men of military age perished in the war. No other soldiers in American history could match the commitment of both the Union and Confederate rank and file.

As one Northern soldier commented in a letter to his brother in January 1863 during the darkest days the Army of the Potomac was to experience: "Though my nightly prayer is for peace, yet 'tis for an honorable peace. I would rather live a soldier for life. Yes! Rather see this country made a mighty sepulcher in which should be buried our institutions, our nationality, our flag and every American that today lives, than that our Republic should be divided into little *nothings* by an inglorious and shameful peace."[13] Some Confederates breathed defiance as late as 1865; one South Carolinian woman from its planter aristocracy even boldly told Union officers who pointed to all the destruction Union forces inflicted on her state that it "would make us more determined & drive every man into the field with feelings more embittered & intense than ever."[14] For the authors, the Vietnamese general Võ Nguyên Giáp best encapsulated the extent of a similar kind of commitment in a passionate soliloquy he delivered on the French Revolution in reply to a question about how he felt about his nation that a Vietnamese American interviewer posed. It was clear that he was willing to live up to John F. Kennedy's challenge that the American people should "bear any burden, pay any price" and believed his countrymen should as well. That was certainly the level of commitment of the great majority of Union and Confederate soldiers throughout the conflict.

Civil War soldiers, however competent on the battlefield, never became automats. To the end of the conflict they remained citizen-soldiers, obedient to officers when it mattered, contemptuous of military pedants, and at times dangerously disobedient when pushed too far by officers who thought their troops should behave like European regulars. Nevertheless, whatever their appearance, one should not for a moment think that the disciplining of Civil War soldiers was in any fashion soft or lackadaisical or that they were not subject to ruthless discipline by their officers. Stonewall Jackson inflicted draconian punishments on deserters and stragglers throughout his campaign in the Shenandoah Valley in 1862. Grant's description of "a bit of regular army discipline" to bring his first command, the 21st Illinois, around indicates methods that would make modern-day drill sergeants shudder. For the most part, discipline aimed at providing the glue required for the actual business of war: the long tough marches essential to military campaigns, the dull wearisome duties of camp and training, and above all the ferocious days of what Civil War soldiers referred to as "seeing the elephant"—combat.

From today's perspective, Civil War soldiers were exceptionally hardy. Admittedly, the bringing together of large numbers of young men reared in the relative isolation of farming communities resulted in the spread of disease that decimated whole regiments at the war's outbreak. The primitive state of the era's medical science exacerbated problems, and roughly two-thirds of the war's fatalities resulted not from battle, but from disease. But once the initial wave of sickness and death had passed, soldiers on both sides proved extraordinarily tough. They were capable of long marches on wretched dirt roads, turned to mud by driving rain or stifling dust by relentless heat, or extraordinary physical labor to build fortifications and other vital military infrastructure, all while subsisting on rations largely consisting of hard tack (an unappetizing cracker used as a substitute for bread) and salted meat.

By present standards, Civil War medicine was primitive. Louis Pasteur's work had yet to discover the existence of germs, so there was no sterilization of instruments or wounds. A Confederate doctor, who practiced medicine until the end of the century, noted that had he known about medicine what he learned after the war, he could have saved hundreds of thousands of lives. Nevertheless, doctors at least knew of anesthetics such as ether. At the beginning of the war surgeons argued the question of whether anesthetics harmed patients, because they interfered with the processes of shock, or whether they helped the patient survive the pain. By the midpoint of the conflict, doctors no longer doubted that anesthetics represented a major help in keeping the wounded alive, especially during amputations.

Moreover, wartime experience significantly advanced the art of surgery so that by 1864 surgeons could attempt unprecedented operations. Doctors saved Joshua Chamberlain's life in 1864, when they repaired a wound that had damaged his bladder, one of the first successful operations of this type in history—an operation successful enough to keep him alive until 1914 despite constant infection. As for the terrible wounds inflicted by minié balls on the human frame, there was little doctors could do except ease the patient's dying. For wounds on the extremities, minié balls inevitably did so much damage that even today amputation would be the only choice. By the end of the war, scientific medicine had appeared in the medical units supporting the armies, replacing an appalling lack of medical organization and support at the start of the war in both armies.

Leadership

Perhaps the wisest and most quoted of Clausewitz's aphorisms is that war is "a continuation of political activity by other means."[15] Thus, political and strategic direction represent the most important element in the conduct of war. In a multivolume study on military effectiveness in the first half of this century, Allan Millett and one of the authors of this volume commented that, "it is more important to make correct decisions at the political and strategic level than it is at the operational or tactical level. Mistakes in operations and tactics can be corrected, but political and strategic mistakes live forever."[16] Here in the long run lay one of the North's greatest advantages. As a political leader and strategist, Abraham Lincoln earned his reputation as the greatest of all American presidents—a man who restored the Union without in the end destroying the compact that the Founding Fathers had made. To again quote Clausewitz, "Everything in strategy is very simple, but that does not mean that everything is very easy . . . [G]reat strength of character, as well as great lucidity and firmness of mind, is required in order to follow through steadily, to carry out the plan, and not to be thrown off course by thousands of diversions."[17] What Lincoln had in the political and strategic realms was an ability to focus on the essential political aim, for which he and the North were fighting the war, no matter how dim the course might appear, and then, follow that aim to the end whatever the difficulties.

Ungainly, extraordinarily ugly, not only a self-made man, but a self-educated one, and a man of the frontier with little polish or sophistication, Lincoln appeared to have few of the qualities the crisis of secession and civil war demanded. But beneath the surface, the president possessed intelligence, common sense, an eloquence as striking as it was straightforward, and political acuity. Perhaps his most important quality lay in his willingness to endure the insults of others without blinking. Nor was Lincoln upset when most who met him underestimated his abilities. In fact, he turned their condescension to his advantage. Early in 1862, when it had become apparent that Simon Cameron, the secretary of war, was making a hash of the North's mobilization, Lincoln without hesitation fired Cameron and appointed Edwin Stanton to the post despite the fact that the lawyer had egregiously insulted the future president in the McCormick reaper trial in Cincinnati in the late 1850s. To Lincoln that past mattered not a wit, if Stanton could bring order to the War Department. He did and in the process became one the president's most loyal supporters.

Nothing better underlines Lincoln's political acumen than his selections for positions in his cabinet. He simply chose all of his major rivals for the Republican nomination, predating by a century Lyndon Johnson's comment that it was better to have George Ball inside the tent pissing out, than on the outside pissing in. Moreover, Lincoln tolerated considerable dissension within his cabinet. William Seward, Lincoln's secretary of state, caused great difficulties during the Fort Sumter crisis by pursuing a course diametrically opposed to the president's. Nevertheless, Seward was invaluable for the North's foreign policy as well as for his political connections. He stayed. Salmon Chase consistently told everyone who would listen, particularly radical Republicans, that he was more suited for the presidency than Lincoln. But Chase proved invaluable in keeping the North's financial affairs on an even keel. Lincoln eventually nominated Chase to be the Chief Justice of the Supreme Court after he had left the cabinet in July 1864 to replace Roger Taney, after that wretched wreck from the past died that October.

American mythology pictures Lincoln as some sort of long-suffering saint. Admittedly, he had his troubles—a somewhat difficult marriage, the devastating death of a young son during the war, a deep sense of the cost the war was inflicting on the common people of the North. Yet underneath the exterior of a joke-telling midwesterner was a hard man, a man willing to see the struggle through to its terrible conclusion. Above all, Lincoln aimed at preserving the Union, what he so aptly termed "the last, best hope of mankind." To do so, he was willing to let slavery alone where it already existed, if necessary; to abolish slavery, if necessary; to preserve peacetime constitutional protections, if possible; and to maintain the struggle by ruthless measures such as the suspension of habeas corpus, if necessary. Thrust into the maw of civil war, Lincoln grappled with the vexatious issues war raised. Revealingly, in the early days of his presidency, he asked the Library of Congress to send over the most important books on war in its catalog. He was never too proud to learn. Throughout the war the president navigated the shoals of wartime leadership and politics, always observant, always sharp, and always learning.

In almost every respect his opponent, Jefferson Davis, was the opposite. Davis's background ought to have been ideal for the position he assumed as president of the Confederacy. He had an impressive combat record during the Mexican War, a successful tenure as a reformist secretary of war, and extensive experience as a politician in Congress. However, he bore the great defect of a fractious, quarrelsome personality. The Confederate president never admitted to a mistake or forgave what he considered a wrong or an insult, no matter how trivial. In the prewar period, a comment Davis made to a fellow representative in the House upon receiving a proposal that each support the other's proposed water improvements suggests much about his personality: "Sir, I make no terms. I accept no compromises. If when I ask for an appropriation, the object shall be shown to be proper and the expenditure constitutional, I defy the gentleman, for his conscience's sake, to vote against it. If it shall appear to him otherwise, then I expect his opposition, and only ask that it shall be directly, fairly, and openly exerted. The case shall be presented on its single merit; on that I wish to stand or fall. . . . I abhor and reject all interested combinations."[18] The British soldier and military theorist J.F.C. Fuller best summed up Davis's personality: "Davis, artificial, autocratic, and forever standing on the pedestal of his own conceit. A man of little humour, who could dictate, but who would not argue or listen, who could read but who could not penetrate deeply. Logical, inflexible, inhuman, a man who scorned advice, for he could not tolerate either assistance or opposition."[19] Not surprisingly, Davis soon acquired a host of political enemies not only among the politicians in Richmond but also the state governors, upon whose cooperation and goodwill so much of the Confederacy's war effort would depend. Equally disastrous to the Confederacy's fortunes was Davis's penchant for making enemies among his senior military leaders, with the notable exceptions of Robert E. Lee and Braxton Bragg.

How the two presidents judged and picked the commanders of their armies suggests much about their relative competence. Here, the Confederacy should have enjoyed every advantage, for as a West Point graduate and former secretary of war, Davis had worked closely with the antebellum army's senior officers. But after some initial success, Davis proved far less competent in choosing his senior commanders than Lincoln. A number of his appointments proved disastrous. Here, Braxton Bragg, John Pemberton, and John Bell Hood spring to mind. Compared to Davis, Lincoln knew little about military affairs and nothing about the regular army's officer corps. Like Davis, he underestimated the complexity and difficulty of the coming war. Thus, he had no choice but to accept what the regular army and the North's political system initially threw up in terms of military leaders. Thereafter, Lincoln's common sense and ability to judge people resulted in a slow but steady improvement in the leadership of Union armies, especially in the Western theater, where Grant, Sherman, Sheridan, Thomas, and McPherson would emerge by the end of 1863. But even the leadership of that strange military organization, the Army of the Potomac, would show improvement by the war's last year.

The War's Geography

The eleven states that made up the Confederate States of America controlled a vast expanse of territory, some of it accessible to invasion, other portions of it offering a nightmarish terrain covered by mountains, swamps, and broken up by rivers. In total, those eleven states consisted of approximately 780,000 square miles, although much of the lands lying to the west of the Mississippi were fated to play a relatively small role in the war. In comparison Britain today occupies only 80,823 square miles. Moreover, the area encompassed by the Confederate states is greater than the territories of Britain, France, Spain, Germany, and Italy combined. Throughout the territory the Confederate states claimed in 1861, primeval wilderness remained interspersed among the ground settlers had cleared for farming, plantations, towns, and villages. Running from northeast to southwest, the chain of the Appalachians separated the coastal settlements of the first English settlers from the great inland expanses of North America. Only in the years following the American Revolution had that dam broken, and a flood of immigrants and Americans seeking their fortune moved west to turn the land east of the Mississippi River into relatively settled country. In the 1840s and 1850s, even as the land between the Appalachians and the Mississippi was blossoming into America's heartland, pioneers were pushing west across the river to create the states of Texas, Arkansas, Missouri, Iowa, and Minnesota.

To a considerable extent the barrier of the Appalachians divided the Confederacy into the two main theaters of war: the first, the Eastern theater, consisted of Virginia, Maryland, and Pennsylvania; the second, the Western theater, consisted initially of the Mississippi River and the states of Missouri, Kentucky, and Tennessee. Eventually Union military operations would move past the initial battlegrounds in the west into Mississippi, Alabama, and Georgia. But there was also a third theater of operations, the lengthy coasts of the Confederacy and their associated seaports. The length of that coast was to provide the blockading ships of the Union Navy with a nightmarish problem in shutting down innumerable blockade-runners, which brought desperately needed supplies to the hard-pressed armies of the Confederacy.

The choice of Richmond as the Confederate capital provided the Eastern theater of operations an initial pride of place that it retained in the writing of the war's history for nearly a century. Nevertheless, whatever Richmond's prominence as the capital and political symbol, there were other reasons why the state of Virginia became the war's first battleground. Politically that state's leaders had been at the heart of both the American Revolution and the effort to build a lasting government in the writing of the Constitution. Moreover, the fact that Washington lay so close to Virginia also inevitably made Richmond, with its defending Confederate armies, a Union military objective for the simple need to protect the nation's capital. The Union could not possibly allow Confederate armies to remain near Washington for political as well as military reasons. Richmond's great Tredegar Iron Works, the most important center for the manufacture of arms and ammunition in the Confederacy, also gave the state and city an importance beyond that of the symbolic. Moreover, Richmond was seemingly within easy range of the primitive armies the Union put into the field in 1861.

Nevertheless, Virginia's geography presented a number of problems to the conduct of operations. Its rivers, actually mostly large streams and creeks, ran from west to east. Thus, they provided little help to the movement of armies from north to south or to their logistical support. In addition, running from the southern to the northern part of the state and then across the Potomac into Maryland and Pennsylvania, the Blue Ridge Mountains separated the Shenandoah Valley from the rest of Virginia. That Valley provided a wonderful shield not only for Confederate military operations against Union armies in the central and northern parts of the state but also for a thrice-used invasion route into the north—the most famous leading to the Battle of Gettysburg in 1863. The other states along the Atlantic coast—North Carolina, South Carolina, and Georgia—all presented similar difficulties of terrain. The rivers also ran from west to east and offered little access to the interior. The miserable state of the road system only added to the difficulties of movement throughout the eastern Confederacy. The state governments in the east had done little to improve the north–south roads, because riverine traffic and railroads could move agricultural products to ports on the coast. Finally, forts, built at considerable cost by the Federal government, protected these Confederate outlets to the Atlantic.

West of the Appalachians lay an entirely different topography. There, great river systems, all of which drained into the Mississippi and its basin, created a land of enormous fertility, providing unheard-of agricultural wealth to the states in the area, north as well as south. East of the Mississippi three major rivers, the Ohio, the Cumberland, and the Tennessee, ran westward from the Appalachians. These rivers were far larger than eastern rivers and therefore navigable for considerable distances. The Ohio provided a highway for the movement of Northern military power, armies as well as supplies, from the midwestern states to the battlefront. As such it augmented and extended the strengths of the North's modern railroad system. To its south, the Cumberland allowed those who held it access to as well as control over Nashville, central Tennessee, and virtually the whole state of Kentucky. Finally, the Tennessee provided navigation all the way to Muscle Shoals in northeastern Alabama. Possession of these rivers would eventually provide the North control over Kentucky and Tennessee and create the base for Union forces to move deep into Mississippi, Alabama, and Georgia.

Early in the war, the great prize in the west appeared to be the Mississippi River. For the North, and particularly the farmers of the Middle West, it was of crucial importance for the movement of agricultural products to foreign markets. For the Confederacy, control over the lower Mississippi represented the vital connection to states on the other side of the river—namely, Louisiana, Texas, and Arkansas. But beyond the political significance of that connection, the western states of the Confederacy provided important foodstuffs, particularly cattle, to feed its armies fighting in northern Mississippi and Tennessee. The key piece of terrain that kept the lower Mississippi in the hands of the Confederacy for the first two years of the war was the town of Vicksburg, Mississippi. Its bluffs dominated and thus controlled movement on the river. Much like West Point's geography during the Revolutionary War, Vicksburg and its surrounding terrain allowed those who held it to dominate the river that ran past it. General "Gentleman Johnny" Burgoyne's invasion of the Hudson River Valley from Canada had aimed at seizing West Point and splitting New England off from the other colonies. British strategy failed, because the British never managed to capture and hold that key piece of terrain and strike a blow at both the physical and psychological integrity of the American nation-in-waiting. Now in the Civil War, Vicksburg held a similar strategic value to the invader, whatever the actual value of trans-Mississippi supplies to the larger Confederate war effort.

The war's third crucial geographic theater was the Confederacy's lengthy coast, and those associated seaports substantial enough to provide an entry point for the blockade-runners that provided the new nation with the weapons, medicines, ammunition, and raw materials its armies desperately needed. There was only a limited number of such ports: New Orleans, Mobile Bay, Savannah, Charleston, and Wilmington. The Union failed to close Mobile Bay until August

1864 and Wilmington until January 1865, despite the US Navy's overwhelming naval superiority—perhaps the North's single greatest strategic failure during the war. While joint army-navy operations provided their own special challenges, the promising start to the Union's naval campaigns in 1861–62, which included the fall of North Carolina's Outer Banks, the capture of Port Royal as an important Federal blockading base, and most importantly, the conquest of New Orleans, suggests that a combination of insular service cultures and unimaginative leadership left this promising line of Federal operations unexploited for far too long.

Above all the Confederacy's geography presented a complex set of strategic problems. It was not so much that those problems were difficult to see or discern, rather, to paraphrase Clausewitz, in war strategy is a simple matter, but in the real world it is extremely difficult to execute. For the North the conduct of a successful strategy required the creation of vast armies and navies and then their projection into the Confederacy. Thus, before the North's leaders could turn to the articulation of successful strategy, they had to mobilize and develop the forces and military leaders to execute that strategy. For Confederate leaders, geography provided a welcome aid in the defense of Virginia. However, the geography between the Appalachians and the Mississippi was as much an enemy as an ally for the Confederates. In the end, the west's river system would provide Northern armies and their supporting gunboats ready access into the Confederacy's heartland.

Conclusion

And so the war came. Few saw the future with any clarity. The political and military choices of the early days of the conflict do not seem to have been the wisest, but that is only in retrospect. To judge the past fairly, one must take into account the perspectives of the time, the onrush of events, the political pressures of the day, and the estimates at the time of what was possible. What was possible was eventually reflected in the projection of Northern power over continental distances and the preservation of the Union along with the abolition of slavery. But it was to prove a long, hard, dark road, as the Union's final casualty bill of more than 300,000 dead would eventually underline.

CHAPTER 3

"And the War Came"

No one starts a war—or rather, no one in his senses ought to do so—without first being clear in his mind what he intends to achieve by that war and how he intends to conduct it.

—Carl von Clausewitz, *On War*

The white South's political counter to Lincoln's election came immediately. South Carolina seceded on 20 December 1860. In January and February 1861, Georgia, Alabama, Mississippi, Florida, Louisiana, and Texas followed, uniting the Deep South's state governments in an outright rejection of the Constitution and the Federal government. At the heart of secession lay the belief that the 1860 election represented a Northern rejection of slavery as the bedrock institution on which the white South's economy, culture, and way of life depended. As Alexander Stephens, the first and only vice president of the Confederacy, declaimed soon after he assumed office: "Those ideas [of the founding fathers that slavery would fade away] rested upon the assumption of the equality of races. This was an error. . . . Our new government is founded upon exactly the opposite ideas . . . its corner-stone rests upon the great truth that the negro is not equal to the white man; that slavery, subordination to the superior race, is his natural and normal condition. This, our new Government, is the first in the history of the world, based upon this great physical, philosophical, and moral truth."[1]

Thus, Buchanan confronted a full-blown crisis, which his own ineptitude, incompetence, and machinations had helped create. Exacerbating the difficulties confronting the nation was the fact that Lincoln would not take office until 4 March 1861, thus creating an interregnum of four months. If Buchanan had showed few signs of either statesmanship or toughness so far during his presidency, he was to display even fewer as he entered the secession winter.

In the immediate weeks after the election, Confederate sympathizers, aided and abetted by those in Congress who supported secession, dominated the cabinet and the president. But slowly the tide turned, so that the administration was under less and less pressure to surrender to those favoring the destruction of the national government. In late December 1860, John Floyd, Buchanan's secretary of war and a secessionist from Virginia, attempted to ship 125 cannon from Pittsburgh to the government's arsenals in Texas and Mississippi. That, along with his own corruption, terminated his career. Floyd then headed south to accept a commission as a brigadier general in the Confederate army, a position in which he was to render service to the Union by his incompetence in early 1862. Buchanan's legal analysis of the crisis was that while secession was unconstitutional, the Constitution did not provide Congress "the power by force of arms to compel a State to remain in the Union."[2] By early February 1861, secessionist sympathizers had left the cabinet, but the president's opinions did not match the firmer stance of his remaining senior officials. Nevertheless, in the face of the collapse of Unionist sentiment in the South, the administration stood steadfast in its inaction, strong in its inability to defend the interests of the national government, and firm in its unwillingness to support its own principles.

The Ignition of War: Sumter and Its Aftermath

By early January 1861 it was apparent that Fort Sumter, located in the middle of Charleston Harbor, represented a bone of immediate contention between the Federal government and the state of South Carolina and later the newly inaugurated Confederate government. In 1860 a small Federal garrison, two companies of regulars and an assortment of bandsmen, occupied Fort Moultrie at the northern side of the entrance to Charleston Bay. On 21 November 1860, the Kentucky-born, former slaveholder, and staunchly Unionist Major Robert Anderson arrived to take command. Anderson, a reformist protégé of Winfield Scott, had played a crucial role in creation of the field artillery branch that had made victory in Mexico possible, where he had served with distinction despite his own opposition to the conflict.

Anderson immediately realized that he could not defend Moultrie. Over the night of 25/26 December 1860, he moved his troops, officers, and officers' wives with provisions for four months to the more secure Fort Sumter, the construction of which was still incomplete. There he intended to await instructions from Washington as to the fate of his minuscule force. Not surprisingly, there was outrage in Charleston, but the locals were not yet capable of taking action against the Federal garrison in their midst. Once ensconced in the fort, Anderson and his garrison were safe, at least as long as their food held out. The Federal presence in Charleston soon became a problem for both Union and Confederate leaders.

Initially, the South Carolinians attempted to force Anderson to return to Moultrie by bluster. Governor Francis Pickens declared that a state of war existed between his state and the Federal government in Washington. Buchanan, berated by leading Southern senators, including Jefferson Davis, almost collapsed when he heard the news. The lame-duck president then pursued a course where he refused to support the stolid Anderson but also refused to order the major to return to Moultrie. In the end, those in the cabinet who supported a stronger course persuaded him that the government must not surrender Federal property to a secessionist state. Buchanan did attempt to reinforce and resupply Sumter. The *Star of the West* was sent to Charleston, but after being fired on it turned back. In sight of the growing Confederate deployment of artillery, Anderson accurately described his position as "a sheep tied watching the butcher sharpening a knife to cut his throat."[3]

Pickens almost initiated an attack on Sumter with inadequate forces, so eager was he to end the insult of seeing the Stars and Stripes displayed in the center of Charleston's harbor. Most South Carolinians were even more eager than their governor for direct military action, should Anderson refuse to surrender. Eager for military confrontation with the "mudsills" of the North, the South Carolinians could hardly wait to display their newfound freedom by military action. James Petigru, one of the last unionists left in the state, summed up the situation: "*South Carolina is too small for a republic, and too large for a lunatic-asylum.*"[4] Nevertheless, Jefferson Davis, sworn in as provisional president of the Confederacy in February 1861, at last managed to rein in the governor by sending P.G.T. Beauregard, West Point graduate and the first general officer in the Confederate army, to assay the situation in South Carolina and take command of the militia troops preparing to attack Sumter.

With his military experience, the Louisianan promptly took matters in hand as he made military preparations against the man who had been his artillery instructor at West Point. He ensured the locals deployed their available guns to destroy the fort, while preventing its resupply. Beauregard also discovered the wretched state of training and discipline among the state's militia. He warned his superiors in Montgomery: "I find a great deal of zeal and energy around me but little professional knowledge and experience"—a remark that many of his fellow regular officers would echo throughout 1861.[5] To the extent possible, the Creole initiated a regime of training in gunnery and tactics, while slaves dug the complex system of artillery emplacements to cover Sumter and the entrance to Charleston Bay through which a relief expedition might approach. To his annoyance, and presaging problems even Lee would have in 1862, Beauregard had to force Pickens to dragoon local slave owners into supplying the forced slave labor needed to dig the artillery positions, because the white militia believed it beneath their dignity to perform manual labor.

On 4 March 1861 Lincoln took the oath of office as president of the United States, thus inheriting the problems his predecessor had failed to address. Furthermore, even within the North, uncertainty prevailed as to how to respond to secession. A substantial minority, mostly Democrats but including some Republicans, believed the North should let the South go with an attitude resembling the old saw: "good riddance to bad rubbish." Furthermore, Lincoln stood at the head of a political party with little institutional continuity and multiple internal rivalries that had been held together in 1860 by an hostility to slavery's extension in the territories—a policy made increasingly irrelevant by secession. In a stroke of political genius, Lincoln had named his main rivals in the Republican Party to the most important cabinet posts— William Seward as secretary of state, Salmon P. Chase as secretary of the treasury, and Simon Cameron as secretary of war. The other major appointments were also men of stature and competence. Montgomery Blair, Lincoln's postmaster general and son of the influential Francis P. Blair, proved a particularly wise counselor, while his brother, Francis P. Blair Jr., would make major military contributions to winning the war as a general. Gideon Welles would become a fine secretary of the navy. Only Cameron would prove a failure. In the long run, the cabinet turned out to be an exceptionally effective tool through which Lincoln ran the war as well as the country. In the short term, however, that strength posed difficulties. Seward, Chase, and Cameron, but especially Seward, each believed that but for bad luck at the Chicago convention, he would have received the nomination and won the presidency, a position each believed himself better suited to hold than Lincoln.

Like most new administrations, especially one containing such high-powered politicians, there was considerable muddle as to responsibilities. That muddle showed most clearly in the effort to get supplies and reinforcements to Fort Sumter before the garrison ran out of food and had to surrender to the Confederates. The choices were grim: pull the garrison out and provide legitimacy to the Confederacy, while damaging Northern morale, or send a military expedition, which would ignite popular feeling in those slave states still sitting on the fence to join the Confederacy, while giving the North the opprobrium of having started the war. Seward urged Lincoln to withdraw the garrison from Sumter, while using back-channel connections to Confederate officials to assure them of this outcome. When it became clear Lincoln would guide policy himself, Seward even suggested starting a war with France and Spain as a means to bring the seceded states back in to the Union. Lincoln immediately made clear that was not in the cards. In the end the president settled on sending an unarmed ship to resupply the Sumter garrison with food. Moreover, Lincoln informed the governor of South Carolina of the coming effort to resupply Sumter's garrison peacefully. At the same time, the president intended a relieving force to stand by. The ball was now in Jefferson Davis's court.

Ironically, it was probably a good thing that due to bad weather the expedition to resupply Sumter failed to reach Charleston before the Confederate bombardment began. An attempt to force the narrows into Charleston, even after the Confederates had opened fire first, would have left the question as to who started the war open to doubt. As Lincoln and his cabinet wrestled with the problem of how to relieve Sumter without earning the opprobrium of starting the war, the Confederates took matters into their own hands. The new Confederate president and his advisors focused on the need to push the slave states in the Upper South, Virginia, North Carolina, Tennessee, as well as hopefully Kentucky and Missouri into secession. They feared that unless they maintained the momentum, the Lower South might find itself without the participation of the northern slave states. Moreover, Davis and most of his cabinet substantially underestimated the reaction of a divided Northern population to an aggressive move against Sumter.

In fairness to Davis, the slave states remaining outside of the Confederacy possessed two-thirds of the South's white population, an even larger percentage of its industrial capacity, 50 percent of its horses and mules, and the majority of its agricultural production. The Tredegar Iron Works at Richmond represented the only location for the production of major artillery pieces in the South. It was an absolute necessity for the Confederacy's survival that Virginia, North Carolina, and Tennessee join the rebellion. Whether they realized it or not, Confederate leaders were revolutionaries, and the more thoughtful recognized at least some of the challenges they would face. The bombardment of Sumter represented a considerable gamble, but it was one Davis and his cabinet felt they had to take. Thus, the word went out from Montgomery that if Anderson failed to surrender immediately, Beauregard was to begin the bombardment. What is astonishing about the decision is that the Confederates knew Sumter was almost out of rations. In fact, Anderson had indicated to the last officers sent from Charleston to demand the fort's surrender that Sumter possessed only sufficient foodstuffs for a few more days.

Early on the morning of 12 April, the Confederates began their bombardment. That well-known antebellum advocate of secession, Edmund Ruffin of Virginia, fired one of the first shots. He would also fire one of the last shots of the war, when he blew his brains out in June 1865 in despair over the collapse of the Confederacy. The bombardment and the reply by the Sumter garrison produced much light and smoke, but little blood. To minimize his casualties, Anderson had his gun crews return fire only with Sumter's lower guns. Sumter's main artillery pieces, the large caliber Columbiads on the parapets, remained silent. The first Federal reply came from a cannon fired by Captain Abner Doubleday, future major general and division commander in the Army of the Potomac. One of his lieutenants was the aforementioned Jefferson Davis of Indiana, who eventually commanded a corps during Sherman's march through Georgia and the Carolinas. Heavily outgunned because of their commander's decision, the garrison replied in a leisurely fashion. Sumter's garrison did manage to put a shell into one of the beachfront hotels to which large numbers of locals had retired to observe what most South Carolinians regarded as the festivities. Those civilians rapidly decamped to safer ground.

The damage to the fort's exterior was considerable, but the garrison suffered little. All through the 12th and into the 13th the bombardment continued. Meanwhile, relieving ships had arrived outside the harbor, but without pilots and lacking armored protection the relief expedition's officers refused to force their way into the bay. By the morning of the 13th, Confederate heated shot had caused a number of fires throughout the fort, which, while contained, forced Anderson to close the magazine doors and then pile dirt around the doors to prevent the fort from blowing up. Nearly out of ammunition and despairing of receiving reinforcements or resupply, Anderson surrendered on the 13th after Beauregard had granted the garrison the honors of war. The only serious casualties, one soldier killed and one mortally wounded, occurred when a pile of cartridges exploded during the salute as the garrison lowered the national colors. Anderson would eventually raise those colors over Sumter again at the war's end. After being properly paroled (pledging to stay out of the war's fighting, until they were "exchanged" for an equivalent number of Confederate prisoners), Anderson and his garrison then boarded the relief fleet and sailed north.

The attack on Sumter settled much of the doubts about which way the Upper South's states of Virginia, North Carolina, Tennessee, and Arkansas would go. Some have suggested Lincoln's call for troops two days after Sumter's surrender precipitated their secession. The historical record suggests otherwise. Upon receiving word of the attack on Sumter on the afternoon of its surrender—well before Lincoln's call went out—large prosecession crowds surged into the streets in Richmond, Nashville, Memphis, and Raleigh to greet the news of a "great" Confederate victory. In Richmond a vast throng of enthusiastic supporters of secession marched through the streets to the capitol. There, with cheers, they lowered the Stars and Stripes and replaced it with the new Confederate flag, while cannons boomed out a 100-gun salute.

Virginia, Tennessee, North Carolina, and Arkansas all quickly moved to secede from the Union and join the Confederacy. Davis's gamble in bombarding Sumter had seemingly paid off. Within two days of the news of Sumter arriving in Richmond, Virginia's "Spontaneous Rights Convention" passed an ordinance of secession. The state's population voted on that ordinance on 23 May, but by that time the state's leaders had already invited the Confederate government to move the capital from Montgomery to Richmond. Given the dilapidated and primitive surroundings in Alabama's capital, Davis and the Confederate congress delightedly accepted the offer on 21 May. Moreover, before Lincoln acted in response to Sumter, the former governor of Virginia, Henry Wise, had dispatched militia units to seize the Federal arsenal and its machinery at Harper's Ferry, one of the two major sites for the production of arms in the United States (the other located in Springfield, Massachusetts). Other militia forces moved against Norfolk, one of the US Navy's main bases. The two expeditions proved eminently successful and added considerably to the Confederacy's war-making capabilities.

The minuscule garrison at Harper's Ferry, surrounded by a hostile countryside, proved incapable of defending the factory and its machinery. On hearing that units of Virginia's militia were approaching in substantial numbers, Lieutenant Robert Jones ordered his men to prepare demolitions to fire the works and destroy the machinery. On the evening of 18 April, his soldiers fired the two warehouses which stored substantial amounts of ammunition and then the workshops which manufactured weapons. The former supplied a massive explosion that lit the way for the soldiers to retreat into Maryland from whence they marched to Carlisle Barracks in Pennsylvania. Unfortunately, the fires in the armory failed to disable much of the machinery, and those machine tools would provide a welcome addition to the Tredegar Works in manufacturing weapons for Confederate armies.

The fate of the Gosport naval base near Norfolk was an even sadder tale. While the ships in the yard were in a state of dismal repair, the yard itself was the most modern the navy possessed. Gideon Welles, the new secretary of the navy, made considerable efforts to persuade Lincoln to safeguard the base, but the president had hesitated to make an overt move that might further encourage secessionist sentiment in Virginia. Welles and the naval officers on his staff had worried particularly about the *Merrimack*, the navy's most modern ship. Unfortunately, the officer commanding the yard was an aged captain named Charles McCauley. In every respect, he was a peacetime military bureaucrat, incapable of making decisions and worried about provoking locals who needed no further reasons to be hostile to the Union. He conceived of his duties as filling out the paperwork so beloved by the prewar navy's shore establishment.

In the aftermath Welles described McCauley as "faithful but his energy and decision had left him."[6] The secretary had sent the navy's chief engineer to repair the *Merrimack*'s steam plant, so that it could escape. But when ready to sail, McCauley refused to allow her to leave the yard. At the last moment, he ordered the ships scuttled. The scuttling of the *Merrimack* was so inadequate that by spring 1862, the Confederates had turned her into an ironclad that would ravage the Union's blockading squadron outside Hampton Roads until the timely arrival of the *Monitor*. Even more damaging was the loss of a large number of heavy cannons McCauley failed to prepare for demolition. No fewer than 1,200 of these weapons fell into Confederate hands, while the yard's machinery escaped serious damage due to the late and ineffectual efforts at demolition. Moreover, the Union Navy lost ten vessels, all of which would have been of considerable use to its blockade efforts. The captured cannon equipped Confederate forts along the Atlantic and Gulf coasts with an impressive array of armaments to thwart later Union efforts to seize the ports and close them off from blockade-runners.

While the Confederacy gathered in weapons from the government's arsenals scattered throughout the South, the countervailing costs of Davis's gamble in bombarding Sumter were becoming clear. There was a massive surge of anger throughout the North. Huge crowds gathered throughout Northern cities to decry the attack. Much like Pearl Harbor in 1941, the bombardment unified what had been an uncertain and divided Northern population. Horace Greeley's *New York Tribune*, which had advocated allowing the South to "go in peace," now sounded the trumpet of national honor and demanded war to crush the secessionists. Even in New York City, which had been a stronghold of Confederate sympathy, vast numbers poured into the streets to support the Union. Douglas hastened to the White House, where he assured Lincoln of the loyalty of the Democratic Party to the Union. He then left for Chicago, where he stressed his support for whatever steps the administration felt necessary. Before huge crowds, he proclaimed: "There are only two sides to the question. Every man must be for the United States or against it. There can be no neutrals in this war, *only patriots—or traitors*."[7]

Lincoln's response to Sumter came the day after the fort surrendered, when he issued a proclamation calling for 75,000 militia to address a rebellion "too powerful to be suppressed by the ordinary course of judicial proceedings, or by the powers vested in the Marshals by law." Not surprisingly, the governors in the Upper South responded with a unanimous *No!* Historians' claims that Lincoln's call for volunteers somehow provoked the secession of Virginia, North Carolina, Tennessee, and Arkansas miss the fact that Davis had as one of his first acts as provisional president called for 100,000 volunteers to man his new armies. Thus, the Confederacy was already mobilizing for war, and Lincoln had no choice but to call for volunteers to protect the Union and particularly those slave states that remained loyal (Kentucky, Missouri, Maryland, and Delaware). Given the North's outrage, it is not surprising the Northern governors pledged more volunteer regiments than Lincoln had requested. The larger problem, of course, was how to train, equip, supply, and support the masses flocking to join.

Even more welcome news for the administration, isolated as it was by secessionist sentiment in Virginia and substantial portions of Maryland, came with a telegram from Governor John Andrew of Massachusetts that his state had already dispatched three regiments of volunteers, two to Washington and one to Fort Monroe at the entrance to the Chesapeake. Those regiments were the first of a flood of Union troops who were to travel to the nation's capital and the battlefields that would come on both sides of the Potomac. The great majority of Northerners, Democrats as well as Republicans, now committed themselves to opposing the Confederate attempt to destroy the *Union*. Admittedly, it would take more than two years before the North could mobilize the full potential of its human and material resources.

Strategy and the Contest for the Border States

Strategy, particularly at the highest levels, is more often than not a matter of personality. Here lay one of the Union's greatest advantages, because Lincoln was in every respect an extraordinary individual with a flexible and perceptive mind. His appearance and habit of interspersing his conversation with jokes gave most who met him for the first time a tendency to underestimate his intelligence and toughness, and Lincoln happily used that to his advantage in the interplay of politics and personality every president faces. Above all, the new president possessed excellent political sensibilities and learned quickly and perspicaciously. When necessary he could be ruthless, but he never

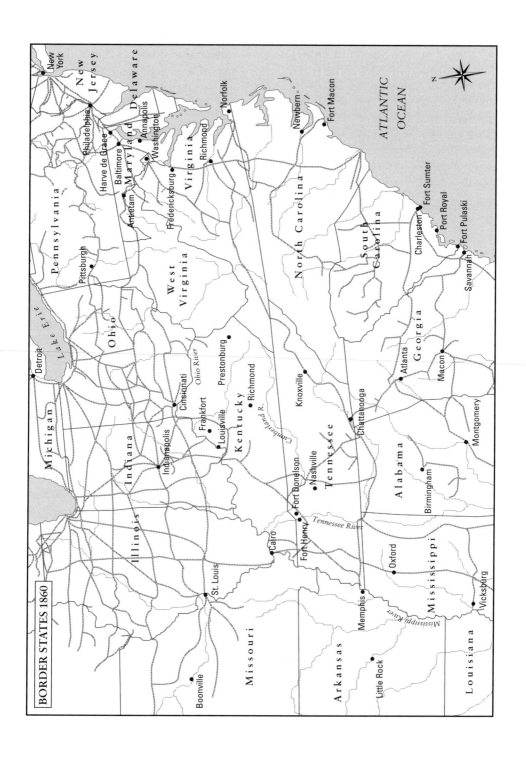

BORDER STATES 1860

New York
New Jersey
Delaware
Maryland
Philadelphia
Harve de Grace
Baltimore
Annapolis
Washington
Antietam
Fredericksburg
Virginia
Richmond
Norfolk
Newbern
Fort Macon
Pennsylvania
Pittsburgh
West Virginia
North Carolina
South Carolina
Charleston
Fort Sumter
Port Royal
Fort Pulaski
Savannah
Detroit
Lake Erie
Michigan
Ohio
Ohio River
Cincinnati
Frankfort
Prestonburg
Richmond
Louisville
Kentucky
Cumberland R.
Knoxville
Chattanooga
Georgia
Atlanta
Macon
Montgomery
Indianapolis
Indiana
Illinois
Nashville
Fort Donelson
Tennessee
Alabama
Birmingham
Fort Henry
Tennessee River
Cairo
Oxford
Mississippi
St. Louis
Memphis
Mississippi River
Vicksburg
Missouri
Arkansas
Little Rock
Louisiana
Boonville
ATLANTIC OCEAN
N

acted in such a fashion unless necessity demanded he do so. From the beginning of the war, he had a better grasp of strategy than did any of his generals with the exceptions of Scott and Grant.

James Wolfe, the conqueror of French Canada in the Seven Years' War (the French and Indian War to Americans), commented during the most trying time of his campaign that "war is an option of difficulties." One might say the same about grand strategy, which demands an understanding of the political complexities involved in a war, of one's own present and potential capabilities, and particularly of the nature and commitment of one's opponent. For Lincoln and his advisors, the first great hurdle was to establish a coherent understanding of their opponents. In spring and summer 1861 they understood little about the extent of the rebellion throughout the South. They believed, as did most of the North's political, intellectual, and military leaders, in the dangerous illusion that only a small group of fire-breathing radicals had been responsible for the launching of the Confederacy.

Matters were little different in the South. Most Confederates held equally flawed perceptions of their former countrymen. They believed that soft, city-dwelling mudsills inhabited the cities and towns of the North, men who were incapable of standing up to the rigors of war and who could not match the toughness of Confederate soldiers. As the *Raleigh Banner* proclaimed in late April 1861: "The army of the South will be composed of the best material that has ever yet made up an army; whilst that of Lincoln will be gathered from the sewers of the cities—the degraded, beastly off-scourings of all quarters of the world, who will serve for pay, and run away . . . when danger threatens them."[8]

Even more out of touch with reality, many Confederates believed that European, and especially British, textile manufacturers depended so heavily on "king cotton" for their economic livelihood that their governments would intervene in the conflict on the side of the Confederacy. While Davis and his cabinet never officially declared an embargo of cotton, they certainly encouraged an unofficial embargo. Thus, for most of 1861 a self-imposed blockade closed off the cotton trade to Europe. In fact, the blockade rebounded on its authors, because the British had little desire to involve themselves in the war, particularly given Canada's vulnerability, Britain's historic role in the antislavery movement, and the large stocks of cotton that remained in British warehouses due to the previous year's bumper crop. The Confederacy thus discarded the opportunity to maximize its cotton exports to pay for the imports of war material its armies needed so desperately during the crucial first year of the war, when the Union's blockade of Southern ports was at its least effective.

With such skewed views firmly set in Northern and Confederate minds, one can be hardly surprised at the paucity of strategic thinking in the opposing sections of what only a few months before had been a unified country. The aged commander in chief of the Union's army in the first months of war, General Scott, articulated that period's most sophisticated attempt at a larger military strategy. His design, eventually called the Anaconda Plan, rested on two assumptions, one accurate, one false. The false one was that there remained substantial Union sentiment in the South, and that once the North brought pressure on the slave states, their leaders would see the errors of their way and agree to the Union's restoration. The other of Scott's assumption was on the mark: a war resulting in the invasion of the Confederacy would eventually turn into a war of conquest, resulting in bitterness that would last for generations. Here Scott was undoubtedly drawing on his experiences in the Mexican War, where the occupation of Mexico City and its surrounding territory had done little to endear the Americans to the Mexicans.

What Scott proposed was an aggressive policy of blockade to shut off the Confederacy from economic contact with the world, coupled with a major campaign down the Mississippi River to split the Confederacy in two and open up that important waterway for the upper Midwest. Both elements would eventually form key parts of the military strategy that would win the war for the North. What was missing in Scott's strategy and would emerge during the war's course was the contest for control of Virginia and the invasion into the Confederacy's heartland that would come through Tennessee beginning in 1862. Those relentless campaigns would eventually exhaust the Confederacy's material and human resources and break its will to continue the struggle.

Scott's strategy in 1861 had several major flaws. First, while it aimed at achieving a reunion without the damage an invasion of the Confederacy by Union armies would incur, it also depended on waging a sustained struggle. In 1861 the North's population was simply not willing to consider, much less engage in, a long war, especially when most Northerners believed that an immediate invasion of Virginia would result in a quick and decisive victory, followed shortly thereafter by the Confederacy's collapse. Second, Scott assumed that only the actions of a few firebrands had resulted in secession and that the population of the Confederacy was lukewarm in its support for secession.

However, in the border states Lincoln could truly draw on the Unionist sentiment he still believed might exist in the seceded states. Inevitably, the political and military contexts within which wars occur shape grand strategy as well as military strategy. Statesmen must react to the demands of current events as well as considering the long term. Now that Virginia, North Carolina, Tennessee, and Arkansas had seceded, Lincoln perceived the securing of the border slave states of Delaware, Maryland, Kentucky, and Missouri as his highest priority. Delaware was not a problem, given its location and political and economic ties to the North. Missouri was important only in terms of St. Louis and the state's potential contribution to the war along the Mississippi. In contrast, Maryland occupied a geographic position central to keeping the nation's capital out of Confederate hands. Kentucky occupied a strategic position, because its northern frontier ran along the Ohio River, while it bordered on Tennessee to the south. Perhaps even more important was the fact that its western counties provided access to the mouths of the Cumberland and Tennessee Rivers, the latter particularly important because its course provided direct access to central Tennessee as well as northwestern Alabama and northeastern Mississippi. In effect the two rivers represented a dagger pointed at the Confederacy's heartland.

A tabulation of those who served in the regiments of the border states suggests where the loyalty of their populations lay at the war's beginning. In Missouri, two-thirds wore Union blue, while only one-third served in the Confederate armies. In Maryland nearly three-quarters of those who fought served in Union regiments, while only a quarter went South to fight for the Confederacy. But Kentuckians split almost evenly between Confederates and Unionists. Of all the states involved in the war, Kentucky would most resemble a civil war with brother fighting brother and father fighting son.

Matters sorted themselves out rather quickly, but rather messily in Maryland and Missouri. In Maryland trouble began as soon as Northern regiments, traveling south in response to Lincoln's call for 75,000 volunteers, arrived by train in Baltimore. No through route by rail to Washington existed. Instead, passengers had to detrain on Baltimore's north side and then cross its streets running south to the nation's capital. The first regiment, the 6th Massachusetts, encountered a mob of secessionists, who began to throw rocks, bricks, bottles, and other items, while a few even fired shots at the troops. The infuriated troops fixed bayonets and fired back. By the time the fracas ended and the troops had fought their way to the waiting trains on Baltimore's south side, twelve citizens lay dead with scores wounded. The 6th Massachusetts suffered four dead.

Some of Baltimore's more outraged pro-Confederates then burned the railroad bridges leading into the city. With its rail and the telegraph connections cut, Washington stood isolated and vulnerable in the eyes of nervous Union leaders. But Benjamin Butler, a brigadier general in the Massachusetts militia, as well as a major politician in the Democratic Party, displayed considerable initiative. He ordered his troops to detrain at Havre de Grace at the northern tip of the Chesapeake, embark on steamboats, and travel by water to Annapolis. In Annapolis the troops repaired the railroad to Washington. By that route a steady flow of troops reinforced the nation's capital, relieving its fears of a sudden Confederate invasion rather than averting an actual danger. As Union troop strength built up in Maryland, secessionist sympathy gradually muted. It was one thing to fly the Confederate flag; it was another to decide to fight for the Confederacy. One month after Union troops arrived in Baltimore, Butler occupied the city with troops, while at the same time declaring martial law. The state legislature declared that Maryland would have no part in the war, but at the same time refused to consider an ordinance of secession.

With Union troops occupying much of the state, Lincoln was in no mood to tolerate those still flirting with disloyalty. The obvious move, besides posting large numbers of troops in the state, was to suspend habeas corpus. The officer imposing martial law in Baltimore then arrested a number of leading Confederate sympathizers, including a certain John Merryman. That gentleman's lawyer immediately brought his client's arrest before the federal circuit court in Baltimore. Roger B. Taney, chief justice of the Supreme Court, presided over the case and ordered federal officers to appear before him and show cause for Merryman's arrest. Once again, as with the Dred Scott decision, the chief justice displayed his pernicious prejudices in an effort to undermine the Federal government. However, the officer in charge of the prison where Union authorities had incarcerated Merryman refused the summons, because Lincoln had suspended habeas corpus throughout much of Maryland. Two days later, Taney denied that the president had the right under the Constitution to suspend habeas corpus, since the article under which that right was stated occurred in the section dealing with the powers of Congress. Lincoln simply ordered his subordinates to ignore Taney's ruling. As he commented in an address to Congress in July 1861: "Are all the laws, *but one* [the right of habeas corpus], to go unexecuted, and the government itself go to pieces, lest that one be violated?"[9]

The Union defeat at Bull Run that month excited another wave of pro-Confederate sentiment in Maryland. But now, worried about a possible Confederate attack on Washington and sure Northerners would support harsh action against secessionist sympathizers, the administration cracked down harder. When a special session of the state legislature was to meet at Frederick in September, at the same time reports reached Washington of a possible Confederate invasion, the administration stepped in to arrest thirty-one members of the legislature as well as the mayor of Baltimore. It held them for two months until matters cooled. To those sitting on the fence the message was clear: The Federal government would not tolerate further babbling about support for the Confederacy. There were howls of outrage throughout the Confederacy at Lincoln's disregard of constitutional rights. Nevertheless, the Confederate authorities expressed no qualms later that year in hanging Unionists in eastern Tennessee without reference to habeas corpus.

In the end, while there was considerable sympathy in Maryland for the Confederacy, economic, political, and military realities overbore that sentiment. Moreover, the actions of Stonewall Jackson in seizing and shipping south fourteen locomotives, while destroying forty-two more along with 386 cars and twenty-three bridges in Maryland, convinced those who owned the Baltimore & Ohio Railroad that their financial interests lay with the North. It also calmed secessionist sentiment in Baltimore. Nevertheless, there remained a belief among Confederate leaders that, given the opportunity, Marylanders would support the Confederacy. The reality, however, was that prosecessionist sentiment existed largely in the southern and eastern portions of the state, regions of little strategic significance, while the northern and western portions of Maryland, where slavery was less prevalent, stood with the Union. The Army of Northern Virginia would discover that reality in its three invasions of the state in 1862, 1863, and 1864.

The question of loyalty played out quite differently in Missouri. In Maryland the Federal government, with Lincoln taking the lead, drove matters to a successful conclusion. In Missouri, two pro-Union individuals played key roles in thwarting secessionists. Representative Francis P. Blair Jr., of the influential Blair family, his brother, postmaster general in the cabinet and himself a future Union general, maneuvered Captain Nathaniel Lyon into command of the garrison guarding the arsenal in St. Louis. Lyon was not a typical army officer. He was a free-soiler and Republican. Unlike many officers commanding garrisons in the South, Lyon refused to surrender the arms the government had placed in his charge to secessionists. In the middle of the night of 25/26 April, he slipped the most modern, rifled muskets out of St. Louis to safer locations in Illinois.

Confronted with pro-Confederate militia drilling in the outskirts of the city, Lyon led four militia regiments of German Americans (many former Radicals who had fled Europe after the collapse of the Revolution of 1848) out to disarm and arrest them. As he marched his captives back into the city, a mob of bottle- and rock-throwing civilians greeted them. As in Baltimore, the soldiers responded with deadly force. After the firing ceased, the pro-Union militia had killed twenty-eight civilians, while only losing two of their own number. Attempts at mediation soon collapsed. In a meeting with his Southern opponents in June, Lyon underlined the depth of his feelings: "Rather than concede to the State of Missouri for one single instant the right to dictate to my Government in any matter however unimportant, I would see you . . . and every man, woman, and child in the State, dead and buried."[10]

The result was all-out civil war. As the fierce fighting over the summer indicated, both sides were willing to pay a high price. At the Battle of Wilson's Creek in August the opponents suffered heavier casualties in percentage terms than had the armies that fought at Bull Run. A Confederate bullet hit Lyon in the heart, and his dispirited troops collapsed against their numerically superior opponents. Franz Sigel, second in command, who had possessed some military experience in Germany in the late 1840s, then displayed the same utter incompetence that was to mark his battlefield performance throughout the war, with the one notable exception of Pea Ridge. But the defeat of Lyon's army failed to change Missouri's overall political and strategic situation.

In July 1861 Lincoln had handpicked John C. Frémont, an officer who had spent his military career in the topographical engineers and who had been the Republican candidate for the presidency in 1856, to command Union forces in the West. Despite the fact that Lyon's army faced increased numbers of Confederates reinforced from Arkansas, Frémont had failed to reinforce him. The "Pathfinder," a nickname earned by his explorations in the west, then failed to reinforce the Union garrison at Lexington, which the Confederates promptly gobbled up, because he and his staff were dreaming of far-flung operations down the Mississippi to open the river to Union commerce. Finally, after gathering 38,000 soldiers to deal with the Confederate army in Missouri, Frémont so overawed his opponents by his army's numbers that they melted away.

The result of the campaigning in 1861 left Missouri under formal Union control and established a pattern of conflict that continued throughout the remainder of the war. The Confederates could never pose a serious conventional threat to the Union position in Missouri, because the area west of the Mississippi simply lacked the strategic importance for them that other areas possessed, given the mounting threats posed by multiple Union armies. Thus, in Missouri the Confederates had to wage a war of raids and guerrilla activities. On the other hand, the only thing that mattered strategically in Missouri to the Union was St. Louis, now firmly in Northern hands, and the right bank of the Mississippi. Thus Northern military leaders never felt it necessary to deploy sufficient troops to bring the remainder of the state under their control.

A vicious war resulted between those who supported the Union or the Confederacy, and the ensuing disorder made way for a number of thugs to seize the opportunity to murder, rape, and plunder. In remarking about the nature of civil war, the great historian of the Peloponnesian War, Thucydides, noted that "with the ordinary conventions of civilized life thrown into confusion, human nature, always ready to offend even where laws exist, showed itself proudly in its true colours, as something incapable of controlling passion, insubordinate to the idea of justice, the enemy of anything superior to itself; for if it had not been for the pernicious power of envy, men would not so have exalted vengeance above innocence and profit above justice."[11] The war in Missouri lived up to his expectations. Confederate guerrilla leaders, typified by the murderous William Quantrill, waged a murderous war on everyone, while the James and Younger brothers survived the war to gain their deserved reputation for homicidal behavior. Nevertheless, one should not believe that only one section's partisans committed atrocities. The postwar victors among Union irregulars could escape into less violent pursuits after the war.

With his failure to bring the Confederates to battle, the "Pathfinder" discovered that he was holding an empty bag. Military victory would have restored his position in the west, but the collapse of Confederate forces in Missouri meant that Frémont would pay for his political sins. In response to his military difficulties, he had mistakenly issued a proclamation announcing that henceforth Union armies would shoot guerrillas out of hand. In addition, Frémont also declared martial law and began seizing the property, including slaves, of those Missourians in rebellion. The former declaration threatened to exacerbate a civil war spiraling out of control, but from Lincoln's point of view the threat to free the slaves carried more serious political dangers. In particular, if implemented it would have caused serious, if not disastrous, difficulties in Kentucky, which was the key strategic piece in the west. Moreover, Lincoln perceived that a direct attack on slavery might also weaken support for the war among Northern Democrats. Thus, it was not surprising that Frémont's days in the west were numbered. But his term in command was to make one major contribution to the Union cause. Thinking in terms of a great campaign down the Mississippi, he set in motion the construction of a large number of gunboats and transports that would in 1862 begin to play a major role in the campaign. Those vessels would not only carry Union forces down the great river, but also deep into Tennessee on the Tennessee and Cumberland Rivers.

On 2 November 1861, Lincoln officially replaced the "Pathfinder" with Henry Halleck, who had left the army in the 1850s and settled in California. Halleck had the distinction of having been one of the army's few intellectuals, with published works on what passed for strategic thought in the antebellum army and on the law of armed conflict. His brother officers had nicknamed him "old brains," a sobriquet that was not always meant favorably. Throughout the war in various positions, Halleck confused his ideas with military reality. He had little feel for or understanding of strategy. In his one active campaign, he thoroughly botched the opportunity to open up the Mississippi River in the spring of 1862. Moreover, jealous of Grant's successes, he would make considerable efforts to sidetrack his subordinate's career. Halleck was, however, a skilled and careful bureaucrat. Thus, he would not make the kind of political mistakes that had marked Frémont's 100-day tenure in command.

The third state caught between North and South was Kentucky. In the muddle of the politics in a state divided almost entirely down the middle, Kentuckians announced their desire to remain neutral. Lincoln recognized the delicate balance and at the end of April informed Kentucky Unionists that while he believed the Federal government possessed the right to march its troops over the state's territory anytime it wished, he had no intention of doing so at that time. Over the summer the president tolerated Kentucky's pretense of neutrality. Again, as with the Sumter quandary, Lincoln understood that in the long run it was to the North's advantage for the Confederates to make the first move. He was even willing to turn a blind eye to the movement of goods through the state by unscrupulous Northern businessmen to the Confederacy. Kentuckians eager to join the fray emigrated either north or south to join the state's regiments that the Federal government and the Confederacy were already enlisting in camps lying beyond the state's borders. Nevertheless, elections over the summer to fill Kentucky's congressional seats and then the legislature resulted in major victories for Unionists.

In early September, the Confederates blinked first. Leonidas Polk, bishop in the Episcopal church and now general in the Confederate army, decided to move north to occupy Columbus, Kentucky, located on bluffs dominating the Mississippi River. The good bishop feared Union forces in Illinois and Missouri were about to strike and seize Columbus before the Confederates could get there. Polk's decision was a serious political mistake in the short term, but more important, it proved to be an even greater strategic mistake in the long run. Kentucky now joined the war as a member of the Union. Ironically, Columbus was of little geographic or strategic importance, because the side that controlled the Tennessee River would control that position from the east.

Foreign Relations

Many in the Confederacy expected European intervention on their side. They believed the embargo on the export of cotton would so impoverish the vital English textile industry that Her Majesty's Government would find itself forced to use its naval power to break the blockade. What they failed to consider was how unpopular slavery was among the British. Moreover, even should they consider intervening in the conflict, the British would face a serious strategic conundrum.

While the Royal Navy could undoubtedly easily blockade the North's ports, Canada represented a hostage to fortune. No British government had the slightest hope of defending America's northern neighbor, once the North's mobilization of its military power was in full flood. Admittedly, Lincoln had commented to Seward when the latter had proposed declaring war on France and Spain, "one war at a time," and a British intervention represented a serious danger from the North's perspective. But the reality was that Union military power was concentrated in North America, while the North's railroad system insured that it could rapidly redeploy to the Canadian frontier.

Even with the absence of direct military conflict, the Union blockade strained Anglo-American relations. Throughout the war the North maintained the fiction that a mere insurrection plagued the South and that the Confederacy was not a nation. However, by declaring a blockade of Southern ports, the North conferred upon the Confederacy belligerent status—a point the British did not hesitate to point out. Ironically, the North relied on legal precedents the British had used during their previous blockades of the European continent, which the United States had traditionally opposed as an affront to neutral shipping—going as far as to cite the principle of freedom of the seas for neutrals as one cause of the War of 1812. With their characteristic sense of history, the Foreign Office put away the arguments used by Northern diplomats for future use. And indeed they would raise those same arguments with Woodrow Wilson's administration during the First World War, when the Americans chafed at the blockade the British imposed on Imperial Germany in 1914.

The one major incident that came close to precipitating British intervention came at the end of 1861. It originated in Richmond with the decision to send a commission headed by William L. Yancey to London in search of diplomatic recognition in spring 1861. Davis could not have made much worse of a choice, because Yancey held such radical proslavery views that he had even called for the resumption of the slave trade—a grim form of commerce that the British government had suppressed for decades. Lord Russell, Britain's foreign secretary, did receive the commissioners, but they heard only platitudes. In September Yancey resigned, and Davis replaced him and the commissioners with ministers plenipotentiary. Thus, James Mason and John Slidell departed for London and Paris respectively in late fall. They slipped through the blockade to Havana and then departed for Britain on the British mail packet *Trent*. Shortly after the *Trent* departed Havana, the USS *San Jacinto* under command of Captain Charles Wilkes intercepted her. Wilkes claimed that since maritime law authorized the seizure of diplomatic dispatches, he was seizing Mason and Slidell as "dispatches."

Not surprisingly, the Northern press took great delight at this twisting of the lion's tail, while the British public roared in outrage. The government in London immediately sent an ultimatum to Washington demanding the release of the Confederate diplomats. At the same time, they strengthened their fleet in the western Atlantic and announced the preparation of reinforcements to strengthen their garrison in Canada. The latter move, however, was simply a diplomatic ploy, because the St. Lawrence River had already begun freezing over and troops would not be able to arrive until late spring 1862. Nevertheless, the crisis abated. Under Lincoln's guidance, Seward found a way for the administration to release Mason and Slidell without losing too much face.

From this point on, relations between the two great Atlantic powers mirrored the progress of Union arms. British annoyance with the blockade and American fury with British tolerance of Confederate purchase of commerce raiders from British ports upset relations throughout the war. Nevertheless, the strategic realities were such that only major mistakes on the part of either side could have led to a British intervention. Both sides had too much to lose in any potential conflict. Ironically, by 1862 the mills of Lancashire were employing many of the workers, heretofore employed in manufacturing cotton fabric, now to clothe Union soldiers with uniforms made of wool, while the British were also drawing on supplies of cotton from alternate sources such as Egypt and British India. The North, on the other hand, had more than enough trouble on its hands in attempting to crush the Confederacy without adding the formidable power of Britain to the strategic complexities it faced.

Paying for War

It takes money to wage war, a fundamental reality that has plagued statesmen and military leaders from the beginning of history. The financing of the war presented one of the most difficult problems the

Confederacy and the Union States confronted at the war's outset. By the end of the conflict the North had spent $3,000,000,000 to support the war. Yet in 1861 the Federal government's income had been less the $40,000,000. In addition, not only had the Buchanan administration proven one of the most corrupt in American history, but the president and his cabinet were also profligate with their expenditures. Each year the administration had seen large deficits, which the president did nothing to ease. Thus, when Lincoln arrived in office he found government coffers virtually empty, its financial reputation in shreds, and no obvious means to raise the sums war would demand. As Senator John Sherman of Ohio, brother of William T. Sherman, recalled: "None of us appreciated the magnitude of the contest—the enormous armies demanded and the vast sums required. . . . [W]hen the war came we were without a currency and without a system of revenue."[12] Adding to the new administration's difficulties was the fact that there was no national banking system. Andrew Jackson had seen to that with his destruction of the Bank of the United States.

There were, of course, precedents in how the major European powers had financed great wars. As early as the War of Spanish Succession in the early eighteenth century, the British had paid for their military operations through the selling of easily traded securities, which owners could sell to each other in a flexible and liquid market, as opposed to being required to sell them back to the government. The costs of that conflict had been monumental in comparison to earlier times, but were minuscule compared to the sums the British government spent to fund the wars against the French Revolution's governments and Napoleonic France. During that conflict, the British had even resorted to an income tax. So there were precedents.

Nevertheless, the voracious demands for industrial products, the maintenance of military railroads in areas of the Confederacy Union troops occupied, and the logistical costs of supporting military forces over great distances, not to mention paying the troops and providing bounties for those who joined or reenlisted in the last years of the war, made the cost of the war to the Union on a per-year and per-capita basis greater than the wars the British had waged against Napoleon. The Confederacy benefited from a higher degree of social cohesion among its white population that allowed for a more aggressive program of conscription, but its export-dependent economy proved more financially vulnerable than the more balanced economic regime of the

North. How to pay for the war, thus, raised a number of difficulties, and the Northern and Confederate governments approached the financing of the war in different fashions.

Of all the serendipitous contributions Lincoln made to winning the war, one of the most important was appointing Salmon Chase as the secretary of the treasury. Lincoln appears to have made the appointment on the basis that Chase could do less damage to the administration, if he were a member of the cabinet, than if he remained on the outside in the Senate, where he might have provided a powerful and critical voice. Indeed, Chase performed admirably, although he hated the job and disagreed with many of the steps that the exigencies of the war forced the treasury to take. In his first months of the war, he secured loans from major banks to keep the government afloat until Congress met in July 1861. He spread the government's expenses as widely as possible, and here, beside his own populist instincts, he drew on the example of how the French had financed their war against the Russians in the 1850s. He intended to support the government's regular expenditures through increased taxes and the war through borrowing.

The first step in raising the money needed to prosecute the war came with a direct tax of $20,000,000, which the states were supposed to collect. Not only was it a paltry sum considering the looming expenditures, but the states hardly represented an effective means to collect taxes. In summer 1861 Chase asked for and received authorization from Congress to borrow $250,000,000. Even with that authorization, the Lincoln administration soon found itself forced to introduce an income tax for the first time in American history. While the method proved successful, it raised only a quarter of the sums required to support the war. Not surprisingly, by late 1861 Lincoln and Chase faced a desperate financial situation as war expenditures spiraled ever higher. As the president commented to the army's quartermaster general, Montgomery Meigs, early in 1862, "The people are impatient; Chase has no money and he tells me he can raise no more; the General of the Army [McClellan] has typhoid fever. The bottom is out of the tub. What shall I do?"[13] There appeared few palatable solutions to the financial difficulties.

Nevertheless, to meet the shortfall, Chase resorted to a number of imaginative and effective measures that placed the Union's finances on a more even keel. At the end of 1861, one of the most important led to the creation of a national banking system. Not only did Chase work out many of the details for that system, but he also used his connections with the Senate and the House of Representatives to pass the necessary legislation. In addition, in February 1862 Congress authorized the treasury to print paper money, the "greenback." By war's end the printing of greenbacks had doubled the North's supply of money. The administration also pushed through Congress in early 1862 an income tax, using as a template the British income tax laws of the early 1800s. Admittedly, the printing of paper currency did increase the rate of inflation, but nothing like what was occurring in the South. With a far larger economic base the North printed only half of the sum of paper currency the Confederate government created by similar means. The increased money supply helped fuel an expansion of the North's economy to the extent that by war's end the economy had increased by an amount equivalent to the cost of the war, similar to what would occur during the Second World War. Chase even put his face on some of the denominations, supposedly to make them more attractive to the public. Undoubtedly he was also hoping to further his own political future, and he would not have done so if the greenbacks had proved economically disastrous and politically unpopular. Lincoln tolerated such egomania, because he recognized the outstanding work Chase was doing in the treasury as well as the fact that he did not find it difficult to outmaneuver the Ohioan politically.

In order to help keep inflation under control and raise the needed funds, Chase turned to one of the financial geniuses of the nineteenth century, Jay Cooke. The New York financier, a patriot, initially helped Chase secure major loans from the major bankers in the North. So successful was Cooke in these efforts that Chase authorized Cooke to serve as the special agent for the distribution of $500,000,000 in bonds the government would issue to finance the war. In return, Cooke received a commission, but he plowed much of the resulting return into hiring agents and launching a propaganda campaign to persuade large numbers of Americans to invest their savings in these bonds. In fact, so successful were Cooke's efforts that he sold substantially more bonds than the initial offering that Congress had authorized. In 1865 Cooke and his propaganda machine, which used the power of Northern newspapers to great effect, persuaded the loyal population to buy $830,000,000 in bonds to keep the armies running through to the war's end. In effect, what Chase and Cooke created was the model the United States would successfully use to finance the cost of the two great world wars of the twentieth century. Indeed, Cooke did make money off selling the government's bonds, but his firm's profits amounted to only $200,000 after expenses, a paltry sum given the amounts he was able to raise.

The Confederate government followed a substantially different path, partially due to the states-rights' ideology that helped justify secession and partially due to Davis's own obdurate, straitlaced personality. The initial move of embargoing the export of cotton to Europe in 1861, when the Union blockade leaked like a sieve, was only the first in a number of false moves. But the embargo had relatively little impact at first, because the 1860 crop had proven particularly large. By the time reduced supplies of cotton began to affect European manufacturers in 1862, the Union was well on its way to mobilizing its naval strength to close down Confederate imports and exports. Obviously an increasingly effective Northern blockade resulted in the collapse of import duties collected in Southern ports, and those duties had provided the bulk of the Federal government's income before the war. By late 1861 such duties had almost entirely disappeared from the Confederacy's coffers. Unwilling to use the powers of the central government, Davis's administration could raise barely 8 percent of the war's financial burden by direct taxes, one-third in percentage terms of what the North raised. The conundrum of a regime founded on the principle of states' rights made the imposition of direct taxes unpalatable to say the least. Moreover, the Confederacy's increasing isolation and lack of access to large money markets over the course of the war, such as those the Union possessed on its own territory and abroad, meant that the Confederacy was incapable of borrowing the sums it needed to support the war.

Finally, in the spring of 1863 the Confederate Congress authorized a "tax in kind" on agricultural goods to provide foodstuffs for its armies. But that tax, while collectable in the vicinity of individual field armies, proved less than successful, not because the locals were unwilling, but because the Confederacy's deteriorating railroads could not connect its armies with the best sources of agricultural goods. In the end, the Confederacy resorted to paying for the war by printing money. At the war's end, the printing of paper money had paid for 60 percent of the war effort. At least through the defeats at Gettysburg and Vicksburg, inflation remained at relatively acceptable levels, but thereafter it ran rampant, destroying the population's confidence in paper money. Union counterfeiters printed their own copies of the badly printed Confederate bills, further adding to the rate of inflation. Nevertheless, the fact that it took so long for Confederate currency to collapse completely is one more indication of the depth of commitment of white Southerners to the Confederate cause.

Conclusion

In the largest sense round one of the political/strategic contest went to the Union. It was not so much that the Lincoln administration made the right decisions, but rather that it avoided making major strategic and political errors that would have haunted the Union's cause later in the war. Especially important was the fact that the new administration acted cautiously in its efforts to resupply Sumter. Had Union vessels forced their way into Charleston's harbor, the issue as to who was responsible for starting the war would have been murkier. Instead, Davis initiated the attack on Sumter and thereby provided the Northern public with the powerful image of a needless secessionist attack on brave Union soldiers only attempting to replenish their food supplies. That was indeed a costly mistake.

The response to Sumter also clarified a number of issues, foremost among which was the weakness of Unionist sentiment in Virginia, Tennessee, North Carolina, and Arkansas. There was never any hope those states would remain loyal in the long run, and the reaction of their populations to the bombardment made it clear on which side they stood. As for the other four slave states, the Confederate attack on Fort Sumter gave Lincoln running room to suppress Confederate sentiment in Maryland and defy Taney's efforts to place an irresponsible interpretation of the law above the desperate necessity of the hour. Equally important for the North's strategic situation was the disastrous error Polk made in deciding to violate Kentucky's neutrality. Not only had the bishop made a political mistake, but it was to prove an error of the greatest strategic significance.

The partial embargo of cotton exports must also count as a major error, in this case one made by Confederate society as well as Davis. In the largest sense, the embargo represented a miscalculation as to the position of the South in international affairs. Most Confederates never seemed to have grasped how negatively Europeans viewed slavery. Thus, the embargo not only reflected that miscalculation but also bolstered popular attitudes abroad that opposed any support for a slaveholding rebellion. Admittedly, there were some in the British upper classes who were favorably inclined to the Confederacy, but even they were not about to be blackmailed. In retrospect, secessionist hopes that Britain and France would intervene were a mirage. Only an egregious miscalculation by Lincoln would have resulted in intervention, and the president was far too clever to make such an error.

One final advantage in 1861 accrued to the North from the political fallout of military events. The defeat at Bull Run (see the next chapter) reinforced the Confederate belief in the inherent superiority of Southern white manhood over the mudsills of the North. Thus, it would not be until the spring of 1862, when a string of military disasters threatened to overwhelm the Confederacy, that it would begin a full mobilization of its resources and strength. Mary Chesnut, that perceptive Southern diarist, recognized the danger: "[Bull Run] will be our ruin. It lulls us into a fools paradise of conceit at our superior valor. And the shameful farce of their flight will wake every inch of their manhood. It was the very fillip they needed. There are a quieter sort here who know the Yankees well. They say if the thing begins to pay—government contracts and all that—we will never hear the end of it."[14] But then Chesnut was a woman, who saw things more clearly than the men who inhabited the circle of her friends at the heart of the Confederate ruling elite.

Thus the Confederacy lost at least a half a year of time, an irredeemable factor in the interplay of human events. As Omar Khayyám wrote: "The moving finger writes and, having writ, moves on: nor all your piety nor wit shall lure it back to cancel half a line, nor all your tears wash out a word of it." By the time the white South woke up, it was too late to take advantage of its victory at Manassas to maximum advantage, because the humiliating defeat on the banks of the Bull Run Creek had galvanized the North into taking the conflict seriously.

CHAPTER 4

First Battles and the Making of Armies

This, then, is the kind of city for which these men, who could not bear the thought of losing her, nobly fought and nobly died. . . . To me it seems that the consummation which has overtaken these men shows us the meaning of manliness in its first revelation and in its final proof. Some of them, no doubt had their faults; but what we ought to remember first is their gallant conduct against the enemy in defence of their native land. They have blotted evil out with good, and done more service to the commonwealth than they did harm in their private lives. . . . So and such they were, these men—worthy of their city. We who remain behind may hope to be spared their fate, but must resolve to keep the same daring spirit against the foe.

—Thucydides, *The History of the Peloponnesian War*

The Making of Soldiers and Armies

In 1861 both sides confronted the monumental task of creating effective military forces out of whole cloth. At the end of 1860, the regular army of the United States numbered only 16,367 men, including officers. Much of the rank and file consisted of the incompetent and inept of civilian society, men who had enlisted for drink and to escape their pasts. Desertion plagued the service, despite a harsh disciplinary regimen. Nevertheless, the "Old Army" had served well as a constabulary force policing Indians and unruly frontier settlers, while standing ready as the leadership and training cadre for a small-scale conflict with either a regional rival such as Mexico, or a European expeditionary force limited by the tyranny of distance. Unfortunately, no American leader, military or civilian, had intended for the US Army to organize, train, and lead mass citizen-soldier armies capable of waging war over continental distances against committed and tenacious opponents. The size of the Union armies in 1864 suggests the scale of the challenge. By 1864 the North would have 1,000,000 soldiers in arms with over 600,000 combat soldiers in the field—many now battle-hardened veterans as proficient as any other troops in the world.

As the two sides absorbed vast numbers of citizen-soldier volunteers in 1861, they had to mold their nationalist fervor, so reminiscent of the French revolutionaries of 1792, into something that resembled a disciplined and well-trained army, rather than an armed mob. The French revolutionaries were able at least to fold their enthusiastic but ill-trained volunteers into a preexisting army comprised of professional soldiers led by many of the junior officers of the monarchy's substantial regular army. Nevertheless, the new revolutionary armies of the French Republic experienced several years of hard fighting, defeats, and heavy losses before they could field the formidable armies of 1795 and 1796. The Americans only possessed a very small cadre of relatively well-trained officers, but unlike the French revolutionaries, neither Union nor Confederate armies had to take the field immediately against a hostile professional military.

Furthermore, both sections' distribution of their preexisting military expertise depended more on institutional inertia and bureaucratic happenstance than any rational program of mobilization. In the North, the continued need to maintain the regular army's frontier garrisons helped restrict officers, especially early in the war, to their old regiments, already staffed with officers and NCOs, as opposed to newly raised volunteer regiments bereft of leaders with meaningful military experience. In the Confederacy, former US Army officers unfettered by a prewar military establishment naturally gravitated toward the Eastern army massing in Virginia, where graduates of Virginia Military Institute (VMI) and the Citadel also naturally congregated—in the case of VMI, due to deliberate policy on the part of the Virginia state government. What later became the Army of Northern Virginia thus received a far higher share of available military expertise than did the western Confederate field armies, which may partially explain their widely diverging combat records over the course of the war.

One must not ignore how raw and untutored the volunteers were as they moved to their initial encampments. Adelbert Ames, the newly appointed commander of the 20th Maine, found himself, upon arrival at his new command in Augusta, confronted by a guard who failed to salute and who greeted his new commanding officer with "How do you do, Colonel?"[1] Although the 20th Maine was about to receive a thorough introduction into military life from its new commander, many volunteer regiments lacked experienced officers capable of providing useful instruction in the day-to-day necessities of military life, much less tactical competence on the battlefield. Furthermore, for West Pointers such as Ames, discipline in battle required iron discipline in camp—an association that citizen-soldiers rejected, and arguably with some claim to justice. Regular army veterans such as Ames would have to adjust some of their "Old Army" standards to the democratic and undisciplined inclinations of the volunteers, while those citizen-soldiers would prove resilient enough on the field of battle. For example, the Union's Western armies proved more successful on the battlefield than did the Army of the Potomac, despite the Army of the Potomac's more respectful attitude toward traditional Old Army standards of cleanliness and parade ground discipline. As Tocqueville observed, "the soldiers of a democratic army . . . do not consider themselves as seriously engaged in the military profession and are always thinking of quitting it . . . Among democratic nations the private soldiers remain most like civilians."[2]

Nevertheless, the dismal record of military ineptitude on the part of both sections' armies at the start of the war showed that the much maligned regulars had the better part of the argument between the volunteer's ethos of freedom and the Old Army's preoccupation with discipline. Even the famously "unmilitary" Grant, well known for his indifference to uniform standards and his antipathy for West Point's rigid ways, looked back to his cadet days when he first took command of the 21st Illinois. Prior to his arrival, the regiment had in its few short weeks of active service established a reputation for bad behavior and ill discipline. Grant took only a matter of days to whip the regiment into shape. "I found it very hard work for a few days to bring all the men into anything like subordination; but the great majority favored discipline, and by the application of a little regular army punishment all were reduced to as good discipline as one could ask."[3] Grant only used a "little regular army punishment" because many soldiers would have agreed with the volunteer who declared that "a West-Point officer and a strict disciplinarian may make good machine soldiers, but to us free born citizens of a free republic, we could not present him the affection that men give toward a real commander."[4]

Nevertheless, even the volunteers recognized the value of military knowledge and training, allowing individuals such as Patrick

Cleburne—who, as a young Irishman, had joined the British Army and risen to the rank of sergeant—to rise to positions of prominence. Cleburne, a graduate of a military tradition and disciplinary regime even harsher than the American "Old Army," performed so spectacularly in helping to train the Confederate regiment he joined that he was soon its commander and eventually gained command of a division before being killed at the Battle of Franklin in late 1864. Finally, one should also not overstate the advantages West Pointers possessed over their counterparts drawn from civil life. One suspects that the majority of regular officers who remained in place watching the plains far from the sound of shot and shell might have helped in whipping Union volunteer regiments into shape at the war's outset, but would not have displayed significant competence in higher positions later in the war. Those officers with ambition and initiative managed to wriggle their way out of the regulars shortly after the outbreak of the sectional conflict, despite considerable efforts by the army to prevent officers from moving to command volunteer regiments.

Yet, the escapees from the regular army were too few to provide much help in whipping the Northern armies into shape. Many regiments suffered considerably from the failure to provide the modicum of military training that a singular regular officer could provide. One Union officer despaired that "I don't meet a man once a month who knows anything about [the] military. I have not seen a field officer who can drill a regiment, or a General who can review a brigade but McCown, who is an old artillery captain."[5] The sad results during the war's initial months were epitomized by a cavalry officer: "the blind led the blind, and often both fell into the ditch, though not always at the same time."[6] Thus, many Union regiments learned the importance of proper instruction in drill *after* their first experience in combat, a costly school of instruction, and one that resulted in the poor showing many Union units displayed even in the first half of 1862. That was also true for Confederate regiments lacking experienced officers, especially in the west. Even in the Army of Northern Virginia, a soldier who had enlisted in May 1861 admitted after the war that he had not set foot on the drill field during his first full year in uniform.

The tactics the regiments employed at the war's beginning were not overly complex, especially compared to those of today. Basically, tactical effectiveness in 1861 required that regiments gain sufficient proficiency in drill to allow their soldiers to deploy with other regiments from marching column to line as quickly as possible, and to be able to use their weapons competently enough that they presented a greater danger to the enemy than to themselves. Anyone with real experience with firearms realizes that the achievement of such a standard under combat conditions required either rigorously repetitive training or hard-won battlefield experience.

Civil War regiments generally moved in columns with a frontage of four men—a manageable size for the rudimentary roads on most Civil War battlefields—but such a column masked most of a regiment's firepower. For that reason, when encountering the enemy, regiments deployed into long lines of battle only two deep, which allowed every man to bring his musket to bear. To use Longstreet's vulgar but apt turn of phrase, Civil War soldiers were as self-conscious of their flanks as a virgin. When the enemy's formation by virtue of superior numbers or position could extend beyond one's own line of battle, the overlapping units could subject one's own flanks to deadly fire, while one could only effectively respond to one's own front. Worse yet, if the enemy gained a position enfilade, that is, standing astride one's flank, he would be able to fire down the length of one's line, negating the common mistake of soldiers to either aim too high or too low. If the enemy could also work its way around the rear of a line of a battle, they could threaten to cut off retreat. Due to poor fire discipline and dismal marksmanship, Civil War combat need not be dramatically deadly—one must remember that two-thirds of Civil War deaths came from disease—but the psychological effect of being flanked could threaten the all-important cohesion that allowed a Civil War line of battle to fight and survive.

Preceding a line of battle, a select number of men—perhaps two companies out of the ten who comprised a regiment—would deploy as skirmishers. Skirmishers advanced and fought in "open order," leaving intervals of roughly five paces between each other. While effective skirmishers maintained a rough alignment with one another, they also exploited terrain and fired independently at targets of their choosing, unlike a line of battle, which would mass its firepower together at the direction of officers. A skirmish line would aim to provoke an enemy response, thus unmasking their dispositions and providing commanders critical intelligence on the enemy, while harassing its opponents with aimed fire. As the war progressed, skirmishing in loose order became more important, with an increasing number of troops placed on skirmish lines, but even at the end of the war, any decisive offensive action eventually required a line of battle formed in close order, elbows touching elbows, to move forward and seize a position.

While hand-to-hand combat with bayonets rarely occurred, even battered and wavering troops (if competently led) would not usually abandon a defensive line until a surging line of closely packed infantry approached its front. In contrast, skirmishers would by definition never attempt to make close contact with the enemy line and would instead break contact to rejoin the primary line of battle for the decisive assault, because even the increased accuracy of the rifle musket over the smoothbore had not yet created the "empty battlefield" of twentieth-century ground combat, where increasingly lethal weapons made close-order infantry formations suicidal. Instead, when a line of infantry began its charge to determine the test of wills that determined the outcome of tactical engagements, either the attacker's offensive momentum would stall and peter out, with more or less disorder, or the defenders would retire in the face of a seemingly implacable assault, in either an orderly withdrawal or chaotic rout.

Competent commanders used terrain to their advantage, knew how to place infantry regiments and artillery batteries in the most advantageous positions, and understood the importance of timing in ordering an assault. But antebellum army officers had no institutionalized process where they could learn such skills. At West Point, they received ample instruction in "minor tactics"—in other words, the basic mechanics of moving infantry, artillery, and cavalry formations to and fro on the battlefield—but their official tactical manuals provided no guidance on *when* a commander should use a specific evolution. A small minority of officers read widely enough to understand in theoretical terms more sophisticated problems such as battlefield deployments and the coordination of different combat arms. Those officers who had served in Mexico had observed large unit maneuvers as junior officers, but the average West Pointer was for the most part nothing more than a competent drillmaster who understood the basics of army administration.

Indeed, we should not overstate the importance of mastering the intricacies of the era's tactical manuals. Grant shrugged off the army's major revision of infantry tactics in the 1850s after he left the service. He spent hardly any time on the matter and recalled after the war that "I perceived at once, however, that Hardee's tactics—a mere translation from the French with Hardee's name attached—was nothing more than common sense and the progress of the age applied to Scott's system. The commands were abbreviated and the movement expedited. . . . I found no trouble in giving commands that would take my regiment where I wanted it to go and carry it around all obstacles. I do not believe that the officers of the regiment ever discovered that I had never studied the tactics that I used."[7]

Whatever the limits of the average West Pointer's military knowledge, basic proficiency in minor tactics and the mundane, but crucial, routine of army bureaucracy set former regular army officers apart from their civilian peers. Even the best eye for battlefield deployments would flounder, if one's troops could not execute the basic movements of close order drill under fire, and only substantial time on the drill ground produced such basic military competence. Even the most brilliant general could not win battles if his army could not perform basic administrative functions, such as accurately counting its own manpower, managing large amounts of war matériel, tending to its sick and wounded, and feeding and paying its soldiers. Mid-nineteenth-century Americans lived in a predominately rural society, with little need for complex organizations and bureaucracies, and former army officers composed the only substantial and well-defined group of Americans with extensive managerial experience. Veterans of the "Old Army" thus became indispensable to both sections' military organizations, and they in turn dominated early appointments to senior positions in both the Union and Confederate armies.

Unfortunately, there never has been any clear criteria for picking competent generals for command positions. Few officers possess the abilities and confidence to make great commanders. There are intangibles that appear significant in retrospect, but none are obvious. More often than not, achievements in lower ranks provide an incomplete guide to superior performance at the highest level. Indeed, if one examines Grant, Lee, and Sherman, there are few similarities in their personalities or methods of command. Grant in his memoirs compared the two great American commanders of the Mexican War, underlining that they had little in common except that they were great battlefield generals: "I had now been in battle with the two leading commanders conducting armies in a foreign land. The contrast between the two was very marked. General Taylor never wore uniform, but dressed himself entirely for comfort. . . . General Scott was the

reverse in all these particulars. He always wore all the uniform pre-
scribed or allowed by law when he inspected his lines. . . . In their
modes of expressing thought, these two generals contrasted quite as
strongly as in their other characteristics. General Scott was precise in
language, cultivated a style peculiarly his own; was proud of his rheto-
ric; not averse to speaking of himself, often in the third person. . . .
Taylor was not a conversationalist, but on paper could put his meaning so plainly that there could be no mistaking it. . . . But with their
opposite characteristics both were great and successful soldiers."[8] And
so Lincoln and Davis had to find their leaders on the basis of performance on the battlefield—a task made more difficult by the fact that
peacetime service or duty at lower levels of command could only serve
as an inadequate guide.

Even Lee had considerable difficulty in 1861 in his efforts to coordinate ill-trained citizen-soldiers and political generals in the western part of the state (now West Virginia). In his memoirs Grant put
his finger on his own fears in the summer of 1861 when given his
first independent command. He had received the task of leading several ill-trained regiments to drive the Confederates off a position they
held. He recounts: "As we approached the brow of the hill from which
it was expected we could see Harris' [the Confederate leader] camp,
and possibly find his men ready formed to meet us, my heart kept
getting higher and higher until it felt to me as though it was in my
throat. I would have given anything then to have been back in Illinois, but I had not the moral courage to halt and consider what to
do; I kept right on. When we reached a point from which the valley
below us was in full view I halted. The place where Harris had been
encamped a few days before was still there . . . but the troops were
gone."[9] Grant then added the lesson he drew from his experience that
explains why he proved so exceptional in independent command.
"My heart resumed its place. It occurred to me at once that Harris
had been as much afraid of me as I had been of him. This was a view
of the question that I had never taken before; but it was one I never
forgot afterwards. From that event to the close of the war, I never experienced trepidation upon confronting an enemy, though I always
felt more or less anxiety. I never forgot that he had as much reason to
fear my forces as I had his."[10] Grant had discovered a basic military
reality that most generals missed—that the enemy always has his own
problems.

Field army commanders needed such equanimity to succeed, because the uncertainty of war could easily cripple a commander's capacity to make even the most basic decisions. Competence is a rare phenomenon at the highest levels of responsibility in any profession, but particularly so among generals, who so rarely have the opportunity to engage in the tasks for which they train. In retrospect only three men fully mastered the art of commanding major Civil War armies: Lee, Grant, and Sherman. Lee may have had the ability to recognize that the enemy also had concerns in western Virginia in 1861, but the fighting was so amateurish it is difficult to tell. However, by the time he assumed command of the Army of Northern Virginia in 1862, he had grown into the position of independent army command. Grant's near defeat at Shiloh in the spring of 1862 showed that he may have been *too* confident, and he still had considerable learning to do. Sherman had a bad year initially in command in western Kentucky in 1861, as the torturous uncertainties of such responsibilities frayed his nerves, but he gained both confidence and understanding under Grant in the 1862 and 1863 campaigns. As Sherman himself put it, "Grant don't care a damn for what the enemy does out of his sight, but it scares me like hell."[11]

Among the corps commanders, only a relatively few displayed a high level of competence. James Longstreet and Thomas "Stonewall" Jackson most famously served the Confederate cause and Robert E. Lee well in the east, while Winfield Scott Hancock would be one consensus pick among historians for a strong corps commander in the Army of the Potomac. George Meade proved an excellent corps commander, regardless of how we might wish to assess his tenure as an army commander. The wide dispersal of Federal operations in the west blurred the line between corps and independent army command. Its distance from the war's strategic cockpit between Washington and Virginia, which loomed so large in the politics and perceptions of Union, Confederate, and international public opinion, also gave Union and Confederate commanders more discretion in their operations. In the West, the Union benefited from such minor army commanders as George Thomas, John "Black Jack" Logan, Samuel Curtis, and James McPherson. Among Confederate generals at this level of command in the West, only Nathan Bedford Forrest distinguished himself, and his force of cavalry raiders had a specialized and limited function. Nevertheless, on both sides, most corps commanders ranged from average to terrible.

By the last two years of the conflict, the fighting had eliminated a substantial number of the incompetent, while a few young West Pointers like Emory Upton and James Wilson had risen to the cusp of corps command as leaders of divisions. Others who had no prewar experience, such as Confederate generals John B. Gordon and Wade Hampton, and the aforementioned Union general John "Black Jack" Logan,[12] rapidly rose to the top on the basis of outstanding combat records. But, of course, their education required a terrible bloodletting of soldiers to determine who was competent and in what positions.

Clearly the Peter Principle was at work throughout the war. Joseph Hooker, who served well enough as a corps commander, froze as commander of the Army of the Potomac at Chancellorsville even before a Confederate cannon ball affected his decision making. Warren was outstanding as the Army of the Potomac's chief engineer but proved an indecisive and overly cautious corps commander. Longstreet displayed outstanding qualities as a corps commander in the Army of Northern Virginian, but failed in his one opportunity at independent command in the West—although perhaps he would have learned from the experience if he had not been needed with the Army of Northern Virginia. Jackson never had such an opportunity before his death, but his personality quirks probably would have led to no better result. John Bell Hood peaked as a hard-hitting division commander, but failed miserably as a corps and army commander.

Furthermore, the relatively primitive state of both Union and Confederate staff organization overemphasized command in the field and neglected strategic planning and coordination. If he could have restrained his tendencies to interfere in politics, McClellan could have served as a superb chief of staff in charge of training, army organization, and overall strategy. But both civilian and military leaders had a cultural fixation that idealized field command at the expense of critical staff work. McClellan thus found his real military talents masked and limited to the management of the Army of the Potomac, while exposing his own overriding flaw as a general—the absence of the sort of moral courage in the face of uncertainty that Grant exemplified. One wonders if on the Confederate side Johnston could have competently fulfilled a similar function in the Confederate command structure—but such a hypothetical scenario would not have cured Davis of his penchant for micromanagement of minor administrative details best left to competent subordinates.

Perhaps the greatest weakness of the war's political and military leadership lay in the failure to remove from command those who failed. Most spectacularly, Davis and Lincoln allowed Braxton Bragg and Nathaniel P. Banks to remain in positions of command long after they had established their ineptitude—Bragg as commander of the Confederate Army of Tennessee and Banks in various capacities as commander of minor Federal field armies. In the end, Lincoln proved a better evaluator of military talent than Davis. Lincoln supported his commanders in the field to the fullest extent, and he tolerated failed commanders such as Banks, Sigel, and Butler for the sake of the important Northern political constituencies they represented. Nevertheless, for crucial commands such as the Army of the Potomac, when generals proved incapable of handling their responsibilities, Lincoln fired them. Thus, Irvin McDowell, John Pope, George McClellan, Don Carlos Buell, Ambrose Burnside, Joseph Hooker, and William Rosecrans fell by the wayside in Lincoln's search for commanders who could perform competently. In the end, he arrived at Grant and Sherman.

In contrast, Davis proved dangerously indecisive in his handling of Bragg's tortuous relationships with his corps commanders in the Confederacy's most important western army, when the conflict reached untenable proportions in 1863. Instead of choosing one side in the dispute and restoring order to the Army of Tennessee, Davis vacillated and kept Bragg in command due to his personal partiality to this much-maligned general, but he left in place Bragg's insubordinate corps commanders—including Leonidas Polk, one of Davis's personal pets. Davis thus managed to combine the vices of *both* micromanagement of military affairs *and* indecisiveness in the resolution of crucial personnel choices. The catastrophic defeat at Missionary Ridge in November 1863 finally forced Davis's hand, and Bragg departed the scene, but Davis never found a way to resolve the Confederacy's command problems in the West. Davis himself had helped create those problems, because while he did not bear complete responsibility for his poor relationships with Johnston and Beauregard, he bore much of the burden for not finding a way to utilize the real military skills of those two senior Confederate generals in a theater bereft of competent army commanders.

By the end of the war, Lincoln proved the more capable judge of military talent, but in the war's first year, neither Lincoln nor Davis nor anyone else had developed effective criteria for selecting generals. In the Confederacy, Davis, with his prior familiarity with many officers due to his service as secretary of war in the 1850s, more or less respected Old Army seniority and prior reputation in his selection of generals. It was thus reasonable to give such figures as Lee, Johnston, Beauregard, and Albert Sidney Johnston senior positions. Lincoln did not defer as much to Old Army reputations, and political influence played a larger role. Irvin McDowell thus gained command of the Union's main Eastern army due to the sponsorship of Secretary of the Treasury Chase, despite his middling reputation and lack of command experience.

However, we should not assume prewar reputations to be an accurate predictor of success at the highest levels of military responsibility—neither Grant nor Sherman had notably successful prewar military careers, and Grant in particular left the Old Army under a cloud due to his problems with alcohol. Both McClellan and Henry W. Halleck had sterling prewar reputations, and both proved to be failures as field commanders. Of the four prewar Confederate luminaries previously mentioned, only Lee had the unambiguously successful record. In the end, success as a field commander depended on a trait Clausewitz associated with "genius"—the coup d'oeil that allowed a general to survey the chaos of a battle and a campaign and do "precisely the right thing at precisely the right moment," to use the crucial quality Thucydides attributes to the Athenian general Themistocles.[13]

The mysterious origins of such a talent makes a mockery of those historians who try to reduce wars to comparative tables of economic capacity or impersonal social forces. Nevertheless, even a Grant could not manifest his genius unless he already possessed a baseline of military competence, and it was only West Point graduates who at the war's outset possessed that minimum body of knowledge. Furthermore, even the most talented citizen-soldier would not have enough time to rise through the ranks to obtain army command by the war's crucial middle years, unlike a West Pointer like Grant who would begin the conflict as at least a regimental commander. For that reason, for all their faults, only Old Army men could serve as the recruiting pool for the war's most senior military leaders.

The Conduct of Military Operations in 1861: The East

In response to Lincoln's call for volunteer regiments, the loyal citizens of the North responded with enthusiasm, but with little organization or discipline among the troops organized by state governors.

Sherman, appointed a colonel in command of a new regiment of regulars in Washington, recalled in his memoirs the mixture of confusion, enthusiasm, and lack of serious preparation: "The appearance of the troops about Washington was good, but it was manifest they were far from being soldiers. Their uniforms were as various as the States and cities from which they came; their arms were also of every pattern and caliber; and they were so loaded down with overcoats, haversacks, knapsacks, tents, and baggage, that it took from twenty-five to fifty wagons to move the camp of a single regiment from one place to another, and some of the camps had bakeries and cooking establishments that would have done credit to Delmonico."[14]

Those with any military background—and there were not many—recognized that this armed mob was hardly capable of conducting serious military operations. The problem was that the country at large did not, while the newspapers of the day screamed for action. The banner headlines on Horace Greeley's *New York Tribune* proclaimed, "Forward to Richmond!" Perhaps more important, the politicians in Washington expressed their fury at the fact that the Confederate seat of government stood so close to the nation's capital. Furthermore, the troops Lincoln had mobilized in early April served on a ninety-day term of enlistment (stipulated by Federal laws that had never foreseen such a crisis), whose end now quickly approached. These so-called soldiers were hardly enthusiastic about facing battle in their last days on active duty. Indeed, decades earlier, their citizen-soldier forebears had ignored Scott's pleas to stay beyond their service contract when his small army invaded Mexico, forcing a pause in the earlier war's decisive campaign.

Thus, the ill-prepared forces of the Union ambled into Virginia on their way to Manassas and the Confederates, who were hardly much better prepared. Two Confederate forces guarded northern Virginia from an invasion. In the Shenandoah Valley, General Joseph E. Johnston commanded 12,000 Confederate soldiers. Against him, an aged veteran of the regular army, General Robert Patterson, led an army of 18,000. His mission was to hold Johnston's forces in the Valley, so that they could not unite with Beauregard's army, which had concentrated with 20,000 men around Manassas. McDowell led the main Union army of 35,000 men out of its encampments near the nation's capital. Thus, he possessed a substantial advantage over the Confederates, as long as Johnston remained in the Valley. But Patterson failed in his assignment, and Johnston not only moved out of the Valley but also

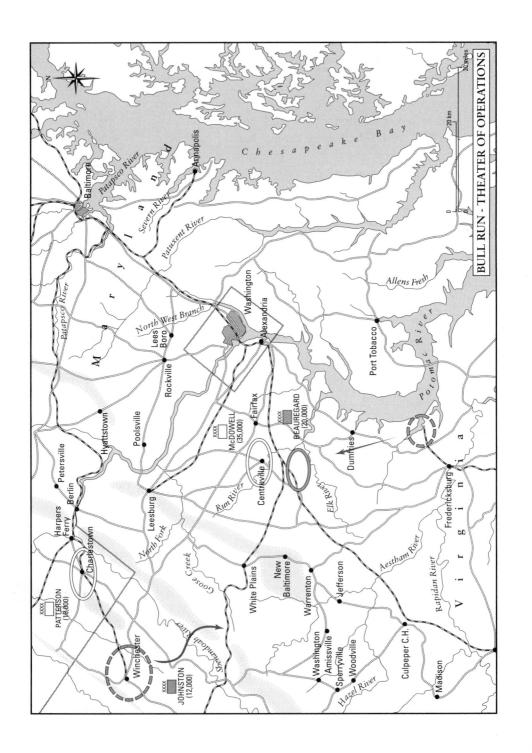

BULL RUN - THEATER OF OPERATIONS

arrived on the battlefield in the nick of time. As was typical of Union commanders in the east, Patterson believed the Confederates outnumbered his force, while he had little faith in the ninety-day wonders who made up the bulk of his army. Because he failed to pressure Johnston, the Confederate general was able to move virtually all his troops out of the Valley to reinforce Beauregard.

It might not have mattered, had McDowell's army moved with dispatch. But his troops moved at a snail's pace. The fault lay in the general inexperience of the officers and ill discipline of the troops. Marching along a route familiar today among those condemned to live in Washington, DC's suburbs—Vienna, Fairfax Courthouse, Germantown, and Centreville—McDowell's army crept toward the Confederates. According to Sherman, the march of his brigade "demonstrated little save the general laxity of discipline; for with all my personal efforts I could not prevent the men from straggling for water, blackberries, or anything else on the way they fancied."[15] By the time the Union army approached Manassas, Johnston already had three of his four brigades approaching or already in the area.

Early on 21 July 1861, the two armies came into contact along the muddy banks of a Virginia creek known as Bull Run. The stream runs from the northwest to the southeast with significant banks on the south side. Nevertheless, a number of fords and stone bridges offer access to the stream's south side. The terrain was heavily wooded with vines, brush, and poison ivy, which made movement difficult and confusing. Both Beauregard and McDowell planned to outflank and then attack their enemy with strong right wings. Because of misunderstood orders, Beauregard's attack on the southern flank of the Union advance never got started, which proved eminently fortuitous, because the Union attack on his left soon threatened to overwhelm the Confederates. Moving beyond the bluffs covering the northern enemy flank, nearly 15,000 Union troops had crossed the stream well to the northwest of Confederate positions. They ran into no opposition and advanced south to gobble up the Confederates.

Captain Edward Porter Alexander, serving as signal officer and soon to make a name for himself as the commander of Longstreet's artillery, sent a message to Colonel "Shanks" Evans, responsible for defending the Stone Bridge. Alexander warned that Union forces were about to smash into the northern flank of the Confederate army. Evans, leaving a handful of soldiers to guard the bridge, hastened north to meet the

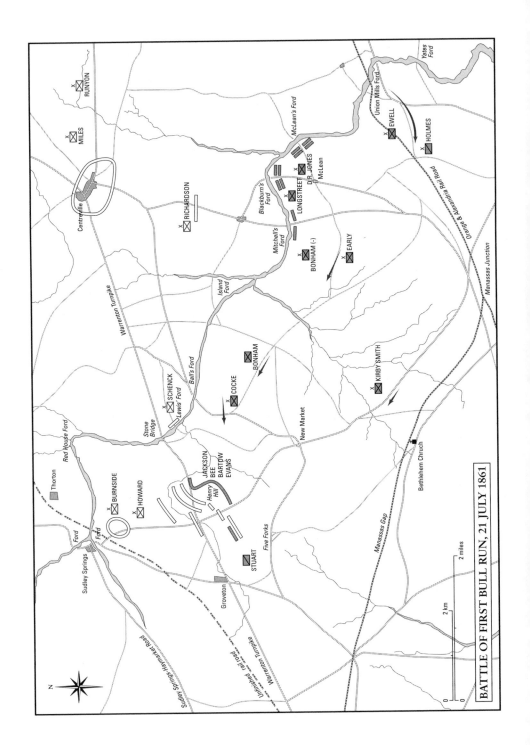

BATTLE OF FIRST BULL RUN, 21 JULY 1861

Union advance. His troops slowed the Union advance sufficiently, so that two more brigades, led by Brigadier General Barnard Bee and Francis S. Bartow, could reinforce the desperate situation on Beauregard's northern flank. The Confederate position eventually collapsed and the disorganized troops fell back on Henry House Hill. However, foreshadowing the inability of the Army of the Potomac to act with dispatch, Union troops failed to take advantage of the favorable tactical situation. Instead of driving the outnumbered Confederates from their new positions, McDowell paused to bombard them. A Virginia brigade now arrived on the field, where its steadfastness won its commander the nickname of "Stonewall" for its steadfastness under fire.

Thwarted by the heat, their inexperience, and the inability of their commanders to coordinate their effort, Union forces launched a series of uncoordinated, weak attacks. The battle then settled down into a series of nasty firefights. By afternoon the momentum of the Union drive had dissipated, as Beauregard fed Johnston's reinforcements into the fight. At approximately 1500 the Confederates launched a counterattack against the exhausted Union troops. They drove Union troops off Henry House Hill, but the real damage occurred on the far right of the Union line. Two of Johnston's brigades from the Shenandoah, under Jubal Early and E. Kirby Smith, smacked into O. O. Howard's flank. Howard's troops dissolved, their collapse soon followed by the rest of the Federal army despite the best efforts of officers. After the war Sherman commented on the reasons for the humiliating defeat: "It is now generally admitted that [Bull Run] was one of the best-planned battles of the war, but one of the worst-fought. Our men had been told so often at home that all they had to do was to make a bold appearance, and the rebels would run; and nearly all of us for the first time heard the sound of cannon and muskets in anger, and saw the bloody scenes common to all battles, with which we were soon to be familiar. We had good organization, good men, but no cohesion, no real discipline, no respect for authority, no real knowledge of war. Both armies were fairly defeated, and whichever had stood fast, the other would have run."[16]

Sherman's recollections sum up the military outcome. The casualty figures were heavy, but nothing close to those suffered in later battles: 387 Confederate dead with 1,582 wounded (225 of whom would die of wounds). Union losses were 625 killed or mortally wounded, nearly 1,000 wounded, many maimed for life, and more than 1,200 captured. But no matter how incompetent and ill disciplined the opposing sides, the battle underlined that even without discipline and training, Americans, on both sides, were willing to stand in the open in a terrifying environment and kill large numbers of their fellow countrymen. The feelings on opposing sides underlined a commitment to the war not seen since the early days of the French Revolution. McClellan, a West Point graduate and veteran of the Mexican War who had left the army in 1857 for a successful railroad career, would write later that fall that "the rebels have displayed energy unanimity & wisdom worthy of the most desperate days of the French Revolution—should we do less?"[17] Bull Run was a foretaste of what was to prove a bitter cup.

At our distance, it is often hard to capture the pain and suffering the war cost those who fought as well as the impact it had on those at home, hoping for the survival of those they loved. Major Sullivan Ballou of the 2nd Rhode Island regiment wrote to his wife on 14 July 1861, shortly before the move to Manassas: "Sarah, my love for you is deathless; it seems to bind me with mighty cables, that nothing but omnipotence could break; and yet my love of country comes over me like a strong wind and bears me irresistibly on. . . . The memory of all the blissful moments I have spent with you come creeping over me . . . And how hard it is for me to give them up, and burn to ashes the hopes of future years, when, God willing, we might have still lived and loved together. . . . If I do not [return], my dear Sarah, never forget how much I loved you. . . . But, oh! Sarah, if the dead can come back to this earth, and flit unseen around those they love, I shall always be near you; in the gladdest day, in the darkest night . . . *always—always*; and if there be a soft breeze upon your cheek, it shall be my breath."[18] Ballou was killed on the field at First Bull Run.

Jefferson Davis was on the scene as the battle ended and urged an immediate pursuit to capture Washington. However, there was no possibility of such a move, because the Confederates were almost as fought out and disorganized by victory as their opponents had been by defeat. Moreover, a heavy rainstorm the next day turned the roads into slick mud bogs. Nevertheless, Union troops took the defeat hard, and there were a number of mutinous acts. Sherman found himself facing down soldiers, led by a captain, of the 69th New York, who announced their ninety days were up, and they were going home. Sherman replied they were not going home until the War Department said their ninety days were up and then threatened to shoot their captain, if he persisted. The captain and his men returned to camp. Later that day Lincoln visited the camp. The aggrieved captain approached the president with his tale of Sherman's threatening to shoot him "like a dog." In a stage whisper, Lincoln replied: "Well, if I were you, and he threatened to shoot, I would not trust him, for I believe he would do it." According to Sherman, "the officer turned about and disappeared, and the men laughed at him."[19]

The question on the Union side was what was to do with this ill-trained conglomeration of men pretending to be soldiers. In western Virginia, soon to break away and become a separate state, McClellan seemingly won a signal success against an equally ill-trained but numerically inferior group of Confederates. When Lincoln announced his call-up of the militia, McClellan had volunteered his services to the governor of Ohio and had ended up commanding the Ohio regiments in a campaign along the Ohio River and into what is now West Virginia. Ironically, given his politics both before and during the war, he owed his position to a considerable extent to the efforts of Chase, who had come to know McClellan in the 1850s.

McClellan had earlier exhorted his troops in western Virginia to maintain the highest standards of "discipline, courage and mercy," and that "rights in person and property shall be restricted." Paired with a conciliatory approach to secessionist civilians that would shortly prove politically controversial, McClellan grandly pronounced, with words that echoed those of the great Napoleon: "Soldiers! I have heard that there was danger here. I have come to place myself at your head and share it with you. I fear now but one thing—that you will not find foemen worthy of your steel."[20] It was a pronouncement of a general taken in by his own self-importance. Yet, the newly minted major general would prove lacking in the moral courage required to assume the crushing responsibilities of commanding men in battle. There would always be some excuse as to why he could not act, always someone else's fault why he could not move, always the need for more reinforcements, more supplies, more men. In effect, he would find himself frozen in the fear that had gripped Grant in his first command in Missouri. The difference was that that fear of what the enemy might do gripped him from the beginning to the end of his short military career. To paraphrase Clemenceau's comment about the French general Georges Boulanger, who, having failed to overthrow the Third Republic, then committed suicide on the grave of his mistress: McClellan wore the uniform of a general, but possessed the soul of a second lieutenant. In fact,

McClellan's subordinates were largely responsible for his supposed successes in western Virginia. But that did not matter in a Washington desperate to restore luster to the North's military effort after Bull Run.

In some respects, McClellan was the perfect choice, because he was a masterful trainer and administrator. Upon arrival in the nation's capital, he set about using soldiers of the regular army as military policemen to clear out Washington's bars and brothels. The "Young Napoleon," as his troops soon characterized him, did a magnificent job in establishing a disciplined, well-trained body of soldiers. Yet, he also set about establishing a culture in the leadership of what was to become the Army of the Potomac that was to exercise a baleful influence on its performance throughout the war. In August 1861, he established brigade and division organizations for the army. Excluding three divisions (commanded by non–West Pointers Nathaniel Banks, Louis Blenker, and Frederick Lander), which did not deploy to the Peninsula between the York and James Rivers in the spring 1862 campaign against Richmond and did not become part of the core of the Army of the Potomac (which later became Corps I-VI), every single division commander assigned to these eight divisions between their organization and the move to the Peninsula had served at some point in the Old Army as officers, and only two were not West Pointers (Edwin V. Sumner and Philip Kearny). Of the forty-five brigade commanders assigned during this period, only sixteen came from civilian life. Two were Old Army officers who were not West Pointers, while the remainder had all graduated from the Military Academy. Three of these divisions at one point or the other during this time period were commanded by engineers (either Corps of Engineers or Topographical Engineer officers)—Rufus King, William B. Franklin, George W. Morell, and William F. Smith. Considering the miniscule size of the engineering branches in the Old Army, this was a striking share of senior command positions. One other division commander, Charles P. Stone, was an Ordnance officer, a staff bureau that inhabited the second run of West Point's academic elite, but which by definition did not serve in the line. Thus McClellan's selection of brigade and division commanders reflected a strong preference not only for Old Army men, but also for the technical elite created by West Point's engineering-heavy curriculum. Like their chief, ten had taught at the academy. Nearly all of them would share McClellan's caution, unwillingness to take risks, and preference to do things by the book.

Interestingly, and revealingly, as the commander responsible for training and leading this great army, McClellan chose to live in Washington in a comfortable house, well removed from the humdrum business of soldiering, as Sherman, serving in the first months of McClellan's command, noted. Slowly, but steadily, McClellan and his subordinates turned an armed mob into a reasonable approximation of an army. Nevertheless, the dark side of McClellan's personality soon exhibited itself. He mounted a sustained and nasty campaign of backstabbing to remove Scott from overall command of the army and replace the general with himself. McClellan let everyone know that the aged general represented an impediment to his efforts to organize and train the army. On 1 November 1861, he achieved his goal. Queried by Lincoln whether with Scott now gone he could handle his new responsibilities that included not only managing the campaign in Virginia, but the whole of the Union's war effort as well, McClellan confidently replied, "I can do it all."

While McClellan developed some strategic ideas of real imagination during his first fall in command (to be discussed in the following chapter), at night the ghosts of doubt beset the Young Napoleon in spite of the fact that tens of thousands of new volunteers were arriving every month in response to Lincoln's calls for three-year volunteers. In August, he had written his wife: "I have hardly slept one moment for the last three nights, knowing well that the enemy intend some movement & fully recognizing our own weakness. If Beauregard does not attack tonight I shall look upon it as a dispensation of Providence—he *ought* to do it."[21] The cause of McClellan's disquiet: the supposed host the Confederates had deployed in northern Virginia, forces which far outnumbered his. "I am here in a terrible place—the enemy have from 3 to 4 times my force."[22] While McClellan might have had more reasons for these anxieties in the chaotic aftermath of First Bull Run, he never escaped this clawing fear of what the enemy might do to him, which lay at the heart of his difficulties. Stephen Sears sums up McClellan as a commander: "The enemy confronting him was invariably a host. Thus every act of war must be perfected, with every man and gun and wagon in place, before risking a move against such odds; thus nothing dared be hurried nor any chances taken."[23]

As the seemingly endless reviews and parades continued, Washington's political leaders grew increasingly uneasy. McClellan displayed little disposition to come into contact with the Confederate army deployed on the other side of the Potomac. As the number of troops under his command grew, so too did his estimates of Confederate strength. By November the Army of the Potomac, as it was now titled, had an end-strength of 168,000 soldiers. As early as mid-August 1861, McClellan was estimating Confederate strength as 150,000 men. In fact, by late fall Johnston and Beauregard could put barely 60,000 effectives in the field. The second factor in Washington's unease was McClellan's attitude toward his political masters. Not only did he make vulgar remarks about the nation's political leaders—he called Lincoln a baboon—within the confines of his headquarters, but also he was downright rude to the president. As for his politics, McClellan made those crystal clear. As he wrote to one of his influential friends outside the army, "help me to dodge the nigger—we want nothing to do with him. *I* am fighting to preserve the integrity of the Union & the power of the Govt—on no other issue."[24]

Over the course of the past two decades, political scientists and historians have built an academic cottage industry with their arguments that there is supposedly a serious rift today between military and civilian leaders. In reality, nothing comes close to replicating the rift in fall 1861. In mid-November, Lincoln arrived at McClellan's house to talk to the general, who was attending a wedding. When the general returned, he was told the president was waiting to see him. Instead of meeting with Lincoln, he went straight upstairs to bed, refusing to spend even a few moments with his commander in chief. Lincoln as always suppressed his own feelings in the face of the country's larger interests. But if the president tolerated the rudeness of his army commander and allowed him great latitude to complete his plans for the future, many in Congress did not.

What instigated the politicians to act decisively was a relatively small action that occurred up the Potomac from Washington at a place called Ball's Bluff on 21 October 1861. In a nutshell, a division commander, believing that McClellan had already launched a reconnaissance in force on the Virginia side of the Potomac, made his own reconnaissance effort. His brigade commander, with too few boats on hand, ordered his troops to cross the Potomac. The Confederates in the vicinity responded quickly. The result was a rout, as desperate Union troops tried to swim the river, which was in full flow due to fall rains. The Confederates captured nearly 700 soldiers. The disaster might not have mattered except for the fact that the brigade commander was Edward D. Baker, a United States senator and a close friend of the president. To make matters worse, McClellan, who had issued confusing orders, attempted to absolve himself of blame. The uproar in Congress led to the creation of the Joint Committee on the Conduct of the War, which was to belabor Union generals throughout the remainder of the conflict.

Moreover, as we shall see later, McClellan's management of the battle's aftermath would reveal much about the lack of mutual trust and confidence among the leaders of the Army of the Potomac. Baker's division commander, Charles P. Stone, became a target for the Joint Committee due to his outspokenly conservative politics. He would eventually be held for six months without charges (two in solitary confinement), even as his former patron, McClellan, abandoned him to his fate. Stanton and the Joint Committee deserve the bulk of the blame for this miscarriage of justice, but McClellan had not helped matters when he set a poor example for his subordinates with indiscrete declarations of conservative and antiradical politics. Not only did the army's commander prove unable to protect his subordinates fully, but also ambitious subordinates, such as Joseph Hooker outside McClellan's circle, would learn the value of Washington intrigue. In the end, the result was a high command predominantly McClellanite, but one riven by faction and intrigue.

While McClellan was busily engaged in creating an army out of the mass of willing volunteers, Johnston and Beauregard were doing the same with fewer troops. Nevertheless, they proved adept at inflating their numbers. They received considerable help from Allan Pinkerton, who headed up a private detective agency in Chicago and whom McClellan had picked to serve as his chief of intelligence. Not for the last time, McClellan swallowed inflated estimates, hook, line, and sinker. Moreover, by the skillful use of logs made to look like cannon, the Confederates inflated their artillery as well as numerical strength. Beauregard, at least, dreamed of a great invasion of the North, if Confederate armies in Virginia received major reinforcements. He proposed such an effort to Davis, who visited his troops at Manassas in September. But as the Confederate president informed his commanders, there were too many threats elsewhere, particularly in terms of Union amphibious operations, and the Confederacy had too few troops to cover all the various danger areas.

In spite of the success at Bull Run, Davis displayed the prickly side of his personality in his relationship with the generals who faced the Union hosts gathering around Washington. On 31 August 1861, the Confederate president nominated five officers to hold the rank of full general in the armies of the Confederacy. He ranked Samuel Cooper, Albert Sidney Johnston, and Robert E. Lee above Johnston, who believed that based on the rank list of the Old Army, he should have received the first position. Not surprisingly, in terms of the Old Army's culture, Johnston sent the president a letter that complained at length about the injustice of his being placed fourth on the list. As his biographer notes, it contained more than the usual "fatuous verbiage" that officers of the nineteenth century were capable of spewing out. It was a letter he never should have sent, but it was also a letter to which Davis should not have replied. The president's reply was just plain nasty: "I have just received and read your letter of the 12th instant. Its language is, as you say, unusual; its arguments and statements utterly one-sided, and its insinuations as unfounded as they are unbecoming."[25] Davis's cold reply resulted in a rift between the two men that the exigencies and necessities of defending the Confederacy were never to heal and that were to have a considerable impact on the war's course. It was one more instance in the annals of the past underlining that war is a human endeavor, and that interpersonal relations among leaders cast and will continue to cast an indelible shadow over the course of events.

Conclusion

And so the first year closed. There had been one major battle in the East, Bull Run, but in comparison to what was to come, it was small potatoes. Nevertheless, the smaller skirmishes in Missouri and western Virginia had set the stage for the Union control over those areas. The first moves into Kentucky had also set the basis for what was to be the most important strategic move of the war: the attack on the river system that reached deeply into the heartland of the Confederacy. That move would come early in 1862, but events in 1861 had laid the groundwork. Moreover, the debacle at Bull Run had awoken the Lincoln administration and much of the North to the fact they were engaged in a serious struggle. On the other hand, the Confederate victory at Bull Run allowed too many Confederates to hold to the comfortable delusion they could humble the North without much of a fight.

Thus, the North began the hard process of mobilizing its strength for the struggle. Nevertheless, that process had barely begun, and sloth, corruption, and incompetence were already apparent. By year's end Lincoln had recognized that Cameron was not suitable as the secretary of war. It was not necessarily that the secretary was corrupt, but rather that his political machinations, coupled with incompetence, had created scandal in his department. If the North were to mobilize effectively, Cameron could not remain. Lincoln informed the Pennsylvanian that he was being sent to St. Petersburg as the US ambassador—a position similar to one that the German statesman Otto von Bismarck had held for the Prussian government in the 1850s, for which he noted that he had laid awake at night "hating." The president graciously allowed Cameron to resign before accepting his new appointment.

In Cameron's place, Lincoln selected a man he had every right to hate, but who was to prove a crucial tool in the Union's arsenal, Edwin M. Stanton. Stanton was a well-known lawyer; he had been the attorney general in the last days of Buchanan's administration, where he had resolutely defended the interests of the United States against the president's pusillanimity and the efforts of secessionist sympathizers to undermine the government's credibility. In the end Stanton proved an outstanding and ruthless manager of the effort to mobilize the North's strengths as well as an excellent judge of those conducting the military effort. On the occasion of Stanton's death after the war, the lawyer George Templeton Strong best described the secretary of war's strengths and weaknesses in his diary: "Good and evil were strangely blended in the character of this great War Minister. He was honest, patriotic, able, indefatigable, warm-hearted, unselfish, incorruptible, arbitrary, capricious, tyrannical, vindictive, hateful, and cruel."[26] But for all his faults Stanton proved to be an extraordinarily competent manager of the Union's war effort.

By the turn of the year, the armies were also in a state of flux. Their leaders were beginning to bring discipline and organization to what in the summer fighting had been armed mobs. On both sides Confederate and Union soldiers had displayed a deep commitment to the concept of what the French revolutionary patriots of 1792 had termed *la patrie*—the nation—in spite of their lack of training and general ill discipline. For Confederates, it was their new nation and its long-standing institutions, particularly slavery. For Northerners it was the Union, the nation their forefathers had created in 1776 and 1787. Only that level of commitment explains the fact that both sides were willing to see the struggle through to the bitter end in 1865—a standard never seen before or after in American history. Not surprisingly, Ulysses Grant depicted best those who had borne the burden of saving the *nation* in a speech given after the war: "What saved the Union was the coming forward of the young men of the nation. They came from their homes and their fields, as they did in the time of the Revolution, giving everything to the country. To their devotion we owe the salvation of the union. The humblest soldier who carried a musket is entitled to as much credit for the results of the war as those who were in command."[27] But the road ahead was long and uncertain. While discipline was spreading through the ranks of the newly formed regiments, the business of leading the increasingly impressive armies remained uncertain.

CHAPTER 5

Stillborn between Earth and Water:
The Unfulfilled Promise of Joint Operations

Wilson, I am a damned sight smarter man than Grant; I know a great deal
more about war, military history, strategy, and grand tactics than he does; I
know more about organization, supply, and administration and about everything else than he does; but I'll tell you where he beats me and where he beats
the world. He don't care a damn for what the enemy does out of his sight, but
it scares me like hell!

—William T. Sherman (Wilson, *Under the Old Flag*)

It would take until the winter of 1863/64 for Grant to formulate a
victorious Federal military strategy of overwhelming and coordinated
military pressure across the whole breadth of the Confederacy's land
and sea frontiers, and a full year's worth of campaigning between 1864
and 1865 to execute that strategy. Nevertheless, one should not believe
that the Federal cause saw a complete absence of strategic planning at
the outset of the war. In what the Northern press later dubbed the Anaconda Plan, Scott had proposed a Union military strategy early in the
war combining a naval blockade with a waterborne expedition down
the Mississippi "to clear out and keep open this great line of communication in connection with the strict blockade of the seaboard, so
as to envelop the insurgent States and bring them to terms with less
bloodshed than by any other plan."[1] Union naval power would also
seize New Orleans at the Mississippi's mouth, while riverine transport
would allow the proposed expeditionary force to turn Confederate
positions. Scott estimated in May 1861 that the Mississippi expedition would require approximately 60,000 soldiers, supported by forty
steam transports and twelve to twenty gunboats.

Later that month, in a missive to his future replacement, McClellan, Scott adjusted his estimate and called for a slightly larger force—roughly 80,000 men, divided into two columns, one spearheaded and supported by gunboats, while the second column marched in parallel via land. Scott asked McClellan for his military opinion on how many troops would be necessary for this campaign, and for advice on the composition of the proposed river fleet, but McClellan never properly replied.[2] Perhaps the senior general, however, had reminded the self-styled "Young Napoleon" of how he had utilized sea power to great advantage during the Vera Cruz campaign, in which McClellan had served as a lieutenant.

Whatever the source of the idea, the younger general early on recognized the potential advantages of Union sea power. He called for a naval force to help protect Cairo as early as April,[3] and he also supported Commander John Rodgers's early efforts to build a fleet of river gunboats.[4] Shortly after he moved east to take command of the Army of the Potomac, McClellan also proposed in his first written campaign plan of 2 August that "an essential feature of the plan of operations will be the employment of a strong naval force, to protect the movement of a fleet of transports, intended to convoy a considerable body of troops from point to point of the enemy's seacoast; thus either creating diversions and rendering it necessary for them to detach largely from their main body in order to protect such of their cities as may be threatened; or else landing and forming establishments on their coast at any favorable places that opportunity might offer. This naval force should also cooperate with the main army in its efforts to seize the important seaboard towns of the rebels."[5]

In his use of sea power, McClellan revealed a skepticism of the value of committing all military efforts to a decisive and climactic battle and a recognition of the importance of mobility and logistics. He recognized that Union naval superiority, if coastal defenses could be overcome, gave its armies secure lines of communications to the Confederacy's littoral regions, including many of its most important cities. Even more importantly, mastery of the sea could provide Federal forces both operational flexibility and the potential for surprising Confederate defenders, which could help compensate for the Confederacy's interior lines of communication (that is, the Confederacy's ability to use its internal rail network to reinforce threatened points more quickly than could the Union mass its forces in response). During both their prior wars with

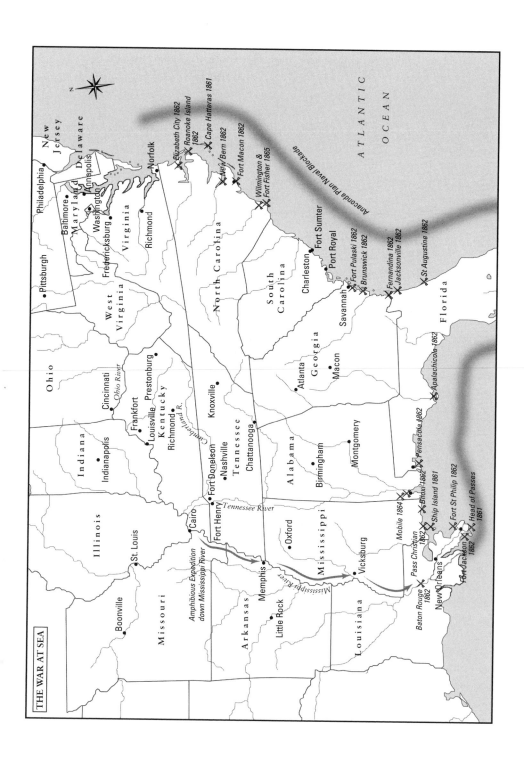

THE WAR AT SEA

the United States, the British had ably exploited such advantages. In the Revolution, the Royal Navy had doomed George Washington's defense of New York City in 1776, and in the War of 1812, its domination of the Chesapeake had played a crucial role in Washington's fall. The US Army Corps of Engineers (of which McClellan had been a proud member as a lieutenant) had constructed a system of seacoast fortifications designed in large part to defend the republic from British joint operations in the event of a third war with England. While the British example indicated that sea power could not by itself win a war, the Union's final set of victorious campaigns in 1864–65 included operations to capture the important port cities of Mobile and Wilmington, and Grant's original campaign plan included an important subordinate expedition to attack Richmond from the southeast via a seaborne expeditionary force, led by Butler.

The Richmond expedition of 1864 followed in broad terms McClellan's own strategy for a seaborne invasion force to turn the Confederate defenses between Washington and Richmond and allow the Union to advance on the secessionist capital from the direction of the Peninsula between the York and James Rivers southeast of Richmond. However, despite the promise of that line of operations, Butler's expedition failed in large part due to the same reasons McClellan's Peninsula Campaign collapsed after the Seven Days battles—namely, both generals proved ineffective field commanders. While McClellan had real strategic vision, his August memorandum also revealed the tendency to overestimate his opponents' strength that would help sabotage his own march on Richmond. McClellan's memorandum called for a great host of 273,000 men with 600 guns—a fantastic and unrealistic figure. In his mind, such numbers were a necessity, since less than a week later, he assessed Confederate strength opposite his to be at least 100,000 men, outnumbering his own 2-1. In reality, the Confederates would exert great energies to their numbers, but could not even manage to attain a goal of 60,000 soldiers. While McClellan's defenders continue to cite the faulty intelligence estimates provided to Little Mac on Confederate dispositions,[6] the Union commander should have realized that in light of the Confederacy's material inferiority, it was fantastic to believe Confederate forces severely outnumbered his own.

In this original formulation, McClellan planned that after everything had been prepared, his vast army would move on Richmond and then on to Charleston, Savannah, Montgomery, and New Orleans.

Additional supporting troops would follow to occupy the cities that fell into Union hands and secure lines of supply. While McClellan aimed to coordinate the primary army's campaign with other separate Federal efforts down the Mississippi River, along the Confederacy's coast, in the Tennessee-Kentucky area, and in Missouri, those operations would be purely subsidiary campaigns to draw Confederate attention away from the main effort under McClellan's personal command. While Grant's winning strategy would eventually balance both the Eastern and Western theaters, McClellan, even at his most innovative, tended to overprioritize Eastern operations. The pressures of the Peninsula Campaign would only exacerbate his problematic tendency to focus on operations he personally directed.

Finally, like his former commander, Scott, McClellan did not neglect political prerogatives in the planning of his military campaign. During his great campaign, McClellan intended that his Northern troops would leave Southern civilians, their property, and slaves untouched, so that the Union would be restored to its antebellum state without bitterness. Historians continue to debate the depth of antislavery sentiment among Northerners at this early stage of the war, but while McClellan's conservative views on slavery and emancipation represented a sizable proportion of public opinion in the loyal states, it also clashed with the antislavery tendencies of Republicans, whose views hardened after secession. More importantly, McClellan's political assessment assumed more Unionist sentiment in the Confederacy than actually existed. Lincoln himself had acknowledged during the 1860 presidential election the constitutionally protected status of slavery in the states where it already existed, and simply protecting slavery from military force during the war would do little to allay Confederates' long-term concerns about the safety of their institution. Regardless, whatever the exact state of public sentiment in the Union and the Confederacy at the start of the war, McClellan himself recognized that his conservative political strategy could only succeed if the war did not become a prolonged and bloody struggle. To prevent that outcome, McClellan's military strategy would have to bring the war to a successful conclusion during the 1862 campaigning season.

However, in late summer, Scott remained general in chief, and McClellan's views of strategy remained private advice he furnished the president. McClellan would spend months undermining his superior's position, but Scott would not finally depart the scene until

1 November. Furthermore, while McClellan early on recognized the value of joint operations and the flexibility provided by mastery of the sea, he never fully appreciated the strategic potential of a blockade of the Confederacy. Fortunately for the Union, Scott retained his position as general in chief long enough to set in motion joint army-navy operations in fall 1861 that would have important long-term results in supporting the Union blockade of the Confederacy.

While the grizzled War of 1812 veteran had provided the initial impetus of making a naval blockade a crucial part of the Union's larger military strategy to win the war, the joint Army-Navy Blockade Board that met in the late summer of 1861 provided crucial planning for such an enterprise. The brainchild of Alexander Bache, West Point graduate and head of the United States Coastal Survey, and a close associate of both senior army and navy officers, the Blockade Board deliberated on what coaling stations the navy needed to support the complicated logistics of the planned blockade. Blockading the South represented an immense task, given the 3,500 miles of coastline and ports at the disposal of Confederate blockade-runners, along with the hardly impressive naval forces at the disposal of the Union at the war's outset—barely forty-two ships in April 1861. The major ports were New Orleans, far and away the most important, Galveston, Mobile, Savannah, Charleston, and Wilmington. There were, of course, other possibilities along the coast, but without access to the docks and railroads available in major ports, the Confederates could import only minuscule tonnage at other locations.

Union naval officers realized that they did not need to cover the entire coastline, but even the closure of the Confederacy's major ports would require coaling stations to sustain the Union naval forces gathering together to enforce the blockade. The fact that the steamships of the time had to burn a ton of coal for every five to seven miles they steamed underlines the logistical importance of gaining such bases. Once in Union hands, colliers could stockpile coal for blockade vessels to replenish their supply of fuel and then return to station outside the port they were blockading, thus allowing them to remain on station for long periods of time.

Utilizing extensive information on such factors as coastal conditions, transportation links, availability of fresh water, and preexisting Confederate defenses, the board determined that the navy should establish coaling stations on the Atlantic Coast at Fernandina, Florida, and Bull's Bay, South Carolina. Welles approved these initial recommendations, which Scott and most importantly Lincoln endorsed in late July, shortly after the defeat at Bull Run. Scott provided feedback on operational timing in a meeting on 1 August and ordered Brigadier General Thomas Sherman to organize an expeditionary force of 12,000 men to cooperate with Samuel F. Du Pont, reassigned from heading the Blockade Board to command the naval component of the expedition, whose objective would eventually shift to Port Royal, South Carolina. Later in August, after an extensive survey of the complex Mississippi Delta, the board recommended the capture of Ship Island, Mississippi, located between Mobile and New Orleans, as a base for a Gulf blockading squadron. The board argued against making New Orleans an immediate Federal objective, as Scott had originally argued in his Anaconda Plan, until the navy could acquire greater resources to contend with the city's fortifications. Whatever the merits of either case, Federal forces seized Ship Island on 17 September. The Confederates were not even in a position to defend the half-finished fort. The campaign against New Orleans would wait until the following spring.

Meanwhile, both Welles and Scott continued to act independently of the Blockade Board in accordance with their own strategic instincts. In an effort to interdict Confederate privateers harassing Union shipping from bases in the Outer Banks, Welles asked Scott to provide army troops to cooperate with a naval expedition to Hatteras Inlet. Scott ordered Major General John F. Wool at Fort Monroe on 13 August to provide the ground forces necessary for the expedition. On 29 August, the combined army-navy force under Flag Officer Silas H. Stringham and Butler seized the barrier islands that protected Pamlico and Albemarle Sounds from the raging storms that move up the coast of North Carolina. Two forts, recently built by the Confederates, had guarded the entrance to the sounds. The troops had floundered ashore on 28 August, while Butler remained on board ship and the navy reduced Fort Clark, while steaming in circles to avoid Confederate gunnery—one of the advantages steam propulsion provided that overturned the old rule that one land-based gun could match four afloat. In the age of sail, land forts had possessed a substantial advantage, because sailing ships were slow and, therefore, wonderful targets. However, steamships could escape the tyranny of winds and currents, and as swiftly moving targets they were more difficult to hit.

The navy turned its attention to Fort Hatteras the following day, as wet and bedraggled troops then dragged themselves across the island to watch the surrender of the fort. The swift and easy nature of the Federal victory surprised both Union and Confederate high commands.

The Unfulfilled Promise of Port Royal

Wrangling between Scott and McClellan, the absence of institutionalized coordination between the land and sea services (the Blockade Board disbanded after submitting its last report on 19 September), and a lack of direction from a Lincoln still learning the position of commander in chief prevented the Union from taking advantage of the weakness of Confederate coastal defenses in fall and winter 1861. Even the one great victory of the season—the capture of Port Royal—faced a near stillbirth when Lincoln canceled the expedition on 14 September. Preoccupied as he was with the Army of the Potomac, and not in command of the larger military effort, McClellan had increasingly clashed with Scott over the safety of Washington's defenses, while doing his best to undermine his superior's authority. An exasperated Scott had gone so far as to offer his resignation on 9 August, which Lincoln initially refused. However, McClellan still had the ear of the president, who canceled the Port Royal expedition to take a mid-Atlantic coaling station in order to divert those troops to McClellan's field army.

Welles immediately raised the issue at a cabinet meeting on 17 September, after which Lincoln reversed himself. On 18 September, Du Pont had a private evening meeting with McClellan, where, in Du Pont's account, "McClellan . . . repelled with some feeling an impression that had got abroad that he was opposed to expeditions—but for the moment Washington was paramount." Furthermore, McClellan "thinks the war in the West should be mainly defensive. . . . The great wave must role from Washington, clear Virginia, and take every seaboard capital, one after the other."[7] Nevertheless, even McClellan's attempts to support combined operations caused problems in this confused command environment. In early September, he proposed the formation of a special amphibious division recruited from New Englanders, and to be "particularly adapted for coast service." He appointed Ambrose Burnside to head this new force, and he requested the attachment of a naval officer to Burnside's staff. That request triggered a comical cabinet meeting on 1 October where the secretary of war and the president only learned of McClellan's scheme after Burnside began recruiting the force. Burnside's proposed marine division caught the attention of an irate Gustavus Fox, former naval officer and assistant secretary of the navy, who wanted nothing to interfere with the Port Royal expedition.

Despite his later checkered career, Burnside's amphibious division would prove useful in North Carolina the following spring. More importantly, the Port Royal expedition survived the Union's confused command situation, but its objective was far more formidable than that faced by the Hatteras Expedition. Indeed, the Blockade Board had earlier deemed its defenses too powerful. But the powerful personality of Assistant Secretary of the Navy Gustavus Fox played a major role in fixing the expedition's objective on such an ambitious target. Port Royal Sound, lying inland from Hilton Head, already possessed two major forts guarding its entrance, Forts Walker and Beauregard. Each held approximately twenty cannons. The capture of the forts and islands would provide Union ships with a wonderful base for blockading Charleston and deny the Confederacy one of the major ports for its blockade-runners, since Port Royal was one of the finest natural harbors on the east coast.

In mid-October a fleet of naval vessels and transports left New York with 12,000 soldiers on board. The trip to Norfolk and Hampton Roads was easily made. However, the journey to South Carolina ran into a fall nor'easter off the coast of Cape Fear, North Carolina. The storm dispersed the fleet and damaged a number of ships. But Flag Officer Du Pont gathered the fleet back together and proceeded south. Even though the expedition would shortly display the new tactical possibilities produced by steam propulsion, naval operations remained prey to inclement weather, just as Xerxes's fleet had suffered serious losses due to a storm shortly before the Battle of Artemisium in 480 BC.

While naval operations still had to cope with unpredictable weather, Du Pont would shortly show the new possibilities provided by steam propulsion to an even greater degree than what the Union navy had achieved at Hatteras Inlet. Du Pont arranged his ships in column formation and sailed by Fort Beauregard, blasting that fort as his ships passed by. Then, once in the sound, his fleet swung around in a turn of 180 degrees. This time his warships passed by Fort Walker, to which they also gave a good dose of Union medicine. Thus, with his ships moving in an elliptical orbit, Du Pont passed by each fort several times, each time approaching the Confederates at a closer distance. Under this intense bombardment, the Confederates manning the guns ran away, and the forts fell into Union hands. With Hilton Head Island and the sound firmly in their hands, Union gunboats moved up the rivers and creeks that fed into the sound, while the ground forces soon had Beaufort and Port Royal in their hands. The plantations in the area, many of which the most rabid supporters of secession owned, immediately fell into Union hands. The owners decamped and the slaves ran away to the protection of Union troops. This underlined how little the plantation owners of South Carolina had calculated their vulnerabilities, and how eager their slaves were to gain their freedom. The navy now had another coaling station, this one less than fifty miles from Charleston.

Both Sherman and Du Pont, to their credit, saw that Port Royal's fall had potential that went far beyond serving as a logistical base for the navy's blockading operations. A few months later Du Pont wrote that "the occupation of this wonderful sheet of water, with its tributary rivers, inlets, outlets, entrances and sounds, running in all directions, cutting off effectually all water communications between Savannah and Charleston, has been like driving a wedge into the flanks of the rebels between these two important cities."[8] The Confederate high command agreed with this assessment, and Davis dispatched Lee to take command of the Confederacy's south Atlantic coast. Lee consolidated the region's limited military resources to defend its most important points, but warned in January that "the forces of the enemy are accumulating, and apparently increase faster than ours. I have feared, if handled with proportionate ability with his means of speedy transportation and concentration, it would be impossible to gather troops necessarily posted over a long line in sufficient strength, to oppose sudden movements."[9] Lee himself certainly recognized the dangerous flexibility Union sea power provided his adversaries.

Du Pont's counterpart, Thomas Sherman, also saw the new strategic possibilities opened by the Union victory at Port Royal. Unfortunately, Fox remained fixated on the capture of Fernandina, in accordance with the recommendations of the Blockade Board. Both Du Pont and Sherman recognized that the dispatch of a large ground force to Port Royal threatened both Charleston and Savannah. On 14

December, Sherman requested reinforcements for a major campaign, writing that, "I am firmly convinced that an operation of this sort would not only give us Savannah, but, if successful and strong enough to follow up the success, would shake the so-called Southern Confederacy to its very foundation."[10] Unfortunately, Fox had little interest in supporting an army-led campaign on the south Atlantic coast, despite Du Pont's sympathy and support for his army counterparts.

By this point, McClellan had officially replaced Scott as general in chief. Despite his recognition of the value of sea power and his organization of Burnside's amphibious division, McClellan had always conceived of any seaborne campaign as subordinate to his primary campaign against Richmond. In late November, he began the planning of the first version of what would become the Peninsula Campaign—the Urbanna Plan, which aimed to land McClellan's army at the mouth of the Potomac to outflank the Confederate defenders and march swiftly on Richmond. Scott's successor was thus loath to divert resources away from the Army of the Potomac, and he allowed Sherman to wither away unreinforced at Port Royal. In March 1862 McClellan finally ordered Sherman to support a naval expedition against Fernandina and another that captured Fort Pulaski guarding the Savannah River in April, which in effect blockaded Georgia from the sea. The city itself, however, would not fall to the Union until shortly before December 1864, and Confederate forces would only evacuate Charleston in February 1865 after Sherman's march through South Carolina cut off the cradle of secession from Confederate lines of supply—although Union operations virtually closed the port to blockade-runners by September 1863.

In retrospect, given what the Confederates were able to import through the blockade, it is surprising Northern leaders failed to mount a more sustained campaign to capture these ports earlier in the conflict. But here, one is dealing with the reality that most army and naval officers regarded their domains as separate preserves of sea and land, in or on which the other service was not to interfere. Furthermore, after Scott's departure, the Union high command lost the sort of strategic perspective that might have fully utilized Union advantages in sea power. While the Port Royal expedition did at least show how army and navy leaders could cooperate and succeed together, if both set their minds to such a task, army and navy field commanders frequently found more hindrance than aid in conducting joint operations from their respective service's high commands. Indeed, even Port Royal showed how Washington's refusal to resolve the question of unity of command in joint operations institutionalized interservice division and rivalry.

In his instructions to Du Pont for the Port Royal expedition, Welles himself had declared that "no officer of the army or the navy, whatsoever might be his rank, can assume any direct command, independent of consent, over an officer of the other service."[11] Absent local commanders determined to sort issues out among themselves, this was an obvious recipe for potential disaster—as a succession of fiascoes in Charleston in 1863 and Wilmington in 1864 displayed, where the army and navy acted at cross-purposes. Sherman found no sympathetic ears among his own service's leaders for a potential army-navy campaign on the south Atlantic coast, while Du Pont himself had to contend with Fox, an archnavalist who wrote Du Pont in June 1862 that "my duties are two fold; first, to beat our southern friends; second, to beat the Army."[12] Fox's fixation on Fernandina reflected in part a reasonable desire to support the blockade, which Scott had argued to be an important part of a larger Union strategy for victory, but it also originated in an unseemly preoccupation with the sea service's public prestige. With Confederate commerce raiders wreaking havoc on Union shipping, Welles and Fox felt considerable political pressure either to prevent the raiders from reaching open water, or to hunt them down on the high seas. While obviously reasonable to some degree, such demands distracted the navy's leadership from the strategic potential of joint operations.

New international prohibitions on privateering hindered this time-worn American form of naval warfare, but it did not stop ambitious Confederate naval officers such as Raphael Semmes from attacking Union merchant shipping. Semmes's case is instructive. An Alabamian who resigned from the US Navy in 1861, he first captained a converted merchant vessel, the CSS *Sumter*. Between the summer of 1861 and January 1862, when Semmes abandoned the vessel in Gibraltar, he had captured eighteen merchantmen. Semmes would go on to skipper the even more infamous CSS *Alabama*, which captured sixty-four merchantmen and sank the USS *Hatteras*, before the USS *Kearsarge* hunted it down and sank it outside Cherbourg, France, in the summer of 1864. Confederate commerce raiders savaged the Union's merchant marine and diverted scarce naval resources away from the blockade, but these tactical successes could not have a decisive effect on the Union war effort.

Nevertheless, outside of commerce raiding—one example of what military writers would now call asymmetrical warfare—it is hard to speak of a naval war in 1861, because the South had neither the ships nor the shipyards and industrial capacity to build vessels that could threaten the ability of the North to blockade the Confederacy. Yet Davis and his naval advisers would expend approximately 25 percent of the iron produced by Southern industry during the war in attempting to build ironclads, which were to have little impact on the war's course. Like the Germans in World War II, who would have done far better not to have invested in their vast U-boat fleet and used those resources elsewhere, the Confederacy would have done better to have ignored efforts to build a naval capability and used the iron to replace the deteriorating rails on its collapsing railroad system. Nevertheless, the conduct of strategy is a matter of difficult choices, choices that, once made, close off other options. Lacking an understanding of the basic principle of industrialized war—that investment in the repair of infrastructure is often more important than the production of weapons and armaments—Confederate leaders consistently made the wrong decisions in these areas. But then, coming from a slave-holding and agricultural elite, their choices are not surprising. More damning, however, was the Union's inability to take full advantage of its insuperable massive advantages in naval power, due not to a deficit of material resources, but to an absence of sufficient strategic imagination among most Union naval and military leaders until Grant took the reins of the Union war effort in the winter of 1863/64. It was no surprise that Grant's willingness to support joint army-navy operations in the East found precedent in his own masterful use of naval power in the spring of 1862.

Northern Industrial Might and the River War

Outside of the skirmishing in Missouri, there was relatively little fighting in the west in 1861, as Grant began his important education in command. The major cause lay in Kentucky's self-proclaimed neutrality, although McClellan actually hoped Union forces could take the offensive in Unionist eastern Tennessee shortly after he took command of Union armies.[13] However, he had installed a kindred spirit, Don Carlos Buell, as commander of the Department of the Ohio, and Buell proved as cautious as his chief. Furthermore, like McClellan, Buell emphasized meticulous preparation in the military sphere and conservative protection of civilian private property (including slaves) in the political arena. However, Buell lacked McClellan's charisma and powerful rapport with his rank and file.

Thus, the armies of the two sides could not get at each other. Nevertheless, both sides prepared for the struggle they knew was coming. But here the substantially greater resources available to the North came into play. As mentioned earlier, one of the most sensible acts undertaken by Frémont during his 100 days in command had been to authorize construction of a gunboat fleet in order to control the Mississippi. The strange-looking vessels that resulted were the product of the inventive mind of James B. Eads, who had received an army contract to construct them in August 1861. His boats were 175 feet in length with a 50-foot beam. Armor plating two and a half inches thick, canted at a 35-degree angle, covered their vulnerable engines, while each carried thirteen guns. Despite their considerable weight they drew only six feet and were astonishingly maneuverable for their size. In other words, they were the perfect vessels to fight for and control the western rivers. By November 1861, less than four months after he had received the contract, Eads and his workmen had produced a fleet of eight armored gunboats with more on the way.

The production and manning of the North's gunboats in the Midwest underlines the immense superiority the North enjoyed in manufacturing strength as well as the ingenuity and competence of its engineers. The Confederates, lacking the resources and perhaps more important the imagination, had nothing comparable. Indeed, the Confederates were at work constructing ironclad vessels along sections of the Mississippi, the Tennessee, the Cumberland, and in the east. Nevertheless, when the crucial naval clashes occurred in spring 1862, with the exception of the *Merrimack*, most were not ready to fight, and those that were proved distinctly inferior in engineering and design.

But it was not just the army that was building up capabilities in what today's parlance would term riverine warfare. Others interested themselves in preparing the logistical and combat basis for a move down the Mississippi, including the navy. Supported by Lincoln, one naval project created of a set of flat-bottom boats that could fire mortar shells into Confederate forts along the river. The navy took over responsibility for Eads's turtle fleet of gunboats, even though the majority of the men manning them were soldiers. Here the advantage the North possessed in its workforce of grubby mechanics, so derided by Confederates, again worked to its advantage. Scattered throughout the Northern volunteer regiments in southern Illinois and Indiana were large numbers of railroad workers and other mechanics, who were ideal candidates to work on and repair the steam propulsion systems of the fleet. War in the nineteenth century was becoming a war of technology, and the side that could utilize technology fully would enjoy a substantial advantage. Thus, the gunboats and transports that assembled to support the drive down the Mississippi already possessed the manpower necessary to man and repair the machinery.

In summer 1861 Ulysses Grant found himself assigned to Cairo, Illinois, where the Ohio and Mississippi meet. He was particularly assiduous in whipping into shape the volunteer regiments assigned to his command. In terms of chance and fortune, of which Grant had little thus far in life, the luck of the draw placed him, as a newly minted brigadier general, in the most important geographic position in the war—namely, where the four great rivers of the Midwest—the Mississippi, Ohio, Cumberland, and Tennessee—all come together. Both Grant and his counterpart Polk, the latter based on the Mississippi in western Tennessee, were poised to move into Kentucky to seize Columbus, whose bluffs dominated the river below.

Polk moved first in early September to grab the town, which he believed to be the key geographic and strategic real estate in the area. But that small city did not turn out to be all that strategically important. Instead, the real prize was control over that portion of the Ohio into which the Tennessee and Cumberland Rivers flowed, because those two rivers led directly to control of most of Tennessee and Kentucky. Moreover, whoever controlled the Tennessee River possessed a back door entry into Columbus and the ground surrounding the town from the east. In other words, Columbus was indefensible if Union forces controlled the Tennessee. But virtually everyone, North and South, was looking at the Mississippi rather than at the river systems that fed into it from the east.

For one of the few times in Grant's military career an opponent moved first. In response, Grant moved up the Ohio River and seized Paducah, Kentucky, which possessed nothing of importance except geography. He who held Paducah controlled the entrance to the Tennessee River, which was only twelve miles up the Ohio from Cairo. Not much farther up the river, the Cumberland flows into the Ohio. Control of the Tennessee River would allow Union gunboats to move deep into central Tennessee and on into northeastern Mississippi and northwestern Alabama to Muscle Shoals. Control of the Cumberland would render Nashville defenseless. Initially Grant does not seem to have recognized why Paducah was more significant than Columbus, but was more than willing to grab the town, if he could not reach Columbus before the Confederates. Once ensconced in Paducah, it quickly became clear to him that the town provided an ideal jumping-off point to seize control of the Tennessee and Cumberland Rivers.

In November, Grant led a small raid of several regiments to attack the Confederates at Belmont, Missouri, across the Mississippi from Columbus. At first, his troops enjoyed considerable success, but matters then fell apart as the inexperienced and somewhat ill-disciplined Union troops paused to loot the Confederate camp. Grant and his little force were lucky to get away, but at least he had blooded his troops. Not only had Andrew Foote's gunboats transported his troops, but they also provided crucial artillery support, including covering fire for the Union withdrawal (Foote was commander of the navy's Mississippi River Squadron). Most importantly, Grant had learned an early lesson in the benefits of joint operations with the navy. The education of Ulysses Grant, having begun earlier in the summer, thus continued.

There had been relatively little movement and even less fighting in the West throughout 1861. But all that was about to change. While the political and strategic focus of the opposing sides remained largely on the Eastern theater throughout 1862, Union forces in the West were to win victories that laid the foundation for the North's victory. Unfortunately for the Union's prospects for 1862, Lincoln had a far better idea of what needed to be done than did his generals in the various theaters. In letters to Major General Don Carlos Buell and Halleck at the beginning of 1862, the president made clear his conception of how he believed the Union should conduct the war at the operational level: "I state my general idea of this war to be that we have the *greater* numbers, and the enemy has the *greater* facility of concentrating forces upon points of collision; that we must fail, unless we can find some way of making *our* advantage an over-match for *his*; and that this can only be done by menacing him with superior forces at *different* points, at the *same* time; so that we can safely attack, one, or both, if he makes no change; and if he *weakens* one to *strengthen* the other, forbear to attack the strengthened one, but seize, and hold the weakened one, gaining so much."[14]

In command of the Confederate Western theater of Kentucky and Tennessee was General Albert Sidney Johnston. Of all the officers from the regular army joining the Confederacy in 1861, Johnston had the highest reputation. At the outbreak of war, he was in command of the Federal troops in California. He resigned his commission when Texas seceded and then led a group of like-minded officers and civilians in a desperate journey across Arizona and New Mexico to reach Richmond after Bull Run. There, Jefferson Davis, an old friend, conferred on him command of Confederate forces responsible for defending Tennessee and eventually Kentucky, if that state were to abandon its self-professed position of neutrality. Thus, the Confederate president charged Johnston with the responsibility of defending a span of territory reaching from the Mississippi River to eastern Kentucky, where that state touched Virginia. Unfortunately for the fate of the Confederacy, Davis failed to provide Johnston with the means. That failure reflected the fact the Confederate leadership devoted too much attention to Virginia and the defense of Richmond and too little to the West. Exacerbating the difficulties Johnston confronted was the fact the Confederates chose to defend forward in Kentucky, once Leonides "Bishop" Polk had breached that state's neutrality. The addition of a star for Kentucky to the Confederacy's new flag, the Stars and Bars, symbolized Confederate aspirations as well as political aims.

The distribution of Confederate forces in the West underlined the lack of means. In western Kentucky Polk possessed approximately 17,000 troops near Columbus, overlooking the Mississippi. Their mission was to block the river. Major General William J. Hardee defended forward in central Kentucky at Bowling Green. His army had a strength of approximately 25,000 soldiers. In the far eastern reaches of the state, Felix Zollicoffer held the Cumberland Gap with 4,000 ill-trained and badly equipped soldiers. Johnston's distribution of forces represented a cordon defense, which attempted to defend everything and thus defended nothing. At least the Confederates had one commander in the West. Nevertheless, by failing to provide a strategic focus, Johnston forfeited that advantage. It is hard to estimate what sort of commander he was, given how briefly he remained in command. His death at Shiloh in April 1862 allowed white Southerners after the war to claim his death as one of the major catastrophes to happen to the Confederate cause, a death on the battlefield some ranked with that of Stonewall Jackson's at Chancellorsville. Yet, both the dispositions of Confederate forces in early 1862, as well as Johnston's conduct of the Battle of Shiloh, hardly suggest a great general.

The key strategic piece of geography the Confederacy absolutely had to defend to protect Tennessee was the area where the Tennessee and Cumberland Rivers converged on the Ohio River. The first two of those rivers provided direct access into the Confederacy's heartland of central Tennessee as well as northern Alabama and Mississippi. Thus, the location where they converged represented a geographic feature of the greatest strategic importance. During the period of Kentucky's neutrality, the Confederates had begun construction of two forts to protect the rivers: Fort Henry on the right bank of the Tennessee and Fort Donelson on the left bank of the Cumberland. The distance between the rivers at that point is approximately eleven miles, so that from their outer defenses, only nine miles separated the two forts. However, in Kentucky the two rivers move even closer, within three miles of each other. Forts there would have been mutually supporting. When Southern troops moved into Kentucky, however, Confederate commanders failed to take advantage of geography and continued work on Donelson and Henry.

Adding to the weakness of the forts, the Confederates had constructed Henry on such low ground that the Tennessee would inevitably flood the post when the fall and winter rains arrived. In addition, high bluffs stood directly across from Henry, which, if Union troops seized them, would render the fort defenseless. Johnston could have corrected this, but in fact did nothing, since he was focusing his attention on the Mississippi River and Bowling Green. He did send an engineering officer to examine the state of the forts. Brigadier General Lloyd Tilghman arrived in November and reported that matters were most discouraging, but that he would not give up. Nevertheless, he appears to have done little to fix the perilous state of Henry's defenses.

Three Union armies opposed the Confederates in the West. Major General Henry Halleck had assumed command of the military district comprising Missouri and western Kentucky on 2 November 1861 as Frémont's replacement. He and his former West Point instructor,

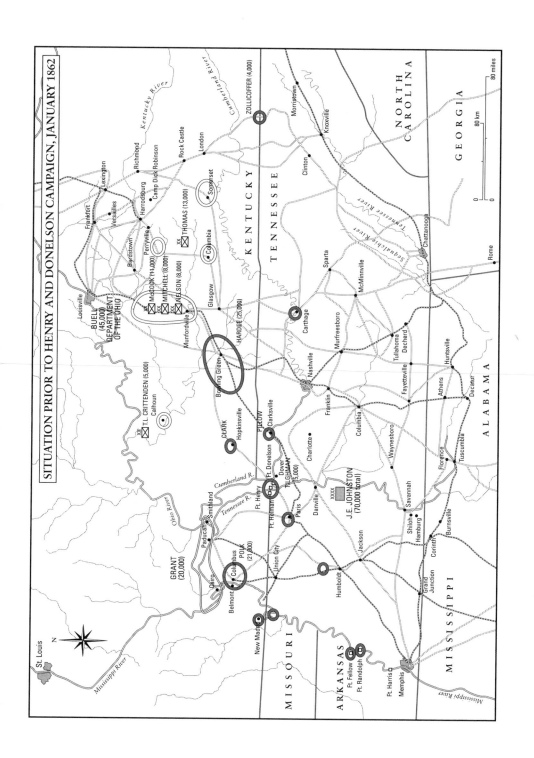

SITUATION PRIOR TO HENRY AND DONELSON CAMPAIGN, JANUARY 1862

Dennis Hart Mahan (father of Alfred Thayer Mahan, the future naval theorist), were the only military intellectuals the regular army produced. In fact, he had even written a book, *Elements of Military Art and Science*, a work that was not much more than a regurgitation of Jomini's dicta, and had translated the Swiss theorist's work on Napoleon from the French. Halleck was also ambitious, but at the same time cautious and unwilling to make decisions, particularly those involving risk. His ambition as well as his personality led him to attempt to rid the army of Grant, and when Grant's success made that impossible, he minimized Grant's opportunities in 1863 after Vicksburg. He was a nasty, arrogant man, sure of his own abilities, but at best a military administrator without either imagination or strategic intuition. Farther east was an equally cautious general, Don Carlos Buell, who reflected the weaknesses of the regular army. Like Halleck, he too was cautious and unimaginative without a shred of leadership ability. However, both generals possessed outstanding subordinates: Halleck with Grant and Buell with George "Pap" Thomas, a Virginian, who, unlike many other officers from his state, had believed in 1861 that he could not simply dismiss the oath he had sworn to defend the Constitution by resigning his commission. And so to his family's fury, he had remained an officer in the US Army, in which he would serve the Union loyally and competently.

Thomas achieved the first success in the West. Marching south in nasty, raw weather, his small army caught Brigadier General Felix Zollicoffer's troops deployed with their back to an overflowing creek, which rendered their position hopeless. Johnston sent General George Crittenden—his brother would prove a more competent Union general—to bring experience to Zollicoffer's command. But Crittenden arrived too late to repair the faulty dispositions. The result was a disaster. In the skirmish at Mill Springs, Thomas smashed the badly deployed Confederates, his victory proving his loyalty to the Union and justifying the strong recommendation that Sherman had given to the president on his behalf in July 1861. Thomas's victory yielded little in physical terms, because the rain and mountainous terrain of eastern Kentucky soon halted his advance.

Thomas's success finally pushed Halleck into authorizing Grant to visit his headquarters in St. Louis. In mid-January Grant arrived to propose a general movement forward. As Grant records: "I was received with so little cordiality that I perhaps stated the object of

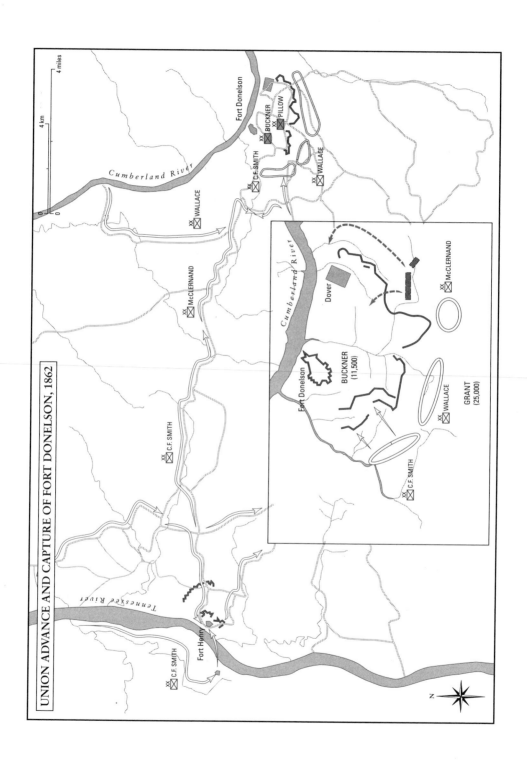

UNION ADVANCE AND CAPTURE OF FORT DONELSON, 1862

my visit with less clarity than I might have done, and I had not uttered many sentences before I was cut short as if my plan was prepos-
terous."[15] But shortly after this meeting Lincoln gave his order that
Union commanders were to begin a forward movement against the
Confederates in all the theaters of operation. Grant had already established a close working relationship with Flag Officer Andrew Foote,
commander of the navy's Mississippi River Squadron.

Lieutenant Seth L. Phelps, skipper of the timber-clad *Conestoga* in
Foote's flotilla, had discovered the haphazard state of Forts Henry and
Donelson through aggressive reconnaissance operations, and Grant
lobbied Halleck for authorization to begin a campaign against both.
As it turns out, both Buell and McClellan had recognized to some degree the importance of gunboats on the rivers, and the importance of
Forts Henry and Donelson, but they lacked Grant's determination to
act.[16] But Thomas's victory at Mill Springs and the pressure from Lincoln finally persuaded Halleck to act. Thus, he gave a surprised Grant
the green light to move against Fort Henry. Grant was delighted. He
had already established an outstanding working relationship with
Foote, responsible for the gunboats and other vessels on the Mississippi and Ohio Rivers, and the two formed an army-navy team even
more potent than the partnership established by Du Pont and Thomas
Sherman.

Never one to lose an opportunity, Grant moved. Led by Foote's
gunboats and loaded on the flag officer's transports, Grant with
twenty-three regiments departed for Henry. His plan was simple and
straightforward, but, to paraphrase Clausewitz, the simplest thing in
war often proves difficult in execution. Grant planned to land one division on each side of the Tennessee, a short distance downriver from
Henry. While Foote's gunboats bombarded the fort, the troops would
work their way up the river to seize the west bank, where the bluffs
overlooked the fort and its defending garrison. In this case, the operation turned out to be easier than expected. The river was in full flood,
so that only nine of the fort's fifteen guns remained above water; water
was already lapping at the doors of the magazine; and the garrison
possessed a motley collection of arms. At first Tilghman, now garrison commander, thought of fighting, but the flood of reinforcing
troops that Grant and Foote were landing downstream quickly
changed his mind. That night he ordered the fort abandoned and left
only a token force to cover the retreat to Donelson. After a two-hour

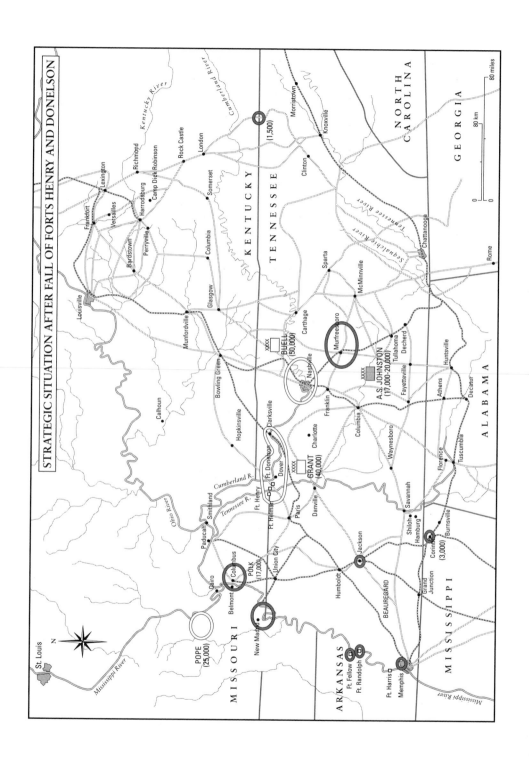

STRATEGIC SITUATION AFTER FALL OF FORTS HENRY AND DONELSON

bombardment, the rump garrison surrendered. On 6 February 1862 the Tennessee River was open to Union naval movement all the way to Muscle Shoals in northeastern Alabama.

The navy immediately underlined how crucial Fort Henry was. Keeping the ironclad turtles for the assault on Donelson, Foote dispatched his three wooden gunboats up the Tennessee into the central portion of the state and on into Mississippi and Alabama. With minimum cost, the joint operation had opened up a 150-mile highway into the South's heartland and placed much of central Tennessee in Union hands. Thus, Union military forces could move into portions of the state close to the river and then supply them for further operations inland. Its strategic effect represented a deadly stroke, perhaps the deadliest of the war. Underlining the river's strategic importance, the three gunboats had a field day on their raid. Not only did they destroy the key railroad bridge over which the Memphis and Charleston Railroad ran—one of the most important links in the Confederacy—but they also captured or destroyed every steamer on the river, including an ironclad on which the Confederates had been desperately at work, and which they had been unable to complete, in sharp contrast to the large riverine fleet of armored gunboats Foote already possessed.

The loss of Henry represented a disaster of the greatest magnitude to Johnston's strategy of holding Union forces north of the Tennessee state line. It made Columbus untenable, which underlined the disastrous mistake that Polk had made in moving into Kentucky the previous September. Hardee had to abandon Bowling Green and fall back to Nashville, since Buell's army was threatening to move on that city. Nor were the Confederates in a position to regain Henry and control of the Tennessee, while Henry's fall indicated Donelson was next. Albert Sidney Johnston had few illusions; he reported to Richmond that Donelson had as little chance of holding out as had Henry. In fact, he had decided to abandon that fort almost immediately. His subordinates, however, had other ideas.

On 12 February, Grant, reinforced by Halleck, struck at Donelson. As the soldiers marched, Foote and his gunboats turned down the Tennessee. When they reached the Ohio, they took a right, sailing up the Ohio until they reached the Cumberland, where they turned south to move up the Cumberland to support the assault on Donelson. Foote's fleet carried 10,000 of Grant's soldiers. Grant with another 15,000 marched across the twelve miles to the Confederate fort. On the way, during a balmy late winter day, the soldiers, still raw in their first months of service, discarded their coats and blankets, a move they would deeply regret. The next day a Canadian air mass chilled Tennessee with below freezing temperatures. Moreover, three inches of snow covered the shivering soldiers. Grant's troops arrived at Donelson before Foote's fleet, leaving Grant uncomfortably outnumbered for a night by the fort's garrison. But Foote arrived the next day, and Grant had three divisions with 25,000 soldiers, one division under Brigadier General Charles Smith, Grant's mentor when he had been at West Point; one under the politician John McClernand; and another under an aspiring writer and lawyer from Indiana, Lew Wallace, who would later write *Ben Hur*.

Unlike Henry, the Confederates had built Donelson on defensible terrain. Johnston had wanted the garrison to hold out long enough for Hardee to retreat from Bowling Green, and for Beauregard, now assigned to the West, to pull the Confederate troops back from Columbus, Kentucky. In fact, the Donelson garrison stayed too long. In overall command of approximately 17,000 Confederate soldiers was Brigadier General John B. Floyd, the corrupt and traitorous secretary of war in the Buchanan administration. His subordinates were Brigadier General Gideon Pillow, another Southern politician and just as incompetent as Floyd, and Brigadier General Simon Bolivar Buckner, who at least had regular army experience and ironically was an old friend of Grant.

On 13 February Smith and McClernand launched unsuccessful probing attacks. By the afternoon of the 14th Union lines entirely surrounded the fort with Smith on the left, Wallace in the center, and McClernand on the right of the Union lines. At 1500, Foote's gunboats opened up with a furious bombardment, but this time Confederate return fire inflicted crippling damage on the Union gunboats and forced Foote to retreat downriver, some of his boats no longer able to get up steam. The repulse of Foote's gunboats showed the limits of naval power, and only truly joint operations with strong army and navy components could overcome competently sited and well-positioned fortifications. Nevertheless, despite their success in driving the gunboats off, the Confederate generals decided their position was hopeless, and they began to plan a breakout.

Pillow was responsible for launching the initial attack. It hit McClernand on the far right of the Union line. Awake after a freezing night, McClernand's division put up a stiff fight. Nevertheless, the Confederates gradually opened the way for a breakout from the encirclement. McClernand sent desperate messages to Wallace, in which he requested reinforcements. However, as he was to do at Shiloh two months later, Wallace hesitated to move his division without direct instructions from Grant. Moreover, Grant was not present, having ridden off to visit the injured Foote. Luckily for Union fortunes, the Confederates failed to take advantage of their enemy's discomfort. Wallace finally reinforced McClernand, and their combined forces beat back several Confederate attacks. Nevertheless, the Confederates had succeeded in opening an escape route, their primary goal.

In the early afternoon, Grant arrived. As he was to do at Shiloh, he immediately took command. He recognized what those on the spot had not; the Confederates were not trying to defeat their besiegers, but rather were attempting to escape. As he noted later, "the one who attacks first now will be victorious and the enemy will have to be in a hurry if he gets ahead of me."[17] Sending word to Foote to restart the bombardment, Grant prepared a counterattack. He did not have to, because Pillow and Floyd lost their nerve and retreated. Meanwhile, Smith had launched his division against the northwestern portion of Donelson's defenses. His attack drove through Confederate lines, denuded to make the breakout. Late in the afternoon, Wallace launched the counterattack that Grant had ordered and retook virtually all of the ground Pillow's troops had seized in the morning.

The day's fighting left the Confederates in a hopeless position. Buckner, the one professional soldier among the senior officers (whose son, the commander of the US Tenth Army on Okinawa, the Japanese would later kill in April 1945), argued that his troops could not hold a determined attack for more than half an hour. He then received the dubious honor of surrendering the fort the next morning, since Pillow and Floyd decided to fly the coop, Floyd being especially worried about talk in the North about a trial for his "treasonable" activities as secretary of war. Nathan Bedford Forrest, the cavalry commander at Donelson, announced that, "he would prefer that the bones of his men should bleach on the surrounding hills rather than they should be carried to the North and cooped up in open prison-pens during mid-winter," and stomped out of the council of war.[18] He proved a man of his words, as he took his cavalry out of the fort during the night and through Union lines to escape the surrender. Buckner wrote out a message requesting an armistice from his old friend. Grant's reply could not have been colder: "Yours of this date, proposing armistice and appointment of Commissioners to settle terms of capitulation, is just received. No terms except unconditional and immediate surrender can be accepted. I propose to move immediately upon your works."[19] There it was: Grant in all his simplicity and directness. His announcement stands in stark contrast to McClellan's mock heroic copying of Napoleon.

Halleck's attitude toward Grant was immediately apparent. Not only did he assume much of the credit for Henry and Donelson, but also he telegraphed Foote congratulations on his "splendid victory." He sent no similar message to Grant. Worse was to follow. Part of the problem in the Halleck-Grant relationship at the time was that a Confederate sympathizer was in the telegraph loop between the generals and had been dumping Grant's messages, leaving Halleck with the impression that Grant was ignoring him. Grant's earlier problems with the bottle, which surely reached Halleck's ears through the small and gossipy world of Old Army officers, could only have fed into Halleck's perception of Grant as unmilitary and undisciplined. Halleck mounted a surreptitious campaign to rid himself of this subordinate. He passed along to McClellan, still the army's commander in chief, rumors Grant was again drinking, a refrain that those who wanted to rid the army of Grant used throughout the war. Halleck also claimed that "satisfied with his victory, he sits down and enjoys it without any regard to the future."[20] In fact, almost immediately after Donelson fell, Grant had requested permission to move up the Cumberland to seize Nashville. However, Halleck, ever cautious, had ordered Grant to proceed no farther than Clarksville, Tennessee.

There is no doubt Halleck was eager to rid himself of Grant, but the administration in Washington was not about to remove a general who was willing to fight. It squashed Halleck's efforts by telling him that if he had serious issues with Grant, he should prefer charges. Halleck was not about to do that, because he knew that any inquiry would make him, not Grant, look bad. Nevertheless, Halleck received most of the credit for the victories. Lincoln and Stanton placed him in command of the Western theater of operations in the same order that stripped McClellan of overall command of the Union armies. That his rival Buell was now his subordinate may have assuaged Halleck's annoyance at the fact that Lincoln placed Grant first on the promotion list to major general.

The opening of the Cumberland River immediately resulted in the fall of Nashville. Johnston had no hope of holding the city with Buell's approach from the northeast and Grant and Foote from along the river. The Confederate failure to emphasize the defense of the lower Cumberland and Tennessee Rivers had come home to roost. Grant and Foote had achieved the key breakthrough of the Confederacy's cordon defense in the West. The results of the campaign deprived the Confederacy of most of her significant economic resources, but the loss of much of Tennessee stung all the more due to its commitment to secession. In addition to losing the iron-rich regions of the lower Tennessee valley, the Forts Henry and Donelson campaign also won for the Union the same part of the country that had supplied one-third of the Confederate army's pork in 1861, along with various supply and ordnance depots. One historian argues that "the consequences that followed the loss of Forts Henry and Donelson may well have been the greatest single supply disaster of the war."[21]

Moreover, at Donelson, Grant bagged an entire Confederate field army and obtained a decisive military outcome, without having to commit to a risky pitched battle against a massed army. He thus achieved the outcome McClellan would later attempt but fail to obtain during the Peninsula Campaign, where the latter also hoped to use joint operations to attempt to trap Confederate defenders in a siege that would force their eventual capitulation. Grant would duplicate this feat, albeit on a far more impressive scale, at Vicksburg the following year. In both campaigns, Grant utilized the strategic flexibility provided by the Union's dominance of the rivers while recognizing the limitations of sea power, and the necessity of hard fighting on land to complete tasks that the navy could only begin.

The disaster at Donelson was bad enough for the Confederacy's strategic position, but it was accompanied by a series of other military failures in spring 1862. Almost concurrently with Donelson's fall, Burnside's unused amphibious force finally got into the fight as part of a combined army-navy task force that seized Roanoke Island inside of North Carolina's barrier islands, thereby insuring that Northern gunboats could dominate Albemarle and Pamlico Sounds. Whatever his other faults, McClellan had helped conceive of this expedition and deserves some credit for it. This strike along the coast tightened the blockade, insuring that North Carolina's inland waters would not be a haven for blockade-runners. But the situation in the West appeared the most threatening to the South's strategic position. The Confederate reaction underlined Lincoln's strategic grasp of the war. As he had pointed out to Halleck and Buell, when pressed on all sides, part or all of the Confederate defenses were going to snap. The focusing of Confederate strength to meet the desperate situation in Tennessee was going to have the unintended consequence of denuding strategically important areas elsewhere of their defenders—the most important being New Orleans. However, as the Confederacy would again attempt later that fall and in summer 1863, it would commit itself to an offensive that aimed at obtaining a decisive Napoleonic battle.

Shiloh: The First of the Killing Battles

The Confederates now attempted to patch together a military force to prevent further Union gains in Tennessee and win back a portion of what they had lost. Beauregard helped Polk pull back the 17,000 Confederates deployed near Columbus. The next Union target was obviously going to be Corinth, Mississippi, a crucial railroad center. The Mobile & Ohio ran from the Gulf Coast to Columbus, Kentucky, while the Memphis & Charleston ran from east to west, both running through Corinth. Thus, the town was one of the most important railroad centers in the Confederacy. Admittedly, Foote's gunboats had already cut the Memphis & Charleston by destroying its bridge across the Tennessee, but the Confederates certainly aimed to regain that territory.

Throughout March, Johnston and Beauregard concentrated their dispersed forces in Corinth. Polk with his 17,000 was the first to arrive. Initially, Beauregard was in charge, but when Johnston arrived with Hardee's bedraggled force of 10,000 soldiers, who had retreated to Decatur from Bowling Green and then on to Corinth, he assumed command with Beauregard as his deputy. Additional forces poured in from the South: Bragg with 10,000 men from the Gulf Coast and Brigadier General Daniel Ruggles with 5,000 men from New Orleans arrived. Their exodus would leave the Gulf Coast largely undefended. Altogether, Johnston and Beauregard assembled an army of slightly over 40,000, many of whom were poorly trained and equipped. Thus, the two generals undertook what measures they could to correct tactical deficiencies. The threat was immediate, because Grant's army

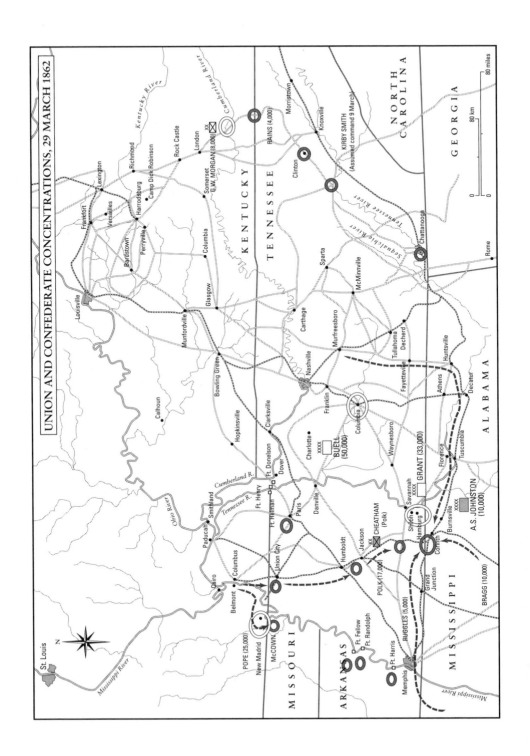

UNION AND CONFEDERATE CONCENTRATIONS, 29 MARCH 1862

had already deployed on the left bank of the Tennessee at a place called Pittsburg Landing. The Confederates knew that Buell was on the march from Nashville to join Grant and that the combined Union force would so outnumber them that there would be no chance of victory. Thus, the Confederate generals had to strike before the Union armies combined.

Grant commanded six divisions with a total strength of slightly over 33,000. To a certain extent he and his subordinate commanders were suffering from "victory disease." The successes at Henry and Donelson had imbued them with an overconfidence that whatever might happen, the Confederates could not launch a major attack. Thus, the division commanders spread their regiments out over the open and flat landscape lying west of the river. Grant had picked Pittsburg Landing precisely because it offered open terrain, on which his officers could train their inexperienced troops. Two creeks bounded the position, Owl Creek on the right and Lick Creek on the left. In effect, the streams narrowed the battlefield to less than seven miles so that the Confederates had no chance of outflanking Union forces, but considering the training of their troops and leaders, they could not have launched an outflanking move anyway.

Within the Union encampment there was a solitary wooden chapel, named by the locals Shiloh Church, which gave the battle its name. Sherman was now one of Grant's division commanders, brought back by Halleck from his near breakdown in eastern Kentucky. The Union deployment was as follows: Lew Wallace's division deployed at Crump's Landing approximately six miles down the Tennessee. The other five divisions spread themselves out over the area between Shiloh Church and the river. Looking to the west from the river, Sherman was on the right, McClernand in the center, slightly to Sherman's rear, and General Benjamin Prentiss slightly forward of McClernand on the left. William H. L. Wallace's division was to the rear behind Prentiss with General Stephen Hurlbut's division to his left, close up on the river. As the Union commanders were confident the Confederates would not attack, they failed to fortify their position. In other words, they deployed as if they were on peacetime maneuvers, rather than deep in Confederate territory with an enemy army numbering at least 25,000 men, if not more, a mere twenty miles distant.

If the Union deployment displayed a certain carelessness, the Confederate planning, deployment, and conduct of the Battle of Shiloh was amateur hour from beginning to end. Johnston and Beauregard understood they had to move quickly before Buell arrived. They possessed seventy-one regiments organized into four corps, which Hardee, Polk, Breckinridge, and Bragg led. There were two tracks, called roads, leading from Corinth to Pittsburg Landing. Hardee and Polk were to take the northern road with Hardee's troops leading the way; Bragg's corps was to lead Breckinridge on the southern route. The movement to contact suggests how unprepared the Confederates were to undertake a serious military operation.

The march began on 4 April. Staff work was appallingly bad, so that confusion, delay, and snarls of units, artillery, and accompanying wagons immediately occurred, as the troops tried to sort themselves out. Early spring showers deluged the troops and muddied the roads into morasses. To make sure their weapons worked, a number of Confederate soldiers test fired their muskets along the way, while others took to shooting stray animals stirred up by the noise of tens of thousands of human beings invading the wilderness between Corinth and Pittsburg Landing. Scheduled to begin in the early morning, the march started four hours late. The army was to cover the twenty-odd miles to Pittsburg Landing by midmorning the next day. In fact, the lead troops were still straggling along the roads to the west of Shiloh early in the afternoon of the 5th. At a conference of senior Confederate generals, Beauregard argued for returning to Corinth, because surely the shooting and noise of the troops had appraised the Union army of the Confederate approach. But his colleagues overruled him. The attack would now begin at dawn on 6 April.

The plan, as with the march, exposed the lack of understanding among Confederate commanders of what complex military operations required. Hardee's corps was to deploy as a solid front line; Bragg's corps was to follow in a second wave behind Hardee. A third wave consisting of Breckinridge's corps and Polk's corps would then follow the first two waves. If the deployment made sense in providing the raw troops and commanders with a simple plan to deploy during the evening and night of 5/6 April, it guaranteed that once launched, command and control would collapse on contact with Grant's troops. Moreover, if the first rush failed to overwhelm the defenders, then it would be impossible to concentrate a coherent drive on any portion of the Union line, because Confederate regiments and divisions would find themselves intermingled. Thus, it would prove almost impossible

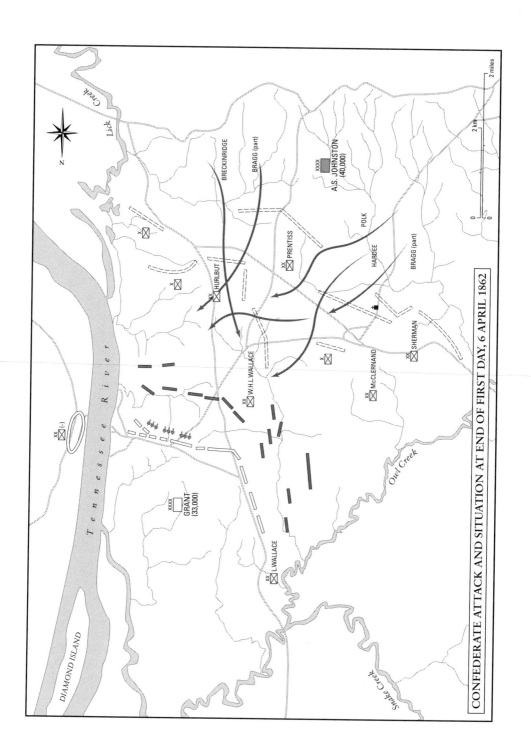

CONFEDERATE ATTACK AND SITUATION AT END OF FIRST DAY, 6 APRIL 1862

BRECKINRIDGE

BRAGG (part)

A.S. JOHNSTON
(40,000)

PRENTISS

POLK

HARDEE

HURLBUT

BRAGG (part)

W.H.L WALLACE

SHERMAN

McCLERNAND

Tennessee River

DIAMOND ISLAND

GRANT
(33,000)

L. WALLACE

Owl Creek

Snake Creek

Lick Creek

N

2 km

2 miles

0

0

to pull the troops out of the line for redeployment. Properly planning the follow-through after even a successful offensive action would remain a chronic problem for both the Union and Confederate armies as late as 1864, but Shiloh was to provide a particularly egregious example of this problem. Altogether the Confederates brought approximately 40,000 men to the battlefield.

To a considerable extent, the Confederate attack caught the Union troops by surprise. There was some initial warning. Before dawn one of Prentiss's regimental commanders sent out several companies to examine the noise to their front. They immediately came scampering back yelling that massed Confederate regiments were bearing down on the Union encampments. With that warning, Prentiss's and Sherman's regiments formed a serviceable defensive line to blast the first wave of Confederate attackers. Sherman, who had dismissed warnings of a Confederate attack over the past several days, came forward and recognized that he did indeed face a major Confederate attack. Some of his troops fled, but the majority stayed to fire at succeeding waves of Confederates. The fact that Sherman's division suffered over 2,000 casualties over the two days of fighting suggests the tenacious nature of its resistance.

Thus, there was no Union collapse. Instead, a series of firefights broke out as the Confederates drove Grant's troops back. Predictably, Southern command and control broke down as the soldiers of Hardee's and Bragg's corps became intermixed. The fact that many Confederate soldiers stopped to loot further added to a loss of control. McClernand, despite his faults and overweening ambition, was no coward, and he gamely inserted his division into the gap between Prentiss and Sherman. Meanwhile, two hours into the attack, Beauregard launched Polk's and Breckinridge's corps into the melee, adding further to the loss of control. Grant, who was downstream, heard the sound of artillery and rushed back upstream. As his steamboat passed Crump's Landing, he yelled at Lew Wallace to prepare to move out, if the artillery firing in the distance indicated a major attack.

By midmorning the Confederate attack had lost cohesion. The corps commanders then assumed responsibility for different sections of the field. Polk and Hardee on the left, while Bragg and Breckinridge covered the center and the right. But, as with Tolstoy's description of Borodino, about all they could do was to urge units forward and attempt to shame shot-up and dis-spirited units to attack again. Beauregard attempted to provide some guidance from the rear, while

Johnston exposed himself in the front lines in pushing the troops forward. He was certainly not acting as an army commander, directing the overall movement of his corps and divisions—although little in his background and training had prepared him for such responsibilities. His soldiery instincts pushed him into harm's way. The original plan had called for a strong attack from the right (south) of the Confederate line to separate Grant's troops from the river. Nevertheless, whatever the initial hope, matters degenerated into a simple straightforward push toward the river. The attack, however, squeezed Grant's army into a narrower and narrower defensive position with its flanks covered by the creeks. That in turn increased the lethality of Union fire and the strength of the resistance of the troops, pressed into an ever tighter and more defensible front. One Confederate soldier moving forward into the battle with his regiment in midmorning recalled: "I had heard and read of battlefields, seen pictures of battlefields, of horses and men, of cannons and wagons, all jumbled together, while the ground was strewn with dead and dying and wounded, but I must confess that I never realized the 'pomp and circumstance' of the thing called glorious war until I saw this. Men were lying in every conceivable position; the dead lying with their eyes wide open, the wounded begging piteously for help."[22]

Upon arrival, Grant took control, providing calm and a perception of what needed to be done in the midst of confusion and terror. He sent word back to Lew Wallace to move immediately from Crump's Landing to the battle to reinforce Sherman's right flank—a distance of barely six miles. Wallace was slow in moving out and took a road that led toward what he thought was Sherman's flank. However, when he had almost reached the battlefield, he discovered Sherman was no longer in his original position, but had fallen back toward the river. Instead, Wallace was almost in the rear of the Confederate attackers. Given the rawness of the enemy troops, had his division attacked, there was a good chance the Confederates would have collapsed. As he hesitated, Lew Wallace received another message, which indicated that his division had taken the wrong road. Instead of ordering the regiment to about face and march in reverse order, Wallace countermarched by having his regiments at the front lead the division back along the road it had traversed. Thus, the following regiments turned one after the other to follow those who had been to their front. The end result was that Wallace failed to arrive on the battlefield until nearly 1900, after most of the first day's fighting had ended. Lew Wallace was never again to receive an important combat command, although he would play a significant role in delaying Jubal Early's raid on Washington in 1864 by leading a scratch force of Union soldiers at Monocacy Junction in Maryland.

Meanwhile, the battle raged. Both Hurlbut and W.H.L. Wallace had manned their own lines by the time Grant arrived and were feeding reinforcements into the heaviest fighting, initially on the Union right. Constant Confederate pressure forced Sherman and McClernand steadily back. Several green regiments, particularly in Sherman's division, broke and ran, usually when their immediate commanders panicked. But most steadied and reformed farther back, soon to find themselves once again sucked into the fighting. Sherman took a bullet in the hand, but simply wrapped a handkerchief around the wound, as James Wolfe had done on the Plains of Abraham a century earlier, and continued directing his troops. By the end of the day the Confederates had shot three horses out from underneath him. But caught up in the adrenalin of the fight, he continued to rally and exhort his remaining troops to stay the course. His steady performance on the field made up for his earlier overconfidence. One of the attacking Confederate units on Sherman's side of the field, the 6th Mississippi, launched three attacks and found itself thrown back each time. Of the 425 who had been on its rolls in the morning, only 125 survived without being wounded or killed.

Grant initially told Prentiss to hold the position his troops had established along a road, today called "the sunken road." In fact, it was just a track, along which Prentiss, W.H.L. Wallace, and their brigade commanders found it easier to align their troops. The terrain in front of their position gradually sloped away from their position across open fields and woodland toward the Confederates. The open areas provided clear fields of fire for Union infantry and artillery; the artillery on a number of occasions took the Confederates under enfilade fire, which decimated the attackers. Steadied by their commander and having the road as a psychological line to defend, Union soldiers refused to break. Confederate attacks forced McClernand and Sherman back and eventually exposed Prentiss's and W.H.L. Wallace's position, soon to be called the "hornets' nest," to Confederate fire from three sides. The retreat of Hurlbut's divisions further exposed the "hornets' nest" to Confederate fire. Yet, the soldiers held.

Somewhere around midday, Albert Sidney Johnston took a bullet in the knee, which cut the artery to his foot. He bled to death. Leadership now devolved on the Confederate generals in different parts of the field. The troops attacking the "hornets' nest" came under Bragg, who proved an incompetent tactician, as he was to do on a number of other battlefields over the next year and a half. Instead of attempting to overwhelm the "hornets' nest" with a massed attack supported by artillery, Bragg persisted in launching uncoordinated attacks, none supported by artillery, and none of which possessed sufficient strength to break Union resistance. Altogether he launched somewhere between ten and twelve attacks, all of which failed with heavy casualties. Moreover, Bragg turned down the request of his brigade commanders for artillery support.

Reflecting the tendency of Civil War officers to continue to rely on controlled volleys that harked back to the dawn of the gunpowder revolution in Europe (one natural product of Union troops' inexperience and lack of training), the colonel commanding the 14th Iowa opposite Bragg ordered his men to lie down until the Confederates were at point blank range. Then he ordered them to stand and fire, and they blew the attackers away: "When the order to fire was given, and the Twelfth and the Fourteenth opened directly in their faces, the enemy first line was completely destroyed. Our fire was returned by only a few, nearly all who were not killed or wounded by it fleeing in every direction."[23] W.H.L. Wallace was badly wounded during the fighting and left for dead so that command of the "hornets' nest" devolved on Prentiss. Since the "hornets' nest" lay in the rear of much of the Confederate advance, it added to the confusion in Confederate ranks. Only when Beauregard concentrated no fewer than sixty-two artillery pieces on the "hornets' nest" did the Union position collapse, a collapse aided by the fact Union troops were running out of ammunition. But Union troops held out until 1730; they had delayed the Confederate advance for most of the afternoon.

By the time Prentiss surrendered, the drive had gone out of the Confederates, while the first of Buell's regiments was already crossing the Tennessee. Brigadier General William "Bull" Nelson's division had reached the river on its east bank across from Pittsburg Landing in the late afternoon and began flowing his regiments across the river. As his regiments crossed to Pittsburg Landing, they found nearly 5,000 shirkers from Grant's army huddled along the river's bank in abject fear, the flotsam of those who had collapsed under the terror of the Confederate attack. By 1900 Lew Wallace's division finally arrived to buck up Sherman's badly battered division. One last attack on the Union left flank occurred in the early evening across the deep ravine leading down into Lick Creek. Attacking up a steep incline, the Confederates not only ran into massed fire from the Union artillery, which Grant had placed on his left flank, but also fire from the navy's gunboats. The huge naval guns smashed those Confederates still willing to attack, while Union infantry and artillery blasted them mercilessly. Hurlbut's soldiers also found themselves supported by the first arriving regiments of Nelson's division. Not only had the Confederates been attacking all day, but some were entirely out of ammunition. This final attack represented the last desperate gasp of an army that had shot its bolt.

In the early evening hours, Grant's army had taken a terrible pounding. But unlike many of his fellow Union commanders in the war, he understood the battle had been equally damaging to the Confederates, while his army was in the process of receiving major reinforcements from Buell's army. Lew Wallace's division had also finally arrived. Buell added 17,000 soldiers; Wallace's division 7,000 more. Thus, at the beginning of the second day, Grant possessed 24,000 fresh troops. Against nearly 50,000 Union troops, Beauregard, Johnston's successor, had barely 25,000 men. With the Confederates in his clutches, Grant refused to let them go. Sherman later recalled that, as he searched for Grant the evening after that first grim day, his own spirits flagged. "It was pouring rain and pitch dark, there was considerable confusion, and the only thing just then possible, as it seemed to me, was to put the river between us and the enemy and recuperate." When he found Grant, "some wise and sudden instinct impelled me to a more cautious and less impulsive proposition than at first intended." Instead of proposing retreat, Sherman commented to his chief, "Well, Grant, we've had the devil's own day, haven't we?" Grant replied, "Yes, lick 'em to-morrow, though."[24]

For the Confederates the second day at Shiloh proved a nasty shock. One private recalled: "Now, those Yankees were whipped, fairly whipped, and according to all the rules of war they ought to have retreated."[25] Nearly everyone among the attackers, including the Confederate generals, believed they had won a great victory and that in the first light of dawn they could destroy the Union army. Only

Nathan Bedford Forrest, already displaying an intuitive grasp of soldiering that bordered on genius, pushed out scouts that evening that discovered the arrival of Federal reinforcements. While searching for higher headquarters, he warned a brigade commander, "If the enemy come on us in the morning, we will be whipped like hell."[26] The night was dismal, with the cries of the wounded, the blood-smeared surgeons amputating limbs, and the ghoulish surroundings of the dead lying across the smashed-up landscape. To compound the suffering, a spring rainstorm poured cold, hard rain on the dismal scene. Those who had survived unharmed were hardly in a position to rejoice. Grant initially sought shelter in one of the few houses in the area, but, as it was also a hospital, the agonies of the wounded drove him into the rain.

The rain affected the Confederates to a greater extent than was the case with the Union units. Southern officers faced an almost impossible task of putting units back together whose soldiers were scattered over considerable territory. Union commanders, their units crowded in the tighter space between the creeks, had an easier time in reconstituting their regiments. In the early morning hours, the Union counterattack began. There was hardly any art to the attack, no attempt to outflank, no heavily reinforced attempt to break through a particular sector. The counterattack caught the Confederates completely by surprise, since they believed they would be doing the attacking. Undeterred, they mounted a spirited resistance that brought the Union advance to a halt by 0800. The fighting on the Union left recovered the "hornets' nest," Bloody Pond, the peach orchard, and the sunken road. Thus, the fighting took on a macabre visage as the soldiers fought over ground on which the human wreckage of yesterday's fighting still remained. And, of course, the renewed battle only added to the horror.

By early afternoon, persistent Union attacks brought the Confederates to the brink of collapse. One officer commented to Beauregard: "General, do you not think that our soldiers are very much in the condition of a lump of sugar thoroughly soaked with water, but yet preserving its original shape, though ready to dissolve?"[27] The withdrawal began shortly thereafter. Not surprisingly, the pursuit was halfhearted. Grant picked Sherman and his division to lead what pursuit there was. That ended abruptly when Forrest led his men in a charge that scattered Yankee cavalry before running into Sherman's formed up infantry. Forrest continued his charge right into the infantry formation, but his men, falling back on that old military saw that sometimes discretion is the better part of valor, failed to follow. Forrest should have been killed, or at least captured. Instead, he whirled his horse around, grabbed a Union soldier to cover his back, and rode back out. One Union soldier managed to wound Forrest, but it was not the last Union troops would hear of the Confederate cavalryman.

In every respect Shiloh had been a murderous battle, unlike anything that had ever before occurred on the North American continent. The casualty bill was unprecedented, although not out of line with the battles that were to follow. Union losses were 13,047, of which 1,754 were killed, 8,408 wounded, many of whom soon died or were maimed for life, and 2,885 captured, most of the last from Prentiss's division. The Confederate losses were almost a carbon copy of the Union losses, except for prisoners: 1,723 killed, 8,012 wounded, but only 959 missing. The combined losses for both sides in two days of fighting exceeded losses in all previous American wars (the Revolutionary War, the War of 1812, and the Mexican War). In retrospect, the generalship on both sides was not impressive. But in spite of ill training, flawed leadership, and the murderous nature of the two-day-long battle, most of the troops displayed extraordinary steadfastness and courage. They stayed the course and showed that they made up for lack of professionalized European-style training with the resolution and staying power of ideologically committed volunteers. Their tenacity underlined the commitment to the cause on both sides of the fighting lines, a commitment every bit as strong as that which had motivated the armies of Revolutionary France.

Shiloh thus achieved the dubious honor of being the first of the war's great killing battles, but since it was the first, its casualty figures reverberated throughout the North. Newspapers throughout the Midwest assailed Grant for the casualties his army, largely recruited from that region, had suffered, while senators and representatives denounced him in Congress. And of course, the stories of Grant's drinking problem surfaced. It was at Shiloh that Grant began to acquire the reputation of being a butcher. In fact, he was anything but a butcher. He alone had kept his head when virtually everyone, with the possible exception of Sherman, was losing theirs. Moreover, Grant assumed responsibility for what had happened, especially the fact that his army had been caught by surprise. A McClellan, a Halleck, or a Bragg would have happily placed the blame for the disastrous first hours on Sherman. But Grant, honest and conscientious, was too big a man to blame others for what was his responsibility. His refusal to blame his subordinate began to forge the deep personal and professional link between the two generals, a link that played a key role in the Union's victory.

Above all, Grant was a learner. Shiloh gave him a sense of the dimensions of the emerging war more advanced of that of the other generals and most politicians with the exception of Lincoln. In a brilliant insight in his memoirs, he noted: "Up to the battle of Shiloh I, as well as thousands of other citizens, believed that the rebellion against the Government would collapse suddenly and soon, if a decisive victory could be gained over any of its armies. Donelson and Henry were such victories. An army of more than 21,000 men was captured and destroyed. Bowling Green, Columbus and Hickman, Kentucky, fell in consequence, and Clarksville and Nashville, Tennessee, the last with an immense amount of stores, also fell into our hands. The Tennessee and Cumberland Rivers, from their mouths to the head of navigation, were secured. But when Confederate armies were collected which not only attempted to hold the line farther south . . . but assumed the offensive and made such a gallant effort to regain what had been lost, then. Indeed, I gave up all idea of saving the Union except by complete conquest."[28]

Four days after the battle, Halleck arrived to take command of Grant's and Buell's armies. He proceeded to place Grant where he believed he deserved to be: namely, in the closet. He appointed the victor of Shiloh to serve as his deputy and then gave Grant nothing to do. If rumor and backstabbing could not rid him of Grant, then Halleck was going to insure that his deputy would not receive further opportunities to redeem himself. Meanwhile, he brought John Pope's Army of the Mississippi south from its victory at Island Number 10 in the Mississippi River—another triumph for joint operations against formidable Confederate fortifications, although Halleck remained incapable of understanding the long-term potential for such movements even as they occurred under his nose. Bereft of Pope's troops, the Union's riverine fleet paused its advance down the Mississippi at Fort Pillow. Halleck was taking no chances the Confederates would launch a surprise attack on his massive accumulation of military power. Thomas assumed command of Grant's army, Pope kept command of his Army of Mississippi, and Buell commanded the third forward element of three divisions. Halleck, ever distrustful of volunteer generals, placed McClernand in command of the reserve. Altogether Halleck's force numbered 120,172 supported by more than 200 artillery pieces.

Having assembled this great army, he now began a ponderous advance on Corinth on 30 April despite outnumbering the Confederates by nearly two to one. The advance began with Pope surging forward seven miles. But even that was too much for Buell, who warned Halleck of the dangers lurking ahead. Halleck had the troops entrench every night, as the advance crept ever closer to Corinth. Even reconnaissance parties were warned not to bring on an engagement and that it was better to retreat than fight. Halleck was sure Beauregard would make a desperate defense of the town, if not launch a sudden attack. He determined to be prepared for that eventuality. It took Halleck's army almost a month to reach Corinth from Pittsburg Landing, a march that should have taken three days at most, if the commander were cautious. Halleck's approach to what should have been a straight-through drive on Corinth disgusted Grant, who suggested a more vigorous advance. For his troubles, Grant records, Halleck silenced his deputy "so quickly that I felt that possibly I had suggested an unmilitary movement."[29] In fact, outnumbered as he was, Beauregard had no intention of defending Corinth. At the last moment he pulled out, bamboozling his overly cautious Union commander. As every empty train arrived in Corinth, Beauregard had his troops cheer, as if new reinforcements had arrived. When the trains pulled out filled with troops, there was silence.

The seizure of Corinth was useful, but looking back at the campaign, Grant later wrote "the victory was barren in every . . . particular."[30] At a minimum the army that Halleck had assembled was in a position to seize the remainder of the Mississippi valley. In fact, all it accomplished after Corinth's fall was the capture of the remainder of western Tennessee, including Memphis. But the navy's victory upriver from Memphis over a weak Confederate river fleet had made the fall of the city inevitable. As he was to do with Grant's army after the fall of Vicksburg in July 1863, Halleck broke up his army and dispersed it over the landscape to seek after places and locations of no great importance. Even more seriously, Halleck even refused to provide ground forces to support David Glasgow Farragut's naval expedition against Vicksburg later that summer.

Halleck's weakness as a strategist resulted from his inability to differentiate between the essential and the insignificant. His performance as a field commander suggests that he was just as incompetent as McClellan, but luckier in that Beauregard was no Lee. The capture of Corinth represented an anticlimax to the casualties Union troops had suffered at Shiloh. Grant was so disgusted by the treatment he received as well as the general incompetence of the campaign waged by "old brains" that he thought seriously of going on a leave of absence with no firm plan for the future. Sherman, however, helped persuade Grant to remain with the army, while Halleck's dispersal of his forces allowed Grant to resume an independent command and raised his spirits considerably. Ironically, Grant was not to understand the mendacity of Halleck's behavior until after the war.

New Orleans

New Orleans was the most important port and the largest city in the South. Its mixture of cultures and races and its economic vitality gave it an allure that no other Southern city could match. It was, moreover, of great economic significance for the North, since it was the terminus of the trade that made its way down the river from the Midwest. Its vulnerable location on the Mississippi delta that reached out into the Gulf made it an obvious target for Union attack. The idea of moving against New Orleans emerged in early 1862 as Lincoln contemplated pressuring the Confederacy from several different directions. Just as the great Union expedition to take the city arrived in the Gulf, the Confederate high command had denuded the city and its outlying forts of troops to reinforce Albert Sidney Johnston's counteroffensive that precipitated the Battle of Shiloh. Two forts, Jackson and St. Philip, lay at the end of the delta and barred entrance to the river and access to New Orleans. They would have to be suppressed, captured, or bypassed. Like the attack on the forts guarding Port Royal, bombardment appeared the easiest approach. In early 1862 the secretary of the navy, Gideon Welles, along with a naval officer, David Dixon Porter, had persuaded the president that the use of mortar boats would help suppress the forts guarding the entrance to the Mississippi. Always an enthusiast for technology—the only president ever to hold a patent—Lincoln enthusiastically adopted the idea of using mortars to suppress the forts. McClellan at first opposed the operation, because he believed it would require 50,000 soldiers, but he capitulated when Welles and Porter suggested that the expedition would only need 10,000 men.

Picked to command the expedition was one of the navy's more se-nior officers, David Glasgow Farragut. Farragut had gone to sea at the age of nine and served on board the frigate *Essex* during the War of 1812 and was sixty years old. Although at the start of the war some in the administration had doubts about his loyalty, since he was from Tennessee and had married a Virginian, he proved the most distin-guished naval officer in the Civil War. His reply to white Southerners who had tried to persuade him to go join the Confederacy was direct: "Mind what I tell you: You fellows will catch the devil before you get through with this business."[31] Butler received command of the land forces of 15,000 soldiers for any land fighting that might be necessary and for occupation duties.

The attacking fleet consisted of eight steam sloops, one sailing sloop, and fourteen gunboats. Porter commanded nineteen mortar boats. Initially, he had difficulty in maneuvering his heavier ships over the bar, but once into the river, the fight began. Porter's mortars fired somewhere around 3,000 shells a day against the forts. They obliterated the insides but inflicted little damage to the main guns. After six days, with no signs the Confederates were considering surrender, Farragut decided to run the forts at night after his gunboats had dislodged the chain blocking the river's entrance. At 0200 on 24 April, Farragut's warships sailed through the opening. A furious gun battle erupted. The small fleet of Confederate gunboats managed to sink one Union warship. Three others turned back, but most of the fleet got through. The Confederate ironclad *Louisiana* added nothing to the struggle, be-cause the Confederates had not managed to get her engines to work—yet another indication of the weaknesses of the their industrial and engineering base. The Union ships that evaded the Confederate gun-fire suffered some damage, but Farragut's crews quickly repaired the damage and sailed up the river. New Orleans was defenseless; the few soldiers left had no chance of opposing the Union fleet and prudently withdrew. The inhabitants were anything but happy. One observer described the scene in the following terms: "the crowds on the levee howled and screamed with rage. The swarming decks answered never a word; but one old tar on the *Hartford*, standing with lanyard in hand beside a great pivot-gun, so plain to view that you could see him smile, silently patted its big black breech and blandly grinned."[32]

The occupation of New Orleans ended the resistance of Forts Jackson and St. Philip, and Butler, the "Beast," then brought the army of occupation upriver. The population displayed a thoroughly hostile attitude toward the occupation. One mob tore the Stars and Stripes down, while local women took to such outright acts of rudeness as spitting at the troops and dropping the contents of chamber pots on senior officers. Butler, however, soon put paid to such acts. He hanged one of the perpetrators of the flag burning incident. As for the excessive rudeness of the women to Union soldiers, he issued a proclamation that declared such women "shall be regarded and held liable to be treated as a woman of the town plying her avocation."[33] At the time, Butler's actions led to outrage not only throughout the South but also in Britain's House of Commons. Nevertheless, his less than velvet glove acts reined in the populace. In comparison to the methods the British would use in South Africa during the Boer War or the Germans in France in 1871 and in the areas they occupied of Europe in two world wars, Butler's methods were tame.

While Butler was bringing order to New Orleans, Farragut took his ships up the Mississippi twice in an effort to open up the river. His sailors and accompanying army troops seized Baton Rouge and Natchez, but efforts to seize Vicksburg failed. A second attack on Vicksburg at the end of June involved a bombardment of the city by gunboats from up the river as well as Farragut's ships. However, Confederate guns on the bluff held a formidable position that defied the naval attack. Had ground troops been available, it is probable that the "West Point" of the Mississippi would have fallen, but as mentioned earlier, Halleck had little interest in cooperating with the navy, despite the fact that his success in the West had in large part hinged on successful joint operations conducted by Grant and Pope.

Farragut came to the conclusion that a purely naval effort against Vicksburg's defenses was simply not in the cards. The naval bombardments of the Mississippi town did have the consequence of awakening the Confederate high command of the danger to Vicksburg. Thus, by the end of June nearly 10,000 Confederate soldiers were solidly entrenched around the town, while fortifications on the landward side were under construction. Moreover, alarmed by the reach of Farragut's fleet, the Confederates soon had fortified Port Hudson well south of

Vicksburg, so that a substantial portion of the river would remain in their hands for another year. The main culprit in the failure to achieve the possibilities that a more rapid seizure of Corinth and then pursuit of Beauregard's army would have bestowed on the Union cause was, of course, Halleck and the failure of his generalship.

Conclusion

Unlike the Eastern theater, military operations in the West chalked up major gains in 1862. Those gains laid the basis for the successful prosecution of the war and the eventual Union victory. The most important of these victories was Grant's brilliant seizure of Forts Henry and Donelson, which at one stroke moved the war into the South's heartland. For many in the North, Shiloh came as a terrible shock with its terrifying casualty bill, which obscured its strategic significance. Admittedly, Grant and his generals had found themselves caught by surprise, but the signal fact was that they had held, and on the second day they had come close to smashing the Confederate army. Ironically, New Orleans' fall several weeks later made a bigger splash in both the North and South than did the results of Donelson, Henry, and Shiloh. As Mary Chesnut recorded in her diary: "New Orleans gone—and with it the Confederacy. Are we not cut in two? That Mississippi ruins us if lost."[34] Yet, Union armies failed to capitalize fully on the spring's victories. Halleck frittered away the advantageous strategic situation after Shiloh, first in his egregiously slow advance on Corinth, Mississippi, and second in his dispersal of the Union armies after Corinth had finally fallen. He also failed to recognize the opportunity presented by Farragut's arrival at Vicksburg.

In early April 1862, Stanton had closed down the recruiting offices in the belief the Union needed no more troops. Given the successes attending Union arms during this period, this seemed a reasonable decision. But events in the summer underlined how overoptimistic that decision had been. In July the administration had to eat crow. Lincoln issued a call for 300,000 volunteers, all to serve for three years. One month later the War Department issued a call for 300,000 more volunteers, these to serve for nine months. It was the first group, the three-year volunteers, who were clearly needed to support the increasing demands of an ever-expanding war effort as well as the casualties of the first great battles. Unlike 1861, 1862 saw little eagerness in the North to fill up the new regiments, even as the Federal government offered bounties, while some states supplemented those cash awards.

By the end of the year, the government had enlisted 421,000 three-year volunteers in the new regiments. Thus, it had more that met its goal. Instead of funneling these volunteers into veteran regiments, the government placed most of them in new outfits. That may well have encouraged the recruitment of young men from small towns and increased the cohesion of the new regiments in the battles in which they were fated to fight, but it certainly maximized the casualties as these regiments deployed and then fought. The new regiments would not tip the scales toward the Union in the last six months of 1862, but in 1863 they provided the key supporting element that enabled the Union to launch three great campaigns against the Confederacy: the first in Virginia, the second down the Mississippi, and the third deep into Tennessee, reaching all the way to northeastern Georgia.

In 1862 the Union had lacked the manpower to conduct major campaigns against Vicksburg and Chattanooga at the same time. Nor were there sufficient troops to protect the vulnerable supply lines that ran through western and central Tennessee from Confederate raiders led by Forrest and John Hunt Morgan. However, the addition in 1863 of a further 421,000 troops to Union strength provided the manpower to mount two great efforts in the West as well as to support the war in Virginia. While the drive into southeastern Tennessee and northwestern Georgia would run into some considerable difficulties in fall 1863, it too would succeed once Grant was placed in charge. Finally, in 1863 the production base in the North would reach the point where it could support the increasingly impressive field armies of the Republic.

Thus, 1862, much like the American effort in the Solomon Islands in the last half of 1942, which broke Japanese air strength and opened the way for further advances, was the year that provided the jumping-off positions for the North to drive deep into the South as well as the time to mobilize the North's strength more fully to meet the demands of a war combining the passions of the French Revolution with the material power of the Industrial Revolution. In 1862 the armies of the Confederacy and those of the North had found themselves evenly matched. That would not be the case in the years following 1862. And like the Pacific campaign waged by the Civil War's descendants, Union army and naval forces would display the mutually reinforcing potential of army-navy cooperation. However, in the absence of institutionalized interservice cooperation, Civil War joint operations would never reach their full potential due to the blinkered perspectives of army and navy leaders such as Fox and Halleck. The Union would thus find itself forced to use its superior material resources to wear down Confederate resistance, as opposed to achieving a swift victory in 1862. Ironically enough for the Confederacy, the longer the war lasted, the more certain it was that Union victory would result in the destruction of the very institution Confederates had seceded to protect.

CHAPTER 6

The Confederacy Recovers, 1862

Alexander, if there is one man in either army, Federal or Confederate, who is, head & shoulders, far above every other one in either army in audacity that man is Gen. Lee, and you will soon live to see it. Lee is audacity personified. His name is audacity, and you need not be afraid of not seeing all of it that you will want to see.

—Edward Porter Alexander, *Fighting for the Confederacy*

[The blast] seemed to shake the very earth. Then the dull thud of the balls as [they] tore . . . through the bodies of the men—then the hiss of the grape—and mangled screams of agony and rage. I looked around me. The ground was filled with the mangled dead and dying.

—Quoted in John Hennessy, *Return to Bull Run*

In late December 1861, Senator Benjamin Wade, a member of the increasingly Radical Republicans, commented to Lincoln: "Mr. President, you are murdering your country by inches in consequence of the inactivity of the military."[1] Undoubtedly, Lincoln agreed, but, of course, he had to dissemble in public. For eight months, the North had been building great armies. Yet, its generals seemed incapable or unwilling to attack the Confederacy. Moreover, the soldiers of the Republic were consuming vast sums of money as well as the nation's resources. And for what? By the end of 1861, the North was becoming less enthralled with the splendid parades and military displays McClellan was mounting week in and week out. All the while, a Confederate army under Joe Johnston remained at Manassas. Parades were fine, but the public and many of the solders wondered why McClellan seemed unwilling to mount any sort of military operations against the Republic's enemies, who remained untouched within sight of the nation's capital. Mc-Clellan fell ill with typhoid fever in December, further compounding problems, since his illness stalled planning and confined the general to his bedside during a crucial political moment when congressional Republicans began to question his military leadership.

Well might Lincoln bemoan on 10 January 1862 to Montgomery Meigs, the army's quartermaster general, that "the bottom is out of the tub."[2] Lincoln's frustration with the military at the turn of the year showed in a number of ways. Displaying a feel for strategy, the president suggested that if all the Union armies were to move at the same time, they would place such pressure on the Confederacy with its fewer resources that somewhere the enemy would break. On 6 January, Halleck had pedantically lectured the president that he could not act in the West because "to operate on exterior lines against an enemy occupying a central position will fail, as it has always failed, in ninety-nine cases out of a hundred. It is condemned by every military authority I have ever read."[3] Lincoln's reply—quoted in the last chapter in full—was clear and to the point: Since the Union has greater numbers and the Confederates "*greater* facility of concentrating," the Union needed to remove that advantage by "menacing him with superior forces at *different* points, at the same time" thus weakening the Confederates at some critical point.[4] Not for the last time, Halleck displayed his inability to match military theory with operational reality.

Unlike Halleck, McClellan valued coordinated operations across the Confederacy's frontiers, but his preoccupation with the Army of the Potomac's supposed weakness vis-à-vis Johnston demanded that his army monopolize the Union's resources, and all other operations support his own primary line of effort. Furthermore, his caution and prejudice against action weakened his earlier attempts to cajole Buell and Halleck into action in the West—although he did attempt to no avail to get both generals to move. Most importantly, McClellan never understood that the Confederacy had its own vexatious resource problems, exacerbated in the West by its choice of a cordon defense and compounded by the overconfidence produced by the early victory at First Manassas. Indeed, the Confederacy would not belatedly institute conscription until spring 1862, after the catastrophic defeats in Tennessee and the Western theater.

In the end, Lincoln was right and Halleck wrong. In fact, operations in the West in 1862 would crack the Confederacy's cordon defense and create the basis on which the North's eventual victory rested. Nevertheless, military operations west of the Alleghenies were far from Washington and Virginia. Even to the amateurs of 1861, it was clear that no decisive victory was possible in the west where Union armies confronted the logistical problems raised by that theater's distances and where there was no single city matching Richmond in its political and economic importance. Thus, military operations there could not achieve the decisive victory needed to bring an increasingly costly war to the quick and successful conclusion, for which Lincoln, the Congress, and the people of the North still fervently hoped. Such a victory could come only in the east.

The problem in Virginia in fall 1861 was that McClellan was already giving wild overestimates as to the size of Johnston's army. Equally distressing to the administration was that McClellan seemed to have no plans for future military operations. As we have seen, McClellan had in fact made plans—and ones with merit no less—but his contempt for Lincoln and obsession with secrecy caused him to withhold his plans until his political position became virtually untenable. In early January Lincoln even had to admit to Congress's Committee on the Conduct of the War that he had no idea of McClellan's plans. To some more cynical or impatient observers, it appeared McClellan's objective was to avoid battle with the Confederates. For most in Washington, the obvious solution was for the army to march out and destroy the Confederates who stood at Manassas on the capital's doorstep. But McClellan continued to emphasize the superior numbers Johnston supposedly possessed. Moreover, the fact that the Union commander was seriously ill further complicated his relations with Lincoln and the administration.

At least the fact that McClellan was bedridden allowed the president to seek advice from several other generals. On 10 January, after a long conversation with Meigs, Lincoln invited two of the Army of the Potomac's more senior officers to a discussion. So McDowell and Franklin accompanied Seward to a meeting with the president to examine the army's options. Thus, Lincoln had the opportunity to discuss the situation with individuals who had some grasp of military matters as well as an opportunity to vent to his frustrations. He commented to the group that "he would like to borrow [the Army of the Potomac], provided he could see how it could be made to do something."[5] Alarmed by the possibility the president was seizing the reins of military strategy from his hands, McClellan roused himself from his sickbed to attend the next meeting. Nevertheless, outside of several arrogant interventions, he added little to the discussions. Bon mots that he threw out—such as "the case was so clear that a blind man could see it"—provided no insights into his thinking.[6] Asked about his plans by Chase, he refused to answer, only stating that he awaited Buell to act first in Kentucky. He even whispered to Meigs that he dared not tell the president anything, because it would immediately appear in the papers.

Lincoln adjourned the meeting without showing obvious anger, but McClellan had once again harmed his own political situation through willful obstinacy. Not surprisingly, his position in Washington continued to deteriorate. Thoroughly frustrated with his senior generals, Lincoln took matters into his own hands. At the end of January, he issued General Order No. 1, in which he ordered that by 22 February 1862, the armies of the United States were to begin a forward movement. Although the order was unrealistic, especially considering the time of year, it did reflect Lincoln's strategic conception. On 31 January, Lincoln, further annoyed by McClellan's obfuscations, specifically ordered the Army of the Potomac to move on Manassas and the Confederates. The threat of action galvanized McClellan, who objected violently and replied with a verbose, twenty-two-page letter to Stanton, proposing an alternative. Lincoln had finally smoked the general out. McClellan informed his commander in chief of his plan to move the army down the Potomac and land at the mouth of the Rappahannock River at Urbanna, thereby outflanking Johnston's position at Manassas. Lincoln had little enthusiasm for the idea, because with the enemy army directly in front of Washington, it seemed McClellan could attack the Confederates any time he wished. The president also feared such a move might leave Washington undefended.

Events in early March settled the matter in McClellan's favor. Johnston, quite rightly, believed that, in view of the numerical superiority of Union forces as well as the logistical difficulties of supplying his troops in northern Virginia, it made sense to withdraw from Manassas. The Confederate retreat revealed how wildly McClellan had overestimated the enemy. The fortifications in front of Manassas were almost entirely a sham, armed with large logs, while the size of Johnston's abandoned encampment showed the Confederates had possessed a troop strength of no more than 50,000 soldiers. Despite this indication of Confederate weakness, McClellan would persist throughout spring and summer 1862 in overestimating his opponents by a wide margin.

Johnston's retreat then led McClellan to propose a riskier strategy of moving most of the Army of the Potomac to the York Peninsula, which the York and James Rivers bounded and which led directly to Richmond. Lincoln was even less enthralled by the new proposal, but at least McClellan was suggesting action. The president agreed, provided sufficient troops remained to defend the nation's capital. Therein lay the seeds of a major blowup in the future between president and general. On 9 March, the fortuitous arrival of the Union ironclad *Monitor* at Fort Monroe, at the tip of the York Peninsula across from Norfolk, checkmated the Confederate ironclad *Merrimack* and opened the way for a land assault on Richmond.

The Peninsula Campaign

Before the move against Richmond began, Lincoln himself stepped in to force a corps organization on McClellan. The president named the Army of the Potomac's initial corps commanders for Corps I-IV on the basis of seniority. McClellan had preferred to wait until combat revealed which division commanders had the highest potential, but Lincoln had good reason to force the issue, since managing so many divisions without an intermediate echelon of command defied a well-known lesson of the wars of the French Revolutionary and Napoleonic Wars. Furthermore, it was apparent the absence of corps commanders in the army was exacerbating McClellan's tendency toward micromanagement.

However, McClellan did have more control over the composition of what eventually became the Army of the Potomac's V and VI Corps, because unlike the first four corps, he named both of their corps commanders. Looking at the composition of these corps, one sees again a preference for engineers—William B. Franklin had been a topographical engineer in the Old Army, along with one of his two division commanders, William F. Smith. In the V Corps, one of the two division commanders, George W. Morell, had graduated from West Point, like McClellan, into the Corps of Engineers. The two new corps also reflected McClellan's preference for the regulars, since the V Corps included a new division of regulars, headed by George Sykes, who had started the war commanding a regular army battalion in the First Battle of Bull Run.

The combat performance of the generals McClellan handpicked for the V and VI Corps also reflected the weaknesses of the command culture he was creating, although there were some redeeming elements. Franklin would have a poor record as a corps commander, and his indecisiveness, combined with Burnside's failings, would contribute to the Union catastrophe at Fredericksburg. Fitz-John Porter, whom McClellan prized above all his other subordinates, would vindicate his superior's confidence by fighting off successive assaults by Lee during the Seven Days battles, and unlike his chief, he proved willing to stand and fight after the Confederate repulse at Malvern Hill. However, like McClellan, Porter wore his conservative Democratic politics on his sleeve, and this clearly contributed to his unwillingness to cooperate wholeheartedly with Pope at the Battle of Second Bull Run. When combined with his extraordinary political indiscretions, his military errors during the Second Bull Run led to his eventual expulsion from the service, to the detriment of the Army of the Potomac's weak bench of capable corps commanders.

Of the division commanders in V Corps, Sykes would eventually prove a competent corps commander, although not an exceptional one. Morell, the former engineer, would top out at division command. In the VI Corps, Henry W. Slocum, as we shall see, would rise to corps command, but prove unworthy of that responsibility. Smith would prove a fine senior engineering officer who helped Grant open the cracker line to relieve Chattanooga in fall 1863, but a mediocre corps commander in summer 1864. In this respect, he was similar to Gouverneur Warren, who served as a brigade commander in V Corps, and who later did fine service as an engineering officer at Gettysburg, but who would falter as VI Corps commander in the 1864 battles.

From Lincoln's perspective, the decision to allow McClellan to embark on the Peninsula campaign rested on his understanding that the general would leave sufficient forces to guarantee the capital's safety. McClellan, however, believed that it was up to him to decide on the size of that force, but from the president's point of view the administration was not about to trust an officer who seemed to be playing games with numbers. On that difference of opinion rested the quarrel that soon erupted between Washington and the Army of the Potomac's commander.

The move to the York Peninsula underlined the size of the mobilization of the North's resources over the war's first year. The Union's extraordinarily capable quartermaster general, Montgomery Meigs, had assembled a fleet sufficient to transport McClellan's 100,000 men; 300 artillery pieces, including siege artillery; the assorted mules and horses the army required; and the vast impedimenta of ammunition, rations, and other supplies necessary for the conduct of military operations on the Peninsula. But at the last moment, Lincoln and Stanton discovered that McClellan had assigned far fewer troops to Washington's defense than promised. Alarmed, they ordered McDowell's corps of some 35,000 troops to remain in northern Virginia, thus robbing McClellan of a substantial body of troops. In fact, McClellan had more than sufficient troops to launch his campaign, but that was not how he saw matters. In retrospect, no matter how many soldiers McClellan received, nothing would have changed his unwillingness to engage the enemy. Nevertheless, the presence of McDowell's Corps with the Army of the Potomac during the Seven Days battles might have shattered Lee's army, in spite of McClellan's distaste for the tactical offensive.

As the first contingents of the Army of the Potomac arrived at Fort Monroe, the Confederate leaders puzzled over their enemy's intentions: were the Federals moving against North Carolina, or Norfolk, or did this arrival herald a move up the York Peninsula against the Confederate capital? But as more Union forces arrived, uncertainty about McClellan's intentions dissipated. A major offensive against Richmond was clearly in the offing. And Richmond was vulnerable. Major General John Magruder, an officer renowned in the Old Army for his thespian talents, guarded the city's approach with slightly fewer than 15,000 troops, a number hardly sufficient to put up token resistance, had McClellan moved quickly. But Lee, acting as Davis's military advisor, recognized that Union forces were coming in strength and detached three divisions from Johnston's army now on the Rappahannock and sent them to reinforce Magruder.

On the other side, McClellan had hardly arrived on the Peninsula when he learned that McDowell's corps of 35,000 troops would not reinforce him and that the administration had removed Banks's army in the Shenandoah from his command. Lincoln attempted to invigorate his commander in the field with words which even in the twenty-first century ring with political and strategic wisdom: "Once more let me tell you, it is indispensable to *you* that you strike a blow. *I* am powerless to help this. You will do me the justice to remember I always insisted, that going down the Bay in search of a field, instead of fighting at or near Manassas, was only shifting, and not surmounting a difficulty—that we would find the same enemy, and the same, or equal, intrenchments, at either place. The country will not fail to note—is now noting—that the present hesitation to move upon an intrenched enemy, is but the story of Manassas repeated. . . . I have never written you, or spoken to you, in greater kindness of feeling than now, nor with a fuller purpose to sustain you, so far as in my most anxious judgment, I consistently can. *But you must act.*"[7]

But McClellan failed to act with dispatch. Not far from the Yorktown battlefield of the Revolutionary War, Magruder constructed a line of fortifications across to the Warwick River, which he had his engineers dam. The fortifications may have looked impressive to McClellan, but as Johnston commented when he first saw them, "no one but McClellan could have hesitated to attack."[8] Adding to the show, Magruder marched his soldiers into the fortifications during the day and then snuck them out during the night, to repeat the exercise day after day. Magruder's antics thoroughly entranced McClellan, who spent a month preparing to conduct a needless siege, as horses and mules dragged the siege artillery up the primitive, muddy roads, made worse by heavy spring rains. It took nearly a month to complete his preparations.

Finally, on 3 May, with McClellan ready to bombard Magruder's fortifications, Johnston ordered a retreat up the Peninsula to the defenses on Richmond's eastern side. Lee had organized and sited those defenses during April. Davis was furious at the withdrawal, particularly because Johnston had informed the Confederate president only at the last moment. Davis, with bad news flooding into Richmond from other fronts, desperately needed aggressive action to defend the capital. Whatever difficulties the Confederates faced, McClellan had done nothing to prepare for the possibility the Confederates might withdraw from their fortifications. Ever cautious, he trailed the retreating Confederates at snail's pace. In a short skirmish near Williamsburg, advancing Union troops ran into James Longstreet, already achieving a name for himself as a combat commander. Both sides suffered several thousand casualties, but more importantly the fight slowed McClellan's advance even further. An incident involving McClellan and his staff best sums up the Union approach to the campaign, as it crawled slowly toward Richmond. Coming across a stream, McClellan

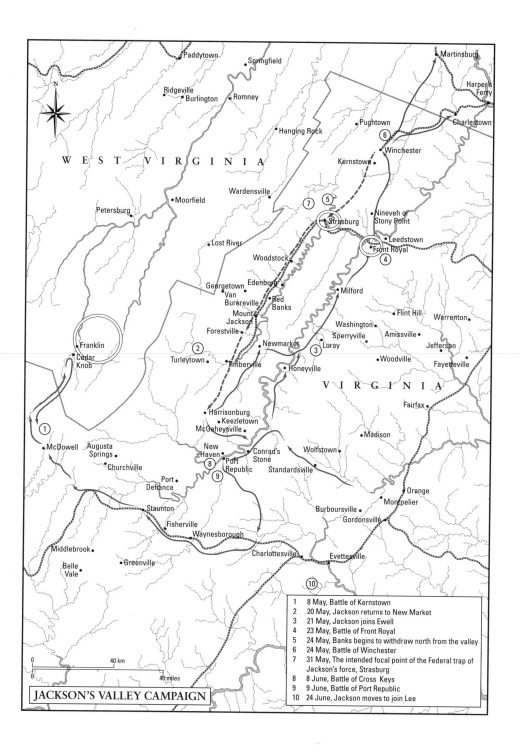

JACKSON'S VALLEY CAMPAIGN

1	8 May, Battle of Kernstown
2	20 May, Jackson returns to New Market
3	21 May, Jackson joins Ewell
4	23 May, Battle of Front Royal
5	24 May, Banks begins to withdraw north from the valley
6	24 May, Battle of Winchester
7	31 May, The intended focal point of the Federal trap of Jackson's force, Strasburg
8	8 June, Battle of Cross Keys
9	9 June, Battle of Port Republic
10	24 June, Jackson moves to join Lee

and his staff halted to debate its depth. After ten minutes or so, an impatient staff officer, a certain Captain George Armstrong Custer, rode into the middle of the stream and turned to his commander with the comment: "That's how deep it is, General."[9]

By the end of May, two months after landing on the Peninsula, the Army of the Potomac was only six miles from Richmond. Moreover, Lincoln had released McDowell's corps to march south, cross the Rappahannock, and then join McClellan's right wing, thus providing the general with the troops he claimed he needed. But fate in the guise of Thomas "Stonewall" Jackson intervened to launch a series of brilliant strokes in the Shenandoah Valley. Jackson with his small army had suffered a nasty rebuff in March 1862. Moreover, his harsh, unbending personality hardly endeared him to the troops. Grim, dour, humorless, Jackson was all of that, but a military genius as well. Yet, Lee had recognized the qualities of command behind one of the strangest personalities ever to command a major force in the war. Jackson also had a thoroughly unromantic understanding of war. When one of his colonels praised the valor some Union cavalry had displayed, Jackson simply commented: "Shoot them all: *I* do not wish them to be brave."[10] Now in May Jackson struck again, this time with devastating success.

Surreptitiously Lee had fed Jackson reinforcements. On 16 May, as the Army of the Potomac approached Richmond with the possibility that Washington would release McDowell's corps to join McClellan by marching across central Virginia, Lee urged Jackson to launch a full-scale attack on the Federals in the Valley, as well as to strike all the way to the Potomac, so that the Federals would conclude the Confederates were about to strike into Maryland, and perhaps even against Washington. Thoroughly familiar with the Shenandoah due to his extensive journeys throughout the area before the war and possessing excellent maps, Jackson utilized his knowledge of the Valley as well as his ability to drive troops to the brink of exhaustion and beyond. The Valley's complex geography aided his campaign. To the west lay the formidable Allegheny Mountains. To the east bounding the Valley was the Blue Ridge, while a thin ridge, Massanutten Mountain, divided the east fork of the Shenandoah River from the west fork. Only a narrow gap with a narrow road ran through Massanutten Mountain.

At the beginning of his campaign, Jackson had already struck the lead elements of Frémont's forces, which were advancing through the Alleghenies toward Staunton and the upper (southern portion) Valley on 8 May. The outnumbered Union troops put up solid resistance and fell back into the mountains after inflicting as many casualties on the Confederates as they suffered. But Jackson had achieved his goal of ejecting Frémont from the complex equation of Union forces in the Valley. He then turned north, and after feinting as if to join Johnston near Richmond, he marched north to burst on Nathaniel Banks's corps guarding the northern part of the Shenandoah. Banks had already divided his forces to handle guerrillas, since he did not believe Jackson represented much of a threat, while Union intelligence had reported Jackson on his way to reinforce Johnston.

Like the Assyrian sweeping down "like the wolf on the fold," Jackson destroyed Union positions in the Valley in a matter of weeks.[11] By forced marches, he drove his troops to Front Royal, where on 23 May he destroyed the outnumbered garrison. Out of 1,000 Union troops, 904 were either dead, wounded, or captured. Jackson suffered fewer than fifty casualties. Banks possessed approximately 6,000 troops just down the road from Front Royal at Strasburg, while his main supply dump lay up the Valley Pike at Winchester with 1,500 more soldiers. Jackson, however, had over 17,000 soldiers, far better trained and led than Banks's motley crew. Banks almost made the mistake of holding Strasburg, which would have put his entire force in the bag, but at the last moment his subordinates persuaded him to retire.

It did not matter, because Jackson caught up with the retreating Banks and his troops at Winchester and in a short decisive battle on 24 May smashed the outnumbered and badly deployed Union troops. Jackson captured a mountain of supplies, which led his troops to refer thereafter to the defeated Union general as "Commissary Banks," and pursued the Federals to the Potomac. But to Jackson's disgust most of the beaten army escaped. Banks attempted to cover up the extent of his defeat by reporting to Washington that "it is seldom that a river-crossing of such magnitude is achieved with greater success."[12] Jackson's campaign in the Valley has drawn the praises of military historians since the war's end. It was indeed a piece of tactical virtuosity, but its real impact was political and operational. On the political side, it restored Confederate morale after the string of stinging defeats in the west over the previous five months. Equally important it had a significant impact on decision making in Washington. Lincoln and Stanton halted McDowell's march to reinforce McClellan just over the Rappahannock and concentrated Union forces in the Shenandoah to assuage the humiliation of the last several weeks by destroying Jackson before he could do more damage.

At the end of May McClellan had reached Richmond's outskirts. He deployed two of his corps, the II Corps under Samuel Heintzelman, and the IV Corps under Erasmus Keyes, neither particularly competent officers, south of the Chickahominy Creek, a muddy stream that ran southeastward from north and east of the Confederate capital. The two corps numbered approximately 31,500 men. McClellan kept the other three corps, led by Fitz-John Porter (V Corps), William Franklin (VI Corps), and Edwin "Bull" Sumner (II Corps), on the north side of the stream. At least to McClellan, there did not appear to be any danger in splitting the army in such a fashion, but it was in fact a piece of bad tactics. The creek was a languid, insignificant body of water, over which Union engineers had constructed a number of bridges, facilitating the transfer of troops back and forth across the Chickahominy. But on the last day of May, the skies opened up and a raging torrent swept most of the bridges away.

On that day Keyes's corps was in the lead south of the Chickahominy and was approaching the hamlets of Fair Oaks Station and Seven Pines, only seven miles from Richmond, when Johnston struck. To do so Johnston concentrated twenty-three of the twenty-seven brigades under his command on the south side of the Chickahominy. McClellan's decision to divide his troops gave the Confederates the opportunity to destroy one-third of the Army of the Potomac. If things had gone right, the Confederates might well have destroyed the entire left wing of McClellan's army. But the fight was one of the most badly botched battles of the war. From its opening moments, the Southern attack got off on the wrong foot. Longstreet was the author of much of the delay by changing Johnston's orders and placing the focus of the Confederate attack on the center. D. H. Hill, Stonewall Jackson's brother-in-law, conducted most of the fighting on the first day. Floundering through knee-deep mud, the Confederates found themselves engaged in a furious firefight and eventually drove Keyes's men from their positions.

But the cost was heavy. In the lead, Robert Rodes's Confederate brigade suffered 50 percent casualties. Heintzelman had proved sluggish during the fighting, but "Bull" Sumner, charged by McClellan with providing reinforcements if necessary to any threatened sector, displayed unusual initiative for the Army of the Potomac—although

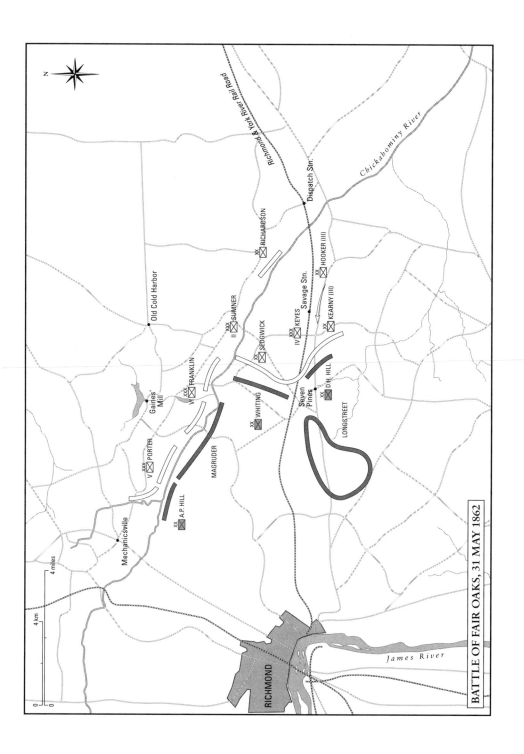

BATTLE OF FAIR OAKS, 31 MAY 1862

he owed his position as a corps commander not to McClellan but to his prewar seniority. Not only had he prepared his troops to move, but he then led them across the flooding waters of the Chickahominy on the rickety bridges over the creek. While the generalship on both sides was less than impressive, the fighting was fierce, as the enlisted ranks on both sides savaged each other. The Confederate success was less than expected: 6,000 casualties with 5,000 on the Union side.

The most significant event of the battle was that Johnston had ridden forward to see how matters were progressing as the fighting died out. Moving too close to Union lines, the Confederate commander was severely wounded by shrapnel and a bullet. Davis had no choice but to name Lee as Johnston's replacement. In a letter to Lincoln in late April, McClellan had assessed his new foe in the following terms: "I prefer Lee to Johnston—the former is *too* cautious & weak under grave responsibility. Personally brave & energetic to a fault, he yet is wanting in moral firmness when pressed by heavy responsibility & is likely to be timid & irresolute in action."[13] The president and "Young Napoleon" were about to discover how flawed McClellan's judgment was on the capabilities of officers he should have been thoroughly familiar with from his days in the regular army.

As soon as he assumed command of Confederate forces in Virginia, Lee set the stage for the destruction of part, if not all, of McClellan's army and the achievement of what he believed would be the decisive victory to gain Confederate independence. For most of the rest of June he annoyed his troops by having them extend and deepen Richmond's defenses by day after day of digging. Although it seemed to the soldiers that Lee was preparing to fight a defensive battle, he had no such intention. Instead, the purpose of such defensive works was to free up troops so that he could launch killing blows at the Army of the Potomac. However, until Jackson could move out of the Valley to reinforce Lee, the Confederates would lack sufficient troops to achieve the kind of victory Lee was seeking.

In the Shenandoah, Jackson, whose advance had carried his army almost to the bank of the Potomac, had placed himself and his army in a dangerous position. Lincoln recognized the possibility of trapping the Confederates in the lower Valley near the Potomac. Using the telegraph, the president and Stanton attempted to coordinate Union armies to trap Jackson. For the Confederates, only the gap between Front Royal and Strasburg remained open. Their escape depended on whether Jackson's soldiers could outrace Union attempts to close the gap. Jackson won the race with the "Stonewall" Brigade, Jackson's old command, which he had left behind as a rear guard, marching through the gap before Union troops arrived.

Jackson had barely escaped this pincer movement when Frémont's command moved south on the Valley Pike and attacked from the northwest near Port Republic. At the same time James Shields's division attacked from the northeast on the southern side of the south fork of the Shenandoah. The fighting on 8 June saw the Confederates drive off both Union armies with relative ease, since neither Frémont nor Shields possessed the toughness to drive home their attacks. A second fight the next day saw the same result, with another tactical victory for Jackson, although Union troops drew off in relatively good order. In tactical terms, Jackson's two victories gave the Confederates control of the upper and central portions of the Shenandoah. But the strategic aspects of his success were of greater importance. The defeats so bruised Union troops and their commanders that they no longer posed a threat to the Confederate position in the central and southern (upper) portions of the Shenandoah. With the Union threat neutralized, Jackson was now able to move from the Valley to reinforce Lee outside Richmond.

Lee had set the stage for what he hoped would be the decisive battle of the Civil War. On taking command, he had informed Davis as to plans to hold south of the Chickahominy with a small part of the army, which also consisted of his weakest troops. Meanwhile, he planned to use the bulk of his army, reinforced by Jackson, to destroy the force McClellan had deployed north of the Chickahominy. The Confederate president had doubts. He feared that with Lee concentrating on Mc-Clellan's northern flank, McClellan would launch an overwhelming attack on the southern front that would break through and capture Richmond. Nevertheless, Lee was persuasive.

On the other side, McClellan again played into Confederate hands. Despite the dangers of splitting his army that Seven Pines/Fair Oaks should have suggested, he now concentrated four corps south of the Chickahominy, while only Porter's corps remained north of the river in case McDowell's corps were to be released from its position along the Rappahannock and advance south to link up with McClellan. However, Union supply lines still ran from White House near the York River. Thus, an attack on the Union right (northern) flank, might separate the Army of the Potomac from its key base. McClellan did take the precaution of preparing to move his logistical base from the York River to the James, the Peninsula's southern boundary. But for all of McClellan's caution, Porter's flank remained up in the air, virtually inviting a Confederate attack. J.E.B. "Jeb" Stuart confirmed these weaknesses during a reconnaissance that took his cavalry entirely around the Army of the Potomac with the loss of only one soldier.

McClellan deployed his corps as follows: Porter's V Corps north of the Chickahominy, holding positions along Beaver Dam Creek, well in advance of the remainder of the army's corps on the other side of the Chickahominy. Franklin's VI Corps held positions closest to the south bank of the river, while to its south Sumner's II Corps, Heintzelman's III Corps, and Keyes's IV Corps deployed in that order. In retrospect, what remains astonishing is that while McClellan believed the Confederates outnumbered him (he wired Stanton the enemy possessed 200,000 men), his dispositions suggest he lacked the imagination to consider the possibility the Confederates might attack *him*.

As was to occur later in the summer during the Antietam campaign, McClellan possessed an excellent piece of intelligence prior to battle. A Confederate deserter reported that Jackson with three divisions would soon arrive and that Lee was about to launch a major attack on the Union right. McClellan paid not the slightest attention. By 0800 on the morning of 26 June, Lee was ready. He had positioned A. P. Hill's division to strike Porter directly across Beaver Dam Creek, while Longstreet and D. H. Hill were to support when needed. But the main blow was to be Jackson, whose troops had arrived from the Valley and were to attack Porter's exposed right flank. The Confederate attack on 26 June represented a situation in which Lee had positioned the pieces of his army for a devastating blow with every chance of destroying Porter's entire V Corps. It never happened, because Jackson never arrived. The best guess is that the dour general had so exhausted himself by a lack of sleep that he had severely diminished his capacity for clear thinking. Thoroughly annoyed by having to wait for seven hours in the boiling sun, A. P. Hill launched his men in a straight-ahead attack across Beaver Dam Creek. The attackers, 11,000 strong, had little chance against 14,000 Union troops, some of whom had entrenched. Jackson's troops finally arrived late in the afternoon but failed to involve themselves in the fighting. The casualty figures

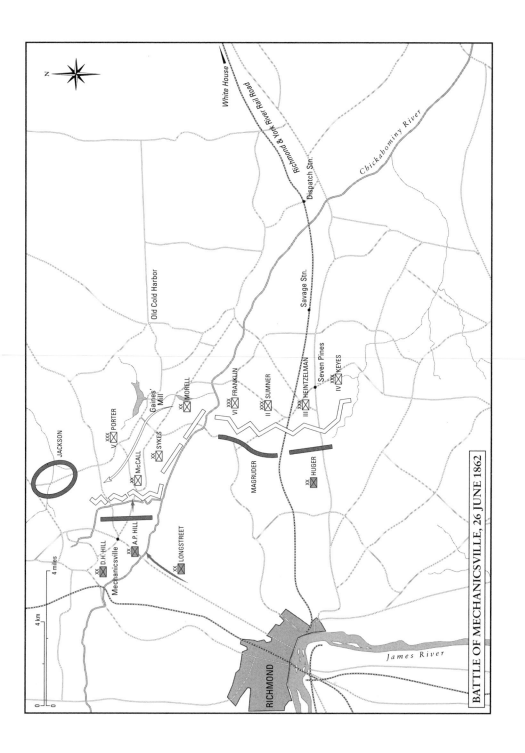

BATTLE OF MECHANICSVILLE, 26 JUNE 1862

reflected a less than auspicious start for Lee's offensive: Confederate 1,475, Union 361.

In retrospect, Lee had lost his best chance to deal a killing blow against McClellan. The frontal attacks had set Porter up for the sort of fierce flanking attacks which Jackson had launched against his enemies in the Valley and which he was to launch at Chancellorsville ten months later. In fact, Jackson would have had an advantage that he would not possess in 1863—namely, major Confederate forces would be holding the V Corps on its front, while the flank attack could have rolled Porter's troops back on the Chickahominy. Such an attack would have destroyed the V Corps, since it had no possibility of retreat or reinforcements to save it from destruction. But Lee was never one to focus on past failures, and so the Confederates moved on. On the other side, McClellan proved why he was a poor tactician as well as moral coward as the commander of an army (McClellan had shown plenty of physical courage as a junior officer in Mexico). First of all, he merely sent Porter congratulatory messages. With massive superiority south of the Chickahominy, he failed to attack on that sector, undoubtedly reinforced in that decision by his continued overestimations of Confederate strength. Magruder's theatrical displays south of the Chickahominy convinced Union corps commanders that McClellan was right in his estimates. McClellan ordered Porter to fall back from his Beaver Dam defensive position, while the latter transferred the V Corps' supply train across the creek. Most importantly, while he instructed Porter to remain on the north bank in a holding action, McClellan neglected to send Porter any reinforcements. For all his faults, Porter fought his corps well, and he retreated to an even stronger position to the rear of Botswain Swamp two miles to the east of Gaines Mill, but his right (northern) flank remained up in the air.

Having seen his plan to have Jackson crush the V Corps flank fail, Lee, ever the gambler, determined to try again on the 27th. Despite the fact that Porter was fully alert, Lee determined on a repeat of the previous day's plan. However, Jackson, as had been the case the day before, was late. The initial Confederate attacks collapsed before devastating fire from Porter's newly dug-in positions. Jackson finally arrived late in the afternoon to attack the Union flank, but Major General George Sykes's regulars on the right of Porter's line held their positions. At that point, Brigadier General John B. Hood's brigade of Texans, supported by another brigade, charged into the middle of

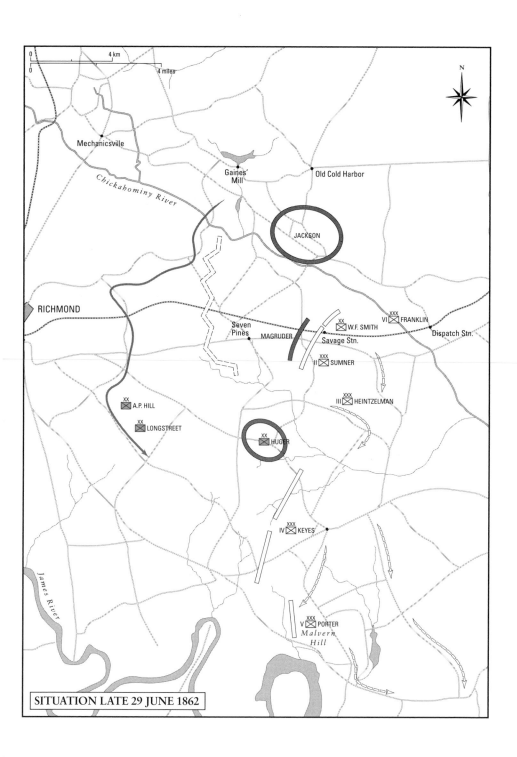

SITUATION LATE 29 JUNE 1862

the Union lines and succeeded in smashing their way through. But the Confederates were facing different troops than they had faced the year before at Manassas. The Union troops on the flanks of the breakthrough did not collapse, but pulled back in a disciplined fashion. Moreover, it was already twilight, McClellan had finally sent reinforcements, and the broken troops soon reformed. In the gathering gloom, the Confederates had to call a halt to their attack. Over the night, the V Corps retreated across the Chickahominy. The fight represented a Confederate victory, but only a tactical one. Porter and his V Corps had escaped.

On the 28th Lee hesitated, because he was not sure whether McClellan, positioned with his army on the right bank of the Chickahominy, might not launch a devastating blow against Richmond. It was not until the next morning that he felt sure that McClellan was pulling back to the James River to change his base. On the 29th Lee's plan called for Magruder, with strong support from Jackson, to attack the rear of Union forces retreating toward the James and force McClellan to stand and fight. Meanwhile, A. P. Hill and Longstreet were to move rapidly across the Confederate rear from the left (northern) flank to the right (southern), where they would hit the head of the Union column marching toward the James. Again, Lee's plans went awry. Jackson failed to appear. Magruder's attacks amounted to little more than skirmishing. Hill and Longstreet managed to cover the eighteen miles to put themselves close to the head of the retreating Union forces, but they were not yet in position to launch effective attacks. Nevertheless, the pressure of Confederates hanging on his rear forced McClellan to abandon the hospital at Savage Station with its 2,500 wounded.

On the 30th, matters proved more favorable for the Confederates. By that point Lee had five divisions south of the White Oak Swamp, positioned to attack the head of McClellan's army, while Jackson could hit the retreating Union forces north of the swamp. A. P. Hill and Longstreet would direct the main blow, one which Lee aimed to break the Union column so that the Confederates could defeat the Army of the Potomac in detail. Brigadier General Benjamin Huger was supposed to begin the attack in the center to the left side of the main attack. But busily engaged in chopping their way through the tangled growth of southern Virginia, because the Federals had obstructed the road he was to take, Huger and his men failed to reach their attack position until midafternoon. When Huger finally ran into

Brigadier General Henry Slocum's outnumbered division, he fired a few artillery shells and then retired.

Meanwhile, Brigadier General Theophilus Holmes's division, the southernmost of the attack, ran into serious opposition. Approaching Malvern Hill, Holmes's division spied large numbers of Union troops crossing the hill. After siting his division's artillery, he proceeded to open up a bombardment. That proved to be a serious mistake, because superior Union artillery on the hill, as well as the massive artillery pieces on Union gunboats in the James, blasted the Confederate attackers. Union naval power once again proved its value. Meanwhile, at the rear of the Union column, Jackson did little more than count prisoners, write to his wife, and take a nap. The course of the fighting over the Seven Days battle proved the most unsatisfactory of Jackson's career. At least Huger's skirmishing made enough of a racket to alert Longstreet that it was time to launch the main blow. It was Lee's last hope of dividing the Union army, but it had no chance of success. Longstreet and Hill launched a series of stand-up attacks against four Union divisions, all of which failed dismally. The Confederates did manage to capture eighteen Union guns and a few prisoners, but achieved no substantial tactical success at the cost of 3,500 casualties.

What happened next had a great deal to do with the frustrations that had beset Lee over the past six days as he had watched his subordinates botch his plans. By morning on 1 July, the Union commanders had entrenched a massive array of artillery on the slopes of Malvern Hill. Two corps under Porter and Keyes had deployed their infantry among the artillery, while the corps of Heintzelman and Sumner were in immediate support. Early that morning, warned by D. H. Hill that it would be dangerous to attack the hill, Longstreet (reflecting his commander's own attitudes) had casually replied: "Don't get scared, now that we have him whipped."[14] Lee and Longstreet were right in terms of McClellan, who would spend the day on a gunboat in the river, but he was wrong in referring to the soldiers of the Army of the Potomac. The opening stage of the battle involved the Confederates attempting to set up their artillery to suppress the Union batteries on the hill. That effort failed almost before it began, but what followed was a disaster. Three Confederate divisions, D. H. Hill's, Huger's, and Magruder's, moved out into the open and attempted to attack up the slope of the hill, and Union defenders slaughtered most. By the time it was over 5,500 Confederates were dead or wounded.

Nevertheless, in spite of the heavy casualties the Army of the Potomac inflicted on the attacking Confederates at Malvern Hill, McClellan failed to authorize a counterattack. Instead, he ordered a retreat back to Harrison's Landing. One of the most interesting soldiers among the generals in the Army of the Potomac was Philip Kearny. As a youth, he had wanted to attend West Point and become a soldier. However, his guardian grandfather, one of the richest men in New York, had forbidden such a career and shipped his grandson off to Columbia to prepare for a career in the law. But his grandfather died, and Kearny joined the army. His performance in the Mexican War was outstanding, although he lost an arm. After resigning his commission, he served in the French Army with distinction at Solferino, where he won the *Légion d'honneur*. Now as the Union army retreated from its victory, he made a devastating, but all too accurate, comment on McClellan's leadership: "I, Philip Kearny, an old soldier, enter my solemn protest against this order for retreat. We ought instead of retreating should follow up the enemy and take Richmond. And in full view of all responsible for such declaration, I say to you, such an order can only be prompted by cowardice and treason."[15] Even Porter, McClellan's most loyal subordinate, considered the retreat a mistake.

The irony of the Seven Days battles was that, while Lee had bested McClellan psychologically in every way, the Confederates had still failed to destroy the Army of the Potomac. While the morale of that army's soldiers had suffered a severe shock, it was not permanently shattered. In addition, the casualty figures for the fighting represented a burden that, in the long run, the Confederacy with its smaller population and more limited resources could not bear. In the Seven Days battles, Union casualties were 15,855 with 1,734 dead, 8,066 wounded, and 6,055 missing including those captured. On the other hand, Confederate losses were 20,204 with 3,494 killed, 15,758 wounded, and 952 missing (most dead).

To all intents and purposes, by July 1862 with the conclusion of the Peninsula Campaign, McClellan had set the Army of the Potomac's command culture. That culture, largely formed by the Old Army's attitudes—rigid obedience to orders, a general lack of initiative and aggressiveness, an emphasis on date of rank, and an unwillingness to cooperate—would dominate the Army of the Potomac long after McClellan had left its command in November 1862. When Grant arrived in the East to take command of all the Union armies in spring 1864 he was to discover that culture still in place, and it would take the costly battles in Virginia for him fully to realize how different the Army of the Potomac's culture was from that with which he was familiar in the West.

Second Bull Run

The incompetence of Union generals in chasing Jackson back and forth across the Valley finally persuaded Lincoln that he and Stanton could not run the war from Washington. Thus, in late June they brought Major General John Pope from the West to assume control of the northern Virginia theater, and to command what was now to be called the Army of Virginia. Politically, Pope possessed excellent connections. In the West he had achieved a measure of success in capturing Island No. Ten in the Mississippi with no casualties. He had then commanded one of the wings in Halleck's tortuous advance on the railroad center of Corinth, Mississippi. But Pope had not distinguished himself against first-rate opponents. He was bombastic and aggressive, but at least Shiloh's casualty bill had not tarnished his reputation.

In retrospect, that bloodbath may well have saved Grant from a transfer East, where the culture of the Eastern armies could have destroyed his future usefulness to the North. Instead, Grant remained in the West, where he would grow into a formidable commander and strategist. Pope arrived in Washington at the end of June 1862. The War Department promulgated his new command on 26 June, which consisted of what had hitherto been three separate commands, led by as unimpressive a group of senior officers as the Eastern armies possessed: Franz Sigel, Nathaniel Banks, and Irvin McDowell. The first two were politicians and well connected, which explains why they were to hang around for another two years, while McDowell was an unimaginative regular officer who had displayed little skill thus far in the war. Sigel claimed some training in the army of the princedom of Baden, Germany, where he had participated in the Revolution of 1848. However, none of that experience had imparted the slightest battlefield wisdom. Banks's prewar experience had been in Massachusetts politics, which, whatever its combative nature, had not prepared him for war. The troops McClellan took to the Peninsula and which became the core of the Army of the Potomac inherited many of its chief's flaws, but it did possess a strong esprit de corps and corporate identity. Unfortunately, that same sense of camaraderie suppressed, as we shall see, any desire on the part of McClellan's forces to cooperate with Pope.

Instead of attempting to pull his new command together, Pope spent most of July politicking and hobnobbing with Washington's elite. He strongly recommended the administration bring Halleck to Washington as the army's general in chief, a position McClellan had held until his demotion in March 1862. Pope's efforts coincided with Lincoln's belief that he and Stanton needed sensible military advice. They ordered Halleck to Washington, and on 23 July, that general assumed the position of commander of Union armies. One recent author has described Halleck in the following terms: "Beneath the dome of his high forehead, the general would gaze goggle-eyed at those who spoke to him, reflecting long before answering and simultaneously rubbing both elbows all the while, leading one observer to quip that the great intelligence he was reputed to possess must be located in his elbows."[16] Lincoln later accurately described Halleck as the army's chief clerk.

While in Washington, Pope issued a proclamation to his soldiers that infuriated McClellan and most of the senior officers in the East. He deliberately aimed at that result: "Let us understand each other. I have come to you from the West, where we have always seen the backs of our enemies; from an army whose business it has been to seek the adversary and to beat him when he was found; whose policy has been attack and not defense."[17] Such hubris proved a terrible mistake, not necessarily because it annoyed McClellan, Porter, and their ilk, but because it forced Pope to act too aggressively when confronting Lee. In addition, the commander of the Army of Virginia issued General Order No. 5, which provided his troops with carte blanche to live off the countryside. That order outraged the Confederates, but it did have the beneficial result of stripping the countryside of northern and central Virginia bare, thus creating a logistical burden on the Army of Northern Virginia.

Halleck's arrival in Washington heralded a fundamental shift in Union strategy. One of his first acts was to visit McClellan, who had hunkered down on the Peninsula after his humiliation of the Seven Days battles. McClellan argued that he needed extensive reinforcements if he were to resume the offensive against Richmond, but Halleck warned that, considering other commitments, he could only provide 20,000 troops. McClellan indicated that would suffice. But upon Halleck's return to Washington, McClellan telegraphed that he required 50,000 more troops to resume the offensive. That was enough of McClellan's obfuscation for Halleck. On 4 August the army's new general in chief, with Lincoln's support, ordered McClellan to pull his army from the Peninsula and return it to northern Virginia. Up to this point the Army of the Potomac had been holding Lee in front of Richmond. Admittedly, Lee had already released Jackson with 12,000 men to protect the railroad junction and supply depot at Gordonsville. Then, on 27 July, he added A. P. Hill's division of 13,000 to Jackson's command, perhaps influenced by the fact McClellan remained quiescent. Nevertheless, the bulk of Lee's army still faced Union forces on the Peninsula.

However, once McClellan's army began returning to Washington, Lee, with a shorter distance to reach the Rappahannock, could reposition his army more quickly to northern Virginia than the Army of the Potomac could make the move, especially under McClellan's dilatory leadership. Having received the order to abandon the Peninsula, McClellan waited no less than ten days before the first units of the Army of the Potomac clambered on board steamboats to head down the James River. As he wrote his wife on 10 August, "I have a strong idea that Pope will be thrashed . . . such a villain as he is ought to bring defeat upon any cause that employs him."[18] Beyond the normal snail's pace characterizing the Army of the Potomac's movements, it appears McClellan and his subordinates did everything they could to insure Pope would fight Lee on his own. Whether their actions were the result of deliberate malfeasance or incompetence is difficult to say. As of 18 August, two weeks after receiving the order to withdraw from the Peninsula, McClellan had not moved a single soldier beyond Fort Monroe at the Peninsula's tip.

But the true author of John Pope's misfortunes was the general himself. He was one of those officers who knows everything and so refuses all advice or intelligence that contradicts his assumptions. On 9 August Jackson moved. Hearing that Banks's corps was in the vicinity of Culpeper, Jackson struck north from the Rappahannock. For once he found himself surprised, when Banks attacked first. After several hours of tough fighting, Jackson launched Hill's division against the Union flank and drove the outnumbered Banks off the field. By the time it was over, Union losses totaled 2,353, while the Confederates suffered 1,000 fewer casualties. Nevertheless, Jackson, lacking the strength to withstand Pope's full strength, retreated back behind the

Rappahannock. The battle achieved little, either in an operational or strategic sense, but psychologically it put Pope on notice the Confederates were in strength on his front.

By 7 August Lee was piecing together an intelligence picture that suggested McClellan was about to withdraw from the York Peninsula. A week later he was sure. Longstreet moved with ten brigades to Gordonsville; Stuart with his cavalrymen also moved to that junction, while Anderson's division, which held Drewry's Bluff, eventually followed. Lee was bringing north over 30,000 men to link up with Jackson. The Confederate commander's express aim was to destroy Pope before McClellan returned to northern Virginia. Unlike its opponents, nearly everything in the Army of Northern Virginia was done with snap and speed—especially since Lee had reorganized the army after the Seven Days battles to remove commanders he found wanting. On 15 August Lee arrived at Gordonsville to confer with his chief subordinates. Out of that meeting emerged one of the boldest campaigns of the Civil War.

In mid-August the Army of Northern Virginia was spread out between Gordonsville and the Rapidan River, while much of Pope's Army of Virginia lay between the Rapidan and Rappahannock. Early morning on 18 August, Pope encountered one of the few pieces of luck he received during the campaign. During the night, the Confederates had neglected to picket Raccoon Ford on the Rapidan, and a Union cavalry raid waltzed in and hit Stuart's headquarters. Stuart escaped, but the Union troopers captured orders indicating Lee was up on the Rapidan and intended to smash the Army of Virginia. Pope immediately moved his troops out of danger by retreating across the Rappahannock. Meanwhile, in preparation for the advance north, Jackson decided to instill additional discipline in his troops. He had three deserters brought in, tried by drumhead court-martial, and sentenced to death. When one of their officers interceded on behalf of two of the men, Jackson announced: "Sir! Men who desert their comrades in war *deserve* to be *shot!*—and *officers* who intercede for them *deserve* to be *hung!*"[19] Jackson then had his divisions formed up on three sides of a square. The miscreants were led out by their own companies, which acted as executioners. After proper pronouncements, they shot the malfeasants.

Thwarted in the effort to destroy Pope between the Rapidan and the Rappahannock, Lee opted for a truly risky strategy. Time was slipping, and despite McClellan's best efforts, it was clear the Army of the

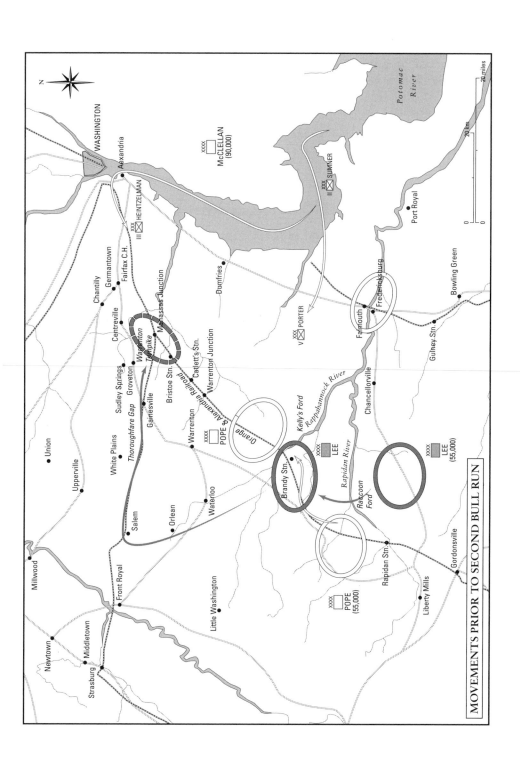

MOVEMENTS PRIOR TO SECOND BULL RUN

Potomac would arrive in northern Virginia in the near future, which would weigh the correlation of forces heavily against the Confederates. On 24 August, after conferring with Jackson, Lee split the army in half and launched Jackson on a deep sweep behind Union lines to strike at the Orange & Alexandria Railroad and Pope's logistical depots. Lee explicitly ordered Jackson not to bring on a general engagement, but rather to entice Pope forward, thus lengthening the time before his troops could combine with the Army of the Potomac. The risk Lee was taking was greater than risks he would take the next year at Chancellorsville, because nearly sixty miles would separate the two halves of his army. As had occurred in the past and would occur in the future, Lee was counting on the lethargy of Union commanders and the sloppiness of their reconnaissance.

Well before dawn on 25 August, Jackson's foot cavalry were marching to the northwest, a march that took them to Orlean and Salem, before they turned east to follow the roadbed of the Manassas Gap Railroad. By early evening the lead soldiers of Richard S. Ewell's division arrived at Salem after a twenty-five-mile march. Jackson's last units straggled in at midnight. Thus, Jackson had positioned his force approximately twenty miles from the Orange & Alexandria Railroad. Sigel on the far right of the Army of Virginia apprised Pope that a major Confederate movement had passed by his troops to the west, headed northwest. Pope, who throughout the campaign displayed an eagerness to believe the enemy was doing what was convenient to his plans, dismissed the threat in his belief Jackson was returning to the Shenandoah. Before dawn on the 26th Jackson headed his troops through Thoroughfare Gap in the Bull Run Mountains, the ridge running east of the Blue Ridge. Meanwhile, Longstreet kept Pope's attention focused on the Rappahannock.

By 1600 on the 26th the Confederates had reached Gainesville less than five miles from Bristoe Station. Sending Ewell's division and Stuart's cavalry ahead, Jackson struck at one of the main transportation centers for Pope's army. Smashing up trains and destroying the rails, the Confederates had a field day. The real prize, however, was five miles farther up the tracks at Manassas Junction, which served as the Army of Virginia's main supply base. Guarded by a few infantry and Union cavalry, who had never seen combat, Manassas Junction too soon fell into Confederate hands. In a march of over fifty-four miles in thirty-six hours, Jackson had wrecked trains, disrupted the

Army of Virginia's supply system, captured immense stores, which fed his weary troops for the next week, and thoroughly embarrassed Pope. Most importantly, Pope had lost control of the campaign. Jackson pulled back as soon as his troops had packed their blankets with everything portable and disappeared toward the northwest; what the Confederates could not carry, they destroyed. The purpose of the raid, however, had not been to wreck Union logistics, or to gather in loot, but rather to draw Pope's Army of Virginia into a major fight before McClellan arrived. In fact, Jackson's humiliating success had done everything necessary to set the stage for the drama Lee set in motion.

Believing Lee had divided the Army of Northern Virginia, Pope set off in pursuit of Jackson. For the next week he focused almost exclusively on Jackson, as if Lee and Longstreet did not exist. Pope even boasted to his staff that he was going to bag Jackson's entire force. Meanwhile, Porter's V Corps had already arrived at Aquia Creek and was moving to Kelly's Ford on the Rappahannock. Porter brought little except his outstanding troops. He had proved on the Peninsula that he could fight when pressed, but like his beloved chief, McClellan, he would take no risks for John Pope, whom he deeply distrusted. Halleck was supposed to try to coordinate the movements of Pope and McClellan, but, of course, he did nothing of the kind. By now Heintzelman's III Corps was also arriving with two of the best division commanders in the Army of the Potomac, Hooker and Kearny. The latter would characterize his corps commander with this scathing description: "His small quanteen [sic] of brains have been fossilized by near 40 years of small garrison routine at the head of 100 foot, in some western outpost."[20]

Meanwhile, Pope had no idea of Jackson's location. On 27 August, the Union general ordered his army to march on Manassas in hopes of catching the Confederates. But as Pope and the Army of Virginia marched north, while Jackson disappeared seemingly into the mists of northern Virginia, Longstreet was also marching. The crucial area through which he had to move was also Thoroughfare Gap. Had Pope paid attention to the larger framework within which operations were unfolding, he would have made an effort to insure that sufficient Union troops held the gaps through the Bull Run Mountains. McDowell did warn Pope of the danger of not reinforcing the gaps, but the Union commander again paid no attention. Thus, Longstreet pushed the relatively weak Union force aside in moving through the gap.

Jackson awaited the Union attack with the calm of a general who had great confidence in himself and his troops. Pope's search finally ended in success. Late on 28 August, Major General Rufus King's division found the Confederates ensconced north of Groveton on the Warrenton Turnpike, not far from the old Bull Run battlefield. In fact, it was Jackson who found them, for after studying the Union column, he ordered his troops to attack from their shelter in the woods north of the turnpike. From the Union perspective, it was an encounter battle, in which both sides steadily fed in regiments. From the Confederate point of view, it was a matter of keeping Pope's attention centered on the fight until Longstreet arrived. The arrival of two regiments from Abner Doubleday's division allowed Union forces, despite their being outnumbered nearly two to one, to fight Jackson to a stalemate.

By evening the fighting was dying down. In spite of the gathering gloom, Jackson ordered his troops to launch one last attack. It was no more successful than the initial engagements, but substantially added to the number of Confederate casualties. Overall on the 28th, the Union probably had the advantage in the casualties. But that was not what mattered. During the night, as King's division abandoned the battlefield, other Union forces were on the way. What mattered was that Pope's attention now centered on Jackson. During the night he issued orders to concentrate Union forces to the west of Manassas near Groveton. The fighting on the 29 August underlined his inability to concentrate on the larger operational framework, or the nature of his enemy. Sigel's corps was closest to Jackson, and both he and Kearny, located to the west of Centreville, received a demand from Pope to attack immediately. Kearny, who was as sick of Pope as he was of McClellan, exploded: "Tell General Pope to go to Hell. We won't march before morning."[21] Disastrously Pope deluded himself that Jackson was retreating, while at the same time he paid no attention to Longstreet's ominous approach.

Jackson deployed his three divisions along an uncompleted railroad cut, which its builders had abandoned. Swinging from the northeast, it crossed Bull Run Creek and then ran in a southwesterly direction, paralleling the Warrenton Turnpike. Behind the unfinished embankment, Jackson stationed A. P. Hill's division, his strongest, on the left, because that position held the key fords over which the Confederates would have to retreat, if Pope pushed too hard. Two brigades of Ewell's division held the center, behind the embankment, while

Brigadier General William Starke's division held the right. By itself, the position was not innately strong, but the terrain, broken up by woods and ravines, made it difficult for Union commanders to control their troops in the heavy fighting.

Sigel's corps began the fighting on the 29th by attacking Hill's positions along the railroad cut on the left (northern) portion of Jackson's deployment. After enjoying an initial success as the Union attack ran into Confederates on the eastern side of the railroad cut, it collapsed when its troops hit the well-protected Confederates behind the embankment. Had Jackson wanted to launch a major attack, Hill's division was in a position to wreck Sigel's corps, but Jackson was waiting for Longstreet's arrival. The division of the German expatriate Carl Schurz bore much of the fighting. For a moment there appeared an opportunity to break through Hill's division, but Kearny, who bore a grudge against Sigel, refused to cooperate and failed to support the first attack. Unfortunately, Sigel dispersed the arriving support from Reno's and Heintzelman's corps in higgledy-piggledy fashion, so that by afternoon, the organization of the three Union corps on the battlefield had broken down. That made command and control of the corps difficult, if not impossible, for the remainder of the battle.

At 0800, a courier arrived at Jackson's headquarters with the report that Lee and Longstreet were only several hours from the field. Stuart, who had been up with Jackson during the raid, now made contact with Lee to guide Longstreet's troops onto Jackson's southern flank. As he returned to Jackson, Stuart spied the dust cloud raised by a large Federal force approaching the left (south) of the Union line and Jackson's right. It was Porter's V Corps, but the Confederates had no idea of the strength of the Union force except that it was large. Stuart immediately deployed skirmishers, while his cavalry stirred up dust to indicate that large numbers of Confederates were in front of Porter's line of advance.

That action was sufficient to stop Porter and allow Longstreet to complete his arrival. According to Pope's orders, he was supposed to pile into Jackson's right flank. Instead Porter stood frozen, hanging to the southeast of Longstreet's deploying troops. Nevertheless, the V Corps was in a position to attack Longstreet's Confederates, should they attempt to attack Pope's southern (left) flank. Thus, the mere presence of the V Corps southeast of the battlefield forced Lee to hesitate in committing Longstreet's divisions to the fight. Admittedly,

Porter failed to attack Jackson's flank, and for both this failure and the sin of his indiscreet politicking with conservative Democratic politicians, Porter would find himself court-martialed and cashiered after Antietam. Due to his able service during the Seven Days battles, and Pope's own self-inflicted errors at Second Bull Run, it was an unfair decision in purely military terms. Nevertheless, Porter had exposed himself to Radical Republican wrath, which sought to make an example of a member of McClellan's clique.

While Longstreet drove his troops on the road northeast from Thoroughfare Gap at a furious pace, another major corps of the Army of the Potomac was available to reinforce the Army of Virginia. On the 27th, late in the afternoon, McClellan informed Halleck that Franklin's VI Corps was ready to march. Nevertheless, although he received three direct orders for the corps to march to Pope's aid, twenty-two hours later McClellan telegraphed Halleck to report the troops might be ready to march the following morning on the 29th. Franklin's VI Corps finally marched at 0600 on the 29th, but only managed to crawl forward ten miles. On the 30th, the VI Corps reached Centreville after a march of only twelve miles. McClellan's correspondence throughout the period suggests a general willing to allow his countrymen to die to promote his own position. On the 29th, he telegraphed Lincoln: "I am clear that one of two courses should be adopted—1st To concentrate all our available forces to open communication with Pope—2nd To leave Pope to get out of his scrape & at once use all our means to make the Capital perfectly safe."[22] As a highly decorated marine officer suggested to us, it is enough for one to wish he could reach back in time and strangle the "dishonest, pusillanimous son of a bitch."

What was Pope doing on the 29th? Until the early afternoon, Sigel had handled the fighting in his usual disorganized fashion. Pope arrived in the early afternoon, while his rambling, incoherent orders, written at 1000 on the 29th, indicate he believed that Longstreet "is moving in this direction at a pace that will bring them here by to-morrow night or the next day."[23] In fact, Pope wrote those orders almost at the moment when Longstreet's troops were deploying on Jackson's southern flank. But Pope was a stubborn man, and in spite of repeated warnings from those on his southern flank, he held to his faulty assessment. He now launched a series of attacks on Jackson. Moreover, much as McClellan was to do at Antietam three weeks later, these attacks went in individually, allowing the Confederates to respond to each. The first came from one of Hooker's brigades under Brigadier General Cuvier Grover, which achieved a signal success when its attack uncovered a hole in Jackson's lines. But Grover failed to receive support, and the Confederates quickly closed up. Similarly, an attack by John Reynolds's division on Jackson's right (southern) flank failed. But Reynolds did discover, lying beyond his final position, masses of Confederate infantry, undoubtedly Longstreet's, farther to the southwest. Pope simply dismissed the warning that one of Reynolds's staff officers brought him: "You are excited, young man; the people you see are General Porter's command taking position on the right of the enemy."[24]

The next Union attack again gained initial success but after pushing across the unfinished railroad embankment collapsed under counterattacks on its flanks. Because of the failure to provide supporting troops, each brigade-sized attack inevitably failed against Jackson's veterans. The collapse of Colonel James Nagel's brigade for a time opened a hole in the Union center, but Jackson was still playing for time. By now Pope was thoroughly annoyed that Porter had yet to launch his attack on Jackson's right. At 1630, he issued another set of orders, directing Porter to attack Jackson's right. At the same time, he ordered Kearny, who had contributed little thus far, to attack the Confederate left, which had been under pressure all day. Kearny struck with his full division of nearly 3,000 men and put heavy pressure on Hill. For a time, it appeared the attack would break through Jackson's left, but Kearny had only one division, while Jackson had three. Thus, he was able to throw Jubal Early's brigade, one of his largest and best, into the fight. It was more than enough to break the Union attack.

The final fighting of the day came when Lee ordered Hood's division forward to set the stage for the next day's fight. Hood's men ran into John Hatch's smaller division in the twilight. Pope and McDowell had ordered Hatch to attack, because the two believed the Confederates were retreating down the Warrenton Turnpike. Nothing could better underline their flight from reality. One of the great failings of incompetent generals lies in their penchant for attempting to adapt the real world to their preconceived notions, rather than adapting their assumptions to reality. Both Pope and McDowell paid for that inability to recognize reality with their reputations. Their soldiers paid with their lives.

Pope still had the opportunity to pull back to Centreville in the night and wait for the rest of the Army of the Potomac to arrive. The evidence certainly indicated Longstreet had arrived and Lee had united his army. But convinced that Longstreet remained at least a march away and that Jackson was on the brink of retreating, Pope stood his ground. On the other side of the hill, Lee and Longstreet considered continuing Hood's attack during the night, but their subordinates, including the always aggressive Hood, talked them out of such a move. Instead, Lee decided to await Pope's first moves the next day, before launching the kind of slashing attack that had already made the Army of Northern Virginia famous during the Seven Days battles fighting.

Well past midnight, Richard Anderson's division of some 6,000 soldiers, whom Longstreet had left behind to cover the Rappahannock, reached the main army. Unlike Franklin's VI Corps, which could barely make ten miles a day, Anderson's division covered over twenty miles a day, the last segment in seventeen hours of marching. As Lee waited for his opportunity, Pope dithered. At 0700, he met with his senior officers. They warned that the Confederates were not retreating; they also argued that the best option was to launch a better-coordinated and larger assault on Jackson's left, given Kearny's temporary success the evening before. But having agreed with them, Pope issued no orders. Instead, he and his confidant McDowell, according to a staff officer, "spent the morning under a tree waiting for the enemy to retreat."[25] The most reasonable explanation is that the two generals still believed the Confederates were retreating in spite of the evidence. On the other side, Lee expected Pope would make the mistake of attacking Jackson again and that an opportunity would arise for Longstreet to attack Pope's southern flank.

In the early morning hours of the 30th Porter, having pulled back from his position on Longstreet's flank, had finally arrived with his V Corps. Along the way he also lost one of his divisions, which wandered off to Centreville and spent the day acquiring new shoes from supply dumps. Into the early afternoon, Pope persisted in his assumption the Confederates were not in strength on his southern flank. He would only send a single brigade to reinforce Reynolds's division, which had deployed on Chinn Ridge to guard the Union flank in front of Longstreet's masses of infantry and artillery. Meanwhile, Pope finally ordered Porter to attack with the V Corps and its 10,000 men against Jackson's right. As the attack would go in against Starke's division, it would not only strike relatively fresh troops but would also expose its flank to enfilade fire from a portion of Longstreet's and

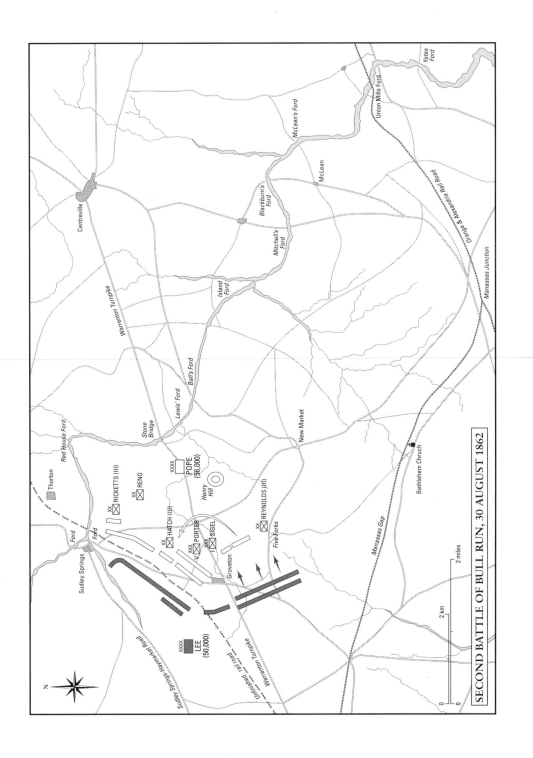

SECOND BATTLE OF BULL RUN, 30 AUGUST 1862

S. D. Lee's artillery battalions. Moreover, Pope ordered no supporting attacks to distract Confederate attention.

The result was predictable. Starke's division was fully prepared. Almost immediately, Confederate artillery fire hit Porter's attack from enfilade positions and inflicted devastating casualties. It was a turkey shoot. Nevertheless, some of Porter's men came close to breaking through Starke's position, but as had been the case throughout the battle, Union commanders, in this case Porter, refused to reinforce success. The fighting was as fierce as anything yet seen on the field of Second Bull Run. One Union soldier recounted: "Regiments got mixed up—brigades were intermingled—all was one seething, anxious, excited mass. Men were falling by scores around us, and still we could see no enemy. . . . Some officers were yelling 'Fire!,' others were giving the command, 'Cease fire, for God's sake! You're shooting our own men!'"[26] The attack collapsed into a rout that, for a moment, spread disorder to the center of the Union line.

At this point McDowell intervened. Seeing the disorder caused by Porter's collapse, he ordered Reynolds's division to leave its position on Chinn Ridge and move to reinforce the V Corps' badly shaken troops. He thereby reduced Union forces standing to the east of Longstreet's massed divisions to two brigades. It was the single most incompetent decision made during the battle and reflected the fact that this late in the battle McDowell, like Pope, still believed Longstreet had yet to link up with Jackson.

Shortly after 1600 Lee and Longstreet struck. Even then Pope failed to recognize the gravity of the situation. McDowell, however, immediately recognized the disaster that confronted the Army of Virginia. Hood's division stepped out of the woods to the west of the Union position with his brigade of Texans leading the way. Longstreet's attack hit the Union flank with the full power with which Hood's Texans and assorted other Confederates were capable. Following to the right of Hood's division and slightly behind them were the men of James L. Kemper's and D. R. Jones's divisions. Only four Ohio regiments and a single battery of Union artillery held Chinn Ridge against the mass power of Longstreet's attack. As Longstreet advanced, Pope finally awoke to the reality that the Confederates were in strength on his exposed flank in a position to destroy the Army of Virginia. It was now a desperate matter of moving sufficient troops onto Henry House Hill, and to do that, the Ohioans were going to have to mount an effective defense of Chinn Ridge, which is precisely what they did.

The Confederates helped. Disordered by the staunchness of the Union stand and the bombardment of Union artillery from the left of Pope's position, they launched a series of attacks that initially failed. The Union position on Chinn Ridge finally collapsed when Kemper's division caught up with Hood's men. Leading the charge that eventually swamped the Union defenders was the commander of the 7th Virginia, Colonel W. T. Patton, grandfather of General George Patton. Eventually, the overwhelming Confederate numbers swamped the Ohioans and they collapsed, but they had taken a heavy toll of their attackers, and perhaps more importantly, they had bought time. As the Ohioans broke, two more Union brigades, rushed over from Sigel's corps, joined in the fight. They, too, went down to defeat, but not before adding to the swelling Confederate casualties. The defenders suffered just as heavily, their most famous casualty the eldest son of Daniel Webster. It was not until the Confederates had broken them that the Stars and Bars flew over the ridge.

While the Ohio regiments were fighting and dying, Pope, McDowell, and Sigel scrambled to mount a makeshift defense along Henry House Hill. If successful, defense of that position would keep the Warrenton Turnpike open, which would provide the Army of Virginia a route to retreat. Should they fail, the Confederates would gain control of the turnpike and be in a position to destroy Pope's entire field army. One of the key elements in Lee's plan, which might have achieved that aim, was for Jackson to mount major attacks to hold the Union center and right (northern) divisions in place. But as in the Seven Days battles, Jackson remained largely quiescent. Thus, the fighting that day was in Longstreet's hands.

In effect, Pope conceded retreat by ordering the divisions that made up his right wing to pull back. The fact that Jackson made only halfhearted efforts to impede their withdrawal aided the pull out of Union troops on the right. By the time the Confederates had taken Chinn Ridge and were ready to continue their advance, Pope had assembled four brigades with two additional brigades, including one of regulars and considerable artillery, on Henry House Hill, extending to the south. It was a strong position, and it would have to hold if the Army of Virginia were to escape back to Centreville. For a period, the Confederates threatened to break through the center of the position, but a brigade of regulars, which had not participated in Porter's debacle, counterattacked. Longstreet's attack finally ran out of steam, and the Union line held. The road to Centreville remained open, and by morning the only Yankees still on the battlefield were either dead or wounded. For the Union troops the retreat continued through Centreville to the defenses of Washington. It was a dark and dismal retreat, made worse by a nasty little skirmish at Chantilly in the midst of a ferocious thunderstorm. The chaotic conditions in that fight were such that the indomitable Phil Kearny rode into the midst of a Confederate unit and then tried to escape, only to be shot down and killed.

The Second Battle of Bull Run had been a disaster. Pope's performance had been abysmal, while McDowell had acted as the court jester, adding to the disaster with bad advice and a lack of understanding of the enemy. The fact that it took the two generals over thirty hours to recognize that Longstreet had arrived on the field in spite of solid intelligence to the contrary speaks volumes as to their generalship. On the other hand, Union soldiers, often placed by their leadership in impossible positions, gave as good as they got. Nevertheless, the Confederates displayed a dash and responsiveness at the highest levels that almost brought about the destruction of the Army of Virginia.

Conclusion

Despite his lethargic pace, McClellan had advanced his army to the gates of Richmond by summer 1862, only to see Robert E. Lee achieve a sudden reversal of Confederate military fortunes after the Seven Days battles. With the Union's Eastern army reeling after Second Manassas, Lee would sense the potential for a war-ending blow and invade Maryland to achieve just such an outcome. In the West, Union momentum had stalled, not so much from Confederate military prowess as the bureaucratic maneuvering of Henry Halleck that stymied the efforts of the Union's best Western commander, Grant, and which also failed to exploit the potential of riverine operations in neglecting to reinforce Farragut's failed naval attack on Vicksburg. The Confederacy would also take advantage of passivity in this theater to embark on a bold invasion of Kentucky, supported by aggressive operations in northern Mississippi. These two paired counteroffensives represented the Confederacy's best, but not final, opportunity for victory.

CHAPTER 7

The Confederate Counter-Offensives, 1862

Fellow-citizens, we cannot escape history. We of this Congress and this administration, will be remembered in spite of ourselves. No personal significance, or insignificance, can spare one or another of us. The fiery trial through which we pass, will light us down, in honor or dishonor, to the latest generation. We say we are for the Union. The world will not forget that we say this. We know how to save the Union. The world knows we do know how to save it. We—even we here—hold the power, and bear the responsibility. In giving freedom to the slave, we assure freedom to the free—honorable alike in what we give, and what we preserve. We shall nobly save, or meanly lose, the last best, hope of earth. Other means may succeed; this could not fail. The way is plain, peaceful, generous, just—a way which, if followed, the world will forever applaud, and God must forever bless.

—Lincoln, Annual Message to Congress, 1862

The Confederate Counterattack: Bragg and Buell

What to do after the fall of Corinth was the crucial strategic question confronting Halleck. Washington was hardly in the position to offer guidance, since Lincoln and Stanton remained preoccupied with the increasingly serious situation in Virginia, where Jackson was wrecking Union forces in the Shenandoah. The most obvious choice would have been for Halleck to move his great army against Vicksburg, clean up the Mississippi River valley, destroy Beauregard's army, soon to be led by Bragg, and then focus on the problem of destroying the Confederate cavalry bands spreading havoc in central and western Tennessee. Admittedly such an effort would have encountered considerable difficulties. The summer of 1862 proved exceptionally dry. Supplying the army as it moved south toward Vicksburg would have depended on increasingly vulnerable supply lines running back to Memphis;

however, the troops could have lived off the countryside, as Grant was to do in his retreat to Holly Springs in December 1862, but Union commanders may not have been ready for such an approach. In retrospect, the fundamental question was whether the navy possessed the logistical strength to support such a drive. Our estimate is that it did, but Halleck had no interest in taking the risks that such a move would involve.

Thus, instead of focusing his strength on the most important objects at hand—the destruction of the Confederacy's main Western army, or capturing Vicksburg, the two aims potentially intertwined—Halleck dissipated his forces on a number of separate objectives. The result was that he broke up the great army that the combination of Grant's, Buell's, and Pope's forces had represented. Halleck instead chose a path that achieved little of strategic value. He left Grant with a shell of an army and the responsibility of controlling western Tennessee and the Mississippi and Tennessee Rivers. Grant's responsibilities involved suppressing guerrilla war in western Tennessee and thereby keeping the lines of communications open between Memphis and Nashville. To Buell, Halleck handed the bulk of forces available, some 40,000-plus soldiers, with the order to push on to Chattanooga from Corinth. At the time, the title of Buell's army was the Army of the Ohio, but it soon changed to the Army of the Cumberland.

Even after the allocation of responsibilities, Halleck could not resist interfering. Instead of allowing Buell to pull back to Nashville and advance toward southeastern Tennessee from that starting point, Halleck made the mistake of ordering Buell to push straight across the state. Such an advance made little sense in terms of either logistics or the state's geography. Buell objected, but Halleck overruled him. Halleck's conception of moving across southern Tennessee rested on his belief that Union troops could repair and then use the Memphis & Charleston Railroad. But that railroad was far more vulnerable to Confederate raiders than the rail link from Nashville south. Thus, Buell's troops spent much of the summer rebuilding bridges on that line, bridges which Confederates destroyed almost as quickly as Union troops reconstructed them, when raiders were not ripping up the rails.

The appointment of Halleck to the position of commander of Union armies in Washington lifted his baleful influence from the Western theater. Lincoln and Stanton appear to have believed Halleck's reports, in which he had awarded himself most of the credit for the successes in the West. What they received was an officer who did not understand the advantages that railroads or sea power provided to the movement of troops and supplies, who generally avoided responsibility and was incapable of swift decisions, and finally who had little understanding of how to conduct operations. But Halleck was also a skilled bureaucrat. He consistently provided military advice that fit in with what his superiors wanted to hear. When Lincoln and Stanton came up with proposals that made little strategic sense, Halleck was not the kind of officer to propose alternative courses of action. It would take Lincoln and Stanton until 1863 to divine his actual abilities. By summer 1863, they were largely using him as a clerk, which was how Grant would also use him when he became the commander of Union armies in spring 1864.

As Buell struggled across southern Tennessee, he found himself beset by logistical problems, the constant harassment of Confederate cavalry raiders, and his own perverse nature. In many respects he was almost as inept a commander as McClellan, but unlike his counterpart in the East, he did not look like a general, instead going around in a shabby overcoat. Buell summed up his approach to war in the following terms: "The object is not to fight great battles, and storm impregnable fortifications, but by demonstration and maneuvering to prevent the enemy from concentrating his scattered forces."[1] McClellan would have agreed with every word.

Buell spent an uncomfortable summer. The march eastward was bad enough. Because of the drought, water and food were in short supply. As he moved eastward, Confederate raiders attacked the bridges and supply convoys in his rear. By nature he was cautious, sure that large forces of Confederates were hiding behind every bush, while Halleck constantly hectored him up to speed up his march on Chattanooga. For their part, Lincoln and Stanton were threatening to transfer 25,000 troops from the Western armies to reinforce McClellan's campaign, which clearly was in trouble. Only Halleck's promise that Buell would move into eastern Tennessee and protect its largely pro-Union population kept the administration from transferring those troops. Adding to Buell's troubles was a serious dispute with his subordinate commanders as to how the occupying Union troops should treat Southern civilians. In one case, the commander of the 8th Brigade, Colonel John Turchin, a former czarist officer, announced to his troops that he was going to close his eyes for two hours, and they were free to take whatever measures they felt necessary to clean out the Confederates. The methods of the czarist army were not yet those of the Union army and certainly not those of Buell, who was a firm believer in McClellan's approach of treating the civilians with kid gloves. Initially, even the Northern newspapers were unhappy about the incident, but the mood shifted within and outside the army, especially after Buell's dismissal of Turchin despite the contrary recommendation of a board of inquiry.

The Turchin affair was only one indication of Buell's growing unpopularity among the troops, while disaffection and indiscipline among the officer corps grew as well. In fact, as did his counterpart Bragg, Buell headed an increasingly dysfunctional command structure among his division and corps commanders that spread to middle-level officers as well. Relations among a number of officers grew so poisonous that a bloody blow-up eventually occurred. In late September, shortly before the Battle of Perryville, a dispute between Major General William Nelson and Brigadier General Jefferson Davis (no relation to the Confederate president) reached the point where Davis shot his superior at point blank range. Davis then escaped the consequences of murdering a superior officer by the fact that the administration had temporarily relieved Buell of command during the period when the murder occurred and then reinstated him. As a result, Buell refused to convene a court-martial because technically he had not been in command when Davis had murdered Nelson. Thus, Davis never stood trial and eventually was to command a corps in Sherman's March to the Sea.

Nevertheless, the incident reflected an army whose commanding general could neither discipline its senior officers nor run a competent campaign. So riven was the Army of the Cumberland with dissension that Nelson had defenders along with opponents, and William Rosecrans would both inherit and exacerbate this poisonous atmosphere, as we shall see at Chickamauga. The patience of officers in the army's III Corps reached the point that twenty-one of them signed a petition that urged the president to remove Buell from command. Buell's decision to replace Nelson with Charles Gilbert to command the army's III Corps again reflected how little in touch he was with reality. Gilbert had been nominated, but not confirmed, as a brigadier general of volunteers. In fact Congress never did confirm him. Nevertheless, Buell appointed an officer who was in fact a mere captain in the regular army and bestowed on him a major general's commission, none of which was legal. That might not have mattered had Gilbert been competent. He was not.

One of Gilbert's first acts was to order an artillery battery to fire on the mutinous 10th Indiana, which had not been paid and had fixed bayonets and then stuck their rifles in the dirt. Major General "Pap" Thomas intervened to prevent a disaster. As the army moved out of Louisville, Gilbert rode by that regiment in the middle of the night and halted to demand why its colonel had not called the troops to attention. Bruce Catton records the exchange that then followed: Gilbert: "Damn pretty regiment. Why the hell don't you get up and salute me when I pass?" Officer: "Who in the hell are you?" Gilbert: "Major General Gilbert, by God, sir, Give me your sword, sir, you are under arrest." The regiment's colonel then entered the argument to announce that he was not going to "hold a dress parade at midnight for any damn fool living." Gilbert then announced that he was going to take away the regiment's colors, to which the color sergeant announced that he would shoot the general if he attempted to seize the regiment's colors.[2]

Whatever difficulties Buell confronted, it was the pace of his movements that provoked increasing unhappiness in Washington. Halleck constantly transmitted the signs of the administration's displeasure to the Western commander, none of which exercised much influence. Part of the difficulties lay in the fact that the rear area troops seemed congenitally incapable of protecting the bridges, supply dumps, and railroad infrastructure on which Buell's logistical system depended. The Confederate raids were so successful that Lincoln acidly telegraphed Buell: "They are having a stampede in Kentucky. Please look to it."[3] The president had been so annoyed at the pace of Buell's advance that on 8 July he instructed Halleck to wire Buell that "the long time taken by you to reach Chattanooga will enable the enemy to anticipate you by concentrating a large force to meet you."[4] That was precisely what happened.

In early June 1862, shortly after the retreat from Corinth, Bragg assumed command from Beauregard of what became the Army of Tennessee. At once he determined to bring "real" discipline to the army. His approach included the flogging of soldiers, but it also involved a considerable number of executions for various offenses. One soldier recalled, "Almost every day we would hear a discharge of musketry, and knew that some poor, trembling wretch had bid farewell to mortal things here below. It seemed to be but a question of time with all of us as to when we too would be shot. We were afraid to chirp. So far now as patriotism was concerned, we had forgotten all about that, and did not now so much love our country as we feared Bragg."[5] While Bragg led a disciplined army, it was hardly a happy one. Moreover, like his Union counterpart, Bragg presided over and exacerbated a senior leadership cadre prone to feuding and backbiting. While "Pap" Thomas would eventually straighten out the command culture in the Army of the Cumberland, the Army of Tennessee would never recover from the poisonous culture that Bragg had done so much to create.

By mid-July Bragg recognized the scale of Buell's problems with his advance across Tennessee to get to Chattanooga, especially in light of reports of the successes that Forrest and Morgan were having. The Confederate commander then took a major gamble and transferred the bulk of his army from western Tennessee to Chattanooga, from whence he planned to drive north, either against Nashville or into Kentucky. Bragg left Earl Van Dorn and Sterling Price with 32,000 soldiers, to defend northern Mississippi and contest a Union advance against Vicksburg. He took the remainder, some 30,000, to join Edmund Kirby's 18,000, who were defending east Tennessee. Bragg's and Kirby's armies were then to invade Kentucky, which, on the basis of reports from Confederate raiders, Bragg believed was on the verge of revolution against the Federal occupation. In that belief he took 15,000 Enfield rifles along with the invading army to equip the thousands of Kentuckians, whom he anticipated would flock to the Confederate colors.

Bragg's move from northern Mississippi to Chattanooga represented one of the logistical triumphs of the Civil War. The troops began the move on 23 July. The journey took them by rail to Mobile, then north through Alabama, eventually reaching Chattanooga. The Union capture of the rail hub of Corinth as well as the gaps in the Southern rail system turned what should have been a 225-mile journey by rail into a 776-mile journey. Corporal Watkins described the movement: "We took the cars at Tupelo and went to Mobile, from thence across Mobile Bay to Montgomery, Alabama, then to Atlanta, from there to Chattanooga."[6] However, Bragg's artillery and wagon train had to move along the roads of northern Mississippi and Alabama. By mid-August his army had completed its move and was ready to join Kirby Smith in moving across eastern Tennessee to invade Kentucky.

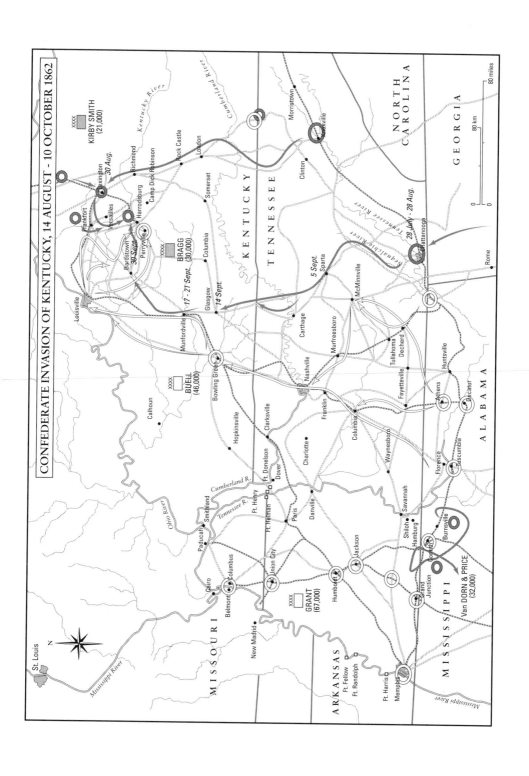

CONFEDERATE INVASION OF KENTUCKY, 14 AUGUST – 10 OCTOBER 1862

Bragg's arrival in Chattanooga made him the ranking Confederate general, but by moving to eastern Tennessee he had taken himself outside his department and area of responsibility. He believed he was not in a position to give orders to Kirby Smith but could only coordinate with him. Smith for his part had every intention of waging an independent command in search of glory. Moreover, while Bragg was supposedly in command of Price and Van Dorn, they were on the other side of the state and following their own agendas. Thus, from the campaign's outset, fault lines existed at the highest levels of the Confederate command in the West. Moreover, no clear goals animated the campaign, because Bragg possessed neither strategic nor operational vision. At best, he appears to have hoped that Van Dorn and Price would move against Nashville, thus fixing Buell, while he and Smith liberated Kentucky.

Bragg and Smith met on 31 July in Chattanooga, and Bragg attached two of his brigades to Smith's Army of Kentucky, which now numbered 21,000. Bragg himself controlled approximately 30,000 men in the follow-up invasion force. Davis provided little guidance to the commanders who would lead the expedition into Kentucky except to warn Bragg that he must not lose his army, which added to Bragg's inherent caution. The plan of the campaign ran along the lines that Smith would either cover Bragg's army or drive Union forces out of the Cumberland Gap, while Bragg took advantage of whatever situation arose to move against Nashville, or Buell, or Kentucky. But such on-the-spot decision making required that Bragg possess the flexibility to adapt to actual circumstances on the ground. He lacked such dexterity.

On 14 August Smith and the Army of Kentucky departed from Chattanooga. Two weeks later Bragg moved out. As the Confederates advanced north from Chattanooga, Buell's response was anything but aggressive. Instead of moving forward to meet the advancing Confederates and thus block their invasion of Kentucky, he fell back on Nashville, which he believed was Bragg's objective. Part of his caution lay in the fact that, like McClellan, Buell consistently exaggerated Confederate superiority in manpower despite the fact that, on Halleck's orders, Grant had sent three divisions to reinforce the Army of the Cumberland. Nor did Buell move with speed, so that on 20 September even Halleck urged him to move faster to intercept Bragg: "I fear that here as elsewhere you move too slowly, and will permit the junction of Bragg and Smith before you open your line to Louisville. The immobility of your army is most surprising. Bragg in the last two months has marched four times the distance you have."[7] Nevertheless, since he was inside of the arc of the Confederate advance, Buell had the option of either covering Nashville or moving north to cover northwestern Kentucky. He was certainly not interested in seeking a fight. Buell made that clear when Bragg began moving northeast. Instead of moving forward Buell retreated to Nashville. One discouraged officer commented that, "the whole army is concentrated here, or near here; but nobody knows anything, except that the water is bad, whiskey scarce, dust abundant, and the air loaded with the scent and melody of a thousand mules."[8]

As they crossed into Kentucky, the Confederates found a less than enthusiastic welcome in the state's hill country. One obviously pro-Union observer noted the Confederates were "ragged, greasy, and dirty and some barefoot, and looked more like the bipeds of pandemonium than beings of this earth. . . . They surrounded our wells like the locusts of Egypt and struggled with each other for the water as if perishing with thirst, and they thronged our kitchen doors and windows, begging for bread like hungry wolves."[9] Buell and Bragg were now following each other on parallel courses as their armies entered Kentucky. At almost the same time that Bragg entered Glasgow, Buell's troops were entering Bowling Green thirty-five miles to the west. In fact, the Confederates were in the lead in the race to reach Louisville, where large numbers of new and largely green Union volunteer regiments had concentrated.

Bragg and his Confederates were still moving faster than their Union opponent. Worried the Confederates were capable of concentrating greater numbers, Buell pulled two divisions away from Nashville's defenses. Bragg, however, was still not interested in fighting his Northern opponent. Instead he moved on Munfordville, where one of his brigades had initially received a bloody nose at the expense of its Union garrison, commanded by Colonel John Wilder of the 17th Indiana. Bragg then moved against the town with a whole division on 15 September 1862. Wilder had as of yet little military experience, and when confronted with the overwhelming strength of Bragg's army, he had charmingly sought out the Confederate general Buckner, who had a reputation for honesty and had recently returned from POW status in the North, for advice as to whether he should surrender. Convinced that the Confederates possessed overwhelming strength, Wilder surrendered with the honors of war. The Confederates captured 4,267 prisoners, ten guns, and 5,000 rifles.

Instead of turning on Buell at this point, Bragg, however, continued north. In line with the thinking of his opponent, Bragg commented: "this campaign must be won by marching, not by fighting."[10] Worried by reports of tens of thousands of Union troops gathering in Louisville, Bragg turned east toward Bardstown instead of continuing on his northern track. By this point Kirby Smith was at Lexington, fifty miles north of Bragg. Bragg allowed Buell to move unimpeded on to Louisville and join his army with the large number of new regiments in the city. Kirby Smith still displayed little interest in uniting his Army of Kentucky with Bragg's Army of Mississippi, which was soon to be renamed the Army of Tennessee. Thus far in their march through Kentucky, both commanders heard a great deal of cheering, but few Kentuckians displayed much inclination to join the Confederate armies.

With Confederate forces spread over much of northern Kentucky, the two Southern commanders engaged in a bit of theater—namely, the inauguration of J. W. Hawes as Confederate governor at Frankfort, Kentucky's capital, which Kirby Smith's troops had occupied. Farce met reality on 4 October as Bragg gave the opening remarks. While he attempted to provide his audience with something resembling oratory, he hid the fact that, should the Confederates gain control of the state, they intended to introduce conscription. Hawes then stepped forward to accept the position. However, no sooner had he finished his oration than couriers arrived with news that Union troops were across the Kentucky River in force and headed toward Frankfort. Bragg then panicked and ordered a retreat before determining the size of the Union force. In fact, Kirby Smith had more than enough troops to defend Frankfort.

For both sides the ensuing Battle of Perryville resulted from tactical miscalculations as well as gross incompetence. Bragg's problem was that once he formed a conception of reality on the strategic or tactical map, he would not or could not change his mind. Thus, his shock at the Union feint toward Frankfort led him to believe Buell was moving against Kirby Smith. He, therefore, determined the Confederates should concentrate their forces on Frankfort. Kirby Smith further reinforced Bragg's misconceptions by reporting major Union deployments between Shelbyville and Taylorsville west of Frankfort. Bragg dismissed reports of major movement of Union troops down the three roads toward Perryville as a feint and left Hardee's and Polk's corps to face overwhelming Union numbers. Buell's feint had set the Confederates up for the Union commander to launch a devastating blow with virtually the whole Union army against Bragg's southern wing.

On the other side, Buell had convinced himself not only that the Confederates outnumbered him, but also that the green regiments that made up a large percentage of his force were incapable of putting up a reasonable fight. However, he still faced intense pressure to act from Washington and from Indiana and Ohio politicians, whose states the Confederate drive seemed to threaten. The Indiana politicians and newspapers were outraged by what they felt had been Buell's negligence in allowing Bragg to gobble up the garrison at Munfordville. Thus, Buell moved out of Louisville, but much like McClellan in his advance from Frederick to Antietam, Buell moved with great caution. He added to his difficulties by managing his cavalry as badly as McClellan was managing his in the East, so that he had no clear conception of Confederate dispositions. Bragg intended to concentrate at Versailles, Kentucky, and strike at what he believed was the main Union drive out of Louisville that had so startled him at Frankfort. In fact, three Union corps were approaching Perryville on three different roads: Alexander McCook's I Corps from the northwest, Gilbert's III Corps from the west, and Crittenden's II Corps from the northwest. Buell was bringing approximately 55,000 troops to Perryville, while Bragg had less than a third of his army, Polk in overall command with Hardee up front.

At dawn on 8 October, the fighting began when Brigadier General Philip Sheridan moved forward in the first gray light to drive the Confederates off Doctor's Creek, one of the few water sources in the area. Sheridan had spent the first year of the war as a quartermaster captain before finally escaping the clutches of the regular army in early 1862. Achieving command of a Michigan volunteer regiment and the rank of colonel on 27 May 1862, he had risen spectacularly. Four months later, he was a brigadier general in command of a division. Sheridan's attack was completely successful, but Gilbert immediately sought to rein in his subordinate's aggressiveness, because Buell had ordered the corps commanders not to bring on a general engagement. Sheridan, nevertheless, repelled a Confederate attack and seized the northern portion of the heights overlooking Doctor's Creek. After bringing up his other two divisions to align them south of Sheridan's position, Gilbert rode off to lunch with Buell.

While Buell and Gilbert comfortably settled down to eat, they missed the sound of a major battle exploding to their north. A rare occasion, an acoustical shadow, shielded them from the roar of the fight. On the night before, Bragg, still in ignorance that Buell was gathering his whole army in front of Perryville, had ordered Polk to destroy the Federals to his front and then move north to join up with the concentration around Versailles. That morning Bragg arrived to approve Polk's concentration of Benjamin Cheatham's and Simon Buckner's divisions under the cover of the woods lying to the front of McCook's I Corps. On the other side, McCook had ordered Brigadier General William Terrill, another Virginian who had remained loyal to the Union, to advance to the Chaplin River. His troops never reached the river as two Confederate divisions attacked. Union artillery slaughtered the first wave. But a flow of more Confederates into the battle drove the Union troops back. By evening they were three-quarters of a mile from their initial position. Only a stand by John Starkweather's brigade prevented McCook's left from collapsing.

On the left of the Confederate attack against the I Corps, Hardee had the greatest success. His soldiers battered McCook's troops back, but never quite succeeded in breaking them. Union artillery again took a heavy toll on the attackers and eventually broke the momentum of Hardee's attack. For a period, the fighting was heavy. Private Sam Watkins remembered that "I was in every battle, skirmish and march that was made by the First Tennessee Regiment during the war, and I do not remember of a harder contest and more evenly fought battle than that of Perryville. If it had been two men wrestling, it would have been called a 'dog fall.' Both sides claim the victory—both whipped."[11] Meanwhile, the other two Union corps did nothing. One could excuse Crittenden, because the acoustic shadow prevented him from hearing the fighting several miles away. However, Gilbert's corps in the center failed to move, although Sheridan used his artillery to enfilade Hardee's attack on McCook's right. The brigade on Sheridan's left happened to be commanded by McCook's younger brother, who recalled after the battle that his regiments had been in a position to attack the Confederates on the flank and roll them up. What were Gilbert and Buell doing while the battle raged? They were eating lunch, although they could hear some of the noise of cannon fire in the distance. Buell's contribution to the day's fighting was to send a message to Sheridan to "stop that useless waste of powder."[12]

By late afternoon 8 October the Confederate attack had burned itself out. It had badly battered, but not broken, Buell's left wing, while Sheridan's line had easily repulsed a halfhearted attack by a single brigade. But it sufficed to prevent Gilbert from sending aid to the hard-pressed McCook. Reinforcements finally reached McCook at 1730. By then the fighting was nearly over, although the other corps were in a position to grab Perryville and make a Confederate escape difficult. But Buell failed to grasp either how heavily the Confederates had attacked McCook or the opportunity that Bragg had offered him. When the Union commander finally realized that a serious fight had taken place, he decided to wait until the following morning to attack. By then, the Confederates were gone. At day's end, Bragg, Polk, and Hardee had time to realize from captured soldiers Union strength. To their shock, they realized that Buell's whole army lay to their front and they faced overwhelming odds. On the following morning Buell's scouts discovered the Confederates had abandoned the battlefield.

The Battle of Perryville settled nothing and everything. For those engaged in the fighting, casualty figures were heavy: Union losses 894 killed, 2,911 wounded, 471 captured or missing, for a total of 4,276. Confederate casualties were 532 killed, 2,641 wounded, 228 captured or missing, for a total of 3,401. Bragg pulled back and determined not to fight. Buell proved no more willing to resume the fight elsewhere in northern Kentucky, but at least he was close to his logistical bases. On the other hand, the Confederates had only the most tenuous of supply lines, while the drought had robbed northern Kentucky of much of the foodstuffs it normally produced. Thus, the Confederate thrust into Kentucky foundered on a logistical system incapable of supporting Bragg's advance over the substantial distances involved.

To Bragg's disgust, hardly any Kentuckians rallied to the Confederacy. He ordered a retreat back to Tennessee, during which Buell made only the most grudging pursuit. In Washington, Lincoln had watched Buell's incompetent efforts to prevent Bragg's advance into Kentucky and then his failure to fight—the Confederates had entirely initiated the Battle of Perryville. Certainly, the campaign, however inconclusive, proved that the North was not in a desperate situation. Lincoln replaced Buell on 24 October, just as he would later replace McClellan, two commanders who had consistently displayed a marked unwillingness to, using Lord Nelson's famous formulation, "engage the enemy more closely." As Buell's replacement, the president chose Major General William Rosecrans, who, along with Grant, had been fighting in western and central Tennessee.

The Confederate Counterattack: Price and Van Dorn

When Halleck took up his new assignment in Washington, he left Grant in charge of western Tennessee and the Mississippi River. He instructed Grant to remain on the defensive and keep the Confederates out of western Tennessee. With the breakup of the Western army after Corinth, Halleck had regarded the troops under Grant's command as a reserve to support other areas. Thus, when Kirby Smith and Bragg moved north from Chattanooga, Grant supplied the reserves that bolstered Buell's forces. The outcome of the summer's campaign underlined that, given Union strength at the beginning of the year, there was only sufficient force in the West for one major effort and that effort had fallen to Buell, since Halleck was suspicious of Grant's aggressiveness.

Meanwhile, neither Price nor Van Dorn on the Confederate side had displayed much disposition to cooperate. Admittedly Bragg was in overall command of both, but once he had departed for Chattanooga, he was far away. At least he had left instructions that the two Confederate generals were to press forward together toward Nashville to keep Buell's attention on central Tennessee. With Bragg out of sight, Van Dorn floated the idea of pressing forward in western Tennessee and grabbing Paducah. This, however, was only to be the first step in a megalomaniacal conception that his army, supported by Price, could drive on to St. Louis smashing Union armies as it moved forward. Van Dorn had no clear conception of what was possible and certainly not what he might do to help Bragg. He did persuade Davis to give him formal command over Price's army as well as his own. There was, of course, the problem of Grant, who soon wrecked Confederate hopes to achieve something in western Tennessee.

Furthermore, Price had ideas of his own. Without clear directions from Bragg, he struck at Iuka, where he chased the small Union garrison away and appropriated its supplies. He then received word that he was under Van Dorn's command as well as orders that he was to join in a drive against western Tennessee, which directly contradicted his instructions from Bragg. Instead of obeying Van Dorn, Price dawdled and almost found himself trapped. Grant immediately recognized that situation could destroy Price before Van Dorn could intervene. In his memoirs Grant noted: "It looked to me that, if Price would remain in Iuka until we could get there, his annihilation was inevitable."[13] With Major General Edward Ord advancing from the northwest from Corinth with two divisions totaling 9,000 men and Rosecrans advancing from the south with another 8,000 Grant's forces had an advantage of 2,000 soldiers, but more importantly he also possessed surprise.

Rosecrans was to open the Union attack from the south, while Ord waited for the sound of cannons before attacking. On 17 September Grant sprang the trap. But Rosecrans, as typical of his career, was late. On the 19th he finally attacked. But an acoustic shadow screened Ord from the noise of the fighting. He and his officers did note clouds of smoke coming from south of the town but assumed Price was burning the stores in Iuka. In fact, it was the cannon and musket fire of the fight on the southern outskirts of the town that was causing the smoke. Rosecrans lost 790 men, while the Confederates only 535. That night Price, recognizing the precariousness of his position, escaped on a road Rosecrans had neglected to cover, but it had been a narrow escape, while the slowness of Rosecrans's pursuit aided the Confederates.

Van Dorn finally forced Price to unite with his force near Ripley, Mississippi; Van Dorn moving from Holly Springs in the west, while Price moved from Iuka in the east. By 1 October the combined armies had reached Pocahontas on the Memphis & Charleston Railroad. They turned south to move against Corinth. However, Rosecrans had not only picked up Van Dorn's move but also believed the Confederates were moving against Stephen Hurlbut's division at Bolivar northeast of Corinth. Ironically, he concentrated his forces around Corinth in preparation to go to Hurlbut's relief. As a result, Van Dorn's Confederates ran into a fully prepared Union army that also happened to outnumber them. Alerted by his scouts that the Confederates were approaching, Rosecrans deployed his three divisions on the outer set of entrenchments dug by Beauregard's defenders the previous May against Halleck's drive.

The Battle of Corinth lasted two days. On the first, Union troops had lost the outer entrenchments at midday, but in a fighting retreat they fell back to an inner line of fortifications and steadily exhausted the attackers. On the second day Van Dorn launched a direct attack on the inner lines of entrenchments, which were bristling with guns. After an opening gun duel, the all or nothing Confederate attack began. In the center the Confederates broke into the Union lines and reached the town, but they soon were driven out. Everywhere else Union cannon and infantry fire forced the Confederates to ground. A few brave souls, some driven mad by the 90-degree heat and lack of water, renewed the attack, only to find themselves either dead, wounded, or persuaded to bury themselves again in the Mississippi clay.

As the Confederates retreated after their crushing defeat, Rosecrans, much to Grant's disgust, failed to pursue. Altogether, Van Dorn's effort to replicate the Battle of Balaclava with infantry against cannon had resulted in a disastrous slaughter. The Confederates lost 4,233 men compared to 2,520 Union casualties. The outcome of Van Dorn's brief campaign to drive the Union out of western Tennessee led one Confederate senator to complain: "He [Van Dorn] is regarded as the source of all our woes and disaster, it is prophesied, will attend us so long as he is connected with this army. The atmosphere is dense with horrid narratives of his negligence, whoring, and drunkenness, for the truth of which I cannot vouch; but it is so fastened in the public belief that an acquittal by a court-martial of angels would not relieve him of the charge."[14]

On 14 October, Major General John Pemberton arrived in Jackson to take command of the new Department of Mississippi, a department that included all of that state and the eastern portion of Louisiana lying on the left bank of the Mississippi. Davis had handpicked this former West Pointer and Pennsylvanian largely on the basis that he was a Northerner. The Confederate president believed Pemberton's presence in the Confederate high command would suggest that secession was not just a Southern affair. Nevertheless, Pemberton had yet to participate in major field operations. The other fallout from Iuka and Corinth was that Rosecrans, on the brink of being fired by Grant, found himself appointed to replace Buell.

Antietam

On 2 September 1862, Lincoln confirmed to his unhappy cabinet that he had asked McClellan to assume command over Pope's badly beaten Army of Virginia as well as continuing in command of the Army of the Potomac. As he commented, "we must use what tools we have."[15] Late that afternoon, McClellan rode out of Washington to meet the beaten Pope and McDowell, both who now deservedly headed off to assignments that bore little responsibility. Pope assumed command of troops on the Minnesota frontier to crush an uprising by the Sioux. McClellan would follow him into exile from the army within a matter of months, but for the moment he regarded himself as divinely commissioned to save the Republic. He set about displaying his greatest military talent—to bring order out of the chaos of a defeated army.

Meanwhile, Lee and Jackson were already plotting an invasion of northern Maryland and Pennsylvania, an invasion that at least in Lee's mind would reach as far as Harrisburg. But he also made clear to Jefferson Davis a larger aim. Besides bringing the war home to the North, he was seeking a decisive victory over the Army of the Potomac before the fall elections in the North. If such a victory proved insufficient to force the North to make peace, then surely it would push the Europeans off the fence to come to the Confederacy's aid. Writing in Maryland nine days before Antietam, Lee boldly suggested that Davis offer peace: "Being made when it is in our power to inflict injury upon our adversary, would show conclusively to the world that our sole object is the establishment of our independence and the attainment of an honorable peace. . . . The proposal of peace would enable the people of the United States to determine at their coming elections whether they will support those who favor a prolongation of the war, or those who wish to bring it to a termination, which can but be productive of good to both parties without affecting the honor of either."[16]

While Second Bull Run had been a Confederate success in humiliating the Army of Virginia, it had been a costly affair. Confederate casualties in percentage terms had been almost as high as those of their opponents with approximately 1,553 dead and 7,812 wounded. Thus, an invasion of the North with an exhausted army involved major risks. Among a number of issues was the fact that the corps McClellan had taken to the Peninsula remained relatively fresh with the exception of Porter's V Corps. Yet, Lee could not resist the temptation of overestimating the capabilities of his subordinates and soldiers. He also knew McClellan well and believed his opponent would move with glacial slowness and the Army of Northern Virginia could take substantial risks. As to McClellan's generalship in the upcoming campaign, the Union general was to miss extraordinary opportunities. For now,

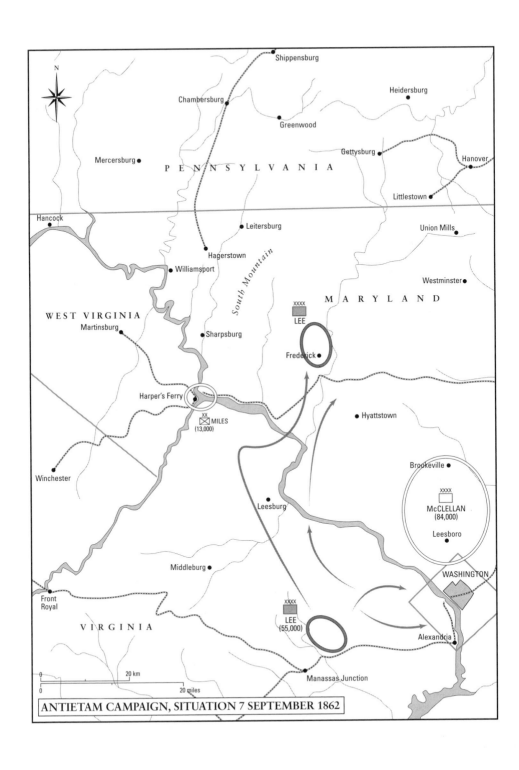

N

Shippensburg

Heidersburg

Chambersburg

Greenwood

Mercersburg

P E N N S Y L V A N I A

Gettysburg

Hanover

Littlestown

Hancock

Leitersburg

Union Mills

Hagerstown

Williamsport

South Mountain

M A R Y L A N D

Westminster

WEST VIRGINIA

Martinsburg

Sharpsburg

XXXX
LEE

Frederick

Harper's Ferry

XX
MILES
(13,000)

Hyattstown

Brookeville

Winchester

XXXX
McCLELLAN
(84,000)

Leesburg

Leesboro

Middleburg

WASHINGTON

Front
Royal

XXXX
LEE
(55,000)

V I R G I N I A

Alexandria

0   20 km
0   20 miles

Manassas Junction

ANTIETAM CAMPAIGN, SITUATION 7 SEPTEMBER 1862

he resumed his tiresome game of overestimating Lee's numbers. Lee not only divided his army but also placed half of it in Virginia and half in Maryland with the Potomac separating them.

The first troops of the Army of Northern Virginia crossed into Maryland on 4 September. Their first stop was Frederick, Maryland. The area surrounding the town was rich farmland, which, unlike northern Virginia, marauding armies had yet to plunder. The soldiers had a field day, but Lee, Jackson, and Longstreet had other matters on their mind. Lee divided his army into four separate commands. Jackson commanded twenty-six of the army's forty infantry brigades and was to strike at Harper's Ferry and its garrison of 10,500. Meanwhile, Longstreet would take much of the remainder north to Hagerstown to gobble up the foodstuffs in the region. Finally, Stuart would deploy his cavalry, supported by D. H. Hill's infantry division, to cover South Mountain, the extension of the Blue Ridge that runs first into northern Maryland and then flows into Pennsylvania between Chambersburg and Gettysburg.

As had been the case in the Valley campaign, the Confederates, abandoning Frederick, would shelter behind a mountain range. The Army of the Potomac's slowness seemed to guarantee the time required to reunite scattered Confederate units, if necessary. Lee and Jackson, both great risk takers, were responsible for the plan, while Longstreet found himself informed later. On 9 September, Lee signed Special Order 191, specifying the roles his commanders were to play in upcoming operations. Jackson would recross the Potomac and swing through the Shenandoah Valley before sweeping down on Harper's Ferry from the northwest. Meanwhile, Lafayette McLaws's division would seize Maryland Heights, the southernmost extension of Elk Ridge on the Maryland side of the Potomac, which looked down on the junction of the Shenandoah and Potomac Rivers. Finally, Brigadier General John Walker's division would seize Loudoun Heights, which lay on the right side of the Shenandoah and which also looked down on the two rivers and town. The plan involved a complex movement of pieces that only the Army of Northern Virginia could have accomplished at this point in the war.

McClellan had suggested the removal of the Martinsburg and Harper's Ferry garrisons, but Halleck, always eager to defend places and positions on the map, demurred. As a skilled bureaucrat, he had then left the decision as to whether to withdraw the garrison to the departmental commander, who grasped little of the operational situation. The garrisons remained in place. While Harper's Ferry possessed an impressive number of defenders, only two regiments had had combat experience. In command was Colonel Dixon Miles, who was not only inept, but also had nearly been cashiered for being drunk at the First Bull Run. Harper's Ferry, lying as it did in a valley, was obviously indefensible, if the Confederates seized the heights and deployed guns along the ridge lines. Nevertheless, Miles had done nothing to defend the heights, or for that matter the town's defenses. At the last moment he assigned four regiments to defend Maryland Heights, only one of which had combat experience, and one of which, the 126th New York, had been in Federal service for three weeks.

On 13 September, the Confederates snapped the trap shut. Two of McLaws's brigades attacked the inexperienced soldiers on the heights. Miles refused to send reinforcements, and the Confederates easily captured that crucial position. They then faced the difficult task of dragging their guns up the mountain to bombard the garrison and town below. Across the Potomac, Walker's soldiers clambered up Loudoun Heights and to their astonishment found no Union troops defending that key piece of terrain. Meanwhile, Jackson arrived from the northwest and blocked the garrison's escape route. That night Miles sent a message that the Confederates had surrounded Harper's Ferry and that he could hold out for only forty-eight hours. Had he done so, he would have rendered McClellan an enormous service. But he failed to do even that.

As dawn broke on the 14th, other issues were breaking that threatened the Confederates on the Maryland side of the Potomac. As a result, Jackson received orders from Lee to finish with Harper's Ferry as quickly as possible. As the Confederates positioned guns on Maryland Heights and Loudoun Heights, which took most of the day, Jackson's artillery began a desultory bombardment. That night the commander of Union cavalry at Harper's Ferry, Colonel Benjamin "Grimes" Davis, a Mississippian who had remained loyal to his oath, engaged in a furious row with Miles over Grimes's plan to escape with his 1,300 cavalrymen. Grimes finally announced he would go whether or not Miles authorized the breakout, and Miles relented. That night Grimes, leading the way and using his Southern drawl to calm Confederate pickets, extracted his cavalry. On the way north to Williamsport, his troopers captured Longstreet's reserve ordnance wagons. Arriving back in Union lines, Grimes reported Miles would surrender the garrison that day.

That is precisely what happened. With the Confederate artillery positioned on the two heights, the Confederates opened up with a thunderous bombardment early on the morning of the 15th. At 0800, as Jackson's infantry massed, the artillery opened up. Miles promptly surrendered, only to be mortally wounded by one of the last shells fired. Union casualties, including those on Maryland Heights on the 13th, barely reached 200 killed or wounded, but the Confederates captured 11,000 prisoners, 13,000 rifled muskets, which reequipped a number of Jackson's regiments still using smoothbore muskets, 200 wagons, and 73 artillery pieces with their caissons, along with assorted other booty. Jackson's soldiers had to spend much of the 15th paroling their prisoners and distributing the plunder. Their commander could only begin speeding his first units on the road to reunite with Lee on the next morning.

As the Confederates began their invasion of Maryland, the Army of the Potomac had moved north. Given his consistent overestimation of Confederate numbers, McClellan advanced with excruciating slowness. However, for one of the few times in the war, fortune shone on the Army of the Potomac. On the morning of Saturday, 13 September, Sergeant John Bloss and Corporal Barton Mitchell of the 27th Indiana, XII Corps, discovered a parcel of three cigars. Delighted with their find, they casually glanced at the paper wrapping. The title read simply "Headquarters, Army of Northern Virginia, Special Orders, No. 191."[17] Despite their lowly rank, the two soldiers immediately recognized the paper's importance.

The find quickly found its way to XII Corps headquarters, where Major General Alpheus Williams's aide recognized the handwriting of Lee's chief of staff, with whom he had served in the Old Army. By the morning of the 13th, Special Orders No. 191 was in McClellan's hands. About the only thing the order failed to spell out was the size of the rebel army, an issue that was to cloud McClellan's actions over the coming days. His estimate remained that the Army of Northern Virginia possessed approximately 120,000 men. In fact, Lee's army numbered 55,000, which soon shrank because of straggling, as Jackson marched his men past exhaustion. Incredibly, even possessing such valuable intelligence, McClellan took eighteen hours before the first of his corps began their march north from Frederick toward

South Mountain. From that moment on, the words Churchill used to describe the escape of the German battle cruiser *Goeben* in the early days of the First World War, "the terrible ifs accumulate," echo again and again.[18] The nearest Union corps, near Frederick, received orders to move only early on the morning of 14 September. Its task was to cross South Mountain. Here Union forces would run into the holding force Lee had left behind in the unlikely happenstance McClellan moved quickly. However, within a day of the discovery of Special Orders 191, Lee had received warning from a sympathizer in Frederick that McClellan had good intelligence as to the Confederate dispositions.

What took place over the next forty-eight hours was a race between the tortoise and hare, with the tortoise having all the advantages, but the hare winning. There were two major passes through South Mountain: Turner's Gap and Crampton's Gap. The latter was close to the Potomac and offered the opportunity of relieving Harper's Ferry, if Union troops moved quickly, which, of course they did not. Turner's Gap ran through South Mountain and opened the way to Boonsboro and the plain beyond. McClellan ordered Franklin's VI Corps with its 19,500 soldiers to break through Crampton's Gap and, if possible, trap McLaws's divisions, which Lee's orders had indicated would be on Maryland Heights. Meanwhile, the remainder of the army under McClellan would attack Turner's Gap with 70,000 men. Astonishingly, the Union troops made no attempt at concealment, so that D. H. Hill at the top of the Turner's Gap could see the IX Corps' campfires below. That alerted him that trouble was brewing.

The movement of Franklin's VI Corps toward Crampton's Gap caused McLaws's difficulties, because it threatened his position before completion of the Harper's Ferry operation. Consequently, he had to move a portion of his two divisions to cover the gap, which a far more numerous Union force threatened. On the morning of the 14th, Franklin moved with two of his VI Corps divisions. His lead division arrived at Burkittsville at the bottom of Crampton's Gap at noon, but a third division under Major General Darius Couch, which McClellan had attached to the VI Corps, failed to show until late that evening. It should not have mattered, because Franklin with 12,000 soldiers had more than sufficient force to break through the gap. However, instead of pushing forward, he sat down, fed his troops, and attempted to decide what to do. There were only four Confederate regiments defending the gap, fewer than 1,000 soldiers altogether. Thus, Franklin had more than a twelve to one advantage. Three hours later, he reported to McClellan that his corps was heavily engaged against unknown numbers of Confederates. Eventually, the men of Major General Henry Slocum's division got tired of waiting, and at 1600, displaying unusual initiative, they charged, overwhelmed the Confederates, smashing two more arriving Confederate regiments in the process, and took the gap. With the valley below open to exploitation, Franklin again halted and waited for Couch to arrive.

The operation to take Turner's Gap and Fox Gap, both close together, was almost a carbon copy of what had happened at Crampton's Gap, except that in this case there were more Confederates. Throughout the day McClellan remained in Frederick attending to paperwork and writing to his wife. He did nothing to speed the advance. Initially, D. H. Hill defended the gap with only two of his division's five brigades and a smattering of cavalry. But if he were not ready to defend the gap, Union troops proved less ready to attack, despite the fact that they had marched hardly any distance the day before. Major General Jesse Reno's IX Corps was near the gap, but McClellan, almost as if he were trying to slow movement to a crawl, ordered Hooker's I Corps to fall in behind Reno, and the I Corps was the farthest away of all of the corps. (Hooker had replaced McDowell as I Corps' commander.) McClellan did not expect a fight, despite the fact that a paroled Union officer warned that Hill was deploying in strength.

Major General Jacob Cox's division was at the front with George Crook's brigade of Ohioans leading the way. Ohio was the only state to send large numbers of regiments to both the Eastern and Western theaters of operations. Thus on this field, there were two future presidents of the United States in Crook's brigade, Rutherford B. Hayes, commander of the 23rd Ohio, and William McKinley, at the time a mere sergeant, but by war's end a major. However, Cox's division received little support from the other divisions in IX Corps. As in so many of the Army of the Potomac's operations, senior officers were in no hurry. Major General Orlando Wilcox's division, the second division in Reno's corps, failed to move from its encampment until nearly 1100 and did not arrive to support Cox until 1400. By then Hill had summoned his other three brigades. Two of Longstreet's brigades had also arrived to add to those on South Mountain. Late in the afternoon, Hooker's I Corps arrived, as well as McClellan. As the I Corps deployed, a soldier of the 9th New York, at the tail end of Reno's corps, noted that the march of Hooker's troops resembled "a monstrous, crawling, blue-black snake, miles long, quilled with the silver slant of muskets at a 'shoulder,' its sluggish tail writhing slowly up over the distant eastern ridge, its bruised head weltering in the roar and smoke upon the crest above."[19]

Only late in the afternoon of the 14th did the Army of the Potomac finally launch a major attack to take the gaps with two full corps against a single reinforced Confederate division. Admittedly, the Confederates held the high ground, but slowly and steadily Union numbers told. At the end of the day, Burnside, whom McClellan had appointed to lead one of the army's wings, consisting of the I and IX Corps, sent John Gibbon's "iron brigade" of slouch-hatted midwesterners straight up the road leading through Turner's Gap. The Confederates brought them to a halt as darkness settled over the battlefield.

The Confederates had held, but barely. That night Lee, Longstreet, and Hill decided they lacked sufficient troops to hold the gaps, and therefore Lee ordered a retreat. On the face of it, they had suffered a defeat, both in terms of their casualties and in losing the gaps, which would allow McClellan to deploy the Army of the Potomac on the plain below South Mountain. The casualties on South Mountain had been heavy on both sides, the Confederates losing 2,300 soldiers killed, wounded, or captured; the Union 1,800. The Union attackers did suffer one serious casualty, when Reno, IX Corps commander and one of the more competent corps commanders in the Army of the Potomac (and one who had not been part of the army McClellan had organized in 1861), went down with a mortal wound.

But Lee had gained another day to unite his army. On which side of the Potomac, however, remained uncertain, because he considered pulling back to northern Virginia. Late in the evening of the 14th, he informed Hill and Longstreet of his intention to pull back across the ford at Sharpsburg to northern Virginia, while a dispatch went to McLaws to fall back across the Potomac. In retrospect, that was clearly the right decision. Yet, the next day Lee changed his mind and decided to stand at Sharpsburg. Here indeed was the man named "audacity." Lee was taking an enormous gamble in deploying portions of his army east of the Potomac in the belief McClellan would fail to attack until Jackson had rounded up the Harper's Ferry's booty. He also counted on Jackson being able to drive his troops to Sharpsburg in time to meet a potential Union attack. The gamble came within hours of destroying the Army of Northern Virginia.

As McClellan deployed his troops over South Mountain and onto the plains below, he received intelligence as to the weakness of Confederate forces. The defense of South Mountain suggested that Lee had at most 25,000 troops. Moreover, both Hooker and McClellan's young aide, Custer, reported the Confederates had barely 15,000 deployed around Sharpsburg. But McClellan moved cautiously. On the 15th, Franklin and his VI Corps moved not at all, in spite of the fact that he outnumbered McLaws at the foot of Crampton's Gap by nearly four to one. Franklin refused to attack and reported to McClellan that the Confederates outnumbered him by at least two to one.

Throughout the 15th the Army of the Potomac crept into position along the east bank of the Antietam creek. It took the army most of the day to move the eight miles from Turner's Gap to the creek's east bank. Across the way, its soldiers could see Confederate artillery deployed, but encountered no action. Nevertheless, McClellan refused to attack until he had fully deployed his army. It was an engineering mentality; yet, it was also more. It reflected a general afraid to make a decision or to take a risk. Sixteen September was a repeat of the 15th. Confronting approximately 15,000 Confederates with 60,000 soldiers, McClellan watched and evaluated, and calculated, and ruminated, and rode around the periphery of the future battlefield, and did nothing. As Porter Alexander acidly commented: "not only did McClellan bring upon the field his 87,176, well equipped men, against Lee's 35,255 ragged and poorly equipped; but he brought *himself* also."[20] And all the while, Jackson was disengaging his soldiers from Harper's Ferry and sending them, after filling their knapsacks, trundling as fast as most could tolerate up the road to Sharpsburg.

How to explain McClellan's behavior? In probing this strange general's mind, the historian finds himself led to the conclusion the general lacked the moral courage to launch his troops against the Army of Northern Virginia. But if moral cowardice resulted in a failure to attack on the 16th, what then led him to launch the great attacks of the next day? Probably, McClellan finally realized that not to attack Lee would permanently brand him among the commanders, officers, and soldiers of the Army of the Potomac, not to mention outside observers, as an out and out coward. The disparity in numbers suggests it all. During the 16th Lee had barely 15,000 on the field at Antietam. Over the night of 16/17 September, McClellan issued no order to his subordinates as to his intentions, nor did he call a conference of corps and divisions to discuss their role in the battle. This lack of guidance suggests that only at the last moment did he realize Lee was going to remain on the hills above Sharpsburg and that to save his own reputation the Army of the Potomac had to attack. Meanwhile, his commanders, in the best traditions of that army, did little to acquaint themselves with the terrain over which their men would fight. The IX Corps, confronting a strong Confederate position across Antietam Creek, failed to locate a usable ford farther down the creek which the Confederates had not guarded and which would have allowed Union troops to outflank enemy positions immediately.

The opposing sides deployed in the following fashion. On the Confederate side, Jackson held the Confederate left, which ran from Stuart's positioning of his artillery near the Potomac, east through the West Woods, along what is now known as "the Cornfield," and then southeast down a steep incline to the Mumma Farm. In the center and south, Longstreet's corps deployed along the Sunken Road and then on the top of the rise to the east and south of Sharpsburg. Poorly disguised Union movements on the evening of the 16th provided Lee a clear idea of where the first Union attacks were going to come—namely, against Jackson. That evening Hooker moved his I Corps across the Antietam Creek to a position north of the Miller house and "the Cornfield." Over a mile to the northeast, Major General Joseph Mansfield, assuming command of the XII Corps the day before, deployed his troops well back from the East Woods and the Cornfield behind the I Corps. The reader, of course, will not find it surprising to learn that Hooker and Mansfield made no effort to coordinate their plans.

Directly to the east of the Confederate positions, but behind Antietam Creek, McClellan deployed the main part of his strength, Porter's V Corps and Sumner's II Corps. Alfred Pleasonton's cavalry division of 4,500 remained near the Union headquarters. McClellan saved his cavalry for a charge, perhaps to emulate the great Napoleon at Eylau, if he were to be confronted with defeat. Finally, well to the south, Burnside's IX Corps positioned itself near the Rohrbach Bridge, today called Burnside Bridge. Additional Union troops were in the neighborhood. Franklin's Corps of 19,000 remained at South Mountain, less than seven miles away, and only began arriving with two of its divisions on the morning of the 17th, while one of Porter's

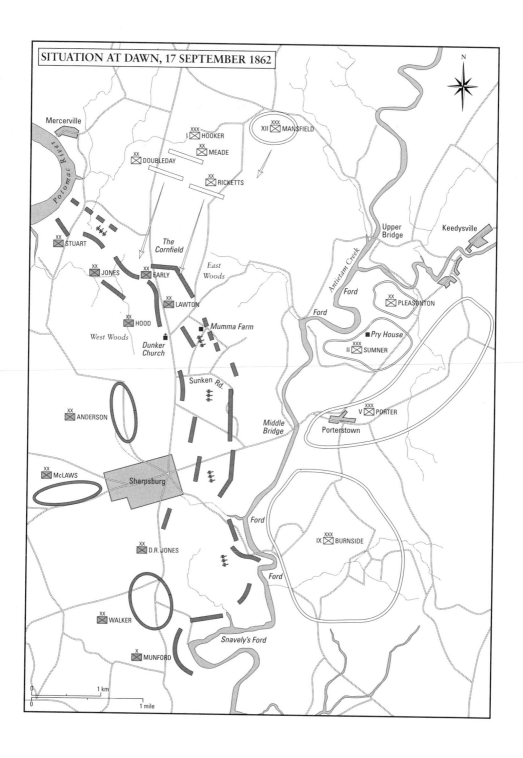

SITUATION AT DAWN, 17 SEPTEMBER 1862

Mercerville

Potomac River

XXX I HOOKER
XX MEADE
XX DOUBLEDAY
XX RICKETTS

XXX XII MANSFIELD

Upper Bridge

Keedysville

XX STUART

The Cornfield

East Woods

Antietam Creek

Ford

XX JONES
XX EARLY
XX LAWTON
XX HOOD

Ford

XXX PLEASONTON

West Woods

Mumma Farm

Dunker Church

Pry House

II SUMNER XXX

Sunken Rd.

XX ANDERSON

Middle Bridge

V PORTER XXX

Porterstown

XX McLAWS

Sharpsburg

Ford

XX D.R. JONES

XXX IX BURNSIDE

Ford

XX WALKER

Snavely's Ford

X MUNFORD

0   1 km
0   1 mile

divisions remained back at Frederick. McClellan placed himself at the Pry House on a hill up from Antietam Creek, where for virtually the whole battle he remained, well removed from the fighting and where he exercised little or no control over the army's movements, except to interfere when opportunities arose.

And so McClellan launched the Army of the Potomac early on 17 September against the Confederates, who were slowly but steadily gaining in strength, as Jackson's weary regiments trickled in from Harper's Ferry. As dawn was breaking in the eastern sky, the worst day in American military history began. Hooker with the I Corps attacked directly south. He had earned the sobriquet of "Fighting Joe" because a newspaper editor had left the comma out of a headline that was to read: "Fighting, Joe Hooker . . ." But certainly in comparison to the Army of the Potomac's other corps and division commanders, it was a deserved title. As the I Corps advanced past the Poffenberger farm on the Hagerstown Turnpike, its soldiers ran into galling fire from Nicodemus Hill to the west where Jeb Stuart had placed guns. Union commanders never bothered to take out that Confederate position during the remainder of the day, an important oversight. As the soldiers moved through the Cornfield, Hooker's soldiers took fire from Confederates along a fence running east and west between the East Woods and the West Woods. As an indication of how raw both sides remained, the Confederates had failed to build any kind of breastworks to cover themselves. They gave Hooker's troops emerging from the Cornfield a devastating volley, but one their opponents replied to in full measure. Then both sides stood out in the open and slaughtered each other, first by the hundreds and then by the thousands.

Hooker's attack quickly became chaotic, and a Confederate counterattack drove the lead units of the I Corps back to the Cornfield, which was fast becoming a jumble of stalks, covered by the dead and moaning wounded. Losses were horrendous; when the 12th Massachusetts pulled back, it had lost 224 of the 334 men with which it had begun the day two hours earlier. On Hooker's left, Abner Doubleday's division ran into a Confederate counterattack, launched out of the West Woods. Both sides blazed away at each other at thirty yards. For a moment, Lee's left flank appeared on the brink of collapsing. At that point, John Bell Hood threw his division of 2,300 men onto the scale with an attack that brought the Union attack to a halt and then drove the Union troops back through the Cornfield. There Hood's Texans ran into the reformed soldiers of Hooker's I Corps. Receiving double rounds of canister fire, they too reeled back after taking heavy losses. The 1ˢᵗ Texas lost four out of five men in a fight that had lasted only twenty minutes. When an officer queried Hood shortly after his attack as to his division's condition, his reply was simple and eloquent: "Dead on the field."[21]

Believing himself in serious trouble, Hooker asked Mansfield for help. Reflecting his lack of experience, Mansfield had done little that morning to prepare his troops to move toward the sound of fighting, although his recent appointment to corps command causes us to judge him less harshly. He now moved south to bolster the badly battered I Corps. The XII Corps, formerly the II Corps of Pope's Army of Virginia, added 7,200 infantrymen, half veterans, to the attack on the Confederate left. Nevertheless, the fighting in the East Woods was thoroughly confused. At one point Mansfield attempted to stop the 10ᵗʰ Maine from firing at the Confederates on their front because he believed they were firing at their own troops. He had hardly absorbed the reality that they were the enemy before both he and his horse went down. Mortally wounded, he died on the 18th after two days in command. Nevertheless, the arrival of substantial numbers of Union troops sufficed to halt the Confederates and drive them back.

Alpheus Williams replaced Mansfield, and he and Hooker confronted demands from front-line units, which were under intense pressure. Both sides were feeding in reinforcements at a rate sufficient to keep the killing and wounding going without being able to achieve a tactical advantage. Moving out of the East Woods, Brigadier General George Greene's Division in the XII Corps caught Samuel Garland's brigade of North Carolinians on the flank and sent the Confederates in a desperate rush to the rear. Greene, in temporary command of the division, was one of the oldest generals in the army. Born in 1801, he had graduated from West Point in 1823 and left the army in 1836 to embark on a highly successful career as a civil engineer. We will meet him again at Gettysburg. Colonel Hector Tyndale commanded Greene's lead brigade with one Pennsylvania regiment that had never been in combat and three smaller veteran Ohio regiments. Yet, the Pennsylvanians fought as well as the Ohioans. Greene's drive not only unhinged the Confederate line running to the west in the Cornfield but also carried them to within 200 yards of Dunker Church, where they would remain, hunkered down, for a considerable period.

Hooker quickly reinforced Greene with artillery, but shortly afterward he too went down with a wound.

As Hooker left the battlefield at approximately 0900, he was sure the Confederates were on the brink of defeat. They were not. Lee was already hurrying McLaws's division up the road from Sharpsburg, the division arriving after an exhausting march from Harper's Ferry. The Union attack on Lee's left flank was on the brink of success, but with the loss of both corps commanders, there was a lack of focus as to the next move. With McClellan failing to provide guidance of any sort, it was as if a great piece of machinery had been set in motion, but with no one directing matters, it careened over the landscape with murderous results.

At this point, the Union commander committed Major General Edwin "Bull" Sumner's II Corps. Sumner had acquired his nickname for his extraordinarily loud voice, but it reflected his command personality as well. He possessed aggressiveness by the bushel full but lacked the dexterity required by a corps commander. His II Corps was one of the largest corps in the Army of the Potomac with 15,200 infantrymen, nearly the equal of Hooker's and Mansfield's corps combined. McClellan had kept the II Corps deployed on the east bank of Antietam Creek, and it was not until shortly after 0700, as Hood's counterattack drove the I Corps back, which McClellan observed from the Pry House, that he finally ordered Sumner to cross with two of the three divisions of his corps. McClellan kept the third division, under Major General Israel Richardson, as a reserve, not to be released until one of Porter's divisions had moved forward to replace it.

The II Corps crossed the ford lying in the valley between the hill in front of Dunker Church and the hills on the other side of the creek. The first division to cross was John Sedgwick's, which formed up on the lower slope of the swale rising up toward the East Woods. As soon as the division formed up, Sumner ordered it to march. Sumner himself rode off with Sedgwick; thus, he left William French's division still forming up. Moreover, since Sumner had no clear idea until he reached the top of the rise as to where he was going, he left no orders for French other than to advance when his men were across the creek and formed up. As a result, the II Corps found itself committed in driblets. As his men reached the southern end of the East Woods, Sumner confronted the chaos of the furious fighting that had lasted for over three hours. He could discern Greene's men deployed east of the Dunker Church, but everywhere else death and confusion lay across the landscape. It appeared to the old regular officer that the Union army's right wing had collapsed. Only Williams, who had assumed command of the XII Corps from the mortally wounded Mansfield, could have briefed him, but Sumner was not interested. Instead, with little knowledge of Union or Confederate dispositions or of the tactical situation, Sumner deployed Sedgwick's division in three long lines separated by approximately twenty-five yards.

Once the division had completed its deployment, he marched it straight toward the West Woods. The advancing troops of Sedgwick's division took heavy casualties, as they moved across the wide fields lying between the East Woods and the West Woods. Leading the last brigade was Brigadier General O. O. Howard, who was about to find himself outflanked for the second time in the war. As the division piled into the West Woods, command and control collapsed. At that point, McLaws launched a devastating attack from the south into Sedgwick's flank. Sumner finally realized the fix he had gotten Sedgwick's division into, but it was too late to do anything but run. The result was a complete collapse. Only the speed with which Sedgwick's soldiers ran limited his division's casualties. The destruction of Sedgwick's division represented more than just a tactical disaster. Had Sumner waited for French to deploy and then launched the two divisions in an attack along the whole of the West Woods, the II Corps might well have broken through Lee's center and smashed the Army of Northern Virginia. It did not happen, because Sumner had launched off with one-third of his force, while providing no guidance or direction to his other two divisions.

As McLaws's soldiers wrecked Sedgwick's division in the West Woods, they also hit Greene's unsupported division of the XII Corps. With Confederate attacks on both of his flanks, Greene's position in front of the Dunker Church collapsed, but his troops were not in nearly so perilous a position as their comrades in Sedgwick's division. The Confederate success was short-lived. Almost immediately they ran into Alpheus Williams's well-posted batteries. His description of the resulting carnage was chilling in its simplicity: As the batteries hit the rebels with double canisters, the blasts "fell in the very front of the line and all along it apparently, stirring up dust like a thick cloud. When the dust blew away no regiment and not a living man was to be seen."[22] With the collapse of Sedgwick's attack, the fighting on the battlefield's north end settled down in exhaustion.

It was now shortly after 1000 as the fourth major Union attack of the day began. French had received no clear orders from Sumner, as Sedgwick's division had started off. With his division across Antietam Creek and deployed for combat, French hesitated and then moved off in the general direction that Sumner had followed. The division's deployment was somewhat to the left of Sedgwick's division, and here the ground interfered. For those who have walked the ground, a gentle ridge curves away to the southwest. The lay of the ground pulled French's division in that direction, tugging French's advance almost 90 degrees away from Sedgwick's line of march. Thus, French's attack headed straight toward Lee's center. The last division in Sumner's corps, Richardson's, naturally deployed behind French's troops, and so it too pulled away from that of Sedgwick's advance. It was indeed an extraordinary comment on the sloppiness of McClellan's control of the battle as well as the inability of his corps commanders to control their divisions.

Lee had had to drain some of the strength off the center to bolster the desperate efforts to hold his left flank against the attacks that Hooker, Mansfield, and Sumner had launched. Longstreet commanded the center, and although he had precious little to hold the line, the terrain, with one exception, seemed to provide substantial advantage to the defense. Running from the southeast on a small hill not far from Antietam Creek up to the Hagerstown Turnpike, the constant traffic of heavily laden farm wagons had created a sunken road that providing a natural trench, which sheltered the defenders. Major General D. H. Hill deployed the brigades of Robert Rodes and George Anderson along the road. Their soldiers ripped down the rail fencing along the Sunken Road from whence any Union attack would come to make breastworks. However, they neglected to build traverses perpendicular to the sunken road to protect themselves from enfilade fire—an error that survivors would not repeat later in the war.

As French's brigades marched over the brow of the hill, they took a deadly volley from the Confederates sheltered in the Sunken Road. Yet with the exception of a few raw troops, the attacking Union troops stood and fought and, as a result, suffered heavy casualties. French, nicknamed "old blinky" by his men for his penchant of blinking furiously when excited, urged his troops forward. Meanwhile, Richard Anderson's division was arriving from Harper's Ferry and rushed into line to reinforce Hill's division. To do so it had to cross open ground behind the Sunken Road, and thus came under heavy fire from French's troops. Some of Anderson's troops reaching the Sunken Road made the mistake of crossing the road and into the open field beyond, where French's soldiers mowed them down. Moreover, Confederate soldiers in the central segment of the Sunken Road where, after sloping down to the east, it then rises towards the southeast, became easy targets for Union soldiers on the rise to the east.

At approximately the same moment, shortly before 1300, two events occurred which turned the Confederate advantage into a disaster. One of the regimental commanders, misinterpreting his orders, ordered a pull back, which other units then replicated. Moreover, some of Richardson's units worked their way around the Confederate line so that they were now looking directly down the southeastern end of the Confederate position. Panic spread, as Confederate soldiers scrambled to clamber up the blood-soaked bank to the rear, which was difficult to climb because it was covered from the slime of the dying and wounded. As they reached the top, the fleeing Confederates found themselves exposed to the fire of French's troops to the front of the Sunken Road. The collapse and losses broke both Hill's and Anderson's divisions.

The Union attack had succeeded in punching a hole in the Confederate lines, but no reinforcements were on the way from McClellan, nor would he make further efforts to reinforce the units involved in the fighting. Richardson at least recognized a glittering opportunity with a gaping hole in the center of the Confederate line. On the other side, Longstreet also realized the danger and with Hill attempted to patch together a defensive line with artillery units. He even had his staff officers man one of the batteries to show that the Confederate center was still holding. Richardson's problem was that the units involved in breaking the Confederate line along the Sunken Road had suffered heavily and were in considerable confusion. Moreover, his request for the support of rifled artillery was turned down by those across the creek. Then, as Richardson was reorganizing his units, a Confederate shrapnel shell exploded close enough to wound him; he would die a month and a half later. His wounding removed the only Union officer on that part of the field with the vision and drive to resume the attack on the Confederate center. Richardson had been one of McClellan's original brigade commanders and would have risen far, had he survived. McClellan, however, with no knowledge of the situation, saw fit to replace Richardson with Winfield Scott Hancock and gave him orders to hold his positions at all costs. The commander of the Army of the Potomac made no mention to Hancock of launching an attack. Thus, the fighting in the center died down, and another major opportunity for a Union victory disappeared.

As Sumner began his attack with Sedgwick's division at 0900, McClellan had received news that Franklin's two divisions were approaching the battlefield. He then ordered Burnside to advance the IX Corps across Antietam Creek against Lee's far right. The last act of the drama now unfolded, but had it not been for the fact that men were soon to die in large numbers, one might suggest it unfolded as farce. At the beginning of the march north, Burnside had commanded one of the army's wings, consisting of the I Corps and the IX Corps. But on arrival at Antietam Creek on the 15th, McClellan pulled Hooker's Corps away to launch its attack on the Confederate left. Thus, Burnside found himself in the anomalous position of commanding a wing of one corps, which already had a commander, Brigadier General Jacob Cox, Reno's successor after the latter's fatal wounding at South Mountain.

Whatever the difficulties of their military relationship, the two generals had no clear idea of the terrain surrounding the Rohrbach Bridge. Some of McClellan's staff had reconnoitered the area on the 16th, but they had botched their assignment. Burnside and Cox determined to force a crossing at the Rohrbach Bridge, since they had not bothered to reconnoiter the creeks path farther south where fords existed within easy reach. Because Lee had pulled off most of the Confederates defending his southern flank, only two Georgia regiments, with slightly more than 400 soldiers, defended the bridge from positions on the hill above. One can still see the outlines of their positions today, which made them almost invulnerable to Union fire from the other side of Antietam Creek. The stream at this point in its flow south is approximately three to four feet deep, but the banks on both sides are steep and slippery. Thus, an infantry formation crossing the creek by wading would have found it difficult to maintain its cohesion.

After receiving orders from McClellan to cross the creek and move against Lee's southern flank, the IX Corps' leaders tried a number of alternatives, all of which failed with considerable losses. It was not until shortly after noon that Brigadier General Edward Ferrero's brigade, under cover of artillery and infantry fire, managed to cross the bridge and drive the Georgians from their rifle pits. Ferrero's promise to restore the 51st Pennsylvania's whiskey ration had added to the attack's impetus. Having thus succeeded in breaking Confederate defenses in the south and opening the way into Lee's rear, the IX Corps' lead units then sat down to resupply themselves with ammunition and eat their lunch. As a result, the IX Corps lost an hour, which did not seem much at the time.

Cox and Burnside finally finished their preparations before moving out toward Sharpsburg and its vital ford across the Potomac, Lee's only escape route. Brigadier General Orlando Wilcox's division advanced on the right, up the sloping hill toward the backside of Cemetery Hill. On the left Brigadier General Isaac Rodman's division advanced toward the Harper's Ferry road that ran down into Sharpsburg. Together the two divisions numbered 5,500 fresh troops, while another 3,300 of the Kanawha Division, which had handled the fight at Rohrbach Bridge, were in reserve. At 1500 the advance began. Opposing them, Confederate Brigadier General Davis Jones had approximately 2,700 men, dispersed to take advantage of the broken, hilly ground, divided by stone walls and rail fences.

The attack drove the Confederates steadily backward. Wilcox's men reached the cemetery and, had they been reinforced by Sykes's regulars, who formed the lead portion of Porter's corps, they might have broken through the center and taken Sharpsburg. Rodman's troops actually reached the southeastern outskirts of the town and caused a momentary panic among Confederate teamsters, stragglers, and wounded. But the Union success, as had been the case throughout the day, was momentary. A. P. Hill's division arrived at precisely the right moment from Harper's Ferry. There was none of the marshaling of units, dressing of lines, checking of equipment that typified the Army of the Potomac. Instead, Hill pushed his brigades immediately into the fight, deploying them from march to combat formations as they arrived from Harper's Ferry. Caught by surprise by Hill's flank attack, the IX Corps, with some units routed, others putting up stout resistance, retreated back to their bridgehead on the west bank of Antietam Creek. Overall, the corps suffered 2,350 casualties; the Confederates barely one thousand. The major fighting was over, and the battle had ended in a draw.

Yet, other possibilities still existed. Franklin, having just arrived on the field, suggested to McClellan that he launch his two divisions of the VI Corps in another attack on the West Woods. Sumner would have none of it, since he believed the Army of the Potomac was barely hanging on, a view McClellan shared. One of the veterans of the II Corps noted that Sumner possessed "the courage which would have borne him calmly up a ravine swept by canister at the head of the old First Dragoons, but [he had lost] the courage which, in the crash and clamor of action, amid disaster and repulse, enables the commander coolly to calculate the chances of success or failure."[23] Porter was no more sanguine about Union chances, in contrast to the aggressiveness he had shown after Malvern Hill. He strongly urged McClellan not to launch another attack. In his case, it is perhaps understandable that he believed Lee was still capable of launching another devastating blow against his corps as had happened at Second Bull Run.

Matters were different on the other side in spite of the terrible pounding that the Army of Northern Virginia had taken. Late in the afternoon with the major fighting over, Jackson had a young private climb one of the trees near his position to count the number of Union flags—each one denoting a unit—to his front to see whether a Confederate attack might be feasible. When the private reached thirty-nine, suggesting at least several Union divisions lay to the north, Jackson had the soldier climb down and abandoned further ideas of attacking. Even more strikingly, Lee, with every unit in his army shot to pieces, remained on the field for another day and did not pull back across the Potomac until 19 September.

The casualty bill for the one-day battle was extraordinary. It was the single worst day in the military history of the United States. The Army of the Potomac suffered 12,401 casualties, of whom 2,108 were killed, 9,540 wounded, and 753 missing. Confederate casualties were 10,316, of whom 1,546 were killed, 7,752 wounded, and 1,018 missing. But many in the wounded and missing categories were dead or soon to die. The surrounding area reflected the murderous meeting of two great armies. Dr. Oliver Wendell Holmes arrived two days after the battle in search of his son, the future Supreme Court justice, and described the landscape: "There was something repulsive about the trodden and stained relics of the stale battle-field. It was like the table of some hideous orgy left uncleared, and one turned away disgusted from its broken fragments and muddy heeltaps."[24] Everywhere, unmentioned by the doctor, hung the stench of the decaying flesh of men, horses, and mules.

It is extraordinary that McClellan sat unmoving throughout the entire 18th of September with Lee still on the east side of the Potomac.

One can best sum up Antietam by noting that the side with the leaders capable of winning a decisive battle lacked the troops, while those who possessed the necessary troops, lacked the martial drive to win such a battle. The fighting on the 17th had battered every single one of the units in Lee's army. However, McClellan still possessed over 30,000 fresh troops who had not been committed to the battle on 17 September and were ready for action. As Porter Alexander noted in his acerbic account of his experiences in the Army of Northern Virginia: "For Common Sense was just shouting: 'Your adversary is backed against a river, which has no bridge & only one ford, & that the worst one on the whole river. If you whip him now, you destroy him utterly, root & branch & bag & baggage. Not twice in a lifetime does such a chance come to any general. Lee for once has made a mistake, & given you a chance to ruin him if you can break his lines, & such a game is worth great risks.'"[25]

Had McClellan driven forward on 18 September, he had every possibility of winning a great victory, which would have destroyed the Army of Northern Virginia utterly and completely. Growing anti-slavery appetite in the North, in conjunction with slaves themselves taking advantage of the war to find freedom behind the lines of Federal troops, probably made McClellan's dream of a peace that restored the antebellum Union and left slavery untouched out of reach, even if McClellan had impaled Lee's army against the Potomac. Nevertheless, as conquering hero, he might well have gone on to become president of the United States, with profound consequences for Reconstruction. The legal basis of the civil rights movement of the twentieth century, the Fourteenth and Fifteenth Amendments, could not possibly have arisen out of a McClellan presidency. Instead, McClellan's failure to seize the many advantages Lee offered insured the conflict would turn into a terrible, long-drawn-out war of attrition, the utter and complete destruction of the Confederacy, and the violent abolition of slavery. As he had done throughout his tenure as commander of the Army of the Potomac, McClellan hesitated, and Lee escaped. McClellan's fitting reward would be the governorship of the state of New Jersey.

With the ability to claim a victory of sorts, Lincoln issued the Emancipation Proclamation. The president announced that if the Confederacy did not quit its rebellion, the slaves would be free as of 1 January 1863. Of course, the codicil was that the troops of the United States of America would have to occupy the whole of the South, destroy the

Confederate armies, and break the will of Southern whites to continue the struggle.

Fredericksburg

McClellan's unwillingness to use his army for anything other, as Lincoln noted, than his bodyguard, finally forced the president's hand. In the period after Antietam, the usual obfuscation and wearisome excuses followed one upon another. If the Confederates lacked superiority in numbers, then the horses of the Army of the Potomac had all broken down. That excuse led Lincoln to inquire of McClellan: "Will you pardon me for asking what the horses of your army have done since the battle of Antietam that fatigue anything?"[26] Lincoln finally reached the point of such exasperation that McClellan had to go and go he did.

The problem then, and for another year, was finding a suitable replacement. David Lloyd George noted in the index of his memoirs about Field Marshal Douglas Haig, commander of the British Expeditionary Force, "no conspicuous officer better qualified for highest command."[27] In a nutshell that sums up Lincoln's problem in finding a replacement for McClellan. Given Pope's disastrous failure, it was not possible to bring a general in from the outside. Halleck with his dithering in the aftermath of Second Bull Run had indicated he was not a suitable replacement. Thus, it had to be one of the corps commanders of the Army of the Potomac, and they were hardly an impressive lot. Porter had the strongest combat record, but his questionable conduct at Second Manassas and reckless political intriguing with Democratic partisans disqualified him. The choice ended up falling on Burnside, a nice, honest officer whose abilities topped out at division command. His incompetence soon showed in the logistical and administrative spheres as well as in tactics and operations. In fairness, that was Burnside's evaluation of his own abilities, as he warned the president before his appointment.

For Lee, the post-Antietam period began with ideas about launching another invasion of the North. However, the sorry state of the Army of Northern Virginia, badly battered by Antietam and beset by desertion, disabused him of such notions. Instead, it was more a matter of rebuilding the army, rather than of invading the North. To that end, the Confederates abandoned the defense of northern Virginia and retreated behind the Rappahannock and Rapidan Rivers, where supply became less of a problem. Across these two rivers, little more than streams, the two armies confronted each other.

For Burnside, pressured by Lincoln and a Washington political scene eager for action, the operational problem seemed easy enough. Simply move directly against Lee's extended lines along the Rappahannock, attack before the Confederates could concentrate, smash through the enemy's defenses, and then see what happened thereafter. Indeed, Burnside's move south to Fredericksburg caught the Confederates by surprise. But the move had one essential piece missing. To cross the Rappahannock at Fredericksburg, the Army of the Potomac required pontoons, and unfortunately the army's quartermasters had left them behind. Halleck apparently had promised his help in getting them forward, but whoever was responsible, it was one more case of the Army of the Potomac getting a major detail wrong. By the time the army's engineers had moved the necessary pontoons forward, a week had passed, and the Confederates were fully alerted. Moving with speed, Lee concentrated his troops along the heights looking down on the town of Fredericksburg and the Rappahannock, which lay on the town's north side.

At this point Burnside should have abandoned his plans to attack and attempted some other move to get the Confederates onto more suitable terrain. But he lacked both imagination and tactical sense. In the end, he decided to undertake that most difficult of military operation, an opposed river crossing. If such an effort did not provide a sufficient challenge, the Confederates looked down from impregnable positions on Marye's Heights to the gentle sloping fields that ran to the town below. By now Jackson had joined Longstreet, and the Confederates had deployed their troops on the heights. Altogether Lee possessed approximately 75,000 soldiers. Longstreet was on the Confederate left on the heights, while Jackson's troops held the right flank along Prospect Hill. Jackson as usual was spoiling for a fight, and he suggested that as soon as the Army of the Potomac was across the Rappahannock, he should attack and force Burnside's army into the river. Lee demurred and was right, because if Jackson had come out into the open, his divisions were bound to lose in a stand-up fight against the more numerous Federals with their supporting artillery directly across the river.

Against the Army of Northern Virginia, Burnside brought an army of 110,000 men, all volunteers, the best the North had to offer. Burnside's plan was straightforward and about as realistic as Haig's attack on 1 July 1916 on the Somme. He ordered his engineers to build two sets of pontoon bridges, three in front of Fredericksburg and three farther down the river over which the army would cross. Winter ice was already beginning to spread from the banks of the Rappahannock, which would have made the engineers' task difficult in the best of times, but to add to their discomfort, Lee had deployed Brigadier General William Barksdale's Mississippi brigade throughout Fredericksburg to snipe at the Union engineers as they attempted to build the pontoon bridges. Stung by mounting losses, Burnside ordered the artillery deployed along Stafford Heights on the other side of the river to blast Confederate snipers out of the lairs in Fredericksburg. When that failed, three regiments of Union infantry, one from Michigan and two from Massachusetts, used the pontoon boats to ferry their soldiers across. After fierce fighting, the town was in Union hands but a complete wreck.

A heavy fog enshrouded the Rappahannock River valley in the early morning hours of 13 December. On the right-hand side of the Union line, Sumner held nearly 60,000 troops to assault Longstreet's line; south of the town, Franklin held close to the same number to attack Jackson's troops. Burnside intended Franklin's assault to be the primary effort, with Sumner's attack only designed to fix Longstreet in place. Due to Franklin's own passivity and a lack of clarity in Burnside's orders, what happened was not a battle, but rather a slaughter. Only on the Federal left did one of the smaller Union divisions, led by George Meade, break through a swampy area that Jackson had believed impassable. But Franklin, committing only half his troops, refused to support Meade, whose troops a counterattack from Jubal Early's division drove back. Meanwhile, on the right, Sumner launched one failed attack after another, which added steadily to a growing casualty bill.

As the French Marshal Pierre Bosquet commented about the charge of the Light Brigade at Balaclava during the Crimean War: "*C'est magnifique, mais ce n'est pas la guerre . . . C'est de la folie.*" In all, fourteen brigade assaults by Sumner's troops attempted to take Marye's Heights. None got close. Hooker, whose corps crossed at the end of the day, recorded in his official report: "Finding that I had lost as many men

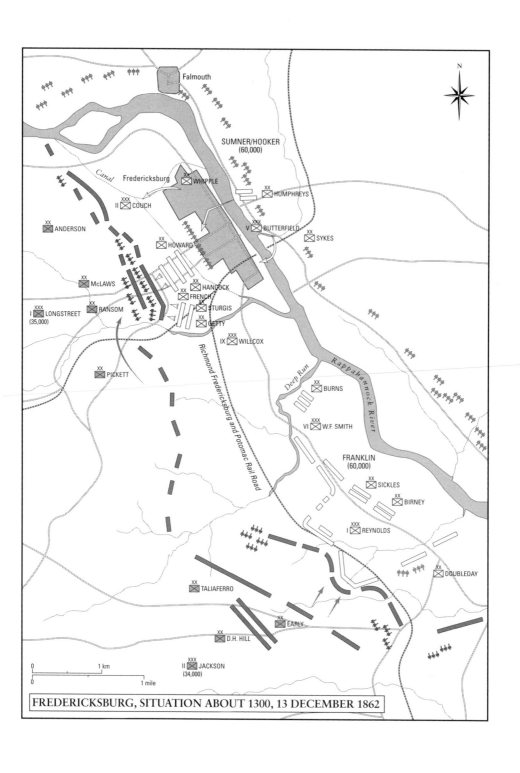

Falmouth

SUMNER/HOOKER
(60,000)

Canal   Fredericksburg

XX WHIPPLE

XX HUMPHREYS

XXX
II COUCH

XX ANDERSON

V XX BUTTERFIELD

XX SYKES

XX HOWARD

XX McLAWS

XX HANCOCK

XX FRENCH

XXX
I LONGSTREET
(35,000)

XX RANSOM

I XX STURGIS

XX GETTY

XXX
IX WILLCOX

XX PICKETT

Richmond Fredericksburg and Potomac Rail Road

Deep Run

Rappahannock River

XX BURNS

VI XX W.F. SMITH

FRANKLIN
(60,000)

XX SICKLES

XX BIRNEY

XXX
I REYNOLDS

XX DOUBLEDAY

XX TALIAFERRO

XX EARLY

XX D.H. HILL

XXX
II JACKSON
(34,000)

0   1 km
0   1 mile

FREDERICKSBURG, SITUATION ABOUT 1300, 13 DECEMBER 1862

as my orders required me to lose, I suspended the attack."[28] A reporter summed up the sorry show: "It can hardly be in human nature for men to show more valor, or Generals to manifest less judgment."[29]

Late in the afternoon, Jackson considered an attack on Franklin, but he had no sooner rolled his artillery out to bombard the Union troops below than Union artillery on the other side of the Rappahannock blasted his artillery back into the woods from which it had emerged. That was more than enough to convince even Jackson that a counterattack was not in the cards. The next day saw Burnside consider more attacks, but his subordinates vociferously argued against additional efforts. So the day passed, but it was not until the second day after the disaster that Burnside arranged a truce with Lee to bury his dead and pull the few wounded who were still alive back to the hospitals. Over the night of 15/16 December a fierce storm with sleet and wind swept across Virginia, and under its cover the Army of the Potomac slipped away. It had suffered 12,653 casualties: 1,284 killed, 9,600 wounded, and 1,769 captured or missing. Confederate casualties were less than half that: 5,377 total: 608 killed, 4,116 wounded, and 653 captured or wounded.

Conclusion

Despite the Union catastrophe at Fredericksburg, Lee knew that such a defensive victory would not by itself gain independence for the Confederacy. He grumbled to his wife on 16 December that "they suffered heavily as far as the battle went, but it did not go far enough to satisfy me."[30] Revealing the mindset that had led him to later attempt another invasion of the North, Lee wrote after Gettysburg that at Fredericksburg "we had really accomplished nothing; we had not gained a foot of ground, and I knew the enemy could easily replace the men he had lost."[31] He remained deeply concerned about Confederate shortages in manpower, and exhorted Secretary of War James Seddon in January to mobilize Confederate resources to a greater extent than had heretofore occurred. He feared that Confederate successes might "betray our people into the dangerous delusion that the armies now in the field are sufficient to bring this war to a successful and speedy termination."[32] As disastrous as Fredericksburg had been, Lee remained aware of how it did not completely make up for opportunities he believed he missed during the offensive into Maryland. Confederate victory at Fredericksburg also could not compensate for the Emancipation Proclamation's strategic blow to the Confederacy's long-term fortunes, although Lee would not have so readily seen the danger of a measure he viewed as villainous. Regardless, he would not hesitate to take the offensive again.

In the West Confederate travails went beyond missed opportunities. Bragg's failed invasion of Kentucky had greater strategic effects than the simple termination of his campaign and the preservation of Kentucky for the Union. From now on, Confederate forces would be on the strategic defensive in the West, attempting (and failing) to hold on to key terrain such as Vicksburg, Chattanooga, and Atlanta. After Grant broke the Confederacy's early attempt at a cordon defense, its Western armies had attempted to regain the initiative through counter-offensives at Shiloh, Van Dorn's operations in northern Mississippi, and, the boldest move of all, Bragg's invasion of Kentucky. Each effort had failed, and with Bragg's defeat at Perryville, the window of opportunity for the Confederacy to more than simply hold the line in the West closed. Confederate losses in manpower and economically valuable territory had been too grievous for them to mount an effective offensive in the West, and Hood's disastrous attempt to regain the initiative with an invasion of Tennessee in 1864–65 would show the folly of anything but a Fabian strategy there after 1862. Nevertheless, the guerrilla-infested expanses of the region, combined with the challenging terrain that protected Vicksburg, would present serious challenges to Federal military forces that hoped to regain the offensive momentum that had been achieved by Union arms in the opening Western campaigns of 1862.

Whatever disappointment Confederate military leaders, such as Lee, felt should have been overmatched by an astute Union observer's frustration with the campaigns of 1862, especially in the Eastern theater. The Peninsula Campaign had been a dismal failure, while what had transpired in the spring in Jackson's thrashing of assorted Union armies had been a disgrace. The Peninsula Campaign showed McClellan at his worst: hesitant, cautious, fearful, wildly exaggerating enemy numbers, and in the end pusillanimous. The administration's effort to introduce reasonably competent generalship into the Eastern theater by bringing John Pope from the West to command the cobbled together Army of Virginia almost resulted in catastrophic military defeat. And then McClellan had discarded all the advantages Lee had provided to turn what should have been a smashing victory into a murderous draw at Antietam. The Young Napoleon's behavior finally led to his removal from command and the war, but his replacement was no improvement. Rather, Burnside led the Army of the Potomac to its worst defeat in the war. Besides his inability to fight, McClellan proved incapable of understanding the nature of the war in which his army was engaged. As he told his troops, "we are not engaged in a war of rapine, revenge, or subjugation; that this is not a contest against populations."[33] But that was precisely the point where he diverged from the reality of the war, for the Civil War was above all a war of populations, North as well as South.

From our perspective there were brighter spots, but those would hardly have encouraged the Northern population. In fact, with the exception of Fredericksburg, Confederate battle losses had been almost as heavy as Federal casualties. The fact was that the combination of the French and Industrial Revolutions was leading this war, as it would the First World War, toward a murderous, drawn-out bloodbath. In such a war, attrition, not battlefield virtuosity, would determine the outcome. The Confederacy's only hope lay in its ability to break the North's will to continue the struggle. In 1864, Lee, forced by Grant's aggressiveness to fall back on the defensive, imposed casualties on the Army of the Potomac that came close to breaking that will. But in the end, the huge casualties the Army of Northern Virginia suffered in pursuit of decisive victory in 1862 and 1863 were to rob the Confederacy of the manpower needed to hold back the North's overwhelming strength in 1864. In the end brilliant victories could not defeat the side with the bigger battalions.

For Lincoln, the problem he had confronted after the defeat at the First Bull Run remained. How was he going to find the competent, driving leadership needed to defeat the Confederates in Virginia? Pope had failed. McClellan had failed. In barely two months Burnside failed. That general's successor in January 1863 would also fail. Lincoln's ruthlessness in removing generals who failed the basic test of military leadership, victory in war, should have represented an example for the first American president in the twenty-first century. Unfortunately, it did not. Unlike Davis or the second Bush, Lincoln would not tolerate failure from his generals.

Moreover, he was willing to make an example of those who had failed. Shortly after McClellan was relieved, the War Department convened a court-martial to try Fitz-John Porter for refusing to obey a lawful order of his superior—namely, John Pope at Second Manassas. In fact, Porter was innocent of the charges, but Lincoln and Stanton could have cared less; they were more interested in sending a message to the generals of the Army of the Potomac that they would not tolerate incompetence or disloyalty. With a verdict of guilty, Porter found himself cashiered from the army. He was lucky that he was fighting in the armies of the United States, because in the French Republic of 1793 or 1794, he would have lost his head. Lincoln would shuffle the deck until he came up with a winning team. What annoyed the president more than anything else about generals were two things: a failure to act aggressively and an inability to get all of their troops into the fight. Behind the president's intuition lay an understanding that one of the North's greatest advantages lay in its numbers. But he still had to find the generals who would be willing to put those numbers to good use.

CHAPTER 8

The War in the East, 1863

Yet a small remnant remained in desperate struggle, receiving a fire in front, on the right and on the left, many even climbing over the wall, and fighting the enemy in his own trenches until entirely surrounded; and those who were not killed or wounded were captured, with the exception of about 300 who came off slowly, but greatly scattered, the identity of every regiment being entirely lost, and every regimental commander either killed or wounded. . . . The brigade went into action with 1287 men and about 140 officers . . . and sustained a loss . . . of 941 killed, wounded, and missing.

—Edward Porter Alexander, *Military Memoirs of a Confederate*

The turn of the year into 1863 represented the nadir of the North's fortunes. In the east Lee's Army of Northern Virginia had just humiliated the Army of the Potomac in the murderous Battle of Fredericksburg. In the West Grant and Sherman had failed in their efforts to attack Vicksburg—the former was forced to retreat back to Memphis after Confederate cavalry raiders had cut his supply lines, while Sherman's attack on Chickasaw Bluffs in front of Vicksburg was no more successful than most such frontal attacks. And in central Tennessee, Union forces, having beaten back Bragg's offensive into Kentucky, remained stalled.

For Lincoln, who saw matters clearly, the purpose of Union armies was to *fight*, a reality that McClellan and all too many Northern commanders had failed to grasp. The president had recognized early in 1862 that the clearest path to victory lay in Union armies pressing the Confederacy from all sides. At least McClellan had been relieved first as commander of Union armies and then as commander of the Army of the Potomac. Nevertheless, his replacement at the top of the military pyramid, Halleck, was hardly an improvement, functioning more as a clerk than director of the Union's military strategy, when he was not bombarding commanders in the field with senseless instructions or even undermining their capacity to fight. Thus, there would be no coordination of the Union offensives in 1863.

It was in the east that Lincoln confronted the most serious difficulties. The Army of the Potomac's morale had reached its lowest point by January 1863. Fredericksburg, along with Burnside's appalling mismanagement and terrible leadership, was undermining the army's soul. Pay was in arrears as much as seven months; soldiers were subsisting on hard tack and salted meat; uniforms were in tatters from the fierce campaigning of the previous year; and, most distressing of all, a significant number of officers had gone home with or without leave, abandoning their men to their own devices. To cap this dismal situation, a cabal of senior officers was working to undermine Burnside's position and bring McClellan back as the army's commander.

Lincoln would have none of that. "Little Mac" had thoroughly discredited himself in the president's eyes with his unwillingness to fight. On 26 January 1863, the president acted. He chose "Fighting Joe" Hooker, who had proven himself to be one of the more aggressive corps commanders in the army. However, he was not popular among his peers. He had a dubious reputation as a drinker and womanizer, in other words, an individual who stood outside the staid moral standards of the time. In particular, he had a long-standing quarrel with Halleck that went back to their California days in the Old Army. So deep was the antagonism between the two that when Lincoln appointed Hooker to command the Army of the Potomac, the general requested that he only deal with the president and have nothing to do with Halleck, a command relationship which was to exercise a baleful impact on the spring campaign. But at least Hooker had earned his nickname on a number of battlefields. However, he had also declaimed to the *New York Times*'s correspondent with the Army of the Potomac that the country needed a dictator. After Lincoln made the momentous decision to appoint Hooker, he wrote the general a letter that put the president's cards on the table: "I have heard, in such a way as to believe it, of your recently saying that both the army and the Government needed a Dictator. Of course it is not *for* this, but in spite of it, that I have given you the command. Only those generals who gain successes, can set up dictators. What I now ask of you is military success, and I will risk the dictatorship."[1]

Hooker immediately tackled the Army of the Potomac's administrative and logistic difficulties. With the administration's help, he cleaned house: he relieved Sumner and Franklin and divided Burnside's old command, the IX Corps, with one division under William "Baldy" Smith sent off to the Peninsula and two divisions deployed west to reinforce Union forces in Kentucky. In the East, Hooker persuaded the administration to relieve him of responsibility for protecting the capital with that duty turned over to Heintzelman, under whom Hooker had served as a division commander. In terms of unintended effects, while the IX Corps achieved little on the Peninsula, its movement alarmed the Confederates. Lee moved Longstreet and two divisions to watch Union forces in the area and ensure the latter did not interfere with the Confederacy's north–south communications or threaten Richmond. Thus, the Army of Northern Virginia faced Hooker with only two of its three corps when the Army of the Potomac moved south in early May.

Hooker also straightened out the administrative and supply mess Burnside and others had created. Whatever Hooker's weaknesses, he was a superb administrator. He solved the desertion problem through a reimposition of discipline and security measures that made it more difficult for soldiers to leave their units without permission. At the same time, he instituted a furlough policy that allowed soldiers leave to return home for short periods. Rations almost immediately improved, including fresh vegetables and soft bread in place of hard tack. Hooker received considerable help from a logistical system organized and run by two of the unsung heroes of the war, Herman Haupt and Daniel McCallum, first-class railroad men. Here, in sharp contrast to the Confederacy's situation, the North's railroad infrastructure supported the front at the same time that it kept the Northern economy running at full speed. By late winter, Hooker had restored the Army of the Potomac's discipline and pride. For that contribution alone he deserves a place as one of the war's more significant generals.

Hooker also carried out a thorough reorganization of the army's command structure. His most important move was to concentrate the cavalry into a separate branch. Through January 1863, the Army of the Potomac had assigned its cavalry regiments higgledy-piggledy to the various corps and divisions. However, while the creation of a cavalry command represented a major step forward, Hooker made the mistake of appointing Major General George Stoneman to command the new force. Stoneman was the worst sort of Army of the Potomac general officer, brave, but devoid of imagination, initiative, and the capacity to adapt to unforeseen circumstances. The change in the Union cavalry became apparent in mid-March when a force under Brigadier General William Averell caught Confederate Fitzhugh Lee's cavalry brigade by surprise and gave the Confederate troopers a bloody nose at Kelly's Ford. Nevertheless, while the engagement was a tactical success, Averell botched the advantage of surprise and failed to wreck Lee's brigade, which he was in a position to do. Again, the excessive caution that marked so much of the Army of the Potomac's history reared its ugly head. Averell reinforced the disastrous penchant of Union subordinate commanders to await orders rather than display initiative by making clear that his regimental commanders were not to act unless they received explicit orders.

Hooker also made the significant mistake of stripping the army's artillery chief, Brigadier General Henry Hunt, of much of his authority. In Hunt's place he dispersed authority over the combat power of the army's artillery arm, which was one of its most important material advantages over the Army of Northern Virginia, which suffered from comparative defects in both numbers of guns and ordnance. In terms of command of the various divisions and corps, Hooker confronted the difficult task of shuffling corps and division commanders to replace those killed or maimed in the fighting in 1862, or those whose incompetence had proved them incapable of serving in the field. The most important command shifts came with the corps commands. Major General Dan Sickles, a New York politician, infamous for having killed his wife's lover and then having been found innocent on a plea of temporary insanity (Stanton was his lawyer), became the head of the III Corps as Hooker's replacement. One of the other division commanders, O. O. Howard, complained that he had date of rank on Sickles. Hooker then appointed him commander of the XI Corps to replace Major General Franz Sigel, who had resigned his command in a huff. Howard was never to be popular with the German immigrants, who made up the great majority of the corps, partially because he was a religious do-gooder who passed out prayer books to the beer-drinking Germans. Howard would have a better war in the West in 1864 under Sherman, but he proved a disastrous choice for corps command in 1863.

South of the Rappahannock, Lee faced the problem of replacing a number of division and brigade commanders. He did possess three supremely talented subordinates to command his far larger corps: the steady Longstreet, the ferocious Jackson, and the mercurial Stuart, whose cavalry was organized formally as a division but acted as a corps. These were men on whom he could depend to display initiative, not only to see but also to capitalize on any opportunity. Lee's problems were, not surprisingly, quite different from Hooker's. Sending much of Longstreet's corps south to watch the IX Corps and the approaches to Petersburg and Richmond relieved him of a considerable logistical burden. Quite simply, the South's antiquated railroad system and its incompetent commissary authorities were incapable of keeping Confederate troops on the Rappahannock sufficiently supplied. Longstreet's troops could correct some of the deficiencies of the supply system by foraging for themselves and their comrades to the southeast of Richmond. Nevertheless, by early spring rations in the army had fallen to four ounces of bacon and eighteen ounces of flour a day—hardly enough to keep body and mind together.

Whatever his supply difficulties, Lee, ever aggressive, was already thinking of launching the Army of Northern Virginia on another invasion of the North. He clearly hoped to achieve the decisive victory that had eluded him in 1862 and which, like Napoleon's victories at Austerlitz and Jena-Auerstedt, he believed, would bring the war to an end. Nevertheless, he might have taken a lesson from Napoleon's experience with multiple recurring wars. Regardless, he would have to wait for Longstreet to return and for the late spring with its grass to repair the famished condition of the horses in his command. Nevertheless, he was confident that Hooker and the Army of the Potomac would remain on the defensive, displaying the lack of initiative and drive that had so characterized that organization during the campaigns of 1862. His underestimation of his opponent would prove a serious miscalculation. Whatever his state of mind, Lee's health had seriously deteriorated in March, when he suffered what appears to have been a mild heart attack. At fifty-six, Lee was long in the tooth for a Civil War field commander in contrast with Grant who turned forty-one in late April. Whether it was a heart attack or not, Lee continued to suffer attacks of angina, which makes his performance in the coming campaign that much more impressive.

By late April Hooker was ready to move. For one of the rare occasions in the war, the Army of the Potomac achieved surprise at the operational level against its nemesis. Hooker's plan was straightforward:

Stoneman's massive force of nearly 10,000 cavalry would swing around Lee's flank and drive deep into the Confederate rear, where its mission was to cause general mayhem: destroy the rickety rail lines (especially the bridges north of Hanover Junction on which Lee depended for his supplies), cut the telegraph lines, and intercept whatever supplies might move across the area's road network. As soon as Stoneman moved out, a portion of the Army of the Potomac would execute a deception operation to suggest that Hooker was about to repeat Burnside's disastrous attempt to break through the Confederate positions on Marye's Heights overlooking Fredericksburg. At the same time, two corps would move under cover of night and the terrain to the northwest and cross the Rappahannock at Kelly's Ford and then the Rapidan at Germanna Ford; a third corps would accompany them crossing at Kelly's Ford and then Ely's Ford. Two corps would be available as a swing force. If Lee fell for the deception, those corps would follow the move around Lee's flank; if he did not and shifted swiftly to his left, they would be in position to take Fredericksburg from its undermanned Confederate defenders. It was a brilliant plan, and it caught Lee off guard. As the Southern artilleryman Porter Alexander noted: "On the whole I think this plan was decidedly the best strategy conceived in any of the campaigns ever set foot against us."[2]

Nevertheless, to paraphrase Clausewitz, war is a simple matter, but its execution, more often than not, is exceedingly difficult. The layout of the Army of the Potomac's winter quarters, resulting from the retreat across the Rappahannock after Fredericksburg, was such that its strongest corps lay to the east and along the river, where they were readily in sight of the Confederates. Any major movement of these units would alert Lee that something was afoot. Thus, Hooker could not use them to lead his outflanking move. Instead it would be Howard's XI and Slocum's XII Corps, followed by Meade's V Corps, which would make the flanking move, the former two led by the least competent corps commanders in the Army of the Potomac. Moreover, the army's system of seniority ensured that Slocum would be the senior officer leading the flanking move, while Sedgwick would be responsible for independent operations around Fredericksburg, in which the VI Corps would cross the river and persuade the Confederates that another major attack was coming on that front. Sedgwick, while beloved to his men, would prove congenitally incapable of independent command. Perhaps the wisest advice Hooker and Darius

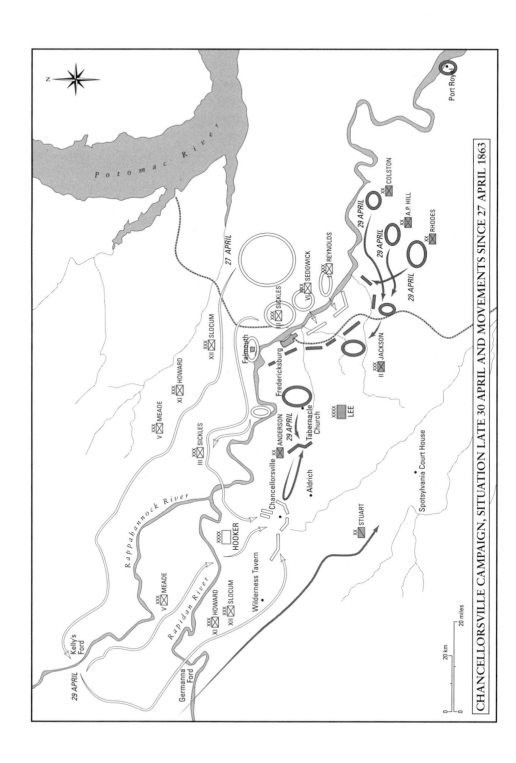

CHANCELLORSVILLE CAMPAIGN, SITUATION LATE 30 APRIL AND MOVEMENTS SINCE 27 APRIL 1863

Couch, senior corps commander in the Army of the Potomac, received before the campaign was the president's: "I want to impress on you two gentlemen in your next fight, put in all of your men."[3]

Hooker expected much from Stoneman's cavalry raid on Lee's rear that was to initiate the campaign. Because it was an independent operation on which much depended, it is worth discussing its course before turning to the fight around Chancellorsville and Fredericksburg. Having done little to prepare despite being provided with thorough instructions, Stoneman gathered his forces at the last moment and ended up having to wait for the infantry corps to cross at Kelly's Ford. Then having wasted most of 28 April in getting to the ford and crossing, he sat down as his official report records: "I assembled the division and brigade commanders, spread our maps, and had a thorough understanding of what we were to do, and where we were each to go."[4] One might have expected him to have accomplished the planning before the move began, admittedly a quaint approach in the Army of the Potomac. By being late Stoneman failed to screen the movement of the XI and XII Corps. As a result, a small Confederate raiding party captured prisoners from both corps, providing the first warning that a major Union move was afoot to the west of the main Confederate positions.

From that point, the Union cavalry raid moved at a snail's pace. Stoneman divided his force, thereby decreasing its striking power. The portion under Averell moved a grand total of twenty-eight miles in the first five days of the campaign. At least that officer informed Hooker where he was, and Hooker curtly noted to the cavalryman that he did "not understand what you are doing at Rapidan Station."[5] On the 30th Stoneman managed to march the remainder of the raiding force a grand total of ten miles; one gets the feeling that infantry, led by a competent commander, could have moved faster. Stoneman's subordinates proved even more cautious, swallowing supposed intelligence that Stonewall Jackson was immediately to their front.

Four days into their slow-motion raid, Stoneman's troopers tore up five miles of the Virginia railroad, subsidiary to the movement of supplies to Lee. When Stoneman finally got around to attacking the Richmond, Fredericksburg, and Potomac Railroad, he did so below Hanover Junction, where Lee's main supply depots lay, and then only inflicted minimal damage. Finally, Stoneman's troopers failed to destroy a single one of that railroad's major bridges, three of which lay immediately to the north of Hanover Junction. Cautious, unimagina-tive, lacking in initiative, and incapable of following clear, unambigu-ous instructions, Stoneman failed to live up even to Hooker's minimal expectations. The cavalryman certainly fit within the Army of the Po-tomac's profile of senior officers. Hooker accurately put it after the campaign: "No officer ever made a greater mistake in construing his orders, and no one ever accomplished less in so doing."[6]

If Stoneman failed to distract Confederate attention, Sedgwick and Reynolds certainly managed their portion of the deception plan to a T. In the early morning hours of 28 April, Reynolds's troops crossed the Rappahannock south of Fredericksburg after a massive artillery barrage; the movement gave every impression that this was where the main blow was coming. For three days the Confederate high com-mand remained largely in the dark. Meanwhile, the XI and XII Corps crossed the Rapidan at Germanna Ford on the 29th while Meade's V Corps moved cross country to cross the river at Ely's Ford. At Ger-manna Ford, the Federals were helped by the fact that Lee had sent a small force of engineers to rebuild the bridge destroyed the year before—a sure indication of his plans to move north as soon as Long-street and his two divisions returned to the Army of Northern Virginia. The Confederates were quickly chased away. As a bonus, Union engi-neers used the materials the Confederates had cut and prepared for their own bridge. Union forces now crossed into the Wilderness. That inhospitable area lay south of the Rapidan from west of Germanna Ford to the east of U.S. Ford. It was a flat, miserable landscape of tangled undergrowth, vines, scrub oaks, poison ivy, and few roads. In other words, it was an area where movement was difficult and commu-nications among units almost impossible.

By 30 April the Union forces gathering on Lee's left flank to the west represented a major threat. Meade, Howard, and Slocum had all reached the outskirts of Chancellorsville with their advanced units pushing down the Orange Turnpike and the Orange Plank Road to-ward the Confederate dispositions near Fredericksburg. Moreover, Couch's II Corps had already crossed at U.S. Ford and was just north of Chancellorsville. At midafternoon, the lead corps commanders conferred. Given the lack of response by the Confederates, Meade proposed they continue the advance with all their forces. Slocum, however, was the senior officer present and demurred, his own cau-tion reinforced by Hooker's instruction that no advance beyond

Chancellorsville occur until arrival of the II and V Corps. By nightfall on 1 May Hooker had nearly 80,000 troops on Lee's western flank, while there were a further 40,000 troops pressing on Fredericksburg to the southeast with approximately 7,000 Union cavalry loose in the Army of Northern Virginia's rear. To oppose that host, Lee had barely 56,000 soldiers. But war is always more than a matter of numbers.

While Slocum was living up to the Army of the Potomac's culture of caution, the reaction in the Confederate high command underlined the difference in competence as well as culture between the two armies. By the 30th, Lee had sufficient intelligence to determine that Hooker's main effort was on his left flank to the west and that the crossing south of Fredericksburg represented a feint. The response was swift and risky, but Lee knew his opponents. Jubal Early with his reinforced division of approximately 12,600 men remained as a holding force on Marye's Heights overlooking Fredericksburg. Meanwhile, the rest of the army under Jackson and Lee moved directly against the the Union corps at Chancellorsville.

The fighting on 1 May underlined Lee's swift response and Hooker's tentativeness. Union forces had moved out in three columns to the east: Two of Meade's divisions on the left flank up River Road, Sykes's division of Meade's corps up the Orange Turnpike, and Slocum's XII up the Orange Plank Road on the right. Sykes moved quickly; Slocum, living up to his name, moved slowly, so that when the two corps ran into the buzz saw of Jackson's advancing units, Sykes, with no support from XII Corps, was almost immediately in trouble. At that point, Hooker pulled his advance units back. It may well be that he feared an encounter battle. Unfortunately, the Union retreat ceded key ground to the east of what would become the front line between the armies. Ironically, having deceived Lee completely, Hooker abandoned that advantage and chose to fight in the Wilderness, thereby minimizing the Union superiority in numbers. The initiative had swung to the Confederates.

The major effort that most of the Army of the Potomac expended on constructing breastworks and abatis to protect their positions suggests the degree to which the war was changing. There would be no standing out in the open to receive Confederate attacks, as had occurred in the Peninsula and at Antietam. Experienced corps commanders, like Meade and Couch, were not about to take chances. By going over to the defensive around Chancellorsville, Hooker was daring Lee to attack him, which is what the commander of the Army of Northern Virginia had already decided to do. Still, Hooker also worried about his right flank, which was dangling with virtually the entire XI Corps facing south. He urged Howard on the night of 1 May to contract his line and swing it back so that a substantial portion of the XI Corps would face west rather the south—the precise direction from which Jackson's devastating attack would come the next day.

But Howard demurred, missing entirely the purpose of Hooker's suggestions. Such a move, he replied, would be bad for morale, and, anyway, he was strengthening his positions. Late in the morning on 2 May, Hooker was equally explicit in his instructions: "The disposition you have made of your corps has been with a view to a front attack by the enemy. If he should throw himself upon your flank, he wishes you to examine the ground and determine upon the position you will take in that event, in order that you may be prepared for him in whatever direction he advances. . . . The right of your line does not appear to be strong enough. . . . We have good reason to suppose that the enemy is moving to our right."[7]

Howard paid not the slightest attention. Thus, due to sheer carelessness, the XI Corps commander put the entire army at risk. As Stephen Sears, the premier historian of the battle, has noted: "unimaginative, unenterprising, uninspiring, a stifling Christian soldier, Otis Howard was the wrong general in the wrong place with the wrong troops that day."[8] That said, there was a general unwillingness of too many senior officers throughout the XI Corps to believe there was a threat gathering on their flank to the west. Howard was not the sole cause of the disaster, simply a reflection of the Army of the Potomac's culture. Furthermore, exacerbating the dangerous situation into which the army was falling was the fact that a communications snafu—Hooker's communications with his widely dispersed forces would generally fail the general and the army throughout the battle—led the I Corps to begin its march from Fredericksburg to Chancellorsville three hours late, thus preventing Reynolds from being on the scene near the XI Corps when Jackson struck.

On the evening of 1 May, after driving the Yankees back to Chancellorsville, Jackson met with Lee. During the meeting, Lee indicated he had had no intention of pushing up the Orange Turnpike and the Orange Plank Road directly against the Army of the Potomac. Instead, he had already decided to move against Hooker's right flank. Jackson delightedly acceded to his chief's conception. By the end of their con-ference, the two had decided to take a major gamble—namely, to split the army into three parts: Jubal Early with his 12,400 men would re-main on Marye's Heights above Fredericksburg and pull back in a holding action, if pressed. Lee would hold in front of Hooker's right flank with the 15,000 soldiers of McLaws's and Anderson's divisions, while Jackson took the bulk of the army, more than 26,000 soldiers, on a flanking march. To reach Hooker's flank was going to take an all-day march, during which Lee's small force would face overwhelming numbers. It was risky, but great victories are not won without risks.

Once Lee had determined the operational approach, the Confeder-ates acted with a dispatch that stands in stark contrast to the patterns of their opponents. Jackson's troops were ready at first light on the morning of the 2nd. Urged on by their officers, they began the long march to move around Hooker's flank. Jackson moved up and down the column, spurring the troops with laconic encouragement: "press forward, press forward. . . . See that the column is kept closed and that there is no straggling . . . press on, press on."[9] For Lee, it was a time of uncertainty; he wrote Davis that he was moving on Hooker's flank and that if that attack did not go well, he would pull back along one of the railroad lines, but would insure that his army remained between Hooker and Richmond. Jackson's advance went largely unhindered except for a brief foray by Sickles.

The Confederate move to the west was in plain view of the III Corps, and its commander, Sickles, urged Hooker to allow his corps to attack Jackson's flank. Hooker only relented when most of the Confederate column had already passed. There was some serious skirmishing, but it was already too late, and Jackson's lead units were already approach-ing their deployment positions on Howard's flank. While Sickles had seen the opportunity, he had failed to act on his own. The result of that failure partially explains his more aggressive actions on the second day at Gettysburg, where he would take the entire III Corps out of the line along Cemetery Ridge in direct contravention to his orders, because he thought the ground in front of him offered better defensive positions.

In the early afternoon Confederate cavalry found the end of How-ard's line, and Jackson, at the front as usual, found himself looking down the whole line of the XI Corps. At 1500 he dispatched a mes-sage to Lee that one of his divisions was up and the other two were following closely. Still, whatever Jackson's efforts to speed things up, it took time to deploy divisions through the tangled mess of the Wilderness. Nevertheless, not all were caught by surprise; Carl Schurz, refugee from the 1848 Revolution in Germany and now a politician and volunteer general in America, had redeployed three regiments and made as many obstructions in his rear as he thought he could get away with, given Howard's orders.

At 1730 Jackson asked General Rodes on his right wing whether his troops were ready; "Yes, sir!" came the reply. And so Jackson launched the devastating attack that came close to destroying the Army of the Potomac. The storm broke on an unprepared XI Corps; even Schurz's three regiments could only delay the Confederates for a few moments as the tide swept eastward, not surprisingly led by Jackson himself, urging his soldiers "press on, press on." Hooker was alerted to the disaster at 1830 when a broken mob of XI soldiers boiled down the road from the west to his headquarters. Howard's corps broke so completely that nearly 80 percent made their escape, while half the casualties were prisoners; in other words, there was little time to fight, so complete was the surprise.

The distance Jackson's troops had to cover, the confusion caused in advancing through the Wilderness, as well as resistance by small groups of Howard's soldiers, allowed Hooker and his subordinates to patch together a line. Hooker ordered Reynolds's corps, still on the other side of the Rapidan, to hurry forward as quickly as possible; Meade, on his own initiative, shifted his V Corps to cover the lines of communications to the river. As dusk approached, Jackson, with a small party, accompanied by A. P. Hill and his staff, rode forward to sort out the confusion and keep the drive going. It was a fateful decision; in the darkness, North Carolina infantry mistook the staff riders for enemy cavalry. A volley of musket fire then devastated both parties, killing or wounding a number of officers. Jackson went down with a severe wound in the arm, an injury further aggravated by being dropped by the soldiers carrying him to the rear. Amputation followed and the inadequate medical care of the time eventually led to his death from pneumonia. Hill was also wounded, which meant no one was available to take command until Stuart could arrive. Jackson's wounding and the lack of a replacement to command the left wing halted the fighting, and quiet settled over the broken and bleeding soldiers.

While Hooker's troubles on his right flank had exploded, he took some comfort in believing that if Sedgwick's VI Corps moved with alacrity, it could drive the Confederates up the Orange Plank Road and catch Lee's right flank in a vice. But Sedgwick displayed not the slightest willingness to move, even when Early pulled most of his division off Marye's Heights and moved off to the northwest. Only a direct order forced Sedgwick to cross the Rappahannock. He then halted despite the fact that there was only a single Confederate brigade holding the heights. By the time he moved against Marye's Heights, Early was back in position. Hooker would get little help from that quarter.

The fighting that occurred on Sunday 3 May proved among the worst killing days of the Civil War, ranking with Antietam and Fredericksburg. For ferocity of fighting, it may have been the worst day of the Civil War, for the battle was largely over by early afternoon, while the other two battles lasted all day. The day also marked Jeb Stuart's greatest hour. As a result of the previous evening's fighting, a dangerously thin salient poked out of Hooker's lines, a salient largely held by Sickles's III Corps to the west and Slocum's XII Corps on the east with a portion of Couch's II Corps at the eastern base. Here Hooker's decision to remove Hunt as commander of the army's artillery exacted a heavy price, because, while Union artillery was superior in every category, it fought in a disjointed fashion throughout the day without the centralized control that would have allowed Union guns to focus on the Confederate artillery. Moreover, even before the fighting started, Hooker abandoned the crucial high ground at the salient's tip, called Hazel Grove. In Confederate hands, it allowed Lee's gunners to enfilade Union positions.

Lee's orders to Stuart were straightforward: attack to your front and drive "those people" (Lee's characterization of Federals) off the ground. Stuart launched his attack with his forces echeloned to hit the west side of the salient. Almost immediately Union gunners at the center of the salient were in trouble from converging fire. Had Hunt been in command, given his expertise and ability to concentrate artillery, he would have dueled with the Confederate batteries and eventually silenced them. But he was not on the scene, and local Union battery commanders, responding to individual brigade, division, and corps commanders, focused on the infantry battle. What is most remarkable about the fighting is that Hooker fought the battle with the three corps in the salient, while Meade's V Corps, backed by Reynolds's I

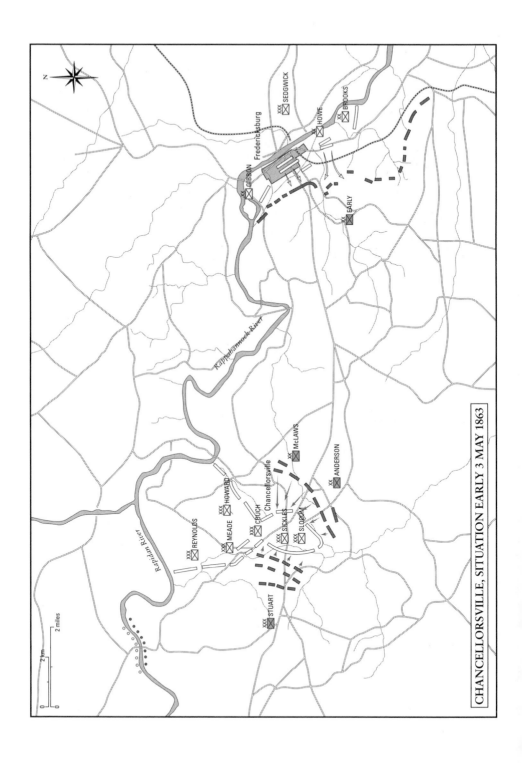

CHANCELLORSVILLE, SITUATION EARLY 3 MAY 1863

Corps, was immediately available to the north. The Federals success-fully halted and then drove back the initial Confederate attack. Never-theless, the salient slowly constricted as Stuart threw everything he had into breaking the Union lines. The casualties were frightful. Typi-cal of Confederate losses was the fate of Brigadier General Stephen Ramseur's brigade, which lost 788 out of 1,509 soldiers.

In the midst of the fighting, a Confederate cannon ball hit a post on the porch of the Chancellor house against which Hooker was leaning. Concussed and badly bruised from his fall off the porch, Hooker was knocked out for nearly half an hour and for the remainder of the battle failed to recover his equilibrium. For a short period, Darius Couch, as senior officer, assumed command, but felt constrained by what he regarded as Hooker's intentions. Shortly thereafter Meade arrived at the army's headquarters to urge that his fresh corps attack Stuart's flank. Here Lincoln's words, urging Hooker and Couch, to "put in all of your men," still haunts the historian. In every sense Meade was in a position to do to Stuart what Jackson had done to Howard the day before. Had Hooker accepted Meade's proposal, Stuart and the whole Confederate position on Lee's left flank would have been in desper-ate straits. If he had then thrown in Reynolds's corps, history might well have recorded Hooker's victory at Chancellorsville. In Hooker's concussed situation, he turned the Pennsylvanian down. Instead, he ordered Couch to pull the three corps out of the salient, while under heavy fire. In desperate straits the Union troops accomplished that dif-ficult maneuver. The Army of the Potomac now retreated into a well-protected and fortified position, hoping that Sedgwick had achieved something. The casualties suggest the ferocity of the morning's fight: Confederates 8,962 killed, wounded, or missing; Union 8,623—over 17,500 casualties in a little over six hours of fighting.

While this murderous fighting was going on over the morning of the 3rd, Sedgwick's VI Corps prepared with exquisite slowness to storm Marye's Heights. With Early back on the heights, it appeared as if Union troops were again to suffer heavy casualties on the killing ground of December's slaughter. In fact, Union casualties would prove heavy, but not nearly as heavy as they might have been had Early de-ployed his troops effectively. As Union troops took the heights, Early pulled back, while Sedgwick leisurely advanced toward Lee's rear. In another of those incidents that typified the incapacity of Army of the Potomac commanders to display initiative, Brigadier General John

Gibbon, with a detached division of the I Corps and not under Sedgwick's command, followed his orders and occupied Fredericksburg and its bridges, while the VI Corps meandered off to the northwest. Neither commander provided troops to garrison Marye's Heights, which the Confederate promptly reoccupied.

For Lee the next two days were frustrating. For once his subordinate commanders failed to move with dispatch, a reflection perhaps of the stress they and their troops had been under over the previous two days. On the 4th, with Hooker driven back into a bend in the Rapidan, Lee moved against Sedgwick to destroy the VI Corps. The result was some sharp fighting, but for once the Confederates failed to "put in all of your men." By the end of the day Sedgwick's troops had given the Confederates a bloody nose; to Lee's immense frustration, Sedgwick, having pulled his corps back into a hedgehog position with the Rappahannock to its rear, retreated across Bank's Ford to the north side of the river and out of danger.

Frustrated in his attempt to destroy Sedgwick, Lee turned back against Hooker and the Army of the Potomac. At this point one is struck by the similarities between Chancellorsville and Gettysburg, especially when one considers what might have happened on 5 May. On the night of 4/5 May, Hooker conferred with his corps commanders. By a vote of three to two they had elected to remain on the south side of the Rappahannock and Rapidan and fight it out with the Confederates. But Hooker had made up his mind in spite of the vote and the fact that his army held a strongly fortified position with its artillery skillfully deployed now that Hunt was back in charge. In fact, the ground held by the Union troops on 4/5 May still displays the outline of the major earthworks after more than 150 years. Nevertheless, Hooker ordered preparations to withdraw across the Rapidan and Rappahannock on the next night. The Union commander had lost the battle in his mind.

While Hooker's corps commanders were preparing to withdraw, Lee was hurrying his troops back to launch a major attack. To Lee's fury, nothing seemed to work quite right. To add to his difficulties a major spring storm pelted the armies. In the end the Confederates had to postpone the attack until the morning of 6 May, by which time Hooker had slipped back across the Rapidan and then the Rappahannock. Thus, on the morning of 6 May Lee found no one to attack. Had Hooker not retreated but remained in his defensive position, with two

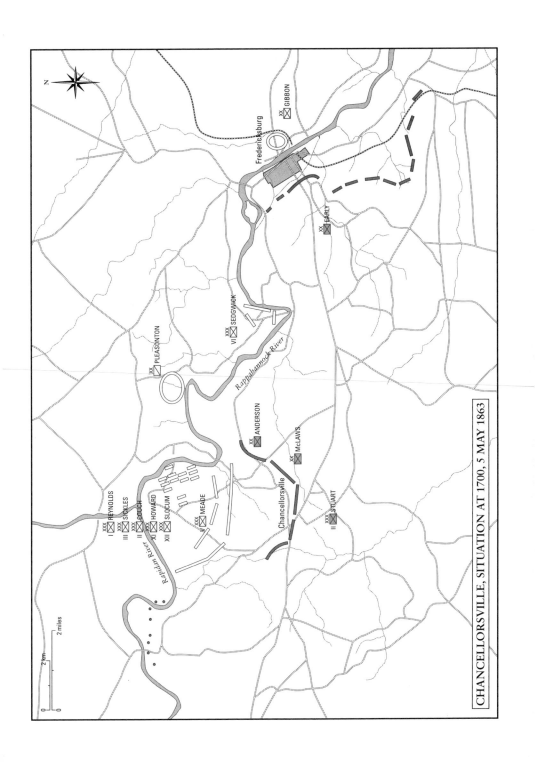

CHANCELLORSVILLE, SITUATION AT 1700, 5 MAY 1863

of his best corps (Reynolds and Meade) untouched by the fighting thus far, Lee might well have suffered an even more disastrous defeat than Pickett's charge at Gettysburg. Certainly that was how Porter Alexander felt in his memoirs written after the war.

Who won Chancellorsville? The obvious answer is Lee and the Confederates. Certainly, in considering the slashing attacks he, Jackson, and Stuart had launched against a superior enemy, who had in the first hours of the battle caught them completely by surprise, their performance stands as one of the great pieces of generalship of the Civil War. Yet, the casualty figures on the two sides were nearly equal: a bill the Union with its superior population could afford to pay, but which the Confederacy in the long term could not. Moreover, throughout the battle, Lee had taken chances that had placed his army on the brink of defeat. Perhaps the battle's most significant result was that Lee gained the impression his troops could achieve anything against impossible odds, an estimation that had a disastrous impact on his conduct of the battle the next July at Gettysburg.

The question, as quiet returned to central Virginia, was what alternatives were open to the Army of Northern Virginia, soon to be augmented by Longstreet's return. It was in these days that the Confederate government and its most successful general laid out the future course of the war in both the East and the West. By so doing they ended whatever chances still remained for the Confederacy to win its independence, assuming of course that competent Federal generalship would finally appear in Virginia. Shortly after Chancellorsville, Longstreet, passing through Richmond to rejoin Lee, had an extensive conversation with James Seddon, the Confederacy's secretary of war. While the situation in the West had yet to collapse, Lee's chief lieutenant urged that in view of Chancellorsville the Confederate high command transfer his two divisions along with other reinforcements to restore the strategic situation in Tennessee.

Both Davis and Seddon were sympathetic to Longstreet, and on 16 May they met with Lee. Unbeknownst to the participants, at the time they were meeting, Grant's army was thrashing Pemberton at the Battle of Champion Hill in Mississippi. Perhaps only Lee himself might have saved the Confederacy from the looming disaster, but whatever the fears of his superiors about the strategic situation in the West, Lee had no interest in that theater. The Confederate president asked: Should the Army of Northern Virginia reinforce the West? Lee would have none of it. As he later put it, "I considered the problem in every possible phase, and to my mind, it resolved itself into a choice of one of two things: either to retire to Richmond and stand a siege, which must ultimately have ended in surrender, or to invade Pennsylvania."[10] Thus, Lee argued that the Army of Northern Virginia should invade Pennsylvania to win a battle that would crush Northern morale. Underlying Lee's conception were two dangerous assumptions: first, that Hooker could not concentrate his forces quickly enough against the invasion because of the need to protect Washington; and second, that the Union's soldiers were substantially inferior to those of the Confederacy. Two meetings of the Confederate cabinet then confirmed Lee's strategic analysis. So it was to be an invasion of the North in search of that elusive "decisive" victory.

Before the invasion began, Lee carried out a substantial reorganization of the Army of Northern Virginia, as a result of Jackson's death. Longstreet would lead the I Corps with his divisions commanded by Lafayette McLaws, George Pickett, and John Bell Hood; Richard Ewell would lead the II Corps with Jubal Early, Edward "Allegheny" Johnson, and Robert Rodes as division commanders; and A. P. Hill would lead the III Corps with Richard Anderson, Henry Heth, and Dorsey Pender as division commanders. Astonishingly, considering the defeat, Hooker made fewer changes in the Army of the Potomac. Couch asked to be relieved of command of his corps, given what he considered the general failure of Hooker's leadership. There was no alternative but to fire Stoneman after his appallingly bad leadership, but his replacement was Alfred Pleasonton, an officer of no particular attainment. John Buford, who would win fame at Gettysburg, would have been a superior choice, but Pleasonton had date of rank and in the Army of the Potomac that trumped competence. Astonishingly, Hooker did not fire Howard, who bore so much of the blame for the disaster on the army's right flank; the Army of the Potomac would pay a price for that decision at Gettysburg. Hancock now assumed command of Couch's II Corps, while Sykes replaced Meade in command of the V Corps, when Meade moved up to command of the Army of the Potomac at the end of June.

As Lee gathered his forces for the march north, Union cavalry caught Stuart's cavalry by surprise and initially drove them in disorder to the rear in a skirmish near Brandy Station; the Confederates quickly recovered and after a nasty fight pushed the Union cavalry back. In fact, the tally of Union losses was nearly double those of the Confederates (907 to 523), but the Richmond press was critical, including the *Daily Examiner*'s rebuke that Stuart's "much puffed cavalry of the army of Northern Virginia has been twice, if not three times, surprised since the battles of December, and such repeated accidents can be regarded as nothing but the necessary consequences of negligence and bad management."[11] While the skirmish disturbed Lee not in the least, it did upset Stuart. He persuaded Lee to allow him to attempt a repeat of the raid that had taken him around McClellan's forces the year before. His initial instructions were to shield the passes through the Blue Ridge Mountains to keep Union cavalry from spying out what was afoot on the western side of the mountains. Then, Lee allowed Stuart to undertake a raid behind the Army of the Potomac. But Lee was also explicit that Stuart was not to forego his primary mission to keep the Confederate high command informed of what Hooker was up to, as the main army moved north into Pennsylvania.

One-legged Ewell led the Confederate advance up the Shenandoah. Along the way, his corps scooped up Major General Robert Milroy's division at Winchester in a repeat of Stonewall Jackson's victory the year before. By 24 June Ewell's corps had marched deep into Pennsylvania. From the start Confederate commanders made clear this was more than an expedition to seek a decisive battle. It aimed to feed the Army of Northern Virginia and gather in the riches of Pennsylvania to support the Confederate war machine. Hagerstown, Chambersburg, Shippensburg, Cashtown, and York, all felt the extortionist threats of the invaders. Besides being a looting expedition, the invasion would also involve the rounding up of blacks to be driven south and sold into slavery in Richmond's slave exchange. In Chambersburg a woman solemnly recorded in her diary, "O! How it grated on our hearts to have to sit quietly & look at such brutal deeds . . . they [the local African Americans] were driven by just like we would drive cattle."[12] But while the Confederates ate off the fat of southern Pennsylvania, Lee remained blind; his best guess was that the Army of the Potomac was far behind, struggling to reach Maryland.

He was wrong. In fact, after initial fumbling and talk of moving south against Richmond in response to the Confederate invasion, Hooker had quickly moved his army between Lee and Washington, while at the same time preparing to engage the Army of Northern Virginia in Pennsylvania or Maryland. Starting late, the Army of the

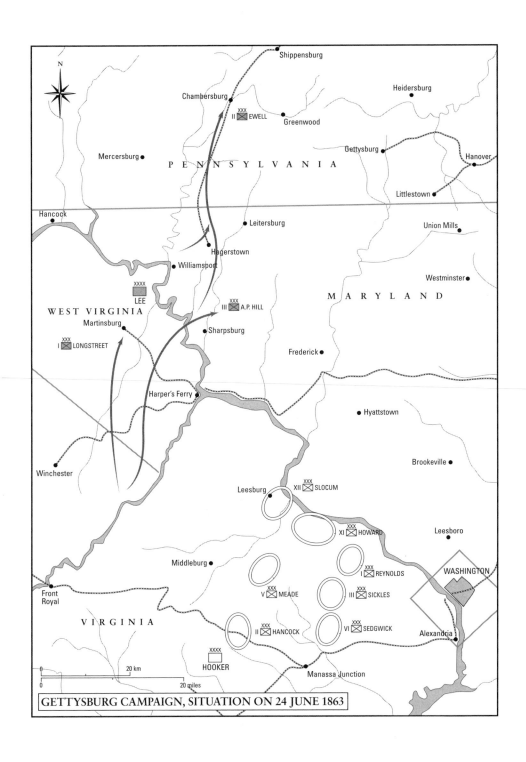

GETTYSBURG CAMPAIGN, SITUATION ON 24 JUNE 1863

Potomac marched rapidly for once in its history as if the war's outcome depended on it. In stifling heat and dust it beat a rapid trail through Virginia to Maryland and on toward Pennsylvania. But Hooker's days as commander of the Army of the Potomac were numbered. Not only had Lincoln lost confidence in the general, but Halleck, as usual placing his personal interests and dislikes above the nation's needs, was undermining Hooker's ability to respond to the invasion. The quarrel between the generals boiled over with Halleck's refusal to release troops from Washington's defense to reinforce the Army of the Potomac as it swung north into Maryland. Moreover, he also refused to put the 10,000 troops guarding Harper's Ferry under Hooker, but left them in as exposed a position as had occurred in September 1862.

The upshot was that Hooker sent his resignation to Halleck, who delightedly sent it on to the president. In the midst of the crisis, Lincoln had enough of quarreling generals, accepted the resignation, and promoted Meade to command the army. Meade was one of its competent and aggressive corps commanders, and so he, once described by one of his soldiers as "a damned old goggle-eye snapping turtle," assumed command of the Army of the Potomac on 28 June.[13] His task: to thwart Lee's invasion of Pennsylvania before it inflicted substantial political damage on the Union's cause.

Without Stuart and his cavalry, Lee remained in the dark as to the approach of Union forces until the night of 28/29 June, when a spy, sent out by Longstreet two weeks earlier, returned with the news that not only were two corps of the Army of the Potomac at Frederick, but also others were poised to cross South Mountain, which would put Union troops astride Lee's line of retreat. While Hill and Longstreet were in the immediate area, Ewell's corps was thirty miles away, threatening Harrisburg, and Early's division was all the way over at York, harassing its staid burgers. Lee immediately dispatched hurried orders for Ewell to pull back and concentrate with the rest of the army, preferably at Cashtown. Lee also warned his subordinate commanders that he did not want them to bring on a major engagement until he was sure of the situation.

Thus, the armies groped toward Gettysburg, where no less than ten roads converged from all points of the compass. Meade had determined to defend what appeared to be an ideal position at Pipe Creek, where his engineers began laying out proposed positions. But he also threw out a cavalry screen and sent Reynolds, his fellow Pennsylvanian, trundling up the roads leading toward Gettysburg with the I Corps, reinforced by Howard's XI, and Sickles's III Corps. By 30 June Union cavalry, under the tough, Indian fighter John Buford, had reached Gettysburg, ready to fight a holding action, should Reynolds deem it necessary. One of Buford's brigade commanders commented that his men could hold the rebels for twenty-four hours. Ever realistic, Buford acidly replied: "No you won't; they will attack you in the morning, and will come booming—skirmishers three deep. You will have to fight like the devil to hold your own until supports arrive. The enemy must know the importance of this position, and will strain every nerve to secure it; and if we are able to hold it, we will do well."[14]

Late on the afternoon of 30 June, Heth sent one of his brigade commanders, Johnston Pettigrew, down the road to Gettysburg from Chambersburg to seize a store of shoes that Early had overlooked on his way to York. West of the town, the advance column ran into a screen of Buford's cavalrymen. Mindful of Lee's stricture not to bring on a general engagement, Pettigrew withdrew, only to meet with derision from Hill and Heth for supposedly mistaking Pennsylvania militia for Union cavalry. The following morning, Heth marched his division in column, confident he would not have to deploy into combat formation to brush the militia away. Instead he ran into Union cavalrymen putting down fearsome fire.

Heth had to deploy his division into combat formation, and while he did so, John Reynolds arrived to meet Buford at the Lutheran Seminary on Seminary Ridge. After a short conversation, the I Corps commander made a series of fateful decisions based on the fact that, like Buford, he believed Gettysburg offered excellent terrain to fight the Confederates. Messengers went out to Sickles and Howard with orders to move as rapidly as possible to support the I Corps; another went posthaste to Meade to inform him that Reynolds had recommended a stand well north of Pipe Creek. Most probably Buford and Reynolds agreed on a holding action on McPherson Ridge with their troops eventually falling back to the more defensible positions on Seminary Ridge, which had the additional advantage of requiring fewer troops to defend.

At the crucial moment when Heth's superior numbers were beginning to overwhelm Buford's cavalrymen, the lead elements of the I Corps arrived. As Reynolds moved forward to guide the deployment of two brigades of James Wadsworth's division into line to bolster

Buford's troopers, a Confederate sharpshooter hit the general in the back of the head. General Abner Doubleday, who, as a captain at Fort Sumter, had fired the first Union reply to the Confederate bombardment in April 1861, assumed temporary command of I Corps. The arrival of Union infantry in substantial numbers turned what had been a large skirmish into a full-scale battle. Heth's right-hand brigade ran into the Iron Brigade of Westerners, the 1ˢᵗ Brigade of the 1ˢᵗ Division of the I Corps, and received a thorough trouncing that included the capture of its commander, James Archer. Heth's other brigade under Jefferson Davis's nephew enjoyed greater initial success because it was farther removed from arriving I Corps infantry. But its attack soon collapsed, when a portion of the advancing Confederates moved into the unfinished railroad cut to the west of town and found themselves looking up at the barrels of Union soldiers, who could have been shooting fish in a barrel so superior was their position. Many surrendered, a few escaped. The survivors fell back, and Davis found himself with barely half the effectives with whom he had started the battle. The initial fighting had nearly wrecked Heth's division.

Doubleday hustled up the other two divisions of the I Corps, and for the moment the Union position appeared secure. Shortly afterward, however, Howard arrived with his XI Corps. As the senior officer present, he assumed command and ordered his corps to deploy to the right of the I Corps, which swung the Union position north to guard the approaches to Gettysburg from that direction. It was noon as the XI Corps's lead division moved into position. Howard also detached one of his divisions to hold Cemetery Ridge on the south side of the town. Nevertheless, while he was supposedly in command, he exercised that duty only in a negative fashion. While Doubleday commanded I Corps with competence throughout the afternoon, he received little support from Howard. Moreover, when Doubleday suggested that his I Corps pull back from McPherson's Ridge to the more defensible Seminary Ridge, Howard turned him down cold. Eventually the I Corps did manage to pull back to Seminary Ridge, but under great pressure and only when it was too late. After the battle, Howard would blame much of the day's failure on Doubleday, when in fact the Union collapse was largely Howard's fault.

Nothing better underlines the differences in the command culture of the opposing armies than the actions of two corps commanders on the opposing sides and their impact—or lack of impact—on the course of the battle. The lead units of Slocum's XII Corps began arriving at Two Taverns along with their general at noon. Two Taverns was *five miles* from Gettysburg. Almost immediately, officers and men heard the heavy rumble of cannon and musket firing indicating a major battle was occurring near Gettysburg. Queried by his staff as to whether the corps should not march to the sound of guns as well as the clouds of smoke on the western horizon, Slocum replied in the negative: his orders required him to go to Two Taverns and indicated nothing else. A messenger from Howard moved him not at all, nor did further reports of the fighting. Charles Howard, the general's brother and staff officer, dispatched to seek Slocum's aid at 1600, as the Union position at Gettysburg was falling apart, reported that the general "in fact refused to come up in person saying he would not assume responsibility of that day's fighting and of the two corps."[15] The explanation for his refusal most probably lies in Slocum's recognition, since the message came from Howard, that Reynolds was down and that, were he to arrive at Gettysburg, he would be the senior officer and responsible for conducting the battle until Meade arrived. Not until late afternoon did Slocum finally order his lead division to march to Gettysburg, while he himself did not arrive until the evening hours. As Howard's brother put the matter: "Slow *Come*, he would not assume the responsibility of *that* day's fighting & of the two corps."[16]

In direct contravention of Slocum's lack of initiative, Ewell and his division commanders, moving from York and south of Harrisburg to concentrate with the remainder of Lee's army near Cashtown, heard the firing from Gettysburg and immediately marched to the sound of guns. The first of Ewell's divisions to arrive was that of Major General Robert Rodes, new to command. Without executing a proper reconnaissance, Rodes launched his brigades independently in an attack from Oak Hill down the Mummasburg Road into what he thought was an open Union flank. In fact, there was a relatively strong Union position along a stone wall directly to his front. Edward O'Neal's brigade on the Confederate left was routed first, while the second, Alfred Iverson's, consisting almost entirely of North Carolinians, was caught while moving past Union troops on their flank. They were slaughtered. One bittersweet story to come out of the battle was that of "Sallie," a bull terrier, and mascot of the 11th Pennsylvania on the I Corps flank, who, when separated from the retreating troops in the afternoon's collapse, returned to the scene and guarded the regiment's

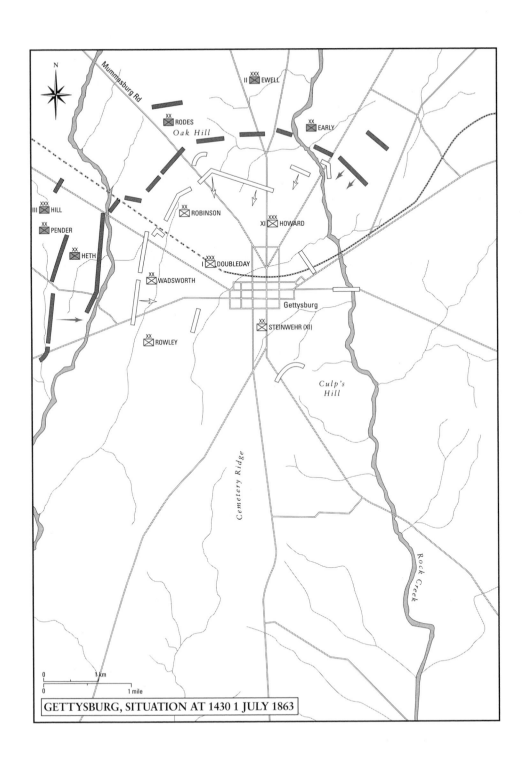

GETTYSBURG, SITUATION AT 1430 1 JULY 1863

dead and wounded until the Confederates withdrew. She was killed by a stray bullet in February 1865 at Hatcher's Run.

At 1430, Lee finally arrived; but this was largely a soldiers' battle, and control of its course remained in the hands of his subordinates. By this point, the arrival of the rest of Ewell's corps spelled the doom of the Union position. Heavily outnumbered, badly deployed with Francis Barlow's division well to the front of the remainder of the corps and with the Howard nowhere to be seen, the XI Corps gave a repeat of its Chancellorsville performance. Early's division smashed into the XI Corps front and soon enveloped its right flank. After some initial attempts to stand, it broke and ran. Its largely German contingent had been known for its slogan of "we fights mit Siegel (its first commander)." Wags in the Army of the Potomac now quipped, "We runs mit Howard." As the XI Corps fell apart, its troops were soon joined by the veterans of the I Corps, who were now under great pressure on their right by a portion of Rodes's division and from their front by Pender and what was left of Heth's division. Exacerbating the disaster was the fact that the number of roads running through Gettysburg created considerable confusion for Union troops desperately attempting to reach Cemetery Ridge.

For Lee, the opportunity to finish the destruction of the two routed Union corps beckoned. But Hill's corps was in bad shape: the fighting thus far had wrecked Heth's division, while it had mauled Pender's. Ewell's corps was in better shape, but deployed directly to the front of Union positions on Cemetery Ridge, which the division that Howard had detached had already turned into a formidable defensive position. Lee's instructions were anything but clear and left considerable latitude to Ewell. He was "to carry the hill occupied by the enemy, if he found it practicable, but to avoid a general engagement until the arrival of the other divisions of the army [i.e., Longstreet], which were ordered to hasten forward."[17] But one of Ewell's divisions was still well to the rear, and he hesitated to attack. Longstreet, who had just arrived, urged an immediate attack, as Union reinforcements were arriving in strength. But Lee refused to order an attack until Ewell was ready.

Longstreet and Lee held a long conversation after Longstreet's arrival. For Longstreet the whole purpose of the campaign had been to seek an excellent defensive position in a strategic location that would force the Army of the Potomac to attack. When he broached the issue, Lee was as usual decisive: "No, the enemy is there and I am going to attack him there." Longstreet was nothing if not persistent. He suggested that the Union troops were there because they wanted the Confederates to attack. Lee was not persuaded: "They are there in position, and I am going to whip them."[18] At that point, Longstreet, seeing Lee's blood was up, rode west to move his divisions along the road from Cashtown.

Meanwhile, Union commanders were also deciding on their strategy. When news arrived at Meade's headquarters in early afternoon that Reynolds was down—from a *New York Times* reporter—the new commander of the Army of the Potomac ordered Hancock to turn over command of the II Corps to one of his division commanders and ride hard for Gettysburg to replace Reynolds as commander of the army's lead units. Immediately on arrival, Hancock found his authority disputed by Howard, who cited his seniority. Hancock, who possessed great bravery as well as common sense, refused to indulge in an unseemly argument, given the circumstances. He simply remarked, "I think this the strongest position by nature upon which to fight a battle that I ever saw, and if it meets your approbation I will select this as the battle-field."[19] The line Hancock laid out extended in a *V* shape based on Culp's Hill and the northern portion of Cemetery Ridge. The fishhook would emerge on the next day as the Union troops filled in the gap and extended the line down Cemetery Ridge to Little Round Top. Howard agreed, and that settled matters, at least as far as the Union was concerned. His mission complete, Hancock returned to Meade.

The fighting was now over as evening descended, seemingly a Confederate victory. Nevertheless, the casualty figures suggest the level of fighting as well as the reality that it was a Pyrrhic victory: approximately 9,000 Union casualties (well over a third of them prisoners), and 8,000 Confederates. Over the course of the evening, Union forces flooded in. Sickles and his III Corps began arriving at 1800. Slocum's XII finally began arriving later that evening. As the senior officer in terms of date of rank, he commanded the forces gathering at Gettysburg until Meade arrived after midnight. After a brief survey of the line, the new commander of the Army of the Potomac confirmed Hancock's decision to stand on the fishhook. By late morning only the VI Corps had yet to come up, but Sedgwick was on the march. At least when he received a direct order, Sedgwick could move with dispatch. Those morning hours provided Meade's troops with the time they needed to prepare their defenses.

In parts of the Union line more substantial work was afoot than in others. What one sees at Gettysburg, as at Chancellorsville, was a transition from the open order of simply awaiting an enemy attack that characterized the fighting in 1862 to the rapid establishment of major defensive works at every opportunity that would occur in the 1864 campaigns. Nothing characterizes this transition more clearly than the work undertaken by Brigadier General George S. Greene's brigade of New York volunteers. Nicknamed "old man Greene" by his soldiers, he was sixty-two and a West Point graduate and had left the army to work as a civil engineer on major projects such as the Central Park reservoir. On the outbreak of the war he had volunteered his service. As we have seen, he had performed in outstanding fashion at Antietam. Now on Culp's Hill, Greene drove his soldiers over the night and morning hours of 1/2 July to dig trenches and build rock embankments as well as a traverse to cover his flank despite the taunts of his division commander, Major General John Geary and, not surprisingly, his corps commander Slocum.

On the Confederate side, Lee had already resolved the question of whether to attempt to maneuver around Meade or stay and fight it out at Gettysburg. In the morning Longstreet again attempted to persuade Lee to change his mind, but to no avail. Lee's initial conception for the second day was a two-pronged attack: Ewell would strike the Union positions at the apex of the fishhook, while the main blow would hit the Army of the Potomac's southern flank. However, in the early morning hours, the conception unraveled. Ewell disliked the looks of Union defenses on his front, defenses strengthened and reinforced during the night. He suggested to Lee that the proper approach would be an envelopment of the southern end of the Union line. However, it was clear that to move Ewell's corps across the Union front would only suggest what was coming. In the center, Hill's corps, immediately to the west of Ewell, had been badly shot up the day before and was incapable of executing a major attack.

Thus, it would have to be Longstreet, but Evander Law's brigade was still far back on the road from Cashtown and had to make an exceedingly long march to reach the far right flank of what would be a massive assault on the southern end of the Union fishhook. Lee then decided that Ewell would make a supporting attack on the Union forces on Culp's Hill, as soon as he heard Longstreet's attack go in, to prevent Meade from shifting troops to meet Longstreet's blow. Almost immediately the frictions of war intervened. Early in the morning Lee sent out one of his staff engineers, a certain Captain S. R. Johnston, to scout the way for the deployment of Longstreet's corps and determine how far south the Union defenses extended. It is difficult to reconstruct what Johnston did during his reconnaissance, because under close questioning by Lee on the captain's return, he reported there were no Federal troops on the southern portion of Cemetery Ridge, nor were there any Union troops on either Little Round Top or Big Round Top. In fact, the whole area was swarming with Union infantry and artillery except on the Round Tops, but there were obviously Union signalers on the smaller hill. On that false intelligence, Lee ordered Longstreet's corps to drive up the Emmitsburg Road and roll up the Union flank. Johnston's after-the-fact excuse, as recorded by R. Lindsay Walker, for his lackadaisical reconnaissance was more typical of the Army of the Potomac than his own army: "he 'had no idea that I (he) [Johnston] had the confidence of the great Lee to such an extent that he would entrust me with the conduct of an army corps moving within two miles of the enemy's line."[20]

Needless to say, Longstreet was not happy with Lee's decision, while Longstreet's failure to begin his deployment for two hours made Lee even unhappier. Lee did agree to allow a further delay to allow the arrival of Law's brigade, which completed its twenty-four-mile march in nine hours and finally arrived at noon. Confederate troubles were, however, not over; the initial route plotted out by Captain Johnston would have taken the troops onto ground visible to Union troops, so the whole column had to backtrack, nearly doubling the distance that Hood's division had to cover. Longstreet's troops would not be in position to launch their attack until late afternoon, well past the time Lee had wished.

On the Union side, Sickles decided the III Corps' position along the Union line running south from Cemetery Hill was not nearly as defensible as it would be if he moved his troops out approximately half a mile to the Peach Orchard on his front and swung it back to a rocky outcropping below Little Round Top. Sickles attempted to get permission from Meade for such a move, who sent the artillery master Hunt to check the ground. Hunt pointed out to Sickles that the move, while it might have some advantages, would spread the III Corps too thinly and thus make its task more difficult. Nevertheless, with no definitive orders from Meade, Sickles took matters into his

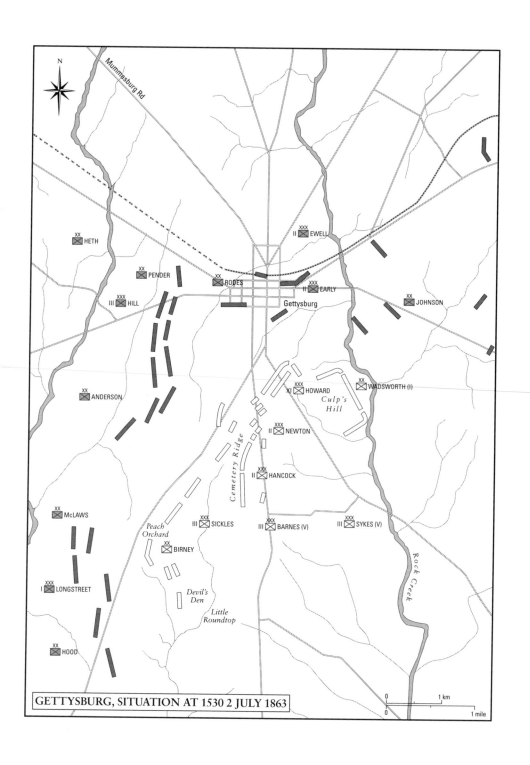

GETTYSBURG, SITUATION AT 1530 2 JULY 1863

own hands, as he had not done at Chancellorsville, and ordered his corps to advance. Watching them move out, Hancock sardonically remarked: "Wait a moment, you will soon see them tumbling back."[21]

As the Confederates massed on the Union left, Hood, the southernmost division commander, urged Longstreet to allow him to move deeper into the Union rear. Longstreet replied that Lee's orders were orders, and Hood was to advance as instructed. At 1600 Hood's division advanced; McLaws's would follow at 1700 and Anderson's at 1800. Ewell would not begin his attack on Culp's Hill with Johnson's division until 1900, while Early would finish off the day with an attack on Howard's XI Corps on Cemetery Ridge. The one advantage that Sickles's advance possessed was that it broke up the coherence of the Confederate attack on the southern portion of the Union line. The artillery battery located on the top of Devil's Den immediately began firing as Hood's troops swept into the open. The ground over which that advance took place has recently been cleared by the National Park Service, and the distance to that point makes clear that it was indeed a lucky shot that hit Hood in the arm and took him off the battlefield. But then as Clausewitz notes, no other human activity is as much subject to vagaries of chance. Hood's wounding threw his division's attack into considerable confusion.

Because of the weakness of the command and control system in Civil War armies, Hood's successor, Law, provided no clear guidance to the division's fight. Most of the division became involved in the fierce fight around Devil's Den, while William Oates and the 15th Alabama clambered up Big Round Top, which was covered entirely with trees. They then moved down into the valley between the two hills only to be greeted by a furious volley as they attempted to move up and seize Little Round Top. Those Federal troops arrived providentially due to the individual initiative of a relatively junior officer. The army's chief engineer, Gouverneur K. Warren, had recognized the vulnerability of the Union position, should the Confederates gain possession of Little Round Top. Galloping to find troops to hold that position, he had run across Colonel Strong Vincent's brigade of Sykes's V Corps moving to bolster the III Corps. Vincent responded by moving his brigade up Little Round Top to hold the hill's left side. Warren continued on his search; he was able to spur two guns and Stephen Weed's brigade of another division of the V Corps to move on the double quick to reinforce Union troops on Little Round Top. Whatever his later failings as a corps commander, Warren showed his considerable worth as a staff officer.

Arriving fifteen minutes before the Confederate attack boiled down Big Round Top and through Devil's Den, Vincent's brigade held long enough for Weed's brigade, the lead regiment led by Colonel Patrick O'Rorke, to hold the right side of the position. On Vincent's left, former Bowdoin College professor Joshua Chamberlain commanded the 20th Maine. Chamberlain is a particularly interesting case of what one might term a natural soldier; by this point in the war he had been in the army for less than eleven months and in command of the regiment for barely a month (appointed to command on 20 May 1863). In the desperate fight on the left flank of the Union line, the soldiers of the 20th Maine were about to run out of ammunition; at that point, Chamberlain ordered them to fix bayonets and charge. The Confederates, exhausted by their lengthy march and climb up Big Round Top in 82-degree weather, and the fierce fighting that followed their descent, broke and ran. Nevertheless, whatever the courage of Chamberlain's men, it was only one action in the defense of Little Round Top that saw Vincent, Weed, and O'Rorke' killed. But the line held, and the Confederates failed to envelop the fishhook.

At 1700 Longstreet launched McLaws's division at the apex of Sickles's salient. For the next hour the fighting wavered back and forth, as Meade rushed reinforcements to hold the exposed positions. Most of Sykes's V Corps was drawn into the vicious fighting centering on the Peach Orchard (recently replanted by the National Park Service) and the wheat field. Sickles went down from a shell that took off most of his leg below the knee; the New York politician, eager as always to embellish his reputation, left the battlefield on a stretcher smoking a cigar so his men would know he was still breathing. After his leg was amputated, he kept the bones on his mantle in Brooklyn. By the time its line collapsed, the III Corps had suffered approximately 4,000 casualties, but with the help of reinforcements had ground Longstreet's attack to a halt.

At 1800 Anderson's division of Hill's corps, temporarily assigned to Longstreet, although neither Hill, nor Longstreet, nor Anderson was sure exactly who controlled the division, went in. The ferocity of the Confederate attack, along with the fact that Meade had sent in most of his available troops as reinforcements to the desperate fight swirling around the III Corps, came close to rupturing the center of the Union line. Hancock, now in charge of the III Corps as well as his own, hurried one of his divisions and an additional brigade south from their emplacements on the northern side of the fishhook to reinforce the line. To his horror he saw a portion of Anderson's division break out into the open. To buy time, Hancock sent the 1st Minnesota into the fray with a suicidal charge that halted the Confederate advance for a few minutes. It was enough. Reinforcements from the II Corps arrived in time to stop the Confederate drive. Ambrose Wright's brigade of Anderson's division had a brief glimpse of the Union rear before Union reinforcements overwhelmed it.

One more fierce fight took place as twilight descended on the broken, bloodied landscape. As was usual with Lee, his orders to Ewell left his subordinate with considerable latitude. When Longstreet's attack went in, Ewell was to launch a powerful demonstration to keep Union forces on Cemetery Ridge and Culp's Hill in place, while if there were prospects for success, he was to launch a full-scale attack. Ewell's demonstration involved moving the artillery from Johnson's division out into the open, where Union guns overwhelmed them. Nevertheless, with the time now approaching 1900 Ewell decided to launch Johnson's division against Culp's Hill. Unbeknownst to him, Slocum, having played a major role in the disaster the day before by not showing up, had decided to display initiative by removing his whole corps to reinforce the Union center, when Meade had asked for only one division. That decision almost lost Culp's Hill. But Slocum did leave Greene's brigade behind in the fortifications the corps commander had ridiculed in the morning. In fierce fighting, Greene's single brigade on the right side of Culp's Hill held its positions against much of Johnson's full division, while Wadsworth's division of the I Corps, badly battered the day before, held the left side. Ewell launched his final attack at 2000 with two brigades of Early's division. The attack came close to driving Howard's XI Corps, once again distinguishing itself for its lack of staying power, off Cemetery Hill, but it was already after dark, and Union reinforcements, flowing back to the northern part of the fishhook, restored the situation.

What had the second day at Gettysburg accomplished? In a tactical sense not much. Meade still held the fishhook; Lee still held the initiative. Once again Union cavalry had done little to screen Meade's forces or alert him to the Confederate move to his left. Needless to say, Stuart's absence—he would not arrive near the battlefield until

1800 that day—had led the Confederates into a number of faulty assumptions. In the end, the second day at Gettysburg had become a terrible encounter battle, where more often than not the troops ran into each other and even when on the defensive fought without cover. Only Anderson's attack had come close to success. On the other side, the Union commanders had displayed considerable initiative; unfortunately, the initiative of Sickles and Slocum had come close to costing Meade the battle. However, at a lower level, the actions of Warren, Vincent, Weed, Chamberlain, Hancock, and Greene had remedied critical situations and turned the course of the battle.

Given the closeness of the fighting on 2 July, Meade was unsure whether he should stand or retreat to Pipe Creek. As Hooker had done at Chancellorsville, he convened a midnight meeting of senior generals. Unanimously they voted to stay, and unlike his predecessor, Meade accepted the result. As the meeting broke up, Meade turned to Gibbon, one of Hancock's division commanders, who held a substantial portion of the center of the Union line, and commented: "If Lee attacks tomorrow, it will be *in your front*." Gibbon confidently replied that he hoped the Confederates would and that "we would defeat [them]."[22]

With the failure of the second day's attack, the choice confronting Lee was whether or not to continue the battle or withdraw, the latter choice an admission of defeat. By now the fighting had savaged every major unit in his army except for Pickett's division. Not surprisingly Longstreet was in favor of maneuvering around Meade to move between the Army of the Potomac and Washington. But the allure of decisive victory, along with the belief that his soldiers could accomplish anything, led Lee to try one more throw of the iron dice. His plan involved three attempts to break the Union line. Johnson's division of Ewell's corps still held portions of the trenches on Culp's Hill, and he was to launch his attack at the same time that the main attack went in. The main attack would come against the Union center with Pickett's division. At the same time, Stuart, who had finally arrived, was to sweep around the Army of the Potomac and drive into its rear to create maximum confusion.

But none of the supporting attacks worked out. Even before dawn's first light, Slocum's corps, returned to its positions on Culp's Hill, had opened up an artillery bombardment on Johnson's position. For nearly five hours, fighting continued until the Confederates, at a huge disadvantage on the lower slopes of the hill, finally broke off the engagement and retreated. The cavalry fight went equally badly for the Confederates. Stuart's ill-conceived raid had exhausted his troopers. However, he still possessed superiority in numbers, because Pleasonton, who had contributed nothing to providing Meade with information, had deployed a substantial portion of his command to tasks other than protecting the Union rear. However, a furious charge by Custer's brigade, consisting entirely of Michigan regiments, brought Stuart's attack to a halt, while Union carbines dominated the small arms fight. Pickett would receive no help from this quarter either.

In the morning the Confederates began massing their artillery facing the Union line on Cemetery Ridge. Having tried both Union flanks, Lee decided he would now smash the Union center. Pickett's division of Virginians would step off on the right with Pettigrew's (replacing Heth who had been wounded two days before) and Isaac Trimble's (Trimble replacing Pender also wounded the day before) divisions of Hill's corps on the left. While Pickett's division was fresh, Hill's selection of Pettigrew's division, badly shot up on the first day, as well as Alfred Scales's brigade, also in bad shape, made little sense. The 26th North Carolina, for example, had lost 624 of its 840 men on 1 July. The initial attacking force numbered approximately 13,000 troops with two brigades in support, some 1,600 additional soldiers. There were a further 3,350 soldiers of Anderson's division available for support, should matters go well.

The concentration of the Confederate artillery took virtually all morning. Unbeknownst to Confederate artillerymen, they would fight under a substantial disadvantage. A fire that spring had damaged the manufacturing center in Richmond that made the fuses for the Army of Northern Virginia; the fuses Lee's artillery now possessed had been manufactured in Charleston and were slower burning. Thus, most of the shrapnel shells fired on 3 July would sail over Union positions protecting Cemetery Ridge and explode harmlessly behind the lines. Moreover, once the Confederate infantry attack began, it would block much of their artillery support from participating in the fight for fear of hitting their own soldiers.

On the Union side, Hunt was also massing Union artillery with the aim of protecting the Union center against the attack which both he and Meade expected. Particularly dangerous for Confederate prospects was the fact that on lower Cemetery Ridge, Colonel Freeman

McGilvery possessed forty-one guns that were out of the Confederate line of sight and hence remained untouched during the upcoming bombardment. Moreover, they were ideally sited to blast Pickett's infantry during most of their advance. Altogether Hunt's batteries possessed 119 guns, and he was explicit that they should only minimally target Confederate artillery and focus on the attacking infantry. Meade's instincts prepared Union forces to meet the Confederate onslaught. Alexander Hays's and Gibbon's divisions of Hancock's II Corps held most of the threatened sector with support from I Corps troops, altogether approximately 8,000 men. Included in that total was what was left of the 1st Minnesota, the regiment sent to the center of the Union line to rest after its extraordinary performance the previous day. Union troops sheltered behind a stone wall that ran along the fish hook but had made few efforts to fortify their positions, a mistake they would not have made in 1864. Behind the Cemetery Ridge line, Meade had 13,000 troops in reserve to counterattack any breakthrough.

At 1307 the Confederate bombardment began. Almost immediately Hunt and Hancock got into a row, Hancock furious the guns in his sector were not firing in reply to the bombardment due to Hunt's plan to conserve long-range ammunition to hit the Confederate infantry when they stepped out. The II Corps guns then began replying, but when Hancock attempted to intimidate McGilvery into firing as well, the II Corps commander met an obdurate refusal. As a result, McGilvery's guns retained their long-range ammunition and remained undiscovered by their opponents. The bombardment, given the fuses and the inability to judge the distance, failed to achieve its purpose. While it was occurring Hays had his men round up abandoned muskets and load them; some of his soldiers had as many as four loaded muskets ready to fire at the Confederates. So ineffective was the bombardment that Gibbon and his aide moved out seventy-five yards in front of the division's position to watch the display. His aide later described the scene: "On either crest we could see the great flaky streams of fire, and they seemed numberless, of the opposing guns, and their white banks of swift, convolving smoke, but the sound of the discharges was drowned in the universal ocean of sound."[23]

Almost out of ammunition, Porter Alexander, commander of Longstreet's artillery, sent word to Pickett to begin the charge. Longstreet himself, fully conscious of what was about to ensue, gave his assent by his silence. The gray line of Confederate infantry swung out into the open, almost immediately to be greeted derisively by some portions of the Union troops shouting: "Fredericksburg! Fredericksburg." More deadly was the fact that Union artillery immediately began firing. From the summit of Little Round Top Battery D, 5th US artillery, opened fire, at first hitting Pickett's right obliquely and then as the advance continued with deadly enfilade fire. At the same time XI Corps' artillery extracted a measure of revenge by firing on the Confederates from the north. And almost immediately McGilvery's artillery began its deadly work. Only in the center were Hancock's guns silent, because they had used up their long-range ammunition and were now loaded up with canister prepared for the moment when the Confederates came within range. The toll on the attacking Confederate infantry was bad enough under long-range artillery fire, but matters became desperate when they approached the killing zone of Union infantry weapons and canister. Moreover, Pickett's division had to execute an oblique march to the left to close with Trimble and Pettigrew, which exposed his brigades to devastating enfilade fire from McGilvery's guns. On the far left, having suffered heavy losses on 1 July, John Brockenbrough's brigade collapsed.

The remainder of Pettigrew's and Trimble's force hardly crossed the Emmitsburg Road so deadly was the Union fire. Hays had packed his front line with all his troops, who, with the additional rifles they had stockpiled, poured a deadly fire into Confederate soldiers attempting to clamber over the stout fence that ran along the road. After the battle Union soldiers examined a board in a fence on the Emmitsburg Road, 16 feet long, 14 inches broad—it had been hit by no less than 836 musket balls. In addition, Hays ordered the commander of the 8th Ohio to advance his troops out on the flank, where in naval terms they crossed the Confederates *T* and poured a deadly fire into the enemy's flank. The same happened on the Union left, where Brigadier General George Stannard took his nine-month Vermont regiments, which had done nothing more so far in their service than guard duty in Washington, out on the Confederate right flank to add to the slaughter. The lead troops of Pickett's division, after terrible losses, eventually broke into the Union position in front of Alexander Webb's brigade, but they remained there either dead, wounded, or prisoners. Their only significant achievement was to wound Hancock, whose later wartime service would be hindered by the painful results. Finally, to no purpose, the brigades of Wilcox and David Lang moved up to support the

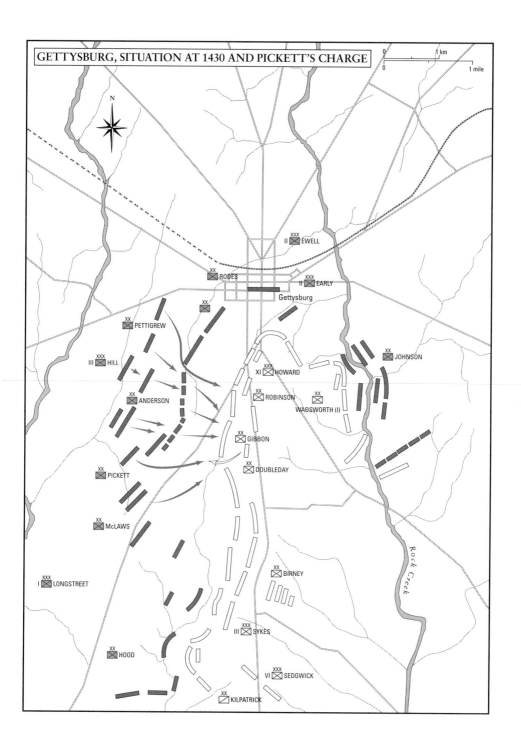

GETTYSBURG, SITUATION AT 1430 AND PICKETT'S CHARGE

N

0   1 km
0   1 mile

II XXX EWELL

XX RODES

II XXX EARLY

Gettysburg

XX PETTIGREW

XX

XI XXX HOWARD

XX JOHNSON

III XXX HILL

XXX ROBINSON

XX ANDERSON

XX WADSWORTH (I)

XX GIBBON

XX PICKETT

XX DOUBLEDAY

XX McLAWS

XX BIRNEY

I XXX LONGSTREET

III XXX SYKES

XX HOOD

VI XXX SEDGWICK

XX KILPATRICK

Rock Creek

attack, where the southern end of the Union line halted their attack before it began.

Thus ended the fighting portion of the Battle of Gettysburg. It was a crucial victory for the Union, especially coming as it did concurrently with the surrender of another Confederate army at Vicksburg on 4 July, the Vicksburg victory the direct result of Lee's and Davis's decision to invade the North rather than to shore up a deteriorating position in the Confederate West. The casualties on the opposing sides were almost even: 22,813 casualties (3,149 dead) for the Union; 22,625 casualties (4,536 dead) for the Confederates. The considerable difference in percentage terms of the dead on the opposing sides resulted from the large number of Union prisoners the Army of Northern Virginia had captured on the first day. The battle had been a soldier's battle; it was perhaps Lee's worst performance, while few of his subordinates had distinguished themselves.

Longstreet's strategic sense to avoid a battle had been correct, but the slowness of his preparations on the second day had robbed the Confederates of what little chance of victory they possessed. Ewell had struck brilliantly on the first day, but had done little thereafter, while the less said about Hill's decisions the better. Considering that he had just taken over command of the army, Meade's performance was competent, which was saying a great deal for the Army of the Potomac. And at least with Lee's help he had put in most of his men. The performance of his corps commanders had varied considerably from that of Slocum and Howard, appallingly bad, to Hancock, outstanding. But the loss of Reynolds and Hancock was one more sign of the bad luck that had plagued the Army of the Potomac throughout its history. Not surprisingly, neither Howard nor Slocum were removed for their failures.

For Lee there was now no choice but a dismal retreat, made more difficult and dangerous by the fact that Union raiders from Harper's Ferry had destroyed the Confederate pontoon bridge across the Potomac. Heavy rains then held up Lee's crossing until 13 July, when the Army of Northern Virginia reached its home ground. Meade's pursuit was not swift, but we can understand his caution. His army had been as badly battered as Lee's; he had lost two of his more reliable corps commanders; and Lee, as always, had taken precautions by building a fortified line to cover his army, while awaiting the floodwaters of the Potomac to recede.

For the next two months the war in the East settled down along the Rappahannock. While Lincoln and his cabinet were none too happy about the lack of activity, they could do little more than push Meade to take the offensive, given the general's popularity in the North. But in late August a deteriorating situation in the West as Rosecrans drove through central Tennessee toward Chattanooga forced Confederate leaders to reconsider their strategic situation. Not surprisingly, Lee once again urged another invasion of the North. This time Davis overruled him and ordered Longstreet with two divisions to reinforce Bragg's forces to hold the heart of the Confederacy. The victory at Chickamauga, the only major Confederate success in the West, was the direct result. That in turn led the Federal high command in Washington to detail two corps from the Army of the Potomac to reinforce Rosecrans's defeated army, now besieged in Chattanooga. Following the long military tradition of sending one's worst when tasked to transfer soldiers or units, the Army of the Potomac sent Howard's XI Corps and Slocum's XII Corps under Hooker to the West. The fact that these corps and their commanders would perform better in the Western fighting over the next two years suggests a great deal about the effectiveness of Confederate commanders in the West in comparison to the leaders of the Army of Northern Virginia.

There would be considerable maneuvering in the east, but no major battles for the remainder of the year. On 9 October Lee moved north around Meade's flank in the hope that he could achieve the kind of victory his troops had achieved the year before at Second Manassas. But Meade moved quickly, carefully retreating up the Orange & Alexandria rail line. At Bristoe Station, just short of Manassas, Hill's lead corps appeared to catch up with the Army of the Potomac's rear guard, which was crossing Broad Run. Hill immediately ordered Heth's division to attack the apparently vulnerable Union troops who remained on the south side of the stream. Heth had some fear his flank might be open to attack and suggested a reconnaissance. Hill would have none of it. In fact, standing to the side was the whole II Corps, now temporarily under Warren's command, which watched as Heth's division charged unsuspecting into the trap and then blasted the Confederates away. In barely half an hour Heth's division lost nearly 2,000 men killed, captured, or wounded; Warren 300 men. Lee's pointed reply to Hill's apology was, "Well, well, general, bury these poor men and let us say no more about it."[24] Unable to support his troops logistically so far north, Lee was back behind the Rappahannock by the beginning of the second week of November. The fighting would not resume until the next spring.

Conclusion

Lincoln's sense of the strategic and political realities of the war never deserted him. Nevertheless, like all individuals in positions of power, he did at times make mistakes. Not surprisingly, given the focus of Northern public opinion, he gave too much attention to the Eastern theater of operations. It was a matter of political pressure as well as Lincoln's geographic location in Washington. Exacerbating that tendency was the fact that he was simply not receiving coherent and intelligent operational and strategic advice from Halleck. Thus, the North's initial impetus to shut down the Confederacy's ports, which had paid such important dividends in 1862, foundered on the inability of the Navy and War Departments to work together as well as Halleck's obtuse theories of position warfare.

Moreover, as we shall see, by focusing on the East, Lincoln failed to recognize Grant's intuitive recognition that the capture of Vicksburg opened up the possibility not only of seizing Mobile but also of contributing indirectly to the advance on Chattanooga. In the East the Army of the Potomac and its commanders continued to be a disappointment. Hooker dismally failed the test of high command at Chancellorsville, while Meade proved unwilling to attack the Army of Northern Virginia once it was back in its lair south of the Potomac. However, his victory at Gettysburg had made him politically invulnerable. Ironically, Lincoln would get that aggressive leadership in the East that he had always desired in 1864, but the cost would come close to causing his defeat in the election.

CHAPTER 9

The War in the West, 1863

That quiet confidence in himself which never forsook him, and which amounted indeed almost to a feeling of fate, was uninterrupted. Having once determined in a matter that required irreversible decision, he never reversed . . . but was steadily loyal to himself and his plans. This absolute and implicit faith was, however, as far as possible from conceit or enthusiasm; it was simply a consciousness, or conviction, rather, which brought the very strength it believed in; which was itself strength, and which inspired others with a trust in him, because he was able thus to trust himself.

—Adam Badeau, *Military History of Ulysses S. Grant*

After Grant's successes at Donelson and Henry in early 1862, the Union war in the West had lost momentum. The death toll at Shiloh in April had shocked the nation, while Confederate counterattacks in summer and fall had reached deep into Kentucky before Union forces drove them back. Certainly the expectations of the North were less than satisfied. What the critics failed to recognize was that the distances in the theater posed logistic difficulties that were more complex and difficult than those Napoleon had confronted in 1812. Only the products of the steam engine, the railroad, and the steamboat would allow Northern armies eventually to overcome the tyranny of distance, and it took the North nearly two years to build the logistical infrastructure to project its military power over the Confederacy's continental distances. On the other side, the Confederates never had the ability to create the logistical infrastructure to launch anything more than raids into Northern territory, which is what Bragg's expedition into Kentucky had been.

It is worth noting that even the reasonably professional (by contemporary standards) French army of the Franco-Prussian War struggled to manage its logistics effectively at the outset of the war, despite access to rail transportation and Europe's superior road network. As Michael Howard notes about its mobilization on its frontier: "Thus a plan already faulty in principle was further marred by faults in execution; and as the army assembled [on the frontiers] it found itself lacking not only men, but the most elementary supplies. . . . The problem lay in the lack of transport and the lack of organization."[1] Nor did the Prussians do much better in supplying their forces during the siege of Paris. Even though the distances between Chattanooga, Tennessee, and Cairo, Illinois, on one hand, and Paris, France, and the German frontier, on the other, were virtually the same, the Prussians found it far more difficult to supply their armies over that distance in 1870 than the Union did in 1863. And the Germans had a far better road system at their disposal.

In fact, in early 1863 the Union's strategic position in the West was much better than it appeared. Two major Union armies were poised to break into the South's heartland. The North's logistical capabilities were slowly but steadily coming into place. Grant's Army of the Tennessee held Memphis and threatened Vicksburg, while Rosecrans's Army of the Cumberland held Nashville and threatened the remainder of Tennessee. In many respects Vicksburg represented a strategic point similar to that of the Hudson Highlands at West Point during the Revolutionary War, which had dominated the Hudson River and prevented the British from breaking the colonies in two. Like West Point, Vicksburg and its bluffs dominated the Mississippi, while at the same time allowing the defenders to create a fortress they could protect from all points.

Moreover, trackless wilderness, bayous, and swamps covered Vicksburg's approaches from the north and west. Five hundred miles to the northeast, the Army of the Cumberland's task was to move across central Tennessee into the southeastern portions of that state, some of the South's richest and most productive agricultural areas. Politically, the capture of Chattanooga would pose a direct threat to the eastern portions of the Confederacy, while at the same time making Confederate communications among the various states more difficult. In the case of the Army of the Tennessee and the Army of the Cumberland, the raids of Confederate cavalry and guerrillas exacerbated the tyranny of logistics. Thus, both Union armies found themselves forced to dilute their strength to protect their lines of communications. Nevertheless,

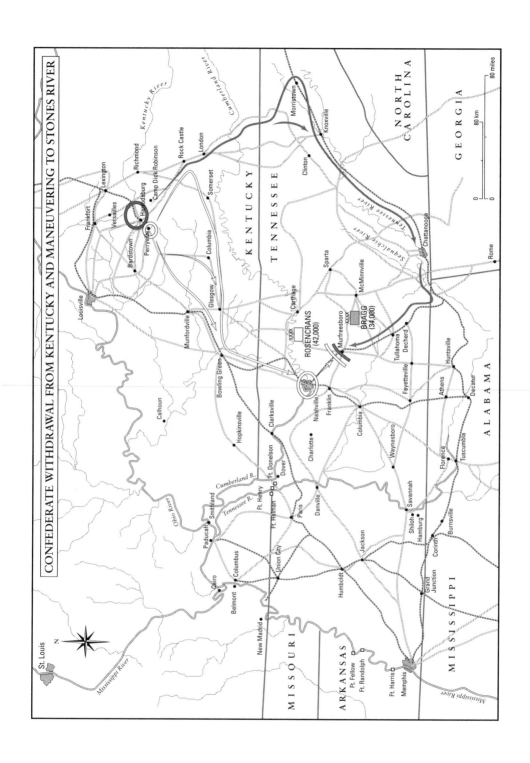

CONFEDERATE WITHDRAWAL FROM KENTUCKY AND MANEUVERING TO STONES RIVER

no matter how successful tactically, such raids failed for the most part to achieve strategic success.

The end of 1862 saw one last battle in the West, a contest that underlined the extent to which the opposing armies were still amateurs. Under pressure from the administration as well as Halleck, Rosecrans finally moved the Army of the Cumberland southeast from Nashville's fortifications on Christmas Day 1862. While his army had an overall strength of nearly 90,000 men, the need to protect Nashville and its lines of communications reaching back to the Mississippi River and the North reduced its battle strength to approximately 42,000 effectives. Bragg's Army of Tennessee numbered 34,000. The Confederates waited for the Union advance on the south bank of the Stones River just north of Murfreesboro. On the evening of 30 December the armies encamped directly opposite each other. After reinforcing his left, Bragg struck the Union right in the first light of dawn on New Year's Eve. Confederate Major General William Hardee's corps caught Major General Alexander McCook's corps by surprise, inexcusably given that McCook's troops were in the presence of the enemy. Two divisions on the Union right collapsed. But the third, Phil Sheridan's division, proved a tougher nut. Under attack by Bishop Leonidas Polk's corps to his front and by Hardee's troops on his flank, the diminutive Irishman fought a delaying action that bought time. When Sheridan's division eventually retreated into the new Union line, three of his brigade commanders were dead, a third of his soldiers casualties.

The day proved to be Rosecrans's finest hour. He was at every critical point, urging his soldiers to hold. With its right shattered, the Army of the Cumberland swung a full 90 degrees so that its back was to the Nashville & Chattanooga Railroad and Stones River, a less desperate situation than it might appear, since a fall drought made the so-called river fordable. Once he recognized the danger, Rosecrans sent two divisions of Major General Thomas Crittenden's corps from his left to reinforce the right flank. As one of the division commanders set out to what was the battle's swelling uproar, he commented to his colleague: "We'll all meet at the hatter's, as one coon said to another when the dogs were after them."[2]

If the morning had gone Bragg's way, the afternoon was different. The hinge in the new Union position lay on a wooded area known locally as the Round Forest. Instead of continuing his outflanking move, Bragg concentrated a series of Confederate attacks on that point.

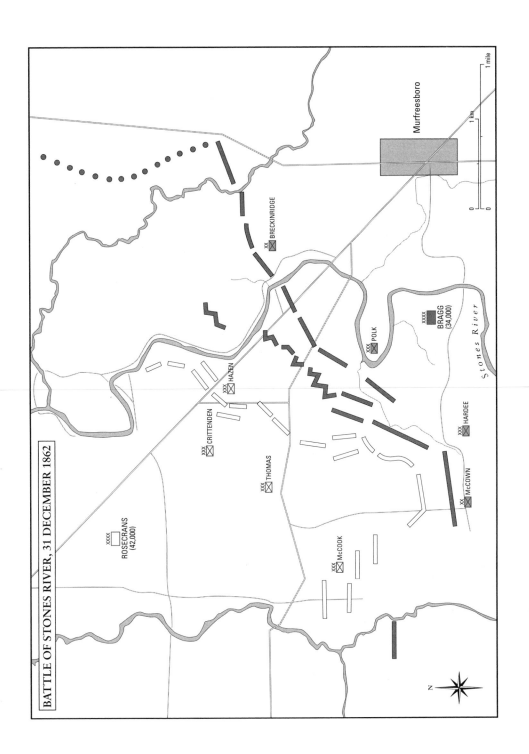

BATTLE OF STONES RIVER, 31 DECEMBER 1862

Murfreesboro

BRECKINRIDGE

BRAGG
(34,000)

POLK

HAZEN

CRITTENDEN

THOMAS

HARDEE

McCOWN

ROSECRANS
(42,000)

McCOOK

N

Stones River

1 mile
1 km

Against the well-prepared Federals, the Confederates launched no less than four separate attacks, each of which suffered heavy losses. Nevertheless, as evening fell Bragg believed he had won a great victory. That was what he reported to Richmond. But Union commanders and their soldiers had a vote, and they refused to retreat. In the words of Major General George "Pap" Thomas, one of the Virginians who had refused to betray their oath to the constitution, "this army does not retreat." The next morning, to his astonishment, Bragg discovered Rosecrans had not retreated, but stubbornly remained in place.

Over the course of New Year's Day, the armies stood glaring, while surgeons desperately repaired the maimed. Rosecrans did abandon the Round Forest, where the fiercest fighting had occurred, but at the same time ordered one of his divisions to cross Stones River and occupy a hill on the river's eastern side, from which its infantry and artillery could enfilade the whole Confederate line. Late on the afternoon of 2 January, Bragg launched Breckinridge's corps of Kentuckians against Union troops holding the hill. It was a serious mistake. Not only did Union infantry and artillery cover the field the Confederates crossed, but also fifty-eight Union cannons on the river's west side had a clear shot at the Confederate's flank. Only two-thirds of the Confederates returned, the remainder dead or wounded.

The battle was over. In terms of percentage casualties of those engaged, Stones River was the bloodiest battle of the Civil War. Moreover, the three-day casualty figures were greater than Antietam. Like that battle, Stones River was a tactical draw—a battle marked by the courage and tenacity of the front-line soldiers, but by a general lack of skill on the part of the opposing generals. Strategically, however, it was a Union victory, because Bragg's army had to retreat south to the Duck River. The Army of the Cumberland held the dismal landscape and thus could claim victory.

The battle had a deeply negative impact on the Army of Tennessee. By this point, its officers and soldiers had had enough of Bragg's leadership and personality, which Grant accurately depicted in his memoirs. Bragg had been a company commander, Grant records, on the Minnesota frontier in the 1850s, when the post quartermaster went on leave. The post commander gave Bragg the additional duty as the quartermaster: "As commander of the company he made a requisition upon the quartermaster—himself—for something he wanted. As quartermaster he declined to fill the requisition, and endorsed on the back of it his reasons for so doing. As company commander he responded to this, urging that his requisition called for nothing but what he was entitled to, and that it was the duty of the quartermaster to fill it. As quartermaster he still persisted that he was right. In this condition of affairs Bragg referred the whole matter to the commanding officer of the post. The latter, when he saw the nature of the matter referred, exclaimed: 'My God, Mr. Bragg, you have quarrelled with every officer in the army, and now you are quarrelling with yourself!'"[3]

One knowledgeable civilian put it pithily later in 1863, when Bragg, unrecognized, asked if he wasn't himself one of Bragg's men: "Bragg's army? He's got no army. He shot half of them himself up in Kentucky, and the other half got killed in Murfreesboro."[4] But the general may not have been the only source of his nasty disposition. His wife suggested to him in spring 1862 that perhaps he needed to "hang or shoot" commanders who failed in their duty.[5] Another veteran of the Army of Tennessee put the attitude of the private soldiers toward their commander in the following terms: "None of General Bragg's soldiers ever loved him. They had no faith in his ability as a General. He was looked upon as a merciless tyrant. . . . Bragg was never a good feeder or commissary-general. Rations with us were always scarce. No extra rations were ever allowed to the negroes who were with us as servants. No coffee or whiskey or tobacco were ever allowed to be issued to the troops. If they obtained these luxuries, they were not from the government. These luxuries were withheld in order to crush the very heart and spirit of his troops. We were crushed. . . . He loved to crush the spirit of his men. The more of a hang-dog look they had about them the better was General Bragg pleased."[6]

The anger throughout the army reached to the highest levels. Bragg made the mistake of not only asking his senior officers to attest that accusations in Southern newspapers that he had overridden his subordinates in ordering a retreat were untrue, but asking as well for their "good opinion." He did not receive their "good opinion." All indicated their dissatisfaction. This sorry state of affairs eventually reached Davis. The Confederate president then passed the ball to Johnston, now overall commander of Confederate armies in the West, as to whether he should relieve Bragg. Johnston, evading responsibility, refused to make a decision. Davis, a notorious micromanager, failed either to remove Bragg's opponents from the army (at least Hardee and Polk), or to replace Bragg with Johnston. Worse yet for the Army of Tennessee, Bragg's subordinates had their own flaws. Both of his senior corps commanders, Polk and Hardee, had an unseemly penchant for playing army politics, and both worked actively to undermine their commanding officer. Polk had the additional defect of ineptitude at his level of command responsibility, while utilizing the protection of Davis's friendship to the full extent. Hardee proved a reliable corps commander but was congenitally unwilling to accept the responsibility of army command. Even after Bragg's departure in November 1863, the army's high command proved incapable of overcoming the combination of incompetence and intrigue that Bragg had set in motion during his tenure.

The Vicksburg Campaign

While Rosecrans was fighting Bragg to a bloody draw in central Tennessee, Grant confronted considerable difficulties in his campaign to open the Mississippi. These were due not only to the problems posed by the Confederates but also to the machinations of his subordinate, the Illinois politician John McClernand. As a Democrat who had supported the war and then joined up, McClernand possessed a political base in southern Illinois of great importance. Grant certainly recognized McClernand's efforts in that regard, not once but twice, in his memoirs. But as events underlined, McClernand was also inordinately ambitious, although he fought well on the battlefield. In October 1862 he had received leave to visit Washington. While in the capital, he persuaded Lincoln and Stanton to allow him to return to Illinois to recruit a large military force, which he intended to lead down the Mississippi to attack Vicksburg.

McClernand was successful in recruiting the promised numbers of northwesterners for what he believed would be *his* military campaign. Halleck, however, got wind of McClernand's efforts. While he had little love for Grant, Halleck disliked political generals even more. So he did everything possible to undermine McClernand, while Grant's subordinates embarked the politician's newly enlisted troops on transports and sent them down the river as fast as they arrived in Memphis. In the end, McClernand received little support from Washington. Instead of possessing an independent command, he found himself in command of the XIII Corps, one of four corps under

Grant's command. Viewing what he regarded as the machinations by West Pointers, McClernand sent Grant a letter bordering on insubordination. Understanding the political dynamite his subordinate represented, Grant merely replied that, "I will take direct command of the Mississippi River expedition, which necessarily limits your command to the Thirteenth Army Corps."[7] As Grant casually remarked in his memoirs, "I had good reason to believe that in forestalling him I was by no means giving offense to those whose authority to command was above both him [McClernand] and me."[8] Events proved him right.

If Grant could outmaneuver McClernand, the Confederates were another matter. In December 1862 Grant launched a two-pronged assault on Vicksburg. From the main supply base at Holly Springs in northern Mississippi, the Army of the Tennessee advanced south into the central part of the state. At the same time Sherman and his XV Corps left Memphis by river transport with orders to land at Chickasaw Bluffs and attack Vicksburg's defenses from the northwest. On 20 December Sherman departed, just before McClernand arrived to find that his "army" had departed for points south. That was about the only success Grant and Sherman would have in December 1862. As Grant advanced south from Holly Springs in northern Mississippi, troubles beset his lines of communications. Nathan Bedford Forrest, undoubtedly the most outstanding combat commander in the war, and his cavalry were loose in northwest Tennessee. Although starting his raid with only 500 men, he added large numbers of volunteers to his raiding force as he moved through Union territory, with his fame preceding him. The damage he did to Grant's lines of communications was out of all proportion to Forrest's numbers.

Moreover, Major General Earl Van Dorn, eager to restore his reputation after his failure at Iuka, carried out a damaging strike. With 3,500 cavalry, he slipped by Grant's army and destroyed the Union supply depot of Holly Springs. Grant had left a certain Colonel Murphy of the 8th Wisconsin in charge of the garrison. Murphy had abandoned Iuka earlier in the year without destroying its supply dumps. Nevertheless, Grant had then given him a second chance. However, despite warnings of Van Dorn's approach, Murphy had done nothing to prepare the town's defenses and had presided over a raucous celebration the night before the Confederates arrived. The sudden Confederate attack convinced him he was facing overwhelming numbers (he wasn't) and, while fleeing the town, he was captured. Murphy then surrendered his command and the depot with its supplies. Grant's acid comment twenty years later, one of the few times in his memoirs that he was brutally harsh about the performance of a subordinate, was that "the surrender of Holly Springs was most reprehensible and showed either the disloyalty of Colonel Murphy to the cause which he professed to serve, or gross cowardice."[9]

Grant viewed his logistical situation as serious enough to warrant retreat to Memphis, as he stood exposed deep in Confederate territory in northern Mississippi. He certainly possessed plenty of fighting spirit, but unlike a figure such as John Bell Hood, he also recognized material realities. The local civilians took great pleasure in ribbing the Union commander as to what he and his soldiers were going to eat with the destruction of their supplies. But Grant, as usual, was resourceful. His army foraged along a wide swath as it retreated north, to the discomfort of those who a short time before had delighted in his predicament. To those who complained, Grant's "response was that we had endeavored to feed ourselves while visiting them; but their friends in gray had been uncivil enough to destroy what we had brought along, and it could not be expected that men, with arms in their hands, would starve in the midst of plenty. I advised them to emigrate east, or west, fifteen miles and assist in eating up what we had left."[10]

While Grant moved back into Tennessee, Sherman's XV Corps attacked Vicksburg's northern defenses. After dragging his wet troops through the river's bottomland to the edge of Chickasaw Bluffs, Sherman found the Confederates behind formidable defenses. Moreover, the enemy had received warning by telegraph that a large force of Federals had headed downstream; not for the last time, a warning of major Union movement arrived in the middle of a ball, being held in honor of Vicksburg's garrison. With no word of Grant's troubles, Sherman attacked. The result was a futile assault. Thus, the December 1862 offensive to take the "West Point" of the Mississippi had failed. The winter campaign now opened; it was to prove to be one damned thing after another. As long as Grant was downriver with the Army of the Tennessee, he was the army commander, and McClernand was merely commander of the XIII Corps. But were Grant to exercise command from upriver at Memphis, then McClernand, as senior officer, would command the army along the Mississippi. That was something that neither Grant, nor for that matter Halleck, was about to allow.

Thus, late on 28 January 1863, Grant arrived to confront the issue of how the Army of the Tennessee would attack Vicksburg. McClernand was not happy at Grant's arrival, but, after writing a letter that most commanders would have used as an excuse to fire an insubordinate general, the Illinois politician sullenly accepted his position. Grant for his part filed the incident away. McClernand's ambitions ran counter to Grant's spirit of trust and solidarity between commander and subordinate that he was creating in the Army of the Tennessee, but he treaded carefully in light of McClernand's political influence in Washington.

There were troubles in the Union command in the West, but the Confederate high command was in even greater disarray. It centered on three individuals: Johnston, in overall command of Southern forces from Tennessee through Mississippi; Bragg with the Army of Tennessee; and John Pemberton in command at Vicksburg. It was not a workable arrangement. Johnston refused to exercise full responsibility for the areas he supposedly controlled. Bragg added nothing in terms of operational or strategic vision. Moreover, far removed from the Western theater but still unable to resist micromanaging, Davis disregarded the chain of command and gave Pemberton instructions without informing Johnston.

Pemberton proved a disastrous choice. He was one of the few regular officers from the North to go south when the war broke out. As Grant laconically commented, Pemberton "was a Northern man & had got into bad company," in this case a Southern wife who talked him out of loyalty to country and family.[11] At least in this case, she did the North a considerable favor. Pemberton's climb to senior command did not result from competence, but simply from service in the backwaters of the war, where he displayed little initiative. In the right place at the right time, he rose to prominence. When in command of Charleston, he had almost abandoned the forts guarding the city's defenses in early 1862 until Lee dissuaded him from such folly. He then found himself transferred to the Mississippi command to defend Vicksburg. Davis moved him for two reasons: first, because the president needed an out of the way place to bury Beauregard, his enemy of the moment, and Charleston fit the bill. Second, he wanted to reward Pemberton as a Northerner for having supported the Confederacy.

The fortified positions surrounding Vicksburg on its river side as well as on the land side were formidable. Well-sited and deeply entrenched, they provided the city with sufficient protection against everything but a siege. In that case, the city would need substantial provisions, a precaution Pemberton failed to take into account in spring 1863, although the Confederate commissary authorities also failed in their responsibilities. Yet, at the highest level, Confederate conceptions about the defense of Vicksburg lacked clarity. Davis and Johnston remained deeply divided about the strategy necessary to defend the Confederacy's hold on the Mississippi. The former placed the holding of the city above all; the latter believed maintenance of Confederate forces in the field represented the key factor in holding open the link to the western Confederate states and closing the river to Northern traffic. Moreover, Davis, despite the fact that he was from Mississippi, failed to grasp the logistical difficulties that the distances in the theater placed on Confederate armies. While Confederate forces possessed interior lines, the decrepit state of the South's railroads and roads, as well as the North's control of the Cumberland and Tennessee Rivers, placed the Confederates at a serious disadvantage. This disconnect between the Confederacy's senior leaders directly affected Pemberton, who was unprepared to act on his own. Rather, he fell into the trap of following the president's directions, when only a willingness to act independently might have saved his army.

As early as January, Grant was turning over in his mind the possibility of attacking Vicksburg from the south, in Churchill's words, "its soft underbelly." But both weather and flooding made that approach impossible until spring. Thus, over the winter Grant pursued a number of unattractive possibilities. As he commented in his memoirs: "I, myself, never felt great confidence that any of the experiments resorted to would prove successful. Nevertheless, I was always prepared to take advantage of them in case they did."[12] On the Mississippi's western bank, Union efforts involved cutting canals through the river's various meanderings to attack Vicksburg's defenses from the south. On the river's eastern bank Union troops attempted to find a way through the Mississippi's tributaries to allow Admiral David Porter's naval power to get at the city's defenses. In both cases, the efforts ran through waterlogged, swampy terrain covered with the tangled growth of the American wilderness and inhabited by creatures that would have delighted Tolkien.

The first of these efforts involved cutting a canal through the almost 360-degree bend the Mississippi River made in swinging by Vicksburg.

However successful it might have proven in getting the Mississippi to bypass the citadel, Confederate guns could still cover the canal's exit. Enthusiastic digging continued until early March, when the rising Mississippi broke the dam and ended the effort. Meanwhile, Grant set Major General James McPherson and his troops to attempt a second route through Lake Providence to the Red River and thus on to its mouth, which reached the Mississippi above Port Hudson. The proposed route, nearly 500 miles, proved impractical, not only due to terrain and distance, but also because it was open to attack by Confederate guerrillas. But Grant let the work continue, "believing employment was better than idleness for the men."[13]

The third route the Army of the Tennessee explored was on the river's east bank, and this effort was led by a newly minted lieutenant colonel and member of Grant's staff, James Wilson, who had been a lieutenant at Antietam, where he had persuaded a journalist to exhort the wounded Hooker to defy orders and resume the offensive in the afternoon. However, attempts to utilize the Yazoo Pass and eventually Steel's Bayou floundered as completely as the efforts to find a way around Vicksburg on the river's west bank. By mid-March, Grant appeared stymied. His subordinates, Sherman in particular, urged a return to Memphis and an advance on Vicksburg through Holly Springs and northern Mississippi, the route used the previous December.

Grant refused. Throughout his life he had avoided retracing his steps. Even more important was his recognition that such a move might have serious political implications for the Union cause. "At this time the North had become very much discouraged. Many strong Union men believed that the war must prove a failure. . . . It was my judgment at the time that to make a backward movement as long as that from [the area of Vicksburg] to Memphis, would be interpreted, by many of those yet full of hope for the preservation of the Union, as a defeat, and that the draft [which was about to be introduced] would be resisted, desertions ensue, and the power to capture and punish deserters lost. There was nothing left to be done but to *go forward to a decisive victory*."[14]

For Grant, this meant an advance south of Vicksburg along the Mississippi's west bank and then across the river to get at the Confederate citadel from the south. His initial conception envisaged a move south after crossing the Mississippi to join Banks and capture Port Hudson before a joint advance against Vicksburg. Success in this approach required three preconditions. First, Porter would have to move his fleet down the Mississippi past Vicksburg to provide shipping and protection for the crossing. To do so, the navy's gunboats and the army's transports would have to run the Vicksburg batteries along the bluffs overlooking the river. Once downriver, they could not return (at least until Vicksburg fell), because the river's flow would so slow their movement upriver as to make them sitting ducks for Confederate artillery at Vicksburg. Second, Grant needed to provide sufficient distractions, as he moved south, to focus Confederate attention away from his main move. And third, the Army of the Tennessee would need a logistical line on the west bank, combining water and land transportation, to build up supply depots south of Vicksburg.

That he was able to achieve all three underlines Grant's qualities as an operational commander: his ability to pick subordinates who could act independently; his willingness to allow them latitude in executing his orders; his ability to work selflessly with others, including the navy; his careful and intelligent planning; and his ability to see the larger issues as well as the possible long-term effects military operations might achieve. All of this required a culture in the Army of the Tennessee that fostered and encouraged initiative. Sherman once commented that "when [Grant] begins a campaign, he fixes in his mind what is the true object point, and abandons all minor ones. . . . If his plan works wrong, he is never disconcerted, but promptly devises a new one, and is sure he will win in the end."[15] In other words, Grant saw the larger design. What made him the greatest general of the war was his ability then to provide the complex details that made a simple operational design work. As Clausewitz noted, "war is a simple matter, but in war the simplest matter is difficult."[16] Grant's conception of decision making in war paralleled that of the Germans in the twentieth century. When queried by a supply officer as to whether he was sure that he had made the right decision over a major expenditure, Grant had replied, "No, I am not, but in war anything is better than indecision. We *must decide*. If I am wrong, we shall soon find it out, and can do the other thing. But *not to decide* wastes both time and money, and may ruin everything."[17]

In April, the administration, unsure how the Mississippi campaign was progressing, sent out two senior officials, Major General Lorenzo Thomas, the army's adjutant general, and Charles Dana, Stanton's most trusted agent, Harvard graduate, and newspaperman of considerable note, to report on the Army of the Tennessee. Dana was clearly the more important of the two, and his reports played an important role in Grant's rise to supreme command. Most commanders might well have taken umbrage at the arrival of two individuals who were clearly the administration's spies. Grant did not. Understanding that his guests could prove a highly useful conduit to pass his views on to Lincoln and Stanton, Grant included both in his official family. Within a matter of weeks, he had completely won Dana over.

In early April Grant began his move. He first had to persuade Porter. In an age when the American military is making Herculean efforts to achieve jointness, Porter stands as a worthy exemplar. He was fully cooperative and willing to put his ships in harm's way despite Vicksburg's strengths and the ingrained interservice rivalries we have seen elsewhere. And there were, of course, none of the doctrinal publications that so beset the modern American military. "Porter fell into the plan at once," only suggesting that he should not only run his gunboats past Vicksburg but also the army's transports as well, to better move the soldiers and their supplies across the Mississippi. Ironically enough a council of war with Grant's army commanders was less successful.[18] All of his senior subordinates disagreed with his approach, Sherman arguing that such a move violated the principles of war, especially Jomini's much-quoted dicta. But when Grant decided, they followed his lead to the best of their abilities. It is a tribute to the army's culture that even McClernand threw his heart into the campaign

Beyond mere principles, Grant recognized that surprise and unexpected movement carried with them incalculable advantages, especially against an opponent whose weaknesses he understood. Grant held firm, ending the meeting with the curt comment that his generals would be ready to move by 1000 the next morning. Thus, the Army of the Tennessee, led by McClernand's corps, moved down the west bank from Milligan's Bend and on to the eloquently named hovel, Hard Times, south of Vicksburg—approximately thirty miles as the crow flies, but double that distance on the tortuous route through the bayous.

Porter began preparation of his gunboats and transports for their journey forthwith. His sailors and army soldiers covered the decks with hay and cotton bales to lessen the impact of Confederate shots; they concealed boiler fires so as not to give away the movement; and coal barges were both towed and lashed to the side of the vessels. With Grant watching with his family from the decks of a steamer upriver, Porter moved south on the evening of 16 April. As in December, the

Confederates were having a ball, no doubt to celebrate their successes thus far. Nevertheless, they responded swiftly. Confederate pickets on the west bank ignited piles of brush to silhouette the Union fleet. A heavy bombardment followed.

It was, however, less than successful, sinking only one of the three army transports—carrying supplies not men—but none of the naval vessels. Nevertheless, the Confederates on the Vicksburg bluffs wildly exaggerated the damage. On the basis of those reports, Lee commented to Davis that the Federals "can derive no material benefit from [their move]."[19] Six days later another contingent of Union ships, this time six unarmored army transports, towing twelve barges, ran the batteries in response to McClernand's warning that failure to do so would add nearly two weeks to the time required for the buildup of supplies. Confederate guns sank one and battered the other five. Still, Porter's men were able to repair the damaged transports. After unloading the supplies, the sailors and their ships provided the means to transport Union troops across to the Mississippi's east bank.

A more perceptive commander than Pemberton would have focused on what appeared to be a dangerous concentration of Union shipping below Vicksburg. Instead, he allowed himself to be caught up with events to the east of Vicksburg. On 18 April Grant ordered one of the more unusual cavalrymen of the war, Colonel Benjamin Grierson, with three cavalry regiments and approximately 1,700 troopers—less than a quarter of the cavalrymen whom Stoneman would lead south several weeks later in Virginia—to conduct a raid. Grierson's path to cavalry command was tortuous. A horse had kicked him in the head when he was eight and for a short period blinded him. Not surprisingly, he hated horses. Moreover, like Grant he had failed at several professions before the war—namely, as a music teacher and store owner. At the war's outbreak, he had tried to join the infantry, but found himself in the cavalry and, while never enthusiastic about horses, he proved a natural cavalry leader. Grierson had come to Grant's attention in 1862, and Grant selected him to lead a raid through Mississippi to Baton Rouge.

Three days into the expedition Grierson detached the sick and the lame to return north, cover his tracks, and cause as much confusion as possible. At midnight on 20 April, Grierson further divided his command; he sent the 2nd Iowa east to attack the Mobile & Ohio Railroad and then return to Union forces in Tennessee, a move that added to the swelling confusion in Pemberton's headquarters as to what was occurring in north-central Mississippi. Meanwhile, Grierson with two other regiments rode south; he dispatched a company to rip up further sections of the Mobile & Ohio; after a wild ride of nearly 200 miles, that small group returned to the main body, just short of Baton Rouge. On 24 April Grierson reached the town of Newton Station east of Jackson, where his troopers captured and destroyed two trains and their cargo. After that, the cavalrymen proceeded to cut the telegraph wires in the neighborhood and burn bridges in both directions, causing further confusion. By now the Confederates were seeing Union raiders everywhere. After considering the possibility of linking up with the Army of the Tennessee at Grand Gulf, Grierson decided there were too many Confederates in the way and turned south to reach Union lines at Baton Rouge eight days later.

Sixteen days after they had started, Grierson and his weary troopers reached Louisiana and the safety of Banks's army. Not only had they distracted Pemberton, but they had disrupted Confederate communications and railroad traffic throughout Mississippi. One of the cavalrymen commented on the exploits of his fellow troopers in words that might have been written about their successors in Normandy 81 years later: "The men who did this work were a year and a half from the plowtail, and their chief claim to consideration is that they were representative men—fair types of our American citizen-soldiery."[20] Grant's laconic tribute was that "Grierson had attracted the attention of the enemy from the main movement against Vicksburg."[21] All in all, the raid had a greater strategic impact than any other cavalry raid in the war.

With the Confederates in disarray from Grierson's raid, Grant and Porter moved. Their first choice for a crossing was Grand Gulf, one that was obvious and against which the Confederates were prepared. Sitting high above the Mississippi, the Confederates drove Porter's gunboats off on 29 April. Nevertheless, the general strategic position remained unclear to Pemberton. Sherman's XV Corps remained in position opposite Vicksburg; there were reports of Federals in the Yazoo; and the fallout from Grierson's raid was still reverberating. With too few resources and soldiers to defend the area from Port Hudson to Vicksburg, Pemberton froze in indecision.

On the night of the 29th, Grant interviewed an escaped slave, who was at first unwilling to talk, but who, after encouragement, revealed there were reasonable roads from the hamlet of Bruinsburg leading northeast to Port Gibson. As in so many other cases, a former slave

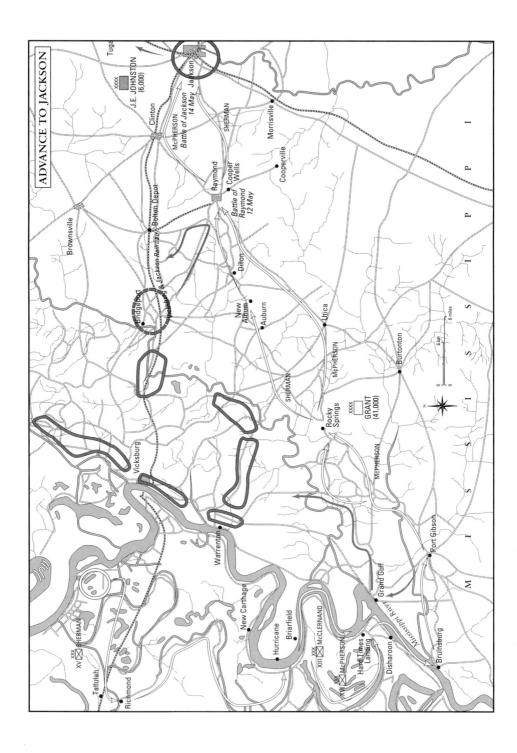

ADVANCE TO JACKSON

found an important way to strike back at the social order that once held him in bondage. There was no hesitation on Grant's part. He ordered McClernand to cross the Mississippi and Sherman to abandon his demonstration across from Haines Bluff and march south to cross the Mississippi after McClernand's and McPherson's corps.

As usual, Porter gave his full support, throwing his gunboats as well as the transports into the task of moving the troops across the Mississippi from Hard Times. To the delight of the Hoosiers who were the first to land, there were no Confederate troops on the opposite shore. There were the normal hiccups in such a move, but within a day McClernand's and McPherson's corps, 22,000 troops, were across. They began the drive into the state's heartland. Sherman, although still opposed to the idea, was moving as fast as he could to reach the crossing. Grant was ecstatic. He recalled twenty years later: "I felt a degree of relief scarcely ever equalled since. Vicksburg was not yet taken it is true, nor were its defenders demoralized by any of our previous moves. . . . But I was on dry ground on the same side of the river with the enemy. All the campaigns, labors, hardships and exposures from the month of December previous to this time that had been made and endured, were for the accomplishment of this one object."[22] The swift movement of the Army of the Tennessee, largely guided by civilian soldiers, stands in stark contrast to those of the Army of the Potomac which, despite its relatively large contingent of McClellan-selected regulars, managed to forget the pontoons at Fredericksburg in December 1862.

What followed was the most impressive campaign of the Civil War. The major problem confronting Grant was that his army was numerically inferior to that of his opponents, if the Confederates united their forces. That proved to be a big "if." Confederate commanders in the West proved unwilling to cooperate, favoring their own interests over larger strategic priorities, as well as proving incapable of timely action. The trouble started at the top with Jefferson Davis, who could not resist meddling in the affairs of his Western operational commanders. Johnston, who refused to provide clear operational guidance to Pemberton, must share in the blame for the Confederate defeats. Finally, Pemberton proved more interested in his administrative duties than in acting as a field commander. Thus, the Confederates failed to unite. Moreover, they were up against a commander willing to *act*. One might say the same about Grant, as one of the members of

Britain's military in World War II noted about Churchill's arrival as prime minister on 10 May 1940: "The days of mere 'coordination' were out for good and all. . . . We were now going to get direction, leadership, action with a snap in it. . . . [As Churchill remarked] it was all very well to say that everything had been thought of. The crux of the matter was, had anything been done."[23] Just as McClellan and Buell had only talked of using the Tennessee and Cumberland Rivers as lines of operations in winter 1861/62, only Grant proved willing to act decisively in an environment rife with uncertainty and risk.

Almost as soon as he had his corps in hand, McClernand pushed inland. Early in the morning hours of 1 May, the lead troops of the XIII Corps ran into Confederates under Brigadier General John Bowen near Port Gibson. Union forces were advancing on two rough tracks running from Bruinsburg through terrain cut by deep ravines and covered by scrub growth, vines, and underbrush. Grant described the terrain in the following terms: "The country in this part of Mississippi stands on edge, as it were, the roads running along the ridges except where they occasionally ran from one ridge to another."[24] Had Bowen possessed sufficient troops, he could have bottled up Grant, but with only a brigade, he was badly outnumbered. After a sharp fight that merely delayed the inevitable, the Confederates retreated. Their retreat allowed Union troops to seize Grand Gulf, which eased the navy's task of building up Grant's supply dumps for the upcoming campaign.

The ensuing Confederate response was defensive. Pemberton interpreted Grant's move as the first step toward a direct assault on Vicksburg from the south. Consequently, instead of acting aggressively, he deployed his forces along the Big Black River to prevent a crossing that would allow a direct approach by Union troops on Vicksburg. Meanwhile, Johnston believed Tennessee was the decisive theater and, therefore, had remained with Bragg. Not until it was apparent in early May that a major crisis was exploding in central Mississippi did he journey to Jackson and only as a result of a direct order from Seddon, the Confederacy's secretary of war. The secretary directed Johnston to take 3,000 troops with him, an indication of how stretched Confederate resources had become. Significantly, Pemberton failed to inform Johnston of Bowen's defeat until 7 May, or that Grant with the Army of the Tennessee was loose south of the Big Black.

Left to his own devices, Pemberton floundered. His problem lay in the fact that he was an unimaginative regular army officer, who found it impossible to interpret his orders in any fashion other than literally. Since Davis had instructed him to hold on to Vicksburg to the last, he was unwilling to maneuver his forces in its defense. Initially, Grant's conception had been that once his forces reached the east bank, he would turn south to join up with Banks to take Port Hudson. But on arrival, Grant discovered that Banks, one of the most hapless of Union political generals, had moved up the Red River. Consequently, there was no union of forces, a thoroughly fortuitous circumstance, since Banks ranked Grant and would have undoubtedly botched whatever campaign ensued. Without hesitation Grant cut his lines of communications, relying for the army's sustenance on local farms and plantations.

The ultimate target was Vicksburg, but the Army of the Tennessee moved first against Jackson, Mississippi's capital, located east of Vicksburg. Grant aimed to split Confederate forces in Mississippi, remove the threat of their uniting by finishing the job of destroying the railroad network that Grierson had begun, and then swing back against Vicksburg after disrupting Confederate defenses in the center of the state. To prevent a combination of enemy forces, Grant launched his army into the state's interior in the belief the Confederates would fail to act in a timely fashion. His assumption rested on his understanding of Pemberton's character, and on Pemberton's performance in Mexico. Long after the war, Grant recalled that an order had come down at some point during the advance to Mexico City that junior officers were not to ride, but march with their men. Soon after, while the order had not been rescinded, junior officers were again allowed to ride. But Grant recalled: "Pemberton alone said, No, he would walk, as the order was still extant not to ride, and he did walk, though suffering intensely the while. This I thought of all the time he was in Vicksburg and I outside of it."[25]

With Johnston not yet in Mississippi, the weight of command fell on Pemberton. Davis provided no help, beyond bad advice. When Pemberton suggested that he abandon Port Hudson and add its garrison to his forces, Davis had replied: "To hold both Vicksburg and Port Hudson is necessary to a connection with the trans-Mississippi."[26] The result was that Pemberton found himself caught between Johnston's orders and Davis's instructions. As his chief engineer put it: Pemberton "made the capital mistake of trying to harmonize instructions from his superiors diametrically opposed to each other, and at the same time to bring them into accord with his own judgment, which was adverse to the plans of both."[27] Johnston later pointed out that Pemberton "can't comprehend that by attempting to defend all valuable points at once he exposes his troops to being beaten everywhere."[28]

Initially, Confederate leaders assumed Grant could only make short forays into the countryside. There is some irony in this belief, because at this time, Lee was considering a deep foray into the North, during which he too would cut himself off from direct supply from the South and depend on what his troops could forage. Similarly, Grant broke with current military thinking in deciding to cut his lines of communications with the Mississippi River and, to the extent possible, live off the land. That decision required careful planning. The army would carry a considerable amount of hard rations and the maximum load of ammunition. While McPherson's and McClernand's spearhead units pushed deeper into the countryside, Grant charged Porter's fleet to bring every army wagon his teamsters could get their hands on across the Mississippi to transport the army's ammunition, medical supplies, and iron rations. In addition, he ordered the troops to scour surrounding plantations for anything that could carry supplies. The resulting supply train was hardly in accordance with army regulations, consisting as it did of plantation wagons, fancy rigs, and anything else that would move. Nevertheless, it underlined how well American soldiers could improvise. For the first week of its advance the Army of the Tennessee continued to receive supplies from Grand Gulf, but as it approached Jackson, Grant cut his supply lines.

By the beginning of the second week of May Grant was ready. On 9 May Sherman and his XV Corps arrived on the east bank, and the army's advance began forthwith. At this point Grant informed Halleck what he was intending, knowing "Old Brains" would disapprove, but by the time Halleck ordered Grant to desist, events, either victory or defeat, would have overtaken his orders. Grant asserts in his memoirs that he received the order to return to Grand Gulf just as the XIII Corps was about to smash the Confederates along the Big Black and shut Pemberton up in Vicksburg. He records that he proceeded to disregard the order to the astonishment of the major who delivered it. As the advance into the interior began, McClernand and Sherman advanced on the eastern bank of the Big Black, while McPherson's corps advanced on Raymond.

In effect, the advance along the eastern side of the Big Black suggested to Pemberton that Grant was searching for a place to cross and drive on Vicksburg, an assumption Union troops advancing along the river reinforced by their actions. In fact, Grant intended first to cut the railroad between Jackson and Vicksburg and divide Confederate forces in central Mississippi. The only effort extraneous to the advance came as foraging parties stripped the country. One planter arrived at Grant's headquarters on a mule to complain that Union soldiers had taken everything except his mule; a division commander denied the complaint and exclaimed, "I know my boys too well. If it had been the 13th Iowa they'd have taken everything."[29]

On 12 May McPherson ran into a Confederate force at Raymond. As his advance units approached the crossroads village, Confederate Brigadier General John Gregg's brigade attacked the lead units of the XVII Corps. Pemberton, under the misperception Grant was about to cross the Big Black, had instructed Gregg to utilize the opportunity to attack what the Confederate commander believed to be Grant's flank. Pemberton's orders were: "Be ready to fall on his rear or flank at any moment. Do not allow yourself to be flanked or taken in the rear. Be careful that you do not lose your command"—not exactly the orders Lee or Jackson would have given.[30] Gregg, however, was spoiling for a fight. Misinformed by both Pemberton and his scouts, he believed he faced a relatively small force. Artillery fire opened the engagement; outnumbered in guns, Gregg launched his brigade against superior numbers. Initially, the Confederates enjoyed some success, but then Major General John Logan, Illinois politician and superb combat commander, arrived to steady the Union line. For two hours the opposing forces engaged in a fight at point-blank range, in some cases even in hand-to-hand combat. In the end tough fighting and numbers told, and Gregg pulled his badly battered brigade back. With Raymond in his hands, McPherson halted for the night.

Apprised that Johnston and Confederate reinforcements were arriving in Jackson, Grant ordered McClernand to move up to Raymond to shield the rear of the Army of the Tennessee from any movement east by Pemberton, not that he expected one, while Sherman's and McPherson's corps moved against the state capital. At almost the same moment, Johnston, arriving in Jackson, believed he had Grant in an ideal position between Pemberton and the Confederate forces gathering at Jackson. But in effect Grant had achieved what the great Napoleonic historian, David Chandler, calls the "strategy of the central position," where Napoleon would split his opponent's forces by moving between enemy armies, a move which then allowed the emperor to defeat the enemy in detail.[31] Pemberton had finally left Vicksburg, but, instead of striking at Grant as Johnston ordered, he was feeling his way cautiously across the Big Black.

Taking advantage of Confederate hesitancy, Grant struck hard. McClernand, outnumbered, pulled back before Pemberton could attack. Meanwhile, throughout 14 May Grant's other two corps slogged their way toward Jackson under a deluge of rain. The next day they arrived on Jackson's outskirts, where they ran into the remains of Gregg's brigade and reinforcements from the Gulf states, one of the brigades under command of a South Carolinian with the wonderful name of States Rights Gist. Under sustained attack, Confederate defenses collapsed by midday. The tactical performances of McPherson and Sherman were less than brilliant, but Grant had concentrated overwhelming numbers on the crucial point. What the German military would call *Fingerspitzengefuhl* (feeling at the end of one's finger) indicated to Grant that he could deal with Johnston and Jackson without interference from Pemberton.

With Jackson in their hands, Sherman's and McPherson's troops proceeded to rip up the railroads that radiated out from the state capital, as well as the factories located in the area. While Grant's twelve-year-old son, Fred, watched Old Glory being raised over the state capitol, his father and Sherman observed seamstresses turning out tent cloth in a factory: "We looked on for a while to see the tent cloth which they were making roll out of the looms, with 'C.S.A.' woven in each bolt. There was an immense amount of cotton, in bales, stacked outside. Finally, I told Sherman I thought they had done work enough. The operatives were told they could leave and take with them what cloth they could carry. In a few moments cotton and factory were in a blaze."[32] That night Grant slept in the hotel room Johnston had used the night before. On leaving the hotel the next morning, Dana paid the bill in Confederate dollars.

Having dispensed with Johnston, Grant reversed course to deal with Pemberton. Receiving intelligence that the Confederates were marching east, he ordered McPherson to hustle down the twenty miles to Bolton Depot from Jackson to prevent the possibility of a juncture between the Confederate armies. At the same time, he ordered McClernand to move on Bolton as well. Early on the 16th, receiving more intelligence that Pemberton was on the march, Grant ordered

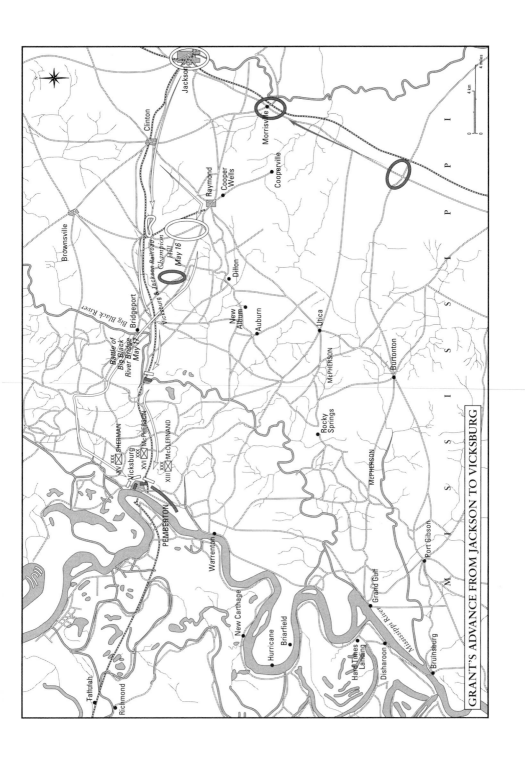

GRANT'S ADVANCE FROM JACKSON TO VICKSBURG

Sherman to desist from smashing up Jackson and move "with all dispatch to Bolton."[33] The crucial battle of the campaign was about to unfold, ironically at the same moment Davis and Seddon were meeting with Lee in Richmond to decide whether troops should be sent west to rescue what appeared even then to be a deteriorating situation, or whether the Army of Northern Virginia should invade the North.

One of the myths of the Civil War is that the Confederates enjoyed an important advantage because they fought on their own turf. Certainly in the Vicksburg campaign, this would not seem to have been the case. Two factors favored Grant: first, his movements were so quick *and* unexpected that the Confederates never grasped his intentions. Second, his intelligence was impeccable, much of it provided by runaway slaves eager to help in their liberation. Above all, Grant was willing to act on such intelligence. By the time the Confederates awoke, Grant had moved on. Such an approach, as with Lee's in the east, depended on trusting his subordinates to act as the situation demanded: in modern terms, to act in accordance with the spirit of his orders. Grant could not be everywhere, and his success rested on the shoulders of his subordinates.

The ensuing Battle of Champion Hill on 16 May had little tactical brilliance but reflected the competence of Grant's system. It was an encounter battle pure and simple. Marching west, with the XIII Corps in the lead, the Army of the Tennessee headed toward the Big Black. McClernand's divisions were on three roads leading from Jackson to Bolton: in the south Brigadier General Andrew Smith's division; Major General Francis P. Blair's division, temporarily assigned to McClernand from Sherman's corps, followed Smith; in the center the divisions of Brigadier Generals Peter Osterhaus and Eugene Carr; and in the north Brigadier General Alvin Hovey's division. Behind Hovey's division, McPherson's corps followed, so that Grant disposed much of his strength on his right. Trundling down the road behind McPherson, but to the rear, were Sherman's divisions, but all driving west.

Pemberton, remaining true to Davis's orders to secure Vicksburg, had left 9,000 soldiers in the city for its defense. On 15 May, he disposed his three divisions of approximately 21,800 men to the west of Champion Hill. Carter L. Stevenson's division was on the north, while Bowen's and William W. Loring's divisions deployed to the south. Pemberton had only been in the field for a few days and so had little grasp of the terrain or the operational situation. The crossroads immediately

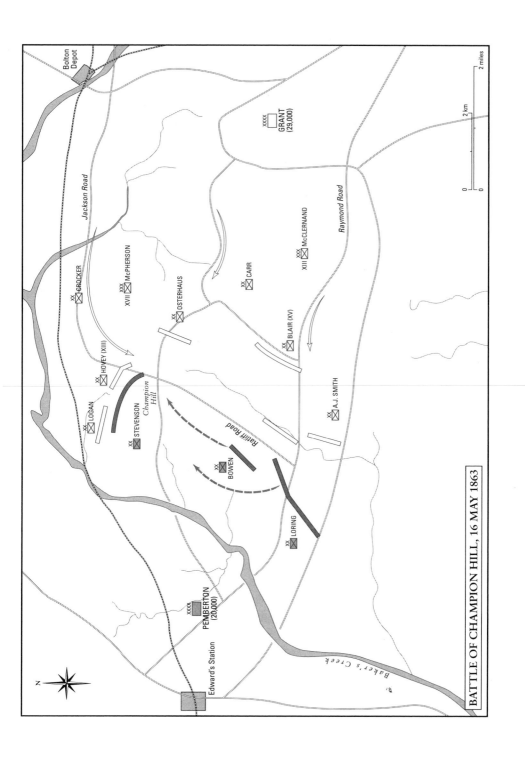

BATTLE OF CHAMPION HILL, 16 MAY 1863

southwest of Champion Hill proved the crucial point around which the battle swirled. Pemberton had initially blundered by moving in the opposite direction from Johnston's instructions to concentrate at Clinton to the northeast. The terrain, while not nearly as dismal as that near Port Gibson and Bruinsburg, was hardly ideal for coordination or tactical movement. On the evening of 15 May, Pemberton held a council with his senior commanders. He failed to persuade them that the army should fall back and defend along the Big Black.

The council itself waffled between urging Pemberton to obey Johnston's orders to concentrate at Clinton to the northeast or move south to cut Grant's nonexistent supply lines. Johnston put the matter accurately in his memoirs: "A majority of the member of the council [of general officers] voted for moving on Clinton in obedience to orders. A minority advocated a plan for seizing the enemy's communications by placing the army on the road from Jackson and Raymond to Port Gibson, to compel General Grant to attack it. Adverse to both opinions, Pemberton adopted that of the minority of his council and determined to execute a measure which he disapproved, and which was in violation of the orders of his commander."[34]

Clearly, Pemberton was uncomfortable with the uncertainties of field command, especially considering the speed and unexpectedness of Grant's moves. Pemberton's discomfort transmitted to his subordinates. In the early morning hours, Pemberton changed his mind and decided to obey Johnston's orders and pull back to Edwards as the first step toward joining up with the theater commander at Clinton. In fact, he may have viewed such a move as a step to pulling back to the Big Black and Vicksburg. As a result, when Union troops appeared first to the east and then to the north, Stevenson's division had already begun its march up the Jackson Road toward Edward's Station. To add to the discord in the higher ranks of the army, Pemberton and his senior division commander, Major General William Loring, had a furious dispute on the morning of the 16th, even as sounds of skirmishing announced the arrival of the Army of the Tennessee.

The first of McClernand's divisions to make contact early on the morning of 16 May was Smith's at the southern end of the advance. Smith wanted to attack, but McClernand hesitated. On the night of the 15th Grant had instructed McClernand "to move early in the morning on Edward's Station, cautioning him to watch for the enemy and not bring on an engagement unless he felt very certain of success."[35]

Thus, for nearly the entire battle, his divisions in the south remained stationary, and he would miss his potential moment of fame.

Meanwhile, to the north, Hovey's division ran into a portion of Stevenson's division lying on the higher portion of Champion Hill. Initially, Hovey held back, following orders. Hurrying forward, but as usual paying attention to details, Grant urged Logan's division, the lead division of McPherson's XVII Corps, to quicken its pace and then ordered Hovey's wagons off the road to speed the movement forward. As he passed one of Logan's regimental commanders, Grant called out: "Colonel, we shall fight the battle for Vicksburg today."[36] Upon arrival at the front, he conferred with Logan and Hovey, a scene a soldier recounted after the war: "I was close enough to see [Grant's] features. Earnest they were, but sign of inward movement there was none."[37] As to an attack, Grant had his doubts, but Hovey, an Indiana lawyer in peacetime, was an aggressive, tough soldier. Dana observed that Hovey "works with all his might and all his mind; and, unlike most volunteer officers, makes it his business to learn the military profession just as if he expected to spend his life in it."[38] He persuaded Grant to unleash the midwestern regiments, most of them from Indiana.

In short order Hovey's troops swept up Champion Hill and then down the other side. Stevenson's division, one brigade of which had barely made it back up the Jackson road, was badly deployed and suffered accordingly. By midday Hovey's division was in possession of the crossroads, while Logan's troops were making their way through heavy wooded terrain to the north. Throughout the morning fight, Pemberton had exercised little tactical control other than to order Bowen and Loring to move north to help bolster an increasingly tenuous situation. Both Confederate division commanders proved recalcitrant, claiming there were major Union forces to their front, and they could not move. By early afternoon one of Logan's brigades, almost reaching the Jackson Road, was in a position to flank Stevenson's division to the northwest, which would have cut the Confederates off from retreat. At the same time, Hovey's division had punched a deep salient across the crossroads behind Champion Hill.

Finally, in midafternoon, Pemberton pushed Bowen into moving north along the Ratliff Road to counterattack Union troops. Bowen's counterattack was only possible because McClernand was applying no pressure in the south or center. Still the Confederate attack almost reversed the tide of battle. Not only did it regain the crossroads, but it also drove on up the Jackson Road, recaptured Champion Hill, and threatened Grant's rear area headquarters. In this serious situation, Grant sent in the two remaining fresh regiments from Marcellus Crocker's division under Colonel Samuel Holmes.

Grant's understanding of what appeared a desperate situation was as usual impeccable. He recognized that "If the enemy has whipped Hovey's division and Boomer's brigade, they are in a bad plight, for these are good troops."[39] He repositioned some artillery batteries and told an officer, "If we can go in again here and make a little showing, I think he will give way."[40] Holmes's charge reinvigorated Hovey's battle-weary units, which proceeded to drive the Confederates back to, and then off, Champion Hill. As they clambered over fences, the 46th and 30th Alabama regiment dissolved under the fire of a six-gun Union battery. One observer of the scene recorded that the guns "completely annihilated men and fence. . . . Such terrible execution by a battery I never saw. It seemed as if every shell burst just as it reached the fence, and rails and rebs flew into the air together."[41]

What was left of the remnants of Bowen's and Stevenson's divisions barely got back to the Big Black. The losses on the opposing sides underlined who had done the fighting. The Army of the Tennessee had suffered 410 killed, 1,844 wounded, and 187 missing with Hovey's two brigades suffering 1,189 casualties. The four divisions that had been under McClernand's command suffered 156 casualties, underlining his inaction. Grant would not forget. As he commented in his memoirs: "Had McClernand come up with reasonable promptness, or had I known the ground as I did afterwards, I cannot see how Pemberton could have escaped with any organized force."[42] Incomplete returns on the Confederate side reported 3,801 casualties, 381 killed, 1,018 wounded, and 2,411 missing (many of the latter either dead or wounded).

The pursuit to the Big Black failed to finish off the remnants of Pemberton's army. But it did bring Union troops up on Confederate defenses before the beaten troops could round into some sort of order. Bowen's division held what appeared to be a well-laid-out bridgehead on the east bank of the river, because Pemberton believed Loring's division would join up with the army after covering the retreat of the army from Champion Hill. In fact, Loring had not covered the retreat at all and was pulling off to the south, eventually to join up with Johnston. In the process Loring lost nearly a third of his men to desertion. Pemberton still controlled two roads leading to the north, by which he might have escaped to join Johnston, but he clearly intended to obey Davis's instructions and retreat to Vicksburg.

Desultory skirmishing occurred on the morning of the 17th, as McClernand's corps came up on the Confederate positions. One of Brigadier General Michael Lawler's regimental colonels soon discovered a weakness in the Confederate positions where recent rains had washed away the tangle of trees and other obstructions the Confederates had emplaced in front of their positions. Lawler, an Illinois farmer, outstanding tactician, and pugnacious Irishman, then organized an assault column of the 23rd Iowa and 21st Iowa with the 11th Wisconsin in support. Taking advantage of the terrain, the attack force approached close enough to blast through the 61st Tennessee, a weak regiment consisting largely of conscripted soldiers from the eastern part of the state, Union country. Lawler's column destroyed the northeastern corner of Confederate defenses, through which Union troops poured. In short order, the defense collapsed as Bowen's soldiers ran for the bridges and, after they were fired, attempted to swim to safety. For a mere 223 casualties, 80 percent in Lawler's brigade, the XIII Corps captured 1,751 prisoners.

For the Confederates the only alternative open was a rapid retreat to Vicksburg. The Army of the Tennessee hounded their footsteps to the city's gates. In the seventeen days from 30 April to 17 May Grant had crossed the Mississippi, disregarded the military maxims of the day by cutting his army loose from its base, marched over two hundred miles, divided the Confederate armies, smashed up the railroads and industrial concerns of central Mississippi, wrecked Pemberton's army, and then set the stage for the capture of Vicksburg and its army. By keeping the enemy off balance, he had concentrated superior strength where it mattered. During this period, Lee was gathering his forces for an invasion of Pennsylvania. Displaying the limitations of his strategic vision, his ill-chosen comment to Seddon in mid-May had been that "the climate in June will force the enemy to retire [whatever happens]," when asked about sending Pickett's division west.[43]

On 18 May Sherman's XV Corps reached the northern flank of Vicksburg and occupied the Chickasaw Bluff overlooking the ground where the Confederates had defeated them the previous December. That position also allowed the Army of the Tennessee to reestablish connections with the North by way of the Mississippi. Grant's umbilical cord to the North reopened and through it he received a steady stream of supplies and reinforcements. Over the next month his army drew major units from throughout the Western theater: Grant's own XVI Corps, guarding supply lines in western Tennessee, provided a considerable body of soldiers; the Department of Missouri provided a division; the Department of the Ohio, the IX Corps—altogether 27,000 soldiers by mid-June. With these forces, Grant could hive off Sherman with 34,000 troops to watch Johnston, while he maintained an ever-tightening grip on Vicksburg.

After the collapse of the Confederates on the Big Black, Grant and his corps commanders had every expectation they could rush the Vicksburg defenses. However, whatever the morale of Pemberton's troops, the fortifications protecting the city's landward approaches were formidable. Anyone who has walked those areas of the siege lines the National Park Service has preserved cannot help recognize the skill with which Confederate engineers had sited the trenches and fortified positions in utilizing the high ground as well as the deep-cut ravines in the area.

A quick Union attack was a failure on 19 May; a more carefully organized effort, beginning with a major artillery bombardment on the 21st, was no more successful on the 22nd. McClernand's attack had some small success, which he magnified. His request for support kept the attacks by Sherman and McPherson continuing beyond the point when both would have halted their attacks. While that miscalculation was not sufficient for Grant to fire him, McClernand then made the mistake of issuing "a fulsome, congratulatory order" to his corps, which Northern newspapers published. Grant had had enough. Because McClernand had violated "War Department orders and also mine," Grant relieved him of command.[44] By sticking to the rule book as well as accumulating a notebook of McClernand's sins, Grant insured there would be no complaint from Washington. In Grant's army McClernand had failed the test of trust and membership in a cooperative enterprise where loyalty mattered.

The Army of the Tennessee settled down for a prolonged siege. Like Caesar at Alesia in 52 BC during the Gallic Wars, Grant confronted the problem of besieging a fortress, while an active enemy army on the outside attempted to relieve those inside. The siege required all the tactical and organizational skills that had accompanied such efforts over past centuries, but none of which were inherent in the backgrounds of the volunteer officers who made up the great majority of the Army of the Tennessee's officer corps. Nevertheless, guided by

West Pointers like Grant, the westerners were quick learners and great improvisers. Over the next seven weeks, Grant's men dug fortified battery positions for their artillery, saps, trenches, parallel trenches, all enveloping the defenders into an ever-closer embrace. All the while a constant artillery bombardment pounded Confederate positions and the town, while sharpshooters picked off those Confederates foolish enough to expose themselves.

Beyond the Vicksburg lines, Johnston faced the problem of how to relieve Vicksburg. The Confederates on the Mississippi's west bank proved of little help, although a Confederate attack on the Union position at Milliken's Bend proved that black soldiers, in this case badly equipped, were more than willing to die for their freedom. Johnston had already lost the possibility of adding the garrison at Port Hudson to his small army, since Pemberton, in accordance with Davis's instructions, had ordered the commander not to leave his fortifications. The arrival of Banks back on the Mississippi allowed his troops to surround the Confederates at Port Hudson. While Johnston received considerable reinforcements, they were never sufficient to allow an attack on Grant. Sherman's force, called the "Army of Observation," insured Johnston kept his distance. Only a Lee, or perhaps a Jackson, would have dared attack Grant's solid lines embracing Vicksburg—and Jackson was dead, while Lee was otherwise engaged.

By the end of June, the Army of the Tennessee was on the brink of launching a massive assault against Vicksburg's half-starved garrison. Its forward trenches were literally up against Confederate defensive lines, while its miners had emplaced no less than five major mines underneath Confederate front lines. Grant indicated to Dana the assault would occur on 6 July. But staring catastrophe in the face, Pemberton and his generals blinked. On 3 July the Confederates asked for terms. Grant initially suggested unconditional surrender, but after conferring with his generals and recognizing the problem of shipping 30,000 Confederate POWs north, he settled on paroling Pemberton's army after its surrender. Afterward Grant justified his decision by arguing that many of the Confederates eventually deserted. Pemberton on his part argued he had achieved better terms by surrendering on 4 July. Both were probably right.

Whatever the justification for paroling Confederate prisoners, the surrender of Pemberton's army, coming on the 4th of July, one day after Meade's victory at Gettysburg, represented a major boost for Northern morale. But for Grant, with his sense of strategy, Vicksburg represented an opening to larger possibilities. He spelled those out to Halleck: the next target for his army should be Mobile, which would close one of the few major ports remaining to the Confederacy and open another major front. As he noted in his memoirs: "Having [Mobile] as a base of operations, troops could have been thrown into the interior to operate against General Bragg's army. This would necessarily have forced Bragg to detach in order to meet this fire in his rear. If he had not done this the troops from Mobile could have inflicted inestimable damage upon much of the country from which his army and Lee's were yet receiving their supplies."[45]

Unfortunately for the Northern cause, Lincoln and Stanton missed the strategic importance of Mobile. It was not just that that port served as a major conduit for the flow of weapons and armaments to Confederate armies in the West, but a major Union force operating from southern Alabama would draw significant forces from Bragg's army in central Tennessee, which would have eased the Army of the Cumberland's advance on Chattanooga. It would also seem that the intervention of Louis Napoleon and the French into Mexican affairs distracted Lincoln from the possibilities that Mobile offered. The upshot was that the Union missed a significant opportunity to undermine the Confederacy's strategic situation. Moreover, by placing Grant on the shelf, the administration was minimizing the impact of its most effective general. Whatever Halleck's role in the discussions, it is certain that he was not providing useful strategic guidance to his political masters. Preoccupied as he was with "clean up" operations to garrison and clear territory, he had no interest in a campaign to attack Mobile and southern Alabama.

Already in July 1863 Union ground and naval forces were closing off Charleston to blockade-runners in a campaign, even though Halleck had argued against providing significant army support. Yet, by September, Union ground forces supported by the navy had captured both Fort Wagner, memorialized in the movie *Glory*, and Battery Gregg on the northern end of Morris Island. Those successes, although they failed to capture the city, effectively closed Charleston to blockade-runners. But Mobile remained in operation despite Grant's vision, only to be closed by the navy a year later. Thus, instead of directing an expedition against Mobile, Grant found himself left to stew in Vicksburg, while Halleck transferred much of the Army of the Tennessee to tasks of little importance. In the meantime, Grant did unleash Sherman's "Army of Observation" on Johnston, who had reoccupied Jackson and its fortifications in the hope of encouraging a direct assault. Sherman had no intention of assaulting those fortifications. Instead, he invested the Mississippi's capital. On 17 July Johnston abandoned Jackson, and Sherman completed the wrecking of central Mississippi.

By this point the war in the West had assumed a more ruthless energy than earlier in the conflict. The governor of Illinois, in speaking to some of his state's troops in May, had noted that the Federal government had spent the nation's treasure on the Louisiana Purchase and then added, *"by heaven we will redeem it, or make it one vast burying-ground."*[46] Among the soldiers, it was Sherman who gave voice to the new, harder turn in the road. In September 1863, in response to Halleck's request for Sherman's views on the war, the fiery redhead commented: "I would ... assert the broad doctrine that ... we will remove and destroy every obstacle—if need be, take every life, every acre of land, every particle of property, everything that seems to us proper; that we will not cease till the end is attained. That all who do not aid are enemies, and that we will not account to them for our acts. If the people of the South oppose, they do so at their peril."[47]

But there was another point of view from that of policy directed at bringing the Confederacy to heel. A young woman, pro-Union in her background and beliefs, recorded the arrival of Union troops in Clinton, Mississippi, in the following terms: "stables were torn down, smoke houses invaded and emptied of all their bacon and hams; chicken houses were depopulated, vehicles of all kind were taken or destroyed, barrels of sugar or molasses were emptied—the sugar carried off, while the molasses ran in streams in the yard. . . . The dry goods stores were broken into, the beautiful goods given to Negroes or destroyed, crockery broken. . . . General Sherman's protection papers proving of very little value."[48] The remorseless civil war that Thucydides had seen in Corcyra now had echoes in the American Civil War.

The Campaign for Tennessee

Nothing better reflects Halleck's failure as general in chief of Union armies than the fact that the Army of the Cumberland remained stationary through the end of June 1863 while the Army of the Potomac and the Army of the Tennessee had moved two months earlier. Admittedly, the Battle of Stones River had shredded Rosecrans's army, but then it had equally damaged Bragg's Army of Tennessee. Halleck might hector his subordinates, but he failed to command them. Thus, despite the flow of resources to Nashville and Murfreesboro, the latter the headquarters for the Army of the Cumberland, Rosecrans refused to budge. Faced with a similar situation in December 1864, when Thomas seemed unwilling to attack the Army of Tennessee in front of Nashville, Grant hopped on a train and headed west to relieve Thomas. Halleck did little more than send telegrams to Rosecrans.

Instead of acting, the commander of the Army of the Cumberland besieged Washington with requests for ever more men, horses, and equipment, as well as excuses as to why he could not yet attack. The first of these was that by holding Bragg in place, the Army of the Cumberland was preventing the Confederates from sending troops to reinforce the deteriorating situation in central Mississippi. Even more bizarre was his argument that the army should not move, since, if Grant were to be defeated, it would represent the last undefeated force available to the Union.

Lincoln's reply to such nonsense was on point: the president wrote to Rosecrans that when he had seen "a despatch of yours arguing that the right time for you to attack Bragg was not before but would be after the fall of Vicksburg, it impressed me very strangely. . . . It seemed no other than the proposition that you could better fight *when* Johnston should be at liberty to return and assist [Bragg], than you could *before* he could so return to [Bragg's] assistance."[49] In too many respects then Rosecrans resembled McClellan. The western general loved the trappings of military organization, parades, uniforms, and visiting with the soldiers. To him one should only wage war when one had insured everything so that no room for error remained.

Matters were more seriously in disarray on the other side. While Davis had decided to retain Bragg, he had not been able to patch over the contempt the Army of Tennessee's corps commanders felt for their commander. It was not just a matter of his fractious personality. Throughout his tenure, Bragg had displayed a penchant for indecision, a general failure to use terrain, a lack of understanding of his opponents, ambiguity in his orders, and a demand that his subordinates follow every minutia of his instructions. To put it bluntly, Bragg never fully grasped the geography of southeastern Tennessee. Admittedly,

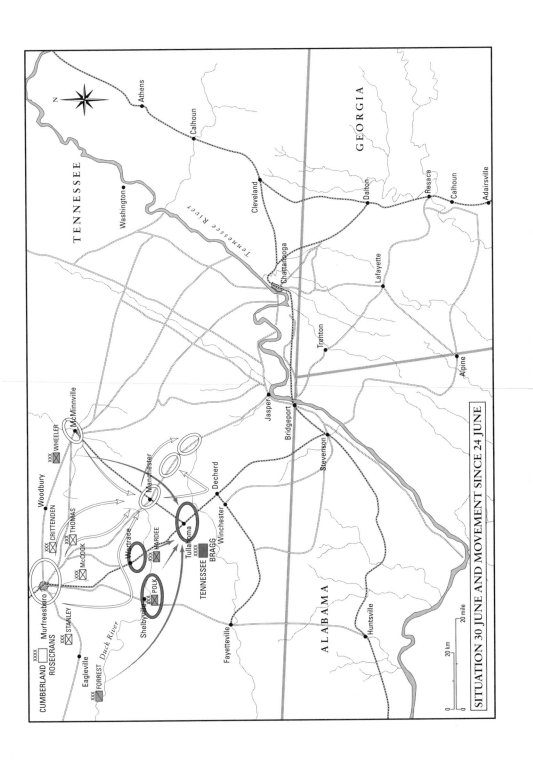

SITUATION 30 JUNE AND MOVEMENT SINCE 24 JUNE

the operational problems he confronted were daunting, but they only magnified his weaknesses. The geography of the region offered his opponent a number of different approaches on a front over seventy miles in length. To add to his problems, instead of using his cavalry to warn of Union moves, he stationed them on the wings with his infantry in the center. Thus, his cavalry failed to elicit usable intelligence, a factor that added to his inability to understand Rosecrans's movements.

Under extreme pressure from Washington, including the threat of imminent removal, Rosecrans finally moved on 24 June. The Army of the Cumberland consisted of the XIV Corps under the Virginian George Thomas with four divisions and 23,166 infantry; the XX Corps under Alexander McCook with three division and 14,096 infantry; the XXI Corps under Thomas Crittenden with three divisions and 15,031 infantry; and David Stanley, who commanded the cavalry with 9,960 troopers. Of the corps commanders, Thomas was the most competent, but better on the defensive than on the offensive. One of Thomas's brigadiers described McCook best: "He looks, if possible, more like a blockhead than ever, and it is astonishing to me that he should be permitted to retain command of a corps for a single hour."[50] McCook's corps had been on the right at Stones River, and it had been he who had failed to take adequate precautions against the possibility of a sudden Confederate attack, even though his troops had been in direct contact with the enemy. Crittenden fell somewhere between Thomas and McCook in terms of competence. A reserve division brought the army's strength to 68,560 men, while Rosecrans's artillery numbered 202 guns. Against that array, the Army of Tennessee numbered considerably fewer. Bragg possessed slightly under 30,000 infantry. His cavalry, diminished by John Morgan's raid across Kentucky into Indiana, numbered 13,000, but were badly mounted, although he did possess the incomparable Forrest. Whatever the weaknesses of the Union corps commanders, the gulf between Bragg and his corps commanders resulted in a completely dysfunctional high command.

Having failed to move through a June of good weather, Rosecrans's troops found themselves deluged by rain, which turned the roads of central and southeastern Tennessee into a mass of glutinous mud. Rosecrans's plan, like Hooker's at Chancellorsville, involved a number of different moving parts. But then the former was not up against Robert E. Lee. One force, consisting of a portion of the XIV Corps, appeared to drive directly south from Murfreesboro toward

Shelbyville. This move confirmed Bragg's belief that the Army of the Cumberland would attack his left. However, the main Union drive came against Bragg's right: two divisions of Crittenden's XXI Corps swung far out to the east with the aim of then driving on Manchester from the north, while Thomas's four divisions of the XIV Corps drove down a macadamized road toward Manchester. With Manchester in its hands the Army of the Cumberland would outflank Tullahoma and Bragg's defensive deployment on the Duck River.

Colonel John Wilder's brigade of mounted infantry spearheaded Thomas's advance. Wilder is one of the most interesting cases of citizen-soldiers in the Union or Confederate armies. Born and raised in Hunter, New York, he had followed Horace Greeley's advice to "go west," where he built an impressive career as an industrialist and an expert on hydraulics. At the war's outset, he enlisted and quickly rose to brigade command. Early in his time in service he had commanded the garrison at Munfordville and surrendered it to superior Confederate numbers—Bragg's whole army—but that had not damaged his career. Along the way, he had become impressed with the possibilities offered by the Spencer rifle, a seven-shot repeating firearm. In early spring 1863, with Rosecrans's support, he used his own promissory note for the private purchase of Spencers for every soldier in his brigade. The soldiers then signed over a portion of their pay to cover the cost of the repeating rifles. His brigade had then been mounted, and Wilder immediately displayed considerable tactical as well as leadership abilities.

Charging through Hoover's gap directly to the south of Murfreesboro, Wilder's mounted infantry brushed the Confederate cavalry screen away before reinforcing infantry could come up. They then held off determined Confederate infantry attacks with the volume of fire their Spencers produced as well as the artillery fire of their one artillery battery, commanded by a certain Captain Eli Lilly, who would eventually found the pharmaceutical firm that still bears his name. The arrival of Thomas's infantry ended the struggle. Thomas himself came up to declare to Wilder and his men: "You have saved the lives of a thousand men by your gallant conduct today. I didn't expect to get this Gap for three days."[51] But Rosecrans, ever cautious, failed to take advantage of Wilder's coup and kept Thomas motionless at Hoover's Gap for two days rather than allowing the XX Corps to push on to Manchester. Wilder's brigade then raided across the Elk River and, after ripping up a portion of the Nashville & Chattanooga Railroad, returned with his mud-splattered infantry troopers with Forrest hot on their heels.

By 29 June Bragg had realized he was in trouble. Outnumbered, in a difficult operational situation, and confused about Rosecrans's intentions, Bragg believed he could still mount a stand at Tullahoma. His corps commanders disagreed. On the afternoon of 30 June, he finally realized he was in danger of being cut off from the Elk River by Rosecrans's seizure of Manchester. Once again he changed his mind and ordered a retreat. Most of the stores and the Army of Tennessee escaped, but the Army of the Cumberland had outmaneuvered the Confederates from their positions along the Duck with hardly any casualties. Thus, it had driven Bragg out of middle Tennessee, one of the Confederacy's most productive agricultural areas. All in all, the Army of the Cumberland had advanced over eighty miles in eight days with fewer than a thousand casualties.

Washington, however, was less than impressed. By now it was dawning on Lincoln and Stanton that the mere occupation of territory and cities would not by themselves achieve victory. The armies of the Confederacy were the most visible representation of the nascent Southern nation, and until Union forces destroyed them, the rebellion would continue. It was not surprising the Union's political leaders were less than enthralled with the fact that Meade had allowed the Army of Northern Virginia to escape from Pennsylvania after Gettysburg or that Rosecrans had not brought Bragg's army to battle and defeat. On 7 July Stanton wired Rosecrans: "You and your noble army now have the chance to give the finishing blow to the rebellion. Will you neglect the chance?"[52] Halleck, undoubtedly also under pressure from his political masters, then resumed his sniping war with Rosecrans. The commander of the Army of the Cumberland replied to Halleck's carping missives that, if the War Department were unhappy with his performance, they could always replace him. And that suggests the nature of the problem Washington faced—one similar to what Lloyd George confronted in 1917 when he thought about replacing Douglas Haig as commander of the British Expeditionary Force in France. One of the entries dealing with Haig in the index of his memoirs simply reads: "no conspicuous officer better qualified for highest command than."[53] Certainly, none of the corps commanders in the Army of the Cumberland had indicated so far they would act more aggressively as an army commander.

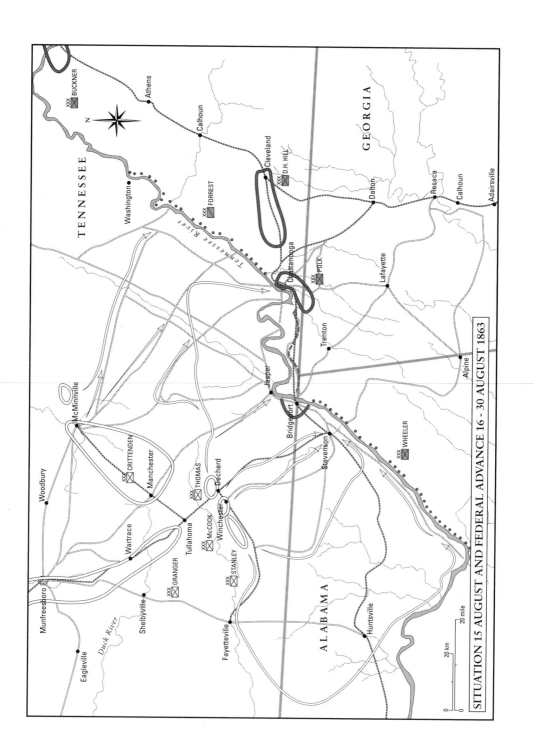

SITUATION 15 AUGUST AND FEDERAL ADVANCE 16 - 30 AUGUST 1863

For six weeks the Army of the Cumberland lingered in the neighborhood of Tullahoma, while Rosecrans repaired his lines of communications and had masses of supplies brought forward and stockpiled for the army's next advance. Only in mid-August did he finally feel he could resume the offensive, the goal being Chattanooga. That city was perhaps the most important rail center in the South. It provided the links to Virginia in the east, Atlanta and Savannah in the south, and Jackson and Nashville in the west. Moreover, in Union hands it would provide the ideal launching point for invasions into Georgia and Alabama and open the back door to the Confederacy's eastern states.

August was a dismal month for Bragg's army, as well as for its commander, whose health apparently collapsed. The army's infantry strength had fallen below 30,000, a situation resulting largely from a swelling number of desertions by soldiers fueled by their commander's harsh style of leadership, a dismally inadequate supply system, and a long series of retreats. Nevertheless, for Rosecrans, just reaching Bragg and the Army of Tennessee represented a major problem in terms of the region's geography, since the lower portion of the Appalachians ran through the area. Heavily forested mountains cut from northeast to southwest throughout southeastern Tennessee and northwest Georgia with few good roads. One potential answer to the problem was a Union advance along multiple axes, but that carried the danger the Confederates could isolate one of the Union corps and destroy it before others could move to its support.

Prodded by threats from Washington, Rosecrans finally ordered the Army of the Cumberland to resume its advance. On 16 August it lurched forward against an Army of Tennessee in even worse shape than it had been in mid-June along the Duck River. Once again, Wilder's mounted infantry, riding all the way to the north bank of the Tennessee opposite Chattanooga, led the advance. There, Wilder's troops bombarded the city with Lilly's artillery, catching the good citizens in their churches in response to Jefferson Davis's request for a day of prayer and fasting throughout the Confederacy.

By 29 August Rosecrans's engineers had bridged the Tennessee River at Bridgeport. Bragg seemed incapable of turning the mountainous terrain to his army's advantage. In a comment that must have made Stonewall Jackson turn in his grave, Bragg noted: "It is said to be easy to defend a mountainous country, but mountains hide your foe from you, while they are full of gaps through which he can pounce upon at you at any time. A mountain is like the wall of a house full of rat-holes. The rat lies hidden at his hole, ready to pop out when no one is watching. Who can tell what lies hidden behind that wall?"[54]

The individual to whom Bragg made these remarks was Lieutenant General D. H. Hill, transferred from North Carolina to take Hardee's place. Like Bragg, Hill possessed a difficult personality, but he was also a competent soldier. The end result of their discussions was that Hill "was most painfully impressed with the feeling that it was to be a haphazard campaign."[55] What is indeed astonishing is that Bragg made no effort to guard the Sand and Lookout Mountain passes, which, if the enemy gained them, provide direct access to his rear in the south. Only on 2 September did the Confederates realize that the Army of the Cumberland was coming at them from the south rather than from the north. By 7 September a Union advance south of Chattanooga completely disconcerted Bragg, since he had expected the Army of the Cumberland to move north of Chattanooga to link up with Burnside's XXIII Corps advancing from Knoxville. In addition, Knoxville's fall to Burnside on 3 September further misled the Confederates and confirmed Bragg's fears about a Union advance coming from the north. As a result, he ordered Chattanooga abandoned and pulled back to the mountainous region lying southeast of the city to meet the Union advance.

Nevertheless, the correlation of forces was changing. Davis and Seddon finally decided to concentrate the Confederacy's effort on the one theater where Union forces were mounting a dangerous campaign. They were able to do so because Meade on the Rappahannock was unwilling to challenge Lee and the Army of Northern Virginia, especially since any renewed fighting would be on the latter's home ground. On the Mississippi front, Lincoln, Stanton, and Halleck had frittered Grant's strength away in penny-packet commitments that gained little. With the Mississippi front quiescent, Johnston, unwillingly, and only as a direct result of orders emanating from Richmond, transferred six of his eleven infantry brigades, altogether approximately 6,000 men, to Bragg. That force had arrived by 28 August. The loss of Knoxville also made Simon Bolivar Buckner's force of approximately 5,000 ill-disciplined troops available in the emergency, since Burnside, never imaginative in the best of times, sat down to enjoy occupying Knoxville rather than advancing south and joining the campaign to take Chattanooga.

But the major decision taken in Richmond was to transfer two divisions of the Army of Northern Virginia, along with Lee's "war horse," Longstreet, to reinforce Bragg. Davis even considered dispatching Lee to command Confederate armies in the West, but Lee talked him out of that possibility. In retrospect, the decision to allow Lee to remain in Virginia was a serious mistake, because only he had the prestige and ability to bring order to the fractious Western command. Not surprisingly, he argued for an aggressive policy in Virginia and against the transfer of Longstreet's corps. But he had already had his chance. This time, unlike May's discussions, Davis and Seddon overruled the commander of the Army of Northern Virginia. But the decision to transfer Longstreet occurred so late in the game that only five brigades of his corps arrived to participate in the battle of Chickamauga, while the other four brigades and Porter Alexander's artillery were still strung out along the South's rickety rail system in South Carolina and Georgia. Again, it was a matter of the Confederacy's weak transportation system.

These augmentations evened the strength between the two armies. By mid-September the Army of the Cumberland numbered 55,799 infantry and artillery and 9,842 cavalry (a total of 65,641); their opponents now possessed 47,520 infantry and artillery with 14,260 cavalry (a total of 61,780). On 9 September the Army of the Cumberland had spread itself over nearly forty miles. In the south McCook's XX Corps was advancing through the southernmost gap in Lookout Mountain; twenty miles to the north Thomas's corps was moving through Steven's Gap with James Negley's division advancing across the valley to Dug Gap in Pigeon Mountain, which ran parallel to Lookout Mountain from southwest to northeast. Finally, fifteen miles to the north, Crittenden's XXI Corps held Rossville and Chattanooga. The dangerous spread of Union corps invited the Confederates to defeat them in detail. But to do so, the Confederates needed to act with dispatch, and Bragg would have to provide clear guidance and leadership. Neither was present in the skirmishing before Chickamauga.

On 10 September Bragg had almost caught Negley's division, but his subordinates botched the job, either through the frictions of war, disobedience, or Bragg's own warnings that Crittenden's corps might be moving down on their rear. Since Bragg remained in the rear, he failed to hurry matters along. When Confederate pincers closed on McLemore's Cove, they closed on thin air. Recognizing the danger,

Thomas had pulled Negley back. On the 13th Bragg had then ordered Polk to attack Crittenden's corps south of Rossville. But Polk demurred. When Bragg arrived the next morning, he discovered nothing had been done. By the time Confederate columns moved forward, Crittenden had pulled back behind Missionary Ridge. Thus the Confederates lost a second opportunity to attack a portion of Rosecrans's army.

It was not until the night of 12 September that the Union commander recognized the imminent danger of defeat in detail and the need to concentrate his army as quickly as possible. Bragg's new aggressiveness was indeed alarming. Thus, the race began to see whether the Army of the Cumberland could concentrate before the Confederates could strike. By 18 September, Rosecrans had nearly completed concentration of his forces on the western side of the West Chickamauga Creek with Missionary Ridge and Lookout Mountain to his rear and Pigeon Mountain on the east side of the creek. The creek itself was deep with fast-running water, while thick stands of trees interspersed with farmer's fields and pastureland covered the valley floor. Thickly forested areas offered less than ideal ground for battle. Command and control of the units engaged in the fight would prove to be a nightmare, as was the case in most battles in the West. With considerable accuracy the Southern diarist Mary Chesnut had described battles in the West as barroom brawls, which fits what was to happen at Chickamauga to a *T*.

On the 18th Bragg attacked. The first brigades from the Army of Northern Virginia were in the process of arriving and would soon be ready. At this point the bulk of the Army of the Cumberland lay to the south of Lee and Gordon's Mills. Bragg planned to seize Alexander's bridge and Reed's bridge, which lay several miles north of Lee and Gordon's Mills. By seizing the ground west of the bridges the Army of Tennessee would have interposed itself between Rosecrans and Chattanooga and cut his supply lines. But the Confederates ran into a fierce delaying action. A portion of Wilder's brigade with its Spencers and a few artillery pieces held Alexander's bridge for five hours against sustained attacks by Confederate infantry. To their north Colonel Robert Minty's brigade of Union cavalry did as well against Bushrod Johnson's division, which had Forrest and his troopers in support. The upshot of the day's fighting was that the Confederates failed to cross the creek in force until late in the afternoon and, thus, could not establish themselves on the Army of the Cumberland's northern flank.

That night Thomas hustled his corps up to the army's northern flank as fast as possible in a demanding march behind Crittenden, whose corps was already in place along Chickamauga creek at Lee and Gordon's Mills. By early morning Thomas had deployed his divisions to the north of Lee and Gordon's Mills, so that Bragg had no chance of outflanking the Army of the Cumberland. Nevertheless, throughout the battle Bragg would persist in his belief that he could outflank the Federals on the northern front despite accumulating evidence to the contrary. The battle opened on the morning of 19 September, when units of Thomas's corps stumbled into one of the Confederate divisions in dense undergrowth.

Initial reports underestimated the size of the Confederate force, and Thomas sent in a brigade to drive the Confederates from their position. Running into a large number of Confederates, the brigade commander sent back a message asking which of the five enemy brigades he was to attack. Thomas quickly dispatched reinforcements, which badly bloodied two Confederate divisions in the battle's opening engagement. Both sides fed increasing numbers of troops into what soon became a furious meeting engagement with little room for maneuver. Thomas's corps succeeded in fending off Confederate attacks in the morning, but after a brief lull at midday, even heavier fighting erupted in the afternoon. Much as he had done at Shiloh, Bragg persisted in throwing his units into the fight in piecemeal fashion—attacks which achieved local successes but which failed in their larger aim of breaking Union resistance. For a time, Confederate attackers in the center closed on Rosecrans's headquarters, but there always seemed sufficient Union troops to fend them off and drive the Confederates back.

Late that afternoon a portion of Longstreet's corps arrived under Hood, who was still recovering from his wound at Gettysburg. The Texas brigade, which had once been Hood's command, participated in a major attack late in the afternoon. As the brigade's soldiers went in, they shouted at a badly shot-up brigade of Alexander Stewart's division: "Rise up, Tennesseans and see the Texans go in." Unfortunately for Hood's command, it ran into Wilder's brigade. As the Hunter Mountain native recorded after the battle, his brigade and Lilly's accompanying artillery gave the attacking Confederates "over 200 rounds of double-shotted 10-pound canister, at a range varying from 70 to 350 yards, and at the same time kept up a constant fire with our repeating rifles." The Texans returned as shattered as their predecessors. One of Stewart's soldiers then shouted out: "Rise up, Tennesseans and see the Texans come out."[56]

The day's major attack came when Patrick Cleburne's well-trained division struck Thomas's weary troops, exhausted not only by the fierce fighting but also by their lengthy night march. Like the other Confederate attacks that day, it too failed with heavy losses. Harvey Hill summed up the Confederate performance as "the sparring of the amateur boxer, and not the crushing blows of the trained pugilist."[57] But then Hill had served throughout 1862 under Robert E. Lee, so he understood what a killing, powerful blow involved. As night settled, with the suffering of the wounded made more agonizing by a scarcity of water, Bragg and Rosecrans had serious thinking to do. For Rosecrans, like Meade at Gettysburg, it was a matter of merely deciding to hold on in the midst of a desperate struggle.

The Union commander decided that Thomas would run the battle in the northern portion of the front, while he directed the southern portion. Thomas suggested at a midnight conference that the Union right swing back to spurs on Lookout Mountain—a position that would have offered more defensible terrain and closed the Army of the Cumberland into a tight hedgehog position. Rosecrans demurred. Whatever the morrow offered, there would be no major Union attacks to shift the battle's momentum. Instead, especially in the area defended by Thomas, Union troops were hard at work throughout the night felling trees and building abatis and strong points, an activity that occasioned considerable dread in Confederate lines.

Without substantive discussion with his subordinates, Bragg came up with an unimaginative plan to attack from north to south in a rolling series of offensives, which represented a replay of the first day. But Bragg still had no real grasp of the positioning of enemy forces. Thus there would be no attempt to cut the Army of the Cumberland off from Chattanooga, but rather a replication of his effort to drive the Federals back into McLemore's Cove. Bragg also decided that Polk would handle the fighting in the north, while Longstreet handled the south. For the northern drive, he placed Hill under Polk's command, but not only were his orders ambiguous, he also neglected to inform Hill he would be under Polk's command. Hill never made contact with either Bragg or Polk, while the latter never received written orders indicating what Bragg expected. To add to these miscommunications, Hill failed to receive Polk's orders. Finally, Longstreet had arrived in midafternoon of the first day's fighting, but Bragg had sent no guides or staff officers to meet him. As a result, in the confused terrain, Longstreet and his staff officers had almost ridden into the Union Army. They failed to link up with Bragg until midnight.

On the morning of the 20th, Bragg awoke before dawn, mounted his horse, and awaited Polk's attack. Two hours later, by now furious, he was still waiting. He then sent a staff officer to find out was going on; none of the various accounts of what then transpired agree, but it was not until nearly 1000, instead of dawn, when Polk finally struck. Hill's corps began a series of attacks that broke themselves on the Union line over the course of succeeding hours. He had already warned Polk and Bragg that there was scant chance of success given the field fortifications Union defenders had emplaced during the night. But Bragg, who had not reconnoitered the ground, ordered the attacks continued. Breckinridge's division managed for a short time to flank Union positions in the north, and by seizing the LaFayette Road, cut the Federals off from the most direct route to Chattanooga. But Polk failed to support Breckinridge with reinforcements, and Union counterattacks drove the attackers back. By noon Union defenses had shattered Breckinridge's division. Only then did Polk commit Cleburne's division. Again the Confederates suffered devastating losses.

But if matters were falling apart in the north, one of the most appalling mistakes made by a Union general during the course of the war occurred on the southern portion of the battlefield. The cause of the disaster lay in a series of relatively minor incidents, which, when combined, led to an error of major proportions. Rosecrans was one of those commanders who believe that the key to command effectiveness lies in humiliating subordinates by lengthy periods of shouting at them. That morning, admittedly under pressure, he had without reason chewed out Brigadier General Thomas Wood with a series of choice swear words in front of his subordinates for not having obeyed orders.

Later in the morning, a newly promoted captain on Thomas's staff, who had transmitted orders moving brigades from the right wing to the left, mistakenly reported that there was a gap in Union lines. When that news reached Rosecrans, he decided to pull Wood's division out of the line to fill the gap. The order was the only one that day not written by Colonel James Garfield, future president of the United States and at the time Rosecrans's chief of staff, who knew the position of every Union division. Garfield would certainly have recognized

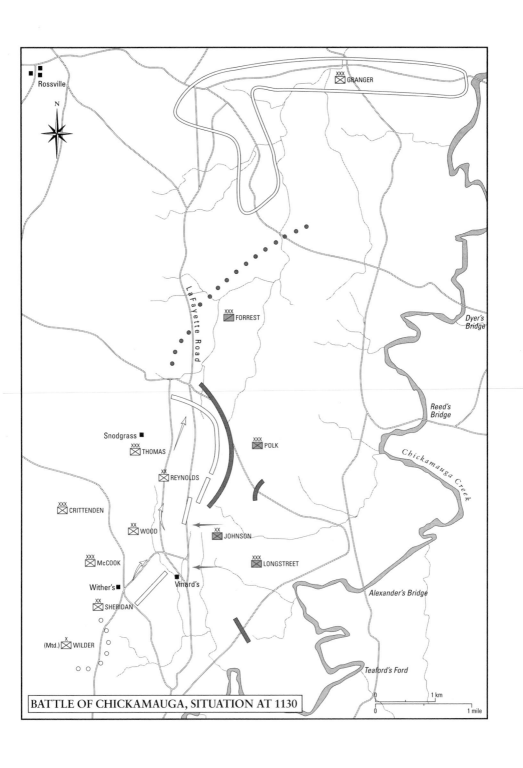

Rossville

N

GRANGER

La Fayette Road

FORREST

Dyer's
Bridge

Reed's
Bridge

Snodgrass

THOMAS

POLK

Chickamauga Creek

REYNOLDS

CRITTENDEN

WOOD

JOHNSON

McCOOK

LONGSTREET

Wither's

Vinard's

Alexander's Bridge

SHERIDAN

(Mtd.) WILDER

Teaford's Ford

0   1 km

0   1 mile

BATTLE OF CHICKAMAUGA, SITUATION AT 1130

the danger of moving Wood's division. In turn, Wood, out of seeming spite after Rosecrans's furious dressing down, read the order and obeyed. Because Rosecrans had done nothing to heal the divisions Buell had left behind in the Army of the Cumberland, disaster now occurred.

In obeying Rosecrans's order, Wood created a major opportunity for the Confederates. At the moment his division was moving back from its defensive position in the center of the Union line and opening a huge hole in the Union line, Longstreet was preparing a massive blow with eight brigades, a force almost as large as Pickett's charge and for the most part consisting of fresh units. Bushrod Johnson's division hit the quarter of a mile gap in the Union line. Not surprisingly, his troops advanced straight through, deep into the Army of the Cumberland's rear. On both sides of the breakthrough, Union positions unraveled. Some units fell apart; others covered the retreat of the collapsing right wing. Wilder's brigade as usual distinguished itself. On at least one occasion it counterattacked, while its Spencers allowed it to inflict grievous casualties on the left of Longstreet's advance. Nevertheless, most of the Union troops on the right (southern) wing fled. The division commanders, including Sheridan, did little to stop the rout. Among those fleeing was Rosecrans, who had the opportunity to join Thomas on the left but chose to flee to Chattanooga, which he entered in a mood of despair.

Thomas, however, refused to panic and pulled his open flank back to the northwest, anchoring it on Snodgrass Hill. There his troops began what proved a heroic tale of resistance. Thomas displayed the qualities that made him one of the first-rate battlefield commanders of the Civil War. He was steadfast, rather than brilliant; tough, rather than aggressive; stolid, rather than imaginative. But one of his division commanders, Brigadier General John Turchin (Ivan Turchaninov), a former member of the Tsar's Guards regiment and veteran of the Crimean War, noted that Thomas had the ability "of foreseeing the moves of the enemy and preparing means to defeat them."[58]

"Old Pete," disobeying Bragg's instructions, turned his troops to the north to sweep up the left (northern) wing of the Union line. The question now was whether the Confederates could destroy Thomas and the northern half of the Army of the Cumberland. Here, Bragg's inability to adapt came into play. The Confederate commander seems almost to have disbelieved his army had achieved a breakthrough, largely because things had not gone according to plan. Instead of rein-forcing Longstreet, who might have outflanked Thomas's right, Bragg sent Polk in against Thomas's left. Without reinforcements, Longstreet had to launch a series of attacks on Snodgrass Hill and Horseshoe Ridge to its west, which Union troops falling back from the break-through had occupied. The defense of Snodgrass Hill and Horseshoe Ridge on Thomas's southern flank is particularly interesting, because the initial force defending the position consisted of individuals and small groups who rallied, not as a coherent unit, but simply as sol-diers. In other words, its defense consisted of soldiers who refused to admit defeat. They held the initial Confederate attacks until reinforce-ments arrived. Turchin noted after the war: "This spontaneous rally on Horseshoe Ridge was an opportunity for just such independent spirits to join the crowd and fight in their own way and not under subordina-tion and strict orders. And they fought splendidly."[59]

The timely arrival of James Steedman's division of Gordon Granger's reserve force stationed to the north of the battlefield saved Thomas's right. Unlike Slocum at Gettysburg, Steedman and Granger marched to the sound of the guns when it was apparent that there was trouble on the battlefield south of their position near Rossville. They arrived at precisely the right moment when it appeared the Confederates were going to seize Horseshoe Ridge and overwhelm Union defenders on Snodgrass. Moreover, they brought their ammunition reserve, 95,000 cartridges, which resupplied Thomas's troops just as they were about to run out of ammunition. At one point, Steedman ordered an artil-leryman to double-shot his guns; the lieutenant replied he had already done that, to which Steedman ordered him to triple-shot the guns.

Underlining the coming revolution in firepower, which had pro-vided Wilder's brigade with lethal doses of firepower, seven compa-nies of the 21st Ohio possessed Colt revolving rifles, which with its seven shots they could load as fast as a rifled musket with its single cartridge. They repelled five separate charges, heavily punishing the attackers. After the war Longstreet claimed that he had launched twenty-five separate attacks on the Union positions. The major at-tacks came close to success, but in the end failed under the punishing firepower of Union guns.

As the battle continued throughout the afternoon, the defenders were constantly at work reinforcing their barricades and defensive positions, which added to Confederate difficulties. In the midst of the battle, Garfield, whom Rosecrans had ordered to report to Thomas, noted "Thomas standing like a rock," which eventually mutated into the Virginian's nickname, "the rock of Chickamauga."[60] As the fighting died down before the sun set, Thomas began his withdrawal through McFarland's Gap. Turchin's brigade had to clear the way by counterattacking St. John Liddell's division of Polk's corps which had almost succeeded in working its way around Thomas's northern flank. The former Tsar's Guards officer's brigade cleared the path, and Thomas's divisions of the Army of the Cumberland escaped into the gathering night.

The Army of Tennessee won its greatest victory, or at least what the Confederates claimed as a victory. But Bragg certainly did not feel victorious. There would be no serious pursuit of the beaten Union army, as some of the Confederate commanders urged. However, when one considers the casualties the Confederates suffered, one can doubt how successful a pursuit might have proven. Out of an end strength of 47,520 infantry and artillery, the Confederates suffered 16,199 casualties: killed, 2,074; wounded, 12,797; and missing, 1,328—34 percent of those present for duty before the battle. The rank and file of the Confederacy's most important western field army had once again shown a fighting spirit its commanders did not deserve. Union losses were also high, but not as high. From an end strength of 55,799 infantry and artillery, Rosecrans's troops suffered 15,696 casualties: killed, 1,625; wounded, 9,618; and missing, 4,453—a loss of 28 percent. Among the generals who went down either killed or wounded, Hood was hit in the upper leg on the second day, necessitating amputation.

Chickamauga ranks with Gettysburg and Antietam as among the worst killing battles of the war. At its end, the Confederates held the battlefield and could claim a tactical victory, one that was certainly Pyrrhic. Some historians have argued the Confederates had the possibility, had they acted quickly, not only to have destroyed the Army of the Cumberland, but also to move forward into Tennessee to regain much of that state. Such arguments represent armchair history at its worst. Bragg's army was badly battered; Union forces were soon flowing into the theater in large numbers; and the Confederates could barely support the move to besiege Chattanooga, considering the state of their logistics.

As to the next step, Bragg decided to besiege the Army of the Cumberland in Chattanooga. In retrospect, it was the only reasonable decision. Given the topography of the mountains surrounding the town, it should have been a relatively easy matter. The Army of Tennessee moved forward to occupy the hills overlooking Chattanooga and the Tennessee River, which, along with the railroad running along its banks, was crucial to supplying of the Army of the Cumberland. At the same time, with a complete lack of sensibility, Bragg relieved and then preferred charges against Polk and one of his division commanders. To further alienate his subordinates, if that were possible, Bragg transferred Forrest's cavalry to Joseph Wheeler, a man whom Forrest detested. At the beginning of October, Forrest went directly to Bragg and, in one of the most stunning conversations between a subordinate and superior, announced: "I have stood your meanness as long as I intend to. You have played the part of a damned scoundrel, and are a coward, and if you were any part of a man I would slap your jaws and force you to resent it. You may as well not issue any more orders to me, for I will not obey them . . . and I say to you that if you ever again try to interfere with me or cross my path it will be at the peril of your life."[61] Forrest's furious diatribe was symptomatic of the poisonous command climate Bragg had fostered.

The wonder of it is that Davis was still willing to stand by Bragg. In early October the Confederate president, despite his health, journeyed from Richmond to smooth over the quarrels among the fractious senior officers of the Army of Tennessee—the quarrels underlined by a savage letter attacking Bragg's competence and signed by a number of the army's senior officers. In meeting with them and Bragg, Davis made every effort "to be serviceable in harmonizing some of the difficulties"[62] that were plaguing the army, but heard Longstreet comment that Bragg "could be of greater service elsewhere than at the head of the Army of Tennessee."[63]

In a strategic sense, Chickamauga led to a strategic defeat for the Confederacy with serious consequences. First, the Confederate "victory" elicited an immediate response from Washington. That response resulted in the decision to send two corps from the Army of the Potomac (Howard's XI and Slocum's XII) under Hooker's command to reinforce the West. What sparked the decision was a telegram from Dana to Stanton that arrived in the evening of 23 September. Dana urged that 20–25,000 men be sent from the East to reinforce the situation in the West. In a meeting that night Halleck estimated such a move would take three months. Wiser heads prevailed, and the president authorized the move. On the next morning Stanton and his staff set about coordinating the move with northern railroad executives. Within forty hours the first trains with the troops of the two corps and their equipment were rolling west. By 8 October the troop movement had been completed in eleven days with Hooker's two corps twenty-six miles from Chattanooga. The journey of over 1,233 miles represented a move that in its sophistication was far beyond anything the Prussian Army would execute in its wars of 1866 and 1870.

Even before Chickamauga, Halleck, apprised of the reinforcements that Bragg was receiving, set in motion a flow of reinforcements from the Western theater of operations to southeastern Tennessee. But even more important was the decision to put everything west of the Appalachians under Grant's command. Dana's report on Rosecrans's collapse after the defeat helped speed the decision; Lincoln was soon convinced the commander of the Army of the Cumberland had to go. As he commented, the general "was acting like a duck hit on the head."[64] Stanton hurried out to meet Grant at Louisville and get some sense of the only Union general who seemed capable of winning. He brought along Grant's new commission. On Halleck's orders, Grant had left Vicksburg to journey to Chattanooga and on the way to meet with Stanton.

It was not an easy trip, because Grant was still recovering from a leg injury resulting from a riding accident. On the way to the front he also met with Rosecrans, who "made some excellent suggestions as to what should be done. My only wonder was that he had not carried them out."[65] The hardest part of the journey was the route into Chattanooga, a circuitous, muddy track over the mountains from Bridgeport on the Tennessee leading through the mountains to the north of Chattanooga and the besieged forces, now under Thomas's command. Upon arrival Grant set in motion the various pieces that would end the siege and result in another major victory for the Union. As one veteran recalled after the war, "you have no conception of the change in the army when Grant came. He opened up the cracker line and got a steamer through. We began to see things move. We felt that everything came from a plan. He came into the army quietly, no splendor, no airs, no staff. He used to go about alone. He began the campaign the moment he reached the field."[66]

Horace Porter, at the time a member of Thomas's staff, but who would soon transfer to Grant's, provides a wonderful picture of Grant at work: "At this time as throughout his career, he wrote nearly all of his documents with his own hand, and seldom dictated to any one even the most unimportant dispatch. His work was performed swiftly and uninterruptedly, but without any marked display of nervous energy. His thoughts flowed freely from his mind as the ink from his pen; he was never at a loss for expression, and seldom interlined a word or made a material correction. He sat with his head bent low over the table, and when he had occasion to step to another table or desk to get a paper he wanted, he would glide rapidly across the room without straightening himself, and return to his seat with his body still bent over at about the same angle at which he had been sitting when he left his chair."[67]

The morning after his arrival, Grant, Thomas, and William F. "Baldy" Smith examined a chink in the Confederate investment of Chattanooga. While the Confederate grip on the town appeared airtight with the exception of the miserable track over the mountains, Smith had discovered a track through Raccoon Mountain, running between Brown's Ferry (down the bend the Tennessee River takes from Chattanooga) and Kelley's Ferry beyond Confederate lines. As Porter Alexander acidly pointed out in his memoirs, "the importance of holding strongly the country between the two ferries . . . seems never to have been appreciated by either Bragg or Longstreet. . . . A full division at least should have guarded so important a point, and one so exposed."[68]

In fact, there were only scattered units of Confederate pickets and sharpshooters on Raccoon Mountain, while the nearest significant force was Law's brigade of Hood's division. As the army's chief engineer, Smith set in motion the construction of flat-bottomed boats to carry a landing force to seize Brown's Ferry after gliding at night past the Confederate pickets on the river's left bank. The boats would then ferry reinforcements across the river and finally serve as the pontoons to construct a bridge for further reinforcements. Turchin's brigade, which had been hiding in the woods out of sight, ferried across after the far shore had been secured. At the same time as the eastern operation was underway, Hooker was crossing the Tennessee at Kelley's Ferry with Howard's XI Corps. The two forces then secured Raccoon Mountain. What soon became known as the "cracker line" opened, and the flow of rations and supplies to the Army of the Cumberland dramatically improved.

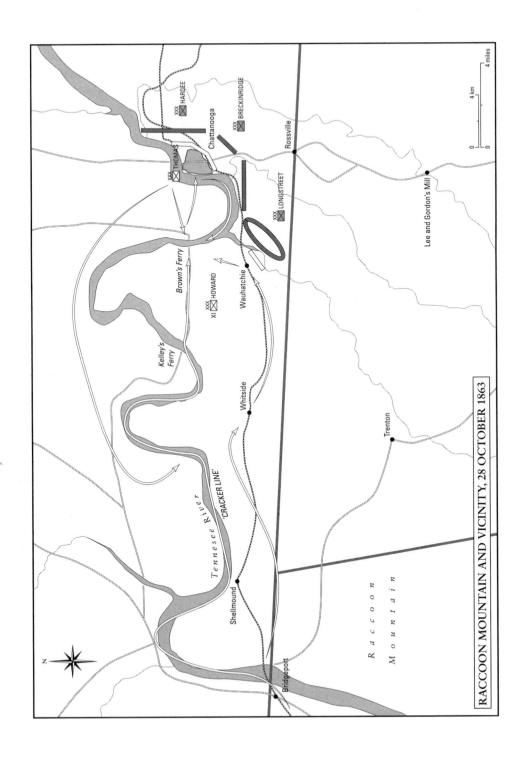

RACCOON MOUNTAIN AND VICINITY, 28 OCTOBER 1863

On the night of 28 October, Longstreet launched a minor attack, which after some initial success was driven off. Astonishingly, Bragg failed to mount a major offensive to cut this new and crucial line of supply to the Army of the Cumberland. The initiative was now in Grant's hands. Still, before he could act, the Army of the Cumberland had to be resupplied, a massive effort over a difficult supply line, while Sherman with his divisions had to come up on their long journey from Mississippi. It took nearly a fortnight for Sherman to reach Chattanooga. On 15 November, he arrived ahead of his troops, who were crossing at Kelley's Ferry. With the Army of the Cumberland largely resupplied and fed, Grant was ready to act.

Bragg in the first weeks of November had made the rash decision to send Longstreet and his troops north in an effort to regain Knoxville. His reasoning is hard to fathom, since it was obvious that Union forces were gathering in and around Chattanooga. The most favorable explanation is that he hoped Longstreet's move against Union forces in Knoxville would draw Grant off. But, given his personality, it is equally possible that the tension and dislike that had grown between the two generals led Bragg to use the Knoxville expedition as an excuse to get rid of another critical corps commander, this one under his command for not quite a month. Indeed, Davis himself may have believed that moving Longstreet to Knoxville would best resolve the friction between the two generals. Having seen the positions on Missionary Ridge, Davis pronounced them impregnable. Grant sarcastically, but accurately, commented in his memoirs was that "on several occasions during the war [Davis] came to the relief of the Union army by means of his *superior military genius*."[69] Finally, Bragg may also have felt his positions holding Lookout Mountain and Missionary Ridge were invulnerable to a Union attack. As Grant admitted after the war, they should have been.

As with most of Grant's operations, his plans were simply a means to feel the enemy out and strike him at his weakest point. His plan called for Sherman to cross Thomas's rear and, once he had gotten his two corps in place on the Union left—to the east of Chattanooga—cross the Tennessee River, and strike Bragg at the north end of Missionary Ridge. For one of the few times in the war, Sherman let Grant down. Admittedly, he had considerable difficulty in getting his troops in place, given the conditions of the ground, pummeled as it had been by fall rains. As a result, the Union offensive failed to open

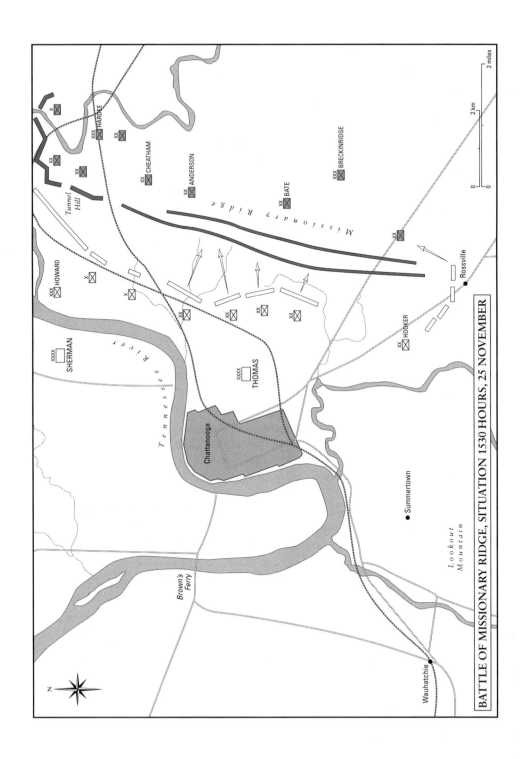

BATTLE OF MISSIONARY RIDGE, SITUATION 1530 HOURS, 25 NOVEMBER

until 24 November with pushes on the flanks of the Confederates by Sherman on the left against the northern tip of Missionary Ridge and Hooker on the right against Lookout Mountain. The day appeared one of success: Sherman reported he had reached Tunnel Hill on Missionary Ridge, while in a fierce fight Hooker, still a competent battlefield leader, drove the Confederates off of Lookout Mountain. Grant was encouraged.

But matters did not go so well on the morning of the 25th. Sherman's troops had not advanced as far as he had thought. In fact, they were nowhere near Tunnel Hill. Moreover, he had Patrick Cleburne's division in front of him. Cleburne, a former sergeant in the British Army, who had immigrated to the United States, had turned his division into one of the best-trained units of the war. Sherman's attack went nowhere. On the right flank, Hooker's attack had no greater luck. Only Thomas's Army of the Cumberland remained, deployed across the valley from Missionary Ridge. At this point Grant, believing Bragg had stripped the troops on Missionary Ridge to support his flanks, decided to launch the Army of the Cumberland across the valley. Its troops were only to seize the gun pits at the bottom of the ridge and hopefully force Bragg to pull units back from the flanks.

As was usually the case with Thomas, preparations took an inordinately long time. For one of the few times in the war, Grant lost his temper. After Grant's annoyed intervention, the attack went forward. It successfully crossed the valley floor under fire from Confederate artillery at the top of Missionary Ridge and reached the rifle pits at the bottom of the slope with relatively few losses. Thomas's troops drove the Confederates out of the rifle pits, and then, the attacking troops, without orders, followed the retreating enemy up the slope. Grant "watched their progress with intense interest."[70] In fact, he did more than watch. He turned brusquely to ask who had authorized the continuation of the attack beyond the rifle pits. No senior officers, including Thomas, owned up.

But the attacking troops were in luck. The Confederates had made several egregious mistakes. First, they had sited their artillery on the geographic crest of Missionary Ridge rather than on the military crest, where they would have had clear shots down the ridge at the advancing Union troops. Second, the Confederates had done little to construct field fortifications and abatis to retard any attack from the valley. As a result, the Union attackers quickly worked their way up the draws, while badly sited Confederate artillery fired over their heads. Finally, with insufficient infantry deployed in the Confederate defenses, there was little possibility of holding a determined attack. Before the astonished eyes of the Union high command, the soldiers of the Army of the Cumberland swarmed over the ridge, as the Confederates ran. One of the heroes of the attack was eighteen-year-old Lieutenant Arthur MacArthur, who would receive the Congressional Medal of Honor for his bravery and within the year would achieve the rank of brevet colonel, the youngest individual in American history to reach that rank, two accomplishments his more famous son would not achieve until he was far older. The Union pursuit was halfhearted, reflecting the astonishment of the troops and their officers at the success as well as the effective rear guard action executed by Cleburne's infantry, as they pulled off the north end of Missionary Ridge. Indeed, the Union victory was one of the most humiliating defeats Confederate armies suffered in the war.

Conclusion

The collapse of the Army of Tennessee was a direct consequence of Bragg's incompetence. At last, Davis had to replace him, in this case with Johnston, which made the decision even more unpalatable to the president. He did keep Bragg on as his chief military advisor, which only serves to underline his unwillingness to recognize that he had ever made a wrong choice. On the other hand, the Union victory was a direct reflection of Grant's extraordinary ability to set things in motion and to energize his subordinates and their troops.

One might note that 1863 was not Lincoln's best year. He had again attempted to get the army commanders to move in unison. Grant and Hooker had moved at nearly the same time, but Rosecrans had remained stationary. Thereafter, Lincoln's attention, understandably, had focused on the war in the East where disaster threatened. That focus partially explains why the president missed the strategic implications of Grant's proposal to move all or part of his army against Mobile and southern Alabama. Whatever the consequences of the French intervention in Mexico, it made little sense to put Grant on the shelf. But Grant's importance to the Union as well as his extraordinary competence in the field would only become fully apparent with his actions in restoring the Union strategic position in the aftermath of Chickamauga.

If there were any year that was decisive in the winning of the Civil War, it was 1863. The two crucial successes of Union forces in the West, which opened the road to victory, were those achieved by Grant. The first of these, the campaign leading to the capture of Vicksburg, was the most brilliant in the war, comparable in many ways to Napoleon's moves that led to the destruction of the "unfortunate" General Mack's Austrian army at Ulm in 1805. In both cases, the result was not only a brilliant battlefield victory but also the surrounding and destruction of an enemy army. Moreover, Grant's destruction of Pemberton's army and capture of Vicksburg represented more than an operational victory. It was a victory with immense strategic and political consequences. As Lincoln noted: "The Father of Waters again goes unvexed to the sea."[71] Confederate public opinion could explain away Lee's defeat in Pennsylvania as a temporary setback. Nothing could mask the Vicksburg catastrophe. Grant's restoration of the Union's fortunes in Tennessee then placed Union military forces in a position to break into the eastern states of the Confederacy by the back door. Had Washington followed Grant's advice to attack Mobile after Vicksburg, the war might well have ended in 1864, with the Confederate military position collapsing in its crucial interior, whatever tactical successes Lee might score in Virginia. All in all, Grant's generalship and leadership in 1863 place him among the great generals in history and as the greatest general of the Civil War.

CHAPTER 10

The Killing Time: The War in the East, 1864

For thirty days, now, it has been one funeral procession past me, and it is too much! Today I saw a man burying a comrade, and, within half an hour, he himself was brought in and buried inside him.—The men need some rest!

—Major General Gouverneur Warren (Lowe and Simon, *Meade's Army*)

I am very sorry to say I have seen but little generalship during the campaign. Some of our corps commanders are not fit to be corporals. Lazy and indolent, they will not even ride along their lines; yet, without hesitancy, they will order us to attack the enemy, no matter what their position or numbers. Twenty thousand of our killed or wounded should to-day be in our ranks.

—Emory Upton (Michie, *Life and Letters of Emory Upton*)

At the turn of 1863 to 1864 the governments of Lincoln and Davis found themselves deeply mired in Clausewitz's trinity. Over the past three years the steadily escalating violence of the war, with its attendant hatred and animosity, was driving those conducting the conflict to move in directions inconceivable in 1861. Moreover, efforts to lay out clear lines of political and military action were floundering on the intractable nature of mankind, while the constant interplay of possibility and chance continued to upset the most carefully laid calculations. From the Northern perspective, it seemed almost inexplicable the Confederacy should continue the war in the face of the pressure and defeats it had suffered in 1863. As Sherman commented in a letter to his wife at the beginning of the campaign against Atlanta: "No amount of poverty or adversity seems to shake their faith—niggers gone—wealth & luxury gone, money worthless, starvation in view within a period of two or three years, are Causes enough to make the bravest tremble, yet I see no signs of let up—Some few deserters—plenty tired of war, but the masses determined to fight it out."[1] Undoubtedly, most Confederates found themselves equally astonished at the resiliency and tenacity their opponents in the North had displayed thus far in the conflict.

In November 1864 the voters of the North would go to the polls to elect their president. Thus, Lincoln confronted the fact that he would have to play a skilled political game against those who continued to underestimate his leadership, while at the same time running a complex and difficult war. The reelection problem was one that Davis did not face, since the Confederate constitution had given him a term of six years. Nevertheless, whatever Lincoln's election problems, both Washington and Richmond confronted noxious political difficulties to which there were no simple solutions.

The war was trying the patience of both North and South. For Davis, there was a constant drumbeat of dissatisfaction with his conduct of the war. Moreover, many Confederates, particularly from those states west of the Appalachians, felt the president and his military advisers had placed the security needs of the East above those of the West. Here they were certainly correct, for Lee's invasion of the North had contributed to the disaster at Vicksburg. Moreover, Davis was now confronting the reality that "states' rights" carried with it implications from which his government could not wriggle. In the coming year, governors from a number of states, Georgia and North Carolina in particular, would place the narrow concerns of their states above the larger strategic needs of a Confederacy facing the storm of a North fully armed and mobilized.

For Lincoln, the victories at Vicksburg, Gettysburg, and especially Chattanooga had dampened the criticism of his conduct of the war as well as the cries of those who believed the war was not worth fighting. Nevertheless, much of the Democratic Party, not to mention many officers and men in the armies, remained unhappy with the Emancipation Proclamation. The enthusiasm for the war itself had declined to the point where the North would have to fill the ranks of its armies, which would soon lose substantial numbers of soldiers who had enlisted for three years in 1861, either through large bounties or conscription. And the July 1863 New York riots had underlined a deep antagonism to the war among substantial numbers of Northerners.

In the end though, Lincoln would handle the Copperheads and other manifestations of dissent as long as Northerners saw indications they would win the war. Nevertheless, the president and his advisers found themselves entangled among the complexities of military operations, the need to encourage political support for the war, and the harsh reality of the war itself. In the case of the last, it was clear by the end of 1863 that the breaking of Confederate resistance would require a hard war that aimed not just at the defeat of Confederate armies, but the carrying of the war to the Confederacy's civilians. Sherman put that reality in his usual harsh terms in a series of letters to Confederate politicians who were complaining about the depredations of his troops in spring 1864: "The Government of the United States has in North Alabama any and all rights which they choose to enforce in war—to take their lives, their homes, their land, their everything—because they cannot deny that war does exist there, and war is simply power unrestrained by constitution or compact. If they want eternal warfare, well and good; we accept the issue, and will dispossess them and put our friends in their place. . . . To those who submit to the rightful law and authority all gentleness and forbearance; but to the petulant and persistent secessionists, why, death is mercy, and the quicker he or she is disposed of the better. Satan and the rebellious saints of Heaven were allowed a continuous existence in hell merely to swell their just punishment."[2]

Preparing for the Next Year of War

The strategic situation at the beginning of 1864 had radically altered from the year before. That change had been almost entirely the result of Grant's brilliant generalship. For many Northerners Gettysburg had obscured Grant's campaign in Mississippi, but nothing could obscure the leadership he had displayed in relieving the Army of the Cumberland and then in wrecking Bragg's army. Admittedly, the victory at Missionary Ridge had largely resulted from the initiative displayed by Union soldiers in storming what should have been an impregnable position, but Grant had provided the drive and will that had restored the Union position in southeastern Tennessee and northern Georgia.

One might have thought that Grant's successes would have led directly to his appointment to command all Union armies as the replacement for the pedantic Halleck. Yet, that appointment would not occur until March 1864, when Congress passed a bill creating the rank of lieutenant general with the provision that only Grant could hold the rank. Ironically, the administration had not been eager to see the bill pass. Lincoln himself appears to have worried Grant might have ambitions to run for the presidency. Having never met Grant, he was unwilling to place the Western general in overall command of the Northern military effort. That unwillingness would have serious consequences, because Grant would not assume that position until too late to prepare fully for the campaigns of 1864. Nor would Grant have the necessary time to repair the severe deficiencies in the Army of the Potomac's culture. Thus, he would have to take that strange organization as it was. One should also not discount the machinations of Halleck in attempting to prevent Grant from becoming commander in chief of Union armies. Grant's actions and comments finally assured the president that the general had no political ambitions. As he told one politician, his only political ambition was to become mayor of Galena "to build a new sidewalk from my house to the depot."[3] Lincoln then signed the bill, promoted Grant to lieutenant general, and appointed him the commander of all Union armies.

In facing election in fall 1864 Lincoln confronted a major problem that Davis did not. With a six-year term Davis had no qualms in simply decreeing that all the soldiers in Confederate service would now serve for the duration. However, facing an election and the fact that three-year terms of enlistment for the regiments that had joined up in 1861 would end in spring and summer 1864, Lincoln and the Congress could not extend the length of service without risking the voters' wrath. The best they could do was to offer attractive inducements for soldiers to reenlist for the duration. Inducements included a $400 bonus (a considerable amount at the time), to which some states and localities added additional bonuses, thirty-day furloughs for those reenlisting, and the promise that regiments that achieved a reenlistment rate of 75 percent would retain their identity. Astonishingly, given the horrors of Civil War battlefields and the medicine of the time, nearly 60 percent of veterans due for release reupped. Numbers in the Army of the Potomac were lower, approximately 50 percent, but, considering the battering it had taken, that was an impressive number. Undoubtedly, close connections among veterans had developed the unit cohesion that contributed greatly to high reenlistment rates.

In the period after Chattanooga, the Union lost five valuable months to continue the heavy military pressure on the Confederacy. Grant did provide suggestions as to how the Union might best employ its forces over the winter. As he had done after Vicksburg's surrender,

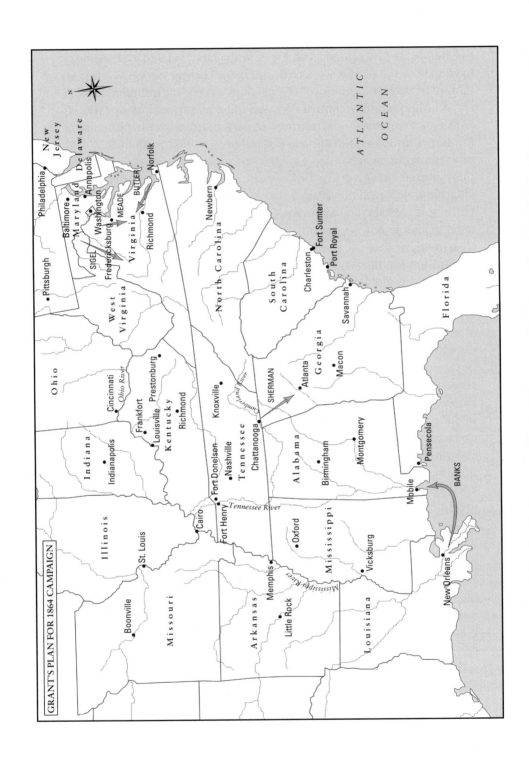

GRANT'S PLAN FOR 1864 CAMPAIGN

he argued that Mobile, as well as southern and central Alabama, should be the next target. Once in Union hands Mobile would not only deny the Confederates the use of one of their last ports but also open up the way for Union forces to strike at Montgomery or Atlanta, the latter which his forces in Chattanooga could also obviously attack. In the Eastern theater, Grant suggested a movement by 60,000 troops from Suffolk in southeastern Virginia to Raleigh, North Carolina, to "destroy first all the roads about Weldon. . . . From Weldon to Raleigh they would scarcely meet serious opposition. Once there, the most interior line of rail way still left to the enemy, in fact the only one they would have, would be so threatened as to force him to use a large portion of his army in guarding it. This would virtually force an evacuation of Virginia and indirectly of East Tennessee."[4]

The Weldon railroad connected the Army of Northern Virginia to North Carolina, and Lee would fight long and hard during the siege of Petersburg in summer 1864 to maintain that crucial supply line. Furthermore, that line of operations "would effectively blockade Wilmington, the port now of more value to the enemy than all the balance of their sea coast." Grant displayed his understanding that the importance of access to waterborne transport extended beyond the inland rivers of the west. His campaign plan would have allowed the Union to use its logistical advantages to pressure the Confederates year-round, "instead of months of inactivity in winter quarters." Most importantly, "it would draw the enemy from Campaigns of their own choosing, and for which they are prepared, to new lines of operation never expected to become necessary."[5]

Halleck contemptuously rejected Grant's suggestions. He wrote his more creative subordinate that "I have never considered Richmond as the necessary objective point of the Army of the Potomac; that point is *Lee's army*. . . . The overthrow of Lee's army being the object of operations here, the question arises how can we best attain it? If we fight that army with our communications open to Washington, so as to cover this place and Maryland, we can concentrate upon it nearly all of our forces on this frontier, but if we operate by North Carolina or the peninsula, we must act with a divided army, and on exterior lines, while Lee, with a short interior line can concentrate his force upon either fragment." Furthermore, Halleck remained wary of Lee's aggressiveness. He asked Grant: "Suppose we were to send thirty thousand men from that army [the Army of the Potomac] to North Carolina;

would not Lee be able to make another invasion of Maryland and Pennsylvania? But it may be said that by operating in North Carolina we could compel Lee to move his army there. I do not think so. Uncover Washington and the Potomac River, and all the forces which Lee can collect will be moved north, and the popular sentiment will compel the Government to *bring back* the army in North Carolina to defend Washington, Baltimore, Harrisburg, and Philadelphia. I think Lee would tomorrow exchange Richmond, Raleigh, and Wilmington for the possession of either of the aforementioned cities."[6] Not surprisingly, Halleck failed to indicate how Lee was going to launch an invasion of the North with his logistical base in North Carolina destroyed.

With Grant's promotion at this point still in doubt, he had no choice but to accept Halleck's verdict. By the time he was promoted to head the Union armies in March 1864, Grant would recognize the political power of Lincoln's desire to take the war directly to Lee as well as the fact that he had precious little time to put into place his larger strategic ideas for winning the war. The only choice on the table was for a campaign to attack Lee directly, a choice that would lead to the horrendous casualties of the Overland Campaign. Halleck, possessing neither strategic imagination nor vision, preferred operations west of the Mississippi of no strategic utility. Such efforts could not possibly have contributed to the winning of the war. Lincoln was probably behind some of these moves, especially in his desire to counteract the French intervention in Mexico and support political efforts at reconstruction in Louisiana with the Red River campaign. Nevertheless, the president was always open to sensible military advice, little of which he got from Halleck. Above all, Halleck was a landlocked soldier with little sense of the importance of both brown- and blue-water strategies. Moreover, he seems not to have grasped the serious leakages that were occurring through the blockades of Mobile and Wilmington. Since the navy and the sea were foreign territory, he had little interest in cooperating with Welles and the admirals beyond what was politically expedient in view of Lincoln's and Stanton's suggestions.

While Grant was proposing his imaginative suggestions, he and Sherman were also making major logistical preparations to launch the follow-up to the Chattanooga victory. This work involved the general repair of the rail and river transportation running throughout Tennessee, as well as the establishment of a truly effective security and repair service that would insure Confederate raiders could not break the Northern logistical and transportation system in Tennessee for sustained periods. These preparations were essential to the most important campaign Union armies would launch in 1864. As usual, it was Grant's thorough understanding of the larger picture and what needed to be done *now* that laid the basis for victory.

In early March 1864 Grant assumed overall responsibility for employment of Union forces and strategy. In effect, he had less than two months to establish his strategic approach to winning the war, reorganize to the extent possible the army's command structure, determine who would command the various Union armies, establish a working relationship with Lincoln and Halleck, and pass his concept of operations along to the senior field commanders. What was done in the time available underlines Grant's ability to get things done as well as his ability to work with others. Moreover, given Halleck's inability to differentiate the essential from the irrelevant, there were issues that Grant could not rectify in the time available.

For the upcoming campaign, he had no intention of chaining himself to a desk in Washington. When asked at Willard's Hotel in Washington whether he planned to have breakfast at that location again before the war's end, Grant's reply was simple: "Not here I shan't."[7] Sherman suggested that Grant might be more comfortable running the war in the West, but the new commander recognized he needed to be with the Union's problem child, the Army of the Potomac, not necessarily to command it, but to insure that Meade and its officers engaged their assets fully in fighting the Army of Northern Virginia, a task at which they had all too often failed.

In terms of strategy, Grant saw things in much the same light as Lincoln had seen them in winter 1862, an approach emphasizing the placing of sustained military pressure on all sides of the Confederacy. On 4 April, he wrote to Sherman, his old comrade in arms: "It is my design, if the enemy keep quiet and allow me to take the initiative in the Spring Campaign to work all parts of the armies together, and somewhat towards a common center. . . . I have sent orders to Banks . . . to finish up his present expedition against Shreveport with all dispatch, to turn over the defence of the Red River to Gen. Steele and the Navy, . . . To abandon Texas, except the Rio Grande and to hold that with not to exceed four thousand men. . . . With all of [his] force he is to commence operations against Mobile as soon as he can. It will be impossible for him to commence too early."[8] Sigel was to move into the Shenandoah Valley, while Butler was to take a newly created force and move up the James to sever the railroad lines from Richmond to the south, thus placing the Army of Northern Virginia in an impossible logistical situation.

As for what Sherman was to do, Grant simply stated: "You I propose to move against Johnston's Army, to break it up and to get into the interior of the enemy's country as far as you can, inflicting all the damage you can against their war resources. I do not propose to lay down for you a plan of Campaign but simply to lay down the work it is desirable to have done and leave you free to execute in your own way. Submit to me however as early as you can your plan of operations."[9] Grant did not expect much from Sigel, given the lines of communications that he had to protect, but he did hope that by attacking up the Shenandoah Valley, Sigel would force the Confederates to send reinforcements to protect what was left of the Valley. And then Grant could not resist a line Lincoln had provided after receiving a briefing on the plans for the upcoming campaign: "In other words, if Sigel can't skin himself he can hold a leg while someone else skins."[10]

In directions to Meade on 9 April, Grant presented much the same information, but added specific guidance for the Army of the Potomac: "Lee's army will be your objective point. Wherever Lee goes there you will go also."[11] Grant determined to retain Meade despite considerable pressure from many in the administration to replace him. In their first meeting, Meade had indicated his willingness to give up his command in favor of any officer Grant might want to appoint and serve in any theater to which Grant might assign him. That act gave him an even higher opinion of Meade than Meade's victory at Gettysburg had earned. As Grant later noted, "it is men who wait to be selected, and not those who seek, from whom we may always expect the most efficient service."[12]

In his military strategy, Grant had devised an approach that should have led to the military and political collapse of the Confederacy in fall 1864. But it did not, because Grant had to devise it at literally the last moment without the time to put some of the necessary pieces in place. The result was that by April 1864 Banks with Halleck's encouragement had already mired his army deep in the muck of the Red River, which meant that there would be no move against Mobile. That in turn meant that Polk's corps, which the Confederates had assigned to protect that crucial port, would be available to support the defense of Atlanta.

But there was a larger problem: the generals who were to pressure the Confederates in support of the major drives of Sherman and Meade (Banks against Mobile, Sigel up the valley, and Butler up the James to Bermuda Hundred) all failed miserably. They were political generals incapable of running an effective campaign. Interestingly, in his memoirs, Grant never blamed the troubles that his strategic approach ran into on these political generals due to their incompetence. Here we are probably dealing with the political sophistication that marks Grant as so unique among the other generals in the war. Whatever their military weaknesses, Banks, Butler, and Sigel were politicians of considerable importance, especially in terms of the upcoming election of 1864, when Lincoln would run as a *Union* candidate rather than as a Republican. To replace such generals might have won the war more quickly, but it also might have led to McClellan's election.

For Southern leaders, the strategic and political situation looked grim. By this point, Davis had alienated nearly all the important Confederate political leaders. As the editor of the *Richmond Examiner* characterized the president's responsibility for Vicksburg: "Serene upon the frigid heights of an infallible egotism sat Mr. Davis, wrapped in sublime self-complacency, turning a deaf ear to all and resolved to maintain his protégé [Pemberton], though the cause should sustain irremediable injury."[13] At least the disaster of the Chattanooga campaign had forced him to remove Bragg. Moreover, the catastrophe had given Davis no alternative but to appoint Johnston, a general for whom he had little respect, particularly given Johnston's unwillingness to attack when the odds appeared unfavorable. Johnston seems to have been the only Confederate general to grasp the reality that Confederate armies could not bear the heavy losses inherent in aggressive tactics. Thus, the result was the considerable caution he took in the conduct of operations. Yet, that strategic insight led Johnston at times to miss tactical opportunities to attack Union forces. Inherent in the relationship between the Confederate president and his commander in Georgia was a deep disagreement as to the need for aggressive action against Sherman. Finally, as if Davis could not resist the opportunity to poke the critics of his handling of the war, he appointed Bragg as his military advisor.

By this point Confederate military leaders no longer held hope for a decisive military victory. They were looking toward the presidential election of 1864 in the hope that, if their armies could win sufficient successes, the Republicans would lose the upcoming election. Longstreet accurately appraised the strategic situation: "If we can break up the enemy's arrangements early, and throw him back, he will not be able to recover his position nor his morale until the Presidential election is over, and we shall then have a new President to deal with."[14] Of all the Confederate commanders in the East, it was "old Pete," the best man at Grant's wedding, who understood the danger that the newly minted lieutenant general represented for the Confederacy. While Lee considered the possibility of attacking the Army of the Potomac, Longstreet understood that the Army of Northern Virginia faced a formidable opponent. At one point before the fighting began, he warned a Confederate officer: "We must make up our minds to get into line of battle and to stay there; for that man will fight us every day and every hour till the end of the war."[15]

For Grant the problem was to keep the Army of the Potomac on track. Unlike Pope when he had come east, Grant made no major moves to replace the army's leadership. Moreover, he never implied he was bringing a Western brand of leadership to fix matters in the east. There were some changes he could make. No one, even in the Army of the Potomac, could quarrel with the assertion that its cavalry's performance had been miserable over the past two years. And so, Grant had Phil Sheridan transferred from the Army of the Cumberland to assume that command. As for command of the Army of the Potomac, Meade had solved that problem in his first meeting with Grant.

Twenty years later in one of those wonderful portraits that he would sketch in his memoirs, Grant described Meade in the following terms: "General Meade was an officer of great merit, with drawbacks to his usefulness that were beyond his control. He had been an officer of the engineer corps before the war, and consequently had never served with troops until he was over forty-six years of age. He never had, I believe, a command of less than a brigade. He saw clearly and distinctly the position of the enemy, and the topography of the country in front of his own position. His first idea was to take advantage of the lay of the ground, sometimes without reference to the direction we wanted to move afterwards. He was subordinate to his superiors in rank to the extent that he could execute an order which changed his own plans with the same zeal he would have displayed if the plan had been his own. He was brave and conscientious, and commanded the respect of all who knew him. He was unfortunately of a temper that would get beyond his control, at times, and make him speak to officers of high rank in the most offensive manner. No one saw this fault more plainly than he himself, and no one regretted it more."[16]

Meade had, as the army's commander, reduced the number of Army of the Potomac's corps commands from five to three, partially because it eased his span of control, but also because there simply were not obvious candidates in his army to fill the responsibilities involved in corps command. Even then there were problems. The II Corps' (26,681 soldiers) commander, Hancock, was the best of the lot, but he would never fully recover from his painful Gettysburg wound. The VI Corps' (24,028 soldiers) commander, "Uncle John" Sedgwick, beloved by his men, was fine in a straight-up fight as long as he received direction from above. But as he had shown at Chancellorsville, he was incapable of initiative. The V Corps' (24,125) commander, Gouverneur Warren, was an unknown quantity; he had replaced Hancock temporarily due to Hancock's wounds suffered on the third day of Gettysburg. Warren had remained in that temporary position until Hancock returned to duty in March 1864, but he had fought no major battles while in that billet. Up to July 1863 he had served as the army's chief engineer but had never led a division, although he had done good service as the army's engineer at Gettysburg. In addition, the IX Corps under Ambrose Burnside (19,250 soldiers) was directly under Grant, because its commander held date of rank over Meade, that arrangement adding unnecessary complexity to the army's command arrangements. Burnside was an affable, pleasant man, but his failures in higher command so far in the war had been glaring.

There were two substantial problems Grant confronted in the coming campaign, which were not apparent at its beginning. He was later to admit that he had not really known either the army or its senior commanders at the campaign's onset. Grant's description of Warren as a corps commander underlines the culture of command that had so thoroughly prevented the Army of the Potomac from realizing its potential: "Warren's difficulty was two-fold: when he received an order to do anything, it would at once occur to his mind how all the balance of the army should be engaged so as properly to cooperate with him. His ideas were generally good, but he would forget that the person giving him orders had thought of others at the time he had of him. In like manner, when he did get ready to execute an order, after giving most intelligent instructions to [the] division commanders, he would go in with one division, holding the others in reserve until he could superintend their movements in person also, forgetting that division commanders could execute an order without his presence. His difficulty was constitutional and beyond his control. He was an officer of superior ability, quick perceptions, and personal courage to accomplish anything that could be done with a small command."[17] Grant would discover almost immediately how deeply ingrained was the culture of rigidity and lack of imagination and initiative throughout the army. In essence, its leaders had none of the qualities of a slashing saber that characterized the Army of Northern Virginia or of his Army of the Tennessee. Rather it was closer to the qualities of a massive sledgehammer, when it moved.

Grant's second problem had to do with the tactics of the war. By 1864 the soldiers on both sides had absorbed the lesson that bullets killed and that needless exposure displayed stupidity rather than bravery. As Grant noted, "in every change of position or halt for the night, whether confronting the enemy or not, the moment arms were stacked the men intrenched [sic] themselves. . . . It was wonderful how quickly they could in this way construct defenses of considerable strength."[18] The same was true for the Confederates. In other words, the tactical framework within which the armies were fighting had altered drastically in favor of the defense, which with its artillery and infantry solidly ensconced behind palisades of logs, branches, dirt, and stones could slaughter attacking formations moving on open ground. This was true in both Eastern and Western theaters. The difference was that there was greater room for maneuver in the West, and Sherman took full advantage of that situation. Grant and Meade, however, had relatively little room for maneuver in northern and central Virginia, and what little there was, its corps and division commanders minimized.

At face value, the numbers available to the Army of the Potomac (approximately 116,000) provided it a considerable advantage over the Army of Northern Virginia (barely 64,000 when Longstreet returned). But the Confederates in Virginia possessed a number of intangibles, the most important being that of a sense of superiority over their opponents that ran from Lee to the lowliest privates. For the most part, its officer corps consistently displayed initiative, and its morale was outstanding. Above all, Lee was the army's greatest advantage. While not a great strategist, he was a superb tactical commander, who inspired extraordinary performances from his soldiers.

The upcoming campaign proved his greatest, because this time the tenacity and mental toughness of his opponent forced him to fight on the defensive against unremitting pressure. Lee's corps commanders were also outstanding: Longstreet among the best in the war; Hill outstanding on his best days, but often sick; and Ewell competent when provided unambiguous directions, but as Lee commented after the war, he suffered from a "want of decision."[19] The incomparable Stuart, who had replaced Jackson at Chancellorsville and might well have better served in 1864 in place of Ewell, led Lee's cavalry.

While the soldiers in the Army of the Potomac had again and again proven willing to sacrifice themselves for the cause, too many defeats and failures had created a frame of mind where officers waited for orders and were unwilling to take risks or display initiative. The army's rigid respect for seniority meant that the leadership cadre put in place by McClellan during the winter of 1861/62 remained highly influential in the Union's most important Eastern field army. Eventually, the army would change, but it would take Grant nearly a year to mold it into a more effective and responsive instrument. Perhaps most important, a general failure to take the initiative, an unwillingness to cooperate, and a lack of understanding of the importance of timely action marked the command culture among the senior officers. For now, there were many in its ranks whom conscription and bounties had dragooned as replacements for the three-year volunteers who had returned home.

Yet, unlike the Army of Northern Virginia, the Army of the Potomac was an extraordinarily well supplied military force. Gone were the corruption and shoddy supplies of the first war year. Secretary of War Stanton insured that what the US government bought met the highest standards. Those who attempted to cheat the government he pursued mercilessly. One historian has noted: "Its quartermaster, Brig. Gen. Rufus Ingalls, believed that probably no army in history 'was in better condition in every respect.' The troops had abundant clothing, good equipment, plentiful rations, and an efficient logistical system from which the North's economic bounty flowed in a continual stream. The supply train supporting the initial movement alone comprised a staggering 4,300 wagons. Moreover, an entire fleet of ships was ready to resupply the army, when necessary, via the great tidal estuaries [of Virginia]."[20] Much as was to be the case in World War II, European observers noted the extraordinary profligacy with which the Union government supplied its soldiers and the attendant waste accompanying that profligacy.

The Wilderness and Spotsylvania Courthouse

So the great campaign began. Meade's initial moves replicated to a considerable extent those of Hooker the year before. Early on the morning of 4 May Hancock's II Corps crossed at Ely Ford, the easternmost of the two fords, and took the lead. Farther to the north Warren's V Corps, followed by Sedgwick's VI Corps, crossed the Rapidan at Germanna Ford. In the long run, it was Grant's intention to outflank Lee to the east so that the Army of the Potomac could maintain contact with its naval and supply forces on the Potomac, an indication perhaps of the influence of his experiences with river transportation in the West. Above all, Grant intended to use the Army of the Potomac aggressively.

There has grown up in the literature of the Civil War an argument that Grant intended to wage a war of attrition in the Overland Campaign. But that misses Grant's hope to maneuver around Lee's flank and force the Confederates to fight on open ground, where his numbers would give his forces a distinct advantage. But were that not possible, Grant then indicated in his report at the end of the war on operations that it had been his aim "to hammer continuously against the armed force of the enemy and his resources until, by mere attrition, if in no other way, there should be nothing left to him but an equal submission with the loyal section of our common country to the constitution and laws of the land."[21] The problem was not that Grant knew only how to bludgeon an opponent into submission, but rather the instrument at his disposal, the Army of the Potomac, was incapable of fighting in any other fashion—a reality that showed up almost immediately.

Unlike 1863, the Federals failed to catch Lee by surprise in their advance south. Confederate signalers on Clark's Mountain picked up the Army of the Potomac's first movements. By early morning they reported Yankee troops were marching west to the Germanna Ford and Ely Ford roads. Lee immediately ordered Ewell's and Hill's corps to move in the hope of tying the attackers up in the Wilderness, where their superiority in artillery would count for less. At the same time, he

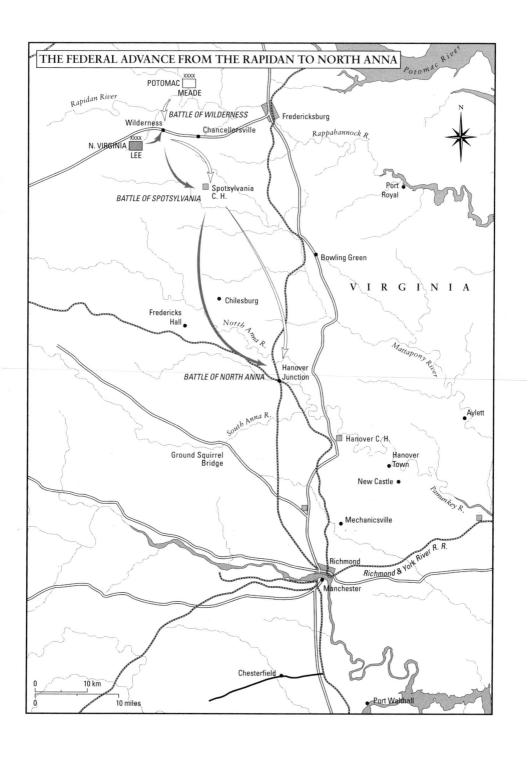

THE FEDERAL ADVANCE FROM THE RAPIDAN TO NORTH ANNA

Potomac River

Rapidan River

POTOMAC
XXXX
MEADE

BATTLE OF WILDERNESS

Wilderness

Chancellorsville

Fredericksburg

Rappahannock R.

N. VIRGINIA
XXXX
LEE

Spotsylvania C. H.

BATTLE OF SPOTSYLVANIA

Port Royal

Bowling Green

VIRGINIA

Chilesburg

Fredericks Hall

North Anna R.

Mattapony River

BATTLE OF NORTH ANNA

Hanover Junction

Aylett

South Anna R.

Hanover C. H.

Ground Squirrel Bridge

Hanover Town

New Castle

Pamunkey R.

Mechanicsville

Richmond & York River R. R.

Richmond

Manchester

Chesterfield

Port Walthall

0   10 km
0   10 miles

ordered Longstreet and his corps, several days' march to the rear, to hustle forward as fast as possible. Lee ordered Ewell and Hill to fix the Army of the Potomac, but not to seek a general engagement, while awaiting Longstreet's arrival. At that point, he intended to launch a devastating attack on one of the Union flanks. He believed the Army of the Potomac, as at Chancellorsville, would remain on the defensive. But this time, he was up against a very different opponent. There would be no waiting and watching, as Union commanders worried about Lee, while the Confederates maneuvered into position for a devastating blow. Instead, with Grant providing the stiffening, the Army of the Potomac would attack, attack, and attack.

There were misconceptions on the other side as well. Astonishingly, considering his opponent's track record, Meade believe Lee would remain on the defensive along the Mine Run position. Thus, he halted his infantry in the Wilderness, admittedly after an exhausting march of fifteen hours. The II Corps halted near Chancellorsville, while the V and VI Corps bivouacked farther west. Most of the Union troops had dark memories of the area, a thoroughly dismal environ, not just because of the terrain, but because of the skeletons scattered throughout the landscape. Meade had ordered a halt to allow his supply trains to close up. Neither side had a clear picture: the Army of the Potomac moving in a southeasterly direction; the lead two Confederate corps moving to the northeast, almost directly perpendicular to the Union movement.

On 5 May the two armies met. Ewell was the first to make contact. Moving up the Orange Turnpike, his troops ran into Union skirmishers. Following Lee's instructions, he deployed his divisions on the western side of an open space known as Saunders Field. His Confederates immediately began work on extensive breastworks. At the same time as Ewell's troops were deploying, Meade and his staff reached Wilderness Tavern just up the road. Despite the fact that a substantial portion of his force was almost through the Wilderness and positioned to get between the Army of Northern Virginia and Richmond, Meade ordered a halt in the move toward the east and a turn to the southwest to meet the Confederates. What he was hoping for was an opportunity to pitch into the Confederates before they could deploy. Contributing to the uncertainty in the Union high command was the fact that once again the cavalry, now under Sheridan, had let the Army of the Potomac down by failing to probe the Wilderness aggressively for the location of Lee's advance.

Warren's V Corps received the task of striking the Confederates along the Orange Turnpike. With Charles Griffin's division in contact on the eastern side of Saunders Field, Warren ordered his other two divisions, which had moved beyond the turnpike, to turn around and move through the deeply forested areas to support Griffin's left. Samuel Crawford's division on Warren's left caught sight of Hill's troops moving along the Orange Plank road, headed toward the intersection of Brock Road and Plank Road. Meanwhile Griffin's right flank was up in the air, a fact that Meade attempted to cover by ordering Sedgwick's lead division to move into position on Griffin's right. While the Union troops arrayed themselves, the minutes passed as the Confederates entrenched behind ever-denser breastworks.

Frustrated by the failure of V Corps to act, Meade ordered the first attack to go forward. Moving toward Saunders Field in dense undergrowth, Griffin's attack lost cohesion. One Union brigade did break through the Confederate field works, but then had to fight its way out when the brigades on its flanks failed to support it. The denseness of the undergrowth led to a general collapse of command and control. As one soldier recalled, "it was simply bushwhacking on a grand scale in brush where all formation beyond that of regiments or companies was soon lost, and where such a thing as a consistent line of battle on either side was impossible."[22] To add to the horror, northern Virginia had had an unusually dry spring, and it was not long before the leaves and undergrowth caught fire, exacerbating the pain and suffering of the wounded.

Farther to the southeast, Lee had queried Hill's leading division commander about the possibility of grabbing the intersection where the Orange Plank Road crossed Brock Road. The Confederates received their answer. Almost immediately heavy firing broke out south of the intersection along Brock Road. For one of the few times in the war, units of the Army of the Potomac had stolen a march on their Confederate opponents. George Getty's division, temporarily assigned to Hancock's II Corps, arrived at the intersection minutes before Heth's men and quickly drove the Confederates back. Initially, the II Corps paused, while it entrenched and organized its units to launch a major attack. Porter Alexander claimed in his memoirs that those entrenchments saved the II Corps on the next day, but that the pause on the first day prevented Hancock's soldiers from overwhelming Heth's division.

While Union commanders were preparing to launch an attack west along Plank Road, an incident occurred that sums up the inability of soldiers in the Army of the Potomac to take advantage of opportunities. A mile to the west of the intersection of the Orange Plank and Brock Roads, a number of the most important Confederate generals were gathering on the open spaces of the Tapp farmyard. Lee, Hill, Stuart, and William Pendleton had assembled with their staffs to consider their opening moves. Suddenly out of the Wilderness's gloom emerged a line of Union skirmishers. Stunned, the Confederate generals barely had begun to move, when the Union line withdrew back from whence it had come without firing a shot. Realizing they were in the wrong place, not a single Union soldier acted. Ironically, by not acting, most had signed their own death warrants. Had they killed or wounded the leading Confederate generals, particularly Lee, the campaign would have taken a decidedly different turn.

Getty arrived at the crucial crossroads and launched an attack down Plank Road. The Union troops had to contend with the denseness of the undergrowth, as well as Heth's well-entrenched soldiers. Pushed by Meade, Hancock fed his units bit by bit into the fight. By late afternoon Hancock had approximately 17,000 men—with two more divisions moving up into position—against Heth's 6,000, and for a time it appeared the II Corps was about to break the Confederates. But at the last moment Wilcox's division arrived and launched a counterattack that halted the Union advance. But the fight was not over; in the early evening Wadsworth's division of the V Corps pushed its way through a mile of the Wilderness to position itself on Heth's left (northern) flank. Had Wadsworth acted decisively rather than tentatively, his division could have broken the Confederates and destroyed much of Hill's corps. But a desperate attack by a small Alabamian battalion, detailed to guard prisoners, persuaded Wadsworth that discretion was the better part of valor. That ended the fighting on the Orange Plank Road on 5 May. With another hour of daylight, Hancock might have crushed Heth and Wilcox, but again the Army of the Potomac was a day late and a dollar short.

Grant and Meade determined to resume the battle the next day with Warren and Sedgwick attacking in the north to hold Ewell on the Orange Turnpike. The southern edge of the battlefield appeared to offer the most enticing possibilities, given the hard knocks Hill had received. They hurried Burnside's corps up to reinforce Hancock. With no sign yet of Longstreet, there appeared to be an excellent possibility of defeating Lee in detail. In fact, Lee got in the first blow with Ewell attacking fifteen minutes before Sedgwick's troops were to move out. "Uncle John" commented to his staff that Ewell's watch must be fast. The Confederates made some minor gains but were quickly halted. Sedgwick and Warren, however, showed little disposition to renew the battle. Meanwhile, late in the day Major General John Gordon launched his division against the far right of the Union line and came close to dealing the Army of the Potomac a devastating blow. But the attack came too late and with insufficient force to achieve anything more than local success. Once again senior corps commanders in the Army of the Potomac had neglected to guard their flanks.

It was another matter in the south where at 0500 Hancock's II Corps launched a furious attack against Hill's two divisions. The attack achieved a stunning success, as the Confederates collapsed. Only two of the eight brigades in the line put up minimal resistance; the remainder hightailed it for the rear. However, what should have been a brilliant success was short-lived, because Burnside was late. Admittedly, his soldiers were tired and hungry, having marched forty miles in the previous thirty-six hours. Nevertheless, despite the fact that Burnside could hear the sounds of Hancock's battle in the distance, he ordered a halt at 0630 so his soldiers could boil coffee and fry their breakfast.

Meanwhile, Longstreet's corps, which had had just as trying a march over the previous two days, arrived to stem the disaster. In the face of the mob that had been two of Hill's divisions, Longstreet deployed a portion of his corps into line and sent them straight into battle; there was no stop to eat breakfast. Lee attempted to join the attack of the Texas brigade, but the brigade's soldiers would have none of it. They were wise to do so for out of the 800 in the brigade that morning only 250 survived unscathed. Longstreet's attack brought the II Corps advance to a screeching halt. He then deployed a scratch force under his chief of staff, G. Moxley Sorrel, to attacked Hancock's flank, while the main force hit the corps with a frontal assault. The rout did not stop until the II Corps' troops were back in their breastworks, from which they had started in the morning. As Hancock noted later, Longstreet "rolled me up like a wet blanket."[23] Luckily for the II Corps, Longstreet was seriously wound in the neck at the height of his success. The steam immediately went out of the drive, and an attack, launched by Lee late in the afternoon into the teeth of the II Corps defenses, collapsed with heavy losses. Porter Alexander, Longstreet's brilliant, young commander of artillery, acidly noted after the war: "This attack ought *never*, *never* to have been made. It was sending a boy to do a man's errand. It was wasting good soldiers whom we could not spare."[24]

To all intents and purposes, the Battle of the Wilderness was over. There would be a flank attack on Sedgwick's VI Corps that achieved some success, but it did not threaten the overall Union position. It did lead to a revealing incident. Throughout the battle Grant had spent most of the two days, when not discussing moves with Meade and the staffs, in whittling, the only sign of his nerves. Confronted late on the second day by a general, who rode up to the headquarters bemoaning the desperate crisis that Lee's attack on Sedgwick was causing, Grant lost his temper for one of the few times in the war: "Oh, I am heartily tired of hearing about what Lee is going to do. Some of you seem to think that he is going to turn a double somersault, and land in our rear and both of our flanks at the same time. Go back to your command, and try to think what we are going to do ourselves, instead of what Lee is going to do."[25]

The next day, 7 May, the two armies remained in place with only some heavy skirmishing. Grant determined not to renew the fighting against the entrenched Confederates, but rather to continue the line of advance on which the Army of the Potomac was moving when the fighting in the Wilderness erupted. The target of the Union advance was Spotsylvania Courthouse, through which a number of roads ran. Should his troops get there first, Grant would be between Lee and Richmond, which would leave the Confederate commander the unpalatable alternatives of either attacking Grant in relatively open terrain, where Union artillery would dominate, or withdrawing without a battle to Richmond against an opponent who would have access to better roads and the inside track.

The broken wreckage, human as well as material, of the intense fighting, not only of the 1864 battles but of Chancellorsville as well, covered the ground Union and Confederate troops now abandoned. A soldier in Burnside's corps noted after spending the night of 10 May near Chancellorsville, "the . . . ground was littered with the accoutrements, arms, and clothing of soldiers, and the bones and skulls of the dead. The stench arising from the mass of decayed human flesh and bone was sickening. The puddles of water made by the May showers were in some places covered with maggots."[26]

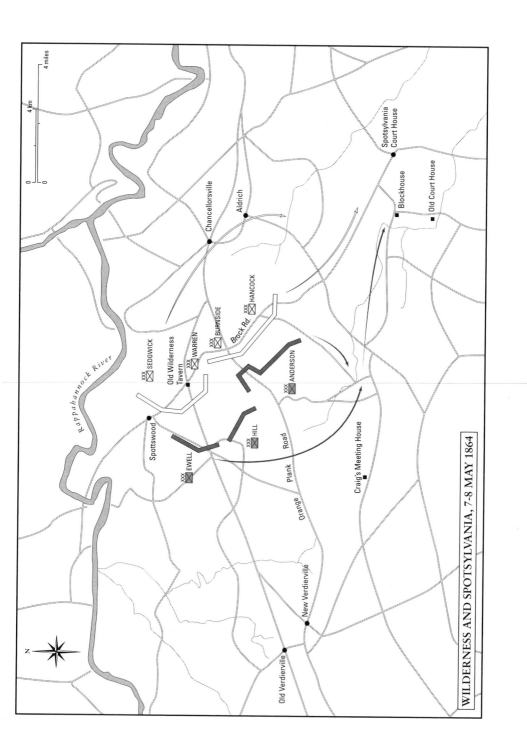

WILDERNESS AND SPOTSYLVANIA, 7-8 MAY 1864

Rappahannock River

Chancellorsville

Aldrich

SEDGWICK

Old Wilderness Tavern

WARREN

BURNSIDE

Brock Rd.

HANCOCK

ANDERSON

Spottswood

EWELL

HILL

Orange Plank Road

Craig's Meeting House

New Verdierville

Old Verdierville

Spotsylvania Court House

Blockhouse

Old Court House

N

4 miles

4 km

Orders went out to the various Union corps on 7 May that the troops should be ready to move as night fell. To most officers and men, it was not clear whether they would move south or whether, like McClellan, Pope, and Hooker, Grant was folding up the tent and retreating. That night, as Hancock's troops prepared to move out, they spied Grant and his staff taking the right-hand turn in the road leading south away from the Rappahannock. They broke out in spontaneous cheers, even though the roads they were now taking led south to more hardships and killing. What those soldiers desired above all else, even at the possible cost of their lives, was victory. One officer noted after the war that "it flashed upon us, like lightning, that there was to no more 'falling back,' and the troops broke into the wildest enthusiasm."[27]

The Army of the Potomac should have reached Spotsylvania Courthouse before the Confederates. The army had a straight run down the Brock Road, while the Confederates had to cut a primitive road, suitable only for infantry, through the Wilderness. But a combination of factors, many reflecting the Army of the Potomac's inability to act with dispatch, as well as the intervention of chance, intervened to give victory in the race to the Confederates. Not fully familiar with the army's corps commanders, Grant picked Warren to lead the advance. That corps commander failed to provide the drive to get his infantry through the congestion caused by units of Sheridan's cavalry, which had engaged with Confederate cavalry earlier in the day. Warren's infantry took their time in moving south—in one case coming to a virtual halt because several inches of water covered a couple hundred yards of the road. In the end, it was the corps commander's responsibility to hurry the men along, which Warren failed to do.

On the other side, Lee had divined that the most dangerous move Grant and Meade could make would be to advance to Spotsylvania. There were other possibilities, but given the road network south of Fredericksburg, Spotsylvania was of critical importance. Lee detailed Major General Richard Anderson, who had replaced the badly wounded Longstreet in command of the I Corps, to make the move. Lee also had the foresight to have his engineers cut a primitive route through the Wilderness's dense foliage to shorten the distance Anderson's infantry would have to move. Initially, Anderson had planned to allow his troops to bivouac along the way, but the woods on both sides of the trail were on fire, and the Confederates plowed ahead with few stops for short rests. They arrived at Spotsylvania only minutes before Union troops.

Warren fed his brigades in slowly against a light screen of Confederate cavalry, which arriving infantry soon bolstered. Then, the division commander went down with a minié ball in the knee, and the attack collapsed. Sedgwick's VI Corps deployed to Warren's left, extending the line to the northeast around Spotsylvania, with both commanders ordered by Meade to attack "with vigor and without delay."[28] By this point Meade found himself furious at V Corps for taking so long to reach Spotsylvania that the Confederates had beaten it to that key road junction. As he did often, he exploded at the nearest target, Sheridan, who admittedly had not sparkled in his task of scouting for the army's advance and whose cavalry had helped slow Warren's advance. The Irishman in turn had as bad a temper as anyone in the Union army, and a furious row erupted between the commander of the Army of the Potomac and his cavalry commander. Finally, Sheridan announced he would whip Stuart and his cavalry, if only Meade would let him. A furious Meade went to Grant, who perked up when Meade reported Sheridan's final comment. Grant's reply, which could not have brightened a furious Meade, was, "Did Sheridan say that? Well he generally knows what he is talking about. Let him start right out and do it."[29]

Meade was now rid of Sheridan, who would launch a fast moving raid to the gates of Richmond. The approach of his troopers caused a panic in the Confederate capital, while they tore up railroad tracks, destroyed much of the Confederate supply base at Beaver Dam Station with 500,000 rations of bread and 1,000,000 rations of meat, and killed Jeb Stuart in a fierce skirmish at Yellow Tavern, where they overwhelmed outnumbered Confederate cavalry. Nevertheless, as with most of the war's cavalry raids, Sheridan's had little long-term impact, other than to kill one of the more competent Confederate commanders. It certainly had none of the strategic and operational impact of Grierson's raid in Mississippi, and it deprived Grant of crucial information on Lee's dispositions later in the campaign.

While Sheridan and Meade were cussing each other out, the V and VI Corps spent the bulk of the day in preparing to launch their attack "without delay." By the time Sedgwick had finally gotten his VI Corps in place at 1800, Ewell's II Corps had arrived on the scene to bolster Confederate defenses. The result of lengthy Union preparations was a snafu. Troops got lost, some never received orders, and the majority never attacked. As one veteran of the VI Corps recalled after the war, "the dim impression of that afternoon is of things going wrong and of . . . much bloodshed and futility."[30] Professional military organizations in the twentieth century have examined their failures as well as their success to correct their mistakes, and when commanders err they are fired. The exact opposite occurred with the Army of the Potomac. In this case, there was no analysis of what had gone wrong, while none of the senior officers or members of their staffs were held responsible for their mistakes. Instead, the army's leadership swept the miserable performance under the rug.

Nevertheless, Spotsylvania underlined that a not too subtle change had occurred in the relationship between the armies. The constant attacks Grant was pushing Meade to launch had robbed Lee of the initiative. The Confederates were finding it difficult to launch the slashing flank attacks marking Lee's operations over the previous two years. Rather, Lee now had to fend off "those people" in a desperate attempt to prevent disaster. As more of the Confederate and Union corps arrived in the vicinity of Spotsylvania, they spread out from west to east with the Confederates holding a semicircular defensive position, forming a salient resembling a mule's shoe to defend the crossroads and a small collection of buildings that marked the county seat. Key to the Confederate defenses was a small rise, known as Laurel Hill, lying west of Spotsylvania and south of the western flank of what became known as the Mule Shoe.

As both sides deployed and entrenched on 9 May, Sedgwick made the mistake of standing on the breastworks of one of his VI Corps units. His men pleaded for him to get down, but he jokingly replied that the Confederates couldn't hit an elephant from their position. Minutes later instead of hitting an elephant, a Confederate sharpshooter hit him full in the face just below the eye. He was dead before he hit the ground. His replacement, Major General Horatio Wright, was a competent division commander who had shown few flashes of brilliance. He was never to enjoy Sedgwick's popularity with the VI Corps soldiers. On the other side, A. P. Hill asked to be relieved from command because of ill health. Lee agreed: his replacement, Jubal Early. Hill would return shortly to active duty, but Early's days as a corps commander were not over. Unlike the Army of the Potomac, Lee possessed a bench of competent division commanders to replace corps commanders when they went down or proved wanting.

Over the course of 9 May the two armies remained on the defensive as they entrenched. One of the key terrain features of the area surrounding the Courthouse was the Po River. It ran in a generally easterly direction until it turned south two miles in front of Spotsylvania and then in a southeasterly direction. Hancock's II Corps arrived during the day and deployed across the stream. In that position, which Grant and Meade believed would allow the II Corps to outflank the Confederates around Spotsylvania, Hancock's corps was also isolated from the rest of the Army of the Potomac. Lee grasped the chance to crush one of the Union corps. But for once, Union fears allowed their commanders to take sensible precautions. Early on the 10th, Grant pulled two of Hancock's divisions back across the Po to participate in the afternoon attack; one division remained, this one under Brigadier General Francis Barlow, one of the army's better combat commanders. Barlow sensed what was coming and prepared his division for a quick retreat. When Lee's counterattack came in midafternoon, Barlow and Hancock got most of the division back across the Po without excessive losses.

The late afternoon attacks on 10 May displayed the usual failures of coordination that marred so many of the Army of the Potomac's tactical operations throughout the war. But there was one stunning tactical success. Colonel Emory Upton, twenty-four years old and an 1861 graduate of West Point, persuaded the VI Corps commander, Wright, to allow him to take advantage of the terrain on the southwest corner of the Mule Shoe. Upton had attended Oberlin for two years before transferring to West Point, where he had engaged in a duel with a Southern cadet over an offensive remark the cadet had made about his attendance at the antislavery and egalitarian Ohio college.

Upton had already displayed outstanding tactical thinking, which would lead in the postwar period to his becoming one of the founding fathers of the US Army's system of professional military education. He had discovered a weakness in Confederate defenses which allowed for an approach by Union troops to within 200 yards of enemy positions before the Confederates could see the attackers. Given command of twelve handpicked regiments, Upton briefed each regimental commander on what he expected and then made sure they understood what they were to do. The regiments formed up in a massive column of four lines with three regiments in each line. Antithetical to Civil War tactics, the troops were not to fire until they were actually over and into the enemy's defenses. The normal tactical practice would have

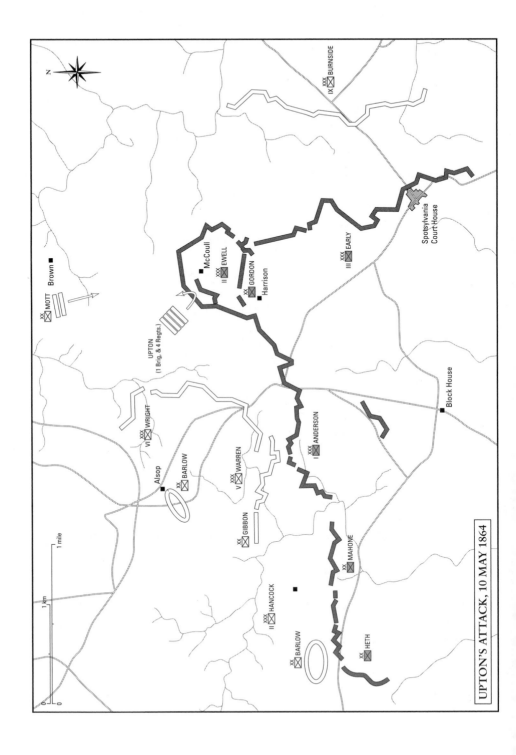

UPTON'S ATTACK, 10 MAY 1864

been for the troops to halt and fire, which inevitably slowed the attack's momentum. Instead, Upton's attacking soldiers were to keep advancing directly into the enemy's fire. To enforce his prohibition against firing, only the first wave of regiments had their soldiers prepare their rifles for firing; the soldiers of the other three waves loaded their rifles, but did not have percussion caps in place.

Upton's attack was an astonishing tactical success. After taking losses from the initial Confederate volleys, the attacking waves with fixed bayonets overwhelmed the defenders. In his after-action report, the young colonel noted, "Numbers prevailed, and, like a resistless wave, the column poured over the works, quickly putting hors de combat those who resisted, and sending to the rear those who surrendered."[31] Unfortunately, Wright and the supporting division commander failed to reinforce Upton's success despite Grant's urgings. Instead, they dithered and sent only one regiment to reinforce those holding open the Mule Shoe.

As usual, the Confederate response was swift; Ewell immediately fed in counterattacking regiments that contained Upton's force and then put it under increasing pressure. In effect, Union commanders were confronting the problem battlefield commanders would face throughout the First World War: how did one know whether a break-in attack had been sufficiently successful to justify funneling further troops into what might well be another tactical failure. The means of communications were not yet available for effective tactical command and control. As a result, increasing Confederate pressure and the lack of reinforcements, as well as declining supplies of ammunition, forced Upton to pull his unwilling soldiers back. For their part, those who had achieved what had initially been a great success were furious at what they regarded as the ineptitude of the generals.

The Army of the Potomac launched four separate attacks at different times on 10 May, including Upton's, of which only Upton's achieved a modicum of success. When it came to coordination among the corps commanders, there was little enough of that, a factor that was as much Meade's fault as it was the corps commanders'. Warren's reply to Meade accurately summed up the general attitude among the senior officers when Meade had asked him to coordinate his movement with that of the VI Corps: "You . . . can give your orders and I will obey them; or you can put Sedgwick in command and he can give the orders and I will obey them; or you can put me in command and I will give the orders and Sedgwick shall obey them; but I'll be God damned if I'll *coöperate* with General Sedgwick or anyone else."[32] The fact that there had been little planning reflected Grant's aggressiveness and desire to attack his Confederate opponent, but it also underlined the army's culture as well as the general immaturity of its staffs. Nevertheless, Grant had no intention of easing his unrelenting pressure on Lee. He noted in a message to Lincoln and Stanton, "I . . . propose to fight it out on this line if it takes all summer."[33]

Upton's attack impressed Grant, who commented: "A brigade today, will try a corps tomorrow."[34] That was precisely what he set in motion. Over the course of the night of 10/11 May, Hancock's II Corps prepared to make the main attack in a corps formation similar, but obviously far larger, to what Upton had launched on the southwest corner of the Mule Shoe. The attack would go in directly to the south at the apex of the Confederate position. The V Corps would shield the positions the II Corps would leave, while Wright's VI Corps would cover the western flank of Hancock's attack. Burnside's IX Corps would cover Hancock's eastern flank and exploit any success. Few Union commanders believed the attack would succeed, and Union commanders did not carefully plan for the attack as Upton had done. The lead division commander, Barlow, fulminated at the lack of any real reconnaissance of the Confederate position, sarcastically asking at one point, "Well, have I a gulch a thousand feet deep to cross?" All the staff officer Barlow queried could say was, "We do not know." But at least Barlow, whatever his doubts, did everything he could to insure his division, as well as the rest of Hancock's corps, were in position to attack. As he commented: "If I am to lead this assault I propose to have men enough, when I reach the objective point, to charge through Hell itself and capture all the artillery they can mass in my front."[35]

A massive thunderstorm aided preparations by muting the noise accompanying the movement of the corps from Confederate ears. All in all, Hancock and Barlow deployed 19,000 soldiers (50 percent more than Lee had launched in Pickett's charge at Gettysburg) before dawn. The attackers found themselves helped by the fact that Lee had ordered the artillery moved out of the Mule Shoe, preparatory to abandoning the salient. Brigadier General "Allegheny" Johnson begged Ewell to return the artillery that night, but that failed to occur before massed waves of II Corps infantry broke on the Confederate defenses.

In the early morning hours of 12 May, the troops of the II Corps attacked directly against the Mule Shoe's apex. They caught the Confederates by surprise. The defending division collapsed. A few Confederates fired off a volley. Some fled, but large numbers surrendered. It was the most outstanding tactical success the Army of the Potomac gained during the war. However, having disordered the defenders, as in most successful attacks in the First World War, the attackers found themselves in chaos. Command and control broke down. Small unit leaders discovered it was one thing to break into an enemy position, quite another to turn the break-in into a break-out. The troops had no clear idea of what to do next; while their commanders had not thought through how to exploit a success, because most believed success impossible.

Almost immediately, problems began. Unlike their opponents, Lee's commanders were always prepared to act. Brigadier General John B. Gordon's division was in reserve, and he immediately launched a brigade into action to hold the attackers, while he prepared his other three brigades for a concerted counterattack. Imbued with the army's aggressive culture, he deployed his troops in minimal time; not all the *T*s were crossed, nor were all the *I*s dotted, but immediate action was preferable to perfect preparations. Lee attempted to lead the counterattack, but the troops refused his aid. The counterattack drove Hancock's troops back to the breastworks, but that was as far as the Confederates reached.

Wright's VI Corps then joined the fight, regaining the breastworks where Upton's attack had achieved its fleeting success. For the remainder of the day masses of Confederate and Union soldiers maintained a tenuous hold along the central and western curve of the Mule Shoe, the soldiers separated by a few yards of logs, stones, dirt, and branches. One veteran officer recalled the fighting in the following terms: "its memories are of bloodshed surpassing all former experiences, a desperation of the struggle never before witnessed, of mad rushes, and of sudden repulses, of guns raised in the air with the butts up and fired over log walls, of our flags in shreds, and at the short intervals which show what small regiments are left."[36] The next morning he found a battery he had sent forward, all dead, horses and men, before they could deploy the guns.

While the fighting continued, Lee had those in the rear prepare a new defensive system that ran across the salient's base. In the early morning of 13 May the Confederates withdrew to new positions. In terms of attrition, the campaign had so far been a mixed success for the Army of the Potomac. Confederate losses by this point of the Overland Campaign numbered nearly 23,000 men, or a third of Lee's army. Union losses exceeded 33,000 men, roughly 28 percent of Grant's forces. Heavy rains interrupted the battle on the 14th, but on the next day Wright's corps attempted to replicate Hancock's attack. Against well-entrenched and prepared Confederates, it was a dismal failure. To this point, much of Grant's aggressiveness had rested on his belief that the Union's subsidiary attacks elsewhere in Virginia would draw strength away from Lee. As the Spotsylvania battle fizzled to a dismal end, Grant received word as to just how badly things had gone elsewhere in the state.

Defeat of the Peripheral Strategy

Grant's approach to the 1864 Eastern campaign had depended on the performance of Union forces not under his direct control. He aimed for them to achieve a number of goals: first, to use Union forces that otherwise were engaged in occupation duties; second, to do substantial damage to the South's infrastructure (railroads), food (the grain of the Shenandoah Valley), and raw materials (the lead and salt mines of southwest Virginia); and third, to tie down substantial numbers of Confederates and deny Lee a pool of reinforcements. These subsidiary campaigns failed to achieve any of those objectives. In fact, so disgraceful was the performance of Union forces, led by regulars as well as political generals, that Lee eventually received substantial reinforcements from elsewhere in Virginia before the end of May.

The smallest operations involved two separate forces, moving out of West Virginia: the first was a cavalry force of some 2,000 soldiers under Brigadier General Averell, who the year before had performed so abysmally in the cavalry raid against Lee's communications. His goal was the salt works of Saltville and the lead mines at Wytheville in Virginia's southwestern corner. After accomplishing the destruction of those Confederate resources, he was to join up with Brigadier General George Crook, who led approximately 6,000 infantry, cavalry, and artillery also out of West Virginia. Crook was to destroy the major railroad bridge across the New River. From there the two forces were to proceed up the Virginia & Tennessee Railroad and destroy the tracks and running stock.

Nothing turned out as Grant had hoped. Averell and his cavalry ran into Confederate cavalry numbering less than half his force. Moreover, Union cavalry possessed seven shot Spencers, while the Confederates only had single shot carbines. But they possessed the superior general in John Morgan. After his capture in summer 1863 the Ohio authorities had housed Morgan in the Columbus Penitentiary, from which he had escaped and returned to Confederate territory. Like McClellan, Averell overestimated Confederate strength, putting it at 4,000 instead of the 750 Morgan actually possessed. As a result, the Union commander failed to attack either of his objectives. Instead, he fled north to join up with Crook at Dublin, Virginia.

Averell arrived at Dublin to discover Crook's troops had just finished destroying the bridge over the New River, but that Crook had not waited. Crook had won a short, sharp skirmish against a ragtag group of Confederates at Cloyd's Mountain. Then, after destroying the New River bridge, he returned to West Virginia. Averell followed hot on Crook's heels, neither one possessing the moral courage for independent command. Thus, they failed to destroy much of the Virginia & Tennessee Railroad. In his report Crook lamely excused himself as having received intelligence that Lee had defeated the Army of the Potomac in the Wilderness. As a result, he had withdrawn from the Shenandoah because of fear the Lee would send reinforcements down the railroad he was supposed to destroy.

In fact, there were no Confederates, outside of Morgan's minuscule cavalry force, within a hundred miles of Crook. The Southern commander in the Shenandoah, Major General John C. Breckinridge, candidate for president in 1860, recognized that he could not protect the Valley from all risks. Hence, he had concentrated much of his forces, some 5,000 soldiers, in mid-valley, north of Staunton to meet the largest invading force—namely, the army under Sigel. Among the defenders was the cadet corps of the Virginia Military Institute, the youngest fifteen years old, whom Breckinridge hoped not to commit to battle. Sigel brought a slightly greater number of soldiers to New Market, some 6,000, but he deployed them in a totally inept fashion. Breckinridge, who was a thoroughly competent civilian soldier, took one look at Sigel's deployment and exclaimed: "We can attack and whip them here," which he and his army proceeded to do.[37]

Tragically, Breckinridge in a crucial point of the battle uttered the fateful command, "Put the boys in, and may God forgive me for the order." Of the 247 VMI cadets who fought at New Market, eight were killed and 46 wounded. Defeat at New Market sent Sigel scurrying back down the valley almost as fast as Banks had run away in 1862. Grant received an acid report from Halleck about Sigel's performance just as the Spotsylvania battle drew to a close: "If you expect anything from him, you will be mistaken. He will do nothing but run. He never did anything else."[38] The outcome of Sigel's dismal performance was that Breckinridge sent two brigades, 2,500 infantry, on flatbed cars to Lee to reinforce the hard-pressed Army of Northern Virginia.

The fourth piece of Grant's peripheral strategy had been the expedition aimed directly at Richmond and the railroad network surrounding the Confederate capital upon which the lifeblood of foodstuffs and reinforcements flowed to Lee's army. It turned into another sorry story of missed opportunities and general incompetence. Political necessity had dictated the selection of Major General Benjamin Butler to head the expedition, and Grant himself had high hopes for Butler's military abilities. The navy provided the transports to get Butler's 36,000 soldiers, made up the of XVIII Corps and X Corps, to their objective. Moving up the James, the invasion flotilla landed troops at City Point, approximately seven miles from Petersburg, but the bulk of the force disembarked at Bermuda Hundred, within twenty miles of the Confederate capital.

Butler, a Democratic politician from Massachusetts, had been one of the first war Democrats to rally to the Union. His continued support for Lincoln was critical to the president's reelection; thus Butler ended up in command of the invading force, even though, unlike many other political generals, he had never held a major combat command. Grant had, therefore, assigned him two senior, regular army generals as corps commanders: "Baldy" Smith, a former disciple of McClellan, who after moving to the Western theater had contributed significantly to the opening of the "cracker line" during the Chattanooga campaign, and Major General Quincy Gillmore. Grant's theory was that the experienced generals would provide intelligent advice, and that Butler would take it. Unfortunately, Smith and Gillmore provided little military advice of use, while Butler had no intention of allowing his regular army babysitters to dictate to him the plan of the campaign.

Thus, as Meade and Grant were moving into the Wilderness, Butler and his force moved up the James to land at City Point and Bermuda Hundred on 5 May. Instead of moving out, Butler had his troops spend their first day and several days thereafter in fortifying the Peninsula's neck. A single brigade advanced from Bermuda Hundred after its landing, but failed to reach the Richmond and Petersburg Railroad. On 6 May four brigades reached the railroad but inflicted only minor, easily repairable damage. Meanwhile, Richmond was in an uproar. There were only 7,000 troops in the military department defending the capital, and they had to cover a number of fronts. The appearance of Sheridan's raiders on 11 May at Yellow Tavern only served to exacerbate the capital's excitement. By accident George Pickett was in Petersburg on 5 May completing his business as the military district commander and waiting to return to his division. There were only 750 men in the neighborhood to defend that key railroad center. Pickett nearly had a nervous breakdown at the responsibility of keeping Butler at bay while preserving Petersburg and its railroads. Butler's force represented the greatest threat Richmond had faced since the grim days of May 1862, when the Army of the Potomac under McClellan had reached the city's gates.

At the heart of the difficulties the Bermuda Hundred effort experienced was the fact that Grant had failed to lay out a clear set of objectives. His miscalculation lay in his understanding that it was impossible to see exactly what the Confederate weaknesses were or what possibilities might exist. But for subordinate commanders to take advantage of the discretion Grant gave them required imagination, intuition, and initiative, qualities none of which those in charge south of Richmond possessed. As a result, drift, uncertainty, and bickering were the order of the day. As a result, constant changes of plan marked Union efforts, until the Confederates arrived to mitigate the danger.

On 9 May Butler moved from his defensive positions to attack Petersburg. His situation was even more favorable than when he had first landed. On 5 May Brigadier General August Kautz had ridden out of Suffolk, Virginia, with his cavalry division to attack the Petersburg & Weldon Railroad, of critical importance to the supplies and reinforcements moving to Petersburg from North Carolina. Unlike most Union cavalry raids in the East, Kautz and his troopers smashed up the railroad, while their destruction of the bridges over Stony Creek on 7 May and over the Nottoway River on the 9th blocked reinforcements and supplies from reaching Petersburg and Richmond except by longer and more difficult routes.

Butler received news of the destruction of the two bridges on 8 May, and so with three-quarters of his available troop strength, he moved against Petersburg—at the same time as Sheridan's cavalry was approaching Richmond from the north. After a tortoise-like advance, Butler and his corps commanders arrived at Swift Creek, two miles north of Petersburg. There, they discovered an unknown number of Confederates in defensive positions on the creek's southern side. In fact, there were hardly any defenders between the Federals and Petersburg, but the best the Union troops could do was to lob a few shells in the enemy's direction. Butler then ordered Gillmore and Smith to attack across the Swift Creek the next morning, while the division remaining at City Point advanced on the city from the northeast. Neither corps commander objected. Instead, after Butler had left, they sat and wrote their commander a proposal, which showed even less disposition to act. They proposed that the army pull back to Bermuda Hundred, move by navy transport back to City Point, and then attack Petersburg from that direction. At that, Butler exploded, furious at what he believed an attempt by his subordinates to usurp his authority. Smith's earlier machinations against Burnside could not have helped his reputation with Butler. Butler's reply was a vituperative piece of writing that only his years of working as a politician and lawyer in Massachusetts could produce. Nevertheless, Butler, perhaps disconcerted by Smith's and Gillmore's opposition, dispensed with the attack and ordered a withdrawal back to Bermuda Hundred.

Having heard from Stanton that Grant was driving south and would soon reach the Confederate capital, Butler decided to move against Richmond. With his quarrelsome corps commanders moving at a snail's pace, the "Army of the James," as Butler had christened it, moved north toward Confederate field fortifications at Drewry's Bluff, which defended the southern approaches to Richmond. On 13 May the XVIII and X Corps launched halfhearted attacks that captured a few outlying works in front of the main Confederate defenses. But Butler was unwilling to launch a major attack, and so the Army of the James entrenched, while its commander pondered its next step. Meanwhile, the correlation of forces was steadily swinging against him. Where the Confederates could barely scratch together 1,000 soldiers when the landing took place on 5 May, by 7 May they had assembled

2,668; by 8 May 7,500. Moreover, as Sheridan's raid disappeared into the dust of southeastern Virginia roads, it freed a further 5,000 soldiers from Richmond's defenses. Finally, despite the damage to the Petersburg & Weldon Railroad, additional brigades began arriving from the Carolinas using longer, but usable, routes that bypassed Petersburg.

By 16 May Beauregard had set the Army of the James up for a disaster. Virtually all of Butler's forces faced the Confederate lines at Drewry's Bluff to the north; he had only a thin screen covering his rear against a southern advance from Petersburg. Early that morning Beauregard struck with his main forces out of Drewry's Bluff. The Confederates achieved some success, although they had considerable difficulty against Smith's lines, where "Baldy" had strung signal wire from stump to stump and tree to tree, which retarded the attackers, a foretaste of the difficulties barbed wire would cause in World War I. By midmorning, the Confederate attack had come to a halt after driving Butler's troops back approximately a single mile.

Beauregard and his commanders then awaited the attack from the south. It never came; Brigadier General W. H. Whiting, commanding the two-brigade force that was to attack from the south, caught a bad case of McClellan fever. He saw Union troops everywhere and after a short advance across Swift Creek, retreated to the creek's south bank. The trap failed to close. Nevertheless, the day's fighting had been more than enough for Butler, who precipitately ordered the Army of the James to return to Bermuda Hundred. There Beauregard somewhat dejectedly—he had hoped to destroy Butler's army and capture the "Beast" who had so egregiously insulted the women of New Orleans—fenced the Army of the James in with a solid line of breastworks. Grant accurately summed up the mess: the Confederates had sealed off Butler's army "as if it had been in a bottle strongly corked."[39] Beauregard could then, somewhat unwillingly, ship 7,000 troops to reinforce Lee, but only after receiving a direct order to do so.

The Denouement of the Campaign against Lee and His Army

Stalemated at Spotsylvania, Grant sidled around Lee's eastern flank with the hope of getting between the Army of Northern Virginia and Richmond, the aim not so much to capture the Confederate capital, but to force Lee to fight in the open. After receiving the depressing news from the Valley and the James, Grant ordered the movement of the Army of the Potomac away from Spotsylvania the following day. Hancock's II Corps was to lead the march south, but immediately after pulling out of the line a Confederate reconnaissance in force hit its flank. To accomplish that mission, Ewell had deployed his entire corps, now down to a paltry 6,000 infantry. The Confederates ran into a Union division, consisting of heavy artillerymen who had been guarding Washington over the previous two years, and whom Grant had ordered converted to infantry. With little or no combat experience, the "heavies" held their own. Having found the Union right, Ewell withdrew, but the engagement at Harris Farm underlined the extent of the losses the Army of Northern Virginia had suffered thus far in the fighting. One year earlier Jackson's corps had attacked at Chancellorsville with more than 20,000 men. Now Ewell with his whole corps had only been able to feel out the Union flank.

For the next day and a half, the two armies marched south: the Confederates taking a straight route to the North Anna River; the Army of the Potomac moving in a southeasterly direction. Along the way, Union troops foraged liberally through the countryside, a portion of Virginia which war had yet to touch. Some commanders attempted to stop that marauding, but Grant was not one of them. One division commander, upon discovering a large number of dead sheep in his path, which a regiment had butchered, commented that "if sheep attack you, you are obliged to fight."[40] Grant determined to pull Baldy Smith's XVIII Corps out of Bermuda Hundred to reinforce the Army of the Potomac. Meanwhile, he ordered Meade to push his corps across the North Anna and pin Lee down.

Beginning on the morning of 23 May Warren got two of his divisions across at Jericho Mill. Confederate skirmishers watched the crossing but did not contest it. But late in the afternoon, after much of the V Corps had crossed, Wilcox's division hit them with a fierce attack. After an initial success, which included scattering the renowned Iron Brigade, Union infantry and artillery brought the attack to a halt after inflicting nearly twice as many casualties on the attackers as the V Corps suffered. At the same time that Warren was fending off Wilcox, Hancock discovered three Confederate regiments on the river's north bank. With a solid dose of artillery fire, II Corps troops charged and overwhelmed the outnumbered defenders. Again what marked the day's fighting was the fact that straight-on attacks inevitably failed

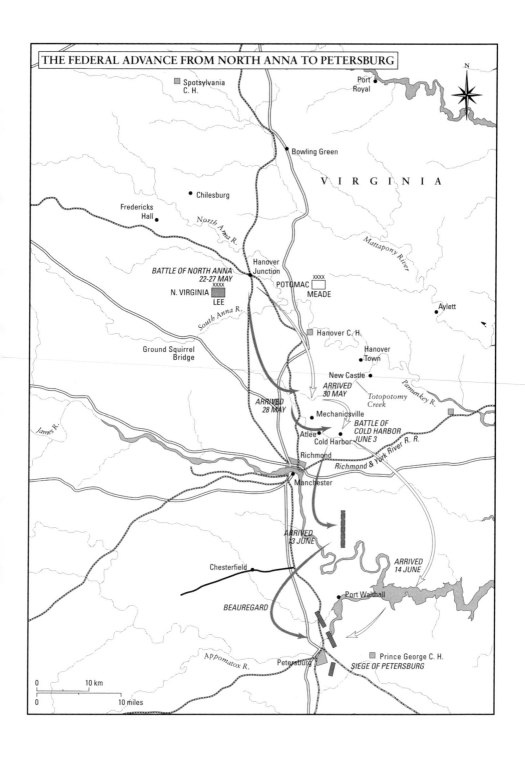

THE FEDERAL ADVANCE FROM NORTH ANNA TO PETERSBURG

Spotsylvania C. H.

Port Royal

Bowling Green

V I R G I N I A

Chilesburg

Fredericks Hall

North Anna R.

Mattapony River

Hanover Junction

BATTLE OF NORTH ANNA
22-27 MAY
XXXX
N. VIRGINIA
LEE

XXXX
POTOMAC
MEADE

Aylett

South Anna R.

Hanover C. H.

Hanover Town

Ground Squirrel Bridge

New Castle

Pamunkey R.

ARRIVED 30 MAY

Totopotomy Creek

ARRIVED 28 MAY

Mechanicsville

James R.

Atlee

Cold Harbor

BATTLE OF COLD HARBOR
JUNE 3

Richmond

Richmond & York River R. R.

Manchester

ARRIVED 13 JUNE

ARRIVED 14 JUNE

Chesterfield

BEAUREGARD

Port Walthall

Appomatox R.

Petersburg

Prince George C. H.

SIEGE OF PETERSBURG

0   10 km

0   10 miles

against firepower and defenses. The only time that reality was not true was when one side possessed overwhelming superiority in numbers or firepower.

Union commanders greeted the next day with some optimism. They were across the North Anna without serious casualties. But then it dawned on them as they pushed forward that they had divided the Army of the Potomac with the Army of Northern Virginia between the two halves of their forces. Lee had deployed his army in strong field fortifications in the shape of a V with its apex resting on the North Anna, the western arm resting on the Little River, and the eastern arm trailing southward a considerable distance. Any Union effort to out-flank the eastern defenses would only separate the Army of the Po-tomac to an even greater extent.

Not only was the Confederate position impregnable, since Lee's soldiers had more than a day to build the breastworks, but they could now concentrate their forces for a major blow against whichever one of the divided portions of the Army of the Potomac they chose. The tactical situation was one that in the past the Army of Northern Vir-ginia would have seized without hesitation. But Lee, incapacitated by dysentery, did not trust his current corps commanders (Anderson, Hill, and Ewell) sufficiently to allow them to supervise an attack on the Union army. Instead, he grumbled in his tent, "We must strike them a blow—we must never let them pass us again—we must strike them a blow."[41]

But the blow never came. It was also a fleeting advantage, because once Union commanders realized their predicament, they immediately fortified their positions. By this point it took the soldiers of the op-posing armies only a matter of hours to build formidable breastworks, which when coupled with their firepower, artillery as well as small arms, were impregnable. Once again it was stalemate, although this time without the casualties of Spotsylvania. What Grant did do was to make a number of operational and strategic decisions. First, he pulled much of Butler's Army of the James, including Smith's XVIII Corps, out of Bermuda Hundred to reinforce the Army of the Potomac. Twenty thousand soldiers went north to join Grant, while 10,000 remained with Butler, who astonishingly believed he had achieved a major suc-cess. Meanwhile, Grant relieved Sigel, a decision with which no one in Washington had the slightest quarrel, given that politician's abysmal performance as a general. Grant informed Sigel's replacement, Major

General David Hunter, to drive back up the Valley to Charlottesville to wreck the transportation infrastructure of canals and railroads in the Shenandoah, while living off the land. After some deliberation on the evening of 25 May, Grant determined to pull out of North Anna and head south, again moving southeast to circle Lee's right.

On the evening of 25 May the Army of the Potomac began its withdrawal to the north bank. Sheridan's cavalry, which had recently rejoined the army, led the way south. Before they left, Grant made sure there was nothing usable left of the Virginia Central Railroad running through the area. It did not take Lee long to discern what was happening; by this point it was clear Grant was not about to retreat. The Army of Northern Virginia also pulled back to Atlee station less than ten miles from Richmond. Unfortunately, Grant was too optimistic about the damage the army had inflicted on Lee. He noted in a letter to Halleck on 26 May, "Lees [sic] army is really whipped."[42] That overconfidence led to the disaster of Cold Harbor.

Having crossed the Pamunkey River, formed by the conjunction of the North Anna and the South Anna Rivers, the Army of the Potomac moved on to the fateful location of Cold Harbor. Near Haw's Shop the cavalry of the two armies, attempting to discover the location of the main armies, ran into each other. After the expenditure of vast amounts of ammunition—one Union cavalryman estimated his outfit of 200 men had expended 18,000 rounds with their Spencers—the arrival of Custer's cavalry brigade broke the Confederates. Interestingly, in comparing the Eastern and Western Union armies, in the West Spencers and other multiple firing carbines appeared in some infantry units, usually as the result of individual initiative, but nevertheless encouraged by senior officers. On the other hand, the Army of the Potomac was content to see the Ordnance Bureau distribute the Spencers solely to the cavalry, while none of its infantry acquired the multiple-shot weapons.

By 30 May it was clear to Lee that Grant was continuing his move around the Confederate right flank. By now he was worrying about the long-term consequences of the Virginia campaign. As he commented to Early in June, "we must destroy this army of Grant's before he gets to [the] James River. If he gets there, it will become a siege, and then it will be a mere question of time."[43] Therefore, he determined to strike "those people" a major blow. Shortly before, he had taken advantage of the fact that Ewell, a disappointment as a corps commander from

Gettysburg on, was temporarily ill. Lee began to rectify the command problems that had crippled his army's movements on the North Anna. He replaced Ewell permanently with Early. Lee had accurately described Early as "my bad old man," given his penchant for quarreling. Whatever his personal defects, Early was a driver, had an outstanding record as a division commander, and would perform more than adequately in independent command. It is worth contrasting Lee's action with the Army of the Potomac's preoccupation with seniority above any measure of battlefield competence in selecting senior positions.

Early launched his attack at Warren's V Corps and achieved an initial success, but once again Union artillery, backed by infantry that had recovered from the initial shock, halted the Confederate attack. A further attack later in the afternoon indicated that the Union right flank was held in strength. One of Early's division commanders, Brigadier General Stephen Ramseur, sent a brigade to clear out Union artillery from his front. By the time it was over Union artillery and infantry had slaughtered the attackers, killing, wounding, or capturing over 60 percent of the lead brigade. Once again, the hard lesson was there for those who chose to see it: against veteran troops in prepared positions there was no hope for attacking infantry, unless they enjoyed overwhelming numerical superiority.

What now happened at Cold Harbor reinforced that harsh lesson to an even greater extent. It also marked Grant's worst performance as a general. As he admitted in his memoirs, "I have always regretted the last assault at Cold Harbor was ever made. . . . At Cold Harbor no advantage whatever was gained to compensate for the heavy loss we sustained. Indeed, the advantages other than those of relative losses, were on the Confederate side."[44] How did this disaster come about then? The battle began ironically, unlike Spotsylvania, with Union forces, in this case Sheridan's troopers, reaching the crossroads of Cold Harbor in strength before the Confederates. Sheridan's cavalry not only took the crossroads but also threw back Confederate infantry and cavalry. Again the superior firepower of the Spencer carbines told against Confederates equipped only with the single shot weapons.

Fearing superior Confederate numbers, Sheridan then withdrew, only to receive orders from Grant to get his troopers back to Cold Harbor immediately. Luckily for him, the Confederates had not noted his withdrawal, so skillfully had his men executed it. The troopers, like their infantry counterparts, then began constructing breastworks and fortified positions against the possibility of a Confederate attack. It came early the next morning. In fact, Lee had ordered a full-scale attack on the Union position in the hopes not only of regaining the Cold Harbor crossroads but also of rolling up the advance corps leading the Army of the Potomac. What was supposed to be a major attack, however, ended up being the disastrous slaughter of a Confederate brigade, led by an inexperienced colonel and consisting of troops who had little experience in combat. Sheridan's troopers allowed the advancing Confederates, who had not even bothered to throw out a line of skirmishers, to advance to within point blank range. At that point their carbines blew most of the attackers away. The devastating results so unsettled Confederate commanders that they failed to patch together an effective attack over the course of the remainder of the day. In that they were probably lucky, because in midmorning Sheridan's cavalry had received infantry reinforcements from the VI Corps.

This initial success turned out to be the prelude to disaster. Meade's orders to Wright and the VI Corps as well as Smith's XVIII Corps, which finally began arriving in midafternoon, had been to launch an immediate attack. This being the Army of the Potomac no such thing occurred. By the time Wright and Smith had things sorted out by early evening on 1 June, the Confederates had constructed effective defensive breastworks. Thus, with one exception, not surprisingly Emery Upton's brigade, the resulting Union attack failed all along the line. Having punched a hole in the Confederate line, Upton finally had to retreat, when it was clear he would not receive reinforcements. To put the icing on the failures that day, Warren's officers had watched a Confederate corps march past their front and failed to inform their commander that a wonderful opportunity existed to slash out at their enemies in the open. In a dispatch from army headquarters to Stanton, Dana reported that Grant and Meade were furious with the performance of Warren and Wright. "Meade says a radical change must be made, no matter how unpleasant it may be to make it." He then added an accurate forecast that Meade would not take "so extreme a remedy" as firing those at the highest level who had botched the attack.[45]

Thwarted in his efforts to launch a devastating counterblow against his persistent opponent, Lee gave orders for his subordinate commanders to lay out a complete set of earthworks. With sufficient time, Lee's engineers established as deadly a set of field fortifications as the Civil War was to see. With a day and a half to improve their breastworks and trenches, the Confederates created a defensive system that no army of the time could have breached. The battle was not as catastrophic a fiasco as Grant's detractors would later claim, but it was still a serious setback. Only one division, not surprisingly Barlow's, got in among the Confederates, but Gibbon's division on his right failed to come up on time—astonishingly a brigade commander had failed to awaken his men. The Army of the Potomac lost around 6,000 men on 3 June, versus 1,000–1,500 losses for the Confederates. Coming at the end of a brutal month of fighting, with Lee still interposed between Grant and Richmond, the grim results reverberated throughout the North and placed Lincoln's reelection in jeopardy. Then to top off one of the most wretched days in American history, Grant and Lee squabbled over the terms a cease fire or truce might require, so that Union soldiers could bring in their wounded, who were suffering immensely from the heat and lack of water between the lines.

In every respect, it was Grant's worst day. In this case, Grant held direct command of the Army of the Potomac but failed to oversee the synchronization of the corps commanders, who certainly were not going to coordinate matters among themselves. The result was a disaster, less excusable even than Fredericksburg. How to explain the decision to attack at Cold Harbor? Perhaps some memory of the success at Missionary Ridge, perhaps sheer frustration at the general incompetence that the Army of the Potomac's leaders had displayed in the campaign, perhaps simply the weariness caused by the constant pressure of the previous four weeks of fighting had impaired Grant's judgment. All are possibilities, but none fully satisfactory.

But as with all great generals, Grant moved on instead of looking back. He now devised perhaps the most innovative and imaginative operational maneuver of the Eastern war. The army would feint a move against Lee's right, threatening Richmond from the east, but instead move across the James River to attack Petersburg and thus cut Richmond and the Army of Northern Virginia off from the sustenance and reinforcements upon which they depended. At the same time, in much the same fashion as he had done with Grierson's raid at the start to his Vicksburg campaign, Grant launched two strikes to draw Confederate attention away from the move on Petersburg. The first involved Major General David Hunter, Sigel's replacement in the Valley. Hunter was to drive up the Shenandoah. On their march from Staunton to Lexington, Hunter's soldiers wrecked much of the countryside, including burning VMI as well as the governor's personal house. Hunter's force then moved on toward Lynchburg. That represented a dangerous move from Lee's perspective. He promptly sent Early with his corps to restore the situation. Confronted with what he believed superior numbers, Hunter slunk into West Virginia, a move which left the Valley denuded of Union troops.

Meanwhile, Sheridan led his cavalry from Cold Harbor northwest to attack the railroad system north of Richmond. There, his troopers got in a fierce fight near Trevilian Station with Lee's cavalry, now commanded by Wade Hampton. With their Spencers, the Union cavalry held Hampton's riders off, while inflicting heavy casualties on their enemies. The days of Confederate cavalry superiority were over. After ripping up some of the Virginia Central Railroad, damage the Confederates quickly repaired, Sheridan returned to the Army of the Potomac. In military and economic terms, neither strike achieved much, but in strategic terms they achieved a great deal. In fact, those operations helped create one of the greatest opportunities the Army of the Potomac would have in its history. While the Confederate high command was looking over its shoulder toward the north and west, Grant stole a march on Lee. Shielded by the cavalry division Sheridan had left behind, the Army of the Potomac slipped away to the south. One corps utilized naval transport to reach the James; the other four marched overland. Once at the James, Union engineers built a pontoon bridge of enormous length (over 2,000 feet) in the face of a four-foot tidal rise and fall—another tribute to the Union Army's logistical sophistication. Troops began crossing on 14 June, while the XVIII Corps, which had arrived by boat to City Point, moved against Petersburg, which was virtually defenseless.

Beauregard, positioned in front of Bermuda Hundred and Petersburg, was in a hopeless military position. But as he had done at Corinth in 1862, Beauregard put on a wonderful show: troops appeared to be marching into the fortifications that surrounded Petersburg—and then snuck out to be seen moving into other parts of the fortifications; whistles blew again and again along with clouds of steam from the few locomotives in the Petersburg station. "Baldy" Smith bought it all; only at dusk did he finally capture a few trenches and guns, not daring to launch a full-scale attack. His lack of action eventually terminated his career. Like Warren, he had proven to be a superb chief engineer on a field army's staff but a poor corps commander in the field. In July

Grant relieved him of command of the XVIII Corps. Grant had nominated Smith for promotion before the campaign began but noted in his memoirs that "I was not long in finding out that the objections to Smith's promotion were well founded."[46] At the same time that Smith was moving out, the II Corps was the first of the overland corps to arrive and cross the James.

But it had lacked rations and halted waiting for resupply. Hancock later claimed that he had never been informed that his corps was to participate in the assault on Petersburg. Not until the 16th did the II Corps arrive to bolster Smith's soldiers. Grant's efforts to hurry the Army of the Potomac into seizing Petersburg failed in muddle, confusion, and bad luck. Smith was sick and Hancock was suffering intensely from the effects of his Gettysburg wound. As the corps commanders dithered, two Confederate divisions arrived to bolster Beauregard. By the 17th the Army of Northern Virginia's units were flowing into the city, and the opportunity evaporated. Some historians have suggested that Cold Harbor had robbed the Army of the Potomac's commanders of a willingness to attack. Perhaps. The unprecedented pace of combat operations during the Overland Campaign had taken a terrible psychological toll; Warren himself seemed close to the breaking point. But their Confederate opponents had if anything suffered even more. Furthermore, where in the account of its activities during the previous month had the Army of the Potomac's commanders displayed the slightest willingness to act with celerity, to display initiative, or to recognize that time was a precious commodity that once lost could not be regained? As the Germans emphasized to their officers in the world wars of the twentieth century, better a faulty decision taken in time than a perfect decision too late.

And so the war in the East between the two great armies settled in to what Lee had feared: a siege. Now reality was at the capital's doorstep. Toward the end of June Lee wrote Davis a despairing note: "I hope your Exc^y will put no reliance in what I can do individually, for I feel that will be very little. The enemy has a strong position, & is able to deal us more injury than from any other point he has ever taken. Still we must try & defeat them. I fear he will not attack us but advance by regular approaches. He is so situated that I cannot attack him." [47]

But the campaign across Virginia had its political costs, particularly for Lincoln. The campaign's enormous cost, with only a siege to show for it, sent chills through the North. Lee knew how dire a military position he held; the voters of the North had no such knowledge. In the harsh balance of attrition, the Army of the Potomac had come out the winner, while Grant's line of operations had answered the public's call for hard fighting to its own unknowing regret. While it had suffered approximately 55,000 casualties, the Army of Northern Virginia had suffered at least 35,000 casualties, and probably considerably more. In the balance of numbers, the North could tolerate such heavy losses, while in the end the Confederacy could not. But, of course, there were political consequences for such losses.

In political terms the issue was much in the air. Lincoln attempted to defuse the growing sense of despondency in the North. In a speech to the Sanitary Commission in Philadelphia, the president noted, "We accepted this war for an object, a worthy object, and the war will end when that worthy object is attained. Under God, I hope it never will until that time. Speaking of the present campaign, General Grant is reported to have said, I am going through on this line if it takes all summer. This war has taken three years; it was begun or accepted upon the line of restoring the national authority over the whole national domain, and for the American people, as far as my knowledge enables me to speak, I say we are going through on this line if it takes three years more. . . . General Grant is this evening with, . . . the brave officers and soldiers with him, in a position from whence he will never be dislodged until Richmond is taken."[48] But Lincoln also understood the thin ice on which he was treading, considering the political costs the campaign in Virginia would impose, unless further military successes by Union armies intervened. Typical of the attitudes of many wafflers in the North, Horace Greeley, always irresponsible, even by the standards of today's media, but a bellwether of Northern sentiment, wrote the president in early July, "our bleeding, bankrupt, almost dying country also longs for peace—shudders at the prospect of fresh conscriptions, of further wholesale devastations, and of new rivers of human blood."[49] For much of the summer, gloom enshrouded the North.

Petersburg, the Shenandoah, and the Siege of Richmond

As the armies settled into the siege of Petersburg, the question was, what next? It was clear that any effort by the Army of the Potomac to punch directly into Petersburg would be of no avail. An attempt to reach out to the west in late June to cut the Weldon Railroad resulted in a disgraceful and humiliating defeat. One of the division commanders, John Gibbon, succinctly characterized the impact of the casualties suffered in the campaign, "troops, which at the commencement of the campaign were equal to almost undertaking, became toward the end of it unfit for almost any."[50]

One further attempt to break into Petersburg occurred in late July, but once again the worst aspects of the Army of the Potomac's culture intervened. In late June one of Burnside's regimental commanders, a certain Lieutenant Colonel Henry Pleasants, whose command came from the coal mining districts of Pennsylvania, suggested digging a mine under one of the main Confederate defensive positions. Burnside found the idea intriguing. Meade agreed to the idea, but his staff, with little mining experience, refused to provide picks and other necessary materials, because they believed such a tunnel would be too long and hence the miners would suffocate. Pleasants's men solved that problem, made their own digging implements, and in slightly more than three weeks completed a mine and chamber filled with 8,000 pounds of black powder.

With time on his hands, Burnside managed to train up one of the new United States Colored Troops (USCT) divisions to exploit the explosion. The division's officers warned the black soldiers not to venture down into the crater, but rather to work their way around the edges, pushing the Confederates away from the giant hole the explosion would cause. Then at the last moment Meade, afraid the abolitionists would accuse him of sacrificing African American troops needlessly, if the attack failed, ordered Burnside to substitute a white division. That division had not received any preparatory orders. Unfortunately, Grant approved the change.

The mine itself was a success. It blew the Confederate defenders, their artillery, and the whole fort to kingdom come. Then the disaster began. Instead of driving through the wreckage into the Confederate rear areas, the attacking troops milled around admiring the miners' handiwork, many of them descending into the gigantic hole the explosion had created. They might have advanced more expeditiously with proper leadership, but the division commander was drunk in the rear. The Confederates acted with usual dispatch and rushed reserves to the crater. Having gained the crater's lip, they fired down into a helpless mass of Union soldiers, many of them USCT troops committed in the last wave of attackers. Union casualties were nearly 4,000; Confederate casualties negligible except for those blown up in the explosion.

Matters in the Shenandoah were faring no better. Hunter's failure in the Valley was bad enough, but his withdrawal into West Virginia opened the lower Valley and Maryland across the Potomac to Confederate operations. Confederate raiders struck at the Baltimore & Ohio Railroad, one of the key transportation links between the East and the West, and kept it closed for substantial periods of the summer. From both the military and political points of view, the situation was unacceptable. For three years, there had been four separate military departments, which in one way or another held responsibility for the Valley and its northern extension. In terms of simple command and control, this was not the way to run a war. There needed to be a unified department, under a single commander, to end the difficulties the Shenandoah had caused, a problem beguiling Northern strategists since the war's beginning

On 13 June, just as the siege of Petersburg was beginning, Lee dispatched Early and his corps to the Shenandoah. Early's instructions were clear: he was to stop Hunter's depredations in the Valley with an aggressive use of the troops available. If possible, he was then to launch those forces into Maryland to cause as much trouble as possible. If the situation were favorable, he was to move southeast along the Potomac, thus threatening Washington. Lee's hope was that Early could cause sufficient difficulties in the Valley so that Grant would have to dispatch substantial reinforcements from Petersburg. In effect, Lee was hoping for a replay of Jackson's attacks in the Shenandoah in spring 1862 that had led the Lincoln administration to withhold reinforcements from McClellan. He may also have thought either that Grant would launch another suicidal attack such as Cold Harbor, or that the withdrawal of Union forces would provide the Army of Northern Virginia with the opportunity to defeat Meade's army and force the Federals to abandon the siege of Petersburg.

With the barn door left open by Hunter's flight, Early began his raid into Maryland on 28 June. On 6 July, having scared Sigel out of Martinsburg, the Confederates crossed into Maryland not far from Antietam. Two days later, marching south, they entered Fredericksburg, while Early's cavalry wrecked substantial portions of the Baltimore & Ohio. By so doing, they insured that Hunter's troops remained out of the picture. Along their march toward Washington the Confederates extorted $20,000 from citizens of Hagerstown and $200,000 from those of Frederick by threatening to burn both towns. By that time Halleck and the thoroughly alarmed politicians in Washington had alerted Grant, who dispatched one division of the VI Corps to Baltimore. Meanwhile, outside Frederick the Confederates ran into an inferior Union force at Monocacy under Major General Lew Wallace, who had failed to appear on the first day of Shiloh. A sharp fight took place, and the Confederates pushed Wallace's smaller force, including the division from the VI Corps, back toward Baltimore and out of the way. Nevertheless, by holding Early up and forcing the Confederates to deploy, Wallace redeemed himself and gained almost a full day for Grant to rush more reinforcements north to protect Washington.

After the fight at Monocacy, Early resumed his march on Washington. There was not much help that Halleck rendered, since apparently he was "in a perfect maze—without intelligent decision or self-reliance."[51] On 9 July Grant shipped the remainder of Wright's VI Corps to Washington and indicated that the XIX Corps, which he had recalled from Louisiana, would also be available to reinforce the forces facing Early. As for the race to Washington's outer defenses, Early seemingly won, but his troops were in such an exhausted state they were incapable of attacking the capital's imposing outer defenses. By the time they recovered, the VI Corps' first troops were arriving. On the evening of 11 July, having received word there were two Union corps arriving in Washington's defenses, Early withdrew.

Skirmishing occurred as the Confederates prepared to withdraw, and Lincoln could not resist the opportunity to observe what was happening. While peering over the parapet, he received a sharp warning— "get down, you damn fool!"—later attributed (probably wrongly) to a Massachusetts captain of infantry, the future Supreme Court justice, Oliver Wendell Holmes Jr.[52] Over the evening of 12/13 July, Early retreated north and crossed the Potomac at Balls Bluff, where the Army of the Potomac had received a nasty rebuff in fall 1861. Grant passed explicit instructions through Halleck that Union troops were not only to crush Early in pursuing him, but also to "eat out Virginia clear and clean as far as they go, so that crows flying over it for the balance of the season will have to carry their provender with them."[53]

The troubles in the Valley and now the raid on Washington led Grant to focus his attention on what was clearly a major operational and geographic problem. The first decision was to merge the four departments. Lee's consistent ability to transfer troops back and forth between the Shenandoah and his main army underlined that the Confederates regarded Virginia as a single theater. Thus, the Union would have to do the same, or it was going to continue to flounder in the area. The second was to place a single commander in charge of the troops, a general directly responsible to Grant, not to Washington. Grant noted in his memoirs: "It had been the source of a great deal of trouble to us heretofore to guard that outlet to the north . . . chiefly because of interference from Washington. It seemed to be the policy of General Halleck and Secretary Stanton to keep any force sent there in pursuit of the invading army, moving right and left so as to keep between the enemy and our capital; and generally speaking, they pursued this policy until all knowledge of the whereabouts of the enemy was lost."[54]

The first problem was solved relatively easily, and Lincoln agreed quickly to the reorganization. We should note the stark contrast here with the disastrous dispute between McClellan and Lincoln over the security of Washington, and how McClellan bore most of the responsibility for failing to win the trust of his commander in chief. The second was more difficult, given the failure of so many commanders. Despite doubts on the part of Lincoln and Stanton, as well as the confusion sowed by Halleck—one is never sure in Halleck's case if it was deliberate obtuseness or simple incompetence—Grant placed Sheridan in command. His force consisted of the Army of the Potomac's VI Corps, the XIX Corps which had just arrived from Louisiana, Crook's two divisions from the Army of West Virginia, and a substantial cavalry force that was largely armed with Spencers.

By now Grant, like Lincoln, had recognized Halleck for what he was, an overpromoted clerk, who quite simply did not understand the war. As Grant's chief of staff, John A. Rawlins, noted: "The fact is, Grant and Halleck have never looked through the same military glasses."[55] On 6 August Grant met with Sheridan at Monocacy station and informed him of his new command. As usual Grant was explicit: "Do not hesitate to give commands to officers in whom you have confidence, without regard to claims of others on account of rank. What we want is prompt and active movements after the enemy in accordance with the instructions you already have." In reference to the previous manner in managing the Shenandoah, Grant added, "I feel every confidence that you will do the best, and will leave you as far as possible to act on your own judgment, and not embarrass you with orders and instructions."[56]

At the same time that Grant was turning the Valley over to one of his trusted subordinates, the first gleam of hope appeared to cut the gloom enshrouding the Northern war effort. Lashed to the mast of his ship, Admiral David Farragut drove his fleet through the minefield—in the parlance of the time, torpedoes—guarding Mobile Bay. When the fleet came to a halt as one of the monitors blew up because of a mine, Farragut reportedly uttered the immortal phrase, "damn the torpedoes, full speed ahead." A brief naval battle followed, in which the navy's ships smashed the Confederate fleet. Three weeks of amphibious operations followed as Union troops subdued the forts guarding the bay. By the last week of August, Mobile could no longer serve as a port of call for blockade-runners. However, the city remained in Confederate hands. As a result, the interior of southern and central Alabama remained untouched by Union troops, largely due to Halleck's lack of imagination, which had thwarted Grant's efforts to launch a major amphibious effort against the port and southern Alabama in summer 1863.

In his initial month in command Sheridan remained relatively cautious. Part of the reason was undoubtedly the fact that Lee had detached an infantry and a cavalry division under Anderson to Culpeper, where they could support the Confederates in the Valley. Nevertheless, contributing to Sheridan's caution was the fact that the administration, and Grant as well, worried that another setback in the Shenandoah would sink Lincoln's prospects for reelection. On the Confederate side, Early continued to play the Confederate shell game by rapid and unexpected moves. Those threatened another raid into Maryland and Pennsylvania, while shutting down the Baltimore & Ohio Railroad.

Sherman's capture of Atlanta on 2 September, which broke the stalemate in the West, ended inhibitions about seeking to destroy the Confederates in the Valley. On 14 September, Grant set off to visit Sheridan. The purpose was solely to meet with his subordinate; the commander in chief had no intention of stopping in Washington to meet with Halleck. Moreover, Grant was not about to attempt to pass orders to Sheridan through Halleck, "because they would be stopped there and such orders as Halleck's caution (and that of the Secretary of War) would suggest, would be given instead, and would, no doubt, be

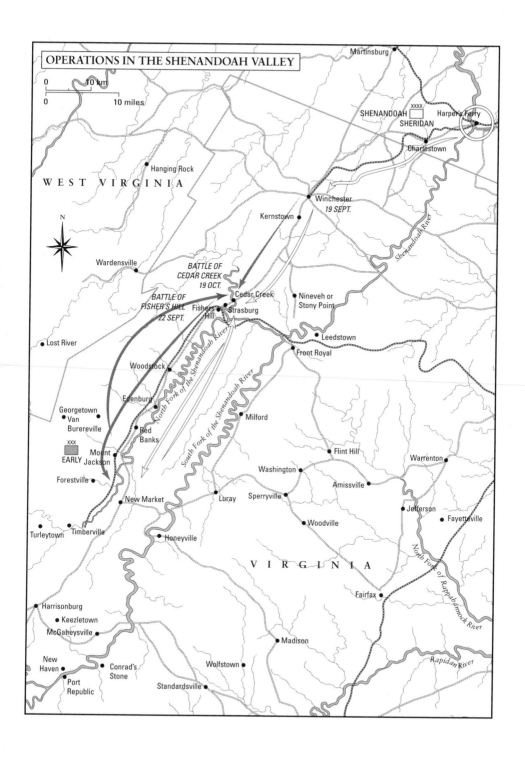

OPERATIONS IN THE SHENANDOAH VALLEY

0   10 km

0   10 miles

Martinsburg

SHENANDOAH   XXXX   Harper's Ferry
SHERIDAN

Charlestown

WEST VIRGINIA

Hanging Rock

Winchester
19 SEPT.

Kernstown

N

Wardensville

BATTLE OF
CEDAR CREEK
19 OCT.

Cedar Creek

Nineveh or
Stony Point

BATTLE OF
FISHER'S HILL
22 SEPT.

Fisher's
Hill   Strasburg

Lost River

Leedstown

Front Royal

Woodstock

North Fork of the Shenandoah River

South Fork of the Shenandoah River

Edenburg

Georgetown
Van
Burereville

Milford

Flint Hill

Warrenton

Red
Banks

Washington

Amissville

XXX
EARLY   Mount
Jackson

Forestville

New Market

Luray

Sperryville

Woodville

Jefferson

Fayetteville

Turleytown   Timberville

Honeyville

VIRGINIA

North Fork of the Rappahannock River

Harrisonburg

Keezletown

McGaheysville

Fairfax

New
Haven

Conrad's
Stone

Wolfstown

Madison

Rapidan River

Port
Republic

Standardsville

Shenandoah River

contradictory to mine."[57] A veteran sergeant, most probably from the VI Corps, watching the meeting between the two generals, sensed what was occurring. He remarked to one of his fellows: "That's Grant. I hate to see the old cuss around. When that old cuss is around there's sure to be a big fight on hand."[58] The sergeant was spot on. The commander in chief brought with him a plan for the campaign, but Sheridan already had one, and Grant accepted the Irishman's concept and returned to City Point after visiting his family in Burlington, New Jersey.

The restrictions were now off Sheridan. On 18 September, two days after meeting with Grant, Sheridan received intelligence that Early had divided his army, two divisions and a cavalry brigade heading toward Martinsburg to strike at the Baltimore & Ohio Railroad, the remainder staying in place around Winchester. Early, believing Sheridan was another one of the cautious losers the Union high command had sent to the Valley, underestimated his opponent. To Sheridan the splitting of the Confederate forces represented a God-given opportunity. He moved quickly; Brigadier General James Wilson's cavalry (Wilson, continuing his meteoric rise, was now a division commander of cavalry) grabbed the road through Berryville Canyon from the surprised pickets. Because the canyon appeared a formidable obstacle, the Confederates had not held it in strength, even though the road led directly to Winchester. Thus, in the early morning hours of 19 September 1864—one day and two years after Antietam—Sheridan surprised his opponent and was in a position to destroy Major General Stephen Ramseur's division, holding the ground east of Winchester.

But having caught the Confederates by surprise, Union forces displayed none of the dash required to destroy the Confederates defending Winchester. The VI Corps led the advance of the infantry, and Wright decided that he would take his wagons through as well. Then in typical Army of the Potomac fashion, Wright, the senior officer by date of rank, refused the pleas of Major General William Emory, XIX Corps commander, to pull the VI Corps wagons off the road so that the infantry of the XIX Corps could deploy into combat formation through the gap. The contrast with Champion Hill in 1863, where Hovey cleared his wagons off the road so that McPherson's troops could close, is instructive.

By the time that the VI Corps wagons had moved through Berryville Canyon, allowing the XIX Corps to deploy in combat formation, Early had had time to reunite his forces. Still the Union army enjoyed a considerable advantage in numbers. Sheridan's force numbered approximately 39,000 infantry, cavalry, and artillery to Early's 14,000 soldiers. At 1140, Sheridan attacked his opponent. As so often happened in the Civil War, the Union generals had not done a careful reconnaissance. Despite galling artillery that hit Grover's division of the XIX Corps on the Union right flank, the initial attacks pushed the Confederates back. Confederate counterattacks then drove the advance Union divisions back to their starting lines. There was now a pause as the combatants caught their breath.

By the early afternoon Sheridan was able to bring up Crook's VIII Corps. Meanwhile, north of the infantry battle, Wilson's cavalry regiments with their Spencers were battering the Confederate cavalry back toward Winchester. By midafternoon, Sheridan was ready to resume the attack. One of Crook's divisions slipped unseen around the Confederate flank. Crossing the swampy morass of the Red Bull Run, a division led by Rutherford B. Hayes, a future president—William McKinley was also present on the battlefield—pried the Confederates out of their positions and forced Early to begin a pullback toward the outskirts of Winchester. The fighting was particularly fierce. One Union officer recalled watching a soldier who "while loading and reciting some prayers in a jumbling sort of way . . . would shout, 'Now Jeff Davis, you son of a bitch, take that,' giving his head a twist at the same time and his eyes looking wildly in front he repeated this several times."[59] The combined effects of the pressure exerted by Union infantry attacks from the east and the cavalry threat in the north, as Union troopers swamped their opponents with numbers and firepower, eventually led to a Confederate collapse.

In the third Battle of Winchester, there was not much generalship, but combat leadership aplenty. Sheridan, himself, played a major role in the afternoon attack by leading his troops as they swamped Confederate defenses. The losses on both sides underlined the fierceness of the fighting. Confederate casualties numbered somewhere around 2,000 or approximately 15 percent. Including the captured raised Confederate loses to nearly 23 percent. Not surprisingly, since the Army of the Shenandoah was attacking, Sheridan's losses were heavier: 697 dead, 3,983 wounded, and 338 missing. Nevertheless, in percentage terms (13 percent) they were less. Most of Early's army escaped, but Sheridan had destroyed the myth of superior Confederate arms in the Valley. For that reason alone, coming as it did seventeen days after

Atlanta's fall, Winchester added to the tide now running in favor of the Union and certainly improved Lincoln's election prospects.

Sheridan underlined the extent to which the Army of the Shenandoah had smashed the myth of Confederate invincibility two days later. As his soldiers fled south up the Valley, Early determined to make a stand at Fisher's Hill. The hill was in fact a ridge that extended nearly four miles east to west, resting on Massanutten Mountain in the east and Little North Mountain in the west. As such, it blocked access to the upper Valley. The position should have been impregnable, had Early possessed sufficient troops. He did not. Moreover, Early in his defensive preparations emphasized defending the eastern side of his line, an impression the Army of the Shenandoah reinforced by its initial movements.

In fact, during the morning and early afternoon of 22 September, two of Crook's divisions climbed the backside of Little North Mountain to the west of the Confederate line and then deployed facing east. At approximately 1600 Crook struck, smashing the Confederate cavalry on the west side of Early's position. Only the rough terrain hindered the advance of the VIII Corps. Meanwhile, on the eastern side of Confederate lines, the rebels fared little better. For one of the few times in the war, Gordon's troops collapsed. This time there was a complete rout. The only thing minimizing Confederate losses was the speed of the collapse and the rapidity with which the defeated headed south. Sheridan's only disappointment was that his cavalry had not closed the trap. On the next day, Averell was one of several Union cavalry commanders who botched the pursuit of Early's beaten army. Sheridan finally took a long overdue decision and removed that incompetent officer from command: "I therefore thought that the interest of the service would be subserved by removing one whose growing indifference might render the best-laid plans inoperative."[60] Fisher's Hill was hardly a battle, so decisive was the Union success. Union casualties were 528; Confederate casualties 1,234.

Now the upper Valley was open to the depredations of Sheridan's troops, and they destroyed the Shenandoah's foodstuffs with delight. That was after all the second major objective Grant had set. On 7 October Sheridan reported to Grant that the "destruction embraces the Luray valley and Little Fort Valley as well as the main valley. . . . Tomorrow I will continue the destruction of wheat, forage, Etc. down to Fisher's Hill. When this is completed the valley from Winchester up to Staunton 92 miles, will have little in it for man or beast." He noted to Grant in October: "the people here are getting sick of war."[61] Along with that destruction went the destruction of much of the valley's infrastructure: Sheridan's troops wrecked woolen mills, railroads, sawmills, tanneries, and anything else that appeared to be of utility. It had indeed become a hard war.

But whatever the level of destruction Union troops inflicted, the fighting had not come to an end in the Shenandoah. After destroying most of the grain and rounding up the animals in the upper Valley, Sheridan moved back north in late October. The attitude not only of the troops but of their commander as well was that they had dispensed with the Confederates in the Valley. As they went into defensive positions along Cedar Creek, which ran into the north branch of the Shenandoah between Strasburg and Middletown, the furthest thing from their mind was that they might face a full-fledged Confederate attack.

On the other side of the hill, Early, always willing to take risks—after all he had been one of Jackson's chief lieutenants—began considering a counterstroke in the aftermath of the Fisher's Hill debacle. Given the balance of forces in the Shenandoah such an attack represented an enormous gamble. In this he received encouragement from Lee, who wrote Early that "I have weakened myself very much to strengthen you. It was done with the expectation of enabling you to gain such success that you could return the troops if not rejoin me yourself."[62] Moreover, Lee had the expectation that Early could crush Sheridan, if Union troops were to move out of the Valley to reinforce Grant.

But as the 9/11 report underlined, the failure of US intelligence about the possibility of an airborne attack on the Twin Towers and Pentagon was not the result of a lack of sufficient information, but rather a lack of imagination. Here in the Shenandoah, Union commanders could not imagine that a major Confederate attack could occur, especially considering the correlation of forces as well as the defeats the Confederates had suffered at Winchester and Fisher's Hill. The fact the Confederates had maintained contact as Sheridan's forces withdrew north should have served as a warning. Moreover, it was clear that the Confederacy was in desperate straits and that the looming election offered up an incentive for a last desperate stab at influencing Northern voters. But so sure that such an attack was not in the offing were senior Union commanders that Sheridan left on

15 October to travel to Washington to confer with Lincoln, Grant, and Stanton as to further operations in the Shenandoah. He left Wright, hardly an imaginative or inspiring general, in command.

Cedar Creek, a relatively fast flowing body of water, stood between Union forces and the Confederates. It flowed west to east and entered the north branch of the Shenandoah to the north of Massanutten Mountain. There was a narrow track on the east bank of the Shenandoah that ran between the river and the mountain, but Union commanders believed that no substantial forces could use that route, then cross the river, and deploy on the eastern flank of their position without being detected. Instead they expected that any Confederate raid—and they could only conceive of the Confederates launching a raid—would cross Cedar Creek west of their main positions, where they would quickly become entangled with Union cavalry.

Having examined the Union position, Gordon proposed to Early that his troops take the risky, difficult route along the northwestern edge of Massanutten Mountain, cross the Shenandoah at Bowman's Ford below where Cedar Creek entered the Shenandoah by wading through chest-deep waters, and then deploy in front of the Union positions. After some thought, Early agreed. An additional move would occur with Major General Joseph Kershaw's division, sent by Lee to reinforce Early, crossing the lower portion of Cedar Creek to link up with Gordon. It was a risky plan that depended on complete surprise.

In the first hours of darkness on 18 October, Gordon moved. Several pickets and junior officers of the XIX Corps observed portions of the Confederate advance. They sensed that something was afoot and warned their superiors, but their senior officers dismissed their worries as the idle imaginings of troops with too much time on their hands. Aiding the Confederate attack was the fact that a heavy fog enshrouded the area in the first hours after dawn. The result was that not only did Gordon and Kershaw gain complete surprise, but that the fog also shielded the movement forward of Confederate infantry up to the last moment. The general confusion that resulted made it impossible for Union commanders to grasp what was happening or develop a coherent response. The XIX Corps collapsed, the soldiers of which had less combat experience than the other troops in the Army of the Shenandoah. Crook's divisions fell apart as well. Wright's VI Corps was the farthest from the Confederate attack and made a fighting retreat north, while Union cavalry, with its lethal Spencers, covered the retreat.

In just under two hours Early's attack had wrecked five Union divisions, driven the remainder of the Union army off the field, and captured nearly 1,500 prisoners and eleven cannons. Nevertheless, troubling signs almost immediately appeared. Reflecting both simple hunger and chronic problems with discipline, a substantial number of Confederate troops stopped to plunder the food and clothing in the Union camp, while others halted from sheer exhaustion of a night-time march and the fact that they had been on minimal rations for weeks. Moreover, Early lacked sufficient troops to crush the Army of the Shenandoah. By midmorning the Confederate attack had come to a halt, literally running out of human capital; Early's soldiers had done as much as one could have expected from a body of men so poorly clothed and fed.

As beaten Union troops straggled north, they ran into Sheridan returning from Washington. The Irishman had no intention of seeing his victorious campaign wrecked by Early's surprise attack. Because the Army of the Shenandoah consisted of so many veterans, it was relatively easy to put the pieces back together again as the pressure from the Confederates lessened. Over the next five hours, the two armies glared at each other, the Confederates in no position to renew their attack, Sheridan on the other hand breathing new life into units humiliated by the morning assault. Early attempted a probe at 1300 with three of his divisions, but it was a miserable failure. The Confederates were psychologically incapable of renewing the battle. Early's best ploy at this point would have been to get off the battlefield as quickly as possible. Yet, a retreat would have been to admit strategic defeat, because the Union troops would have remained in control of the ground.

And so the Confederates watched as the Army of the Shenandoah gathered its strength like a wounded tiger, injured, but not incapacitated. By 1600 Sheridan was ready. He threw much of his strength against the western portion of the Confederate line, which the XIX Corps quickly overlapped. Sheridan may not have been a great tactician, but he was a fearsome battlefield leader. Having restored Union morale in a matter of hours, he threw himself into the battle. One of the cavalry officers described Sheridan's impact in the following terms: "In action, however, or when specially interested in any subject, his eyes fairly blazed and the whole man seemed to expand mentally and physically. His influence on his men was like an electric shock, and

he was the only commander I have ever met whose personal appearance in the field was an immediate and positive stimulus to battle—a
stimulus strong enough to turn beaten and disorganized masses into
a victorious army. . . . [His soldiers] simply believed he was going to
win, and every man apparently was determined to be on hand and see
him do it."[63]

Custer, leading his cavalry division from the front, administered
the decisive blow, as his cavalry outflanked Early's dispositions. What
followed was as substantial a rout of Early's troops as they had caused
among the Union troops in the morning. The defeat at Cedar Creek
broke Confederate military power in the Valley. Sheridan had completed his mission both in military and economic terms. Equally important, the Union victories at Winchester, Fisher's Hill, and Cedar
Creek underlined for the Northern electorate that the war had turned
irrevocably in favor of the Union.

Conclusion

The campaign in the East in 1864 represented as terrible a bloodletting
as the American people have ever experienced. The contest between
the Army of the Potomac and the Army of Northern Virginia was a
duel between the two greatest generals in American history. On the
Confederate side it was Lee's most impressive performance. In spite of
his inclinations, and partially due to Grant's ever-aggressive actions,
Lee fought the campaign largely on the defensive. In retrospect, had
he controlled his instincts to strike at his opponent, he might have
performed at an even higher level. The high casualties his army suffered reflected the fact that at times he could not resist the opportunity
to attack. In the tactical framework of the war in 1864 that invariably
carried with it high casualties. As Porter Alexander noted, some attacks "ought *never, never* to have been made."

Grant confronted substantially greater problems than did Lee, because as commander in chief of all Union armies he was responsible
for the conduct of the whole Union effort. On the political level, he
found himself saddled with a number of incompetent generals in subsidiary but important positions. The generals in those theaters, political as well as regular officers, achieved far less than Grant expected
and had every right to expect. Yet, he also recognized that the support

of political generals like Butler, Banks, and Sigel was essential to Lincoln's reelection. As one of this book's authors has written elsewhere, "Grant's excellent strategic plans could have—indeed *should* have—led to a *decisive* victory in the Eastern theater by the end of the summer. A series of entirely avoidable organizational failures in the Army of the Potomac, along with some plain bad luck, transformed the Overland campaign into an indecisive war of posts."[64]

On the military side, Grant had insufficient time to prepare and direct the various Union armies to work toward the center, since he received his appointment late in the game. Furthermore, Halleck had vetoed some of Grant's most innovative campaign plans, when the former was Grant's superior. With barely two months to develop and articulate Union strategy, it is astonishing what he accomplished. In the West, he and Sherman had laid the logistical and transportation framework for the great campaign against Atlanta and into the South's heartland. Moreover, in turning that campaign over to Sherman, a general in whom Grant had complete faith, the new commander in chief had one rock-solid subordinate in place in the war's most important theater.

The problem was the Eastern theater and in particular that strange military organization, the Army of the Potomac. Arriving in the east, Grant expected a modicum of competence from that army's senior leaders and fighting ability from the soldiers in that army. He got the latter, but not the former. Leadership at the senior levels of the army was appallingly bad. Moreover, chance bedeviled the Army of the Potomac throughout its march to Petersburg. The result was a casualty bill that threatened the political basis on which the North was fighting the war. Nevertheless, Grant understood that as an outsider to the army, he could not execute a wholesale purge of senior officers, who reflected a military culture of caution, lack of initiative, carelessness in planning, and unwillingness to cooperate with colleagues. That culture would change, but at a cost of vast numbers of casualties.

On his arrival in the Eastern theater, Grant lacked an understanding of the geographic connection of the Shenandoah Valley to the operations of the Army of Northern Virginia and the Army of the Potomac. That, of course, had been something the Confederates had understood even before Lee had assumed command of the Army of Northern Virginia. Thus, Jackson's brilliant campaign had upset McClellan's Peninsula Campaign before it had hardly begun by tying McDowell's corps to northern Virginia. In April 1864, Grant had regarded the Shenandoah Valley as a subsidiary theater in which Sigel could hold a leg while others skinned the Confederacy. Sigel's debacle, followed then by Hunter's, followed then by Early's raid on Washington, finally focused Grant's attention on the Valley. Once he focused his attention on a problem, Grant acted. The result was the concentration of four departments into a single department responsible to Grant and not run by out-of-touch Washington. In picking Sheridan, providing him, and then unleashing him, Grant ensured the Shenandoah problem would end. In the smoking ruins left by the progress of the Army of the Shenandoah, there would be no more raids into the North, while one of the major sources of food for the Army of Northern Virginia disappeared.

Finally, we might note that the campaign against the Army of Northern Virginia ended Lee's ability to dictate the pace of the war in the East. There were no more great, slashing attacks by Lee's lieutenants. Instead, the Confederates could only hold on in a desperate struggle for survival. Indeed, the siege of Richmond and Petersburg represented the end of the road, the defense of a symbol rather than the defense of a state, while elsewhere Sherman's armies were ripping the heart out of the Confederacy.

CHAPTER 11

Victory in the West, 1864

I am bound to say, while I deplore this necessity daily [of laying waste to the countryside of Georgia] and cannot bear to see the soldiers swarm . . . through fields and yards,—I do believe it *is* a necessity. Nothing *can* end this war but some demonstration of their helplessness, and the miserable ability of J. D. [Jefferson Davis] to protect them. . . . But war is war, and a horrible necessity at best; yet when forced on us as this war is, there is no help but to make it so terrible that when peace comes it will *last*.

—Henry Hitchcock, *Marching with Sherman*

One of the truisms of military affairs is that amateurs talk about operations, but professionals about logistics. Over winter 1863/64 Grant and Sherman underlined they were modern professional soldiers, because it was to that dismal subscience of war, namely, logistics, that they devoted themselves. They understood that if they were going to project Union military power into Georgia and on to Atlanta from their main bases at Nashville and Chattanooga, their armies had to have a reliable system of supply. Yet, the campaign against Chattanooga in summer and fall 1863 had rested on railroads verging on collapse, a transportation system, moreover, Confederate guerrillas and raiders had disrupted for significant periods. Thus, the first order of business was to insure the coming Union offensive would possess a logistical system that could support Union armies from Nashville to Chattanooga, and then to Atlanta.

Until mid-March, when he moved east to assume his duties as commander in chief of all Union armies, Grant focused on ensuring that the advance on Atlanta would possess the logistical infrastructure, that is, one dependent on railroads, required to support Union forces deep in the Confederacy. Work began on repairing and building that infrastructure almost as soon as the Confederates had fled Missionary Ridge. The distance over which the logistical system had to work was, according to Sherman, 185 miles from Louisville to Nashville, 151 miles on to Chattanooga, and 137 miles from Chattanooga to Atlanta, a total of 473 miles. The distance between the Franco-German frontier and Paris, over which the Prussian Army had such trouble in supplying its army in 1870–71, is 250 miles, approximately half of what Union logistics had to support during the siege of Atlanta. Moreover, the French road network was of a high class by the standards of the time, while the road network in northern Georgia was virtually nonexistent. Sherman's engineers also had to maintain the railroad from Chattanooga to Atlanta and then keep it open under incessant attacks.

Sherman's calculations were that the logistical support necessary to keep his armies in the field required sixteen trains per day pulling a total of 160 cars, which could haul 1,600 tons per day from Nashville to Chattanooga and then on to Atlanta. That effort was sufficient to support his army of 100,000 men and 35,000 animals from 1 May to 12 November 1864. To have had a similar amount of food, ammunition, and forage, according to his calculations, would have required 36,800 wagons, each pulled by six mules, to haul their loads at a rate of twenty miles per day, "a simple impossibility in roads such as then existed in that region of country. Therefore, I reiterate that the Atlanta campaign was an impossibility without these railroads; and only then, because we had the men and means to maintain and defend them, in addition to what were necessary to overcome the enemy."[1] This campaign was war in the industrial age.

There lay the crux of the matter, for it had largely been the result of Grant's planning and energy that created the means "to maintain and defend" this crucial logistical system. The first element in creating this system lay in the repair of the railroads between Nashville and Chattanooga, as well as creation of subsidiary lines. To further the refurbishment of the system, Grant fired the previous director of the line and initially replaced him with Major General Grenville Dodge. Within forty days Dodge's XVI Corps had repaired or relaid a hundred miles of track and repaired or rebuilt 182 bridges. In February 1864, Grant appointed Daniel McCallum, one of Herman Haupt's most competent assistants in running the eastern railroads, as general manager of all military railroads in the West, which consisted of the Southern railroads Union forces controlled.

McCallum created two departments, the first to control rail movements and perform day-to-day repairs. The second department had responsibility for major repair work on bridges and sections damaged or wrecked by Confederate raiders and to build new rail spurs where necessary. This division of responsibility continued through fall 1864. McCallum further divided the construction corps into six separate sections, each with the same organization but responsible for different portions of the line. He also distributed stockpiles of bridging materials, rails, and ties throughout the system, so that his construction divisions possessed the necessary material to carry out major repairs immediately.

Finally, McCallum contracted through Stanton for the purchase of new locomotives and rolling stock from Northern manufacturers. The first twelve new locomotives rolled into Nashville in April, twenty-four more in May, twenty-four in June, and a further twenty-six in July. By year's end Northern manufacturers had delivered 140 new locomotives to the Western theater, while they also built and delivered an average of 202 new freight cars a month. Nothing better underlines the gap between the resources available to Northern military commanders and those available to the Confederacy, which failed to produce a single locomotive during the entire war.

Unlike current logistical practices in a zone of military operations, in the Civil War civilians ran the locomotives, maintained the roadbeds, and repaired the damage caused by Confederate raiders and guerrillas. Their commitment was extraordinary. As McCallum reported, "it was by no means unusual for men to be out with their trains from five to ten days without sleep, except what could be snatched upon their engines and cars while the same were standing to be loaded or unloaded, with but scanty food, or perhaps no food at all, for days together, while continually occupied in a manner to keep every faculty strained to its utmost."[2] McCallum's men confronted not only the balky and often dangerous machinery of the time but also the dangers of guerilla attacks or damage to the rails, which often led to disastrous crashes.

There was one other element in the logistical system of critical importance. While his construction troops refurbished the roadbeds, rails, and bridges, Grant, and then Sherman, ordered construction of block houses to protect the most critical bridges. This involved the detailing of significant numbers of soldiers, but here again the North's manpower advantage told. There were sufficient troops available to protect the logistical infrastructure, while at the same time enabling Sherman to throw a massive military force into Georgia and supply it. That advance to Atlanta would then depend on McCallum's construction crews rebuilding the roadbed, laying new rails, and constructing new bridges, as Johnston's soldiers had destroyed everything of use, particularly railroad tracks and bridges, as they retreated south.

Napoleon's invasion of Russia had failed over distances that were logistically comparable to the task Sherman's armies faced, if one considers the origin of Union supplies. The French march to Moscow failed because animal muscle power could not sustain logistical support at such distances. Nothing better underlines the fact that the North's victory depended on the Industrial Revolution to overcome the continental distances of the South than the logistical support rendered by railroads in 1864. What had been logistically impossible before was now possible.

For those who dismiss the idea that the Civil War was a war of the industrial age, it is well to recall that in September 1914 the German advance in France came to a floundering halt as much for a failure of logistical support as for any other reason. As German troops fought a desperate Battle of the Marne for what the German general staff regarded as the decisive campaign of the war, the German army had barely repaired the railroads through to Brussels. While the Germans kept their troops supplied by living off the countryside of Belgium and northern France at the height of the harvest season, such was the state of their supply system in early September that some troop commanders took the dubious expedient of feeding their troops wine and champagne to keep them going. Admittedly, Grant and Sherman had been at war for three years in dealing with the problems of projecting military forces over great distances. Nevertheless, the care with which they prepared the logistical base for the 1864 campaign in the West stands in stark contrast with the lack of preparations made by the Germans in either 1870 or 1914.

The Opponents

On 18 March, Sherman assumed command of the Military Division of the Mississippi from Grant. By this point the gathering of supplies and troops at Nashville and Chattanooga for the campaign against

Atlanta was in full swing. Grant fully trusted Sherman, and despite the latter's plea that the new commander in chief of Union armies remain in the West, Grant determined that he needed to go east and supervise the Army of the Potomac. He had no qualms about leaving Sherman in charge of what turned out to be the war's decisive campaign—one that would insure Lincoln's reelection and break the Confederacy's will. Sherman, while still displaying the restlessness that had led to his near breakdown in 1861, had now brought a discipline and focus to his energy. Grant's trust, as well as Sherman's experience in the field, provided Sherman with the confidence in his abilities necessary to master the uncertainties, ambiguities, and doubts that confront all those in independent command.

Sherman also had an important advantage over Grant in the 1864 campaigns: he knew and trusted his subordinates, who were for the most part outstanding combat leaders in their own right. They were generals who had grown under Grant's mentorship, and they reflected an organizational culture that emphasized leadership, initiative, and drive. Some historians have ascribed the culture of the Western armies to the peculiarities of soldiers brought up in the hard life of turning a wilderness into civilization. While there may be some truth in that argument, the Confederate Army of Tennessee, an army consisting wholly of westerners, displayed few of the qualities of its Union opponents. Instead, like the Army of the Potomac, it stood the course in spite of an appalling series of defeats.

Sherman divided his forces into three separate "armies," which differed in size. Each possessed differing subcultures, reflecting their origins and the nature of their commanders, who had led them during the war. Each army was capable of acting independently, which provided Sherman greater flexibility than was the case with the Army of the Potomac's rigid structure, while their varying sizes allowed him the flexibility to tailor the army to the task at hand. In effect, Sherman led what we would today term an army *group*.

Major General George "Pap" Thomas, who had won fame for fending off the Confederates at Chickamauga, commanded the largest of Sherman's armies, the Army of the Cumberland. A native Virginian, Thomas had kept his oath to defend the Constitution. After his soldiers had seized Missionary Ridge in the Battle of Chattanooga, a chaplain, charged with laying out the Union cemetery, had asked whether he should have the Union dead buried by states. Thomas replied that they should bury them together, as the division of states had already caused too much trouble. As a commander, Thomas was steady, rather than brilliant, but when he acted, he acted with thoroughness. There was a native caution to his nature, but he held none of the mindless fears that had characterized McClellan. His troops loved him, perhaps because they sensed that he was cautious with their lives. Altogether his army numbered 60,773 (54,568 infantry, 2,337 artillery, and 3,828 cavalry) with 130 cannons. The army was divided into three corps: the IV under O. O. Howard; the XIV under John Palmer; and the XX (a combination of the XI and XII Corps which had come west in fall 1863) under "Fighting Joe" Hooker.

Major General James McPherson led Grant's and Sherman's old army, the Army of the Tennessee. McPherson was new to command and young for his position. He had graduated first in his class from West Point in 1853 along with Sheridan and Hood. Both Sherman and Grant regarded him almost as a son, but his rise to the top reflected considerable military abilities. Like many other successful Civil War generals, McPherson grew into higher position as the war progressed, but from the beginning he had displayed outstanding leadership qualities. Like Thomas, his troops held him in high regard. Attrition and the transfer of some of its divisions to other armies had decreased the Army of the Tennessee from the force Grant had led against Vicksburg. Nevertheless, it was a veteran force with high morale consisting of 24,465 soldiers (22,437 infantry, 1,404 artillery, and 624 cavalry) with ninety-six guns. These were divided into three corps: the XV under "Black Jack" Logan, an Illinois politician of considerable military competence; the XVI under Major General Grenville Dodge; and the XVII under Major General Francis P. Blair Jr. Logan was one of the most outstanding combat commanders of the war, so highly thought of by Grant that he almost became Thomas's replacement at the end of 1864.

The smallest of the armies was that of the Army of the Ohio under Major General John Schofield. Nevertheless, there were times when Sherman detached corps or divisions from other armies and assigned them to Schofield, who had graduated from West Point in 1853. The outbreak of the Civil War had found him on a leave of absence from the army and teaching physics at Washington University in St. Louis. He became Nathaniel Lyon's chief of staff in the desperate effort to keep Missouri in the Union and was later awarded the Medal of

Honor for his bravery at the Battle of Wilson's Creek in August 1861. After extensive service west of the Mississippi, Schofield received command of the Army of the Ohio, which to all intents and purposes was a fleeted-up corps, consisting of 13,559 soldiers (11,183 infantry, 679 artillery, and 1,697 cavalry) with twenty-eight guns. The army possessed one corps under Schofield's command, but also George Stoneman's (another reject from the Army of the Potomac) cavalry division.

Opposed to Sherman was the Army of Tennessee, which Johnston had assumed command of after Bragg's disastrous defeat at Chattanooga. Davis, given the deep antipathy between himself and the general, had not wanted to appoint Johnston, but there was no other choice, since he disliked Beauregard even more. Johnston found the Army of Tennessee in disarray, because Bragg was not only a bad tactician, but a weak administrator. Thus, throughout the winter Johnston confronted much the same task that Hooker in early 1863 had confronted in repairing the administrative and logistical damage his predecessor had caused. To the extent possible, given the shambles which passed for the Confederacy's logistics, Johnston attempted to feed, clothe, and equip the Army of Tennessee adequately. With a lighter hand than Bragg, Johnston restored discipline. He also had charismatic rapport with the soldiers that went beyond simply not being Bragg. By spring he had restored the army's morale.

Johnston's approach to the war was quite different from that of other senior Confederate commanders, for he had the least desire to seek battle for its own sake. There are two possible explanations. The first appears in an entry in 1861 in Mary Chesnut's deliciously sharp diary. She records a story told by one of her male friends about Johnston that underlines Confederate suspicions about the general's willingness to get into a scrap: "Wade Hampton brought him [Johnston] here to hunt. . . . We all liked him—but as to hunting, there he made a dead failure. He was a capital shot, better than Wade or I and we are not so bad—that you'll allow. But then with . . . Johnston the bird flew too high or too low—the dogs were too far or too near—things never did suit exactly. He was too fussy, too hard to please, too cautious, too much afraid to miss and risk his fine reputation as a fine shot. . . . Unless his ways have changed, he will never fight a battle—you'll see. Oh, yes—he is as brave as Caesar. An accomplished soldier? Yes, who denies it? You'll see. . . . [Nevertheless, in war] he is too particular—things are never all straight. You must go at it rash—at a venture to win."[3]

That mentality was precisely the great flaw in the Confederate approach to the war: the desire to attack, attack, and attack with resulting casualty bills that eventually broke the will of the Confederate people. It may be that Johnston was just too fussy about finding the perfect circumstances. Or like Porter Alexander and many modern historians, he believed the Confederacy could not afford the heavy casualties involved in an aggressive approach and that a Fabian strategy aiming at exhausting the North's will was the only route to success—despite the aggressive inclinations of Confederate public opinion. Either explanation helps explain Johnston's generalship, which came close in 1864 to preventing Sherman from capturing Atlanta.

For Johnston the improvement of the army's morale and discipline proved to be the least of his problems. The repair of the command relations among the fractious corps and division commanders proved an insurmountable task. The dysfunctional command culture had been a direct result of Bragg's leadership; about the only thing his subordinates could agree on had been that Bragg must go, but the various plots and efforts to remove Bragg had engendered a climate of suspicion and a lack of loyalty among the senior officers. Not surprisingly, the command climate ended up in poisoning their relations with their new commander as well as among them. Throughout spring 1864, Johnston's corps commanders consistently attempted to undercut their commander's position by reporting maliciously and dishonestly on the army's combat capabilities to politicians in Richmond, including Davis. Admittedly, Johnston did not help matters by the fact that he failed to share his plans and conceptions with his senior generals. Part of the reason may well have been that he caught a sense of the poisonous atmosphere among his senior subordinates. As he noted when he assumed command: "If I were president, I'd distribute the generals of this army over the Confederacy."[4]

Exacerbating the poisonous command climate was the fact that the arguments and disagreements between Bragg and his generals had spilled over into the political arena. During Bragg's tenure as commander of the Army of Tennessee, disgruntled generals had taken to writing their political friends in Richmond, including the president. None of that changed with his relief. Johnston, himself, had played the political game by using surrogates, such as Senator Louis Wigfall, to argue his case, particularly in regard to the Vicksburg campaign. Given Davis's personality and his suspicion of others, except the few he regarded as friends, the result was a deeply fractured relationship among Confederate generals in the West. In such a climate, it was impossible to develop an effective strategy for the 1864 campaign. Adding to the fractiousness of relations among the senior officers was the fact that in January 1864, Patrick Cleburne, former British Army sergeant and outstanding division commander, had proposed enlisting slaves in Confederate armies in return for their freedom. That proposal caused a furor about an abolitionist conspiracy that spread from the senior ranks of the Army of Tennessee to Richmond before Sherman's offensive provided other matters on which the generals could focus.

The appointment of Hood to a corps command in the army only made matters worse. Hood had spent fall and winter 1863/64 in Richmond recovering from the amputation of his leg from a wound suffered at Chickamauga, not to mention an arm so badly injured at Gettysburg as to be largely useless. In the Confederate capital he found himself lionized. Hood enthusiastically courted the president and his wife, Varina, in whose house he became a fixture. Undoubtedly, he was a brave and outstanding division commander, but he had not a clue about strategy, logistics, or operations. Moreover, his physical condition was serious; he could not mount a horse without help, and once on horseback had to be tied to the saddle. Finally, and perhaps most importantly, he was deeply ambitious, ambition fueled by his physical condition. Upon arrival in Dalton, he began writing Davis a stream of letters, all of which confirmed the president's unrealistic hopes that the Army of Tennessee was in the position to launch a major offensive to regain Tennessee. Johnston never caught on to the duplicitous role that Hood was playing. Instead, he regarded him as his most loyal corps commander.

Even before the winter ended, Johnston found himself under pressure from Davis to attack Union forces in Chattanooga and continue on to regain central Tennessee. Hardee had assumed acting command of the army after Bragg's resignation, and astonishingly he had sent Richmond a series of reports indicating the army had rapidly recovered from its defeat. As he turned the army over to Johnston "with great pleasure," he reported it in "fine condition."[5] It was not; it was a broken and fragile instrument. From Hardee's reports, Davis gained an impression that remained with him into the spring. As a result, he bombarded Johnston with proposals of the most unrealistic kind, including one for the army to invade southern Tennessee, in spite of its deplorable state and lack of a supply system to support such a move in the dead of winter. Moreover, such an offensive would have advanced through one of the poorest areas in the South, one consisting of rugged mountains with a few hardscrabble farms the opposing armies had already picked clean. That landscape was one that could hardly supply a brigade much less an army, unless, of course, there was a logistical system capable of supplying the army's needs.

Davis's missives, urging an offensive into Tennessee, received support not only from Bragg but from Lee as well. Bragg, continuing his contributions to the Confederacy's defeat, was now serving as Davis's chief military advisor and delighted in the opportunity to inform the president that the Army of Tennessee was in excellent shape for a drive to recapture Tennessee. Bragg, of course, should have known the state in which he had left his army, but military reality had never interfered with his capacity for intrigue and back stabbing or for that matter in currying favor with the president. Bragg did this despite the fact he had rejected many of those proposals for offensive operations in southeastern and eastern Tennessee when he had commanded the Army of Tennessee, and it had been summertime.

Not until late March did a series of reports, authored by Davis's own representatives, reach Richmond on the real state of the army, particularly in regard to its shortages in artillery, horses, and mules. But none of these made an impression on Davis, who had made up his mind that Johnston possessed the means to attack Grant and Sherman and was obdurately refusing the sensible advice from Richmond. Contributing to Davis's refusal to recognize reality were the reports Hood was enthusiastically writing about the army's state and Johnston's refusal to take the offensive, which Hood deeply regretted, "as my heart was fixed upon our going to the front and regaining Tennessee and Kentucky."[6] The result of Davis's misapprehensions was simple. Because it was politically impossible for him to fire Johnston, he took the disastrous course of refusing reinforcements.

Lee exacerbated Davis's inclinations by arguing that the buildup of Union forces along the Rappahannock River was the result of the transfer of forces from Tennessee. He urged an aggressive move north by the Army of Tennessee to take the pressure off the Army of Northern Virginia. In the face of Lee's arguments, Johnston reported to Richmond the hard reality that Sherman's forces had not diminished in size, but instead were steadily growing. What Lee and Davis failed to recognize was that while there was a major Union buildup occurring in northern Virginia, a similar buildup was occurring in Tennessee as well, as the North, now mobilized, could concentrate overwhelming force not only on two major drives but also on subsidiary offensives. By April the evidence of the Northern buildup in the West was there for all to see. In addition, Lee obviously had no comprehension of the logistical difficulties confronting the Confederates in the Western theater. Perhaps considering the Confederacy's shortages in men and resources in 1864, it is understandable its leaders failed to grasp the extent of the military forces the North was gathering.

Quite simply, Johnston did the only thing he could, which was to remain on the defensive and await Sherman's offensive. He had two infantry and one cavalry corps under his immediate command at Dalton: Lieutenant General William Hardee's corps with divisions under the command of Major Generals Benjamin Cheatham, Patrick Cleburne, William Walker, and William Bate; and Hood's corps with divisions under Major Generals Thomas Hindman, Carter Stevenson, and Alexander Stevenson. Polk's corps was in Alabama to protect Mobile against a potential Union attack on that port, and there it would have remained had not Banks completely floundered in the Red River's mud. Polk's corps would return to Johnston's command at a key point in the campaign. There was one major flaw in Confederate dispositions. Davis and Bragg posted Forrest out in western Mississippi to execute a raiding strategy to carry the war into western Tennessee and along the Mississippi. It was one more indication of Davis's strategy of attempting to strike everywhere rather than focusing on the theater that mattered. As for Bragg, he undoubtedly was paying Forrest back for the furious tirade Forrest had launched at him in his departure from the Army of Tennessee in late 1863.

Forrest's assignment to Mississippi left Johnston with Wheeler to command his cavalry; and while that officer was an outstanding combat commander, he possessed none of Stuart's or Forrest's ability to ferret out the enemy's moves and strike where it mattered. As one commentator noted after the war, "he'll fight; game as a pebble is Wheeler. But there's one trouble with Wheeler's valor. It overruns itself. He'll fight flies as ferociously as he has Spaniards."[7] With only 41,300 infantry available for defense of north Georgia, Johnston stood in danger of being overwhelmed by Sherman's armies, numbering over 100,000 tough, experienced soldiers.

In terms of campaign planning, neither Sherman nor Johnston possessed the immense staffs characterizing military organizations in the twentieth century. The search for Sherman's or Johnston's detailed plans represents an anachronistic search for what never existed. Like Moltke the Elder after the Franco-Prussian War, both generals understood instinctively that plans never survive first contact with the enemy, because the enemy gets a vote. The enemy will always do the unexpected, while a cloud of uncertainty and ambiguity enshrouds the conduct of operations. Both generals undoubtedly held conceptions of how they hoped their military efforts would unfold. Given the expanse of the theater, Sherman aimed to use his superior numbers to outflank the Confederates from their strong defensive positions and hopefully catch them in unfavorable tactical deployments where he could destroy them. For his part, Johnston aimed at conducting a cautious campaign that recognized the disparity in numbers; he too intended to look for favorable moments when he might catch Sherman's forces divided and vulnerable to a riposte.

Making the task of offensive operations more difficult was the fact that both armies, like those in the East, understood the importance of entrenching themselves as quickly as possible, when they came in contact with the enemy. In several cases during the campaign, units even entrenched when they were actually under attack. For Sherman, this meant a war not only of operational movement, but also of tactical defense. Thus, in a tactical sense the war in the West was one dominated by the defense, although on the strategic level it was a war of movement, where Sherman's numbers provided him a distinct advantage.

The Atlanta Campaign

Concurrent with the Army of the Potomac's move into the Wilderness, Sherman arrived at Ringgold, Georgia, on 5 May, and his troops immediately began their drive south. One of the officers, formerly of the XII Corps, which had now been amalgamated with the XI to form the XX Corps, described Sherman in the following terms: "Sherman could be easily approached by any of his soldiers, but no one could venture to be familiar. His uniform coat, usually wide open at the throat, displayed a not very military black cravat and linen collar, and he generally wore low shoes and one spur. On the march he road

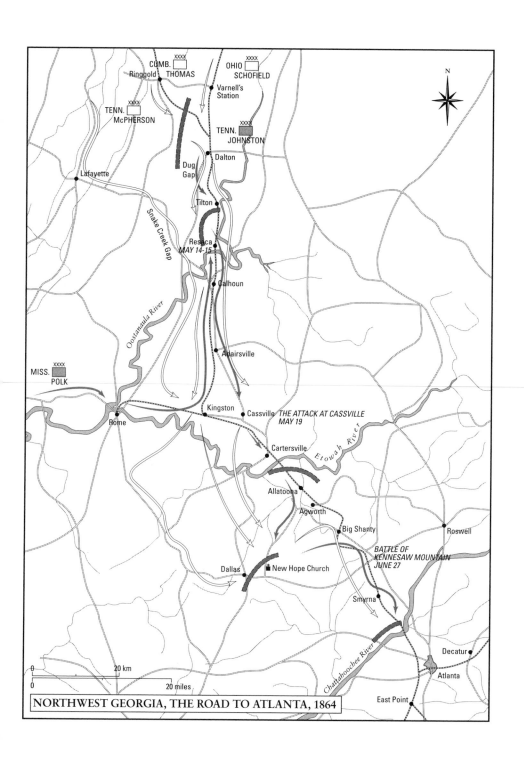

N

CUMB. [xxxx] THOMAS
OHIO [xxxx] SCHOFIELD
Ringgold
Varnell's Station
TENN. [xxxx] McPHERSON
TENN. [xxxx] JOHNSTON
Lafayette
Dalton
Dug Gap
Snake Creek Gap
Tilton
Resaca
MAY 14-15
Oostanaula River
Calhoun
Adairsville
MISS. [xxxx] POLK
Kingston
Cassville
THE ATTACK AT CASSVILLE MAY 19
Rome
Etowah River
Cartersville
Allatoona
Agworth
Big Shanty
Roswell
Dallas
New Hope Church
BATTLE OF KENNESAW MOUNTAIN JUNE 27
Smyrna
Chattahoochee River
Decatur
Atlanta
East Point

0   20 km
0   20 miles

NORTHWEST GEORGIA, THE ROAD TO ATLANTA, 1864

with each column in turn, and often with no larger escort than a single staff-officer and an orderly. In passing us on the march he acknowledged our salutations as if he knew us all, but hadn't time to stop."[8]

The difference between the theater of operations from that of the East was that Sherman had greater room for maneuver. At the campaign's start, Johnston's left flank rested along Rocky Face Ridge, which ran just to the west of Dalton from north to south. There were several gaps through the ridge, but Johnston had them covered. However, he believed Sherman would not attempt to outflank him to the west, but would drive east of Rocky Face Ridge, where the Confederates were best placed to meet his forces. As a growing number of reports indicated Sherman's armies were on the move, Johnston requested aid from Polk, whose corps had remained in southern Alabama to defend Mobile. Richmond agreed to the movement of a single division, but instead Polk moved his entire force of 10,000 infantry and 4,000 cavalry to aid Johnston—a move that proved crucial to Johnston's ability to fend Sherman off, but one that outraged Bragg. Thus, Polk provided Johnston with a third corps, which would not have been available, had Halleck seen the importance of Mobile and had Banks been where Grant had intended him to be. As they had done in April 1862, the Confederates concentrated in the West by taking risks in other areas.

But Sherman had no intention of attacking into the teeth of Confederate defenses. While Hooker probed various gaps in the Rocky Face Ridge and Thomas threatened Johnston's Dalton position from the north, McPherson with the Army of the Tennessee executed a wide swing to the west and an advance that carried his troops to Snake Creek Gap. Johnston picked up little of what Sherman was doing, largely as a result of the fact that Wheeler's cavalry failed to win the fight for information. Confederate cavalry commanders in the West excelled in fighting, like Stuart, but unlike Stuart, they were terrible at gathering intelligence. What became clear at once was the fact that Union soldiers were probing Johnston's left flank west of Rocky Face Ridge for weaknesses in his defenses guarding the gaps through the ridge. On 8 May Hooker's XX Corps hit Dug Gap with a major blow, which the Confederates were barely able to counter by the arrival of two brigades from Cleburne's division.

But on the 8th a more dangerous situation appeared. McPherson and the Army of the Tennessee were moving steadily toward Snake

Creek Gap five miles to the south. Wheeler failed to pick up this move because he had disobeyed his orders. Instead of covering the area west of Rocky Face Ridge and the approaches to the gaps, Wheeler wasted his time in skirmishing with Union cavalry. Not until early on 9 May did the Confederates discover that McPherson's Army of the Tennessee with over 20,000 men was approaching Resaca, the capture of which would have cut Johnston's lines of communications with Atlanta and placed McPherson in his rear. While the defenses of Resaca appeared formidable, there were only 4,000 soldiers manning them. Finally awakening to the danger, Johnston ordered a portion of Hood's corps south, but it would have arrived too late, had McPherson attacked. He did not, because the entrenchments appeared too formidable. The Army of the Tennessee then pulled back to Snake Creek Gap. Sherman's laconic comment in his memoirs on the episode was that "such an opportunity does not occur twice in a life."[9]

Sherman then pulled the full weight of his force down the valley to the west of Rocky Face Ridge in a move to assault Resaca with overwhelming force. Yet, by the time Thomas's divisions had linked up with McPherson west of Resaca, it was too late. By 13 May Johnston had awoken to the danger and pulled out of Dalton. Thus, the Army of Tennessee, including most of Polk's troops, concentrated on Resaca. Combined with the positions surrounding the town, they made Resaca too formidable to risk assault. Sherman's armies then continued their outflanking move to the west and south. Union engineers threw pontoon bridges across the Oostanaula River, and advance units placed Sherman in position to attack Johnston's rail communications. That ended Confederate hopes of attacking Sherman's eastern flank with Hood's corps, although one of Hood's divisions failed to receive the word to pull back, attacked entrenched Union troops, and suffered heavy casualties. Johnston ordered his army to abandon Resaca and retreat. Round one had gone to Sherman. Moreover, he had served in northern Georgia as a lieutenant in the 1840s and knew the countryside well.

There was no terrain south of the Oostanaula on which Johnston could develop defensive positions to stop Sherman until the Army of Tennessee reached Kingston. As the three arms of Sherman's army group advanced southward, Schofield, reinforced by Hooker, moved toward Kingston on both sides of the Western & Atlantic Railroad. Sherman detached two cavalry and an infantry division to wreck the

Confederate industrial center at Rome. Rome fell on 18 May, as the rest of the Union armies drew closer to Kingston. As the march continued, Sherman's construction crews repaired the captured railroad almost as fast as the troops advanced. When Union troops found the bridge across the Oostanaula destroyed, Sherman ordered his chief construction engineer, General William Wright, to rebuild it in two days. It took Wright and his construction crew of 2,000 men three days. As Wright described it: "the work of reconstruction commenced while the old bridge was still burning, and was somewhat delayed because the iron rods were so hot that the men could not handle them to remove the wreck."[10]

By the time the Western armies arrived in front of Kingston, halfway between Ringgold and Atlanta, they had suffered only 4,000 casualties, only slightly more than the Confederates. For his part, Johnston had prepared an ambush by deploying Polk's and Hood's corps east of the Kingston-Cassville line, while Hardee pulled back to the line between those two towns. The aim was to smash Schofield's reinforced Army of the Ohio before Thomas could arrive. Johnston was so enamored of the opportunity that he issued an order of the day to the troops, who responded with considerable enthusiasm for the opportunity to attack. However, Hood, supposedly the spearhead, failed to attack because a report indicated Union troops were outflanking his corps to the east. In fact, a small Union force had taken a wrong turn and simply wandered into Hood's rear. Alarmed by a threat to his rear, but failing to order a more thorough reconnaissance, Hood called off the attack and retreated. Johnston confirmed Hood's decision without checking on the situation despite Hood's inexperience.

The Confederates fell back on the ridge line that ran from east to west behind Cassville. Johnston believed it to be a strong position, but neither Hood nor Polk liked it. In a conference over the evening and night of 19/20 May, the two corps commanders talked Johnston out of defending the position, Hood even claiming the Confederates could not hold the position for two hours. The Confederates retreated across the Etowah River into a strong position at Allatoona. But Sherman had no intention of dancing to Johnston's tune. Instead, he ordered each of his three armies to draw rations for twenty days and set them in motion to cross the Etowah far downstream, Schofield crossing ten miles west of Allatoona, while Thomas and McPherson crossed even farther west. Johnston had no choice but to authorize a retreat from the Allatoona position along the railroad to the southeast, the Army of Tennessee taking up positions near New Hope Church. There the lead division of Hooker's corps, commanded by Brigadier General John Geary, former governor of the Kansas territory under Buchanan, ran into Hood's soldiers near New Hope Church. Hooker's soldiers received a nasty rebuff that cost them 1,665 casualties.

Two days later, on 27 May, Sherman launched another probing attack on Johnston's line, this one by Howard, but one no more successful. A Confederate probing attack on McPherson's Army of the Tennessee at the western portion of Sherman's line also suffered a bloody repulse. At an afternoon conference on 28 May, Hood proposed that his corps pull out of the line and launch a flank attack on the eastern side of Union lines. Johnston approved, but when Hood deployed to attack, he discovered Union commanders had stationed a division guarding their flank in another heavily fortified position. There was no opportunity to launch a Chancellorsville-style attack. Again Hood used his latitude and called off the attack. Nevertheless, in spite of his own unwillingness to attack on several occasions, Hood continued to write Davis that Johnston was failing to use the Army of Tennessee offensively.

Threatened by Sherman's outflanking movements, Johnston ordered another retreat. Despite almost continuous rain, Sherman's troops had reached Big Shanty, halfway between Allatoona and Marietta, by 6 June. Within five days Wright had rebuilt the railroad to Big Shanty, and the flow of supplies continued. In addition, 10,000 of Blair's XVII Corps soldiers returned to McPherson's Army of the Tennessee, the men having completed their reenlistment furloughs. They more than made up for Sherman's losses thus far in the campaign. Nevertheless, Sherman was not happy with the performance of his subordinates. His major criticism was of Thomas. He wrote Grant that "my chief source of trouble is with the Army of the Cumberland, which is dreadfully slow. A fresh furrow in a plowed field will stop the whole column, and all begin to intrench [*sic*]. I have again and again tried to impress on Thomas that we must assail and not defend . . . and yet it seems the whole Army of the Cumberland is so habituated to be on the defensive that, from its commander down to the lowest private, I cannot get it out of their heads."[11] Sherman's impatience undoubtedly helps explain why he was about to make the biggest mistake of the campaign.

Meanwhile, Johnston had had his engineers lay out new and impressive defensive positions. These rested on Kennesaw Mountain with Brush Mountain covered by cavalry to the northeast and Confederate lines swinging to the southwest. Out in front beyond the main positions, the Confederates held a small hillock named Pine Top that provided an excellent view of Sherman's three armies to the northwest. Urged by Hardee to pull the brigade back because Pine Top was too vulnerable to a Union assault, Johnston decided to reconnoiter the position. He, Hardee, and Polk rode to the top, where they dismounted despite warnings of Yankee shelling. At that same moment, Sherman, riding Union lines, saw the group on Pine Top, and, while not recognizing them, but recognizing the uniforms of high-ranking officers, suggested to Howard that his artillery throw a few shells at the Confederate generals. Howard complied, and an Ohio artillery battery hit Polk straight on, splitting the Episcopal bishop nearly in half and thereby removing one of the less effective corps commanders from the Army of Tennessee's order of battle.

Pulling back from Pine Top, and thus shortening his lines, Polk's corps, now under its senior division commander, Loring, held the right along Kennesaw Mountain, Hardee the center, and Hood the left. Confederate positions also covered Marietta, with its factories, one of the several important industrial centers in northern Georgia. For reasons that remain unclear, Sherman believed the Army of Tennessee's center was weak, and on 27 June he launched an all-out assault on Confederate positions, which were not only well entrenched but also strongly held. The results were a disaster. Sherman considered renewing the assault after the first failure, but Thomas persuaded him that further attacks made no sense. Union casualties were over 3,000 compared to barely 1,000 on the Confederate side. However, the day was not an entire failure, because Schofield's Army of the Ohio, only making a demonstration to hold the Confederates west of the battlefield, managed to cross Olley's Creek within five miles of the Chattahoochee River, the last major river between Sherman and Atlanta. It was the second success Schofield had gained against Hood in a week; earlier in the week the latter had launched an ill-considered attack without reconnaissance against Schofield's well-entrenched troops and suffered 1, 000 casualties.

Sherman would not make the Kennesaw Mountain mistake again. Instead, he feinted a move to his left (the east) and moved west. He again loaded up his supply wagons to cut his armies loose. Thomas opposed the move, but after considering the alternatives noted to his commander that, "I think [such a move] decidedly better than butting against breastworks twelve feet thick and strongly abatised."[12] Leaving a strong force of cavalry with their Spencers to cover the railroad, Sherman moved west to outflank the outnumbered Confederates. Once Union troops were across the river, Johnston hurriedly pulled back, and Marietta fell into Union hands. Not surprisingly, Wright's construction crews soon had the railroad rebuilt all the way to Marietta, and supplies flowed unabated to Sherman's troops.

But even more important was the fact that Johnston had no choice, but to fall back on Atlanta and its defenses, such as they were. Johnston's failure to launch a major assault on Sherman's forces during the course of the two-month campaign had come home to roost. From our perspective, the only major error had come in the failure to attack Schofield in the flank at Cassville. It had been Hood who had blown the chance, but Johnston too was at fault for not having checked up on his subordinate. Yet, given the numbers and the competence of Union commanders, it was inevitable that Sherman and his armies would reach the environs of Atlanta. The mark of Johnston's generalship lay in the fact that he fended off Sherman's flanking moves and kept his army intact. In effect, he was prolonging the war, and after the failure of Lee's invasion of Pennsylvania in 1863, a Fabian strategy presented the only possibility for the Confederates to gain their independence. The looming fall presidential election in the North was the last remaining possibility for the Confederacy to survive, and the longer Johnston could draw out the campaign in Georgia, the more doubtful Lincoln's prospects would become.

But that was not good enough for Davis. Despite the fact that Lee had failed to gain a decisive victory over Grant's and Meade's advance, Davis clearly expected something along those lines from Confederate armies in Georgia. Further exacerbating the Confederate president's anger was the flow of reports from those, like Hood, who were dissatisfied with Johnston's failure to show the requisite aggressive style of leadership they believed the Confederacy's situation demanded. Adding to Johnston's problems was the fact that the Confederacy's politicians and newspapers were acting in an even more irresponsible fashion than their Northern cousins. The cry throughout the Confederacy was for action to defeat the Northern vandals.

The final nail in Johnston's coffin came with Braxton Bragg's visit to the Army of Tennessee. On 9 July Davis dispatched his chief military adviser to Atlanta to scope out the lay of the strategic land. Bragg was the last person Davis should have chosen. The general had regarded his relief after the Chattanooga defeat as the result of a cabal of disgruntled generals who had consistently failed him and who had combined with politicians to cause his downfall. Astonishingly, Bragg believed he had been popular with the troops. He also felt the defeat at Chattanooga was not his fault, but rather the fault of the troops who had refused to do their duty. Now as Davis's military adviser, Bragg arrived at Johnston's headquarters to examine the situation in front of Atlanta. Supposedly having done that, which largely involved listening to Hood's poison, Bragg telegraphed to Davis that "as far as I can learn we do not propose any offensive operations," despite being briefed on Johnston's plan to attack Union forces as they crossed Peachtree Creek.[13]

Hood delightedly bolstered Bragg's case against Johnston by accusing his commander of failing "to give battle to the enemy many miles north of our present position."[14] Not surprisingly Hood failed to mention those cases where he himself had not attacked. Finally, Bragg added that Sherman had only 65,000 infantry and 10,000 cavalry instead of the 100,000 Johnston had more accurately estimated his opponent to possess. Bragg's advice persuaded Davis to remove Johnston. The choice of his replacement quickly narrowed to a few senior officers. It was obviously not going to be Beauregard, given Davis's dislike for the creole; Davis probably would have preferred Bragg, but recognized that such a choice would have been disastrous politically; while Hardee had declined the position after Chattanooga. Thus, by default it came to Hood, a general who was the aggressive commander the president and the white South so fervently wanted. Lee, who, whatever his defects as a strategist, was an outstanding judge of military talent, commented on Davis's decision to appoint Hood to command the Army of Tennessee: "It is a bad time to release [relieve] the commander of an army situated as that of Tenne. We may lose Atlanta and the army too. Hood is a bold fighter. I am doubtful as to other qualities necessary."[15]

Lee was right. But Davis had made up his mind. At 2200 on the night of 17 July, Johnston received the telegram announcing the termination of his command and replacement by Hood. It could not have been more curt: "I am directed by the Secretary of War to inform you that as you have failed to arrest the advance of the enemy to the vicinity of Atlanta, far in the interior of Georgia, and express no confidence that you can defeat or repel him, you are hereby relieved from the command of the Army of Tennessee."[16] One corporal in the Army of Tennessee caught the soldiers' attitude toward the relief: "Old Joe Johnston had taken command of the Army of Tennessee when it was crushed and broken, at a time when no other man on earth could have united it. He found it in rags and tatters, hungry and heart-broken, the morale of the men gone, their manhood vanished to the winds, their pride a thing of the past. Through his instrumentality and skillful manipulation, all these had been restored."[17]

Not surprisingly, Sherman and his senior officers were delighted. McPherson and Schofield had been Hood's classmate at West Point. McPherson's tutoring of Hood had kept the future Confederate general from flunking out of the academy. George "Pap" Thomas had served in Texas with Hood in the 1850s. All three informed their commander that Hood was reckless and aggressive and that they would soon have a fight on their hands. Sherman later recalled: "At this critical moment the Confederate government rendered us most valuable service. . . . The character of a leader is a large factor in the game of war, and I confess I was pleased at this change."[18]

The Siege of Atlanta

With Hood's appointment, the period of maneuvering ended and a time of fierce fighting ensued. Hood described himself as cut from the Jackson-Lee mold, but where the former two had a deep perception of the enemy's strengths and weaknesses, Hood had none. He was still living in 1862 when at Antietam armies had stood toe to toe, fought in the open without entrenchments in receiving enemy attacks, and attempted to overwhelm their opponents with their fury, as if firepower did not matter. Hood's personality hardly suited him for high command. He had been dishonest in his relationship with Johnston, had lied to Richmond about the condition of the army throughout the spring, and was to blame others for his mistakes throughout his career in the West. None of those qualities endeared him to subordinates, especially since most were older than he. Moreover, as with too many generals in World War I, Hood calculated military effectiveness in terms of the casualties suffered by the units under his command.

As the Confederate high command changed, Sherman continued his wheel to the left toward the east with the aim of cutting the railroad connecting Atlanta to the eastern Confederate states. McPherson led the advance with Schofield and Thomas following. Hood's first attack came boiling out of Atlanta with the aim of hitting the Army of the Cumberland before Thomas could get his whole force across Peachtree Creek. Alexander P. Stewart's (Polk's replacement) corps and Hardee's corps achieved a degree of surprise, but the Union soldiers had already begun entrenching, when the Confederates attacked. With bare equality in numbers to Thomas, the Confederates had little chance of achieving anything, but they certainly proved they could die in large numbers. Hood blamed Hardee for the defeat. In total, Confederate casualties came close to 5,000, while the Army of the Cumberland barely lost 1,000 killed or wounded.

On 22 July Hood launched his second attack. He chose Hardee to lead the sortie. This time Hood came up with a more imaginative plan than a straightforward lunge. He seems to have hoped to replicate Lee and Jackson's attack at Chancellorsville. During the day Hood pulled Stewart's and Hardee's troops back from Peachtree Creek to the defenses the Confederates were developing on Atlanta's outskirts. After completion of that move Hardee's corps was to move out of the line, march through Atlanta to the city's south, and then swing east and north to catch the Army of the Tennessee in the flank and roll it up. Accompanying Hardee's flanking march was Wheeler's cavalry, which was to attack McPherson's supply train in the rear at Decatur. At the same time Hardee was striking the Army of the Tennessee in the flank, the Confederates manning the fortifications would attack Thomas and Schofield to prevent them from reinforcing McPherson. The attack was supposed to start early in the morning, but a series of delays slowed Hardee's march and deployment. Thus, his corps was not ready to launch its attack until midday. Moreover, his troops had had no rest, were already exhausted by the heat, and had had little to eat during their march to their jump off positions.

When the attack finally began, Hardee had placed his corps to take the Army of the Tennessee in the flank. But again chance intervened. McPherson had detached Dodge's XVI Corps on Sherman's orders to rip up the railroad from Decatur to Atlanta, or at least as close to the city as they could. Dodge's two divisions were on their way back and, thus, were in position to cover McPherson's flank when the Confederates attacked. Moreover, they had sufficient time to form into line of battle. As a result, when the Confederate columns broke into the open after floundering through the woods, they had little chance of success, as an aide to McPherson recalled: "It seemed impossible, however, for the enemy to face the sweeping deadly fire from Fuller's and Sweeny's divisions, and the guns of the Fourteenth Ohio and Welker's batteries of the Sixteenth Corps fairly mowed great swaths in the advancing [rebel] columns."[19] There was, however, a dangerous gap between the XVI Corps and the remainder of the Army of the Tennessee. It was into this gap that McPherson rode from a conference with Sherman only to run into Confederates and to be shot dead, when he refused to surrender. With McPherson down, Major General "Black Jack" Logan assumed command of the Army of the Tennessee. It was to be his finest hour, for while the XVI Corps easily handled the attack on the army's flank, the XVII Corps on the line facing Atlanta was soon in serious trouble from Pat Cleburne's division, which caught Blair's corps flush in the flank and caused a desperate retreat by some.

But these were stout veterans, and they put up serious resistance. In one case an officer observed Union infantry make themselves a palisade in the midst of a fierce firefight: "Some distance to the rear of us was a rail fence. Consternation, I have been told, fell upon General Sherman, as with his glass he saw half of Leggett's division drop their guns and run to the rear. But when he saw them stop at the rail fence, and each man of them pick up two, three, and even four rails, and turn back, carrying them to the place where they had left their guns, he understood what it meant. . . . The operation was repeated, the rails were placed lengthways along their front; with bayonets, knives, and tin plates taken from their haversacks, the earth was dug up and the rails covered until a fair protection for men lying on their bellies was made."[20]

For a part of the battle, portions of the XVII Corps fought in two directions, when Cheatham's (Cheatham having temporarily replaced Hood) corps attacked out of the Atlanta defenses. But Logan's leadership was inspiring and effective, and the Army of the Tennessee not only held but also administered a brutal rebuff to Hood's second offensive. A Confederate brigadier described the defeat of his attack thusly: "All the regiments acted well. Taking the brigade all together, I never saw a greater display of gallantry; but they failed to take the works simply because the thing attempted was impossible for a thin line of exhausted men to accomplish. It was a direct attack by exhausted men against double their number behind strong breast-works."[21] Union troops improvised breastworks throughout the battle, so much had the tactics of the war changed from 1862. By the time the fighting had ended at dusk the Confederates had suffered over 8,000 casualties, while the Army of Tennessee had suffered 3,521—a casualty exchange ratio disastrous for the Army of Tennessee, especially considering the fact that it was outnumbered to begin with. So heavy were the Confederate casualties that Sherman doubted Hood would be able to launch another attack. He was mistaken.

Having wrecked the rail lines between Atlanta and Richmond, Sherman determined to switch his avenue of approach and swing back to the west. Howard, who had replaced the dead McPherson in command of the Army of the Tennessee, led the Union advance. Sherman had decided that Logan did not possess sufficient experience (he was a volunteer officer, as opposed to a West Pointer) to lead the Army of the Tennessee in spite of his brilliant performance in battle as McPherson's replacement. It also appears that Thomas expressed doubts as to whether he could work with the Illinois politician.

Logan would keep his mouth shut and do his duty for the remainder of the war, but after the war he made his feelings known about the "West Point protective association." Grant, however, had none of Sherman's prejudice against volunteer soldiers and, as we shall see, would select Logan for higher command at the end of the year. While Logan was willing to stick it out despite being passed over, Hooker was not. "Fighting Joe" requested to be relieved from command, his pique justified by the fact that Howard's incompetence had been responsible for Hooker's disastrous defeat at Chancellorsville. Meanwhile, McCallum's construction crews had bridged the Chattahoochee, a considerable undertaking which had required construction of a bridge 740 feet long and 90 feet above the river. Sherman's forward supply base had reached his immediate rear.

Sherman had not expected another Confederate attack; Howard knew Hood better and so had his troops ready. Hood's third strike came on 28 July near Ezra Church. The Confederate commander planned his attack on the assumption the Confederates could seize the crossroads at Ezra Church before Sherman's soldiers arrived, which would force the Union soldiers to deploy. Steven D. Lee had

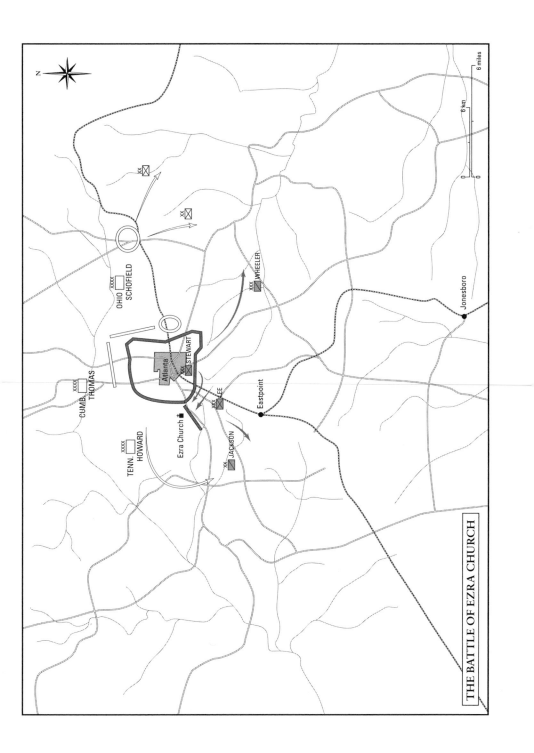

THE BATTLE OF EZRA CHURCH

assumed command of Hood's old corps from Cheatham, and despite his newness to the position received responsibility for the fight at Ezra Church. Meanwhile, Stewart's corps was to swing behind Lee and move rapidly to the west so that it could swing back and catch Howard in the flank.

Howard's men, marching rapidly south from their swing around Atlanta, reached the Ezra Church crossroads first. That completely upset Hood's conception as to what was supposed to happen, and he had made no contingency plans. Lee simply threw his troops into straight-ahead attacks. Logan's men reacted in the following fashion: "During temporary lulls in the fighting, which did not at any time exceed from three to five minutes, the men would bring together logs and sticks to shield themselves from the bullets of the enemy in the next assault."[22] A portion of Stewart's corps then came up to add to the slaughter. Like the chateau generals of World War I, Hood remained in Atlanta out of touch with the battlefield. The attacks at Ezra Church cost the Confederates 3,000 casualties, while Howard lost slightly over 600.

The losses between the beginning of the campaign in May and the end of July underline how disastrous Hood's lunges out of Atlanta had been. Over that period, Confederate casualties had reached nearly 30,000, while Sherman's losses were approximately 26,000. Hood's attacks had added 16,000 to the Confederate casualty bill. Given Northern superiority in numbers not only on the Atlanta front but also overall, these losses represented an exchange ratio the Confederacy could not bear. As one of Hood's soldiers replied to the question shouted across the lines by a bluecoat as to how many men were left in the Army of Tennessee, "oh, about enough for another killing."[23]

Even Hood realized that his army could not stand another killing battle. Nevertheless, his explanation for his defeats had nothing to do with his responsibility for having launched the Army of Tennessee against an immensely superior opponent, but rather focused on the supposed incompetence of his corps commanders and the lack of aggressive fighting ability among the troops, whose spirit, he argued, Johnston's reliance on the defensive had ruined. Even Davis became alarmed at the losses in the three attacks and had ordered Hood to desist. Thus, at the beginning of August the contest between the two great armies settled into a siege. Following Grant's example the year before at Vicksburg, Sherman began a major bombardment of Atlanta in the hope he could pry Hood loose from the city, while looking for a means to cut the lines of communications that supported the Confederates.

On 27 July, Sherman launched his cavalry around the flanks of Atlanta to apply additional pressure on the Confederates. Two columns of Union cavalry, the first of 3,500 troopers under McCook, the second under Stoneman with 6,500 troopers, were to cut the Macon & Western Railroad at Jonesboro so that the Confederates would have to abandon Atlanta. Sherman, who did not hold his cavalry commanders in high regard, had his prejudices confirmed. The raids were an utter failure. Stoneman, paying no attention to his mission, rode off with 2,500 cavalrymen to free the Union prisoners being held in appalling conditions at Andersonville and got himself and two of his three brigades captured or killed for their troubles. McCook's cavalry force wrecked approximately a mile of track, which stopped rail traffic for two days, before fleeing back to the shelter of Sherman's infantry. Sherman's understated report was that "on the whole the cavalry raid is not deemed a success."[24]

Yet there was an unintended effect from the cavalry's defeat. Given the lackluster performance of Union cavalry, Hood decided he could dispense with much of his cavalry. He believed that if Wheeler cut loose and rode north with the purpose of disrupting Sherman's rail lines of communications, Union armies would abandon their efforts to capture Atlanta and retreat back to Chattanooga. Wheeler's raids, however, proved no more successful than the Union raids. Here and there they cut the railroads, pulled down telegraph lines, and captured supplies. But in every case McCallum's crews repaired the damage in short order; there was no stoppage in the flow of supplies. Moreover, as with Stoneman's efforts in the East in 1863 and in the West in 1864, Wheeler failed to concentrate on attacking the enemy's lines of communications, but instead went on a wild ride through the countryside that eventually resulted in the destruction of most of his cavalry by the time he returned to Confederate lines in Alabama. The mistake in sending Wheeler's cavalry off to raid Union communications in Tennessee lay in the fact that it robbed Hood of his reconnaissance force.

In mid-August, Sherman sent another cavalry raid against Hood's rail lines, again with a notable lack of success. Thus, he decided he was going to have to break the Macon & Western himself. On 26 August he pulled his corps away from Atlanta except for Slocum, who now ironically commanded Hooker's old XX Corps. Sherman's intention was

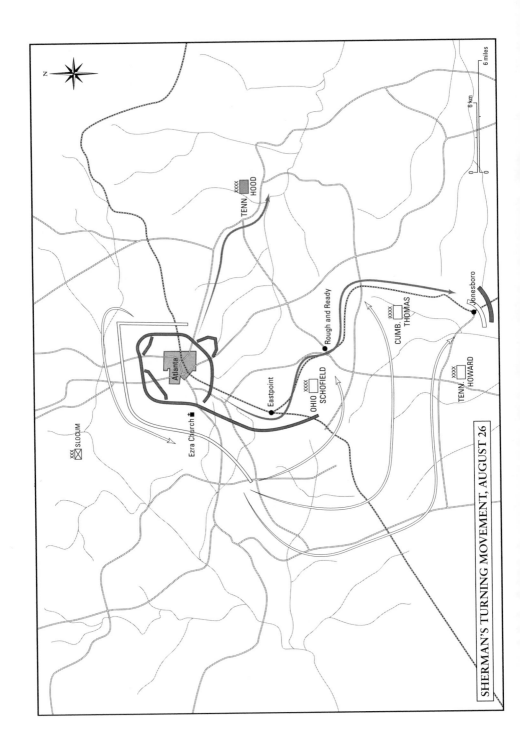

SHERMAN'S TURNING MOVEMENT, AUGUST 26

to swing his entire army around the Confederate defenses. Schofield would command the left wing, which after marching south would swing in toward the railroad station of Rough and Ready. Thomas would hold the center, and Howard's Army of the Tennessee would aim at Jonesboro to destroy a sufficient portion of the Macon railroad to force Hood to abandon Atlanta. There were, of course, risks in such a move, because Hood might strike north at Sherman's lines of supply. But Sherman calculated that Hood had used up the Army of Tennessee. This time he was right.

Considerable confusion marked the Confederate response to Sherman's flanking move. With minimum cavalry available, Hood had no idea of what was transpiring other than the fact that much of the Union host had pulled back from their positions surrounding Atlanta. Was Sherman retreating because Wheeler had cut their lines of supply? Was Sherman moving around the Confederate lines? If so, how far? Where was he planning to strike? Not only was Hood blind, but the advantage in numbers that Sherman possessed was working to an even greater extent, given Hood's profligacy with the lives of his men. By the time the Confederates reacted, it was too late. Howard's men were astride the Macon railroad and wrecking it thoroughly, while comfortably entrenching themselves. Confederate counterattacks on the last day of August were halfhearted, but costly, totaling 1,700 to barely a quarter of that number for the defenders. Further fighting occurred on the next day, when Sherman came close to destroying Hardee's corps, both sides suffering approximately 1,000 casualties.

On 1 September Hood abandoned Atlanta. With Sherman firmly astride the railroads supplying the Army of Tennessee and the town, Hood had no hope of holding the city. The defeat represented a political disaster for the Confederacy. Sherman's announcement that "Atlanta is ours and fairly won" echoed throughout the North and made Lincoln's reelection a near certainty. Ordered in haste and with little preparation, the Confederate retreat from Atlanta resembled a rout. The city's considerable manufacturing establishments producing war material went up in smoke, along with masses of food and military equipment. With Atlanta's capture, the Confederacy lost its second most important industrial center. The destruction of eighty-one carloads of ammunition added to the noise and light show. About the only advantage the Confederate cause gained was the fact that the Army of Tennessee regained its freedom of movement.

The Return to Tennessee

With the fall of Atlanta, Sherman pulled back to the city to give his armies a rest. In retrospect, his decision to reform his armies in Atlanta was a mistake. After all, the campaign's strategic aim was not just to capture Atlanta but to destroy the Army of Tennessee, as well as to inflict as much economic damage on the Deep South as possible. By not moving rapidly to attack Hood's demoralized army as it abandoned Atlanta, Sherman lost the opportunity to finish off his opponent. While Union armies reformed in Atlanta, Hood had equal time to reorganize the Army of Tennessee. Without baggage and with much of its artillery lost, Hood's army represented a force capable of more rapid movement than its Union opponents. Thus, it would fight only the battles that Hood wanted to fight.

In Atlanta, Sherman took one of his more controversial steps by ordering the city's civilians to leave. He decided to expel the city's population partly on the basis that his lengthy logistical lines could only support his armies. But there was another reason. As he explained after the war in his memoirs: "I knew that the people of the South would read in this measure two important conclusions: one, that we were in earnest; and the other, if they were sincere in their common and popular clamor 'to die in the last ditch,' that the opportunity would soon come." Or, as Sherman put it in a wartime letter to Halleck, "if people raise a howl against my barbarity and cruelty I will answer that war is war, and not popularity seeking."[25]

The strategic question facing Sherman was, what next? Considerable reshuffling of senior officers and units took place. Thomas returned to Nashville with two divisions to keep a watchful eye on Forrest. Logan and Blair returned to their states to help in Lincoln's reelection efforts. Sherman, who had none of Grant's political understanding, found electioneering by those officers thoroughly distasteful. For Sherman, there were a number of possibilities such as a drive into Alabama toward Mobile or against Augusta. But Hood's army remained Sherman's main problem. Having finally recognized that he could not defeat Sherman's armies by direct attack, Hood decided to attack the Union supply lines by moving around Atlanta to the west and then advancing northward.

Before he could move, however, Davis arrived to confer with his senior commanders. As usual the high command of the Army of

Tennessee was in turmoil. Hardee in particular was unhappy and made it clear to the Confederate president that either Hood went or he would go. In conference with Davis, the other two corps commanders were no happier with Hood's brand of leadership, while the troops greeted the president with cries demanding Johnston's return. Caught in the web of his prejudices and a personality that refused to admit mistakes, Davis was not about to reappoint Johnston. Instead he cobbled together a command arrangement which shipped Hardee to the Carolinas, while Beauregard received general supervisory command of the Western theater, but no direct command. Finally, the Confederate president gave his blessing to Hood's aggressive plans to take his army back into Tennessee. Both Davis and Hood believed such an invasion would draw Sherman away from Georgia. If Hood were not able to fight a battle to his advantage in Tennessee, then he was to fall back into northern Alabama where he could fight a decisive battle. If Sherman fell back into Tennessee, Hood would pursue him and defeat him there. Such were the plans of desperate Confederate leaders, who much like those in the *Führerbunker* in 1945 failed to recognize that the enemy has a vote as well.

Davis also revealed his increasingly fantastic attitudes toward the course of the war when he gave an address in Macon, Georgia, on September 22: "Our cause is not lost. Sherman cannot keep up his long line of communication, and retreat, sooner or later, he must; and when that day comes the fate that befell the army of the French Empire in its retreat from Moscow will be repeated."[26] Davis's strategy by this point had become one of fantasy and delusion, which he continued to peddle to a Confederate public, increasingly despairing about the war's course. When informed of Davis's remarks, Grant acidly noted: "Mr. Davis has not made it quite plain who is to furnish the snow for this Moscow retreat."[27] In describing Davis's musings, Sherman commented that the Confederate president seemed "to have lost all sense and reason."[28] In fact, Davis was sowing a whirlwind with his challenge to Sherman, whose response the Confederates of Georgia would soon regret deeply.

While Davis was speaking, Hood struck at Sherman's lines of communications. Having gobbled up the garrisons at Big Shanty and Acworth, Hood went after the major Union supply dumps at Allatoona. Sherman watched the battle that ensued from Kennesaw Mountain, as his signalers messaged the Union garrison that help was coming. The commander of the Union force replied to Confederate demands for his surrender with the terse note that, "Your communication demanding the surrender of my command I acknowledge receipt of, and respectfully reply that we are prepared for the 'needless effusion of blood' whenever it is agreeable to you."[29] The fight cost Union defenders 707 casualties; the Confederates 799, but the supply depot remained in Union hands.

The upshot of the attack was a series of skirmishes that forced Hood to retreat into northern Alabama; there he remained a latent threat, but his attacks were more than a mere nuisance, because they left the initiative in Confederate hands. As Sherman fended Hood off from his railroad lines of communications, he contemplated a major change in his strategic approach. As long as he remained tied to Atlanta, his lines of communications would remain vulnerable to Confederate raids. Moreover, given his position in northern Alabama, Hood could attack in a number of directions, any one of which might cause difficulties. The combination of the Army of Tennessee with Wheeler's and particularly Forrest's ability to raid led Sherman to warn Grant and Stanton that the Confederates possessed the ability to inflict up to 1,000 casualties on static Union garrisons each month.

What Sherman proposed as a solution was that his armies abandon Atlanta with a portion falling back into Tennessee. At the same time Sherman would march with 65,000 handpicked troops through central Georgia to bring the war home to the Deep South. As he put it: "On the supposition always that Thomas can hold the line of the Tennessee, and very shortly be able to assume the offensive against Beauregard, I propose to act in such a manner against the material resources of the South as utterly to Negative Davis' boasted threat and promises of protection. If we can march a well appointed Army right through his territory, it is a demonstration to the World, foreign and domestic, that we have a power which Davis cannot resist. This may not be War, but rather Statesmanship."[30] Initially Grant was skeptical, but Sherman soon won him over. After all, had not his Army of the Tennessee lived off much poorer land in Mississippi during the Vicksburg campaign? It took Grant's log rolling to persuade Lincoln and Stanton that Sherman's approach was a war-winning strategy. In the end they too agreed.

For Sherman the immediate task was to clean up the loose ends preparatory to this march through Georgia. Thomas assumed command in Tennessee with Schofield under him. Not surprisingly, the two sub-ordinates Sherman selected to remain behind to defend Tennessee were the two generals most capable of acting on their own. To command the army's wings in the march through Georgia, Sherman selected Slocum and Howard. He would remain with Howard throughout much of the campaign. Given the fact he did not expect serious military opposition on the march to the sea, the distribution of senior officers made sense. As he prepared, Sherman sent the sick, as well as those lacking the fortitude for such a march, back to Nashville. These were to provide Thomas and Schofield with the strength to counter any of Hood's aggressive moves. Thus, through October into November, Thomas received a steady flow of reinforcements. David Stanley's corps moved out of Atlanta to Nashville, while A. J. Smith's divisions returned from Missouri to add to the forces gathering under Thomas in Tennessee.

As he had with the Army of the Potomac's cavalry when he had appointed Sheridan, Grant intervened to fix the cavalry in the West. With few exceptions, Grierson being one, its record had been little better than that of its Eastern brethren, especially against Forrest. As one infantryman acidly commented: "Confound the cavalry. They're good for nothing but to run down horses and steal chickens."[31] So Grant sent James Wilson to shape up the cavalry supporting Thomas. Wilson obviously did not have time to affect matters before Hood crossed into Tennessee, but he was to render a crucial service during the campaign. As for Hood, Sherman caustically commented: "Damn him, if he will go to the Ohio River I'll give him rations. . . . Let him go north, my business is down South."[32] Thus, Sherman changed the basis of Union strategy in the West. It now focused on carrying the war to the Confederacy's civilians, in this case white Georgians, but others would soon feel the power the North was willing to bring to bear to break Confederate will.

Hood's army, unless it was willing to defend Georgia, which its current placement in northern Alabama indicated it was not, was an irrelevancy. Given Union strength in Tennessee, it had little prospect of achieving much, and if it were to seek out battle against Thomas and Schofield, it had every prospect of being destroyed. Yet, Hood was toying not only with invading Tennessee but also with coming to Lee's aid, if Sherman refused to fight. Nevertheless, Hood turned down the possibility of attacking Sherman in mid-October on the advice of his corps commanders, who argued that the shaky morale of their troops and the numbers available made the prospects of success minimal.

Hood, Davis, and Beauregard saw nothing of the possibilities open to Sherman. As is true of much of military history, there was a distinct lack of imagination among Confederate leaders as to the path on which their opponent might embark. Instead of recognizing Sherman's options, they expected Sherman to follow Hood into the rugged terrain of northern Alabama and southeastern Tennessee, where separated from his supply bases, his forces would shrink. At that point, supposedly Hood and the Army of Tennessee could destroy Sherman's armies. Shortly before assuming his new position in the West, Beauregard met with Hood. Hood laid out his plans for an invasion of Tennessee, which sounded much like the course of action Beauregard had been urging on his government over the past two years with one important difference: Beauregard had always urged that major reinforcements be sent West to reinforce the Army of Tennessee, but now the cupboard was bare; Hood was proposing the Tennessee offensive with an army which had suffered heavy losses as a result of his generalship and the morale of which had not yet recovered, if ever it would. Moreover, the maneuverability that had allowed Hood to escape Sherman's grasp was a result of the fact that the Army of Tennessee's logistical system was almost nonexistent.

What is astonishing about Hood's movements at the end of October and into early November is that the crippled general had no clear idea of exactly what he intended to accomplish. He was clearly ad-libbing, making up strategy as he went along. Initially, it appears he hoped to break the railroad lines between Nashville and Chattanooga. Driving Hood was the dream that not only could he defeat Thomas, capture Nashville, and recruit 20,000 volunteers in Tennessee, but also drive all the way to the banks of the Ohio, a goal that Confederate armies had failed to achieve during the heyday of their success in summer 1862. Thus, the Army of Tennessee approached Guntersville, Alabama, with the intention of crossing the Tennessee River at that point.

But a strong Union garrison held the crossing, and Hood decided that his army would suffer too heavy casualties, were it to attempt to force a crossing. Upon reaching Decatur, Alabama, fifty miles downstream, Hood reached the same conclusion, given the strength of Union forces at the crossing. So it was another long march down the swollen Tennessee to Tuscumbia in the northwestern corner of Alabama. Over

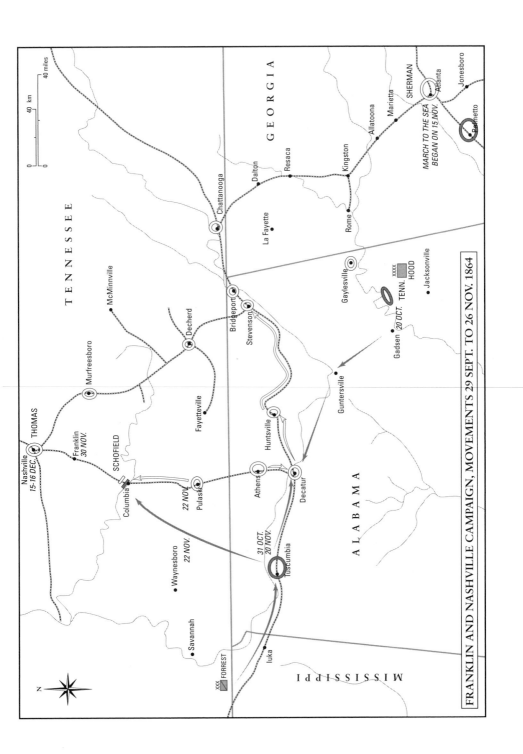

FRANKLIN AND NASHVILLE CAMPAIGN, MOVEMENTS 29 SEPT. TO 26 NOV. 1864

a ten-day period, Hood wandered around northern Alabama looking for a crossing point. At Tuscumbia he wasted more time waiting for Forrest to join up, since Forrest had engaged his troopers in a successful raid in wrecking Union supply depots along the lower Tennessee. The property damage was considerable, but whether the Confederacy gained in strategic terms is doubtful. The delay, however, did allow Union commanders on the other side of the river to prepare themselves to meet the Army of Tennessee.

On 16 November Hood issued his orders for the upcoming campaign, the same day Sherman began his march to the sea. Until the 15th Hood and Beauregard seem to have believed Sherman was moving back into Tennessee. On the 16th and 17th they received reports that Union troops were ripping up the railroad between Atlanta and Chattanooga and that Sherman was marching off into the depths of Georgia with four corps. By then, of course, they were 200 miles away, and it was too late to respond. Confederate leaders were about to pay for the strategic choices they made in underestimating their opponent's strength and intentions. In effect, Hood had left the heart of Georgia defenseless, a terrible miscalculation, because at the most fundamental level the purpose of armies is to defend the citizens of the state from the depredations of enemy military forces. By leaving Georgia defenseless, Confederate leaders had broken that bond between army and people.

Four days after Sherman embarked on his campaign to make "Georgia howl," Hood crossed the Tennessee. His intentions had no connection with the situation he confronted. He had no understanding of the vast forces the Union had deployed in the state. Again, we confront that inability of Confederate leaders to comprehend the scale of Union mobilization. Most probably, Hood believed he could rush Nashville, and its fall would rally Tennesseans to the Confederacy. His unsuitability for the position he had so eagerly sought became even clearer than it had been during his dismal performance in defending Atlanta. To begin with he was not particularly bright, but his terrible wounds exacerbated a personality incapable of recognizing his own weaknesses, thus his constant attempts to blame others for his mistakes. Even more inexcusable was his inability to recognize the tactical realities that charges against entrenched troops possessing Civil War weapons represented a hopeless proposition. Exacerbating these defects was the fact that Hood's amputated leg was not fully healed and his need to ride in order to command must have represented sheer agony.

Schofield had positioned his Army of the Ohio at Pulaski, northeast of Tuscumbia. He possessed two divisions of the XXIII Corps and three divisions of the IV Corps, altogether adding up to nearly 30,000 soldiers including cavalry units, virtually the same strength as the Army of Tennessee. Driven off by Forrest's cavalry, Union scouts failed to warn Schofield that Hood was moving toward Columbia, Tennessee, and was on his way to seizing that crucial town in his rear. But the road Schofield's troops had to traverse was in better shape, and the Union troops not only arrived at Columbia before Forrest's outriders but also had time to entrench. What happened next resembled Chancellorsville, but not its results. Given his remarks at the time it is likely Hood believed Nashville was lightly held and that once around his former roommate's flank he could grab the city along with its supplies and then turn back on the Army of the Ohio to destroy it. In fact, Thomas possessed more troops in Nashville than Hood possessed in his entire army, but such was the state of Confederate intelligence that Hood had no clear idea of Union strength or dispositions.

The Army of Tennessee's opening moves were brilliant. Yet, Hood remained in the dreamy days of 1862. As he described his plans after the war: "The situation presented an occasion for one of those interesting and beautiful moves upon the chess-board of war, to perform which I had often desired an opportunity. . . . I had beheld with admiration the noble deeds and grand results achieved by the noble Jackson in similar manoeuvres [*sic*]."[33] With such romantic notions, Hood sent Forrest to seize a set of fords ten miles upstream, followed in the early morning hours by Cheatham's and Stewart's corps. To speed up the move to outflank Schofield, the units left their artillery behind. Meanwhile, two divisions and the Army of Tennessee's artillery were to keep Schofield's attention focused on Confederate forces directly across from the town. With seven of his ten divisions across the Duck, Hood expected Forrest and then Cheatham would reach Spring Hill on the Columbia Pike before Schofield. After the war he argued that had matters continued as planned, he would have cut Schofield off from Nashville and then destroyed him. In fact, there were other roads farther west that the Army of the Ohio could have taken, which would have allowed it to pull away from the Confederates. However, Hood's remarks at the time suggest he was thinking of seizing of Spring Hill and cutting off the Columbia Pike as the first step in seizing Nashville.

To ensure that matters went according to plan, Hood accompanied Cheatham's infantry and ordered Cheatham to commit his first division as soon as possible to take Spring Hill. Hood then rode back to check how Stewart's corps was progressing. From that point matters went downhill. Cheatham discovered Spring Hill heavily defended not only by cavalry but also by infantry and artillery. Early the previous evening Wilson had accomplished the primary cavalry mission that many cavalry commanders in the war ignored—namely, to feel out the enemy's movements. He had warned Schofield the Confederates appeared unusually active upstream on the Duck River from Columbia. Thus, in the early morning hours, Schofield set his wagon trains and artillery as well as two divisions under Stanley in motion to retreat northward. Immediately before Forrest arrived, Stanley had reached Spring Hill with a full infantry division supported by artillery to reinforce the two regiments in the town. Forrest attempted one of his intimidating moves by launching a full cavalry charge, which might have worked had only two regiments been defending. But against an infantry division supported strongly by artillery, the charge was a disaster. Forrest's horses and men did not stand up well against full loads of canister. Late in the afternoon Cleburne's division launched an attack that was no more successful. Moreover, the Confederates possessed virtually no artillery, since the outflanking corps had left their guns at Columbia to keep Schofield's attention focused on the south.

While the Confederates possessed superiority in numbers, nothing then happened. Because Hood had left the scene, the baleful culture left by Bragg's demand for obedience to orders held sway. The strong breastworks undoubtedly made Cheatham as well as Forrest hesitate. It was almost dark when Confederate reinforcements reached Cleburne's division to make possible a stronger attack. Moreover, there was considerable confusion among the Confederate generals as to what to do. Since Hood had departed without leaving orders, while his verbal instructions had only been to occupy what he believed a lightly held village, none were willing to attack a well-fortified position. Unlike Hood, the generals recognized the casualties involved in attacking an enemy behind well-entrenched breastworks. Yet, the lassitude of the Confederates in the late afternoon and evening is surprising. Even Forrest failed to move up the pike and make a stab at establishing a blocking position.

Thus, the Confederates went into bivouac east of the Columbia Pike, leaving the road to Franklin open, although obviously the Union retreat was vulnerable to Confederate harassing fire. But as Schofield marched his wagons, his artillery, and his infantry past bivouacked Confederates, nothing happened. As an exhausted Hood slept in the comfortable assumption his troops had seized Spring Hill and cut Schofield off from Nashville, his subordinates did nothing. Part of the explanation is that they too were exhausted by the flanking move that had taken all of the previous night, and, like their soldiers, they too were weary and hungry. No one was willing to make a decision independent of the army commander.

When morning came, the Confederates discovered that not only were there no Union troops in Spring Hill, but also that Schofield's entire army had eluded their grasp and moved smartly up the road to Franklin. Hood exploded at the failure of his commanders as well as the soldiers. His memoirs underline how little he understood of how war had changed in the two years since the glorious, "romantic" years of Jackson in the Shenandoah Valley: "The best move in my career as a soldier, I was thus destined to behold come to naught. The discovery that the Army, after a forward march of one hundred and eighty miles, was still, seemingly, unwilling to accept battle unless under the protection of breastworks, caused me to experience grave concern. In my inmost heart I questioned whether or not I would ever succeed in eradicating this evil. It seemed to me I had exhausted every means to remove this stumbling block to the Army of Tennessee."[34] Hood then lashed into his generals and called them cowards—this to men who had risked their lives in battle after battle.

Hood's second effort to fix this "evil" came on the battlefield. He ordered an immediate pursuit of the Army of the Ohio, which was already well down the road. Schofield had every intention of crossing the Harpeth River at Franklin and continuing his march to unite with Thomas in Nashville. But when he arrived at Franklin on the morning of 30 November 1864, he discovered the rising river had washed away much of the wagon bridge. While the railroad bridge remained undamaged, it needed planking laid across its rails to enable the movement of troops, wagons, and artillery. With no pontoon bridge available, he had to wait until his engineers had repaired the pedestrian bridge and fixed the railroad bridge to carry traffic.

Meanwhile, as his divisions arrived at Franklin, Schofield had them entrench, should the Confederates appear before the army crossed. Union breastworks and entrenchments sprang up along a semicircular arc that surrounded the town, anchored on the banks of the Harpeth southeast and northwest of the town. There would be no standing around in unprotected positions while awaiting the enemy's arrival. To make the position even more impregnable, Schofield positioned a division across the river, and his artillery, which crossed first, positioned their guns on high ground immediately on the river's north side, where their plunging fire could cover the open fields lying south of Franklin. Those open fields extended across the entire plain that sloped gradually upward to a circular ridge lying approximately a mile and a half beyond Union positions. Yet, Schofield had no intention of fighting; the deployment and defenses were meant to dissuade Hood from attacking and allow a Union retreat that night.

There was one weakness in the deployment, and that resulted from Schofield's decision at the last moment to deploy two brigades on the Columbia Pike in front of the main positions. The most reasonable explanation is that he never expected Hood to attack, given the strength of the defensive positions. Thus, he probably intended the forward deployed brigades to fall back into the main positions as his army retreated under cover of night. Beyond those positions a brigade commanded by Colonel Emerson Opdycke provided early warning. When it came marching into sight it was clear to Union defenders that the Army of Tennessee was approaching. Opdycke then led his brigade through the gap in the breastworks and halted 200 yards inside the fortified ring.

The anger that had overwhelmed Hood had destroyed all sense of reason or common sense. After a quick survey of Schofield's position, Hood announced to his staff and corps commanders simply "We will make the fight," a decision which he indicated would mean an all-out assault.[35] That was how Hood intended to erase the "evil" of the supposed unwillingness of his officers and soldiers to fight in the open. His subordinates greeted his announcement with disbelief. Cheatham attempted to persuade Hood to change his mind, but met obdurate refusal. Forrest, who knew the area well, suggested that he take his cavalry and a division of infantry to flank Schofield's position on fords up river. Hood would have none of it. He was going to strike the way his Texans had at Antietam. And so the Army of Tennessee deployed for its last major attack.

If Schofield still had doubts his former West Point roommate was about to attack, the soldiers of Wagner's two brigades thrown out in front of the main Union positions had none. They were less than enthralled with their position. They were the last to begin the process of entrenching and were only able to throw together with spades a shallow trench and dirt wall in front of their positions. As the Confederate brigades and divisions deployed approximately 500 yards away, their fears increased. Then the Confederates came on with a rush, screaming the rebel yell. A captain in the 64th Ohio recalled that his soldiers got off five or six rounds before rapidly retreating to the main defensive positions. "I had been glancing uneasily along our line, watching for a break as a pretext of getting out of there, and was looking towards the pike when the first break started. It ran along the line so rapidly that it reminded me of a train of powder burning. . . . [The Confederates] were coming on the run . . . and [were] so close that my first impulse was to throw myself flat on the ground and let them charge over us. . . . I shouted to my company, 'Fall back! Fall back!' and gave an example of how to do it by turning and running for the breastworks."[36]

The problem was that while Wagner's brigades were fighting, the troops behind were never able to fire for fear of hitting their comrades. The result was that much of Cleburne's division reached the Union breastworks and broke through. But that success lasted only a matter of minutes. Opdycke, without waiting for orders, immediately launched a counterattack. His soldiers were fresh; the Confederates were exhausted and winded. The attack's momentum collapsed. Nearly a thousand Confederates surrendered, while the rest threw themselves back over the breastworks. On part of the front, the fighting resembled what had taken place at the "Mule Shoe" at Spotsylvania. In the advance Cleburne had two horses shot from underneath him. He then advanced into the cauldron of fire to be shot down at some point, his body discovered the next morning pierced by forty-nine bullets, at least according to one veteran.

Outside of that success, the rest was slaughter. Plunging fire from the Union guns on the high ground on the other side of the Harpeth began the killing, while cannons and riflemen along the breastworks chimed in. On the right flank, the Confederates ran into Union infantry equipped with repeating rifles, which made their fire even more devastating, while Union artillery stationed across the river took the attackers in the flank and literally blasted them to pieces. Hood continued to commit troops to attack even after darkness. Forrest attempted to ford the river to get at Union artillery, but Wilson was ready and drove Confederate troopers back across the river. By the time the fighting died down, the slaughter had decimated the Army of Tennessee. A Union captain recalled the scene in front of one the artillery embrasures: "I went to a gun of the 6th Ohio Battery, posted a short distance east of the cotton gin. . . . The mangled bodies of the dead rebels were piled up as high as the mouth of the embrasure, and the gunners said that repeatedly when the lanyard was pulled the embrasure was filled with men, crowding forward to get in, who were literally blown from the mouth of the cannon. . . . Captain Baldwin of this battery has stated that as he stood by one of his guns, watching the effect of its fire, he could hear the smashing of the bones when the missiles tore their way through the dense ranks of the approaching rebels."[37] A Confederate recalled the sights of the next morning: "O, my God! what did we see! It was a grand holocaust of death. . . . The dead were piled the one on the other all over the ground. I never was so horrified and appalled in my life."[38]

In a few hours of suicidal attacks, Hood all but wrecked his army. In his memoirs, astonishingly dishonest even by the standards of the genre, he claimed he had been close to victory. Nothing could have been further from the truth. In a matter of three hours the Army of Tennessee had lost 6,200 men out of the approximately 16,000 who participated in the attack. Confederate dead numbered 1,750, more dead than the Army of the Potomac suffered at Fredericksburg or Chancellorsville, while Union losses were barely a third. Union firepower killed six Confederate generals, including the incomparable Cleburne, whose bravery and sagacity deserved better commanders than those under whom he had served, and wounded another five. One general was captured. Altogether twelve Confederate brigade and division commanders were casualties. In the middle command ranks no less than fifty-four regimental commanders were dead, wounded, or captured. Most of the Union losses came in Wagner's two brigades that had been so badly placed at the battle's outset. The fact that Schofield pulled out during the night to join up with Thomas at Nashville allowed Hood to report the Battle of Franklin as a victory. Moreover, he sent an entirely misleading message to Richmond indicating the loss of six generals killed but, astonishingly, suggested the loss of high-ranking officers "was excessively large in proportion to the loss of men."[39] Bragg and Davis did not discover the extent of Hood's losses at Franklin until mid-January.

Even Hood recognized that the Battle of Franklin had exhausted his troops. The Confederates spent 1 December burying their dead and pulling the wounded off the battlefield into some sort of shelter. Nevertheless, in the face of these terrible casualties, Hood resumed the march on the next afternoon in pursuit of Schofield, who had already joined up with Thomas. The combined Union army now numbered over 60,000 soldiers, while Hood possessed 25,000 dispirited men. In his memoirs, Hood suggested his reason for advancing into the maw of disastrous defeat: "In truth, our Army was in that condition which rendered it more judicious that men should face a decisive issue rather than retreat—in other words, rather than renounce the honor of their cause, without having made a last and manful effort to help lift up the sinking fortunes of the Confederacy."[40]

Hood arrived in front of Nashville on 2 December with 25,000 weary, poorly clad and ill-equipped soldiers. It is difficult to figure out what he intended to do. Probably Hood, like Mr. Micawber, hoped that something would turn up. In his memoirs, he suggests that he was hoping for reinforcements from Texas, but that was an idle hope. Underestimating the number of troops available to Thomas now that Schofield had arrived, Hood seems to have believed Thomas would come out from his fortifications where the Army of Tennessee could smash the Union hosts, seize Nashville, and turn around the war's course. In retrospect, his decision making is inexplicable. Not only did he lack sufficient troops to attack the city or for that matter invest it, but he also sent Forrest with two cavalry divisions and an infantry division, nearly 7,000 men, off on an attempt to destroy the Union garrison at Murfreesboro. His lack of troops meant that his flanks were up in the air, while his defensive line was lightly held.

Almost immediately Grant urged Thomas to attack. Some have criticized Grant for his efforts to push Thomas into action. Nevertheless, at the time Grant was under considerable pressure, some of it self-induced, but some of it from Lincoln. First of all, there were worries about Sherman's March to the Sea. As Lincoln commented, "I know what hole he went in at, but I can't tell what hole he will come out of."[41] Southern newspapers were the only intelligence about Sherman's army, and their reporting had no connection with reality. Stuck to the Army of the Potomac, Grant remained uncertain about

Sherman's fate. He worried that Thomas, "old slow trot," would wait too long and allow Hood to slip away on a desperate raid that might undermine much of the success Union arms had won over the past several months.

But Thomas refused to allow pressure from Washington to move him. For nearly a week he continued to report his troops were not ready. Then, beginning on 10 December, one of the worst early winter storms in years hit Tennessee. It blanketed the roads and fields with a thick coating of ice. Again Thomas reported he would have to postpone his attack. At this point Grant lost patience. Logan, still on leave from his efforts to get out the vote in Illinois, happened to be visiting City Point. Grant immediately provided him with a set of orders relieving Thomas and placing Logan in command of Union forces in the West. He was to travel to Nashville immediately, and if he arrived in that city, and Thomas had not yet attacked Hood, he was to relieve Thomas. If, however, he arrived and Thomas had already struck the Army of Tennessee, he was to leave Thomas in command. Shortly after Logan had left, Grant decided to proceed to Nashville himself to see what was preventing the Union counteroffensive. As matters turned out, arriving in Louisville, Logan discovered Thomas had already attacked and events had overtaken his orders. At the same time Grant had reached Washington and on receiving the news laconically commented to his signal officer: "Well I guess we won't go to Nashville."[42]

On 13 December the cold snap that had accompanied the ice storm relented, but that only added to Confederate difficulties. It turned everything into a sea of mud, which meant that Hood could not retreat even had he wanted. By the 15th the weather had warmed, the ice had melted, and the roads had begun to dry. Thomas now called Hood's poker hand, only to discover that Hood, as he had in a card game before the war, was not even holding a pair. The first part of the Union plan involved a feint by Steedman's division against Cheatham's corps on the eastern (right) side of the Confederate positions. The main effort, involving nearly all of Thomas's field soldiers, was a massive wheeling movement from the west of Nashville's fortifications. It took Union commanders all morning to deploy. As a result, it was not until early afternoon that the attack began. The westernmost participants of the Union attack were Wilson's cavalry divisions, 9,000 mounted, 4,000 without horses, all equipped with repeating rifles, and A. J. Smith's XVI Corps. The inward portion of the wheeling attack consisted of

Wood's IV Corps and Schofield's XXIII Corps. Altogether, Thomas threw over 45,000 troops at Hood's left.

As tough soldiers as they were, the Confederates had no hope of stopping the blow at their flank. Nevertheless, darkness fell before Thomas's troops could complete the destruction of Stewart's corps and swamp the entire Army of Tennessee. Hood, however, took the fact that his army had held two-thirds of its line, while only being badly battered on its left, as an indication all was not lost. He would stay and fight. On the second day, his position appeared stronger in terms of the terrain, but in fact it held a major weakness. Cheatham on the far left (western flank) held a position where his line bent back to the south. It was vulnerable to attack on three sides. Schofield's XXIII Corps was to the immediate west of his position, Smith's XVI Corps was to the north, and the artillery of both corps could enfilade Cheatham's defenses, one from the north and one from the west. Moreover, Wilson and his well-armed troopers were feeling their way around the main Confederate positions with only weak cavalry in their path, since Hood had sent Forrest away on the wild goose chase to Murfreesboro.

On the battle's second day, Thomas aimed at achieving a double envelopment of Hood's army. The attack by Steedman and Wood's IV Corps failed against tenacious resistance. Nevertheless, Hood was so impressed by the strength of the Union attack that he ordered Cheatham to send three brigades from the western flank to buttress Lee's corps. But Lee did not need reinforcements, and the removal of the three brigades fatally weakened Cheatham. Late in the afternoon, Thomas finally got his three corps commanders on the western side of the battle to act together. Attacked from three sides, the Confederates on Shy's Hill collapsed, followed by Cheatham's corps, and shortly thereafter by the remainder of the Army of Tennessee. Hood, dreaming of launching a flanking attack on the next day, saw his entire left collapse. He later admitted: "our line, thus, pierced, gave way; soon thereafter it broke at all points, and I beheld for the first and only time a Confederate Army abandon the field in confusion."[43]

The Battle of Nashville represented a disastrous defeat for the Confederacy. Union casualties numbered 3,061, over twice the number of killed and wounded the Confederates suffered. But 4,462 Confederates surrendered, raising Confederate casualties to over 6,000. With considerable help from Hood, Thomas's army had broken the Army of Tennessee's morale, and it never recovered. Thomas's report on the campaign listed no less than 13,189 prisoners captured by his troops. Hood, himself, resigned. As one Confederate corporal noted about Hood: "As a soldier, he was brave, good, noble, and gallant, and fought with the ferociousness of the wounded tiger, and with the ever-lasting grit of the bull-dog; but as a General he was a failure in every particular."[44] Nevertheless, the Union victory did not encompass the complete destruction of Hood's army. The pursuit of the remnants of the Army of Tennessee failed to catch the Confederates before they escaped across the Tennessee.

Perhaps their complete destruction was not necessary in view of the extent of the Union victory and the collapse of Confederate morale, but the conduct of the Union campaign suggests much about Thomas's strengths and weaknesses. Grant put those qualities best in his memoirs: "As my official letters on file in the War Department . . . reflect upon General Thomas by dwelling somewhat upon his tardiness, it is due to myself, as well as to him, that I give my estimate of him as a soldier. . . . He was a man of commanding appearance, slow and deliberate in speech and action; sensible, honest and brave. He possessed valuable soldierly qualities in an eminent degree. He gained the confidence of all who served under him, and almost their love. . . . Thomas' dispositions were deliberately made, and always good. He could not be driven from a point he was given to hold. He was not as good, however, in pursuit as he was in action. I do not believe that he could ever have conducted Sherman's army from Chattanooga to Atlanta against the defences and the commander guarding that line in 1864. On the other hand, if it had been given him to hold the line which Johnston tried to hold, neither that general nor Sherman, nor any other officer could have done it better."[45] It is worth noting the personal price Thomas paid for staying loyal to the Union. His relatives in Virginia, all enthusiastic supporters of the Confederacy, refused to have any intercourse with him after the war for his "disloyalty."

The March to the Sea

While Hood had been destroying what was left of the Army of Tennessee, Sherman had been ripping the heart out of Georgia. A strange, restless character was Major General William T. Sherman. A new arrival to his staff described him in a letter to his wife: "My 'chief' occupies a position and has already done things which certainly invest him with more than ordinary interest; and he impresses me as a man of power more than any man I remember. Not general intellectual power, not Websterian, but the sort of power which a flash of lightning suggests,—as clear, as intense, and as rapid. Yet with all his vigor, his Atlanta campaign showed, as his conversation and dispatches do, abundant caution and the most careful forethought. Without any signs of arrogance, he has complete confidence in himself."[46]

To prepare his army, Sherman had his commanders and surgeons carefully cull the units which were to make the journey of those who were sick or did not have the stamina to stand the rigors of what could be a trying exercise. Sherman's army on its march through Georgia would consist of two wings, each led by the rejects of the Army of the Potomac, Howard and Slocum. Howard would command the southern wing with the XV and XVII Corps, both from the Army of the Tennessee, while Slocum commanded the northern wing with the XIV and the XX Corps. Slocum's newly styled Army of Georgia came from diverse origins. The XIV Corps had been under Rosecrans and then Thomas in the Army of the Cumberland, while the two corps that had come west from the Army of the Potomac formed the XX Corps. As to the political and strategic purpose of his march through Georgia, Sherman was explicit in one of his last telegrams to Grant before his expedition began: "it is overwhelming to my mind that there are thousands of people abroad and in the South who will reason thus: If the North can march an army right through the South, it is proof positive that the North can prevail."[47]

With Hood's army in northern Alabama, Sherman knew his force of some 62,000 soldiers would face no serious opposition in its advance to the Atlantic Ocean. What was totally unexpected by Confederate leaders was the fact that Sherman intended to cut his lines of communications to the North and, having provisioned his army to the extent possible, live off the land. The strategic aim was not military, but political. It was to underline to white Southerners that their "supposed" government could not protect them from the armies of the North. Sherman made clear at the beginning of the march that his men were only to destroy the infrastructure that supported the Confederate war effort—railroads, factories, foodstuffs beyond what the local population needed for its sustenance. Where there was significant resistance or guerrilla attacks, his soldiers would target civilian homes as well.

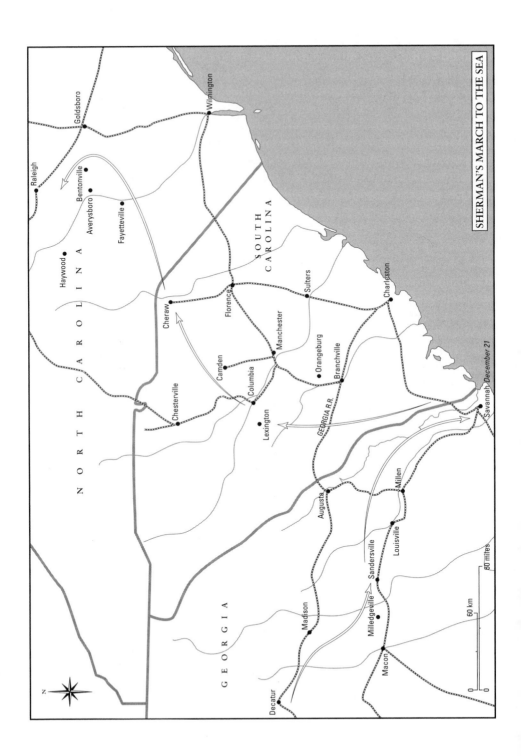

SHERMAN'S MARCH TO THE SEA

Certainly, Sherman himself went to considerable efforts to protect the homes of a number of the civilians, but the strategic purpose of the campaign was to bring the war home to Confederates of all classes.

Moreover, by 1864 we should not miss the fact that Sherman's troops, many of whom had been fighting the Confederates for three years, had hardened in their attitude toward their opponents. News of the massacre of black soldiers at Fort Pillow by Forrest and his raiders had reached much of the Union army by the time the march began. Scattered throughout the evidence left by the soldiers in their letters home, there is evidence of a willingness to use extreme measures against the enemy. One Wisconsin soldier wrote back to his home shortly after the attack at Resaca, Georgia, in May 1964, that "twenty-three of the rebs surrendered but our boys asked if they remembered Fort Pillow and killed all of them. Where there is no officer with us, we take no prisoners. . . . We want revenge for our brother soldiers and will have it."[48] Such paybacks may well have been more common, given the bitterness and anger engendered by the conflict, than the narrative that came to dominate the postwar popular histories of the conflict suggested.

In one of his last messages to Grant, Sherman reported that, "I will give you notice by telegraph of the exact time of my departure. General Steedman is here to clear the Rail road back to Chattanooga, and I will see that the road is broken completely between the Etowah and Chattahoochee including their bridges; and that Atlanta is utterly destroyed."[49] On 16 November the army began its march into Georgia. Behind it, the soldiers left the smoldering wreckage of what had been the Confederacy's second most important industrial site after Richmond: the railroads and their repair facilities wrecked, the iron foundries and factories destroyed along with a substantial amount of collateral damage.

Much of the civilian portions of the city burned as well. A recent addition to Sherman's staff, Major Henry Hitchcock, recorded the burning of the city's industry: "[One-third] of horizon shows immense and raging fires, lighting up whole heavens—probably, says Sherman, visible in Griffin, fifty miles off. First bursts of smoke, dense, black volumes, then tongues of flame, then huge waves of fire role up into the sky: presently the skeletons of great warehouses stand out in relief against and amidst sheets of roaring, blazing, furious flames,—then the angry waves roll less high, and are of deeper color, then sink and cease, and only the fierce glow from the bare and blackened walls, etc.

Now and then are heavy explosions and as one fire sinks another rises, further along the horizon."[50]

Sherman himself explained the destruction of Atlanta in terms that would have been familiar to those who conducted the Combined Bomber Offensive against Germany eighty years later: "this city has done and probably contributed more to carry on and sustain the war than any other, save perhaps Richmond. We have been fighting *Atlanta* all the time in the past: have been capturing guns, wagons, etc., etc., marked '*Atlanta*' and made here, all the time: and now since they have been doing so much to destroy us and our Government we have to destroy them, at least enough to prevent any more of that."[51] In front of Sherman were a few badly trained militia units and Wheeler's cavalry. The latter would behave almost as badly as Sherman's bummers in their treatment of civilians. Sherman's target was Savannah, but the movement of Slocum's northern wing initially suggested the advance was pointing at Augusta. For the first three days it ripped up the railroad between Atlanta and Augusta, but then turned to a more southerly course. From the first, there was a jocularity to the expedition. On the third day out Hitchcock observed a soldier, "buried all but eyes in cup of molasses," call out to Sherman, '[f]orage liberally,'" which was a direct quote from "Special Field Order No. 120." The general was not pleased, but his staff thought the remark hilarious.[52]

The stories told by the local slaves of whippings and mistreatment were an almost constant refrain for those willing to listen. For the most part, Sherman was content to allow subordinate commanders to determine the fate of the houses and villages through which the troops passed, but occasionally he intervened. Such was the case when he found himself in the plantation house of Howell Cobb, at present a general in the Confederate army, but before the war secretary of the treasury in Buchanan's cabinet. Sherman later recounted that, "I sent word back to General [Jefferson] Davis to explain whose plantation it was, and instructed him to spare nothing. That night huge bonfires consumed the fence-rails, kept our soldiers warm, and the teamsters and men, as well as the slaves, carried off an immense quantity of corn and provisions of all sorts."[53]

On the same day that Davis's division was stealing everything not nailed down and burning Cobb's plantation, the only serious infantry engagement of the campaign occurred. The rear guard of Osterhaus's XV Corps (Osterhaus replacing Logan for the campaign), a single brigade, came under an inept attack by several brigades of Georgia militia. Attacking across an open field, the Confederates launched three attacks, all of which the Union defenders repulsed with hardly any casualties. The fact that the brigade was also equipped with repeating rifles made the slaughter that much worse. After the battle, Union veterans surveyed the dead and discovered to their horror that their opponents had been old men and young boys. The 600 Confederate casualties, compared to 62 Union killed or wounded, underlined the inexperience of the Confederate militia and the idiocy of launching them across open fields. Like the Germans of World War II, the Confederacy's hopeless position was leading its leaders to throw boys into the fight.

For a short while, it appeared Hugh J. Kilpatrick's cavalry would hit Macon, but at the last moment it veered off. Georgia's capital, Milledgeville, was not so lucky. After calling on the people of Georgia to resist the Yankee invaders to the last man, the governor and legislature decamped. To Sherman's delight a group of young Union officers occupied the state capitol, declared themselves the legislature of Georgia, and repealed the ordinance of secession. Union troops destroyed state property, the arsenal, and anything that might be of use to the Confederate war effort. Almost immediately, the march resumed. For the most part the advance of Slocum's and Howard's troops was a casual walk through Georgia's heart. One veteran described the advance so: "We can march twenty miles a day whenever we choose, and do march over fifteen. It is a magnificent army of *veterans*, brimful of spirit and deviltry, literally 'spoiling for a fight,' neither knowing nor caring where they are going, blindly devoted to and confiding in 'the old man,' in splendid condition, weeded of all sick, etc., and every man understanding that there is no return but in fighting through."[54]

Yet, the ugly head of racial prejudice among the liberators bubbled up throughout the advance. To rid himself of the clouds of recently freed slaves doggedly following his XIV Corps, the Union general, Jefferson Davis, had his engineers pull up the corps' pontoon bridge after the last soldiers had crossed, leaving the blacks on the other side with Wheeler's pursuing cavalry pressing forward. The result was panic among the blacks and then a mass effort to swim the creek, which resulted in the deaths of many. Sherman, claiming his army lacked sufficient food to feed large numbers of blacks, made extensive efforts to persuade those recently freed to stay where they were, but large numbers refused and followed the army to Savannah.

On 9 December, twenty-five days after they had left Atlanta, the outriders of Sherman's army arrived at Savannah's outskirts. Before he could gain a solid grip on the city, his soldiers needed to seize Fort McAllister on the right bank of the Ogeechee, which would allow direct contact with the navy. Sherman's old division from Shiloh led the attack on the fort, which fell into Union hands on 13 December. That victory connected Sherman and his army to the outside world. Almost immediately, naval supply ships brought in 600,000 rations for the troops, a clear indication of how well the Union's logistical system was functioning by this point in the war. Perhaps even more important to the troops was the fact that the navy also brought their mail, which had accumulated over the past month. Hardee still held the city with 15,000 men, but he had no chance of holding out should Sherman invest Savannah, and if that happened, he would lose his army as well. He appealed to Richmond for reinforcements, which were not forthcoming, given the Army of Northern Virginia's perilous strategic position. On the 21st Hardee abandoned Savannah and retreated north into South Carolina. For Sherman this represented the crowning achievement to what we can only term one of the most brilliant campaigns of the war. Exultantly, he reported to an appreciative president: "I beg to present to you as a Christmas gift the city of Savannah with 150 heavy guns & plenty of ammunition & also about 25,000 bales of cotton."[55]

Conclusion

The decisive campaign occurred in the West with Sherman's efforts in 1864. First, and perhaps most important, it saw the capture of Atlanta, the decisive turning point in Lincoln's reelection campaign to give the president a second four-year term. On 23 August, Lincoln had written a realistic appraisal of his electoral prospects after a summer of military frustration. "This morning, as for some days past, it seems exceedingly probable that this Administration will not be re-elected."[56] So perilous was Lincoln's electoral position that even after the war's turn in the North's military favor, the Democratic Party still received 45 percent of the popular vote in the 1864 presidential election, slightly above the 44 percent the Democrats had won in the free states in 1860.

The fall of Atlanta less than two weeks later turned the political situation around. Admittedly, Hood and Davis contributed mightily to placing the Army of Tennessee in an impossible situation, but it had been Sherman's dogged but competent generalship that had led the Confederate president to make the disastrous decision of replacing Johnston. After Atlanta's fall, Sherman had then made the brilliant decision to take a substantial portion of his forces and launch the campaign through Georgia to the Atlantic Ocean. Again his opponents created the strategic and political opportunity, but it was Sherman who took advantage of the strategic blunder the Confederates made in leaving Georgia undefended. While some historians have found continued defiance among the civilians caught in the path of Sherman's March to the Sea, the campaign raised Union spirits and impressed upon the larger Confederate public the weakness of their cause.

Nevertheless, there was a price to be paid for the hard war that Sherman brought to so much of the South. Some historians have seen in the widespread destruction Sherman's army inflicted as the first steps toward "total war" that was to mark the twentieth century, particularly in the great bombing campaigns that smashed German and Japanese societies. That is a stretch, because Sherman, and Grant, for that matter, were looking backward rather than forward. There were certainly models for their approach to the war in 1864 scattered throughout European history, not to mention the actions of Americans over the centuries of fighting the Indians in North America. Yet, this was not a gentleman's campaign that Sherman's soldiers waged against the citizens of Georgia. Beside the targeted destruction of war-making facilities and the foraging efforts that kept the army quite literally living high off the hog, there was a massive amount of wanton destruction, executed by the fringe elements, aptly termed "bummers."

Sherman himself estimated that the damage his troops inflicted on Georgia reached as high as $100,000,000 (an extraordinary sum for the time), $20,000,000 of which supported his army and the remainder sheer wanton destruction. Where his foragers took or destroyed the excess foodstuffs of various farms they passed like a herd of locusts, they left the population at a subsistence level. In areas where Confederate guerrillas operated or where white Southerners had perpetrated atrocities on the Union soldiers they captured, and there were a number of such cases, the destruction fell on the civilians in the neighborhood. In some ways these actions were equivalent to Bomber Command's "dehousing campaign," with the exception that the inhabitants could leave their dwellings before their houses were torched.

Such cases were relatively rare in Georgia, but became more prevalent when Sherman's army reached South Carolina.

In particular, the destruction of houses fell disproportionately on the upper-class plantation owners. They were the ones who possessed the packs of bloodhounds that they had used before the war to track down runaway slaves and then during the war escaped Union prisoners. The latter cases, not surprisingly, enraged Union soldiers, who delightedly burned down the offending plantation houses. Invariably it was such slave owners who had used the whip liberally on their slaves. The testimony of the blacks they freed added to the enthusiasm displayed by Sherman's soldiers in destroying plantations. Union troops would undoubtedly have tossed such owners into the fire, but invariably the plantation owners had already decamped.

Significantly, those who were to write the white Southern narrative of the war, which dominated and distorted so much of the conflict's history, came precisely from those who had lost the most and in many cases had homes burned by vengeful Union troops. The end result of what historians have termed the *hard war* was that Union armies had destroyed not only the infrastructure of the South but its wealth as well. Because Confederates had invested and reinvested their wealth in slaves, the mere appearance of Union troops destroyed the financial basis on which a postwar recovery of the Southern states would depend. In that sense, the destruction of much of the white South's wealth was a direct result of the decision to secede and then so enthusiastically to challenge the North.

As with Germany and Japan in 1945, the war, and the manner in which Northern armies had waged it, had reduced the South to a bare subsistence economy by 1865. Germany and Japan would recover because the Cold War would bring in massive economic aid from their erstwhile enemies and because both nations had highly educated populations. However, in the case of the South, the North would not provide substantial economic aid in the postwar period. Moreover, the South's educational system, not just for blacks, but for poor whites as well, was virtually nonexistent before the war. Thus, the price white Southerners paid for the Northern hard war may not seem as terrible as that dealt out to the Axis Powers by the Allies in World War II, but its effects would last far longer and resonate to the present.

CHAPTER 12

The Collapse of the Confederacy

We never yielded in the struggle until we were bound hand & foot & the heel of the despot was on our throats. Bankrupt in men, in money, & in provisions, the wail of the bereaved & the cry of hunger rising all over the land, Our cities burned with fire and our pleasant things laid waste, the best & bravest of our sons in captivity, and the entire resources of our country exhausted—what else could we do but give up.

—Sarah Hine (Joslyn, *Charlotte's Boys*)

And so came the war's fifth year, a conflict that had rippled across North America while taking and ruining the lives of those left in its wake. By now in a rational world, the South's leaders would have recognized the Confederacy had no chance of surviving, given the strategic and military situation. Meade's Army of the Potomac had Lee's Army of Northern Virginia in a death grip in its siege of Petersburg. Sherman's armies had devastated Georgia in their advance to Savannah. Union forces under Thomas and Schofield had smashed Hood's Army of Tennessee in the Battles of Franklin and Nashville. Sheridan's cavalry and infantry had ravaged the Shenandoah Valley from the Potomac to its southern extremities. Slavery was dead. Desertion was rife. Inflation had destroyed the last vestiges of a modern economy. What few railroads remained were in the last stages of collapse.

Politically, Lincoln's reelection insured the Federal government would stay the course. There would be no backsliding as to the demand that the Confederacy rejoin the Union on the North's terms. By this point, the North's mobilization had turned what had been mere potential four years earlier into a juggernaut. In January 1865 Union armies could put over 600,000 *effectives* in the field out of the nearly 1,000,000 who wore the blue uniform. Northern industry had equipped these soldiers with state-of-the-art weapons and equipment, while its railroads and steam-powered fleet could project military forces over continental distances. The North's railroad and industrial infrastructure was in better shape than when the conflict had begun. Moreover, there was no hope now that foreign powers would intervene in the conflict. In fact, the French were deeply fearful as to what would happen to their Mexican adventure once Northern armies had finished with the Confederacy.

Yet, for all that reality suggested, Davis and Lee still argued for a continuation of the struggle. In fact, as late as February 1865, Davis predicted to enthusiastic listeners that if those at home capable of bearing arms would only join the Confederate armies in the field, they would, in the words of one newspaper correspondent, "compel the Yankees, in less than twelve months, to petition us for peace upon our own terms."[1] Lee even suggested to members of the Confederate Congress that while the abandonment of Richmond could have negative political consequences, it would be advantageous to his military situation, because it would release him from the need to defend the capital. He could then conduct military operations independently of having to defend a fixed point. From whence his ammunition and supplies would come, he failed to indicate.

Part of this response had to do with the fact that white Southerners would not abandon hope, that most dangerous of illusions. Well might Northern leaders have repeated the cold words Athenian negotiators had spoken to the Melians in 416 BC: "you seem to us quite unique in your ability to consider the future as something more certain than what is before your eyes, and to see uncertainties as realities, simply because you would like them to be so."[2] Yet, such was the desperation of the Confederacy's strategic situation as well as the illusions of its leaders that in mid-March, the Confederate Congress passed a bill to allow the recruitment of African American slaves into its military forces. Davis immediately signed the bill. However, Howell Cobb, that reprobate politician from Georgia, promptly pointed out the illogic of an exercise that never got off the ground: "The moment you resort to Negro soldiers your white soldiers will be lost to you; . . . The day you make soldiers of them is the beginning of the end of the revolution. If slaves will make good soldiers our whole theory of slavery is wrong."[3]

January was a month that brought a cold chill to Confederate hearts. Having dissimulated and lied about the results of his campaign in Tennessee, Hood had at least resigned. On his way to examine the Army of Tennessee and draw some of its strength away to help defend South Carolina, Beauregard received a dispatch from Hood, written shortly after Nashville: "Our loss in killed and wounded is very small. . . . Our loss in prisoners is not yet fully ascertained, but I think it comparatively small."[4] The truth emerged when Beauregard arrived in Tupelo to see the wreck of what had once been the Army of Tennessee. In his search for glory, Hood had reduced it to approximately half its strength when it had crossed the Tennessee River two months earlier—and less than one-third the strength of what he had taken over from Johnston in July. As one of its division commanders noted: "The remnant of my command, after this campaign of unprecedented peril and hardship, reduced by its battles and exposure, worn and weary with its travel and toil, numbered less when it reached its rest in Tupelo than one of its brigades had done eight months before."[5] After he had scratched together approximately 6,000 soldiers to move east to defend South Carolina against Sherman, Beauregard left Richard Taylor to command the beaten remains of a once proud army.

Planning the Last Campaigns

At the end of 1864 and beginning of 1865, Grant possessed the authority to guide Union military strategy in a fashion that had not occurred in previous years. The political generals were now expendable. With Lincoln's reelection, there was no need for the likes of Banks, Sigel, or Butler. Only those political generals like Logan and Carl Schurz, who continued to prove their worth on the battlefield, remained to finish the war. Moreover, Halleck had been reduced to the only position he was worthy of holding—that of an administrator to pass Grant's instructions to field commanders beyond the immediate reach of City Point. Moreover, Halleck could no longer interfere with Grant's conception of using the Union's naval power to project its ground forces against the vulnerable shores of what remained of the Confederacy's ever-shrinking territory. Included in Grant's strategic conception was the aim of bringing the war home to those unregenerate Confederates

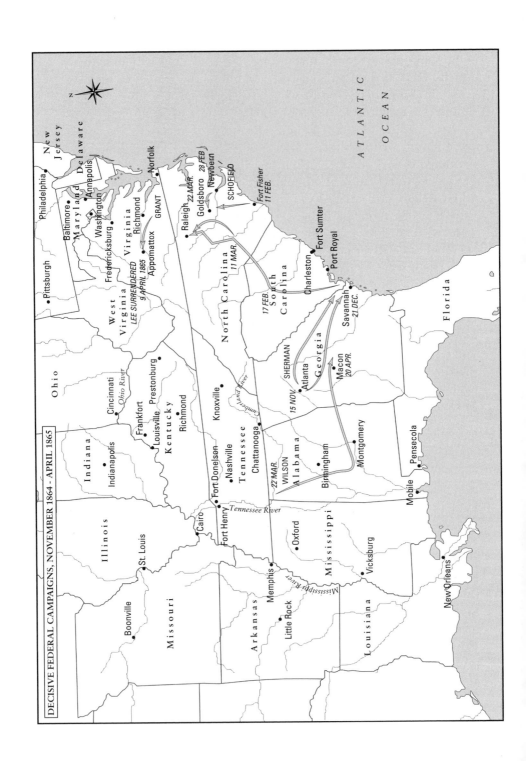

DECISIVE FEDERAL CAMPAIGNS, NOVEMBER 1864 - APRIL 1865

who kept the embers of rebellion glowing. The "hard war" lay at the heart of Union strategy in the war's last months.

As he had the year before, Grant made clear his military strategy to Sherman. On 21 January 1865 he telegrammed his approval of Sherman's planned campaign through the Carolinas. In addition, he put Sherman on notice that he had ordered the transfer of Schofield's corps, some 21,000 men, from Tennessee to Annapolis, from whence it would move to the coast of North Carolina, either to Wilmington or New Bern. Once there, Schofield would reinforce Sherman after he had wrecked South Carolina. The combined force could then more than handle Lee, if the Army of Northern Virginia abandoned Richmond and came south. "A force of twenty-eight or thirty thousand [including troops already in the area] will cooperate with you from New Bern or Wilmington or both. You can call for reinforcements."[6] Schofield's move from central Tennessee to Annapolis by railroad in the dead of winter and then on to North Carolina by steamboat represented a graphic indication of Union logistical capabilities at the war's end. The redeployment was even more impressive than the move of the XI and XII Corps to Tennessee in September 1863. Altogether the deployment from central Tennessee took eleven days to the Chesapeake and a further six to North Carolina—a total of some 1,400 miles.

Grant detached Schofield's corps from Thomas, because he did not believe the latter was capable of undertaking a rapid move south from central Tennessee into northern and central Alabama. After all, as Grant noted, Thomas "is possessed of excellent judgment, great coolness and honesty, but he is not good on a pursuit."[7] In the end, Grant authorized Thomas to launch Wilson in a massive cavalry raid into northern and central Alabama to wreck that last undamaged portion of the Confederacy. By early January, Wilson had completed his reorganization and reequipment of Union cavalry in the West, which now amounted to some 22,000 troopers—a force equipped with repeating rifles and able to hold its own against infantry. Not all of Wilson's refurbished cavalry would make the move south from Tennessee, because Grant siphoned some off for raids into other areas of the South untouched by the war.

In east Tennessee George Stoneman had somewhat redeemed his dismal performance as Hooker's cavalry commander and his capture in July 1864 by leading a raid at the end of December that had destroyed the salt works at Saltville, Virginia, and threatened the lead mines at Wytheville. Thomas now sent Stoneman through the Great Smokies into North Carolina to link up with Sherman and Schofield, while wrecking everything along the way. Sheridan for his part was to complete the destruction of the Shenandoah Valley and at the same time destroy what few forces remained under Early's command. He was then to move south to link up with Sherman. But the bandy-legged Irishman had a mind of his own. Instead of moving south, he turned east to rejoin to the Army of the Potomac to be in on the kill. Meanwhile, Major General Edward Canby and Union forces in New Orleans were to strike at Mobile before driving north to wreck untouched areas of southern Alabama.

Here was a strategy similar to what Grant had developed in 1864, but one Union forces in 1865 employed more effectively. It rested on overwhelming force as well as a utilization of the railroads and steamboats to transport and supply forces over great distances, while also taking advantage of the navy's ability to dominate the South's coasts. These operations aimed at a common purpose: the destruction of the Confederacy's ability to make war and the willingness of white Southerners to continue the struggle. Grant noted these various operations, including "Sherman with a large army eating out the vitals of South Carolina," would "leave nothing for the rebellion to stand upon."[8]

Fort Fisher

The first move came in December 1864, an amphibious assault on Fort Fisher guarding the Cape Fear River and Wilmington, North Carolina, the last port providing a haven for blockade-runners. Union forces should have attempted to seize the fort two years earlier. A report on the cargoes that Confederate blockade-runners managed to slip past the Union navy's patrol ships in the last two months of 1864 underlines its importance: "8,632,000 pounds of meat, 1,507,000 pounds of lead, 1,933 pounds of saltpeter, 546,000 pairs of shoes, 316,000 pairs of blankets, 520,000 pounds of coffee, 69,000 rifles, 97 packages of revolvers, 2,639 packages of medicine, 49 cannon," and a considerable amount of other material.[9]

Even though the attack on Fort Fisher was in Butler's area of responsibility, Grant hoped the Massachusetts general would defer actual command to Major General Godfrey Weitzel. Butler demurred;

he would lead the expedition and gain the glory for one of the war's culminating victories. To support Butler and two divisions of 6,500 troops, Admiral Porter supplied fifty-seven vessels, including five ironclads. In addition, Butler took along the steamship *Louisiana* packed with 215 tons of powder, the explosion of which he claimed would reduce Fisher to rubble. Porter had doubts about Butler's explosive ship, but he certainly believed his fleet sufficient to reduce the defenses.

By December 1864 the Confederate high command had reduced Fisher's garrison by half in its attempt to patch together something resembling a defense in Georgia. At the last moment before Butler and Porter appeared, some 400 North Carolina militia and 450 sixteen- to eighteen-year-old boys had arrived to bolster its defenses. In the early morning hours of Christmas Eve, the *Louisiana* was set on a course to explode against the fort's outer walls. The explosion was spectacular, but did little damage. Grant acidly wrote that, "at two o'clock in the morning the explosion took place—and produced no more effect on the fort, or anything else on land, than the bursting of a boiler anywhere on the Atlantic Ocean would have done. Indeed when the troops at Fort Fisher heard the explosion they supposed it was the bursting of a boiler in one of the Yankee gunboats."[10]

Nevertheless, the *Louisiana*'s failure to damage the fort inhibited Porter not at all. At noon on Christmas Eve, his fleet began an intensive bombardment. Over the course of the rest of the 24th, Porter's ships hurled some 10,000 heavy caliber shells without doing substantive damage to the fort or its defenders. Late in the afternoon Butler arrived with a portion of the amphibious force, but, since it was late, he refused to land. On Christmas Day, the navy began a more intense and accurate bombardment, while landing approximately 2,000 troops under Weitzel. Porter exaggerated the effectiveness of the bombardment thus far, while Union troops ran into resistance. Moreover, some of the Confederate prisoners told their captors Robert Hoke's division from the Army of Northern Virginia would soon arrive in the Union rear. That was enough for Butler. He decided he possessed insufficient troops to capture the fort. Ordering their withdrawal, he skedaddled off to Norfolk, leaving Porter to pull the last Union forces off the beaches. The fact that Union attackers lost one man drowned and fifteen wounded suggests the level of effort.

Porter was furious, but not as furious as Grant, when the latter heard what had happened. His mood did not improve when he read reports in the Richmond papers indicating the Confederates had received detailed information about the expedition even as it was leaving Hampton Roads. On 28 December, the commander of Union armies reported to the president: "The Wilmington expedition has proven a gross and culpable failure. . . . Delays and free talk of the object of the expedition enabled the enemy to move troops to Wilmington to defeat it. . . . Who is to blame I hope will be known."[11] Initially, Grant blamed both Butler and Porter, the latter unfairly, but he could only fire Butler, which he immediately proceeded to do. Six days later Butler had his walking papers. With the election over, Lincoln had no qualms about shipping the Democratic politician back to Massachusetts. However, instead of returning home, Butler headed straight to Washington to decry his removal by Grant before the Committee on the Conduct of the War, a sympathetic audience. He testified that he was not culpable for the failure to take the fort, because it was impregnable. Moreover, ever happy to blame others for his failings, he suggested that Porter had failed to provide the necessary support.

Then in one of those all too rare moments that delight historians when the incompetent receive their due, a newspaper, sold by a boy hawking a special edition outside the committee room, indicated that Fort Fisher had indeed fallen, this time to a competently led and organized effort. Understanding Fisher's importance, Grant had organized and launched another expedition. He appointed Major General Edward Ord to command the Army of the James and Major General Alfred Terry to lead a new amphibious assault. Terry received explicit instructions from Grant that he was to cooperate fully with his naval counterpart, Porter. Terry received some 8,000 soldiers with which to assault Fisher. However, he did not receive word of the objective until he was at sea, when he could at last open his orders. Grant was not going to risk another security leak.

Meanwhile, the Confederates celebrated their victory by reducing Fisher's garrison despite pleas from the garrison's commander the Northerners would soon be back. By the time the second expedition arrived, the young reservists had already departed and the garrison commander, Colonel William Lamb, was down to fewer than 900 men. Lee certainly recognized Fisher's importance with its supplies arriving to support his army and the Confederacy's strategic situation, but Bragg was the area commander. As usual he dawdled, refusing to focus his attention on the most important strategic position in his area. Not until it was too late did he attempt to reinforce Fisher.

Freed from Butler's incompetence, the amphibious assault and co-ordination between army and navy worked like clockwork. Before dawn on 13 January, Porter began a more careful, but heavier and more lethal bombardment. While his ships had fired 20,271 shells with a weight of 1,275,000 pounds in the first bombardment, this time he fired 600 fewer shells, but the weight of the bombardment was 1,652,638 pounds and more accurately aimed. Four hours after Porter's gun crews had begun destroying the fort, embrasure by embrasure, Terry started landing his 8,000 troops, the disembarkation completed within seven hours. In addition to three days of emergency rations and the normal supply of ammunition, the navy brought ashore six days of rations and 300,000 rounds of ammunition.

As the naval bombardment accomplished the fort's slow but steady destruction, Terry's men dug a line of fortifications to cover their rear before advancing against their objective. By this time the Confederates were desperately attempting to funnel reinforcements into the fort, 700 North Carolinians arriving on the second day. But it was too little, too late. On the third day, the bombardment continued until three o'clock in the afternoon. Terry left half his force to cover his rear in the northern portion of Fisher's Island, but the other half launched one of the two assault parties to attack the fort. The second party consisted of 1,600 volunteer sailors and 400 marines, many of the sailors armed with cutlasses. By evening Terry had four brigades inside the fort, and by 2200, it was over and the fort was in Union hands. The cost to the assaulting troops was heavy: 955 killed and wounded, but the South had lost its last window on the world. There would be no more ships cutting through the blockade to bring crucial weapons and supplies to the hard-pressed Confederacy.

Sherman's Winter Campaign

Grant's initial reaction to the news that Sherman had arrived at Savannah had been to have Union troops garrison the town strongly and then bring most of Sherman's forces north to Virginia by sea, where he could fold them into the Army of the Potomac. Then, together, the two armies could crush Lee, capture Richmond, and end the rebellion.

Sherman immediately objected. Instead, he proposed keeping his army intact for a drive north starting at Savannah. From there, his army could push through South Carolina and bring the war home to the state that had so blithely ignited the catastrophe of civil war. He sketched out his intention in a letter to Grant shortly after his arrival at Savannah: "With Savannah in our possession, at some future time if not now, we can punish South Carolina as she deserves, and the thousands of people in Georgia hoped we would do. I do sincerely believe that the whole United States, North and South, would rejoice to have this army turned loose on South Carolina, to devastate that State in the manner we have done in Georgia."[12] Nevertheless, he first replenished his supplies and prepared his troops for what would be an arduous campaign in midwinter.

In a letter to Grant, written on Christmas Eve, Sherman elaborated. From his comments, he had already thought through the next stage of the war as his soldiers were wrecking Georgia: "I left Augusta [Georgia] untouched on purpose, because the enemy will be in doubt as to my objective point, after we cross the Savannah River, whether it be Augusta or Charleston, and will naturally divide his forces. I will then move on either Branchville or Columbia, by any curved line that gives us the best supplies, breaking up in our course as much railroad as possible; then ignoring Charleston and Augusta both, I would occupy Columbia and Camden, pausing there long enough to observe the effect. . . . Charleston is now a mere desolate wreck, and is hardly worth the time to starve it out. . . . But on the hypothesis of ignoring Charleston and taking Wilmington, I would then favor a movement direct on Raleigh. The game is thus up with Lee, unless he comes out of Richmond, avoids you and fights me; in which case I should reckon your being on his heels. Now that Hood is used up by Thomas, I feel disposed to bring the matter to an issue as quick[ly] as possible. I feel confident that I can break up the whole railroad system of South Carolina and North Carolina, and be on the Roanoke, either at Raleigh or Weldon, by the time spring fairly opens. . . . I do not mean to boast, but believe this army has a confidence in itself that makes it almost invincible."[13]

That same day, Sherman wrote Halleck. He underlined that his strategic approach was fully in line with Grant's belief Union armies needed to bring the war to the South: "I am very anxious that Thomas should follow up his success to the very utmost point. My orders to him before I left Kingston were, after beating Hood, to follow him as far as Columbus, Mississippi, or Selma, Alabama, both of which lie in districts of country which are rich in corn and meat. I attach more importance to these deep incursions into the enemy's country, because this war differs from European wars in this particular: we are not only fight[ing] hostile armies, but a hostile people, and must make old and young, rich and poor, feel the hard hand of war, as well as their organized armies."[14] As for the fate of South Carolina, Sherman reported that many of the Georgians he had met on his way to Savannah hoped his army would make their neighbors "feel the utmost severities of war." As for himself, "I look upon Columbia as quite as bad as Charleston, and I doubt if we shall spare the public buildings there as we did at Milledgeville."[15]

Sherman had hoped to begin his harrying of South Carolina in January, but a consistent pattern of storms with their accompanying rains blowing in from the Gulf forced a delay. On 1 February with his army reequipped, resupplied, and well rested, Sherman began his march north into South Carolina. He already knew that Grant had ordered Schofield's XXIII Corps detached from Thomas and sent to North Carolina. There, Sherman's advancing troops were to meet them, increasing the size of his army to approximately 90,000. Moreover, at New Bern Sherman could resupply his army with new uniforms and the necessary supplies to continue the campaign. Sherman also possessed a good sense as to the weaknesses of the Confederate forces in front of him. It was not so much the numbers that represented the enemy's weakness, but rather the command structure. In fact, with a portion of what was left of Hood's army being moved to Augusta, the Confederates possessed nearly 25,000 troops, which if they had been united could have offered substantial resistance, especially considering the terrain, flooded as it was by the overflowing of rivers and streams. The real Confederate weakness lay in a divided command and in the depressed morale of the troops. There were three separate commanders in the Carolinas: Hardee responsible for defense of Charleston; G. W. Smith and the wreckage of two corps from the Army of Tennessee (barely 6,000 men) at Augusta; and Bragg at Wilmington, the latter with a record thus far in the war of refusing to cooperate with others and an extraordinary ability to quarrel with his subordinates. Moreover, the Confederate had no clear idea of where Sherman was headed: Augusta, Columbia, and Charleston were all possibilities.

Davis appointed no overall commander for the defense of South Carolina, partially due to the fact that there was no obvious candidate except Johnston, and he was the last choice Davis wanted to make. As a result, there was little focus to South Carolina's defense, and the Confederate generals went their separate ways. As he began his advance, Sherman feinted at both Augusta and Charleston, leaving the Confederates unsure as to his objective until it was too late. When "Black Jack" Logan's XV Corps approached Columbia, his troops discovered that only light cavalry defended South Carolina's capital.

Throughout the march north, continual rains flooded the rivers, turning the wretched road system into a morass. Consistent cold bothered the troops, while the rain and sleet added to their discomfort. But Sherman and his subordinate generals kept their soldiers busy building bridges over flooded streams and rivers, constructing causeways over terrain that was almost always wet and swampy, and in other areas laying out corduroy roads to hold their artillery and supply wagons over the muddy tracks that passed for roads. Passable roads were an absolute necessity because the army was bringing along sixty-four artillery pieces, their ammunition caissons, and 3,000 wagons with ammunition and hard rations.

The recollections of an officer with the 2nd Massachusetts, describing the efforts required to move through the sodden countryside, underline the toughness of Sherman's troops and the difficulties they confronted as they moved toward North Carolina: "A mile from the Lumber River the country, already flooded ankle deep, was rendered still more inhospitable by a steady down-pour of rain. The bridges had been partly destroyed by the enemy, and partly swept away by the flood. An attempt to carry heavy army wagons and artillery across this dreary lake might have seemed rather foolhardy, but we went to work without loss of time. The engineers were promptly floated out to the river, to direct the rebuilding of bridges, and the woods all along the line of each column soon rang with the noise of axes. Trees quickly became logs, and were brought to the submerged roadway. No matter if logs disappeared in the floating mud; thousands more were coming from all sides. So, layer upon layer, the work went bravely on. Soon the artillery and wagons were jolting over our wooden causeway."[16]

Sherman expected his troops would live off the land, although there were some areas where that was going to be impossible. Jokingly, he commented before the march began that if things got desperate, the army could always eat its horses and mules. More often than not the soldiers found themselves waist deep in the cold muck of flooded terrain as they worked to construct roads and bridges through and over waterlogged terrain. The fact that few of Sherman's soldiers got sick during the march north despite appalling weather underlines their hardiness. The conditions of the Mississippi and Tennessee River campaigns had inured his troops to almost any hardship. As Johnston noted to Union officers as they made arrangements for surrendering his army: "when I learned that Sherman's army had not only started, but was marching through [the Salkehatchie] at the rate of thirteen miles a day, making corduroy road every foot of the way, I made up my mind there had been no such army since the days of Julius Cæsar."[17]

Neither weather nor Confederates stopped Sherman's steady advance. Confused by his intentions, Confederate commanders kept their forces divided and thus incapable of defending anything. On 7 February Sherman's bummers reached the South Carolina Railroad, which ran across the state from Augusta to Charleston. The advance columns of the army soon followed. Together, they immediately began ripping up the rails, heating them to the point where they were red hot and malleable, and then twisting them around trees so that they could not be used again. The soldiers termed the twisted results hanging around trees, "Sherman's neckties."

While Sherman's soldiers had spared most of the houses in Georgia, except of course where they had run into resistance, or where there were suggestions owners had run down slaves and escaped Union prisoners, it was different in South Carolina. From the moment Union troops crossed into the state, they made clear their intention to wreak havoc. One soldier described Robertsville after Union troops had finished with it as "a very nice little village but now there is nothing left to mark the place except one hundred 'monuments' [Chimneys] erected in the memory of Jefferson D."[18] Others of Sherman's troops renamed the town of Barnwell, "Burnwell"—an accurate description of its fate. Many came to call their march through South Carolina the "smoky march."

Some soldiers had sympathy for the suffering of civilians and expressed varying degrees of regret for the devastation. But most approved of the punishment they inflicted on South Carolina. One chaplain, obviously well versed in the Old Testament, wrote to his wife: "You know that from the beginning I have advocated the most rigid measures. . . . But on this raid [into South Carolina] my desires have been *more* than gratified, for there is scarcely anything in our *rear* or *trac[k]s* except pine forests and naked lands and Starving inhabitants. A majority of the *Cities, towns, villages* and *county houses* have been burnt to the ground."[19] Another officer, commenting on the destruction, remarked that "I knew it would be so before we entered the state, but I had no idea how frightful the reality would be."[20] What is clear is that the Union campaign through South Carolina came close to resembling the Royal Air Force's Bomber Command's "dehousing" campaign in World War II, although Union troops still spared Confederate civilians their lives. Or, to use Johnston's comparison of Sherman's army to the legions of Rome, Union forces made a desert and called it peace.

Then Union troops arrived at Columbia. On the approach some of the Union troops had even chanted a ditty based on the unofficial national anthem at the time: "Hail Columbia, happy land, if I don't burn you, I'll be damned."[21] The Confederates remained uncertain as to Sherman's objective almost until the last. Attempting to defend both Augusta and Columbia, they defended neither. Nevertheless, their surprise is partially explicable by the fact that Sherman's columns were moving at astonishing speed, given the conditions. From Richmond Davis added to the confusion among the commanders in South Carolina by demanding they hold Charleston for too long, thus robbing Beauregard of the opportunity to concentrate Confederate forces on Columbia.

Almost until the last, the civilians in Columbia felt secure; then suddenly Sherman and his hordes were at their doorstep. The result was a wild panic, which added to the confusion. Someone ordered the cotton bales stored in the warehouses taken out into the open fields and burned. But Sherman's troops arrived so suddenly there was no time to get the bales off the streets, where they had been dumped. There they sat adding to the vulnerability of a town the buildings of which were largely wooden. When the fires had burned themselves out, some Union officers claimed Wade Hampton's cavalry had torched the cotton bales as they fled. However, there is no doubt that Logan's troops, many of whom became roaring drunk, added to whatever fires had already started. Whether Hampton's men had started fires or not is irrelevant. Logan's troops would have burned the town anyway, and if there were fires when they arrived, they delightedly added to them.

Howard made some effort to get his troops to fight the fires, but by then it was too late. Strong winds that blew embers, sparks, and burning cotton balls from one dwelling to another, turned Columbia into a raging inferno by nightfall.

Sherman's comment after the war was that, "the burning of the private dwellings, though never designed by me, was a trifling matter compared with the manifold results that soon followed. Though I never ordered it and never wished it, I have never shed many tears over the event, because I believe it hastened what we all fought for, the end of the war."[22] If perhaps the damage was excessive even by the standards his soldiers had established thus far in their march through South Carolina, it certainly fit within the context of the war Grant and Sherman were waging. In his memoirs Sherman admitted that he deliberately blamed the Confederates and Hampton for setting fire to Columbia in order "to shake the faith of his people in him, for he was in my opinion a braggart, and professed to be the special champion of South Carolina."[23]

The sun had barely risen on the burned wreckage of South Carolina's capital on 18 February, before Logan's corps began its march out of the city. The right wing of Sherman's forces under Howard moved toward Winnsboro, where the left wing under Slocum was waiting. After a few short days of relatively good weather, the rains came again. Such was the flooding of the Catawba River that the Union XIV Corps under Major General Jefferson Davis found itself stuck on the river's south bank for nearly a week until his engineers and troops could construct a new bridge. That halted the advance, but the Confederates were in no position to take advantage of Davis's vulnerability, because the weather hindered their movements as much as it did Sherman's. Moreover, the Confederate president was still unwilling to create a unified command structure to handle Sherman's advance. By early March Sherman had turned to the northeast to move against Wilmington and the Cape Fear River, where he knew that Grant had placed Schofield's XIII Corps and a complete resupply for his weary troops.

As Sherman approached Cheraw, he interviewed an African American about the best road to take and whether there were any guerrillas up ahead. The freedman replied: "Oh! no master, dey is gone two days ago; you could have played cards on der coat-tails, dey was in sich a hurry!"[24] At Cheraw, Sherman was able to sample some of the outstanding wines that Blair's corps had captured—a supply that wealthy denizens of Charleston had sent north for safekeeping. While the wine was superb, Sherman was not amused to discover a copy of the *New York Tribune*, in which one of the editorial writers commented "that General Sherman should next be heard from about Goldsboro', because his supply-vessels from Savannah were known to be rendez-vousing at Morehead City."[25] Nor could Sherman have been any happier to discover while he was at Cheraw waiting to cross the Pedee River that Johnston was back in the saddle again, having received command of Confederate forces in the Carolinas. That appointment meant that Sherman was up against his old nemesis and that the Confederate forces he now confronted would have first-class leadership. Once Union troops crossed into North Carolina the mass destruction of property ceased, although one could hardly characterize the actions of Sherman's hard-nosed veterans as pacific.

By the time his troops arrived in Goldsboro on 23 March to meet Schofield's corps, Sherman's troops had marched more than 425 miles in a little more than a month and a half. Sherman put the accomplishment of his army in simple terms: "the route traversed embraced five large navigable rivers, viz., the Edisto, Broad, Catawba, Pedee, and Cape Fear, at either of which a comparatively small force, well handled, should have made the passage most difficult, if not impossible. The country was generally in a state of nature, with innumerable swamps, with simply mud roads, nearly every mile of which had to be corduroyed. In our route we had captured Columbia, Cheraw, and Fayetteville, important cities and depots of supplies, had compelled the evacuation of Charleston City and Harbor, had utterly broken up the railroads of South Carolina, and had consumed a vast amount of food and forage, essential to the enemy for the support of his own armies. We had in mid-winter accomplished the whole journey of four hundred and twenty-five miles in fifty days, and had reached Goldsboro' with the army in superb order."[26]

Our account of Sherman's 1865 campaign through South Carolina contained little fighting, because there was little. It was rather an account of a military effort to break the will of the Confederate people by every means except slaughtering them wholesale. Grant and Sherman did not intend these efforts just as a measure of revenge for South Carolina's role in sparking the conflict, although such thinking certainly figured in the actions of Union soldiers. Rather, the *chevauchée* that wrecked South Carolina was part of the larger strategic aim of underlining the compelling power of Northern military force.[27] Nevertheless, South Carolina had paid a terrible price. As a junior officer in a Michigan regiment noted as he left the state: "South Carolina may have been the cause of the whole thing, but she has had an awful punishment."[28]

The Harrying of the South

It was not until March and after Sherman had completed his epic campaign through South Carolina that the other pieces of the Union's military strategy moved forward. Grant had hoped these efforts would support Sherman's drive through South Carolina, but they started so late that Sherman had completed his destruction of the Palmetto State by the time they began. Canby possessed 45,000 men for his drive on Mobile, but he had spent January and February building up the logistical infrastructure for his army, including the construction of seventy miles of railroad. It was of considerable annoyance to Grant, but he was not on the scene. For a short period he thought about sending Sheridan to New Orleans to handle the situation, but then realized he needed the Irishman close at hand.

To make matters worse, Canby ended up quarreling with Grant over the selection of the commanders for the two wings of his army. It was bad enough that he appointed Major Gordon Granger to command one wing, but Grant was not about to allow the appointment of Canby's other nominee, "Baldy" Smith, a major disappointment in the 1864 campaign. In no uncertain terms, Canby was told that "Baldy" would remain on the shelf, while Major General A. J. Smith would command the column. A third force under Major General Frederick Steele was to move on Mobile from Pensacola. A thoroughly annoyed Grant made clear the purposes for which Canby was to conduct his attack on Mobile well after Sherman had wrecked most of South Carolina: "I wrote to you long ago, urging you to push promptly and to live upon the country, and destroy railroads, machine shops, etc., not to build them. . . . Destroy railroads, rolling stock, and everything useful for carrying on war.[29]

In retrospect, Canby was a first-rate administrator, but not a thruster. Grant, who was sharply perceptive in evaluating his subordinate commanders, characterized Canby in the following terms:

"General Canby was an officer of great merit. He was naturally studi-
ous, and inclined to the law. . . . His knowledge . . . made him a most
valuable staff officer. . . . I presume his feelings when first called upon
to command a large army against a fortified city, were somewhat like
my own when marching a regiment against General Thomas Harris in
Missouri in 1861. Neither of us would have felt the slightest trepidation in going into battle with someone else commanding."[30]

The move on Mobile did not start until 20 March, and then despite the fact Union strength was more than four times that of the
Confederate defenders, Canby's army moved with exquisite slowness.
It was not until 26 March that his troops began attacks on the city's
outer defenses. After investing the two major Confederate defensive
positions guarding the city, Spanish Fort and Fort Blakely, Union
troops, including a substantial number of African Americans, stormed
the forts on 8 and 9 April respectively. Losses were heavy. Three days
later Union troops took control of Mobile, but Canby had contributed little to Grant's overall strategy, because of his failure to move
in February, when he was supposed to. According to Grant's original
conception, Canby's army was to advance on and take the important
arsenal and manufacturing center of Selma after seizing Montgomery.
However, due to Canby's slowness, Selma would fall to Union forces
advancing from the north.

While Canby was proving dilatory, Grant was not surprised to discover that Thomas was almost as slow in preparing his forces for a
move across the Tennessee River into northern Alabama. There, they
were to complete the destruction of the Army of Tennessee and the
northern and central portions of Alabama. Forrest, now promoted to
lieutenant general for his exceptional service, led those whom Hood
had failed to kill and what remained after Beauregard had siphoned
off troops to help in the defense of South Carolina. At Grant's direction Thomas prepared two great raids out of Tennessee, the smaller
led by Stoneman to retrace the route of his December raid into southwestern Virginia; the second and major effort under Grant's favorite,
Wilson, to smash into northern and central Alabama to eliminate the
perennial problem of Forrest, while at the same time wrecking one of
the few areas of the South as of yet untouched by the hard war. Stoneman's raid eventually ended up in Salisbury, North Carolina, where he
would capture Pemberton, who had surrendered Vicksburg to Grant
two years earlier, now holding the rank of a lowly lieutenant colonel.

Stoneman would destroy much of the infrastructure in the area before turning back to Tennessee.

Wilson's raid was to be more substantial and destructive. The cavalry commander had been busy throughout the winter months in finishing the job Grant had sent him west to do—namely, to reform, re-equip, and retrain the Western cavalry. Included in that effort was the rearming of Wilson's troopers with repeating rifles, which provided them with a decided firepower advantage over their Confederate opponents. It also meant that they now had the firepower to stand up to any infantry formations they ran into. Thomas's initial plan had been for a combined infantry-cavalry army to move against Forrest. But now impressed with what Wilson had done with the cavalry, Thomas decided to unleash the cavalry in an independent raid aimed at not only reaching Selma and Tuscaloosa but also at driving on to Alabama's capital of Montgomery and finishing up at Columbus, Georgia.

Immediately before Wilson launched south, one of his staff officers met with Forrest under a flag of truce to discuss a prisoner exchange. Forrest's comment on the coming clash of cavalry was that: "Jist tell General Wilson that I know the nicest little place down below here in the world, and whenever he is ready I will fight him with any number from one to ten thousand cavalry and abide the issue. Gin'ral Wilson may pick his men and I'll pick mine. He may take his sabers and I'll take my six-shooters. I don't want nary a saber in my command—haven't got one."[31] Forrest had every right to be optimistic, given his record against previous Union cavalry commanders, but now he was no longer just a raiding cavalry commander but held the responsibility for defending northern and central Mississippi and Alabama. New to such responsibility, he divided his forces, perhaps calculating that once again Union commanders would move with their usual slowness. But that deployment made little sense, if the Confederates were to disrupt Union efforts to break into the last bastion of undestroyed territory the Confederacy possessed; rather, they needed a concentrated force. In fact, once he launched southward, Wilson moved with great speed, and Forrest was never able to recover, as advancing Union forces defeated his units piecemeal.

Rains and bad weather delayed Wilson, and he did not begin his drive until 22 March. In every respect Wilson's command represented a force far superior to anything that Forrest and his men had yet encountered. The Union general accurately described his command as "in magnificent condition, splendidly mounted, perfectly clad and equipped."[32] Beside the quality of the men, Wilson had an outstanding group of division commanders, including Upton, promoted to division command after his impressive performance in the East. Once started, the Union cavalry moved swiftly. Over the first five days Wilson's troopers covered over one hundred miles. Having crossed the Black Warrior River, Wilson detached 1,800 soldiers under Brigadier General John Croxton, the son of a Southern plantation owner and Yale graduate, to strike west toward Tuscaloosa. Croxton's raiding party not only smashed up the town but also, much like Grierson's raid two years before, thoroughly confused the Confederates as to the main objective of Wilson's raiding force. Croxton would not rejoin Wilson for thirty days after an epic ride that covered 653 miles, destroyed much of Tuscaloosa—"making a complete wreck of the place"[33]—and ripped up railroad tracks wherever they found them.

Meanwhile, Wilson had continued his drive toward Selma. After crossing the Cahaba River, his troopers abandoned most of their wagons to speed up their advance. On 31 March, they ran into Forrest's outnumbered troopers; after a sharp skirmish near the town of Montevallo, Upton's division broke the Confederate line and sent Forrest and his soldiers scurrying southward. Capturing a courier on their way, Union forces gained a clear idea of the location of Forrest's dispositions as well as Confederate intentions. On 1 April Forrest again attempted to halt Wilson's advance on Selma, but Union forces had destroyed the bridges to the west at Centreville, thus preventing two of Forrest's divisions from joining up with their commander. Again, Upton's troopers proved decisive in breaking the Confederate lines. The pursuit took Union cavalry all the way to Selma.

The city's defenses should have proved sufficient to hold Wilson, but again Union troops achieved a considerable coup. One of the engineers responsible for designing the city's defenses fell into Union hands and, indicative of the collapse of Confederate morale, willingly sketched out their design. After some heavy fighting, made more difficult by the eruption of Confederate riders attempting to fight their way into the city from the north, Union cavalrymen drove into the city. Forrest's force collapsed, an indication of the weakening of Confederate morale. A portion of the victorious troops, aided by newly freed former slaves, torched Selma in spite of Wilson's efforts. Over succeeding days, the victors carried out extensive demolitions of the city's manufacturing infrastructure. After destroying the arsenal along with a number of other industrial establishments, including the iron-works and a powder mill, Wilson moved on to Montgomery, which his troopers occupied on the fourth anniversary of the bombardment of Fort Sumter. Three days later Union cavalrymen reached Columbus, Georgia. On the 20th, they occupied Macon, where they discovered that Johnston had surrendered the troops under his command, includ-ing those facing Wilson.

There in Macon, Wilson, utilizing Confederate telegraph, received orders from Sherman at Raleigh confirming the Confederate surren-der and informing him, "You will therefore desist from further acts of war and devastation."[34] That phrase underlines the fundamental purpose for which Wilson had been unleashed. In the pursuit of that objective, his cavalry force had been eminently successful. At a cost of only ninety-nine men killed, 598 wounded, and twenty-eight miss-ing, they had destroyed: "seven iron works, seven foundries, two roll-ing mills, seven collieries, 13 large factories, two nitre [sic] works, a military college, three C.S.A. arsenals, a powder magazine, a naval armory, two gunboats, 35 locomotives and 565 cars, several railroad depots and bridges, 235,000 bales of cotton," and considerable other military equipment.[35] They had also ripped up whatever railroad tracks they crossed to add further to the devastation of the infrastructure in northern and central Alabama.

The End in North Carolina

The continuing dissatisfaction with Davis's conduct of the war reached the boiling point in Richmond, as the end drew close. In mid-January 1865 the Confederate Congress passed a bill naming Lee as the com-mander in chief. Incorporated in the bill was a recommendation that Johnston return to command of the Army of Tennessee, a direct slap in the face of the Confederate president. Davis had no difficulty in appointing Lee to the honorific post of general in chief, because he knew that Lee had not had the slightest desire to run the whole war. But as to appointing Johnston, Davis drew the line. In fact, he spent a good deal of time in February drawing up a 4,000 word memoran-dum, detailing Johnston's extensive faults. He particularly empha-sized what he regarded as the general's greatest failing, his supposed unwillingness to fight. He concluded with the comment: "My opinion of General Johnston's unfitness for command has ripened slowly and against my inclinations into a conviction so settled that it would be impossible for me again to feel confidence in him as the commander of an army in the field."[36]

Barely a week later, Davis, however, appointed Johnston to command virtually everything east of the Mississippi with the exception of Lee's army defending Richmond and Petersburg. Johnston was not exactly enthralled. He believed at first that Davis had appointed him as a means to saddle him with the task of surrendering the forces in North Carolina. In fact, that was not Davis's intention, since the president believed the Confederacy should continue the struggle. Rather, it appears that Davis realized that Johnston was the only general outside Lee—and Lee was obviously not available—who could bring some coherence to the defense of North Carolina and that instinctively the soldiers would rally to him, given his popularity. For once, Davis placed the cause above his personal animosities. Yet, it is also astonishing, given the threat Sherman had posed in Savannah in January, that Davis had failed to nominate Johnston to take charge of the defense of South Carolina, when there was some hope of using the flooded rivers and terrain to defend the state.

Johnston assumed his new command at Charlotte on 25 February. He was not in an enviable situation. His subordinates hardly formed an effective team. Both D. H. Hill and Hardee held a deep dislike, bordering on hatred, of Bragg, a dislike more than justified by their past experience with that divisive, quarrelsome officer. Moreover, numerous other general officers, most without commands or with commands that had shrunk to the size of battalions, had arrived in Johnston's area of responsibility. In fact, Johnston had under him no less than two full generals (Bragg and Beauregard); three lieutenant generals (Hardee, Stewart, and Hampton, plus S. D. Lee not recovered from wounds suffered after Nashville); fourteen major generals; and too many brigadier generals to count. As Mary Chesnut observed, North Carolina seemed overrun with generals, but with precious few soldiers.

On 11 March Sherman's advance parties reached Fayetteville. The troops, under close discipline in North Carolina, had had to amuse their arsonist tendencies by slicing open the pine trees and then setting them afire. On the next day they made contact with a steamboat sent upriver by Schofield. Schofield's two corps, increased by two divisions, now numbered some 30,000 men, which provided Sherman with some 90,000 soldiers—more than sufficient to handle Johnston and Lee, should the latter escape Grant's clutches. Sherman then ordered the XXIII Corps to New Bern to open up the Wilmington & Weldon Railroad for a complete resupply of shoes and uniforms for his soldiers, who even by the standards of the Western armies were looking bedraggled. Sherman left Fayetteville in relatively good shape to join Schofield, but he did have the US arsenal destroyed. As he informed Stanton: "This arsenal is in fine order, and has been much enlarged. I cannot leave a detachment to hold it, therefore shall burn it, blow it up with gunpowder, and then with rams knock down its walls. I take it for granted the United States will never again trust North Carolina with an arsenal to appropriate at her pleasure."[37]

In the desperate situation confronting the Confederacy, Johnston acted aggressively. In many respects his efforts in March and early April 1865 resembled those of Napoleon during the emperor's last-ditch efforts to save his throne in early 1814. But as with Napoleon, considering the disparity in numbers, the best the Confederates could hope for were local tactical successes. Despite the fact that Sherman held overwhelming numbers on his front, Johnston, with fewer than 25,000 soldiers at his disposal, moved to support Bragg. He sent Bragg 3,000 soldiers, who had recently arrived from the wreckage of the Army of Tennessee. On 8 March Bragg attacked one of Schofield's corps, moving from New Bern and repairing the railroad as it advanced toward its coming junction with Sherman. By this point, Union commanders were getting sloppy. With no reconnaissance, Cox's division received a bloody nose; altogether it lost over 1,000 prisoners, before Schofield moved the rest of his corps up to fight Bragg to a standstill. Confederate casualties were only 134. The Battle of Kinston was a warning that the fight was not yet out of the Confederates. Having achieved a minor tactical success, Bragg followed his orders and sent most of his troops back to Johnston.

For his part, Johnston prepared a major counterattack in the hope of crushing part of Sherman's army before it could unite with Schofield. Sherman himself was aware that he was now up against a general of considerable competence and that the vacation ride against incompetent, badly led forces was over. On 12 March, in the process of leaving Fayetteville, he wrote Terry who was still at Wilmington: "We have swept the country well from Savannah here, and my men and animals are in fine condition. . . . We must not lose time for Joe Johnston to concentrate at Goldsborough. We cannot prevent his concentrating at Raleigh, but he shall have no rest. . . . I can whip Joe Johnston provided he don't catch one of my corps in flank, and I will see that my army marches hence to Goldsborough in compact form."[38]

Uniting the various Confederate pieces, Johnston prepared a trap for Sherman's left wing, a force of two corps under the command of Henry Slocum, who had had such an undistinguished career with the Army of the Potomac. But since he had come west in September 1863, Slocum had recovered his reputation under Sherman's tutelage. Hardee informed Johnston that the two wings of Sherman's army were at least a day's march apart and that heavy rains had resulted in considerable straggling as well as separation among advancing Union forces. With that intelligence, Johnston concentrated his small forces near Bentonville. Early on the morning of 19 March, he had ridden the lines to be greeted by enthusiastic cheers from the few remaining veterans of the Army of Tennessee. Unfortunately for the Confederates, Hardee was late in arriving. By that time Union pressure had forced the Confederates on the scene to attack.

On 19 March, as Slocum's lead division advanced toward Goldsboro, it had run into a screen of Confederate cavalry and infantry under Bragg. Misinformed by a Union cavalry officer who had escaped from the Confederates that Johnston's main force was still at Raleigh, Slocum and his division commanders pushed forward without reconnaissance. As the initial skirmish unfolded, Slocum believed that "the only force in my front to consist of cavalry with a few pieces of artillery,"[39] and informed Sherman accordingly.

But as the fighting heated up, a deserter informed Slocum that Johnston had concentrated his army of 40,000 men in the neighborhood with the aim of crushing the flank corps of the Union army. While the numbers were nearly twice what the Confederates had available, the intelligence was sufficient to cause Slocum to pull his lead division back, while speeding up his other divisions to deploy in defensive positions. That and the hurried move forward of the other units of Slocum's two corps brought the Confederate advance to a halt. Nevertheless, Confederate commanders persisted in attacking throughout the day. By the time evening ended the Battle of Bentonville, the Confederates had suffered 2,606 casualties, while Slocum's divisions had lost 1,646 men.

Surprisingly, Johnston remained in position the next day despite the fact that Slocum possessed more soldiers with his two corps than the whole Confederate army. Moreover, Sherman was hurrying forward with Howard's two corps, which would provide Union forces with overwhelming superiority. By noon Howard's first divisions were arriving. Nevertheless, Johnston remained a third day. Not until late on that afternoon did Major General John Mower, division commander on the Union right, attack with his division without orders. His attack broke through the Confederate lines. On the brink of capturing the single bridge that secured the only escape route for the Confederates, Mower found himself and his division recalled. In the fighting that day, Hardee had allowed his sixteen-year-old son to participate. Wounded in the fighting, the boy died three days later. By then Johnston had pulled back, faced with the reality that as Schofield's corps approached from New Bern, Sherman had nearly 90,000 men under his control.

Johnston's one hope was that somehow Lee could pull the Army of Northern Virginia out of Richmond and Petersburg and by moving quickly unite with the remaining forces in North Carolina to defeat Sherman before Grant could reach the scene. But he recognized the small forces under his command were in a hopeless situation. As he wrote Lee, "Sherman's course cannot be hindered by the small force I have. I can do no more than annoy him."[40] But there was to be no union of Confederate forces under Lee and Johnston, because events in Virginia would soon remove that possibility. In fact, by the end of March, Sherman was approximately 150 miles from Richmond, in other words, within striking distance for an army that had already covered over 400 miles since the beginning of February.

End Game: Richmond to Appomattox

Not long after the Battle of Bentonville and the union of his two forces with Schofield's two corps, Sherman departed from North Carolina. Taking advantage of the need to refit and rest his troops after their exhausting campaign in South Carolina, he left his reinforced army under Schofield. He made his way to meet up with Lincoln, Grant, and Porter at City Point to plot out the war's last moves. In an extended conversation the four men discussed how to bring the war to a successful close. Both Grant and Sherman suggested that there would inevitably be one last great battle. Lincoln asked: "Must more blood be shed? Cannot this last bloody battle be avoided?"[41] Sherman suggested that events were beyond their control, and he believed Davis and Lee would make a last desperate throw of the dice before the matter concluded. Furthermore, Sherman expected that Lee would escape Grant's clutches and that it would fall to his army to defeat what remained of the Confederate armies. Grant demurred and indicated the Army of the Potomac would move against Lee in the near future and finish the Army of Northern Virginia in its home state. At the least, Meade's soldiers would be immediately on Lee's heels should the Confederates escape from the siege of Richmond and Petersburg.

Throughout the meetings, Lincoln expressed worry about Sherman's absence from his army. As the general was departing, "the last words I recall as addressed to me [by the president] were that he would feel better when I was back at Goldsboro. We parted on the gangway of the *River Queen*, about noon on March 28th, and I never saw him again. Of all the men I ever met, he seemed to possess more of the elements of greatness, combined with goodness, than any other."[42] Grant and Sherman parted immediately thereafter, the former to destroy the Army of Northern Virginia, the latter to destroy Johnston's army.

As spring approached, the pressure Grant and Meade applied to the Army of Northern Virginia became increasingly intolerable for Lee's forces, stretched ever thinner by a steady toll of casualties and deserters, "wastage" in terms of the Western Front fifty years later. By February Lee understood that he needed to abandon Richmond and Petersburg and move south to join Johnston. His hope was that the two remnants of the once great armies would have time to unite and crush Sherman before turning back to destroy Grant. To gain time, Lee prepared a strike at the Union lines surrounding Petersburg. The aim was to inflict sufficient damage to distract Grant's attention. The Confederate president later wrote in his memoirs that the proposed stroke was one to "delay the impending disaster for the more convenient season for retreat."[43]

Lee designated Lieutenant General John Gordon, perhaps the foremost combat commander in Confederate ranks, to lead the assault. Gordon is of particular interest because, like Forrest and Hampton, he was one of the few non–West Pointers to attain high rank in the Confederate army. He had started the war as a captain and company

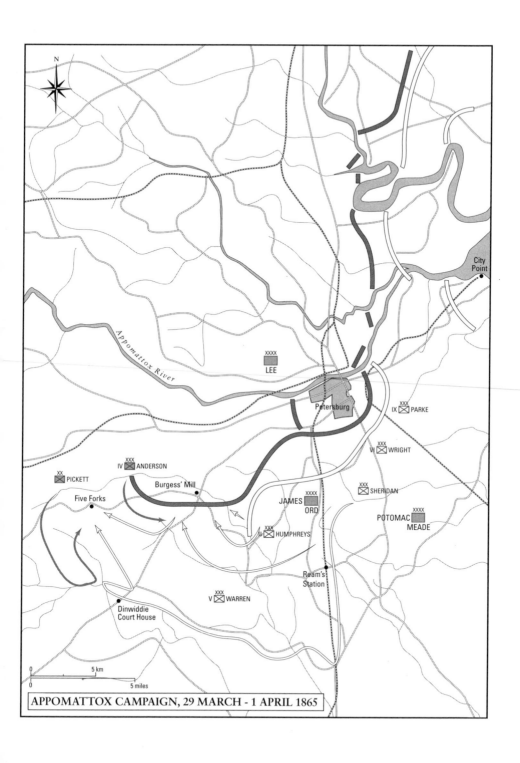

N

City Point

Appomattox River

XXXX
LEE

Petersburg

IX ⊠ PARKE
XXX

VI ⊠ WRIGHT
XXX

XX
⊠ PICKETT

IV ⊠ ANDERSON
XXX

Burgess' Mill

Five Forks

⊠ SHERIDAN
XXX

JAMES XXXX
ORD

POTOMAC XXXX
MEADE

II ⊠ HUMPHREYS
XXX

Ream's
Station

V ⊠ WARREN
XXX

Dinwiddie
Court House

0   5 km
0   5 miles

APPOMATTOX CAMPAIGN, 29 MARCH - 1 APRIL 1865

commander, commanded the 6th Alabama at Antietam where he had participated in the defense of "Bloody Lane," led a brigade of Georgians at Gettysburg and a division in the 1864 campaigns, and now at the end of the war had risen to corps command.

Lee scratched together a force by denuding the defenses holding the perimeter around Petersburg. In the end he gathered a force of 12,000 infantrymen with a cavalry division under his son, Rooney Lee, to exploit a breakthrough. The target of the Confederate attack was Fort Stedman. Gordon planned to have a picked group of engineers remove the abatis that lay in the front works of the fort. A second group of picked men were to seize three smaller forts to the rear and turn the artillery pieces of the Union positions to the left and right, while the main infantry force smashed into the Yankee rear. In particular, the attacking Confederates were to destroy the railroad west of City Point, which was Grant's logistical tether. The attack, if successful, would not directly endanger Grant's center and left wing, but it would certainly delay a further buildup for Union forces preparing to break out to the west. It was an audacious plan but depended on flawless intelligence, swift execution, and the Army of the Potomac to react in its usual lackadaisical fashion.

At 0400 on 25 March, the Confederates attacked. In their first rush, they stormed Fort Stedman with little difficulty, but then everything came apart. They discovered there were no positions with artillery pieces to the rear of the fort, Union batteries to the east and west of Stedman put up stout resistance with devastating artillery fire, and for once the officers and soldiers of the Army of the Potomac acted with dispatch. As was so often to occur in the First World War, an initial tactical success degenerated into a killing zone, where the attackers became the helpless targets of artillery fire. It was all over by 0800, the Confederates having suffered 3,500 casualties to 1,000 for the defenders. Lee had attempted to gain the initiative and had lost it in a matter of hours.

Lincoln had arrived shortly after the collapse of Gordon's attack to meet with his senior commanders. Informed by his son, Robert Lincoln, a captain on Grant's staff, of Gordon's defeat, the president asked to see the battlefield. Even more than his view of the rebuff of Early's raid on Washington from Fort Stevens in July 1864, Lincoln saw the carnage of war firsthand. Thus, after bidding the president adieu, Grant and his staff turned west. Sheridan and his cavalry, refurbished and refreshed from their return from the Shenandoah Valley, had already moved out to the far west of Union lines. At the end of February Sheridan and his cavalry had smashed Early's pitiful force of 2,000 men at Waynesboro. At the time Grant's instructions had been for the Irishman to move on Lynchburg and then on into North Carolina to join Sherman. But Sheridan had no intention of leaving the Virginia theater. When he arrived back with the Army of the Potomac, he claimed that the rivers and streams were too high and that he had been forced to turn east through the Blue Ridge to occupy Charlottesville and return to the Army of the Potomac. More honestly, he admitted in his memoirs that "feeling that the war was nearing an end, I desired my cavalry to be in at the death."[44]

In his succinct fashion Grant had already issued orders on 24 March, the day before Gordon's attack, to his subordinate commanders: "On the 29th instant the armies operating against Richmond will be moved by our left, for the double purpose of turning the enemy out of his present position around Petersburg and to insure the success of the cavalry under General Sheridan, which will start at the same time, in its efforts to reach and destroy the South Side and Danville Railroads."[45] The lead two corps of the Army of the Potomac were to advance as rapidly as possible to support Sheridan's drive toward Dinwiddie Court House. When he issued his orders, Grant had foreseen the possibility Lee might attack first, but by the time the movement began, the Army of the Potomac had beaten back Gordon's attack.

To Sheridan, Grant had been clear in his instructions as to what he expected the Irishman to accomplish: "I mean to end this business here."[46] And that was a sentiment with which Sheridan was in full agreement. On 29 March the Army of the Potomac's move to the west began. Ord's corps of four divisions moved south from the Army of the James to replace the six divisions of Warren's V Corps and Andrew Humphreys's II Corps. The initial move almost immediately ran into heavy rains that slowed matters to a crawl. It was not, however, sufficient to stop Grant's advance. On 29 March, echoing his earlier conversation, Grant ordered Sheridan: "I now feel like ending the matter, if it is possible to do so, before going back. I do not want you, therefore, to cut loose and go after the enemy's roads at present. In the morning push around the enemy, if you can, and get on to his right rear. . . . We will act all together as one army here until it is seen what can be done with the enemy."[47] Thus, the aim of operations was not just to cut the railroad lines supporting the Army of Northern Virginia in Richmond and Petersburg, but rather to accomplish the destruction of the Confederate army. Still, the advance through difficult terrain and over terrible roads in pelting rain was agonizingly slow. On 30 March in his rain-soaked headquarters, Grant considered pulling Sheridan back, but the Irishman, riding back through the rain, persuaded his boss the advance should continue.

Grant now gave Sheridan authority over Warren's V Corps to insure that it would move to secure Five Forks and get around Lee's flank. But once again Lee's sixth sense of what his opponent would do was at work. Recognizing that the reports of scouts that Union cavalry was working its way toward Dinwiddie Court House presaged a larger move to get around his flank, Lee sent Pickett with two infantry divisions and substantial cavalry—over 10,000 soldiers—to secure the vital road junction at Five Forks and insure Union forces would not reach the Southside Railroad.

On 31 March Pickett's soldiers gave Brigadier General Thomas Devin's cavalry division a mauling and drove it back from Five Forks. In the midst of heavy rain, the Confederates administered an even nastier shock to Warren's V Corps, which, seemingly without a care, was marching along, strung out along the muddy Virginia roads as if it had nothing to fear from the Army of Northern Virginia. Pickett's soldiers caught the V Corps by surprise and routed two of Warren's divisions, which, having made no preparations to meet a Confederate attack, departed rapidly for the rear. The Confederate attack, launched by 5,000 soldiers against Warren's 15,000, only came to a halt when it ran into the Union corps' third division, which soldiers from Humphreys's II Corps had to buttress. Union casualties were nearly 2,000. It was not a good show. Bruce Catton described the skirmish in his inimitable fashion: "the poorly handled many beaten by the well-handled few."[48] But it was to be the last of the successes won by the soldiers of the Army of Northern Virginia.

In fact, Sheridan was so unhappy with Warren's performance that he sent a message to Grant suggesting that Wright's VI Corps move forward to replace the V Corps. Given the distances, that was not possible. Grant was even less pleased. In a message to Meade, he queried: "If the enemy has been checked in Warren's front, what is to prevent him from pitching in with his whole corps and attacking before giving him time to entrench or return in good order to his old entrenchments?

I do not understand why Warren permitted his whole corps to be fought in detail. When Ayers [the first division commander to be over-run] was pushed forward he [Warren] should have sent other troops to their support."[49] Grant also provided the authority for Sheridan to fire Warren, if Warren failed to act with dispatch.

In conversation with Warren on the evening of 31 March, it was certainly Sheridan's impression that he had conveyed to the V Corps commander the absolute need for speed on the next morning so that the combined infantry/cavalry force could pitch into Pickett at Five Forks and crush the Confederates. With over 50,000 infantrymen and cavalry, the latter equipped with Spencers and trained to fight as in-fantry, Sheridan had every expectation of victory on the next day, whatever the initial setbacks. He certainly expected that Warren with his corps would be ready on the next morning, April Fool's Day.

But Warren was not ready. It was not until midday the V Corps' lead division began to arrive, while the corps commander was back with the last division. By now Sheridan was furious. To make matters worse, Sheridan found Warren less than enthusiastic about the pros-pects of launching an attack before the day was over. When Sheridan suggested that the V Corps was in a position to strike Pickett's left flank and rear and put the whole Confederate force in the bag, War-ren demurred. Sheridan suggested in his memoirs: "Warren did not seem at all solicitous; his manner exhibited decided apathy, and he remarked with indifference that 'Bobby Lee was always getting people into trouble.'"[50] And then as if the V Corps were practicing for a slow-motion film, it took Warren and his division commanders nearly three hours to deploy their troops over a distance of some two miles. The infantry of the V Corps was finally ready to go into action at 1600.

One of the ironies of Warren's exceedingly slow deployment was that Pickett and his cavalry commander, Fitzhugh Lee, Robert E. Lee's nephew, decided there was little chance the Federals would attack. As a result, in the early afternoon they accepted an invitation to feast on a meal of shad caught in one of the creeks in their rear. To top their irresponsibility, or perhaps their contempt for their opponent's lack of aggressiveness, they neglected to tell their subordinates where they were going. Caught flatfooted by a sudden, massed attack of Union infantry and cavalrymen, there was no one among the Confederates in overall charge of the defense. Exacerbating the situation was the fact that a pine forest muted the sound of the Union assault. Pickett and Rooney Lee only discovered what was happening when groups of Confederate soldiers came scurrying past them headed for the rear.

Still, even with the advantage of surprise, the V Corps came close to botching the attack. Only the left-hand division set off in the correct direction. The middle division eventually sorted itself out and changed direction to join the fight, arriving in time to lap the Confederate line and break into Pickett's rear. Warren eventually caught up with his third division and reported to Sheridan that he was deep in the Confederate rear. Sheridan's reaction was pure Sheridan. He told Warren's messenger: "By G—, sir, tell General Warren he wasn't in the fight."[51] With that he fired Warren as corps commander and replaced him with crusty Major General Charles Griffin. There was, not surprisingly, an outcry throughout the army's officer corps, especially given the role that Warren had played at Gettysburg. In retrospect, the Army of the Potomac would have been a more effective combat force had its commanders been willing to exercise their authority over their subordinates and remove those who failed in the hard test of combat. Or been willing to recognize that Warren, like "Baldy" Smith, was a superb chief engineer on a staff, but ill suited to serve as a corps commander.

Sherman put matters in his usual unambiguous fashion after the war: "It would be an unsafe and dangerous rule to hold the commander of an army in battle to a technical adherence to any rule of conduct for managing his command. He is responsible for results, and holds the lives and reputations of every officer and soldier under his orders as subordinate to the great end—victory. The most important events are usually compressed into an hour, a minute, and he cannot stop to analyze his reasons. He must act on impulse, the conviction, of the instant, and should be sustained in his conclusions, if not manifestly unjust. The power to command men, and give vehement impulse to their joint action, is something which cannot be defined by words, but it is plain and manifest in battles, and whoever commands an army in chief must choose his subordinates by reason of qualities which can alone be tested in actual conflict." Then, he reached the crucial point. "No one has questioned the patriotism, integrity, and great intelligence of General Warren . . . but in the clash of arms at and near Five Forks, March 31 and April 1, 1865, his personal activity fell short of the standard fixed by General Sheridan, on whom alone rested the great responsibility for that and succeeding days."[52] War is not a popularity contest, a game of good sportsmanship where one takes care of those who have contributed in the past. Military organizations must always be prepared to ask the cold, hard question: "what have you done for me lately," as Major General James Mattis, commander of the 1st Marine Division, asked his regimental commanders in the invasion of Iraq in 2003. And it was precisely in that unwillingness to remove those who failed in which so much of the Army of the Potomac's weaknesses had lain.

Five Forks was a great success for the Army of the Potomac. By early evening on 1 April 1865, Sheridan's attacking forces had completely smashed Pickett's divisions. By evening, the Union commander was reporting to Grant that his soldiers had captured nearly 5,000 prisoners. By morning Pickett was able to assemble barely 2,000 infantry out of the 10,000 men Lee had given him to defend Five Forks. It is, however, worth noting that Five Forks represented only the second victory in the long and troublesome history of the Army of the Potomac, Gettysburg being the first. Even then, Warren's tardy approach almost prevented Sheridan from using the numbers available.

Had the officers of the Army of the Potomac missed that wonderful opportunity that loomed on 1 April, it is entirely conceivable Pickett would have held Five Forks sufficiently long for the rest of the Army of Northern Virginia to escape from the trenches protecting Richmond and Petersburg. But Sheridan was a sufficiently ruthless driver to insure the V Corps would do its job, even if it meant firing its commander. What was clear was that the Confederates had suffered a grievous defeat, more than enough to make up for the bloody nose that the V Corps had suffered the day before. Grant immediately ordered an attack across the entire line of Confederate trenches defending Petersburg.

Union artillery opened up with a massive bombardment of Confederate lines on the night of 1/2 April. At 0400, 2 April, Union infantry surged across no-man's land and began to break into and through the Confederate defensive system. Lee had already lost nearly a quarter of his army in the attack on Fort Stedman and Pickett's defeat the day before. Simply put, the Army of Northern Virginia was now stretched too tightly to hold, and in a number of places it broke. On the Richmond front, the Army of the James made significant penetrations, but the real crack came with the breakthrough by Wright's VI Corps along Hill's lines. At the moment the break occurred, Lee, Longstreet, and Hill were conferring about a potential Union attack, when the weight of the Union offensive broke on them. As teamsters and shirkers began to appear moving rapidly to the rear, Hill galloped off to take control of the situation, only to be shot down by Union skirmishers who had advanced behind Confederate lines.

Lee immediately sent a dispatch off to Davis to alert his president that the moment they had dreaded had arrived. The Confederate government was going to have to abandon Richmond. The message came in the midst of services at St. Paul's Church. Davis hurriedly left. There then began a desperate flight from the city, involving attempts to get as much of the government, its finances, and its records out of the city as possible, while at the same time destroying anything of use to the enemy. A combination of the breakdown of law and order along with massive demolitions led to fires throughout the city. With no organized control and looters, black and white, at loose throughout the city, the fires rapidly spread. Those fires had burned most of Richmond by dawn the next day.

In the day's confusion, Lee and his senior officers managed to control the situation sufficiently so that the great majority of what was left of the Army of Northern Virginia escaped Petersburg and Richmond. The defense of Fort Gregg and Battery Whitworth, on the inner line of the Petersburg defenses, was particularly noteworthy for the tenacity of the Confederate defenders. But even while Lee was pulling back to the west, Union forces had a distinct advantage in the positioning of their forces. Sheridan with his cavalry and two corps of infantry was already well to the west of the Confederates, while Union infantry that had finally smashed up the defenses of Petersburg was pursuing what was left of Lee's army. Instinctively, Sheridan recognized that the Army of the Potomac now had the Army of Northern Virginia in its grasp. On 4 April he telegraphed Grant: "Everything was in confusion yesterday, the enemy moving to the north side of the Appomattox. . . . *If we press on we will no doubt get the whole army.*"[53]

For Lee and his soldiers, a twofold race began: first to get to the supply dumps at Amelia Courthouse and then to move around Sheridan to swing south to join up with Johnston. Thus, getting to Amelia Courthouse, where Lee had ordered a full set of rations to relieve his famished troops—their hunger exacerbated by the strenuous fighting and marching they had undertaken since the Union attack on 2 April—was of critical importance. The second was never in the cards, because Sheridan was relentlessly staying parallel to the Confederate movement to the west. Under his driving leadership the Union advance in no respect resembled the lackadaisical approach characterizing the movements of the Army of the Potomac in the past. While Lee was slightly ahead, he had no chance to get around Sheridan's force without a major battle.

Then, to Lee's horror, the rations failed to arrive at Amelia Courthouse. Some clerk in the Confederate War Office had not made the necessary arrangements in the desperate attempt to escape from Richmond. The troops had to continue their march west on empty stomachs. Late on the afternoon of 6 April, Sheridan's cavalry and infantry smashed into the rear of the Confederate army at Sayler's Creek. After a short, sharp fight, Sheridan's forces, which far outnumbered their opponent's, routed the Confederates. The Confederates were in such bad shape that over 6,000 surrendered. Sheridan reported to Grant late on the evening of 6 April: "I attacked them with two divisions of the Sixth Army Corps and routed them handsomely, making a connection with the cavalry. I am pressing on with both cavalry and infantry. Up to the present time we have captured Generals Ewell, Kershaw, Barton, Corse, De Foe [Du Bose], and Custis Lee, several thousand prisoners, 14 pieces of artillery with caissons and a large number of wagons. If the thing is pressed I think Lee will surrender."[54]

Lee won the race to Farmville, but that was the last race the Army of Northern Virginia won. While the II and VI Corps followed him closely, picking up an increasing number of stragglers and deserters, Sheridan's cavalry and the V Corps took a more southerly route. That proved to be the crucial move, because Union cavalry reached Appomattox Station and the crucial supplies Lee's soldiers needed, if they were to continue the struggle. The V Corps infantry then arrived to bolster the hold Union troops had on the Army of Northern Virginia. Once the supplies were in Sheridan's hands, it was over except for the signing of surrender terms on the afternoon of 9 April. There, in the McLean House, Grant and Lee took the first small steps in healing the civil war between the two halves of the nation. Three days later the formal surrender of the Army of Northern Virginia took place.

Eleven days later Johnston surrendered to Sherman, but in between those two dates the assassination of Lincoln put much of what was going to happen politically in doubt, but that story lies beyond the purview of this work. On the military side, Sherman granted Johnston's army terms that went well beyond the military aspects of the surrender of Confederate forces in North Carolina. On receiving the terms, Grant reported to Sherman on his meeting with the new president and the secretary of war, as well as his own reaction: "I read [your message on the surrender terms] carefully myself before submitting it to the President and Secretary of War and felt satisfied that it could not possibly be approved."[55]

In the end, Grant went to North Carolina, and the two Union commanders granted Johnston's soldiers terms similar to those the Army of Northern Virginia had received. There was one last incomplete business that Union soldiers finished in April. On 16 April 1865, a Union cavalryman killed Colonel Charles A. L. Lamar, who had in the late 1850s thumbed his nose at the law of the land, the US Navy, and the Royal Navy by transporting 500 blacks from Africa to the slave markets of Georgia on the fast cutter *Wanderer*, a voyage which saw 100 of the 500 perish. The report of the action by a Union officer made clear that he knew Lamar's history.

The End of the War

It has become fashionable among Civil War historians to suggest that the Confederacy possessed the option of waging a sustained guerrilla war against the Union. Supposedly the failure to take that option resulted from a lack of commitment to the cause of Confederate freedom or to the statesmanship exhibited by Confederate military leaders in spring 1865. Such arguments miss entirely the military and political context of the time. Nor do they understand the correlation of military forces between those available to the North and what few resources would have been available to those white Southerners willing to continue the struggle. In effect, such arguments have emerged from the love affair too many academics have had in imagining a Vietnam War that never occurred, one that was supposedly won militarily by guerrillas, hiding in the countryside of South Vietnam.

Lee, however, did understand the correlation of forces in April 1865, and when he decided to surrender, he made that decision, because he recognized the game was up. A continuation of the struggle would only result in greater suffering and hardship for the Confederate people with no hope for success. Shortly before the surrender took place, Porter Alexander held an extended conversation with his commander. Alexander had suggested that instead of surrendering, the soldiers and officers of the Army of Northern Virginia should scatter to the woods with the aim of carrying on an extended guerrilla war against the armies of the Union. Lee immediately asked: "Well what would you accomplish by that?" Then under more questioning, Lee gave a devastating reply to Alexander that underlined why he surrendered rather than continued the struggle: "There are here only about 15,000 [soldiers] with muskets. Suppose two thirds, say 10,000, got away. Divided among the states, their numbers would be too insignificant to accomplish the least good. Yes, the surrender of this army is the end of the Confederacy. . . . Suppose I should take your suggestion & order the army to disperse & make their way to their homes. The men would have no rations & they would be under no discipline. They are already demoralized by four years of war. They would have to rob & plunder to procure subsistence. The country would be full of lawless bands in every part. . . . Then the enemy's cavalry would pursue in the hopes of catching the principal officers, & wherever they went there would be fresh rapine & destruction."[56]

What Lee saw and what armchair historians seem incapable of recognizing is the reality that the Confederacy had no chance of gaining its independence by continuing the struggle by waging a sustained guerrilla war against the armies of the North. Supposedly, the argument runs, guerrilla warfare throughout history has nearly always been successful. In fact, such a line of argument is entirely fallacious, because it misses the fact that historical outcomes are contingent on the context within which they occur. Certain factors have been an absolute requirement for successful insurgencies, and where they have not been present guerrillas have invariably gone down to defeat at the hands of conventional military forces.

Guerrilla wars in Spain against Napoleon and in Vietnam against the French and the Americans were successful because they received sustained help from outside sources, and that aid more often than not included conventional military forces. Moreover, such successful insurgencies have rarely threatened the essential interests of the state against which the insurgency has been aimed. But where the indigenous guerrillas failed to receive external help and where they have threatened the basic interests of the state, the results have almost invariably resulted in their defeat. The sad tales of Irish insurgencies is a case in point. It was only when the context of Britain's politics changed that the Irish were successful. In the case of South Korea, Kim Il Sung's murderous regime in the north made a number of attempts to start an insurgency, but without an ability to supply guerrillas those efforts failed.

In April 1865, the Confederate states had suffered devastating losses over four years of military operations. Approximately 50 percent of the male population between eighteen and sixty was either dead or maimed. Union armies had just completed wrecking the South's infrastructure. Its economy was a shambles due to the direct and indirect effects of the war. The freeing of the slaves had destroyed most of the region's monetary wealth. Union troops had stripped the countryside of its horses and mules, at least those which remained after the Confederate government had requisitioned what its armies had needed. Nearly one-third of the population consisted of recently freed slaves who had proven enthusiastic supporters of their liberators.

Moreover, from whence was outside help going to come, given the refusal of European powers to intervene when the Confederacy possessed significant military forces and some prospect of success? With an economic base reduced by the war to that of hardscrabble farming, the Confederacy had no chance of sustaining a prolonged guerrilla war against the massive military forces of the North. Reinforcing the belief among Confederate military leaders that the war was over was an understanding that their opponents might be willing to deploy their military forces even more ruthlessly than they had thus far in the war. The fate of South Carolina was a warning of what might happen in the future. Faced with that reality, the surrender of the Confederate armies signaled an end to the conflict over whether the white South could secede from the Union.

Conclusion

Over the last six months of the war, the North brought overwhelming military power to bear on the Confederacy. Not surprisingly, the result was the physical destruction of the main Confederate armies to the east of the Mississippi River. The military defeat was so complete that Nathan Bedford Forrest's comment to his troops as he abandoned the struggle was: "That we are beaten is a self-evident fact, and any further resistance on our part would be justly regarded as the very height of folly and rashness."[57] Certainly, most Civil War historians have emphasized the military nature of that defeat. Some have even suggested that the late start of the great raids launched by Canby, Wilson, and Stoneman failed to provide Sherman with the direct help that Grant had hoped they would provide the drive through the Carolinas. But that is to miss the larger *political purpose* that lay behind the Union campaigns Grant set in motion, beginning with Sherman's drive into South Carolina.

The implicit purpose of these campaigns was not merely the defeat of Confederate armies, but to bring the war home to the Confederate population, to paraphrase Sherman, to make white Southerners realize that it was in the reach of Northern military power to dispossess them of their homes, their lands, and, if necessary, their very lives. As Forrest commented at the end of the war, only those fit for an insane asylum would aim to continue the conflict. Given the nature of the man, it suggests how removed from events are those historians who suggest that Confederates could have continued a guerrilla war for their independence. The experience of 1864 and 1865 took that possibility off the table. There was, of course, a limited political insurgency reliant on terrorist organizations such as the Ku Klux Klan after the war, but that aimed at a far more limited goal—namely, to thwart Northern and Southern Republicans' efforts at reconstruction and to position black Southerners firmly at the bottom of the Reconstruction South's racial totem pole.

There have been those historians who have argued that the "hard war" waged by Grant, Sherman, Sheridan, and others presaged the massacre of My Lai. It did no such thing. My Lai involved the criminal acts of an ill-disciplined company, led by incompetent officers. However, like the bombing of Germany and Japan, the destruction of the white South represented a deliberate and successful strategy to break the will of an intransigent, deeply committed enemy. Historians all too often miss the terrible nature of war, especially when it becomes a life-and-death struggle for survival between two nations. The Union generals of 1865 understood the nature of the problem. As the perceptive Confederate general Porter Alexander noted in his *Personal Recollections*, even in April 1865 a substantial portion of those Confederates still in arms were unwilling to give up the fight. But to continue the fight they needed the support of the Southern population. And after the grim cavalrymen and infantrymen of the Union armies had brought the war to every corner of the Confederacy, they were not going to get that support.

In November 1918 General "Black Jack" Pershing, commander of the American Expeditionary Forces, warned his colleagues Douglas Haig, Philippe Pétain, and Ferdinand Foch that to agree to an armistice with the badly beaten German Army before Allied armies had brought the war home to the German people was to insure that there would be another great European war. The Allies failed to listen to Pershing, and they got a second world war, brought on by a German nation convinced as early as 1919 that its armies had stood unbroken and unbeaten in the field. That was not to be a problem in 1945, because no German or Japanese soldier or civilian could claim in the wreckage of their bombed-out cities that they had not lost the war. In the same fashion, the great destruction of the Confederacy accorded by the military operations of Union armies insured that no white Southerner, no matter how much he or she might despise Yankees, dared raise a real rebellion after the destruction wrought by Union armies in 1864 and 1865. Thus the United States became a singular noun even in the heart of Dixie.

Too much romanticism about the Civil War pervades the present-day view of the conflict. The apocryphal tale of the surrender of the Army of Northern Virginia to a detachment of the Army of the Potomac, commanded by that great hero Joshua Chamberlain, appears often as a representation of the first steps toward the reunion of the two halves of a nation sundered by a great Civil War. In fact, it represented nothing of the sort. The wounds of the conflict only began to heal in the 1960s and 1970s, when the white South finally began to rejoin the United States. Representative of the real attitudes of former Confederates was the Ku Klux Klan, which aimed to retake the political ground lost by the war and to insure that the South's black population would remain in abject servitude, since the war had destroyed the institution of slavery. Most of the whites in the South nursed a dark, abiding hatred of the North in their souls. But they would not resume the war; instead, they would cloak the conflict in a fog of dishonest myths that would cover over and distort the real history of the war until the 1960s.

CHAPTER 13

The Civil War in History

Surely a just God will punish these Northern fanatics for the misery and death they are spreading over our land. Yes, a day of retribution must come when they shall be made to feel the curse of their own evil doing. I sometimes wish that the earth might engulf them as the wicked were in the Red Sea.

—Jesse Sparkman (quoted in Joseph Glatthaar, *General Lee's Army*)

Was the victory of the North inevitable? To look at the results of 1865 and the overwhelming strength that by the war's end the North deployed against the Confederacy and then to conclude that the results were inevitable is to remove the role of contingency and human factors from the history of the war. Viewed from April 1861, the Union's triumph was by no means certain. The Confederacy possessed important advantages. The extent of its territory, continental in its expanse, at least in European terms, the commitment of most of its white population to the cause of independence, and the economic weapon that cotton provided, all represented major advantages. In addition to the distances with which Union armies would have to come to grips, there was the wretched state of unimproved roads throughout the Confederacy.

On the other hand, substantial portions of the Northern population, at least before Sumter, preferred to see the Confederate states go in peace and were hardly willing to support a great war for the Union. As the war dragged on, violent outbreaks of Northern resistance—the most spectacular being the New York City draft riots of 1863—to intrusive military mobilization underlined the limits of Northern commitment. But perhaps most daunting of all was the fact that no one in the North at the war's outbreak had a clue as to the difficulties that the translation of the North's advantages in population and economic strength into military power would confront, much less the price that a successful war for the Union would demand. The political and strategic conduct of the war would require extraordinary leadership and therein lay the great imponderable on which success or failure in the Civil War, as in all conflicts, rested.

Contingency and chance are the great determinants of history. Of all the uncertainties those twin sisters throw in the way of those who conduct war, the most important is that of leadership. The dominant themes among academic historians today are those of social and cultural history, and one of the leading mantras is that leaders matter little in the course of human affairs—a supposition that only those who have spent their lives comfortably ensconced in the gated communities of our colleges and universities could possibly hold. They are wrong. As in all great human trials, leaders, political and military, drove events and outcomes throughout the Civil War. Their strengths and weaknesses, their wisdom and incompetence, their vision or myopia, their understanding of their opponents, or their dogged unwillingness to adapt to war's actual conditions, among a host of other attributes, determined the conflict's outcome.

The great historian of the war, James McPherson, notes four key turning points on which the war's course depended, listing the Union victory at Antietam, the twin Union victories at Gettysburg and Vicksburg, and Atlanta as four moments when the Confederacy could have gained victory. However, we can also find additional important contingent decisions by leaders at a smaller but profoundly significant scale of human action. For example, it is entirely conceivable that in the first half of 1862 Henry Halleck, through either jealousy or dislike, might have removed Grant from the war's chessboard, revealing the worst faults of the insular and personality-driven world of the antebellum Old Army. Indeed, Halleck treated Grant so badly in the post-Shiloh period that only Sherman's intervention and Grant's return to independent command after Corinth's fall prevented the future leader of the victorious Union effort from packing up and leaving the army with consequences impossible to calculate. Grant's absence from the chessboard might well have led to Confederate victory.

Halleck's baleful influence continued into 1863 in spite of, or perhaps due to, his reputation as the Old Army's premier soldier intellectual. His contemptuous dismissal, a dismissal buttressed by Lincoln and Stanton, of Grant's proposal for a move against Mobile after

Vicksburg's surrender in July 1863 prevented a move that would have forced the Confederates to divide their attention between southern Alabama and Rosecrans's move against Chattanooga. Later, again with Lincoln's support, Halleck contemptuously rejected Grant's innovative proposal for alternative lines of operation during the winter of 1863/64 before Grant's promotion to lieutenant general and assignment to become the army's commander in chief. Grant's strategy had aimed at threatening Lee's communication and logistical support by cutting off the crucial port of Wilmington via a major movement directed at Raleigh, North Carolina, starting in southeastern Virginia. Instead, Halleck insisted that the Union army continue to butt its head against the Army of Northern Virginia north of Richmond. Halleck thus managed to marry the worst elements of Jominian "science" and overaggressive civilian public opinion. Grant's unavoidable acquiescence to this approach, thus, led in large part to the 65,000 combat casualties of the Overland Campaign, which produced buyer's remorse among the Northern electorate and almost cost Lincoln the election.

An equally contingent moment came with Davis's decision to replace Johnston with Hood as Sherman arrived at the doors of Atlanta in July 1864. Davis proved incapable of focusing on the larger political and strategic issue—the upcoming presidential election in the North. Instead, like Lee, he was still seeking the mirage of decisive victory, which Johnston, outnumbered by Sherman, understood was impossible. Had Johnston remained in command, he would certainly not have launched the three ill-thought-out attacks Hood launched on Sherman's armies, attacks whose bloodletting began the process of destroying the Army of Tennessee as a viable military force. Moreover, Johnston would most probably have held Atlanta for a longer period, thus exacerbating political dissension in the North. But whatever Johnston might have done, he certainly would not have taken the Army of Tennessee off into Alabama after Atlanta's fall, a move that left Georgia open to Sherman's destructive March to the Sea and his advance into the Carolinas, which ripped the heart out of the Confederate will to continue the war.

Indeed, at critical points, even relatively low-ranking leaders could have outsized influence. For example, as we have seen at First Bull Run, "Shanks" Evans, a relatively junior brigade commander, chose to mount an aggressive defensive action against a superior Federal force, buying another brigade commander, Stonewall Jackson, the time needed to establish a strong enough Confederate position on Henry Hill to allow Beauregard and Johnston to ensure that the Confederacy would not be strangled in its grave.

Also suggestive of how narrow the thread on which events hung are a number of other events, which stem not so much from the conscious decisions of leaders but from fate's capricious cuts. As Clausewitz suggested, the movement of a battalion may well be determined by a single soldier. Friction, the ability of a series of seemingly unconnected and unimportant incidents to combine and in their combination result in disastrous or positive outcomes, continued to dominate the battlefield. A Federal artillery shell wounds Johnston severely at Seven Pines, allowing Lee to take command of what became the Army of Northern Virginia. Jackson's own troops fire at their commander in the gloom of the evening of his greatest victory, and one of their bullets smashes into his arm, creating a wound that will take his life. Reynolds goes down on the first hours of the first day at Gettysburg, turning the conduct of the battle over to a less capable officer. A Confederate staff officer on the second day at Gettysburg executes a sloppy and inaccurate reconnaissance that results in a significant delay in Longstreet's deployment. A report that there is a gap in Union lines leads Rosecrans to order a division commander to move his troops, thereby creating a hole through which Longstreet's corps smashes at Chickamauga. A Union platoon at the Wilderness fails to blow away the leaders of the Army of Northern Virginia when offered an enormous opportunity. As Clausewitz and Thucydides noted, no other human activity is so bound up with contingency and chance as is war. So was it with the American Civil War. Throughout the conflict the course of events often hung by a thread, but eventually they broke in favor of the Union, when finally, the big battalions won. But, as the Duke of Wellington noted about the Battle of Waterloo, for much of the war it was a close-run thing indeed.

As the Prussian theorist had warned about the nature of war, uncertainty and ambiguity ran like a bad movie throughout. Grant at least had glimpsed and then mastered those baleful twin sisters that have bedeviled commanders throughout history; McClellan never did. Historians have distorted too much of the war's history by Monday-morning quarterbacking and their failure to recognize that, living in the present, they can see what was happening on both sides. As a result, they make it seem clear as to what those on the fields of bloodshed and chaos should have seen and understood. But the fog of war cloaked the events of the Civil War in as tight an embrace as it did for those recent Americans who fought in Iraq and Afghanistan.

Many of these random and unpredictable events may not necessarily have changed the war's most important final outcome, the death of the Confederacy and the preservation of the Union, but they still had profound effects on the war's consequences. For example, while Johnston's wound at Seven Pines obviously did not save the Confederacy in the end, the paradoxical result of the Confederacy's longer lease on life helped ensure the death of slavery and a more punitive postwar settlement vis-à-vis the former Confederate states. A McClellan victorious at Antietam could well have gone on to victory in the 1864 presidential election as the hero who had destroyed the Army of Northern Virginia, and while historians can debate whether or not McClellan could have stopped the demise of slavery in a reunited Union, he certainly would not have supported the radical changes to the Constitution found in the Fourteenth and Fifteenth Amendments. The Civil War's many profound effects on American society all flowed from a torrent of individual acts and events diverging in multiple directions, and although random obstructions might not stop the stream leading to Union victory, other important outcomes might have been significantly altered.

The Military-Social Revolution

In retrospect, the American Civil War heralded the dawn of a new age of warfare. Clausewitz would certainly have recognized the mobilization of whole peoples and their resources in both North and South. But he would also have recognized the ability of two sides to harness the Industrial Revolution and its technological manifestations as representing a fundamentally new factor in war that influenced the Civil War deeply. While the Industrial Revolution had begun to emerge in Britain at the end of the eighteenth and beginning of the nineteenth centuries, it had had no direct influence on the battlefields of the French Revolutionary and Napoleonic Wars. We, of course, with the benefit of hindsight, know that the fruits of that revolution allowed the British to maintain their massive navy, support an expensive conflict on the Iberian Peninsula, *and* provide the subsidies that aided the monarchies of Eastern and Central Europe to raise and maintain the armies that finally in the great campaigns of 1813, 1814, and 1815 overthrew Napoleon.

One cannot underestimate the impact of the French Revolution on the conduct of war over the next century and a half. The commitment of the French people to the struggle from 1792 overthrew the framework within which the European powers had waged war for well over a century. As Clausewitz suggested shortly after that quarter century of terrible conflict, "[s]uddenly war again became the business of the people—a people of thirty millions, all of whom considered themselves to be citizens. . . . The people became a participant in war: instead of governments and armies as heretofore, the full weight of the nation was thrown into the balance. The resources and efforts now available for use surpassed all limits; nothing now impeded the vigor with which war could be waged, and consequently the opponents of France faced the utmost peril."[1] In the end it took the massive power of the coalition of Britain, Prussia, Russia, and Austria in 1814 to invade France and break the power of a French people in arms.

It has become popular among some American historians to suggest that the Civil War created something known as the "American way of war." That approach supposedly led to the dreadful, "inhumane" mass bombings of German and Japanese cities in the Second World War. In fact, those bombings were crucial not only to the wrecking of the German war economy, thus easing the task of Allied soldiers on the front lines, but also to the persuasion of German and Japanese civilians that they should not attempt the same course again. What Grant, Sherman, Sheridan, and the hard men who served under them knew by early 1864 was that their armies were going to have to break the popular will of the Confederate people, not only in the present, but also for the future, or the North was not going to win the war.

Ironically, Jefferson Davis in his carping memoirs understood this reality. "At the commencement of the year 1862 it was the purpose of the United States Government to assail us in every manner and at every point. . . . The usual methods of civilized warfare consist in the destruction of an enemy's military power and the capture of his capital. These, however, formed only a small portion of the purposes of *our* enemy. . . . Thus, while the Executive was preparing immense armies . . . with which to invade our territory and destroy our citizens, the willing aid of an impatient, enraged Congress was invoked to usurp new powers, to legislate the subversion of our social institutions [i.e., slavery], and to give the form of legality to the plunder of a frenzied soldiery."[2]

In that sense, the Civil War was the harbinger of war in the twentieth century. Without the destruction of the deep feeling of national identity for which the enemy was waging war, there would be no peace. It was, therefore, a war against the South's white population as well as its armies, a course that the great wars of the twentieth century followed. Thus, the war represented not some peculiar American approach to conflict that emphasized sledgehammer blows, but the political reality that only war waged against the very *idea* of a Confederate nation would break the nationalistic fervor the French Revolution and its successors had called forth.

In the American Civil War, moreover, the French Revolution and the Industrial Revolution came together in a fashion that allowed for the mobilization of great armies in both the North and the Confederacy and the maintenance and projection of Northern military forces over continental distances. The Industrial Revolution allowed for the mass production of everything from uniforms, boots, tents, wagons, and saddles to rifled muskets, rapid-fire weapons, artillery pieces in increasing numbers, and the ammunition that provided the means for killing and maiming soldiers in enormous numbers. It was the capacity of Northern and Confederate societies to put the two revolutions together that created the possibility of massed war, supplied and fought over the distances that delineated the populated sections of the United States in 1860. Moreover, the North's great advantage proved to be its ability to construct and support the infrastructure required by war's new garb. In this respect, the Civil War represented a harbinger of the marriage of the French Revolution with the Industrial Revolution, a marriage that similarly characterized the First World War and did so much to wreck Europe's politics and culture. As Yogi Berra so aptly noted, it was to be déjà vu all over again.

Thus, the ability of Northern industry to mass produce train engines, rails, and ties made the depredations of Forrest and other Confederate raiders largely irrelevant to the ability of the Union logistical system to support the campaign Sherman was waging against Atlanta. In this regard, the Confederacy was hopelessly outclassed. While the Northern economy not only supported the war effort being waged by Union armies, it was also undergoing an expansion that was in every respect extraordinary. A few short statistics indicate the extent of the explosion. By 1864 the North's iron production was 29 percent greater than in any year before the war for the whole nation; its overall manufacturing had increased by 13 percent; Union shipyards produced more merchant vessels than in any comparable period before the war; traffic along Northern railroads increased by 50 percent, as did that along the Erie Canal; and finally, agricultural production not only fed the Union armies and Northern society, but also exported huge amounts of grain and other produce to a Europe suffering from crop failures.

Of the greatest importance was the ability of the Lincoln administration to finance the war, the expenses of which were on a scale unimaginable before 1861. The explosion of expenditures on the Union's military forces suggests the extent of the mobilization. In 1860 the government's expenditures had totaled $66,500,000. In 1862 those expenditures reached $474,800,000, and by 1865 they had reached $1,297,600,000. During the same period expenditures on the army jumped from $23,000,000 in the last year of peace to $394,400,000 in 1862 and by the war's last year to $1,031,300,000. Admittedly there were problems with inflation in the North, but nothing like the inflation in the Confederacy. Particularly impressive was the adaptability and flexibility of the various railroad and steamboat companies, which responded in rapid and effective fashion to emergencies such as the need to move Hooker's two corps from the Army of the Potomac to east Tennessee after Chickamauga.

Equally impressive was the ability of Northern railroads to balance the demands of war with those of the civilian economy. The exact opposite occurred in the Confederacy. Admittedly, through herculean efforts the Confederates kept their armies supplied with ammunition and weapons, but that was about the sum and total of what their logistic system was able to do. It could not even keep its armies supplied with a minimum of clothing or footwear. Even more disastrously, for much of the war it failed to provide its soldiers reasonable rations, an indication of the weaknesses of its railroad and transportation network in an area that possessed enormous agricultural riches.

Grant's victories at Forts Donelson and Henry largely removed the rivers of the west from the support of the Confederate armies and civilian economy. That move represented a strategic thrust from which the Confederacy never fully recovered. But equally disastrously, the slow, steady deterioration of the railroad system, a system that was already inadequate at the war's outset, resulted in the Confederacy's loss of the advantages that interior lines would have provided in the days before railroads. What little industrial potential the Confederates possessed had to focus largely on supporting its armies. There was, in addition, the waste of about 25 percent of the Confederacy's iron production in its attempt to build ironclads. As a result, virtually nothing was left for the manufacture of new railroad engines or cars to replace those destroyed by normal wear and tear or accidents, much less the damage inflicted by Union armies as they moved deeper into the Confederacy. Moreover, the inability to replace the rails on which those trains rode guaranteed an increase in the number of accidents. By 1864 Confederate railroads were in the final stages of collapse, a situation that Union depredations over the war's last year completed and which returned the southern states to their preindustrial state as it had existed in 1830.

But it was much more than just the equipping of soldiers with the accoutrements of war and their support that reflected this revolution in the social and economic framework that undergirded the war's conduct. The fact that considerable portions of the Union and Confederate populations were literate increased the ability of the opposing governments to mobilize popular enthusiasm. Soldiers as well as civilians avidly read newspapers and weekly magazines, a factor entirely new on the human scene. Print journalism had exploded in the decades immediately before the war, and it reflected, as well as molded, public opinion. For the most part it proved a potent weapon in mobilizing support for the war on both sides. And one should not underestimate the sophistication of Northern and Southern politicians in manipulating the narrative. Nevertheless, as is the case today, the participation of the media in the conveying of ideas and news cut both ways. For politicians, it could prove a nasty distraction, then as today, for those unlucky enough to become its targets. Lincoln found himself the focus of as vicious a series of attacks as any president has ever suffered, but he would undoubtedly not have exchanged his position for that of Davis, who was the butt of a constant barrage of negative press. While politicians may not have found themselves delighted by what the press said, they were also quite adept in manipulating the press to their advantage.

Not surprisingly, the press paid generals the same scrutiny it gave politicians. Civil War commanders would undoubtedly have found themselves in considerable sympathy with those in today's military who complain about the media's irresponsibility in revealing state secrets. After all, Lee culled much of his intelligence from the Northern newspapers he avidly read, while Grant found himself outraged to learn that the Richmond newspapers had been reporting about Ben Butler's expedition against Fort Fisher before it had even embarked. As for the media's scurrilous reporting, it was every bit as dishonest as today's tabloids. While Sherman delighted to hear that several newsmen had gone down in a steamship sunk on the Tennessee River, Grant at least understood how important the reporters were to keeping the folks back home informed and the morale of the troops at the front at a reasonable level.

For Clausewitz, the eruption of the technologies of the Industrial Revolution would have come as a surprise, given the fact that it had yet to impact directly the European continent in his time, in contrast to the ideological mobilization he himself had seen during the French Revolution. For example, in 1815 the Ruhr, one of the throwaway provinces the Prussians picked up in return for turning over much of the Polish territory they had controlled before 1806 to Russia, was a sleepy, agricultural valley of little economic worth. Nevertheless, he would have argued that however much the technological framework of the war had changed, the fundamental nature of war had not. For example, the telegraph certainly increased the speed of communications, but at the same time it magnified the potential for misunderstanding between commanders separated in some cases by hundreds of miles. While Hooker found during the Chancellorsville campaign he could communicate with his chief of staff and Sedgwick, all separated by considerable distances, he could not necessarily communicate his intentions. In Iraq 140 years later American commanders discovered that while advanced communications removed some ambiguities, at the same time those systems introduced new and equally distressing indeterminacies. None of this would Clausewitz have found unexpected, and friction then as now continues to impede the machinery of war. "The more things change, the more they stay the same."

Yet, in the largest sense, technology brought an enormous change in the conduct of war—namely, the fact that over the course of the Civil War the opposing armies found themselves forced to adapt to the new circumstances and conditions. In our age of rapid, unceasing, and explosive technological change, the changes of the mid-nineteenth century appear relatively small. Yet, in terms of their impact on the societies of the time as well as the conduct of war, these were truly revolutionary. For the first time in history, man could communicate, move his fellows, and transport his goods at unheard of speeds and volumes. Logistics no longer depended only on muscle power of animals or men, or the wind. The social and economic impact of these changes are difficult for us to access, because change forms an intimate and inseparable part of our lives. The kinds of changes that the first half of the nineteenth century experienced were something entirely new in history.

In terms of the Industrial Revolution's impact on the war, the result was that steady, constant adaptation occurred from the beginning to the end, to a great extent driven by the realities of technological changes that had emerged in the decades before the war. Those changes had to a great extent altered the context of war. On the operational level the most obvious was the symbiosis among railroads, steam-powered ships, and the telegraph. The fact that Halleck would suggest in September 1863 that it would take three months to transport two corps of the Army of the Potomac to the Tennessee theater of operations after the Union defeat at Chickamauga suggests how much some senior officers had to learn about the impact of the transportation revolution on the movement of military forces. Yet, within a year, Grant conceived of an even more ambitious move, this time transferring Schofield and two corps from central Tennessee by rail to the Atlantic coast and then by steamboat to North Carolina. These movements represented logistical feats far beyond anything the Prussian military would achieve in 1866 and 1870.

On the tactical level, there was an even greater revolution. While some historians have overemphasized the introduction of the minié bullet and the rifled musket in changing the battlefield's lethality, the increase in the range of shoulder-fired weapons combined with improvised fieldworks had important implications for the war's tactics. Much of the fighting in the first years involved combat formations standing out in the open toe to toe and blasting away at each other. Nothing better underlined this proclivity than the fight in the cornfield in the first hours of Antietam. There, the Confederates had had all night to entrench themselves, but Jackson and his troops had done nothing until Hooker's corps smashed into them in the early hours of 17 September. The slaughter was then mutual. But by 1864, the armies proved themselves exceedingly skilled at building entrenched positions, in some cases in the midst of battle.

Here the fact that the armies consisted almost entirely of civilian volunteers and individualistic Americans suggests an explanation for the relative speed with which adaptation took place in the war as opposed to the Napoleonic period. In the American case adaptation bubbled up from below, sometimes from the enlisted ranks, as was to occur in the world wars, but mostly from the middle ranks—the regimental and brigade commanders. There was a price, because sometimes the amateur soldiers could make egregious mistakes when not monitored by trained officers. On the other hand, Upton's imaginative tactical approach at Spotsylvania suggested the first glimmering of a solution to the problem of breaking into an entrenched enemy position, a tactical problem that would beset First World War generals fifty years later. The early morning corps' attack several days later that smashed through the Mule Shoe defenses then indicated a second problem that would appear throughout the war of 1914–18: how could attacking troops exploit a break in and turn it into a break out—a problem not solved until Ludendorff's "Michael" offensive of March 1918.

Nevertheless, one should not think of adaptation simply in terms of technology or tactics. Perhaps the most significant adaptations came off the battlefield. The creation of the North's massive logistic system that supported the projection of its armies represents one of the great untold stories of the war. In 1861 the quartermaster and supply system supported an army of fewer than 16,000 men. Admittedly, it had done so over great distances, which provided its officers with some glimmering, however faint, as to how to handle the problems that were to come. But four years later the army's logistical system was supplying forces numbering 1,000,000 men, 600,000 plus in the field, with rations, clothing, horses and mules (and their fodder), tents, ammunition, small arms, and artillery over a military railroad system that covered much of what had been Confederate territory.

Even more extraordinary was the fact that a minuscule number of bureaucrats and officials ran the procurement and logistical systems. Nor should one forget that while this system was whirling away in supporting the armies of the Republic, an equally complex one, if not so large, was supporting the navy in its blockade of the Confederacy. The adaptations required to create and then run that system throughout the vagaries of an ever-changing conflict and its demands represented perhaps the most important contributing factor to the Union's victory. Certainly, Grant and Sherman understood the crucial factor of logistics in laying out the basis for the 1864 campaign in the West. The rebuilding of not only the railroad system throughout Tennessee, but then the stockpiling of engines, cars, rails, and bridging materials, as well as a systematic approach to the protection of those railroads, insured that the depredations of Forrest and others would be of only local significance in the 1864 campaign in the West.

If the armies at the beginning had looked back more to the past and particularly the Napoleonic world of "decisive victories," by 1864 and 1865 they were providing a warning of the nature of the wars that were to plague the first half of the twentieth century. It was also a foreshadowing of the American way of war. In the end, the North had to win the Civil War by crushing the will of the white South. Sheridan's comments to his Prussian hosts in 1870 that they should leave the French "nothing but their eyes to weep with" suggests the extent to which the North had carried out that effort.[3] It also explains Pershing's warning to his fellow Allied commanders in November 1918 that they were letting the Germans off too easily and that only a peace dictated in Berlin—which was to happen in that city's suburbs twenty-seven years later—would prevent the occurrence of another great European conflict.

The movement to a "hard war" represented the most important of all the adaptations that took place during the course of the war. By 1864 Union troops were carrying out the equivalent of the RAF Bomber Command's "dehousing campaign," with the important exception that they were sparing Confederate civilians' lives. While in Georgia and Shenandoah Union troops may have left Southern houses intact, their removal or destruction of the supporting infrastructure for an agriculturally based economy—horses, mules, cows, goats, chickens, barns, plows, and slaves—was perhaps more destructive to the region's economic long-term stability than the economic destruction that the Combined Bomber Offensive dealt out to the Germans in the Second World War. But the greatest impact of these campaigns was the fact that they robbed white Southerners of the capital basis necessary for them to match the North's explosive economic growth after the war.

In the case of South Carolina, Sherman's soldiers burned most of the houses as well. Admittedly, as Mark Grimsley has pointed out, the destruction and killing were certainly not on a level with what was to come in the twentieth century. Nevertheless, for the time they were ruthless and thorough. The aim was the same: to break the political will of the Confederate people to continue. If that were not sufficient, Sherman, at least in his written statements, suggested to those white Southerners who were considering continuing the struggle that there were alternatives available to the North, such as dispossessing them of "their lives, their homes, their lands, their everything."[4] Thus, in the postwar period former Confederates were willing on one level to contest efforts to impose Northern views on the proper place of the freed slaves in Southern society, but few were willing to contest the idea of the recreated Union as an entity, and most of those went into self-imposed exile.

The Warping of the Narrative

Those who do not drink deeply of Clio's meanderings might well find it somewhat surprising that only in the past half century has a more nuanced and realistic picture of the Civil War begun to emerge. That undoubtedly reflects the fact that as events recede into the past, even as those who participated in them grow old and memories fade, it becomes easier to place events in a more reasonable and understanding perspective. In the period after the Civil War, white Southerners increasingly found themselves enwrapped in efforts to explain what they increasingly came to call the "Lost Cause." On the other hand, the victorious North with its massive industrial and financial expansion, while absorbing large numbers of immigrants, did not dwell so stubbornly on memories of a war that had resulted in the deaths of well over 300,000 of its citizens. As a result, it is not surprising that by the turn of the century, white Southern myths about the "Lost Cause" began to envelop the writing of the war's history (or as so many white Southerners termed the conflict that had begun with the Confederate bombardment of Fort Sumter, the "War of Yankee Aggression"). In effect, the Confederate viewpoint captured much of the war's narrative as well as its historiography. Even as late as the 1990s Shelby Foote, that great literary master of the war, claimed that the Confederacy's cause had been hopeless. After all, he noted in an interview recorded by Ken Burns's series on the conflict, the North had fought the Civil War with "one arm tied behind its back."[5]

Simply put, the "Lost Cause" narrative argued that the struggle for Confederate independence had been a hopeless endeavor against the numbers and industrial strength the North had brought to the conflict. Against that massive military power, the brave cavaliers and stalwart farmers of the Confederate armies had waged a brave and noble, yet in the end hopeless, struggle against the "mudsills" of the North. Modern purveyors have reached back to the whiskey drinking mists of the Celtic past to explain the supposed ferocity of Confederate soldiers on the field of battle. Nevertheless, before the myth had set in concrete, a Confederate veteran commented to an English visitor to the United States in the late nineteenth century: "Our officers were good, but considering that our rank and file were white trash and they had to fight regiments of New England Yankee volunteers, with all their best blood in the ranks, and Western sharpshooters together, it is only wonderful that we weren't whipped sooner."[6]

To those white Southern creators of the narrative, only the extraordinary efforts of straight-shooting, hard-charging men, hardened by a life of hunting and adventure and led by noble chivalric knights, staved off defeat. Not surprisingly, they concentrated on the Eastern theater where Lee, Jackson, and Stuart—but not Longstreet who had betrayed the cause in the postwar period—had performed with such brilliance. The narrative downplayed what had happened in the West, given the dismal performance of the Army of Tennessee. What did get mentioned in terms of the fighting in the West, of course, were the depredations of Sherman's barbarians in their march through Georgia. For those who created the Confederate "Lost Cause" narrative, the Union armies supposedly consisted of masses of soldiers drawn primarily from the enervating confines of city life, which ill-prepared them psychologically and physically for the trials of combat. Almost immediately the myth of the hopeless struggle against impossible odds became deeply imbedded in the white Southern psyche: as the great novelist William Faulkner noted, for the Confederacy's heirs, time always seemed to stop at one o'clock in the afternoon of 3 July 1863, as Pickett's troops prepared to step off in their desperate, hopeless attack on Cemetery Ridge.

Moreover, the futile struggle against the Northern hordes had also supposedly destroyed a society of racial harmony, where plantation owners had run agricultural operations that kept "Sambo" not only in his place but also happily engaged in his proper station in life.

Nothing better encapsulated the extent to which that myth had captured American popular culture in the early twentieth century than those two thoroughly dishonest movies, D. W. Griffith's *Birth of a Nation* and Margaret Mitchell's *Gone with the Wind*. The first was a portrayal not of what had actually happened, but of the deeply racist currents swirling through America at the beginning of the twentieth century. Mitchell's novel and the Hollywood box-office production that followed were more nuanced, but no less dishonest.

The victims of the "Lost Cause" myth were, of course, the blacks liberated from the servile conditions of the antebellum South. While white Southerners could not blame them for the defeat of the Confederacy, as so many Germans were to blame the Jews for the smashup of Bismarck's Second Reich, the freedmen were a readily available target for those embittered by the war's result. The well-meaning and idealistic efforts of so many Northerners during the Reconstruction to help in the education and acculturation of freedmen and women only served to exacerbate Southern white antipathy. For freedmen and women, the war did bring an end to slavery, but it was also to see them eventually denied most of the rights supposedly accompanying their freedom.

The poisons of white Southern racism found ready abettors throughout the North, where the Democratic Party, both before and during the war, had formed an avid and enthusiastic supporter of the Southern view of America's racial divide. After Grant left office in 1877, no president of the United States until the election of Franklin Roosevelt displayed any interest in providing either succor or help to America's downtrodden black population. Some like Woodrow Wilson actively participated in the spread of Jim Crow throughout states north of the Mason-Dixon Line. And none attempted to force the South to live up to the rights guaranteed by the Constitution, much less the basic legal protection provided by the laws of the Southern states for their white population.

Nor did those who spun the "Lost Cause" narrative of the war neglect to include in their account the supposed depredations of the Northern barbarians, particularly of Sherman's and Sheridan's armies. As with all myths, there was some truth in the white Southern narrative, as this account has suggested. The war's destructive course did wreck the South's economy, making it a laggard in the swift economic growth that made the United States the great powerhouse of the twentieth century. In their own way that result was something defeated

Confederates did not forget. Unlike the Germans and the Japanese in their year zero in 1945, white Southerners lacked the educational skills and the outside financial aid of an equivalent to the Marshall Plan to crawl out of the dismal poverty the war had left them in by 1865. If on one side of the coin the "hard war" waged by Northern armies in 1864 and 1865 disabused Confederates of the notion that the price to be paid for their independence was worth paying, there was another side of the coin and that was the deep, abiding bitterness toward the North that many white Southerners held into to the twentieth century. The secondary and unintended effects of the war would last until the late 1960s and early 1970s, when suddenly the flag of the United States became as popular as the Stars and Bars throughout the South, undoubtedly as a retort to the flagrant antipatriotism that marked so much of the rest of the country during the Vietnam War.

Those who perpetrated the myth also turned to the Virginia theater of operations, which provided much grist for their mill and enabled them to turn the 1864 campaign into a blackening of Grant's generalship. What better way to explain the defeat of the noble, brave warriors of the Army of Northern Virginia than the merciless throwing of wave after wave of Union soldiers against Lee's army, waves which in the end overwhelmed it. Grant had already received the none-too-tender assaults of the anti-war Northern press, which by July 1864 had hung the title of "butcher" around his neck. Such newspaper commentaries, like those of today, were more interested in ensuring Lincoln's defeat in the upcoming election than in understanding the complex factors that had led to the casualties of the fighting from the Wilderness to Petersburg. Grant, of course, represented the perfect target, because he had also, as president, supported Reconstruction and other efforts to bring a modicum of reasonable treatment to the newly freed former slaves.

Why Did the North Win?

Given the political and strategic framework of April 1861, the Confederate states held the considerable possibility of gaining their independence. Why they failed reflected a number of factors: the context and strategic framework within which the conflict took place, the political and strategic leadership of those at the top, the role of strategic decision making, the incalculable impact of luck in human affairs, the ability and capabilities of the opposing sides to adapt to the dramatic new problems the war raised, and finally the inevitable role that military effectiveness and operational strategy played in the conduct of the war. For those in the twenty-first century, the strategic and operational choices open to the opposing sides appear glaringly obvious, but to those at the time, who had to grapple with the uncertainties and ambiguities of the war, nothing was clear. To paraphrase the King James Bible, they did indeed see through a glass darkly.

The fact the war lasted a sustained period and involved the level of sacrifice reflected in the casualty bills played a major role in the Union's victory and the destruction of the Confederacy. Any Union victory in the first two years of the war would have handed the South a peace that would have largely rested on the status quo ante bellum. That was certainly the end for which many of the Democratic politicians in the North as well as military figures such as McClellan hoped. Even in the case of Lincoln, it appears the president would have settled for such an outcome. Nevertheless, such a peace would not have obliterated slavery, and it would have left secessionists in charge of the former Confederate states. Nor would it have disabused many radicals in the Confederacy of the notion that they might at some time in the future gain their independence.

In retrospect, as was the case with both world wars, there was no chance there would be a short war, once the opposing sides began to draw on the well of nationalistic feelings of their populations as well as their immense resources. The Napoleonic myth of a decisive victory, similar to Jena-Auerstedt that could end the conflict at a single blow, enthralled both sides in the war's first years; it continued to attract Lee and Davis until the end, but perhaps given the growing superiority of Northern military power they had no choice. But it was a myth nevertheless, and Lee's great victories such as the Seven Days battles and Chancellorsville netted him little more than a victory over the minds of McClellan and Hooker, since the Confederates lost at least as heavily in terms of casualties, if not more heavily, than their Northern opponents.

A long war did provide the North with considerable prospects of winning. But a prolonged war also represented a double-edged sword, because Union prospects would depend on the constancy and steadfastness of Northern public opinion. Adding to the complexities of that imponderable was the fact that the Lincoln administration willingly conducted both the congressional elections of 1862 and the presidential election of 1864. But luckily for the North, Union victories kept the ship of state on a relatively stable course. What the long war did allow the Union to do was to bring its greater military power to bear in the conflict's Western theater. That in turn also held the advantage that it caused Union military operations to drive across the heart of the Confederacy, helping bring the consequences of the war home to nearly every village in the South, a reality of great political importance. There would be no *Dolchstosslegende* (stab in the back legend) as was to occur in Germany after the First World War.

LEADERSHIP: POLITICS AND STRATEGY

In the late 1980s Allan Millett and one of this work's authors reflected on the implication of a multivolume study which the two had edited and which dealt with the military effectiveness of the major powers during the two world wars and the interwar period. Their bottom line was that no matter how effective the military institutions might be at the tactical and operational levels, if the strategy and political framework within which they were fighting was flawed, the result was defeat. But if the national approach reflected a realistic appraisal of the political and strategic framework, then victory was a reasonable probability whatever tactical and operational flaws might have existed at the conflict's outset in a nation's military instruments.

What is of crucial importance in weighing the competence and leadership of the opposing sides in the Civil War is the fact that virtually no one at the time could have foreseen the complexities and difficulties that emerged during the course of the conflict. That said, the political and strategic leadership that Lincoln exhibited stands in stark contrast with that of Davis. In the largest sense, Lincoln learned and grew during the war; Davis did not. Moreover, what makes Lincoln's performance so stunning is the fact that his aim was not just the preservation of the Union but also the preservation of the constitutional and legal framework that the Founding Fathers had created in the Constitution. Thus, one of the foremost problems he faced was the maintenance of the North's political will, particularly because it depended on holding together a diverse coalition, within which there were deep political divisions, especially on the issue of slavery.

If the war were to turn into a lengthy struggle, then the weight of Northern superiority in manpower and industrial strength was going to tell. But at the same time the longer the struggle, the greater would be the strain on the North's political stability. Lincoln's political genius was as important as his strategic genius in keeping the Union on a coherent course that combined, to the extent possible, the internal demands of politics with the maintenance of the war effort.

Above all the new president was a keen observer of others as well as the political landscape and the pulse of popular opinion. He was a good judge of the strengths and weaknesses of the politicians and generals with whom he dealt. That ability to observe those with whom he was dealing and absorb the larger import of issues provided Lincoln with the ability to judge his actions carefully but act when necessary with dispatch. He was, moreover, one of those few who saw the larger issues, in other words, what was important and what was not. Finally, he was able to keep his great strategic goal, the reunion of the southern states with the United States, always firmly in mind, whatever the distractions of the moment might be.

Lincoln's political brilliance also allowed him to manage a cabinet composed in large part of his rivals within the Republican Party. Through judicious, effective leadership, he kept the cabinet together, losing only Secretary of War Cameron in the first three years of the war, and replacing him with the far more competent Stanton. Seward's attempt to assume the role as the real leader of the administration during the Fort Sumter crisis occasioned only the slightest tap on the wrist from the president. From that point, the secretary of state remained a stalwart and loyal member of the administration. Chase was another matter, but Lincoln suffered the treasury secretary's political maneuverings and disloyalty in silence, recognizing that he was also of great value in guiding the government's financial policies. Lincoln's efforts to keep the cabinet largely pulling in the same direction reflected the problem of maintaining the support of the various political, social, and religious constituencies in the North. As the leader of a democracy rather than a monarchy or an oligarchy, the president had to balance the needs of the war with the political views and prejudices of the voters. Moreover, he had to explain, defend, and justify not only the financial cost but also the swelling total of casualties as the war progressed. His Gettysburg Address was only one indication of the sophistication and eloquence that Lincoln brought to the task of mobilizing and maintaining support for the war.

Nothing underlines the difficulties this involved more than the problem of what to do about slavery. At the war's outset, the president's overarching goal was the maintenance of the Union. Nevertheless, there were constituencies in the public at large, in Congress, and even among his own cabinet which wanted the immediate abolition of slavery in response to the secession of the Southern states and the outbreak of war. Other important groups opposed such a radical step, because they believed the break was not irremediable and the radical step of freeing the slaves would in fact embitter the conflict and make compromise with the white South impossible. Among those who opposed the abolition of slavery were McClellan and a number of senior officers in the Army of the Potomac, who presented another set of problems Lincoln had to master.

In fact, Lincoln, though deeply opposed to slavery, was in that second group; yet he also needed the support of the abolitionists. The president's apparent equivocation on the issue made neither group happy, but not so unhappy that they turned against the war. It was only in summer 1862, when it was apparent a compromise peace would not bring the South back into the Union and that the freeing of the slaves represented an important weapon to undermine the Confederacy's economy, that Lincoln drafted the Emancipation Proclamation. He recognized not only the importance of the measure but also how the war had changed the political landscape substantially.

Equally important was Lincoln's ability to deal with Congress and its representatives. Here, the fact that Chase, a crucial figure in financing the war, was also playing duplicitous games with the more radical members of Congress represented a dangerous situation. In 1862, having heard that Chase had fed important Republican senators fallacious information that Lincoln was not listening to the advice of the cabinet, Lincoln invited the concerned senators to attend a cabinet conference. Then during the meeting, the president asked his cabinet whether anyone had any criticisms of how he was conducting the war. No one admitted such conflict. And so the secretary of the treasury lost face with the senate radicals not only for the general silence of the cabinet, but also for his lack of moral courage in remaining silent himself.

Cameron's replacement, Stanton, underlines another part of Lincoln's greatness as a political leader: his ability to suppress his own personal feelings for the good of the nation. The president had every reason to despise Stanton, given the contemptuous fashion with which the eastern lawyer had treated Lincoln in the McCormick trial in 1857. Moreover, Stanton was a Democrat who had supported Douglas in the 1860 election. Yet, Lincoln put that political baggage aside to name a man who was to prove a masterful secretary of war over the last four years of the conflict and one of the president's most competent and loyal supporters. Perhaps Lincoln's greatest strength was the fact that he never allowed his ego to obstruct his larger priorities. His appointment of Stanton is a case in point, because virtually every major figure with whom Lincoln dealt tended to underestimate the qualities and sophistication of the president, at least at first. And the president understood that reality was much to his advantage.

Lincoln's difficulties in finding a winning combination of generals took time. Part of the problem was that the president knew so little about the nature of war and the conduct of strategy. Unlike, however, so many armchair generals scattered throughout the North, the president recognized his ignorance. His request to the Library of Congress that its librarians send him books dealing with war reflected an effort to repair a lack of knowledge about strategy and war. Exacerbating Lincoln's difficulties in developing a successful military strategy and military operations was the fact that so many of those who appeared competent, like McClellan, Pope, Rosecrans, and Halleck, eventually proved dismal failures. Yet, here again Lincoln's dealings with his generals as well as his instinct for competence eventually led him to Grant.

But for the first three years of the war, he confronted the difficulty that he rarely received cogent, intelligent, and useful advice from the military figures with whom he interacted. McClellan was the worst. The Young Napoleon contemptuously dismissed the president's advice in February 1862 that it might be best if Union armies struck against the Confederacy simultaneously; the following year, Lincoln attempted to get Rosecrans to move at the same time as Grant and Hooker, but that general refused to budge. Halleck was certainly not much of an improvement over McClellan in tendering sensible military advice. Moreover, he proved less than helpful in his willingness to support Lincoln's less effective strategic notions, such as an excessive commitment to the overland line of operations against Richmond and the persistent attraction that the Red River and Texas exercised on the president's imagination, even after Vicksburg had rendered those portions of the Confederacy west of the Mississippi strategic and military irrelevancies to the war's outcome.

Lincoln's efforts to articulate a sensible strategy eventually found an able helpmate with the emergence of Grant in the last year and a half of the conflict. Like the president, the general understood the importance of political generals to the conduct of the war. The Confederacy's one hope by 1864 was that its resistance could finally wear down the North's willingness to maintain its course. Above all the other political and strategic issues of 1864 was the reality that the presidential election would occur in November of that year and so the war Democrats, like Butler, Logan, and others, along with important constituencies such as Germans loyal to Sigel, were of great importance to how major portions of the Northern population would vote. Grant's strategy for the crushing of the Confederacy in 1864 rested to a substantial degree on how those generals performed. Yet, he never complained then or later about the fact that their dead weight hobbled the conduct of his military operations.

Perhaps the foremost indication of the brilliance with which Lincoln managed the conduct of politics and grand strategy during the war is to consider the distinct possibility of what would have happened had either Seward or Chase won the nomination for president in mid-May 1860. The mere fact that Seward strongly advocated a war with Spain and France in the first days of the new administration as a means to bring the two halves of the nation back together suggests how disastrous his presidency might have been. On the other hand, Chase as president would probably have supported the abolition of slavery before the length and tenacity of Confederate resistance made it clear that there was no alternative but to free the slaves. That alone would have added to the numbers of those in the North who believed the war was not worth fighting. And neither Seward nor Chase possessed the political flexibility or sagacity to balance the contending factions in Congress or the North in a fashion sufficient to keep the majority firmly committed to the conduct of the war.

GENERALSHIP AND THE CONDUCT OF THE WAR

Those who were to lead the armies of the Union and the Confederacy understood little at the beginning of the war about the character and extent of the coming conflict. Not only were the basic tactical and operational conceptions fundamentally flawed, but also virtually no one understood the complexities of the strategic framework as the war unfolded. Moreover, this was a war during which the armies learned on the fly. In other words, they learned by filling graves. And considering the state of military knowledge at the time and the enormous changes that the advent of technology brought in its wake, the extent of the war and the difficulties the opposing sides discovered in waging it should not be surprising.

In the Civil War one can speak of a nascent military profession, molded by a combination of a West Point education, the idiosyncratic experiences of the war against Mexico in the late 1840s, and the isolated, mundane drudgery of service in the forts and posts of the frontier. But even in Europe, the concept of a *military profession*, one that required intellectual as well as physical preparation, was only now beginning to emerge. Given the fact that even at the beginning of the twenty-first century, all too many generals and admirals regard the study of military and strategic history as only of minimal use to their profession, one should not find oneself surprised at the general lack of study among the officers of the United States Army before 1861.

In fact, at that time only the Prussians had established a school for the education of a *very* small group of their officers, who found employment in their army's minuscule Great General Staff. Not until after Prussia's devastating victories over the Austrians in the Seven Weeks' War of 1866 and the French in the Franco-Prussian War of 1870–71 did the world's military organizations take note that the schooling of officers might be of some use in the preparation for and then the execution of military operations. Nevertheless, it would take the First World War before there was some glimmering in the world's military institutions that the profession of arms was not only the most demanding physically but intellectually as well. Competence is a most rare commodity in human affairs—a reality to which too few historians give consideration. Lincoln's search for a competent general who could understand the war's larger strategic framework and at the same time fight it at the tactical and operational levels represented a most difficult task, because the only man in the North or the South who eventually matched that job description could not possibly have been considered for that position at the war's outset. It was only later in the war that Grant grew into the stature and ability to fill that position.

Lee, for all his ability as a tactical commander, never understood the wider parameters of the Confederacy's strategic position. He was right to fear the prospect of a long war that would allow Federal superiority in men and material to make its weight felt, but he underestimated the countervailing effects of Northern impatience. And while Lee's offensive victories, particularly in 1862, provided a huge boost to Confederate morale, Lee's aggressive style of operations had far more to do with his own style and character of command than a deliberate and rational attempt to buttress Confederate public opinion, even if that was the result of his actions. Johnston was an outstanding army commander as long as he was on the defensive, but in 1863 his conduct as overall commander of the Confederacy's Western theater was less than impressive. His retreat to Atlanta in 1864 represented a brilliant defensive campaign, but he never made it clear to the government in Richmond exactly what his military strategy was. By the war's last year, Sherman came closest to resembling Grant's breadth of vision. As a strategist in the largest sense he was brilliant, but while a competent operational commander, he never quite matched Lee's capabilities on the battlefield.

In terms of the other army commanders, the record is dismal. Bragg was the worst in the war at every level, a major contributing factor to Union victories in the West and eventually in the war. Pemberton was no better as an army commander, but unfortunately he had less time to damage the Confederate cause. The Army of the Potomac provides the clearest example of how rare competence at the highest ranks of the opposing armies was. One can count only Meade as reasonably competent; on the other hand, a list of its largely or totally inept commanders would include McClellan, Pope, Burnside, and Hooker, all of whom dismally failed to handle Lee.

At the next level down, that of corps commanders capable of independent action as well as performance under the direction of a superior, the truly competent are not much more numerous. Certainly one would include Jackson, Hardee, Early, Stuart, and Longstreet on the Confederate side (although the last was not impressive in independent command in the West); on the Union side one might count Porter, Sheridan, McPherson, Schofield, Thomas, Logan, Hancock, and perhaps Hooker. Hooker, of course, is a wonderful example of the Peter Principle, since his record as a corps commander was outstanding, while his performance as an army commander at Chancellorsville was dismal. Thereafter, the list is hardly impressive. There is one other additional figure worthy of mention and that is Forrest, whose record for what today might well be termed "special operations" places him without a doubt as the greatest combat leader in the war. Nevertheless, Forrest only got to exercise higher command after Hood had entirely wrecked the Army of Tennessee. Thus, there is little to judge him on beyond his extraordinary record in leading small cavalry forces against more numerous Union cavalry.

Of all the generals in the war Grant is both the most interesting and the most difficult to discern, because behind his mask of simplicity lay an understanding of war that few generals in history have equaled. In his practical rather than theoretical fashion, Grant was groping toward an understanding of generalship from the earliest days in independent command. Shortly before the Virginia campaign of 1864, he gathered together his staff and indicated to them not only how he intended to use them but his expectations for them as well: "I want you to discuss with me freely from time to time the details of the orders given for the conduct of a battle, and learn my views as fully as possible as to what course should be pursued in all contingencies which may arise. I expect to send you to the critical points of the lines to keep me properly advised of what is taking place, and in cases of great emergency, when new dispositions have to be made on the instant, or it becomes suddenly necessary to reinforce one command by sending to its aid troops from another, and there is not time to communicate with headquarters, I want you to explain my views to commanders and urge immediate action, looking to cooperation, without waiting for specific orders from me."[7] In terms of when Grant tendered his views on their role to his staff officers, he undoubtedly was referring to the immediate battles in which the Army of the Potomac would soon find itself involved, but as he steadily recognized his responsibility as the commander in chief of all Union armies, he would extend this staff system to all his various responsibilities and the Union armies under his command.

Like Lee, who learned hard lessons in the complexities of operational command in West Virginia, where he failed, and in the Seven Days battles, where his search for his own Cannae eluded him even as he dominated the cowed McClellan, Grant grew into his role as a great operational commander. This is extraordinarily surprising, considering his starting point as a clerk in his father's dry goods store in Galena, Illinois, in spring 1861. His memoirs, extraordinary for their honesty as well as literary qualities, provide wonderful insights into his growth. Perhaps the most important is his account of his first independent command in Missouri, an account which we quoted in chapter 3. Grant perceptively underlined the psychological demands that confronted him and all those embarking on their first independent command. Some commanders, like Grant, master that fear immediately; some, like Sherman, master it later when given a second chance (and when protected by a superior like Grant); some, like McClellan and Hooker, never master that fear; and some, like Bragg and Burnside, lack the imagination to have that fear. The last two generals, moreover, lacked the ability to conceive of either the range of options either open to them or to their opponents.

Like other commanders in the West, Grant understood little about the complexities of the war he confronted. But he had important advantages over most other Civil War generals. He possessed an instinctive feel for war, particularly in his belief that it was better to move sooner rather than later. Thus, unlike McClellan and Halleck and many others, Grant, like Napoleon, understood the importance of time to the conduct of military operations and that delay was probably as useful to his opponents as it might be to him. Thus, his move against Donelson and Henry in the middle of winter—a move others considered but did not act on—underlined the crucial advantage that acting rather than thinking provided the commander.

Shiloh was the first terrible killing battle of the Civil War. It still provides ammunition for those interested in supporting the thesis that Grant was a butcher. In fact, Shiloh was nothing of the sort. Rather, it reflected the rank amateurism of everybody involved in the Civil War in 1862. Moreover, Grant and his subordinate commanders were clearly suffering from a bout of "victory disease." Neither they nor their Confederate opponents displayed the slightest professionalism at that battle, the Confederates advancing toward Shiloh Church at a snail's pace, firing their weapons as they advanced toward their Union opponents. The Union army was scarcely better prepared, not bothering to entrench in the middle of the enemy's country and ignoring all the reports of a Confederate approach.

But at Shiloh Grant displayed great sangfroid. At the end of the first day, when approached by Sherman in the evening about the dismal results of the fighting, Grant laconically replied: "lick 'em tomorrow."[8] And that was precisely what happened. When it was over, Grant became the target of scurrilous reports that reflected the horror in the North at the casualty bill. There was, of course, an excuse for the

Northern newspapers to display considerable upset at the casualties, but less so for historians. In historical terms Shiloh was only the first of the many terrible killing battles. In reality it reflected the deep commitment of both sides to the struggle, something few on either side of the struggle had yet recognized.

Grant could have escaped much of the opprobrium by blaming Sherman for the fact that Johnston and Beauregard had surprised his troops. If anyone deserved blame for the initial debacle at Shiloh, it was the redhead. But unlike with the probable reaction of McClellan in similar circumstances, Grant took responsibility for the fact that the Confederates had surprised his troops at Shiloh, instead of looking for a scapegoat. Sherman would not forget that fact, which was to create the basis for his lifelong loyalty to Grant. In late 1862 the failure of Grant's initial thrust against Mississippi revealed to him during the course of the retreat the possibility that his army could subsist on its own by living off the countryside. Sherman vociferously argued against that course in April 1863, but having later participated in the Vicksburg campaign and seen firsthand the possibilities of having the South feed Union armies, both he and Grant saw the next step. Thus, in 1864 they moved on not only to having the South provide sustenance to Union armies on the march but also to having those armies wreck its infrastructure as a part of a larger campaign of intimidation to break the will of Confederate civilians to continue the war. In Clausewitzian terms it was war carried out for distinctly political purposes. As we have suggested, it came with a long-term political price, but there was no other choice given the willingness of the Confederate people to bear enormous burdens in the face of terrible defeats.

Grant's generalship shows to its best advantage during 1863, when he was able to articulate two stunning victories, the first of which resulted in the capture of Vicksburg and the capture of most of Pemberton's army, the second such victory Grant had achieved during the course of the war. The second great victory in 1863 saw Grant restore the North's strategic control of southeastern Tennessee after the defeat at Chickamauga. In both campaigns Grant relied on the initiative and drive of his subordinate corps and division commanders to execute, what the US military today terms, his intent. With subordinate army, corps, and division commanders like Sherman, McPherson, Thomas, Hooker, Hovey, Sheridan, and a number of others, Grant's conduct of military operations throughout the year was extraordinary by any standard, especially considering where Grant had started two years before.

In 1864, Grant, however, ran up against the command culture that marred the performance of the Army of the Potomac at every level. For the less than impressive results that army achieved in its Overland Campaign in Virginia, there were a number of major factors that inhibited Grant's ability to influence operations. The first was that, given how little time Grant had to deal with the army's senior leaders after assuming his position in command of all Union armies, he was almost completely unfamiliar with the army, its senior officers, and its culture of command. Thus, after the Wilderness he gave the crucial role of the advance to Spotsylvania Courthouse to Warren, the last individual capable of reaching that critical point with dispatch. As with all things in life, it took Grant time to adjust to his new surroundings; perhaps his clearest insight lay in his understanding that he had to leave the command structure as it was.

In the Army of the Potomac Grant possessed a flawed institution incapable of acting in a fashion similar to the armies and corps he had commanded in the West in 1863. It took Grant time to recognize that there was something wrong in the context of leadership within which the Army of the Potomac worked. As he commented to Wilson, "what's wrong with this army?"[9] But he also understood that as an outsider, he could not act as Pope had in 1862; he had to provide the nudge and the drive to the army, but only through the commanders with whom it was familiar.

The command culture that Grant had created in the West depended on mutual trust and cooperation among senior leaders. An overly intrusive hand in the East in 1864 would only revive the divisions that had bedeviled Pope. As a result, Grant understood that he must provide Meade and his subordinates with the moral support that would provide them the ability to take on "Bobby" Lee and the myth of Confederate battlefield superiority that the Army of the Potomac's culture of command had done so much to create. With Meade, Grant played a role similar to the surrogate figure that he wished he had had on that lonely day in Missouri when he had undertaken his first independent command. Indeed, Grant had great respect for Meade that had begun in their first meeting when the latter had offered without bidding to relinquish his position. Grant understood that he had to run the Army of the Potomac through Meade and that whatever Meade's weaknesses he was the only one of that army's senior officers capable of keeping that army moving forward. In the end, one must evaluate Grant's conduct of the great 1864 campaign from the Rappahannock through to Petersburg in terms of the flawed instrument through which he waged that effort.

Of all the other commanders in the war, Sherman most resembled Grant in his skill and understanding of the nature of the war the Union was fighting. Unlike Grant, Sherman had a most unsteady beginning to independent command. His first independent command came close to giving him a nervous breakdown, but he recovered under Grant's tutelage. Shiloh represented an epiphany for Sherman, and he steadily improved with the Vicksburg campaign providing the final class in generalship. It also provided him an education in how to move an army through enemy territory and live off the countryside. That campaign provided Sherman as well as Grant with insight as to the necessity of destroying the South's industrial infrastructure as well as its agricultural basis. Sherman's conduct of the 1864 Atlanta campaign, followed by the March to the Sea and his march through the Carolinas, represented the war's decisive act. About the only weakness in his conduct of the Georgia operations was that he lacked Lee's innate aggressiveness, but then 1864 was hardly the year for overaggressiveness, as Hood's attacks underlined. But Sherman's capacity to maneuver his armies in the face of as sagacious and dangerous an opponent as Johnston underline why only Grant exhibited greater generalship.

The war against the Confederacy's civilian population signaled how much the war had changed since the early years of the conflict. The historical record of the March to the Sea indicates that it was not nearly as ferocious as the mythmakers of the Confederacy were to make it. Sherman's troops did leave alone most of the houses in Georgia, while their commander and his troops behaved with exquisite politeness to the citizens of Savannah. When it came to South Carolina, it was another matter. Sherman's troops, with the support of their commander, ratcheted the damage up to a new level, a warning to unreconstructed Confederates of what awaited white Southerners should their resistance continue. His unvarnished comments during the war were for the most part aimed at Confederate propaganda and were designed to break the will of the white South. They were at times overstated except perhaps in the case of South Carolina, but those ferocious comments came back to haunt him after the war. The economic and psychological damage Sherman wreaked on the larger Confederate war effort, however, prevented any postwar revival of secession.

On the other side of the hill, Lee was the master of the operational art. Furthermore, Lee had the perspicacity to select Jackson and Longstreet as his two most important subordinates when he reorganized his command structure after the Seven Days battles. From June 1862 through to the end of the war, Lee kept alive among the soldiers of the Army of Northern Virginia the flame of resistance and a belief in their own superiority. But Lee's twin invasions of the North in search of a decisive victory underlines that he greatly overestimated the operational possibilities. The defensive campaign of 1864 against Meade and Grant represented Lee's greatest campaign of the war considering the odds. Yet, there are two significant points to make about that campaign. First, Grant's constant, unrelenting pressure robbed Lee of the opportunity to launch one of those blistering counterattacks that had proven so psychologically devastating during the Seven Days battles, the Second Bull Run, and Chancellorsville. Second, even with the numbers weighing so heavily against the Army of Northern Virginia, Lee could not resist launching weak counterattacks, which, as Porter Alexander noted after the war, simply added to a casualty bill the Confederacy could not afford. In the end, the greatest accolade for Lee's reputation lies in the fact that having fought to the bitter end, he accepted the results with grace and humility *and* urged his countrymen to follow along the same path.

Johnston is the great puzzle among the Confederate commanders. He was not a risk taker, refusing to take the offensive unless absolutely pushed into desperate circumstances. The position of Confederate armies in front of Richmond in late May 1862 represented such circumstances, and at Seven Pines, Johnston struck as hard a blow as any Lee was to strike in succeeding weeks. Whether Johnston would have continued with the hammer blows that his replacement, Lee, was to launch is impossible to answer, although it seems unlikely considering his later record. After Johnston's recovery from wounds suffered at Seven Pines, he moved to the West. He received a position similar to the one Grant would receive in response to Chickamauga, but Davis refused to provide him with the authority Grant received from Lincoln. Moreover, the Confederate president consistently interfered by issuing orders to Pemberton and Bragg, those to Pemberton contributing significantly to the Vicksburg disaster.

Nevertheless, the Vicksburg campaign did not display Johnston in an impressive light. In particular, he underestimated Grant's ability to act with dispatch and overestimated the threat that Rosecrans posed, at least in spring 1863. He even had to be ordered by Seddon to travel to central Mississippi to take charge of what was a rapidly deteriorating situation. As theater commander, he was out of touch with what was happening; his failure to dispatch a liaison officer from his staff kept Pemberton in the dark, while confusing messages and reports from central Mississippi obscured the situation to Johnston himself. Not surprisingly, his arrival at Jackson came too late to repair what was already a disaster in the making. Still, had Pemberton followed Johnston's orders rather than those of Davis, to keep his army in being rather than to hold Vicksburg at all costs, the Confederates might have at least saved the army.

Finally, after Chattanooga, Davis replaced Bragg with Johnston. In his role as army commander of the Army of Tennessee, Johnston put the army back together again. Much like Hooker with the Army of the Potomac the year before, he reorganized the army's administration, saw that his troops were properly fed and clothed to the extent possible, and provided a hands-on leadership that earned the admiration of his troops. His conduct of the 1864 campaign also earned their deep respect, even though their army was retreating, because they now had a commander who was highly skilled in defensive warfare and willing to husband their lives. What Johnston could not repair was a culture of backbiting in the army's high command that Bragg's long tenure had created. Hood's arrival as a corps commander only exacerbated the troubles among the senior officers of the Army of Tennessee. In the end Johnston proved the greatest master of defensive warfare— but that skill put him out of touch with the larger culture of Southern white society.

At the next level down, Jackson and Sheridan were cut from the same cloth as combat commanders. There were few harder men than those two, both as impatient with their subordinates as with the enemy's continued existence. It is no wonder that the Prussians, hardly the humanitarians of the nineteenth century, found Sheridan so congenial. The harshness with which Jackson not only drove himself but also his subordinates and soldiers was something that few of the hagiographies about the general mention. As an independent commander in the Shenandoah in spring 1862, he conducted the most brilliant campaign of the war against far more numerous Union armies. Whether he could have been as effective in the larger arena of the great armies that fought farther east in the Virginia theater can never be known, but of all those at that level of command, Jackson appears as the most likely to have succeeded at the highest level of war. Sheridan was almost as ruthless, as tough, and as effective a commander as Jackson. It took him longer in the war to emerge, and it was not until 1864 after three years of preparation that he got his chance. Sheridan did have the advantage of numbers in the Shenandoah, but then he was up against a far more competent opponent in Early than the fools Jackson had faced in the Valley in 1862. As for unsatisfactory subordinates, Sheridan simply fired them, unlike Jackson who put them under arrest. Sheridan also proved himself an avid pupil of Grant's and Sherman's hard war in his harrying of the Valley at the end of 1864.

Longstreet clearly had less success than either Jackson or Sheridan in his opportunities at independent command. But he may well have been the best corps commander of the lot. He was cautious when there was a need for caution, but furious in the attack when the opportunity presented itself at Second Bull Run, Chickamauga, and the second day of the Wilderness. Moreover, of all the commanders in the war, Longstreet grasped the realities of firepower. Thus, throughout the Gettysburg campaign he warned a Lee unwilling to listen that a defensive stance had a far better chance of success. He lost the argument, and Pickett's charge, against which Longstreet had so strongly argued, was the result.

But if competence played a major role in the conduct of the war, so too did incompetence. Three individuals are deserving of special mention in this regard, because of their positions at senior levels for extended period: McClellan, Halleck, and Bragg. McClellan was an extraordinary bundle of contradictions and personality flaws, all of which were exacerbated by real intelligence. There is no doubt that he was a highly competent administrator. He also displayed more strategic sense than his successors, until Grant stepped on the scene. His preparation of the Army of the Potomac created a force with the discipline and coherence that allowed it to stay the course through four terrible years of sacrifice. Yet, McClellan also did much to imbue that army with a culture that was top down, averse to risk taking, prone to factionalism, incapable of acting with dispatch, and overly insistent on an officer's date of rank in determining who commanded. That culture remained in the fiber of the Army of the Potomac long after McClellan had departed for his home in New Jersey.

McClellan's aptitude as an organizer and trainer is well known, but less widely acknowledged are his merits as a strategist. His plan to take advantage of Federal naval superiority and strike at Richmond via the Peninsula was an inspired choice, vindicated to some degree by Grant's difficulties with the more direct overland approach. However, McClellan's strengths were undone by his political ineptitude and operational incapacity. He consistently overestimated Lee's strength, arrogantly dismissed Lincoln as a fool, and in his letters to his wife, which formed so much of his autobiography (written by others after his death) he revealed a personality always seeking to blame his failings on others. Nothing displays McClellan's weaknesses more than his failure to act with dispatch before Antietam when Lee's plans fell into his hands and the opportunity existed to bag the Army of Northern Virginia. As a field commander McClellan lacked any sense that his opponents had worries of their own. Above all he lacked that German sense that it was better to make a flawed decision in time than to make a perfect decision too late. Undoubtedly, McClellan's faults masked deep psychological weaknesses and insecurities. Despite his obvious physical courage (McClellan had earned a fine combat record during the Mexican War), his unwillingness or inability to lead from near the sharp end of the fighting—his disappearance from the battlefields of both Malvern Hill and Antietam cases in point—suggest a worthwhile human trait—namely, that he could not abide the suffering that is inherent in war, but that is a human quality no successful general can afford.

There was considerable irony in McClellan's time as commander of the Army of the Potomac, because his failings, insured that the Civil War was going to be a long war. If ever there were a chance there might have been a short conflict, it was during the spring of 1862. McClellan's handling of the Peninsula Campaign was so slow and incompetent that the Confederates were not only able to hold on but also eventually dealt the Army of the Potomac a series of blows that broke its commander's morale. A swift Union victory at that point might still have furthered a remorseless process that led to the destruction of slavery, but a President George B. McClellan would not have supported civil rights measures such as the Fourteenth and Fifteenth Amendments. Indeed, a shorter war that did not devastate and exhaust the Confederacy as did the actual war might have made possible a resumption of the fighting at a later date.

In every respect Henry Halleck was a serious impediment to the conduct of the war by Union forces. He was a pedant, enveloped in a warped understanding of Jomini and what Halleck believed was proper military theory. Like McClellan, he was overly cautious as a field commander, and if he did not consistently overestimate the size of the Confederate armies opposing him in spring 1862, he certainly worried incessantly about what his opponents were going to do to his force. His leadership in the advance to Corinth was an appallingly bad piece of overcautious generalship. Luckily, he was not up against Lee. When Halleck moved to Washington in July 1862, he assumed the position as commander in chief of the Union armies. From that lofty perch he provided endless advice but refused to provide clear and sensible direction to the commanders in the field.

There are few positive things that one can say about Halleck. He was certainly an improvement over Frémont in the West when he replaced the latter, but that is damning with faint praise. Halleck did maintain a friendship with Sherman and gave the redhead a second chance after his breakdown at Louisville. He also provided Grant with the warning about McClernand's efforts to create an independent army along the Mississippi. That decision appears to have been motivated more by Halleck's desire to keep volunteer officers from holding the highest positions than by any real desire to help Grant or by an understanding of McClernand's incapacity to conduct major military operations in the Mississippi Valley.

It was in his relationship with Grant that Halleck came closest to wrecking the Union's military effort. One can only characterize Halleck's treatment of his subordinate after the successes of Donelson and Henry as reflecting a general who recognized Grant's competence as a threat to his own position. His dismissal of two major proposals that Grant made after the capture of Vicksburg suggest a great deal about his consistent inability to focus on what mattered strategically. Halleck's contemptuous rejection of Grant's proposal that his Army of the Tennessee move against Mobile by using the navy underlined his inability to see that such a move would add greatly to the impact of Rosecrans's move against Chattanooga. Similarly, his dismissal of Grant's proposal to attack Wilmington in early 1864 again represented a lack of strategic imagination. Unlike his eventual superior, Grant,

Halleck had no ability to see how the combination of joint army and navy forces could contribute to the achievement of the North's larger military goals. Finally, in terms of understanding the transportation revolution, Halleck estimated that the move of Hooker's two corps to the Western armies would take three months. That fact underlines how little he was in tune with the technology and logistical capabilities of the time, even after more than two years of war.

Braxton Bragg's record of command is indeed one of the strangest in American military history. There seems to have been no one who served under his command who did not in a relatively short period of time come to despise him. Longstreet holds the record for the speed with which he evaluated Bragg's dismal talents. Within forty-eight hours of his arrival on the Chickamauga battlefield, Longstreet had recognized Bragg's unsuitability to hold higher command. Yet Davis allowed Bragg to remain in significant positions until the end of the war.

THE CULTURE OF THE ARMIES

One of the major areas of Civil War history that surely is deserving of further study is that of the culture of the main armies that bore the greatest burdens in the fighting of the war. The two most peculiar of those cultures were those of the Army of the Potomac and the Army of Tennessee, which managed through four years of fighting to accumulate the most appalling record of lost battles and yet stay the course until the collapse of the Confederacy and the triumph of the Union. The Army of the Potomac listed in its dismal record, defeats (or, at the very least, severe disappointments) at the First Bull Run, Seven Pines, the Seven Days battles, Second Bull Run, Chancellorsville, the Wilderness, Spotsylvania Courthouse, North Anna, Cold Harbor, Petersburg, and the "Crater." In four years of war, it managed two victories, Gettysburg and Five Forks (the latter at the war's very end) and one tie (Antietam). The Army of Tennessee's record was even worse, one victory (Chickamauga) and perhaps one tie, Stones River.

On the other hand, the Army of Northern Virginia and the Union's Western armies—the Army of the Tennessee, the Army of the Cumberland, and the Army of the Ohio—offer interesting contrasts in terms of their combat performance. In terms of the enlisted ranks, the material in these armies was much the same. What differed were the command echelons and officer corps of these armies. How the armies developed their individual cultures suggests much about leadership and the creation of an effective military culture as well as the difficulties involved in altering a dysfunctional command climate, particularly in the first days when a new general takes command of an organization. This is as true of modern armies as it was of Civil War armies.

Obviously, there are simple but inadequate explanations for the extraordinary differences in the operational performance of these armies. McClellan clearly played a major role in establishing a culture which abjured initiative and emphasized top-down control of virtually everything. Yet, McClellan left the army within little more than a year of assuming command, and the culture of the Army of the Potomac remained as obdurately unimaginative and top down in its Overland Campaign of 1864. His influence lived on through the fact that he had appointed the division and brigade commanders when the army formed up in the months after the First Bull Run. Part of the problem also had to do with the dominance of Old Army, by-the-book, date-of-rank officers, who failed to adjust to the realities of volunteer citizen-soldier armies. It was the exact opposite of the attitudes of the armies led by Grant and Lee in 1863. Warren's punctilious desire to insure that his subordinate division commanders executed his orders precisely, to the point of doing their job for them, is a case in point. However, one should not overemphasize the influence of regular army attitudes—the Army of Northern Virginia possessed more than its fair share of West Pointers, but it displayed none of the Army of the Potomac's characteristic caution. In this case, the character of Lee mitigated decisively the worst influence of the Old Army.

One should not dismiss the role of chance, a factor that both Thucydides and Clausewitz emphasize as among the most important in the conduct of war in determining the command climate that characterized the Civil War armies. Lee's great advantage in the first years of his command was the fact that he possessed an extraordinary group of corps and division commanders to execute his orders, especially Jackson, Longstreet, and Stuart. Yet, here chance played its role, combat removing first Jackson in May 1863 and then Stuart in May 1864 from the table permanently and Longstreet for much of the fighting in 1864. But the Army of Northern Virginia was lucky in comparison to its opponent, the Army of the Potomac, which in 1862 and 1863, lost a number of its most promising and aggressive general officers in combat—Kearny, Reno, Richardson, and Reynolds—leaving

Meade after Gettysburg with a less than impressive team of corps commanders.

In contrast the Army of the Cumberland proved more fortunate. Besides a rough start under Buell, who allowed internal divisions to run rampant, and which were only exacerbated by Rosecrans, the army eventually found a competent commander in Thomas. However, even in its revived state, the Army of the Cumberland would remain a sluggish and blunt instrument when compared to Grant's Army of the Tennessee. Not surprisingly, given the differences in their approach to war, Grant would find himself frustrated by Thomas's inability to move quickly.

The Army of Tennessee would seem to offer the easiest explanation for a culture of command that was to prove so dismal. Bragg is the prime candidate for the dysfunctional culture of command that emerged over the course of his period of command. Moreover, as Grant discovered with the Army of the Potomac, the command culture of a military organization is not easily altered. Clearly, in terms of the Army of Tennessee, that culture did not disappear when Davis sacked the main agent of its creation, Bragg, after the disaster of Missionary Ridge. Johnston found that culture still firmly imbedded in the Army of Tennessee throughout his period in command. And it was not just a matter of Bragg's legacy, because Hood fit right into the persistent pattern of backstabbing that continued through to the demise of the Army of Tennessee in 1865.

In the end both Lee and Grant created and managed effective combat organizations that determined the course of the war. Admittedly, Lee was immensely helped by having such an extraordinary group of subordinates. In the West, Grant created a group of generals who proved capable of absorbing his intent and then acting on it. Admittedly, the process of acculturation took time, partially because Grant himself had to grow and adapt to the difficulties that leading a great army inevitably raised. On the other hand, when Grant moved East, he had to handle the problems that the leadership culture of the Army of the Potomac raised. Not only was he thoroughly unfamiliar with that organization and its leaders, but also the demands of running the larger war inevitably pulled at his time and concentration. Thus, Grant could only encourage Meade to drive the Army of the Potomac forward with the result that the Overland Campaign of spring 1864 ended up in one flawed attack after another. In other words, even for

Grant the Army of the Potomac remained a flawed instrument, so cautious and lacking initiative, as opposed to the Western armies Grant had led in 1862 and 1863.

Conclusion

Grant's difficulties during the Overland Campaign and Lee's masterful fighting withdrawal showed how a Confederate strategist might have eroded the Union's will to continue the war with a defensive strategy of attrition, but only Johnston seems to have had some glimmerings that defensive operations offered up substantial possibilities of success at the strategic level. Nevertheless, such a strategic approach would have been antithetical not only to the leaders of the Confederacy, but to its people as well in the early years of the war. Even as late as summer 1864, Davis's removal of Johnston in July 1864 was popular among most white Southerners until the results of Hood's disastrous offensives became clear.

The failure of the Confederate experiment then lay in several factors. Even with the offensive mentality that characterized so much of its conduct of the war, the rebellion's failure was not foreordained. The defeat of the Confederacy lay in the West with the failures of 1863 and 1864. Lee held the front door with his magnificent leadership until the end. But the collapse of the backdoor resulted in the destruction of the whole enterprise. And there Davis's flawed understanding of the Western theater and its reality consistently contributed to the defeats. The cordon defense established by Albert Sidney Johnston in 1862 failed disastrously. Nevertheless, that did not deter Davis from ordering Pemberton to hold both Vicksburg and Port Hudson.

If that were not enough, Davis's persistent support for Bragg, not only in 1862 and 1863, but also his continued use of that vicious, quarrelsome officer as his chief military advisor in 1864, beggars imagination. Having done so much to make the Western theater of operations a disaster for Confederate arms from Murfreesboro through Chattanooga, Bragg then put the icing on the cake by supporting Hood in his duplicitous and dishonest efforts to supplant Johnston. The fact that the United States Army still has one of its most important military installations named for a racist, vicious incompetent suggests something about the ahistoricism of the politically correct America of the twenty-first century. The collapse of the Confederate military position in the West by the fall of 1864 bought Grant the time he needed to asphyxiate Lee's Army of Northern Virginia in the trench lines of Richmond and Petersburg. And so by disastrous strategic mistakes did Davis minimize the Confederacy's potential to survive its war of independence.

But the great mastermind behind the Union victory was Abraham Lincoln. In no way was Lincoln the kindly martyred saint that has entered too much of the nation's mythology. He was a hard, tough man of great perception, natural talent, and deep political discernment. He also was a deeply decent human being. When he had to, he signed the execution orders for those who had deserted Union armies. He supported the hard war, when there was no other choice. Consistently underestimated by most, he used that fact to his advantage. Lincoln adapted and tacked as conditions demanded, but he never lost sight of his goal: Union. And he supported those who displayed competence on the battlefield, although in the first two years of the war, it was hard to find that quality among Union generals. His assassination at the war's end saved his reputation from the ravages of the "Lost Cause" narrative, because he would undoubtedly have followed a course of reconstruction similar to that pursued by Grant. In the end he deserves the title of the greatest American president because the recreated United States of 1865 was his doing more than that of any other man.

ACKNOWLEDGMENTS

There are innumerable individuals whom I should thank for helping to see me through this long and tortuous effort to write my portions of this history of the Civil War. But in particular let me thank just a few: John Henry Lang, class of 1977, whose history thesis on the Civil War I directed because no faculty members of the Yale history department believed themselves capable of guiding a thesis on the military aspects of the war. John's outstanding work reawakened my interest in the war just before I left Yale for The Ohio State University. I should also like to thank Colonel Len Fullenkamp, US Army ret., and Colonel Robert Gaskin, USAF ret., who through our long conversations, numerous staff rides, and an ongoing dialogue that lasted for nearly two decades pointed me in the right direction. I would also like to thank Generals Bill Mullen and Dale Alford, both still on active duty with the Marine Corps, for the time they spent in reading my chapters and going on staff rides of Gettysburg and Antietam a number of times. I would also like to thank Colonel Rick Sinnreich for his help in reading the manuscript as I produced my portions of it and in giving me carefully crafted criticism, as only he can do. Finally, there is my kind, gentle, ruthless, no-holds-barred editor, Lesley Mary Smith, who now has become deeply knowledgeable about the Civil War through her innumerable readings of various drafts.

WILLIAMSON MURRAY

Recognition should also go to our mapmaker, K. Fitzgerald for Red Lion Mapping.

The younger author would like to acknowledge the continuing support of his employer, the History Department of the United States Naval Academy, which remains hospitable to a historian of the United States Army. Professor Lynn M. Thomas, former chair of the University of Washington History Department, provided invaluable assistance in granting me access to her institution's superb library resources as a visiting scholar during a family leave in the Pacific Northwest, without which this manuscript's completion would have been considerably delayed. Finally, the younger coauthor's family deserves credit for patiently awaiting the completion of this manuscript, despite all its associated distractions away from play dates, library visits, and walks in the park.

WAYNE WEI-SIANG HSIEH

NOTES

Preface

1. Thucydides, *The History of the Peloponnesian War*, trans. Rex Warner (London, 1954), p. 35.

Introduction

1. MacGregor Knox and Williamson Murray, eds., *The Dynamics of Military Revolution, 1300–2050* (Cambridge, 2000), p. 190.
2. Allan R. Millet and Williamson Murray, *Military Effectiveness*, vol. 1, *The First World War* (London, 1988), p. 2.
3. Historians past and present have also chastised Davis for abandoning African American refugees to vengeful Confederate cavalrymen during the March to the Sea at Ebenezer Creek. Davis never received a promotion to major general due to his notoriety for murdering his superior officer. It is telling, however, that he was never court-martialed.

Chapter 1: The Origins

1. Thucydides, *The History of the Peloponnesian War*, p. 49.
2. John C. Calhoun, *A Disquisition on Government and a Discourse on the Constitution and Government of the United States*, ed. Richard K. Cralle (Charleston, 1851), p. 393.
3. William Thomas, *The Iron Way: Railroads, the Civil War, and the Making of Modern America* (New Haven, CT, 2011), appendix.
4. Frederick W. Seward, *Autobiography of William H. Seward from 1831–1834, with a Memoir of His Life, and Selections from His Letters from 1831 to 1846* (New York, 1877), p. 271.
5. Ira Berlin, *Many Thousands Gone: The First Two Centuries of Slavery in North America* (Cambridge, MA, 1998).
6. Ulysses S. Grant, *Personal Memoirs of U. S. Grant*, 2 vols. (New York, 1885), vol. 1, p. 53.

7. Ibid., vol. 1, p. 56.
8. *Congressional Globe,* 29th Cong., 1st Sess., August 12, 1846, p. 1217.
9. Roy P. Basler, ed., *Collected Works of Abraham Lincoln* (New Brunswick, NJ, 1953), vol. 2, p. 323. Henceforth cited as *CWAL.*
10. Allan Nevins, *Ordeal of the Union*, 8 vols.; vol. 2, *A House Dividing, 1852–1857* (New York, 1947–71), p. 446.
11. Quoted in James M. McPherson, *Battle Cry of Freedom: The Civil War Era* (New York, 1988), p. 156.
12. Don E. Fehrenbacher, *The Dred Scott Case: Its Significance in America Law and Politics* (New York, 2001), p. 3.
13. Quoted in ibid., p. 418.
14. James D. Richardson, ed., *A Compilation of the Messages and Papers of the Presidents of the United States, 1798–1897* (Washington, DC, 1897), vol. 5, p. 479.
15. "The Harper's Ferry Outbreak," *New York Herald*, November 3, 1859.
16. Henry David Thoreau, *Essays: A Fully Annotated Edition*, ed. Jeffrey S. Cramer (New Haven, CT, 2013), p. 198.
17. Quoted in Nevins, *Ordeal of the Union*, vol. 4, *The Emergence of Lincoln: Prologue to Civil War, 1859–1861* (New York, 1950), p. 96, n. 37.
18. Ibid., p. 223.
19. Quoted in Eric Foner, *Free Soil, Free Labor, Free Men: The Ideology of the Republican Party before the Civil War* (New York, 1970), p. 223.
20. Jefferson Davis, *Jefferson Davis, The Essential Writings*, ed. William J. Cooper Jr. (New York, 2004), p. 197.
21. Thucydides, *The History of the Peloponnesian War*, p. 82.
22. Quoted in Nevins, *Ordeal of the Union*, vol. 4, *The Emergence of Lincoln*, p. 156.
23. Thucydides, *The History of the Peloponnesian War*, p. 82.

Chapter 2: The War's Strategic Framework

1. Quoted in Stanley Chodorow and MacGregor Knox, *The Mainstream of Civilization since 1660*, 6th ed. (New York, 1994), p. 620.
2. Quoted in ibid., p. 595.
3. Carl von Clausewitz, *On War*, ed. and trans. Michael Howard and Peter Paret (Princeton, NJ, 1976), p. 592.
4. Ibid., p. 609.
5. E-mail from Lieutenant General James Mattis, in possession of the author.
6. Quoted in Thomas, *The Iron Way*, p. 22.
7. Thomas, *The Iron Way*, pp. 130–32.
8. Andrew F. Smith, *Starving the South: How the North Won the Civil War* (New York, 2001), p. 76.

9. Grant, *Personal Memoirs of U. S. Grant*, vol. 1, p. 42.

10. Milo M. Quaife, ed., *From the Cannon's Mouth: Civil War Letters of General Alpheus S. Williams* (Detroit, 1959), pp. 40–41.

11. Quoted in Joseph T. Glatthaar, *The March to the Sea and Beyond: Sherman's Troops in the Savannah and Carolina Campaigns* (Baton Rouge, LA, 1995), p. 37.

12. Mark Grimsley, "Success and Failure in Civil War Armies: Clues from Organizational Culture," in *Warfare and Culture in World History*, ed. Wayne Lee (New York, 2011), p. 124.

13. Gerry Harder Poriss and Ralph G. Poriss, eds., *While My Country Is in Danger: The Life and Letters of Lieutenant Colonel Richard S. Thompson, Twelfth New Jersey Volunteers* (Hamilton, NY, 1994), pp. 40–41.

14. Frances Wallace Taylor, Catherine Taylor Matthews, and J. Tracy Power, eds., *The Leverett Letters: Correspondence of a South Carolina Family, 1851–1868* (Columbia, SC, 2000), p. 387.

15. Clausewitz, *On War*, p. 87.

16. Allan R. Millett and Williamson Murray, "Lessons of War," *National Interest* 14 (Winter 1988): pp. 83–95.

17. Clausewitz, *On War*, p. 178.

18. *Congressional Globe*, 29th Cong., 1st Sess., March 16, 1846, appendix, p. 436.

19. Major General J.F.C. Fuller, *Grant and Lee: A Study in Personality and Generalship* (Bloomington, IN, 1957), p. 28.

Chapter 3: "And the War Came"

1. The title of this chapter comes from Lincoln's second inaugural address. *The American Annual Cyclopædia and Register of Important Events of the Year 1861* (New York, 1864), p. 129.

2. Richardson, *A Compilation of the Messages and Papers of the Presidents*, pp. 633–36.

3. Quoted in Eba Anderson Lawton, *Major Robert Anderson and Fort Sumter, 1861* (New York, 1911), p. 9.

4. Abner Doubleday, *Reminiscences of Forts Sumter and Moultrie in 1860–'61* (New York, 1876), p. 56.

5. United States War Department, *The War of the Rebellion: A Compilation of the Official Records of the Union and Confederate Armies*, 128 vols. (Washington, DC, 1880–1901), Ser. 1, vol. 1, pt. 1, p. 274. Henceforth cited as *OR*.

6. William E. Gienapp and Erica L. Gienapp, eds., *The Civil War Diary of Gideon Welles, Lincoln's Secretary of the Navy: The Original Manuscript Edition* (Urbana, IL, 2014), p. 665.

7. *New York Daily Tribune*, June 13, 1861.

8. Quoted in Marcus Cunliffe, *Soldiers and Civilians: The Martial Spirit in America, 1775–1865* (New York, 1973), p. 344.

9. *CWAL*, vol. 4, p. 430.

10. Thomas L. Snead, *The Fight for Missouri from the Election of Lincoln to the Death of Lyon* (New York, 1888), p. 200.

11. Thucydides, *The History of the Peloponnesian War*, p. 245.

12. Quoted in Jane Flaherty, *The Revenue Imperative* (London, 2009), p. 66.

13. "General M. C. Meigs on the Conduct of the Civil War," *American Historical Review* 26, no. 2 (1921): p. 292.

14. Mary Chesnut, *Mary Chesnut's Civil War*, ed. C. Vann Woodward (New Haven, CT, 1981).

Chapter 4: First Battles and the Making of Armies

1. Ellis Spear, "The Story of the Raising and Organization of a Regiment of Volunteers in 1862," 4 March 1903, p. 9. War papers No. 46, Military Order of the Loyal Legion of the United States, Commandery of the District of Columbia.

2. Alexis de Tocqueville, *Democracy in America* (New York, 1840), pp. 287–88.

3. Grant, *Personal Memoirs of U. S. Grant*, vol. 1, p. 243.

4. Quoted in Steven J. Ramold, *Baring the Iron Hand: Discipline in the Union Army* (DeKalb, IL, 2010), pp. 58–59.

5. Quoted in Wayne Wei-Siang Hsieh, *West Pointers and the Civil War: The Old Army in War and Peace* (Chapel Hill, NC, 2009), p. 144.

6. Wm. Forse Scott, *The Story of a Cavalry Regiment: The Career of the Fourth Iowa Veteran Volunteers from Kansas to Georgia, 1861–1865* (1892; Iowa City, 1992), p. 16.

7. Grant, *Personal Memoirs of U. S. Grant*, vol. 1, p. 253.

8. Ibid., vol. 1, pp. 138–39.

9. Ibid., vol. 1, pp. 249–50.

10. Ibid., vol. 1, p. 250.

11. John Harrison Wilson, *Under the Old Flag: Recollections of Military Operations in the War for Union, the Spanish War, the Boxer Rebellion, etc.* (New York, 1912), vol. 2, p. 17.

12. Logan had served as a volunteer officer in the Mexican War but saw no combat during that previous conflict.

13. Thucydides, *The History of the Peloponnesian War*, p. 117.

14. William T. Sherman, *Memoirs of General William T. Sherman, by Himself* (New York, 1875), vol. 1, p. 178.

15. Ibid., vol. 1, p. 181.

16. Ibid., vol. 1, pp. 181–82.

17. Stephen W. Sears, ed., *The Civil War Papers of George B. McClellan: Selected Correspondence, 1860–1865* (New York, 1989), p. 118.
18. Quoted in Chas. Wadsworth, *War a Discipline: A Sermon Preached in Cavalry Church, San Francisco, on Thanksgiving Day, November 24th, 1864* (San Francisco, 1864), pp. 19–20.
19. Sherman, *Memoirs of General William T. Sherman*, vol. 1, pp. 189–91.
20. Sears, *The Civil War Papers of George B. McClellan*, pp. 35–36.
21. Ibid., p. 81.
22. Ibid., p. 85.
23. Stephen W. Sears, *Landscape Turned Red: The Battle of Antietam* (New York, 1983), p. 6.
24. Sears, *Civil War Papers of George B. McClellan*, p. 128.
25. *OR*, Ser. 1, vol. 1, p. 611.
26. Allan Nevins and Milton Halsey Thomas, eds., *The Diary of George Templeton Strong: Post-War Years, 1865–1875* (New York, 1952), p. 266.
27. Quoted in Gary W. Gallagher, *The Union War* (Cambridge, MA, 2011), p. 161.

Chapter 5: Stillborn between Earth and Water

1. *OR*, Ser. 1, vol. 51, pt. 1, p. 369.
2. *OR*, Ser. 1, vol. 51, pt. 1, p. 387.
3. Sears, ed., *The Civil War Papers of George B. McClellan*, p. 12.
4. Fletcher Pratt, *Civil War on Western Waters* (New York, 1956), p. 19.
5. Sears, *The Civil War Papers of George B. McClellan*, p. 73.
6. Stephen W. Sears, *George B. McClellan: The Young Napoleon* (New York, 1988), pp. 101–2. Sears points out that McClellan's first assessment of Confederate strength occurred before the arrival of Allan Pinkerton, his future intelligence chief, who would continue to feed McClellan inflated Confederate numbers.
7. John D. Hayes, ed., *Samuel Francis Du Pont: A Selection from His Civil War Letters*, vol. 1, *The Mission: 1860–1862* (Ithaca, NY, 1969), p. 160.
8. Ibid., p. 285.
9. *OR*, Ser. 1, vol. 6, p. 367.
10. *OR*, Ser. 1, vol. 6, p. 204.
11. Quoted in Craig L. Symonds, *Lincoln and His Admirals: Abraham Lincoln, the U.S. Navy, and the Civil War* (Oxford, 2008), p. 68.
12. Quoted in Ari Arthur Hoogenboom, *Gustavus Vasa Fox of the Union Navy: A Biography* (Baltimore, 2008), p. 152.
13. *OR*, Ser. 1, vol. 4, 355; Ser. 1, vol. 7, p. 447.
14. *CWAL*, vol. 5, p. 98 (emphasis original).
15. Grant, *Personal Memoirs of U. S. Grant*, vol. 1, p. 287.

16. *OR*, Ser. 1, vol. 7, pp. 451, 458, 488, 521; Sears, *Civil War Papers of George B. McClellan*, pp. 144, 147. On 29 December, Buell wrote McClellan that "the Cumberland and Tennessee where the railroad crosses them, is now the most vulnerable point. I regard it as the most important strategic point in the whole field of operations" (ibid., p. 521).

17. Grant, *Personal Memoirs of U. S. Grant*, vol. 1, p. 307.

18. Thomas Jordan and J. P. Pryor, *The Campaigns of Lieut.-Gen. N. B. Forrest, and of Forrest's Cavalry* (New Orleans, 1868), p. 91.

19. Grant, *Personal Memoirs of U. S. Grant*, vol. 1, p. 311.

20. *OR*, Ser. 1, vol. 7, p. 680.

21. Richard D. Goff, *Confederate Supply* (Durham, NC, 1969), p. 56.

22. Sam R. Watkins, *1861 vs. 1882, "Co. Aytch," Maury Grays, First Tennessee Regiment; or, A Side Show of the Big Show* (Nashville, 1882), p. 34.

23. *OR*, Ser. 1, vol. 10, pt. 1, p. 153.

24. Dan Macauley, "Chestnut Grove," *Washington Post*, 17 December 1893.

25. Watkins, *Co. Aytch*, p. 35.

26. J. R. Chalmers, "Forrest and His Campaigns," *Southern Historical Society Papers* 7, no. 10 (October 1879): p. 458.

27. Thomas Jordan, "Notes of a Confederate Staff-Officer at Shiloh," in *Battles and Leaders of the Civil War*, ed. Robert Underwood Johnson and Clarence Clough Buel (New York, 1887), vol. 1, p. 603.

28. Grant, *Personal Memoirs of U. S. Grant*, vol. 1, p. 368.

29. Ibid., vol. 1, p. 379.

30. Ibid., vol. 1, p. 381.

31. David D. Porter, "The Opening of the Lower Mississippi," in *Battles and Leaders of the Civil War*, ed. Johnson and Buel, vol. 2, p. 26.

32. George W. Cable, "New Orleans before the Capture," in *Battles and Leaders of the Civil War*, ed. Johnson and Buel, vol. 2, p. 20.

33. *Life and Public Services of Major-General Butler (Benjamin F. Butler): The Hero of New Orleans* (Philadelphia, 1864), p. 83.

34. Chesnut, *Mary Chesnut's Civil War*, p. 330.

Chapter 6: The Confederacy Recovers, 1862

1. Quoted in Hans L. Trefousse, *The Radical Republicans* (New York, 1969), p. 184.

2. "General M. C. Meigs on the Conduct of the Civil War," p. 292.

3. *OR*, Ser. 1, vol. 7, pg. 533.

4. *CWAL*, vol. 5, p. 98.

5. Don E. Fehrenbacher and Virginia Fehrenacher, *Recollected Words of Abraham Lincoln* (Palo Alto, CA, 1996), p. 322.

6. Henry J. Raymond, *The Life and Public Services of Abraham Lincoln* (New York, 1865), p. 777.
7. *CWAL*, vol. 5, p. 185.
8. *OR*, Ser. 1, vol. 11, pt. 3, p. 456.
9. Wilson, *Under the Old Flag*, vol. 1, p. 102.
10. Robert L. Dabney, *Life and Campaigns of Lieut.-Gen. Thomas J. Jackson* (Richmond, 1866), p. 397.
11. Lord Byron, "The Destruction of Sennacherib."
12. *OR*, Ser. 1, vol. 12, pt. 1, p. 551.
13. Stephen W. Sears, ed., *The Civil War Papers of George B. McClellan: Selected Correspondence, 1860–1865* (New York, 1992), pp. 244–45.
14. Gary W. Gallagher, ed., *Fighting for the Confederacy: The Personal Recollections of General Edward Porter Alexander* (Chapel Hill, NC, 1989), p. 112.
15. Quoted in J. Watts de Peyster, *Personal and Military History of Philip Kearny* (New York, 1869), p. 350.
16. Steven E. Woodworth, *Nothing but Victory: The Army of the Tennessee, 1861–1865* (New York, 2005), pp. 61–62.
17. *OR*, Ser. 1, vol. 12, pt. 3, p. 474.
18. Sears, *The Civil War Papers of George B. McClellan*, p. 389.
19. Glenn C. Oldaker, ed., *Centennial Tales: Memoirs of Colonel "Chester" S. Bassett French* (New York, 1962), p. 18.
20. William B. Styple, ed., *Letters from the Peninsula: The Civil War Letters of General Philip Kearny* (Kearny, NJ, 1988), p. 146.
21. Quoted in Hennessy, *Return to Bull Run*, p. 195.
22. Sears, *Civil War Papers of George B. McClellan*, p. 416.
23. *OR*, Ser. 1, vol. 12, pt. 2, p. 76.
24. Quoted in John J. Hennessy, *Return to Bull Run: The Campaign and Battle of Second Manassas* (Norman, OK, 1999), p. 259.
25. Cecil D. Eby Jr., ed., *A Virginia Yankee in the Civil War: The Diaries of David Hunter Strother* (Chapel Hill, NC, 1961), p. 95.
26. Quoted in Hennessy, *Return to Bull Run*, p. 356.

Chapter 7: The Confederate Counter-Offensives, 1862

1. Quoted in McPherson, *Battle Cry of Freedom*, pp. 512–13.
2. Quoted in Bruce Catton, *This Hallowed Ground: The Story of the Union Side of the Civil War* (Garden City, NY, 1956), p. 174.
3. *OR*, Ser. 1, vol. 16, pt. 1, p. 738.
4. *OR*, Ser. 1, vol. 16, pt. 2, p. 104.
5. Watkins, *Co. Aytch*, p. 47.

6. Ibid., p. 50.

7. *OR*, Ser. 1, vol. 16, pt. 2, p. 530.

8. John Beatty, *The Citizen-Soldier; or, Memoirs of a Volunteer* (Cincinnati, 1879), pp. 173–74.

9. Quoted in Clement Eaton, *A History of the Southern Confederacy* (New York, 1954), p. 91.

10. David Urquhart, "Bragg's Advance and Retreat," in *Battles and Leaders of the Civil War,* ed. Johnson and Buel, vol. 3, p. 601.

11. Watkins, *Co. Aytch*, p. 52.

12. *OR*, Ser. 1, vol. 16, pt. 1, p. 284.

13. Grant, *Personal Memoirs of U. S. Grant*, vol. 1, p. 410.

14. *OR*, Ser. 1, vol. 17, pt. 2, p. 789.

15. Quoted in David Herbert Donald, *Lincoln* (New York, 1995), p. 372.

16. *OR*, Ser. 1, vol. 19, pt. 2, p. 600.

17. Quoted in Sears, *Landscape Turned Red*, p. 112.

18. Winston Churchill, *Churchill by Himself*, ed. Richard Langworth (New York, 2008), p. 231.

19. David L. Thompson, "In the Ranks to the Antietam," in *Battles and Leaders of the Civil War*, ed. Johnson and Buel, vol. 2, p. 558.

20. Edward Porter Alexander, *Military Memoirs of a Confederate: A Critical Narrative* (New York, 1907), p. 245.

21. J. S. Johnston, "A Reminiscence of Sharpsburg," *Southern Historical Society Papers* 8 (1880): p. 528.

22. Quaife, *From the Cannon's Mouth*, p. 129.

23. Francis A. Walker, *History of the Second Army Corps in the Army of the Potomac* (New York, 1886), p. 117.

24. "My Hunt after 'The Captain,'" *Atlantic Monthly* 10 (December 1862): p. 749.

25. Gallagher, *Fighting for the Confederacy*, p. 146.

26. *CWAL*, vol. 5, p. 474.

27. David Lloyd George, *War Memoirs of David Lloyd George* (Boston, 1936), vol. 6, p. 3478.

28. *Report of the Joint Committee on the Conduct of the War, Part I, Army of the Potomac*, 37th Congress, 34d sess. (Washington, DC, 1863), p. 668.

29. Quoted in J. Cutler Andrews, *The North Reports the Civil War* (Pittsburgh, 1955), p. 331.

30. Clifford Dowdey, ed., *The Wartime Papers of R. E. Lee* (Boston, 1961), p. 365.

31. "Letter from Major-General Henry Heth, of A. P. Hill's Corps, A. N. V.," *Southern Historical Society Papers* 4, no. 3 (September 1877): p. 153.

32. Dowdey, *Wartime Papers*, p. 389.

33. *OR*, Ser. 1, vol. 11, pt. 3, p. 364.

Chapter 8: The War in the East, 1863

1. *CWAL*, vol. 6, pp. 78–79.
2. Gallagher, *Fighting for the Confederacy*, p. 195.
3. Darius N. Couch, "The Chancellorsville Campaign," in *Battles and Leaders of the Civil War*, ed. Johnson and Buel, vol. 3, p. 155.
4. *OR*, Ser. 1, vol. 25, pt. 1, p. 1058.
5. *OR*, Ser. 1, vol. 25, pt. 1, p. 1080.
6. *Report of the Joint Committee on the Conduct of the War at the Second Session Thirty-Eighth Congress: Army of the Potomac, Battle of Petersburg* (Washington, DC, 1865), p. 140.
7. *OR*, Ser. 1, vol. 25, pt. 2, pp. 360–61.
8. Stephen W. Sears, *Chancellorsville* (Boston, 1996), p. 263.
9. Hunter McGuire, "General T. J. ("Stonewall") Jackson, Confederate States Army: His Career and Character," *Southern Historical Society Papers* 25 (1897): p. 110.
10. "Letter from Major-General Henry Heth," p. 154.
11. *Daily Richmond Examiner*, June 12, 1863.
12. James C. Mohr, ed., *The Cormany Diaries: A Northern Family in the Civil War* (Pittsburgh, 1982), pp. 329–30.
13. Jeffry D. Wert, *The Sword of Lincoln: The Army of the Potomac* (New York, 2005), p. 268.
14. James H. Wilson, "Major-General John Buford," *Journal of the United States Cavalry Association* 8 (September 1895): p. 178.
15. Quoted in Sears, *Gettysburg*, p. 241.
16. Quoted in Wert, *Sword of Lincoln*, p. 283.
17. *OR*, Ser. 1, vol. 27, pt. 2, p. 318.
18. James Longstreet, "Lee's Invasion of Pennsylvania," *Century Magazine* 33 (February 1887): p. 626.
19. E. P. Halstead, "Incidents of the First Day at Gettysburg," in *Battles and Leaders of the Civil War*, ed. Johnson and Buel, vol. 3, p. 285.
20. Fitz Lee, "A Review of the First Two Days' Operations at Gettysburg and a Reply to General Longstreet," *Southern Historical Society Papers* 5, no. 4 (April 1878): p. 183.
21. Quoted in Harry W. Pfanz, *Gettysburg: The Second Day* (Chapel Hill, NC, 1998), p. 268.
22. John Gibbon, *Personal Recollections of the Civil War* (New York, 1928), p. 145.
23. Franklin Aretas Haskell, *The Battle of Gettysburg* (Wisconsin, 1908), p. 106.
24. A. L. Long, *Memoirs of Robert E. Lee: His Military and Personal History* (London, 1886), 311.

Chapter 9: The War in the West, 1863

1. Michael Howard, *The Franco-Prussian War* (London, 1961), p. 70.
2. G. C. Kniffin, "The Battle of Stone's River," in *Battles and Leaders of the Civil War*, ed. Johnson and Buel, vol. 3, p. 627.
3. Grant, *Personal Memoirs of U. S. Grant*, vol. 2, pp. 86–87.
4. Willis J. Abbott, *Battle Fields and Camp Fires: A Narrative of the Principle Military Operations of the Civil War* (New York, 1890), p. 120–21.
5. James Lee McDonough, *Shiloh: In Hell before Night* (Knoxville, TN, 1977), p. 8.
6. Watkins, *Co. Aytch*, p. 40.
7. *OR*, Ser. 1, vol. 24, pt. 1, p. 13.
8. Grant, *Personal Memoirs of U. S. Grant*, vol. 1, pp. 430–31.
9. Ibid., vol. 1, p. 434.
10. Ibid., vol. 1, p. 436.
11. "Grant at Vicksburg," *Chicago History* 2, no. 4 (1949): p. 121.
12. Grant, *Personal Memoirs of U. S. Grant*, vol. 1, p. 446.
13. Ibid., vol. 1, p. 449.
14. Ibid., vol. 1, p. 443 (italics original).
15. James F. Rusling, *Men and Things I Saw in Civil War Days* (New York, 1899), p. 146.
16. Clausewitz, *On War*, p. 119.
17. Rusling, *Men and Things I Saw in Civil War Days*, p. 137 (italics original).
18. Grant, *Personal Memoirs of U. S. Grant*, vol. 1, p. 461.
19. *OR*, Ser. 1, vol. 25, pt. 2, pp. 752.
20. Quoted in James Arnold, *Grant Wins the War: Decision at Vicksburg* (New York, 1997), p. 87.
21. Grant, *Personal Memoirs of U. S. Grant*, vol. 1, p. 489.
22. Ibid., vol. 1, pp. 480–81.
23. General Sir Leslie Hollis, *One Marine's Tale* (London, 1956), pp. 66–71.
24. Grant, *Personal Memoirs of U. S. Grant*, vol. 1, p. 483.
25. Quoted in John C. Pemberton, *Pemberton: Defender of Vicksburg* (Chapel Hill, NC, 1942), p. 14.
26. Quoted in Arnold, *Grant Wins the War*, p. 125.
27. S. H. Lockett, "The Defense of Vicksburg," in *Battles and Leaders of the Civil War*, ed. Johnson and Buel, vol. 3, p. 487.
28. Robert M. Hughes, "Some War Letters of General Joseph E. Johnston," *Journal of the Military Service Institution of the United States* 50 (May–June 1912): pp. 319–20.
29. David D. Porter, *Incidents and Anecdotes of the Civil War* (New York, 1886), p. 186.
30. *OR*, Ser. 1, vol. 24, pt. 3, p. 862.
31. David G. Chandler, *The Campaigns of Napoleon* (New York, 1966), pp. 170–74.

32. Grant, *Personal Memoirs of U. S. Grant*, vol. 1, p. 507.

33. Ibid., vol. 1, p. 512.

34. Joseph Eggleston Johnston, *Narrative of Military Operations Directed during the Late War between the States* (New York, 1874), p. 181.

35. Grant, *Personal Memoirs of U. S. Grant*, vol. 1, p. 510.

36. John B. Sanborn, "Reminiscences of the Campaigns against Vicksburg," *Transactions of the Department of American History of the Minnesota Historical Society* (October 1879): p. 98.

37. S.H.M. Byers, "Some Recollections of Grant," in *The Annals of the War Written by Leading Participants, North and South, Originally Published in the Philadelphia Weekly Times* (Philadelphia, 1879), p. 344.

38. Charles A. Dana, *Recollections of the Civil War: With the Leaders at Washington and in the Field in the Sixties* (New York, 1898), p. 64.

39. *Report of the Proceedings of the Society of the Army of the Tennessee at the Seventeenth Meeting Held at Lake Minnetonka, Minnesota, August 13th and 14th 1884* (Cincinnati, 1893), p. 224.

40. Quoted in Arnold, *Grant Wins the War*, p. 180.

41. Osborn H. Oldroyd, *A Soldier's Story of the Siege of Vicksburg from the Diary of Osborn H. Oldroyd* (Springfield, IL, 1885), p. 23.

42. Grant, *Personal Memoirs of U. S. Grant*, vol. 1, pp. 520–21.

43. *OR*, Ser. 1, vol. 25, pt. 2, p. 790.

44. Grant, *Personal Memoirs of U. S. Grant*, vol. 1, p. 547.

45. Ibid., vol. 1, p. 549.

46. Quoted in Arnold, *Grant Wins the War*, p. 233.

47. *OR*, Ser. 1, vol. 30, pt. 3, p. 698.

48. John Eaton with Ethel Osgood Mason, *Grant, Lincoln, and the Freedmen: Reminiscences of the Civil War* (New York, 1907), pp. 79–80.

49. *CWAL*, vol. 6, p. 377.

50. Beatty, *The Citizen-Soldier*, p. 295.

51. Paul M. Angle, ed., *Three Years in the Army of the Cumberland: The Letters and Diary of Major James A. Connolly* (Bloomington, IN, 1959), p. 94.

52. *OR*, Ser. 1, vol. 23, pt. 2, p. 518.

53. George, *War Memoirs of David Lloyd George*, vol. 6, p. 348.

54. Daniel H. Hill, "Chickamauga: The Great Battle of the West," in *Battles and Leaders of the Civil War*, ed. Johnson and Buel, vol. 3, p. 641.

55. Quoted in Shelby Foote, *The Civil War: A Narrative* (New York, 1958–74), vol. 2, p. 691.

56. All quoted in James R. Arnold, *Chickamauga 1863: The River of Death* (London, 1992), p. 45.

57. Hill, "Chickamauga," pp. 650–51.

58. John B. Turchin, *Chickamauga* (Chicago, 1888), p. 165.

59. Ibid., p. 132.

60. Glenn Tucker, *Chickamauga: Bloody Battle in the West* (New York, 1994), p. 359.

61. John Allan Wyeth, *Life of General Nathan Bedford Forrest* (New York, 1899), p. 266.

62. *OR*, Ser. 1, vol. 51, pt. 2, p. 772.

63. James Longstreet, *From Manassas to Appomattox: Memoirs of the Civil War in America* (Philadelphia, 1896), p. 465.

64. Quoted in Donald, *Lincoln*, p. 457.

65. Grant, *Personal Memoirs of U. S. Grant*, vol. 2, p. 28.

66. Bruce Catton, *Grant Takes Command* (Boston, 1969), p. 56.

67. Horace Porter, *Campaigning with Grant* (New York, 1897), p. 7.

68. Alexander, *Military Memoirs of a Confederate*, p. 466.

69. Grant, *Personal Memoirs of U. S. Grant*, vol. 2, p. 87 (italics original).

70. Ibid., vol. 2, p. 80.

71. *CWAL*, vol. 6, p. 409.

Chapter 10: The Killing Time

1. Brooks Simpson and Jean V. Berlin, eds., *Sherman's Civil War: Selected Correspondence of William T. Sherman, 1860–1865* (Chapel Hill, NC, 1999), p. 609.

2. *OR*, Ser. 1, vol. 32, pt. 2, pp. 280–81.

3. Albert D. Richardson, *A Personal History of Ulysses S. Grant* (Hartford, CT, 1868), p. 373.

4. Charles Francis Adams, *Richard Henry Dana: A Biography* (Boston, 1890), vol. 2, p. 272.

5. John Y. Simon, ed., *The Papers of Ulysses S. Grant* (Carbondale, IL, 1982), vol. 10, pp. 39–40. Henceforth cited as *PUSG*.

6. Ibid., pp. 110–12.

7. Adams, *Richard Henry Dana: A Biography*, vol. 2, p. 272.

8. *PUSG*, vol. 10, p. 251.

9. Ibid., p. 252.

10. Ibid., p. 253.

11. Ibid., p. 274.

12. Grant, *Personal Memoirs of U. S. Grant*, vol. 2, p. 405.

13. Frederick S. Daniel, *The* Richmond Examiner *during the War; or, the Writings of John M. Daniel with a Memoir of His Life* (New York, 1868), pp. 107–8.

14. *OR*, Ser. 1, vol. 32, pt. 3, p. 588.

15. Porter, *Campaigning with Grant*, p. 47.

16. Grant, *Personal Memoirs of U. S. Grant*, vol. 2, p. 538.

17. Ibid., pp. 214–15.

18. Ibid., p. 205.
19. William Allan, "Memoranda of Conversations with General Robert E. Lee," in *Lee the Soldier*, ed. Gary W. Gallagher (Lincoln, NE, 1996), p. 11.
20. Ibid., p. 22.
21. *OR*, Ser. 1, vol. 38, pt. 1, p. 2.
22. Augustus Buell, *"The Cannoneer": Recollections of Service in the Army of the Potomac* (Washington, DC, 1890), p. 167.
23. Longstreet, *From Manassas to Appomattox*, p. 568.
24. Gallagher, *Fighting for the Confederacy*, p. 363.
25. Porter, *Campaigning with Grant*, pp. 69–70.
26. Charles A. Cuffel, *History of Durrell's Battery in the Civil War* (Philadelphia, 1904), p. 182.
27. Frank A. Burr, *A New, Original and Authentic Record of the Life and Deeds of General U. S. Grant* (Battle Creek, MI, 1885), p. 59.
28. *OR*, Ser. 1, vol. 36, pt. 2, p. 541.
29. Porter, *Campaigning with Grant*, p. 84.
30. Thomas W. Hyde, *Following the Greek Cross; or, Memories of the Sixth Army Corps* (Boston, 1894), p. 191.
31. *OR*, Ser. 1, vol. 36, pt. 1, p. 668.
32. Wilson, *Under the Old Flag*, vol. 1, p. 396.
33. *OR*, Ser. 1, vol. 36, pt. 1, p. 4.
34. Luman Harris Tenney, *War Diary of Luman Harris Tenney, 1861–1865* (Oberlin, OH, 1914), p. 115.
35. John D. Black, "Reminiscences of the Bloody Angle," *Glimpses of the Nation's Struggle, Fourth Series*, Military Order of the Loyal Legion of the United States, Minnesota (Wilmington, NC, 1992; Saint Paul, 1898), vol. 4, p. 423; 420–35.
36. Hyde, *Following the Greek Cross*, p. 200.
37. John D. Imboden, "The Battle of New Market, VA., May 15th, 1864," in *Battles and Leaders of the Civil War*, ed. Johnson and Buel, vol. 4, p. 483.
38. *PUSG*, vol. 10, p. 460.
39. *OR*, Ser. 1, vol. 46, pt. 1, p. 19.
40. Eugene Arus Nash, *A History of the Forty-Fourth Regiment New York Volunteer Infantry in the Civil War, 1861–1865* (Dayton, OH, 1988; Chicago, 1910), p. 193.
41. C. S. Venable, "The Campaign from the Wilderness to Petersburg," *Southern Historical Society Papers* 14 (1886): p. 535.
42. *PUSG*, vol. 10, p. 491.
43. J. William Jones, *Personal Reminiscences of General Robert E. Lee* (Richmond, VA, 1989, reprint of 1875 edition), p. 40.
44. Grant, *Personal Memoirs of U. S. Grant*, vol. 2, p. 276.
45. *OR*, Ser. 1, vol. 36, pt. 1, p. 85.

46. Grant, *Personal Memoirs of U. S. Grant*, vol. 2, p. 133.

47. Douglas Southall Freeman, ed., *Lee's Dispatches: Unpublished Letters of General Robert E. Lee, C.S.A., to Jefferson Davis and the War Department of the Confederate States of America, 1862–1865*, new ed. (New York, 1957), p. 254.

48. *CWAL*, vol. 7, pp. 395–96.

49. *CWAL*, vol. 7, p. 435.

50. *OR*, Ser. 1, vol. 40, pt. 1, p. 368.

51. Gienapp and Gienapp, *The Civil War Diary of Gideon Welles*, p. 442.

52. Donald, *Lincoln*, p. 672, n. 519.

53. *OR*, Ser. 1, vol. 37, pt. 2, p. 366.

54. Grant, *Personal Memoirs of U. S. Grant*, vol. 2, pp. 316–17.

55. Quoted in Jeffry D. Wert, *From Winchester to Cedar Creek: The Shenandoah Campaign of 1864* (Carlisle, PA, 1987), p. 141.

56. Porter, *Campaigning with Grant*, p. 272.

57. Grant, *Personal Memoirs of U. S. Grant*, vol. 2, p. 327.

58. Quoted in Catton, *Grant Takes Command*, p. 363.

59. Quoted in Wert, *From Winchester to Cedar Creek*, p. 93.

60. Philip Sheridan, *Personal Memoirs* (New York, 1888), vol. 2, p. 45.

61. *PUSG*, vol. 12, pp 269–70.

62. *OR*, Ser. 1, vol. 43, pt. 2, p. 892.

63. E. R. Hagemann, ed., *Fighting Rebels and Redskins: Experiences in Army Life of Colonel George B. Sanford, 1861–1892* (Norman, OK, 1969), pp. 222–24.

64. Hsieh, *West Pointers and the Civil War*, p. 185.

Chapter 11: Victory in the West, 1864

1. Sherman, *Memoirs of General William T. Sherman*, vol. 2, p. 399.

2. *OR*, Ser. 3, vol. 5, p. 1001.

3. Chesnut, *Mary Chesnut's Civil War*, p. 268.

4. Quoted in Foote, *Civil War*, vol. 3, p. 328.

5. *OR*, Ser. 1, vol. 31, pt. 3, p. 860.

6. Quoted in Thomas Lawrence Connelly, *Autumn of Glory: The Army of Tennessee, 1862–1865* (Baton Rouge, LA, 1971), p. 324.

7. John Percy Dyer, *From Shiloh to San Juan* (Baton Rouge, LA, 1961), p. 5.

8. Daniel Oakey, "Marching through Georgia and the Carolinas," in *Battles and Leaders of the Civil War*, ed. Johnson and Buel, vol. 4, p. 671.

9. Sherman, *Memoirs of General William T. Sherman*, vol. 2, p. 34.

10. *OR*, Ser. 3, vol. 4, pt. 2, p. 957.

11. *OR*, Ser. 1, vol. 38, pt. 4, p. 507.

12. *OR*, Ser. 1, vol. 38, pt. 4, p. 612.

13. Haskell M. Monroe and James T. McIntosh, *The Papers of Jefferson Davis* (Baton Rouge, LA, 1971), vol. 10, p. 524.

14. *OR*, Ser. 1, vol. 38, pt. 5, p. 880.

15. Freeman, *Lee's Dispatches*, p. 282.

16. *OR*, Ser. 1, vol. 38, pt. 5, p. 885.

17. Watkins, *Co. Aytch*, p. 156.

18. William T. Sherman, "The Grand Strategy in the Last Year of the War," in *Battles and Leaders of the Civil War*, ed. Johnson and Buel, vol. 4, p. 253.

19. Grenville M. Dodge, "The Battle of Atlanta," in A. Noel Blakeman, ed., *Personal Recollections of the War of Rebellion*, Military Order of the Loyal Legion of the United States, New York (New York, 1897; Wilmington, 1992), vol. 2, p. 245.

20. Henry Steele Commager, *The Civil War Archive: The History of the Civil War in Documents*, rev. and exp. Erik Bruun (New York, 2000), p. 666.

21. *OR*, Ser. 1, vol. 38, pt. 3, p. 732.

22. *OR*, Ser. 1, vol. 38, pt. 3, p. 104.

23. Jacob D. Cox, *Atlanta* (New York, 1882), p. 186.

24. *OR*, Ser. 1, vol. 38, pt. 1, p. 77.

25. Sherman, *Memoirs of General W. T. Sherman*, vol. 2, pp. 111–12. The wartime letter can also be found in *OR*, Ser. 1, vol. 38, pt. 5, p. 794.

26. Charles Carleton Coffin, *Freedom Triumphant: The Fourth Period of the War of the Rebellion from September, 1864, to Its Close* (New York, 1891), p. 66.

27. Porter, *Campaigning with Grant*, p. 313.

28. Sherman, *Memoirs of General W. T. Sherman*, vol. 2, p. 141.

29. Quoted in ibid., p. 149.

30. *PUSG*, vol. 12, p. 375

31. James A. Connolly, *Three Years in the Army of the Cumberland*, ed. Paul M. Angle (Bloomington IN, 1959), p. 335.

32. Quoted in Lloyd Lewis, *Sherman: Fighting Prophet* (New York, 1932), p. 430.

33. J. B. Hood, *Advance and Retreat: Personal Experiences in the United States and Confederate States Armies* (New Orleans, 1880), p. 283.

34. Ibid., p. 290.

35. Quoted in Foote, *Civil War*, vol. 3, p. 665.

36. John K. Shellenberger, "The Battle of Franklin," in J. C. Donahower, Silas H. Towler, and David L. Kingsbury, eds., *Glimpses of the Nation's Struggle*, Military Order of the Loyal Legion of the United States, Minnesota, vol. 5 (St. Paul, 1903; Wilmington, 1992), vol. 5, p. 503.

37. Ibid., p. 513.

38. Watkins, *Co. Aytch*, p. 222.

39. Quoted in Connelly, *Autumn of Glory*, p. 507.

40. Hood, *Advance and Retreat*, pp. 299–300.

41. Fehrenbacher and Fehrenbacher, *Recollected Words of Abraham Lincoln*, p. 403.

42. William Rattle Plum, *The Military Telegraph during the Civil War in the United States* (Chicago, 1882), p. 238.

43. Hood, *Advance and Retreat*, p. 303.

44. Watkins, *Co. Aytch*, p. 230.

45. Grant, *Personal Memoirs of U. S. Grant*, vol. 2, pp. 649–50.

46. Henry Hitchcock, *Marching with Sherman: Passages from the Letters and Campaign Diaries of Henry Hitchcock*, ed. Mark A. De Wolfe Howe (New Haven, CT, 1927), p. 30.

47. *OR*, Ser. 1, vol. 39, pt. 3, p. 660.

48. Margaret Brobst Roth, ed., *Well Mary: Civil War Letters of a Wisconsin Volunteer* (Madison, WI, 1960), p. 57.

49. *PUSG*, vol. 12, p. 375.

50. Hitchcock, *Marching with Sherman*, p. 57.

51. Ibid., p. 58.

52. Ibid., p. 69.

53. Sherman, *Memoirs of General William T. Sherman*, vol. 2, pp. 185–86.

54. Hitchcock, *Marching with Sherman*, pp. 108–9.

55. Quoted in James McPherson, *Tried by War: Abraham Lincoln as Commander in Chief* (New York, 2008), p. 254.

56. *CWAL*, vol. 7, p. 514.

Chapter 12: The Collapse of the Confederacy

1. *Richmond Daily Dispatch*, February 7, 1865.

2. Thucydides, *The History of the Peloponnesian War*, p. 407.

3. *OR*, Ser. 4, vol. 3, p. 1009.

4. *OR*, Ser. 1, vol. 45, pt. 2, p. 699.

5. *OR*, Ser. 1, vol. 45, pt. 1, p. 724.

6. Grant, *Personal Memoirs of U. S. Grant*, vol. 2, p. 405.

7. Ibid., vol. 2, p. 404.

8. *OR*, Ser. 1, vol. 36. pt. 1, p. 50.

9. Quoted in Foote, *Civil War*, vol. 3, p. 741.

10. Grant, *Personal Memoirs of U. S. Grant*, vol. 2, p. 391.

11. *PUSG*, vol. 13, pp. 177–78.

12. Sherman, *Memoirs of General William T. Sherman*, vol. 2, p. 213.

13. Ibid., vol. 2, p. 225.

14. Ibid., vol. 2, p. 227.

15. Ibid., vol. 2, p. 228.

16. Oakey, "Marching through Georgia and the Carolinas," p. 677.

17. Jacob D. Cox, "The Surrender of Johnston's Army and the Closing Scenes of the War in North Carolina," in *Sketches of War History, 1861–1865*, Military Order of the Loyal Legion of the United States, Ohio, Vol. 2 (Wilmington, NC, 1991; Cincinnati, 1888), p. 256.

18. Quoted Mark Grimsley, *The Hard Hand of War: Union Military Policy toward Southern Civilians, 1861–1865* (Cambridge, 1995), p. 201.

19. Quoted in Grimsley, *Hard Hand of War*, p. 202.

20. Angle, *Three Years in the Army of the Cumberland*, p. 387.

21. Taylor, Matthews, and Power, *Leverett Letters*, p. 384.

22. Quoted in James Ford Rhodes, "Who Burned Columbia," in *Historical Essays* (New York 1909), pp. 307–8.

23. Sherman, *Memoirs of General W. T. Sherman*, vol. 2, p. 287.

24. Ibid., vol. 2, p. 290.

25. Ibid., vol. 2, p. 292.

26. Ibid., vol. 2, pp. 306–7.

27. The French word *chevauchée* was what Edward III of England used to describe his destructive marches through the French countryside in the fourteenth century.

28. Quoted in John G. Barrett, *Sherman's March through the Carolinas* (Chapel Hill, NC, 1956), p. 116.

29. Grant, *Personal Memoirs of U. S. Grant*, vol. 2, p. 411.

30. Ibid., vol. 2, pp. 525–26.

31. Lewis M. Hosea, *Some Side Lights on the War for the Union: Paper Read before the Ohio Commandery of the Loyal Legion at Cleveland, Ohio, October 9, 1912* (n.p., 1912), p. 13.

32. Wilson, *Under the Old Flag*, vol. 2, p. 189.

33. Thomas P. Clinton, "The Military Operations of Gen. John T. Croxton in West Alabama, 1865," in *Transactions of the Alabama Historical Society: 1899–1903*, ed. Thomas McAdory (Montgomery, 1904), vol. 4, p. 450.

34. *OR*, Ser. 1, vol. 47, part 3, p. 267.

35. Tabulation in Edward G. Longacre, *Grant's Cavalryman: The Life and Wars of General James H. Wilson* (Mechanicsburg, PA, 1972), p. 215.

36. *OR*, Ser. 1, vol. 47, pt. 2, p. 1311.

37. Sherman, *Memoirs of General William T. Sherman*, vol. 2, p. 296.

38. *OR*, Ser. 1, vol. 47, pt. 2, p. 803.

39. *OR*, Ser. 1, vol. 47, pt. 1, p. 423.

40. *OR*, Ser. 1, vol. 47, pt. 2, p. 1454.

41. Fehrenbacher and Fehrenbacher, *Recollected Words of Abraham Lincoln*, p. 404.

42. Sherman, *Memoirs of General W. T. Sherman*, vol. 2, p. 328.

43. Davis, *Rise and Fall of the Confederate Government*, vol. 2, p. 649.

44. Sheridan, *Personal Memoirs*, vol. 2, p. 119.

45. *OR*, Ser. 1, vol. 36, pt. 1, p. 52.

46. Adam Badeau, *Military History of Ulysses S. Grant, from April 1861, to April 1865* (New York, 1881), vol. 3, p. 451.

47. *OR*, Ser. 1, vol. 36, pt. 1, p. 55.

48. Catton, *Grant Takes Command*, p. 442.

49. *PUSG*, vol. 30, p. 22.

50. Sheridan, *Personal Memoirs*, vol. 2, p. 161.

51. Joshua Lawrence Chamberlain, *The Passing of the Armies: An Account of the Final Campaign of the Army of the Potomac, Based upon Personal Reminiscences of the Fifth Army Corps* (New York, 1915), p. 142.

52. Sheridan, *Personal Memoirs*, vol. 2, pp. 169–70.

53. Henry Edward Tremain, *Last Hours of Sheridan's Cavalry: A Reprint of War Memoranda* (New York, 1904), p. 117.

54. Ibid., p. 163.

55. *OR*, Ser. 1, vol. 47, pt. 3, p. 264.

56. Gallagher, *Fighting for the Confederacy*, pp. 531–32.

57. *OR*, Ser. 1, vol. 49, pt. 2, p. 1289.

Chapter 13: The Civil War in History

1. Clausewitz, *On War*, p. 592.

2. Davis, *Rise and Fall of the Confederate Government*, vol. 2, pp. 158–59.

3. Quoted in Howard, *The Franco-Prussian War*, p. 380.

4. Faunt Le Roy Senour, *Major General William T. Sherman, and His Campaign* (Chicago, 1865), p. 162.

5. Ken Burns, director, *The Civil War*, PBS miniseries, 1990.

6. Quoted in Charles Wentworth Dilke, *Greater Britain: A Record of Travel in English-Speaking Countries* (London, 1890), p. 23.

7. Porter, *Campaigning with Grant*, pp. 37–38.

8. Macauley, "Chestnut Grove."

9. Wilson, *Under the Old Flag*, vol. 1, p. 400.

FURTHER READING

General Studies

Vast does not begin to describe the oceans of ink that writers have expended on the military history of the American Civil War, never mind the nonmilitary topics that academic history in particular has focused on as of late. Nevertheless, in the last decades, only a relative handful of one-volume military histories of the war have appeared amid a plethora of studies focused mostly on individual campaigns and generals. The most recent, John Keegan's *The American Civil War: A Military History* (2009), comes from a British historian of great scholarly stature, but despite some references to the Civil War's geographical scale (a similarity it shares with our own interpretation), it is marred by serious factual errors, and its larger assertion that the war's intensity was "mysterious" really stems from Keegan's unfamiliarity with the larger scholarly literature. While his *Face of Battle* (1976), which aimed at looking at battle from the perspective of the common soldier, remains immensely influential, Keegan's volume of the Civil War has had little impact on scholarly literature of the war. It certainly has not dethroned what has been up to now been the standard one-volume military history of the Civil War, Herman Hattaway and Archer Jones's *How the North Won: A Military History of the Civil War* (1983).

Unfortunately, Hattaway and Jones obviously could not benefit from the decades of scholarship that have followed, and while pathbreaking in many ways, it continues to subscribe to the argument that the rifle musket's increased range by itself revolutionized infantry combat during the Civil War, making battles indecisive and extending the war's length. It thus gives relatively short shrift to the projection of power on a continental scale, unlike our own book, and the question of organizational culture in different Civil War armies (along with general questions of military effectiveness). Moreover, its analytical framework for judging military effectiveness lies in a rigid interpretation of World War I's Western Front that relies on a crude psychological model, and could not benefit from the larger military effectiveness project one of the authors superintended on behalf of the Department of Defense. Russell F. Weigley's *A Great Civil War: A Military and Political History, 1861–1865* (2000) is a more academic tome than Hattaway and Jones's, but it has not had the same influence on either lay or academic historians as that much older volume. Indeed, it recapitulates in large part the Civil War chapters of Weigley's seminal (but decades old) *American Way of War*, published in 1973, supplemented by the interpretation put forth by Hattaway and Jones a decade later.

While not a strictly military history, James McPherson's *Battle Cry of Freedom* (1988) deserves mention as the best one-volume history of the whole Civil War era, in all its aspects. Like this work, it strongly emphasizes the uncertainty of Union victory, but it obviously could not deal with military issues at the same level depth as this work. Donald Stoker's *The Grand Design: Strategy and the U.S. Civil War* (2010) also serves in some respects as a one-volume military history of the Civil War, albeit told from an ostensibly strategic perspective unseen in other scholarly works. While there is some value to Stoker's application of the current US military's scheme of three levels of war—strategy, operations, and tactics—to the military operations of the American Civil War, a large body of work long before Stoker's arrival on the scene covered issues involving Civil War strategy, even if they do not follow current US military definitions. In addition to the abovementioned one-volume military histories, which all deal with strategic issues in one way or the other, there is the important and diverse collection of essays by eminent historians in a slim volume edited by Gabor Boritt and titled *Why the Confederacy Lost* (1992). More broadly, most stronger scholarly works on the Civil War's military history deal with strategic issues in some way, shape, or form, whatever their specific genre—generally, either a battle study or a general's biography.

While we deliberately intended this military history of the war to be one volume, we certainly do not discount the value of multivolume studies of the war—most especially, Allan Nevins's magisterial eight-volume *Ordeal of the Union* (1947–71), which also covers the run-up to the war, and Shelby Foote's *The Civil War: A Narrative* (1958–74). Despite its age, Nevins's treatment of politics and economics remains serviceable, even if it did not benefit from the rise of social and cultural history among twentieth-century academic Americanists. Foote's fine volumes occupy a peculiar place among Civil War historians—while Foote read and drew insights from the academic historians of his era (leading, for example, to his balanced treatment of the Western and Eastern theaters), historians have been reluctant to draw on his work due to the absence of formal citations. Nevertheless, we judge his three volumes to be reliable scholarly accounts, and have drawn widely from his work. Also worthy of mention here is the Military Campaigns of the Civil War series edited at the University of North Carolina Press by Gary W. Gallagher, which are published collections of essays by different scholars on individual eastern campaigns and battles. Those essays run a wide gamut of scholarly approaches, including coverage of strategic issues, questions of command, logistical matters, and the examination of battles in their social and cultural context. It is regrettable that no equivalent exists for the war's western battles, which reveals a continuing imbalance of attention when it comes to the war's Eastern and Western theaters.

Related to this series is the vast number of Civil War battle studies—book-length treatments of single campaigns and battles, or even components of battles (as with the three individual days at Gettysburg). The studies we have used can be found in the notes accompanying our treatment of individual battles, but worth mentioning here are some scholarly studies of individual field armies. Joseph Glatthaar's *General Lee's Army: From Victory to Collapse* (2008) is the current gold standard for a history of a field army, with its comprehensive treatment of campaigns, leadership, culture, and social history, including an extensive demographic study of the Army of Northern Virginia's composition. Steven Woodworth's *Nothing but Victory: The Army of the Tennessee, 1861–1865* (2005) and Larry J. Daniel's *Days of Glory: The Army of the Cumberland, 1861–1865* (1994) deserve special mention, as does the older but still important and useful two-volume account of the ill-fated Confederate Army of Tennessee by Thomas Connelly (1971–85), which also served as a useful and early academic attempt to rebalance scholarly emphases on the Western and Eastern theaters. Bruce Catton's trilogy on the Army of the Potomac (1951–53) remains insightful and a model in terms of style, even if his research methods were not as disciplined as Douglas Southall Freeman's classic command study of the Army of Northern Virginia, *Lee's Lieutenants* (1942–44). Finally, despite its episodic coverage, Stephen Sears's superb collection of essays, *Controversies and Commanders: Dispatches from the Army of the Potomac* (1999) has deep insight into the peculiar culture of that troubled army. Gary Gallagher's collection of essays in *Lee and His Army in Confederate History* (2001) is the counterpart to the Sears volume for the Army of the Potomac's perpetual nemesis. Also worth mentioning are Jeffry Wert's *The Sword of Lincoln: The Army of the Potomac* (2005) and one of the co-author's own *West Pointers and the Civil War: The Old Army in War and Peace, 1814–1865* (2009), the latter situates the Civil War in the context of the US Army's antebellum professionalization. Furthermore, while not a full-length book, Mark Grimsley's treatment of the different command cultures of Civil War field armies in a volume of essays edited by Wayne Lee (2011) deserves mention. Finally, with regard to the naval war, James McPherson's *War on the Waters: The Union and Confederate Navies, 1861–1865* (2012) is the best one-volume treatment of the war's various naval aspects. Daniel T. Canfield's article on combined operations is also immensely valuable (2015).

Related to work on land and naval campaigns are, of course, biographies of generals. For important figures such as Grant, the number of biographies is immense, but especially worthy of mention here J.F.C. Fuller's influential dual biography of Grant and Lee (1933), which did a great deal to rehabilitate Grant's reputation in the twentieth century after it had fallen into a "Lost Cause"–driven nadir of sorts. The modern standard scholarly account of Grant's Civil War career remains Brooks Simpson's *Ulysses S. Grant: Triumph over Adversity, 1822–1865* (2000). Emory Thomas's *Robert E. Lee: A Biography* (1995) is the equivalent for Lee, but Alan Nolan's provocative *Lee Considered: General Robert E. Lee and Civil War History* (1991) is the work that caused waves among historians due its sharp criticism of Lee as both soldier and man. As for other crucial figures, we would like to highlight Stephen Sears on McClellan (1988), John F. Marszalek on Sherman (1993), Grady McWhiney on Bragg (1991), and Craig Symonds on Joseph Johnston (1992).

The authors have also drawn on a select group of primary sources. The first and foremost of them is Grant's *Memoirs* (1885). Other memoirs of note include William T. Sherman's (1875) and James Wilson's (1912). For a common soldier's view in the longest suffering of all Civil War armies, Union and Confederate, there is the peerless firsthand account of Sam Watkins's service in the Confederate Army of Tennessee. Other notable and widely available primary sources include printed collections of correspondence, including the fascinating (if self-damning) collection of George B. McClellan's Civil War correspondence edited by Stephen Sears (1989), a one-volume compilation of Robert E. Lee's wartime papers edited by Clifford Dowdey (1961), and a published volume of selections from Sherman's voluminous wartime correspondence edited by Brooks Simpson and Jean V. Berlin (1999). Standard (and less accessible) collections of documents used by the authors are the standard scholarly editions of Ulysses S. Grant's papers edited by John Y. Simon (1967–2012), Lincoln's public papers edited by Roy P. Basler (1953–55), and, most importantly, the important multivolume *Official Records*, compiled by the US War Department after the war (1880–1901), and which remains the most extensive single compilation of military records, both Union and Confederate.

As for sources not specifically mentioned above or cited in the text, we have relied on the following works regarding individual topics. For the initial confrontation surrounding Fort Sumter, the works by Nelson D. Lankford (2007), W. A. Swanberg (1959), and Maury Klein (1997) have been especially useful. On coercive forms of motivation in the Union army, see Stephen J. Ramold's *Baring the Iron Hand: Discipline in the Union Army* (2010). For more positive forms of commitment, see James M. McPherson's *For Cause and Comrades: Why Men Fought in the Civil War* (1997). On railroads, see the work of Thomas Weber (1952) and John E. Clark, Jr. (2001). While not cited in the notes, Mark Grimsley's one-volume study of the Overland Campaign (2002) is a superb and concise treatment of the campaign. The gold standard on that crucial campaign, however, remains Gordon C. Rhea's multivolume study (1994–2005). For the raw biographical and organizational data that comprised our analysis of the Army of the Potomac's early formation, the sources were Frank Welcher's important reference work on Union Army organization (1989) and the standard reference works of Ezra Warner on Union generals (1964). For the standard work on how Americans have remembered the Civil War, a burgeoning field of scholarship that this work only touches on, see David Blight's *Race and Reunion* (2001).

Primary Sources

Adams, Charles Francis. *Richard Henry Dana: A Biography*. Vol. 2. Boston, 1890.

Alexander, Edward Porter. *Military Memoirs of a Confederate: A Critical Narrative*. New York, 1907.

Angle, Paul M., ed. *Three Years in the Army of the Cumberland: The Letters and Diary of Major James A. Connolly*. Bloomington, IN, 1959.

Allan, William. "Memoranda of Conversations with General Robert E. Lee." In *Lee the Soldier*. Edited by Gary W. Gallagher, 7–24. Lincoln, NE, 1996.

Badeau, Adam. *Military History of Ulysses S. Grant from April 1861, to April 1865*. 3 vols. New York, 1868–81.

Basler, Roy P., ed. *Collected Works of Abraham Lincoln*. 8 vols. New Brunswick, NJ, 1954–55.

Beatty, John. *The Citizen-Soldier; or, Memoirs of a Volunteer*. Cincinnati, 1879.

Black, John D. "Reminiscences of the Bloody Angle." In *Glimpses of the Nation's Struggle, Fourth Series*. Military Order of the Loyal Legion of the United States, Minnesota. Vol. 4, pp. 420–35. Wilmington, NC, 1992; Saint Paul, 1898.

Boyd, David F. "Gen. W. T. Sherman: His Early Life in the South and His Relations with Southern Men." *Confederate Veteran* 18, no. 9 (1910): pp. 409–14.

Buell, Augustus. *"The Cannoneer." Recollections of Service in the Army of the Potomac*. Washington DC, 1890.

Burr, Frank A. *A New, Original and Authentic Record of the Life and Deeds of General U.S. Grant*. Battle Creek, MI, 1885.

Byers, S.H.M. "Some Recollections of Grant." In *The Annals of the War Written by Leading Participants, North and South, Originally Published in the Philadelphia Weekly Times*, pp. 342–56. Philadelphia, 1879.

Cable, George W. "New Orleans before the Capture." In *Battles and Leaders of the Civil War*. Edited by Robert Underwood Johnson and Clarence Clough Buel, vol. 2, pp. 14–21. New York, 1887.

Calhoun, John C. *A Disquisition on Government and a Discourse on the Constitution and Government of the United States*. Edited by Richard K. Cralle. Charleston, SC, 1851.

Chalmers, J. R. "Forrest and His Campaigns." *Southern Historical Society Papers* 7 (October 1879): pp. 451–86.

Chamberlain, Joshua Lawrence. *The Passing of the Armies: An Account of the Final Campaign of the Army of the Potomac, Based upon Personal Reminiscences of the Fifth Army Corps*. New York, 1915.

Chesnut, Mary. *Mary Chesnut's Civil War*. Edited by C. Vann Woodward. New Haven, CT, 1981.

Churchill, Winston. *Churchill by Himself*. Edited by Richard Langworth. New York, 2008.

Clinton, Thomas P. "The Military Operations of Gen. John T. Croxton in West Alabama, 1865." In *Transactions of the Alabama Historical Society: 1899-1903*. Edited by Thomas McAdory, vol. 4, pp. 449–63. Montgomery, AL, 1904.

Coffin, Charles Carleton. *Freedom Triumphant: The Fourth Period of the War of the Rebellion from September, 1864, to Its Close*. New York, 1891.

Commager, Henry Steele. *The Civil War Archive: The History of the Civil War in Documents*. Revised and expanded by Erik Bruun. New York, 2000.

The Congressional Globe. Washington, DC, 1833–73.

Connolly, James A. *Three Years in the Army of the Cumberland*. Edited by Paul M. Angle. Bloomington, IN, 1959.

Couch, Darius N. "The Chancellorsville Campaign." In *Battles and Leaders of the Civil War*. Edited by Robert Underwood Johnson and Clarence Clough Buel, vol. 3, pp. 154–71. New York, 1884.

Cox, Jacob D. *Atlanta*. New York, 1882.

——. "The Surrender of Johnston's Army and the Closing Scenes of the War in North Carolina." In *Sketches of War History, 1861–1865*. Military Order of the Loyal Legion of the United States, Ohio. Vol. 2, pp. 247–76. Wilmington, NC, 1991; Cincinnati, 1888.

Cuffel, Charles A. *History of Durrell's Battery in the Civil War*. Philadelphia, 1904.

Dana, Charles A. *Recollections of the Civil War: With the Leaders at Washington and in the Field in the Sixties*. New York, 1898.

Daniel, Frederick S. *The* Richmond Examiner *during the War; or, the Writings of John M. Daniel with a Memoir of His Life*. New York, 1868.

Davis, Jefferson. *Jefferson Davis: The Essential Writings*. Edited by William J. Cooper Jr. New York, 2004.

——. *The Rise and Fall of the Confederate Government*. 2 vols. New York, 1881.

Dilke, Charles Wentworth. *Greater Britain: A Record of Travel in English-Speaking Countries*. London, 1890.

Dodge, Grenville M. "The Battle of Atlanta." In *Personal Recollections of the War of Rebellion*. Edited by A. Noel Blakeman. Military Order of the Loyal Legion of the United States, New York. Vol. 2, pp. 240–54. New York, 1897; Wilmington, 1992.

Doubleday, Abner. *Reminiscences of Forts Sumter and Moultrie in 1860–'61*. New York, 1876.

Dowdey, Clifford, ed. *The Wartime Papers of R. E. Lee*. Boston, 1961.

Du Pont, Samuel Francis. *Samuel Francis Du Pont: A Selection from His Civil War Letters*. Edited by John D. Hayes. Ithaca, NY, 1969.

Dyer, John Percy. *From Shiloh to San Juan*. Baton Rouge, LA, 1961.

Eaton, John, with Ethel Osgood Mason. *Grant, Lincoln, and the Freedmen: Reminiscences of the Civil War*. New York, 1907.

Eby, Cecil D., Jr., ed. *A Virginia Yankee in the Civil War: The Diaries of David Hunter Strother*. Chapel Hill, NC, 1961.

Fehrenbacher, Don E., and Virginia Fehrenbacher, eds. *Recollected Words of Abraham Lincoln*. Palo Alto, CA, 1996.

Freeman, Douglas Southall, ed. *Lee's Dispatches: Unpublished Letters of General Robert E. Lee, C.S.A., to Jefferson Davis and the War Department of the Confederate States of America, 1862–1865*. New ed. New York, 1957.

Gallagher, Gary W., ed. *Fighting for the Confederacy: The Personal Recollections of General Edward Porter Alexander*. Chapel Hill, NC, 1989.

"General M. C. Meigs on the Conduct of the Civil War." *American Historical Review* 26, no. 2 (1921): pp. 285–303.

Gibbon, John. *Personal Recollections of the Civil War*. New York, 1928.

Gienapp, William E., and Erica L. Gienapp, eds. *The Civil War Diary of Gideon Welles, Lincoln's Secretary of the Navy: The Original Manuscript Edition*. Urbana, IL, 2014.

"Grant at Vicksburg." *Chicago History* 2, no. 4 (1949): pp. 120–21.

Grant, Ulysses S. *Personal Memoirs of U. S. Grant*. 2 vols. New York, 1885.

Halstead, E. P. "Incidents of the First Day at Gettysburg." In *Battles and Leaders of the Civil War*. Edited by Robert Underwood Johnson and Clarence Clough Buel, vol. 3, pp. 284–85. New York, 1884.

Haskell, Franklin Aretas. *The Battle of Gettysburg*. Madison, WI, 1908.

Hayes, John D., ed. *Samuel Francis Du Pont: A Selection from His Civil War Letters*. Vol. 1, *The Mission: 1860–1862*. Ithaca, NY, 1969.

Hill, Daniel H. "Chickamauga: The Great Battle of the West." In *Battles and Leaders of the Civil War*. Edited by Robert Underwood Johnson and Clarence Clough Buel, vol. 3, pp. 638–62. New York, 1884.

Hitchcock, Henry. *Marching with Sherman: Passages from the Letters and Campaign Diaries of Henry Hitchcock*. Edited by Mark A. De Wolfe Howe. New Haven, CT, 1927.

Hollis, Leslie, Sir. *One Marine's Tale*. London, 1956.

Hood, J. B. *Advance and Retreat: Personal Experiences in the United States and Confederate States Armies*. New Orleans, 1880.

Hosea, Lewis M. *Some Side Lights on the War for the Union: Paper Read before the Ohio Commandery of the Loyal Legion at Cleveland, Ohio, October 9, 1912*. n.p., 1912.

Hughes, Robert M. "Some War Letters of General Joseph E. Johnston." *Journal of the Military Service Institution of the United States* 50 (May–June 1912): pp. 318–28.

Hyde, Thomas W. *Following the Greek Cross; or, Memories of the Sixth Army Corps*. Boston, 1894.

Imboden, John D. "The Battle of New Market, VA., May 15th, 1864." In *Battles and Leaders of the Civil War*. Edited by Robert Underwood Johnson and Clarence Clough Buel, vol. 4, pp. 480–86. New York, 1884.

Johnson, Robert Underwood, and Clarence Clough Buel, eds. *Battles and Leaders of the Civil War*. 4 vols. New York, 1887–88.

Johnston, J. S. "A Reminiscence of Sharpsburg." *Southern Historical Society Papers* 8 (1880): pp. 526–29.

Johnston, Joseph Eggleston. *Narrative of Military Operations Directed during the Late War between the States.* New York, 1874.

Jones, J. William. *Personal Reminiscences of General Robert E. Lee.* Richmond, VA, 1989, reprint of 1875 edition.

Jordan, Thomas. "Notes of a Confederate Staff-Officer at Shiloh." In *Battles and Leaders of the Civil War.* Edited by Robert Underwood Johnson and Clarence Clough Buel, vol. 1, pp. 594–603. New York, 1887.

——, and J. P. Pryor. *The Campaigns of Lieut.-Gen. N. B. Forrest, and of Forrest's Cavalry.* New Orleans, 1868.

Joslyn, Mauriel Phillips. *Charlotte's Boys: Civil War Letters of the Branch Family of Savannah.* Berryville, VA, 1996.

Kniffin, G. C. "The Battle of Stone's River." In *Battles and Leaders of the Civil War.* Edited by Robert Underwood Johnson and Clarence Clough Buel, vol. 3, pp. 613–31. New York, 1884.

Lee, Fitz. "A Review of the First Two Days' Operations at Gettysburg and a Reply to General Longstreet." *Southern Historical Society Papers* 5, no. 4 (1878): pp. 162–94.

"Letter from Major-General Henry Heth, of A. P. Hill's Corps, A. N. V." *Southern Historical Society Papers* 4, no. 3 (1877): pp. 151–60.

Life and Public Services of Major-General Butler (Benjamin F. Butler): The Hero of New Orleans. Philadelphia, 1864.

Lloyd George, David. *War Memoirs of David Lloyd George.* Boston, 1936.

Lockett, S. H. "The Defense of Vicksburg." In *Battles and Leaders of the Civil War.* Edited by Robert Underwood Johnson and Clarence Clough Buel, vol. 3, pp. 482–92. New York, 1884.

Long, A. L. *Memoirs of Robert E. Lee: His Military and Personal History.* London, 1886.

Longstreet, James. *From Manassas to Appomattox: Memoirs of the Civil War in America.* Philadelphia, 1896.

——. "Lee's Invasion of Pennsylvania." *Century Magazine* 33 (February 1887).

Lowe, David W., ed. *Meade's Army: The Private Notebooks of Lt. Col. Theodore Lyman.* Kent, OH, 2007.

McGuire, Hunter. "General T. J. ("Stonewall") Jackson, Confederate States Army: His Career and Character." *Southern Historical Society Papers* 25 (1897): pp. 91–112.

Michie, Peter S. *The Life and Letters of Emory Upton, Colonel of the Fourth Regiment of Artillery, and Brevet Major-General, U. S. Army.* New York, 1885.

Mohr, James C., ed. *The Cormany Diaries: A Northern Family in the Civil War.* Pittsburgh, 1982.

Monroe, Haskell M., and James T. McIntosh, eds. *The Papers of Jefferson Davis.* Vol. 10. Baton Rouge, LA, 1971.

"My Hunt after 'The Captain.'" *Atlantic Monthly* 10 (December 1862): pp. 738–64.

Nash, Eugene Arus. *A History of the Forty-Fourth Regiment New York Volunteer Infantry in the Civil War, 1861–1865*. Dayton, OH, 1988; Chicago, 1910.

New York Daily Tribune.

New York Herald.

Oakey, Daniel. "Marching through Georgia and the Carolinas." In *Battles and Leaders of the Civil War*. Edited by Robert Underwood Johnson and Clarence Clough Buel, vol. 4, pp. 671–79. New York, 1897.

Oldaker, Glenn C., ed. *Centennial Tales: Memoirs of Colonel "Chester" S. Bassett French*. New York, 1962.

Oldroyd, Osborn H. *A Soldier's Story of the Siege of Vicksburg from the Diary of Osborn H. Oldroyd*. Springfield, IL, 1885.

Porter, David D. "The Opening of the Lower Mississippi." In *Battles and Leaders of the Civil War*. Edited by Robert Underwood Johnson and Clarence Clough Buel, vol. 2, pp. 22–55. New York, 1884.

Porter, Horace. *Campaigning with Grant*. New York, 1897.

Quaife, Milo M., ed. *From the Cannon's Mouth: Civil War Letters of General Alpheus S. Williams*. Detroit, 1959.

Raymond, Henry J. *The Life and Public Services of Abraham Lincoln*. New York, 1865.

Report of the Joint Committee on the Conduct of the War at the Second Session Thirty-Eighth Congress: Army of the Potomac, Battle of Petersburg. Washington, DC, 1865.

Report of the Joint Committee on the Conduct of the War, Part I, Army of the Potomac, 37th Congress, 34d sess. Washington, DC, 1863.

Report of the Proceedings of the Society of the Army of Tennessee at the Seventeenth Meeting Held at Lake Minnetonka, Minnesota, August 13th and 14th 1884. Cincinnati, 1893.

Richardson, James D. *A Compilation of the Messages and Papers of the Presidents of the United States, 1798–1897*. Vol. 5. Washington, DC, 1897.

Richmond Daily Dispatch.

Roth, Margaret Brobst, ed. *Well Mary: Civil War Letters of a Wisconsin Volunteer*. Madison, WI, 1960.

Rusling, James F. *Men and Things I Saw in Civil War Days*. New York, 1899.

Sanborn, John B. "Reminiscences of the Campaigns against Vicksburg." *Transactions of the Department of American History of the Minnesota Historical Society* (October 1879): pp. 81–111.

Scott, Wm. Forse. *The Story of a Cavalry Regiment: The Career of the Fourth Iowa Veteran Volunteers from Kansas to Georgia, 1861–1865*. 1892; Iowa City, 1992.

Sears, Stephen W., ed. *The Civil War Papers of George B. McClellan: Selected Correspondence, 1860–1865*. New York, 1989.

Senour, Faunt Le Roy. *Major General William T. Sherman, and His Campaign*. Chicago, 1865.

Seward, Frederick W. *Autobiography of William H. Seward from 1831–1834, with a Memoir of His Life, and Selections from His Letters from 1831 to 1846*. New York, 1877.

Shellenberger, John K. "The Battle of Franklin." In *Glimpses of the Nation's Struggle*. Edited by J. C. Donahower, Silas H. Towler, and David L. Kingsbury, vol. 5, pp. 496–521. Military Order of the Loyal Legion of the United States, Minnesota. St. Paul, 1903; Wilmington, 1992.

Sheridan, Philip. *Personal Memoirs*. 2 vols. New York, 1888.

Sherman, William T. "The Grand Strategy in the Last Year of the War." In *Battles and Leaders of the Civil War: The Way to Appomattox*. Edited by Robert Underwood Johnson and Clarence Clough Buel, vol. 4, pp. 247–59. New York, 1887.

———. *Memoirs of General William T. Sherman, by Himself*. 2 vols. New York, 1875.

Simon, John Y., ed. *The Papers of Ulysses S. Grant*. 32 vols. Carbondale, IL, 1967–2012.

Simpson, Brooks, and Jean V. Berlin, eds. *Sherman's Civil War: Selected Correspondence of William T. Sherman, 1860–1865*. Chapel Hill, NC, 1999.

Snead, Thomas L. *The Fight for Missouri from the Election of Lincoln to the Death of Lyon*. New York, 1888.

Spear, Ellis. "The Story of the Raising and Organization of a Regiment of Volunteers in 1862." In *War Papers, Military Order of the Loyal Legion of the United States*. Commandery of the District of Columbia, 4 March 1903.

Styple, William B., ed. *Letters from the Peninsula: The Civil War Letters of General Philip Kearny*. Kearny, NJ, 1988.

Taylor, Frances Wallace, Catherine Taylor Matthews, and J. Tracy Power, eds. *The Leverett Letters: Correspondence of a South Carolina Family, 1851–1868*. Columbia, SC, 2000.

Tenney, Luman Harris. *War Diary of Luman Harris Tenney, 1861–1865*. Oberlin, OH, 1914.

Thompson, David L. "In the Ranks to the Antietam." In *Battles and Leaders of the Civil War*. Edited by Robert Underwood Johnson and Clarence Clough Buel, vol. 2, pp. 556–58. New York, 1884.

Thoreau, Henry David. *Essays: A Fully Annotated Edition*. Edited by Jeffrey S. Cramer. New Haven, CT, 2013.

Tremain, Henry Edward. *Last Hours of Sheridan's Cavalry: A Reprint of War Memoranda*. New York, 1904.

Turchin, John B. *Chickamauga*. Chicago, 1888.

United States War Department. *The War of the Rebellion: A Compilation of the Official Records of the Union and Confederate Armies*. 128 vols. Washington, DC, 1880–1901.

Urquhart, David. "Bragg's Advance and Retreat." In *Battles and Leaders of the Civil War*. Edited by Robert Underwood Johnson and Clarence Clough Buel, vol. 3, pp. 600–609. New York, 1884.

Venable, C. S. "The Campaign from the Wilderness to Petersburg." *Southern Historical Society Papers* 14 (1886): pp. 522–42.

Wadsworth, Chas. *War a Discipline: A Sermon Preached in Cavalry Church, San Francisco, on Thanksgiving Day, November 24th, 1864*. San Francisco, 1864.

Walker, Francis A. *History of the Second Army Corps in the Army of the Potomac*. New York, 1886.

Watkins, Sam R. *1861 vs. 1882, "Co. Aytch," Maury Grays, First Tennessee Regiment; or, A Side Show of the Big Show*. Nashville, 1882.

Wilson, James H. "Major-General John Buford." *Journal of the United States Cavalry Association* 8 (September 1895): 171–83.

Wilson, James Harrison. *Under the Old Flag: Recollections of Military Operations in the War for Union, the Spanish War, the Boxer Rebellion, etc.* 2 vols. New York, 1912.

Wyeth, John Allan. *Life of General Nathan Bedford Forrest*. New York, 1899.

Secondary Sources

Abbott, Willis J. *Battle Fields and Camp Fires: A Narrative of the Principle Military Operations of the Civil War*. New York, 1890.

Andrews, J. Cutler. *The North Reports the Civil War*. Pittsburgh, 1955.

Arnold, James R. *Chickamauga 1863: The River of Death*. London, 1992.

———. *Grant Wins the War: Decision at Vicksburg*. New York, 1997.

Barrett, John G. *Sherman's March through the Carolinas*. Chapel Hill, NC, 1956.

Berlin, Ira. *Many Thousands Gone: The First Two Centuries of Slavery in North America*. Cambridge, MA, 1998.

Blight, David. *Race and Reunion*. Cambridge, MA, 2001.

Boritt, Gabor S., ed. *Why the Confederacy Lost*. New York, 1992.

Canfield, Daniel T. "Opportunity Lost: Combined Operations and the Development of Union Military Strategy, April 1861–April 1862." *Journal of Military History* 79, no. 3 (2015): pp. 657–90.

Catton, Bruce. *Army of the Potomac*. 3 vols. New York, 1962.

———. *The Centennial History of the American Civil War*. Vol. 2, *Terrible Swift Sword*. Garden City, NY, 1963.

———. *The Centennial History of the American Civil War*. Vol. 3, *A Stillness at Appomattox*. Garden City, NY, 1951–53.

———. *Grant Moves South, 1861–1863*. Boston, 1960.

———. *Grant Takes Command*. Boston, 1969.

———. *This Hallowed Ground: The Story of the Union Side of the Civil War*. Garden City, NY, 1956.

Chandler, David G. *The Campaigns of Napoleon*. New York, 1966.

Chodorow, Stanley, and MacGregor Knox. *The Mainstream of Civilization since 1660*. 6th ed. New York, 1994.

Clark, John E., Jr. *Railroads in the Civil War: The Impact of Management on Victory and Defeat*. Baton Rouge, LA, 2001.

Clausewitz, Carl von. *On War*. Edited and translated by Michael Howard and Peter Paret. Princeton, NJ, 1976.

Clinton, Thomas P. "The Military Operations of Gen. John T. Croxton in West Alabama, 1865." *Alabama Historical Society*, Montgomery, 1904.

Connelly, Thomas Lawrence. *Army of the Heartland: The Army of Tennessee, 1861–1862*. Baton Rouge, LA, 1985.

———. *Autumn of Glory: The Army of Tennessee, 1862–1865*. Baton Rouge, LA, 1971.

Cunliffe, Marcus. *Soldiers and Civilians: The Martial Spirit in America, 1775–1865*. New York, 1973.

Daniel, Larry J. *Days of Glory: The Army of the Cumberland, 1861–1865*. Baton Rouge, LA, 1994.

Davison, Eddy W., and Daniel Foxx. *Nathan Bedford Forrest: In Search of the Enigma*. Gretna, LA, 2007.

De Peyster, J. Watts. *Personal and Military History of Philip Kearny*. New York, 1869.

Donald, David Herbert. *Lincoln*. New York, 1995.

Eaton, Clement. *A History of the Southern Confederacy*. New York, 1954.

Fehrenbacher, Don E. *The Dred Scott Case: Its Significance in America Law and Politics*. New York, 2001.

Flaherty, Jane. *The Revenue Imperative*. London, 2009.

Foner, Eric. *Free Soil, Free Labor, Free Men: The Ideology of the Republican Party before the Civil War*. New York, 1970.

Foote, Shelby. *The Civil War: A Narrative*. 3 vols. New York, 1958–74.

Freeman, Douglas Southall. *Lee's Lieutenants: A Study in Command*. 3 vols. New York, 1942–44.

Fuller, J.F.C. *Grant and Lee: A Study in Personality and Generalship*. London, 1933.

Gallagher, Gary W. "Blueprint for Victory: Northern Strategy and Military Policy." In *Writing the Civil War: The Quest to Understand*, edited by James M. McPherson and William J. Cooper Jr. Columbia, SC, 1998.

———. *The Confederate War*. Cambridge, MA, 1997.

———. *Lee and His Army in Confederate History*. Chapel Hill, NC, 2001.

———. *The Union War*. Cambridge, MA, 2011.

Glatthaar, Joseph T. *General Lee's Army: From Victory to Collapse*. New York, 2008.

———. *The March to the Sea and Beyond: Sherman's Troops in the Savannah and Carolina Campaigns*. Baton Rouge, LA, 1995.

Goff, Richard D. *Confederate Supply*. Durham, NC, 1969.

Grimsley, Mark. *And Keep Moving On: The Virginia Campaign, May–June 1864*. Lincoln, NE, 2002.

———. *The Hard Hand of War: Union Military Policy toward Southern Civilians, 1861–1865*. Cambridge, 1995.

———. "Success and Failure in Civil War Armies: Clues from Organizational Culture." In *Warfare and Culture in World History*, edited by Wayne Lee, pp. 115–41. New York, 2011.

Hagemann, E. R., ed., *Fighting Rebels and Redskins: Experiences in Army Life of Colonel George B. Sanford, 1861–1892*. Norman, OK, 1969.

Hattaway, Herman, and Archer Jones. *How the North Won: A Military History of the Civil War*. Urbana, IL, 1983.

Hennessy, John J. *Return to Bull Run: The Campaign and Battle of Second Manassas*. Norman, OK, 1999.

Hoogenboom, Ari Arthur. *Gustavus Vasa Fox of the Union Navy: A Biography*. Baltimore, 2008.

Howard, Michael. *The Franco-Prussian War*. London, 1961.

Hsieh, Wayne Wei-siang. *West Pointers and the Civil War: The Old Army in War and Peace*. Chapel Hill, NC, 2009.

Keegan, John. *The American Civil War: A Military History*. New York, 2009.

———. *The Face of Battle*. New York, 1976.

Klein, Maury. *Days of Defiance: Sumter, Secession, and the Coming of the Civil War*. New York, 1997.

Knox, MacGregor, and Williamson Murray, eds. *The Dynamics of Military Revolution, 1300–2050*. Cambridge, 2001.

Lankford, Nelson D. *Cry Havoc! The Crooked Road to Civil War, 1861*. New York, 2007.

Lawton, Eba Anderson. *Major Robert Anderson and Fort Sumter, 1861*. New York, 1911.

Longacre, Edward G. *Grant's Cavalryman: The Life and Wars of General James H. Wilson*. Mechanicsburg, PA, 1972.

Marszalek, John F. *Sherman: A Soldier's Passion for Order*. New York, 1993.

McDonough, James Lee. *Shiloh: In Hell before Night*. Knoxville, TN, 1977.

McPherson, James M. *Battle Cry of Freedom: The Civil War Era*. New York, 1988.

———. *For Cause and Comrades: Why Men Fought in the Civil War*. Oxford, 1997.

———. *This Mighty Scourge: Perspectives on the Civil War*. Oxford, 2007.

———. *Tried by War: Abraham Lincoln as Commander in Chief*. New York, 2008.

———. *War on the Waters: The Union and Confederate Navies, 1861–1865*. Chapel Hill, NC, 2012.

———. *The War That Forged the Nation: Why the Civil War Still Matters*. Oxford, 2015.

McWhiney, Grady. *Braxton Bragg and Confederate Defeat*. Tuscaloosa, AL, 1991.

Millett, Allan R., and Williamson Murray. "Lessons of War." *National Interest* 14 (Winter 1988): pp. 83–95.

———. *Military Effectiveness*. Vol. 1, *The First World War*. London, 1988.

Nevins, Allan. *Ordeal of the Union*. 8 vols. New York, 1947–71.

Nolan, Alan. *Lee Considered: General Robert E. Lee and Civil War History*. Chapel Hill, NC, 1991.

Pemberton, John C. *Pemberton, Defender of Vicksburg*. Chapel Hill, NC, 1942.

Pfanz, Harry W. *Gettysburg: The Second Day*. Chapel Hill, NC, 1998.

Plum, William Rattle. *The Military Telegraph during the Civil War in the United States*. Chicago, 1882.

Poriss, Gerry Harder, and Ralph G. Poriss, eds. *While My Country Is in Danger: The Life and Letters of Lieutenant Colonel Richard S. Thompson, Twelfth New Jersey Volunteers* (Hamilton, NY, 1994).

Pratt, Fletcher. *Civil War on Western Waters*. New York, 1956.

Ramold, Steven J. *Baring the Iron Hand: Discipline in the Union Army*. DeKalb, IL, 2010.

Rhea, Gordon C. *The Battle of the Wilderness, May 5–6, 1864*. Baton Rouge, LA, 1994.

———. *The Battles for Spotsylvania Court House and the Road to Yellow Tavern, May 7–12, 1864*. Baton Rouge, LA, 1997.

———. *Cold Harbor: Grant and Lee, May 26–June 3, 1864*. Baton Rouge, LA, 2002.

———. *To the North Anna River: Grant and Lee, May 15–25, 1864*. Baton Rouge, LA, 2005.

Rhodes, James Ford. "Who Burned Columbia?" In *Historical Essays*, pp. 299–314. New York, 1909.

Sears, Stephen W. *Chancellorsville*. Boston, 1996.

———. *Controversies and Commanders: Dispatches from the Army of the Potomac*. Boston, 1999.

———. *George B. McClellan: The Young Napoleon*. New York, 1988.

———. *Gettysburg*. Boston, 2003.

———. *Landscape Turned Red: The Battle of Antietam*. New York, 1983.

Simpson, Brooks D. *Ulysses S. Grant: Triumph over Adversity, 1822–1865*. Boston, 2000.

Smith, Andrew F. *Starving the South: How the North Won the Civil War*. New York, 2001.

Stoker, Donald J. *The Grand Design: Strategy and the U.S. Civil War*. Oxford, 2010.

Swanberg, W. A. *First Blood: The Story of Fort Sumter*. New York, 1959.

Symonds, Craig L. *Joseph E. Johnston: A Civil War Biography*. New York, 1992.

———. *Lincoln and His Admirals: Abraham Lincoln, the U.S. Navy, and the Civil War*. Oxford, 2008.

Thomas, Emory. *Robert E. Lee: A Biography*. New York, 1995.

Thomas, William G. *The Iron Way: Railroads, the Civil War, and the Making of Modern America*. New Haven, CT, 2011.

Thucydides. *The History of the Peloponnesian War*. Translated by Rex Warner. London, 1954.

Tucker, Glenn. *Chickamauga: Bloody Battle in the West*. New York, 1994.

Vetter, Charles Edmund. *Sherman: Merchant of Terror, Advocate of Peace*. Gretna, LA, 1992.

Warner, Ezra J. *Generals in Blue: Lives of the Union Commanders*. Baton Rouge, LA, 1964.

Weber, Thomas. *The Northern Railroads in the Civil War, 1861–1865*. New York, 1952.

Weigley, Russell F. *The American Way of War: A History of United States Military Strategy and Policy*. New York, 1973.

———. *A Great Civil War: A Military and Political History, 1861–1865*. Bloomington, IN, 2000.

Weintraub, Stanley. *General Sherman's Christmas: Savannah, 1864*. New York, 2009.

Welcher, Frank J. *The Union Army, 1861–1865: Organization and Operations*. Vol. 1, *The Eastern Theater*. Bloomington, IN, 1989.

Wert, Jeffry D. *From Winchester to Cedar Creek: The Shenandoah Campaign of 1864*. Carlisle, PA, 1987.

———. *The Sword of Lincoln: The Army of the Potomac*. New York, 2005.

Woodworth, Steven E. *Nothing but Victory: The Army of the Tennessee, 1861–1865*. New York, 2005.

INDEX

war: American way of, 11, 514, 521; character of, 1–2, 4–5; civil war, nature of, 82; conduct of, 2, 5, 38, 45, 57, 514, 518–519; contingency and chance and, 512; guerrilla warfare and, 505–506; popular mobilization and, 38; uncertainty in, 2, 512; Western way of, 1
War of 1812, 51, 85
Warren, Gouverneur, 172, 354, 498–501, 545; at Gettysburg, 282–283, 285, 291; leadership of, 365–366; Overland Campaign and, 390, 394, 395, 398; at Spotsylvania Courthouse, 376–377, 381–382; at the Wilderness, 368, 371–373
Webb, Alexander, 288
Webster, Daniel, 21
Weed, Stephen, 282–283, 285
Weitzel, Godfrey, 474–475
Welles, Gideon, 68, 72–73; New Orleans expedition and, 161–162; Port Royal expedition and, 126, 130
West Point (United States Military Academy), 50–51; military leadership and, 95, 104; tactical training and, 98
Western theater of war, 11, 61, 247, 291, 327, 527; Confederate command and control problems in, 212, 218, 303, 311, 336; Confederate cordon defense in, 135, 146, 168, 247, 547; logistics and, 293, 415–418; Union gains in 1862 and, 164; Union operational discretion and, 101. *See also individual campaigns and battles*
Wheeler, Joseph, 345, 428–429, 436, 441, 443, 446, 464–465
Whig party, 19, 23
Whiting, W. H., 389
Whitney, Eli, 17

Wilcox, Orlando, 227, 239, 288, 372, 390
Wilder, John, 213–214; Tennessee campaign and, 331–332, 334, 337–338, 342–343
Wilderness, Battle of the, 368–374, 512
Wilkes, Charles, 86
Williams, Alpheus, 225, 233–234
Wilmot, David, 20
Wilmot Proviso, 21
Wilson, James, 102, 305, 406–407, 447; Carolina campaign and, 473, 486–489, 507; Franklin and Nashville campaign and, 452, 456, 458–459
Wilson, Woodrow, 524
Wilson's Creek, Battle of, 81
Winchester, First Battle of, 177
Winchester, Third Battle of, 406–408
Wise, Henry, 72
Wood, Thomas J., 10, 340, 342
Wool, John F., 125
World War I, 12, 85, 389, 418, 508, 527; command and control breakdown and, 383; communications and, 381; French and Industrial Revolutions and, 5, 248; tactics and, 496, 520; Western Front of, 40
World War II, 468, 482; economic expansion and, 89–90; logistics and, 367; mass bombing and, 467, 482, 507–508, 514, 521; Marshall Plan and, 525; naval investment and, 131
Wright, Ambrose, 284
Wright, Horatio, 378, 381–384, 395, 402, 501; Atlanta campaign and, 430, 433

Yancey, William, 85

Zollicoffer, Felix, 135, 138